NOV 0 8 2001

NO LONGER THE
PROPERTY OF
ELON UNIVERSITY LIBRARY

D1786884

Reflections on the Classical Canon in Economics

In this discipline-defining volume, some of the leading international scholars in the history of economic thought re-examine the concepts of classical economics and the canon, illuminating the roots of the contemporary discipline, and the shape and form of its evolution.

The investigation addresses three related issues. First, the contributors attempt to determine which ideas are vital to classical economics, and whether these ideas distinguish classical economics from other approaches to economic questions. Second, the essays address the development of classical economics over time through sociological and intellectual processes, and attempt to determine why some writers and works are elevated to the canon, while others are not. Third, some contributors examine the intellectual consequences of this inevitable process of canonization.

The book includes examinations of the work of major economists such as Smith, Bentham, Malthus, Ricardo, Mill, Marx and Keynes. Offering new perspectives on the way an intellectual discipline is constructed, this book will be of essential interest to all scholars of the history of economic thought.

Evelyn L. Forget is Professor of Economics at the University of Manitoba, Canada. Her publications include journal articles on various aspects of classical economics and the role of women in the economics profession. She is the author of *The Social Economics of Jean-Baptiste Say* (Routledge 1999).
Sandra Peart is Associate Professor of Economics at Baldwin-Wallace College. She has had articles published on the transition from classical to neoclassical economics in various leading journals, and she is the author of *The Economics of William Stanley Jevons* (Routledge 1996).

Routledge Studies in the History of Economics

1 **Economics as Literature**
   Willie Henderson

2 **Socialism and Marginalism in Economics 1870–1930**
   Edited by Ian Steedman

3 **Hayek's Political Economy**
   The socio-economics of order
   Steve Fleetwood

4 **On the Origins of Classical Economics**
   Distribution and value from William Petty to Adam Smith
   Tony Aspromourgos

5 **The Economics of Joan Robinson**
   Edited by Maria Cristina Marcuzzo, Luigi Pasinetti and Alesandro Roncaglia

6 **The Evolutionist Economics of Léon Walras**
   Albert Jolink

7 **Keynes and the 'Classics'**
   A study in language, epistemology and mistaken identities
   Michel Verdon

8 **The History of Game Theory, Vol. 1**
   From the beginnings to 1945
   Robert W. Dimand and Mary Ann Dimand

9 **The Economics of W. S. Jevons**
   Sandra Peart

10 **Gandhi's Economic Thought**
   Ajit K. Dasgupta

11 **Equilibrium and Economic Theory**
   Edited by Giovanni Caravale

12 **Austrian Economics in Debate**
   Edited by Willem Keizer, Bert Tieben and Rudy van Zijp

13 **Ancient Economic Thought**
   Edited by B. B. Price

14 **The Political Economy of Social Credit and Guild Socialism**
   Frances Hutchinson and Brian Burkitt

15 **Economic Careers**
   Economics and economists in Britain 1930–1970
   Keith Tribe

16 **Understanding 'Classical' Economics**
   Studies in the long-period theory
   Heinz Kurz and Neri Salvadori

17 **History of Environmental Economic Thought**
   E. Kula

18 **Economic Thought in Communist and Post-Communist Europe**
   Edited by Hans-Jürgen Wagener

19 **Studies in the History of French Political Economy**
   From Bodin to Walras
   Edited by Gilbert Faccarello

20 **The Economics of John Rae**
   Edited by O. F. Hamouda, C. Lee and D. Mair

21 **Keynes and the Neoclassical Synthesis**
   Einsteinian versus Newtonian macroeconomics
   Teodoro Dario Togati

22 **Historical Perspectives on Macroeconomics**
   Sixty years after the 'General Theory'
   Edited by Philippe Fontaine and Albert Jolink

23 **The Founding of Institutional Economics**
   The leisure class and sovereignty
   Edited by Warren J. Samuels

24 **Evolution of Austrian Economics**
   From Menger to Lachmann
   Sandye Gloria

25 **Marx's Concept of Money: the God of Commodities**
   Anitra Nelson

26 **The Economics of James Steuart**
   Edited by Ramón Tortajada

27 **The Development of Economics in Europe since 1945**
   Edited by A. W. Bob Coats

28 **The Canon in the History of Economics**
   Critical essays
   Edited by Michalis Psalidopoulos

29 **Money and Growth**
   Selected papers of Allyn Abbott Young
   Edited by Perry G. Mehrling and Roger J. Sandilands

30 **The Social Economics of Jean-Baptiste Say**
   Markets and virtue
   Evelyn L. Forget

31 **The Foundations of Laissez-Faire**
   The economics of Pierre de Boisguilbert
   Gilbert Faccarello

32 **John Ruskin's Political Economy**
   Willie Henderson

33 **Contributions to the History of Economic Thought**
   Essays in honour of R D C Black
   Edited by Antoin E Murphy and Renee Prendergast

34 **Towards an Unknown Marx**
   A commentary on the manuscripts of 1861–63
   Enrique Dussel

35 **Economics and Interdisciplinary Exchange**
   Edited by Guido Erreygers

36 **Economics as the Art of Thought**
Essays in honour of G L S Shackle
Edited by Stephen F Frowen and Peter Earl

37 **The Decline of Ricardian Economics**
Politics and economics in post-Ricardian theory
Susan Pashkoff

38 **Piero Sraffa**
His life, thought and cultural heritage
Alessandro Roncaglia

39 **Equilibrium and Disequilibrium in Economic Theory**
The Marshall–Walras divide
Edited by Michel de Vroey

40 **The German Historical School**
The historical and ethical approach to economics
Edited by Yuichi Shionoya

41 **Reflections on the Classical Canon in Economics**
Essays in honor of Samuel Hollander
Edited by Sandra Peart and Evelyn L. Forget

42 **Piero Sraffa's Political Economy**
A centenary estimate
Edited by Terenzio Cozzi and Roberto Marchionatti

43 **The Contribution of Joseph A. Schumpeter to Economics**
Richard Arena and Cecile Dangel

44 **On the Development of Long-run Neo-Classical Theory**
Tom Kompas

45 **Economic Analysis and Political Economy in the Thought of Hayek**
Edited by Thierry Aimar and Jack Birner

46 **Pricing and Change**
Gunnar Myrdal

Reflections on the Classical Canon in Economics

Essays in honor of Samuel Hollander

**Edited by Evelyn L. Forget
and Sandra Peart**

London and New York

First published 2001
by Routledge
11 New Fetter Lane, London EC4P 4EE

Simultaneously published in the USA and Canada
by Routledge
29 West 35th Street, New York, NY 10001

Routledge is an imprint of the Taylor & Francis Group

Editorial material and selection © 2001 Evelyn L. Forget and Sandra Peart

Individual chapters © 2001 the contributors

Typeset in Baskerville
by Curran Publishing Services Ltd, Norwich
Printed and bound in Great Britain
by St Edmundsbury Press, Bury St Edmunds, Suffolk

All rights reserved. No part of this book may be reprinted or reproduced or utilized in any form or by any electronic, mechanical, or other means, now known or hereafter invented, including photocopying and recording, or in any information storage or retrieval system, without permission in writing from the publishers.

British Library Cataloguing in Publication Data
A catalogue record for this book is available
from the British Library.

Library of Congress Cataloging-in-Publication Data

    Reflections on the classical canon in economics: essays in honor of Samuel Hollander / edited by Evelyn L. Forget and Sandra Peart.
    544 pp. 15.6 x 23.4 cm
    Includes bibliographical references and index.
    1. Classical school of economics. I. Forget, Evelyn L., 1956– II. Peart, Sandra.
    HB 94.R44 2000   00–036595
    330.15'3—dc21

ISBN 0–415–20801–7

This volume includes some of the papers presented at a conference designed to celebrate the career of Samuel Hollander on the occasion of his retirement as University Professor from the Department of Economics at the University of Toronto. We attach, as an appendix, Paul Samuelson's tribute to Samuel Hollander, and Samuel Hollander's response.

The pride and affection of Samuel Hollander's children, Isaac and Frances, characterize their words, which are also appended.

On behalf of all those students who have gained much from the masterful knowledge and very hard criticism of Samuel Hollander, we would like to offer our gratitude and affection.

Contents

List of figures and table	xiv
List of contributors	xv
Acknowledgements	xx

1 **Introduction** 1
   EVELYN L. FORGET AND SANDRA PEART

2 **"Classical economics": a reification wrapped in an anachronism?** 7
   SAMUEL HOLLANDER

3 **Notes towards an un-canonical, pre-classical model of political oeconomy** 27
   A. M. C. WATERMAN

4 **Bentham and the classical canon** 43
   NATHALIE SIGOT

5 **A new institutional perspective on the canonical model: the case of capital markets in *The Wealth of Nations*** 57
   ANTHONY ENDRES

6 **Beyond the canonical growth model: knowledge and learning in classical economics, 1815–34** 75
   MASAZUMI WAKATABE

7 **Reading *The Wealth of Nations* in context: rethinking the canon of mid-eighteenth century British political economy** 125
   RICHARD A. KLEER

Contents

8 Justice versus expediency: *The Wealth of Nations* as an anti-political economy 148
JEFFREY T. YOUNG

9 The canon in the history of the Adam Smith problem 168
INGRID PETERS-FRANSEN

10 The French foundations of the classical canon 185
WALTER ELTIS

11 J-B. Say and the French liberal school of the nineteenth century: outside the canon? 205
RICHARD ARENA

12 Priceless value (or almost so): misunderstood concerns of Marx and Ricardo 224
WILLIAM J. BAUMOL

13 Sraffa's Ricardo after fifty years: a preliminary estimate 241
PIER LUIGI PORTA

14 David Ricardo's contribution to the constitution of the canon of Ricardian economics: a reconsideration of 1970s interpretations of the 1815 debate 270
ANDRÉ LAPIDUS AND NATHALIE SIGOT

15 Ricardian economics: reasoning about counter-intuitive tendencies when system constraints are present 290
LAURENCE S. MOSS

16 Ricardo's use of Say's law: the case of the post-Napoleonic war depression 318
TIMOTHY DAVIS

17 Does Ricardo's theory of money belong to the classical canon? 331
GHISLAIN DELEPLACE

18 On Hollander's and Keynes's "canonical" interpretations of Malthus 346
THOMAS K. RYMES

19 Theory, application and the canon: the case of Mill and Jevons SANDRA PEART	356
20 Canons in the history of economic thought ALESSANDRO RONCAGLIA	378
21 Claiming and reclaiming the past: the legitimizing role of the precursor concept JOHN K. WHITAKER	386
22 Economic texts as apocrypha DAVID M. LEVY	400
23 Women in the canon of economics ROBERT W. DIMAND	451
24 The canon in economics WARREN J. SAMUELS	482
Appendix	500
Index	512

Figures and table

Figures

3.1	Distribution of product in each sector	30
3.2	Interdependence of food and luxury production in population equilibrium	36
3.3	The Adam Smith modification	39
3.4	The canonical classical model in relation to the un-canonical, pre-classical model	41
4.1	Secure regime	52
4.2	Insecure regime	52
4.3	From insecurity to security	53

Table

5.1	Security and institutional factors in *The Wealth of Nations*	67

Contributors

Richard Arena is Professor of Economics at the University of Nice-Sophia Antipolis (France). He is also the director of a national research network in history of economic thought (GDR CNRS "Histoire de la pensée et méthodologie économiques"). He is a member of the Executive Committee of the French Society of History of Economic Thought (Association Charles Gide), the Vice President of ESHET (European Society for History of Economic Thought), and a member of the editorial boards of *History of Economic Ideas*, the *Journal of the History of Economic Thought*, the *Cahiers d'Economie Politique*, *Metroeconomica* and *Revue d'Economie Industrielle*. He has edited various books (including *Etudes d'économie classique et néo-ricardienne*, *Keynes aujourd'hui*) and has published many articles in a variety of journals.

William J. Baumol received his BSS at the College of the City of New York in 1942 and his Ph.D. at the University of London in 1949. His honors and awards include nine honorary degrees, presidency of the American Economic Association, two other professional societies and membership in the National Academy of Sciences. He has served on many boards and committees. He is Professor of Economics and Director of the C. V. Starr Center for Applied Economics at New York University and Professor Emeritus at Princeton University. Dr Baumol is the author of numerous books and over 500 articles published in professional journals. His most recent books include *Contestable Markets and the Theory of Industry Structure* (with R. D. Willig and J. C. Panzar, 1982, 1987), *Productivity and American Leadership: The Long View* (with S. A. Batey Blackman and E. N. Wolff, 1989), *Entrepreneurship, Management and the Structure of Payoffs* (1993), *Toward Competition in Local Telephony* (with J. Gregory Sidak, 1994) and *Transmission Pricing and Stranded Costs in the Electric Power Industry* (with J. Gregory Sidak, 1995).

Timothy Davis completed his Ph.D. in economics at the University of Toronto in 1998, under the supervision of Sam Hollander. For the thesis, he was subsequently awarded the 1999 Joseph Dorfman Prize by the History of Economics Society. At the time of this publication, Dr Davis is reading law at University College, Oxford.

Ghislain Deleplace is Professor of Economics at the University of Paris 8. He previously lectured in France at the Universities of Amiens and Orléans. He has been visiting professor in various countries, including the USA (New School for Social Research), Russia (State University of Moscow), China (Nankaï University, Tianjin), and Mexico (UAM, Mexico City). In English, he has co-authored *Private Money and Public Currencies* and co-edited *Money in Motion: The Post Keynesian and Circulation Approaches*. In addition to numerous papers in French, he is the author of *Histoire de la pensée économique: du "royaume agricole" de Quesnay au "monde à la Arrow-Debreu,"* and the editor of *Monnaie et étalon chez David Ricardo* and *Monnaie bancaire, étalon-or et change: les leçons des Classiques*.

Robert W. Dimand is Professor of Economics at Brock University, St. Catharines, Canada. A graduate of McGill and of Yale (Ph.D. 1983), his main research interests are the history of macroeconomics and monetary economics before 1939 (with emphasis on Irving Fisher), the history of game theory, and the history of women in economics.

Walter Eltis is an Emeritus Fellow of Exeter College, Oxford, and Visiting Professor of Economics in the University of Reading. He was Fellow and Tutor in Economics at Exeter College, Oxford from 1963 until 1986, and Visiting Professor in the University of Toronto in 1976–7, and in the European University, Florence, in 1979. He worked for the UK government from 1986 until 1995, as Economic Director and then Director General of the National Economic Development Office and subsequently as Chief Economic Adviser to the President of the Board of Trade. His books include *The Classical Theory of Economic Growth, Classical Economics, Public Expenditure and Growth*, and with Robert Bacon, *Britain's Economic Problem: Too Few Producers*. In 1997, with his wife, Shelagh M. Eltis, he published the first English language edition of Condillac's *Commerce and Government*.

Anthony Endres is Associate Professor of Economics at the University of Auckland, New Zealand. His current research interests include the treatment of institutions in classical economics, the development of Austrian economic thought, theoretical and empirical approaches to the study of entrepreneurial behavior in the market process, economic thought and policy in international organizations in the twentieth century, and the history of ideas on international monetary reform from the 1940s to the late 1970s.

Evelyn L. Forget is Professor of Economics in Community Health Services at the University of Manitoba. She serves on the editorial board of the *Journal of the History of Economic Thought*, and has published articles on classical economics in *History of Political Economy*, the *Journal of the History of Economic Thought*, the *European Journal of the History of Economic Thought*, the *Canadian Journal of Economics* and *Feminist Economics*. Her most recent book is *The Social Economics of Jean-Baptiste Say: Markets and Value* (1999).

Samuel Hollander is University Professor Emeritus at the University of Toronto and is currently affiliated with LATAPSES (University of Nice-Sophia Antipolis ICNRS), France, and Ben Gurion University of the Negev, Israel. He is a Fellow of the Royal Society of Canada, and Officer of the Order of Canada. He was recently granted an honorary Doctor of Laws degree by McMaster University, Hamilton Ontario.

Richard A. Kleer obtained his Ph.D. in Economic History from the University of Toronto in 1992. His early research concerned the relationship of British classical economics to Enlightenment philosophy. Presenty he is interested in the interconnections between politics and economic thought, institutions and policy, and is writing a book-length study of English finance during the Nine Years War (1689–97).

André Lapidus received his Ph.D. from the University of Paris in 1979. He is currently Professor of Economics at the University of Paris I (Panthéon-Sorbonne) and Chair of the *Centre d'Histoire de la Pensée Économique*. The author of many articles, his research interests include medieval economic thought and British traditions in the eighteenth and nineteenth centuries.

David M. Levy is Associate Professor of Economics at George Mason University. His book *How the Dismal Science Got its Name: Classical Economics and the Ur-Text of Racial Politics* will be published by the University of Michigan Press in 2001. His econometric research interests include the link between exploratory data analysis and non-normal error distribution and bias-seeking estimation procedures.

Laurence S. Moss is Professor of Economics at Babson College. An accomplished magician and past president of the History of Economics Society, he has published several books and many articles on classical and neoclassical economics. He is editor of the *American Journal of Economics and Sociology* and serves on the editorial board of *History of Political Economy* and the *Journal of the History of Economic Thought*.

Sandra Peart is Associate Professor of Economics at Baldwin-Wallace College. She has published *The Economics of William Stanley Jevons* (Routledge) and articles in *History of Political Economy*, the *Canadian Journal of Economics*, *The Manchester School*, the *Journal of the History of Economic Thought* and the *American Journal of Economics and Sociology* on the transition from classical to neoclassical economics. For the past two years, she has chaired the History of Economics Society's "Best Article Competition" committee.

Ingrid Peters-Fransen is a doctoral candidate in economics at the University of Toronto. She is currently teaching economics at the Canadian Mennonite University.

Pier Luigi Porta is Professor of Economics and Director of the Department of Political Economy at the new University of Milano-Bicocca, where he also teaches a course in the history of economic thought. He has been a visiting member of several Faculties and Colleges around the world and is on the board of *History of Economic Ideas* and *Risec*. He is also on the Council of the European Society for the History of Economic Thought. He has worked extensively on the Cambridge School and has edited several volumes of Sraffa's Ricardo in Italian. He is currently working on a new definition of the classical canon in political economy and on issues in the history of economic thought in Italy.

Alessandro Roncaglia graduated in Statistics from the University of Rome in 1969. He is presently Professor of Economics and Chairman of the Department of Economic Sciences at the University of Rome I, and a Member of the *Accademia Nazionale dei Lincei*. He is the editor of *Moneta e Credito* and *Banca Nazionale del Lavoro Quarterly Review*, and on the managing board of editors of the *Journal of Post Keynesian Economics*. His principal publications include *Sraffa and the Theory of Prices* (Wiley 1978), *Petty: The Origins of Political Economy* (Sharpe 1985), *The International Oil Market* (Macmillan 1985) and *Lineamenti di economia politica* (Laterza, 8th edn 1999).

Thomas K. Rymes is Distinguished Research Professor of Economics at Carleton University. He has published widely on the economics of J. M. Keynes, including *Keynes's Lectures, 1932–35: Notes of a Representative Student*.

Warren J. Samuels is Professor Emeritus at Michigan State University. He specializes in the history of economic thought, methodology, and the economic role of government. His principal current interests include the use of the concept of the invisible hand and the publication of selected archival materials. He is a past president and Distinguished Fellow of the History of Economics Society.

Nathalie Sigot is Professor at the University of Besançon, and a member of the *Centre d'Histoire de la Pensée Economique* (University of Paris 1). She earned her *Docteur en Sciences économiques* in 1995, from the University of Paris 1 (Panthéon-Sorbonne). She has published a number of articles on Jeremy Bentham and on classical economic thought, including "*Les principes d'un système monétaire sain selon Bentham*", in *Cahiers d'économie politique* (1998), and "A note on Hollander's 'Notes on a Possible Bentham Manuscript: a Mystery Unresolved'," in the *Cambridge Journal of Economics* (1999).

Masazumi Wakatabe is Assistant Professor at the School of Political Science and Economics, Waseda University, Japan. Samuel Hollander supervised his doctoral thesis on the economics of John Rae. His current research interests also include the history of knowledge-based growth theories and the economic analysis of institutions and entrepreneurship. His most recent publication is "The Creation of Wealth: John Rae's Knowledge-Based Growth Theory," in the *Journal of the History of Economic Thought* (1998).

A. M. C. Waterman is Professor of Economics in the University of Manitoba, Director of the Institute for the Humanities, and a Fellow of St John's College, Winnipeg. He was Reckitt Fellow in Christian Social Thought at the University of Sussex in 1979–80. Since then he has worked on the relation between economics and theology in normative social theory, including history of economic thought, and general intellectual history, 1688-1850. He has written many articles on Malthus and Malthus's immediate predecessors and successors, and his *Revolution, Economics and Religion* (Cambridge 1991) won the Forkosch Prize in 1992.

John K. Whitaker is currently Georgia Bankard Professor of Economics at the University of Virginia, whose faculty he joined in 1969. He was previously

Professor of Economic Theory at the University of Bristol. British by birth, he was an undergraduate at the University of Manchester and pursued graduate studies at the Johns Hopkins University and Cambridge University, obtaining a Ph.D. from the latter in 1962. His interests have focussed increasingly on the history of economic thought, particularly that of the period 1870–1930. He is best known for his work on the economist Alfred Marshall, whose early manuscripts and correspondence he has edited. He was president of the History of Economics Society for 1983–4.

Jeffrey T. Young is the A. Barton Hepburn Professor of Economics at St Lawrence University, New York State, USA, where he has taught since 1980. He received his Ph.D. in economics from the University of Colorado in 1975. He has taught at the University of Colorado in Denver, Marshall University, and St Lawrence University, and he has been a research visitor at the University of Newcastle, Australia. His research interests include the economics and moral philosophy of Adam Smith and David Hume as well as the key figures of the era of British classical economics. His publications include two books and journal articles that have appeared in respected international journals.

Acknowledgements

The chapters in the volume were selected from among papers presented at a conference held to honor Samuel Hollander. We gratefully acknowledge funding for the conference from the Social Sciences and Humanities Research Council of Canada, Routledge, the University of Toronto Press, the Provost's Office of the University of Toronto, the York University–University of Toronto History of Economic Thought Workshop, and the Departments of Economics at the University of Toronto, York University, the University of Manitoba and Baldwin-Wallace College. The conference would not have succeeded without the tireless efforts of Karolina Sygula, who undertook local arrangements with great energy and sensitivity. Jean Wilson's help in preparing the manuscript was indispensable. We especially thank all of the friends who helped to make the conference a joyous affair.

Evelyn L. Forget
Sandra Peart

1 Introduction

Evelyn L. Forget and Sandra Peart

We have chosen the "classical canon" as the theme of these essays, in order to organize our attempts to reclaim a group of writers – writers we refer to as "classical economists" – as vital components of the heritage of contemporary economics. If this reclamation is to be meaningful, rather than empty rhetoric, it requires an ongoing attempt to understand the ideas developed by classical economists, including those ideas upon which they agreed, the context in which the ideas were developed, and their points of dispute. Our purpose is not, therefore, to create exclusive definitions, or to encourage economists or historians of economic thought to embark on the "canon wars" that have infected other disciplines.

Strong feelings, however, are aroused by the notion of a "canon." The very definition is ambiguous, and disputes are generated by questions pertaining to the formation and evolution of a "canon." Therefore, we begin by setting out our definition. By "canon," we mean that essential set of ideas that characterizes an intellectual field, and that we can legitimately attribute to an identifiable group of writings. The "classical canon," we contend, consists of those ideas which are the defining characteristics of an approach to economics by the "classical economists," and which distinguish these works from others. Not surprisingly, given the ambiguity surrounding the notion of the "canon," these definitions beg a number of questions, some of which are addressed in the chapters that follow. What are the defining ideas of classical economics? How many of them must be shared by a work or an author to merit the label "classical"? Why are some works that share these ideas designated important, while others are not? Are these ideas exclusive to classical economics, or are they shared by later writers and writers from other traditions?

We address three related issues in this book. First, most of our contributors attempt to determine which ideas and concepts are vital to classical economics, and whether these ideas distinguish classical economics from other approaches to economic questions. That is, is there a relatively distinct group of ideas that characterize classical economics, and can we find a group of writers and works that embody these ideas? Second, we recognize that the canon is not a static concept, but is developed over time through sociological and intellectual processes that are not well understood. The story of classical economics emerges and is debated and honed through a process of canonization. Some of the chapters in this volume attempt to understand that process, and to determine why some writers and works are elevated to the canon, while others are not. David Levy takes this process one step further, by trying to understand how mistakes – ideas erroneously attributed to a writer – become embedded in the canonical representation of his work. Third, some of the chapters examine the consequences of the inevitable process of canonization. The creation of a canon not only creates canonical works, it also creates heretical works and ignored works. Who gets left out? Who gets ignored? Who founds or contributes to heterodox approaches?

This choice of theme is almost predetermined by the scope of Samuel Hollander's work. He has written massive treatises on every one of the major classical economists: *The Economics of Adam Smith* (1973), *The Economics of David Ricardo* (1979), *The Economics of John Stuart Mill* (1985), and *The Economics of Thomas Robert Malthus* (1997b). His textbook, *Classical Economics* (1987), and his collections of essays, *Ricardo – The New View* (1997a), *The Literature of Political Economy* (1998) and *John Stuart Mill on Economic Theory and Method* (2000) supplement a large number of journal articles. The underlying theme of all his work is the attempt to address our questions. Is it legitimate to speak of "classical economics" as though there were a shared core of ideas that distinguish these writers from others? What are the defining features of the economics of these classical writers, are these features universal to classical writers, and to what extent are they shared by later economists? In the process of answering these questions, he has developed a narrative of the development of economic thought that has occasioned significant interest and a good deal of controversy. If the ideas of classical writers are alive as long as we debate the content and significance of their writing, then Samuel Hollander certainly shares responsibility for their longevity. It seems appropriate, therefore, in a volume honoring Samuel Hollander, to ask ourselves what we mean by classical economics.

This exercise has reminded us vividly of the power that narrative wields in scientific discourse. Paul Samuelson's "On the Canonical Classical Model of Political Economy" (1978) is the most well known attempt to create a simplified narrative of classical economics. He attributes to Smith, Malthus, Ricardo and Mill a growth model incorporating a number of features: a population growth mechanism driven by real wages, a capital accumulation mechanism that ultimately results in a falling rate of profit, a secular growth path that culminates in a stationary state characterized by a socially-determined level of subsistence wages, zero population growth, no net capital accumulation and a zero rate of profit. When land scarcity is added to Marx's scheme, he ends up with the same model. Differences between writers are de-emphasized, and common features emphasized. The result is a simple and coherent story.

Samuel Hollander's essay "'Classical Economics': a reification wrapped in an anachronism?" takes pride of place in this collection, because in it he articulates those ideas he has developed over his career. He develops the analysis by outlining the characteristic features of a "representative" classical economist: a growth theory based upon land scarcity, an adherence to the inverse wage–profit relationship, a pricing model that integrates short and long-run considerations, and an analytical appreciation of a weak version of Say's law. Then he considers the degree to which particular classical writers adhered to this representative analysis, and the extent to which policy considerations reveal the model.

Hollander's narrative is clear: at the core of classical economics, he argues, is a market analysis based upon self-interest and contract. Like those writers who followed them and built upon their ideas, the great classical writers, Adam Smith, David Ricardo, T. R. Malthus and J. S. Mill, all recognized the centrality of price determination based upon demand and supply, or scarcity. All recognized, to a greater or lesser extent, the roles of price elasticity of demand and supply, and distinguished between short and long-run market adjustments. Hollander recognizes the importance of a shared growth model, as did Samuelson, although he attributes more significance to the differences between writers, and particularly the attenuation of Smith's recognition of land scarcity, than did Samuelson. Hollander claims that there is, nonetheless, a core of ideas that characterize classical economics. These ideas are shared, to a greater or lesser extent, by all those writers we generally label classical economists, and by Marx. Moreover, the centrality of microeconomic ideas of price determination in classical economics implies that later writers developed the ideas of classical writers. That is, the development of economics from the time of Adam Smith to the present is a story of continuity or, perhaps, development within a broader field of shared ideas.

This story is not one universally acclaimed by our contributors, although it is considered important by all of them. Anthony Waterman develops the idea, implicit in Hollander's work, that there is a fundamental schism in the development of political economy occurring around 1804. Adam Smith falls on one side of the divide, and Ricardo, Malthus and J. S. Mill on the other. The key difference between the two approaches, he argues, is the explicit recognition by the later classical writers of the implications of scarce land and natural resources for the "canonical" growth model. Nathalie Sigot examines Jeremy Bentham's writing to determine whether he can justly be considered a "classical" economist. Anthony Endres agrees that Samuelson's "canonical classical model" may be a more valid representation of Ricardo's ideas than of Smith's, but nonetheless asks to what extent that model can be made to reflect Smith's concerns. He relaxes the assumption of the given, stable institutional "state of nature" upon which Samuelson's model is constructed, specifically by considering the implications of imperfect capital markets. Masazumi Wakatabe relaxes another of the assumptions of Samuelson's canonical classical model, and asks whether the assumption of a given state of knowledge can legitimately be attributed to classical writers, and what the implications would be of recognizing the impact of learning on productivity.

Richard Kleer attempts to place *The Wealth of Nations* in an appropriate intellectual context, to "consider the conference theme at one remove: the canon not of key works in the history of economic thought, but of contemporary writings considered relevant for interpreting *The Wealth of Nations*." He argues that intellectual history would benefit from an attempt to understand the full range and depth of intellectual and policy issues to which authors were responding, rather than limiting our attention to those influences that we, with the hindsight of time, have determined to be of lasting significance. Rather than seeking a single "source" for ideas that, over time, have been labeled important, he challenges us to attempt to recreate the intellectual environment in which their ideas took shape.

Jeffrey Young and Ingrid Peters-Fransen both address the relationship between *The Theory of Moral Sentiments* and *The Wealth of Nations*. Young argues that economists have been badly served by the "canonical" Smith that emerges from our history of economic thought textbooks that focus on *The Wealth of Nations*. The purpose of *The Wealth of Nations*, Young argues, was to place economic science within the science of jurisprudence. Peters-Fransen presents a review of the vast literature on what is termed the "Adam Smith problem," that is, how are we to understand the relationship between Smith's two great books?

Walter Eltis and Richard Arena both address the question of whether there were distinct French and English traditions, and arrive at somewhat different answers for slightly different periods. Eltis argues that five key aspects of classical economics, first synthesized in *The Wealth of Nations*, were developed initially in France and communicated to Smith by the physiocratic writers with whom he made contact during his European tour. These central ideas are the importance of competition and free markets in a system that protects property rights, the notion that surplus is generated only by "productive" industries, that economic growth depends upon the reinvestment of that surplus, that there is a population mechanism that links growth to real wages, and that market prices will converge upon prices of production. That is, Eltis argues that there is continuity between the physiocratic writers and Adam Smith.

Richard Arena, examining a slightly later period, recognizes that nineteenth-century French liberal economists, beginning with Jean-Baptiste Say, developed an analysis quite distinct from that of the British classical school. The French preoccupation with a value theory based upon utility and with the role of the entrepreneur is well known. Arena points, however, to a further distinction of French liberal thought. Economic agents, according to Arena, are not treated as autonomous decision-making units driven solely by their own self-interest, but rather as socialized human beings embedded in society. He sees this difference as fundamental, and responsible for the persistence of a distinct French liberal school throughout the nineteenth century. In Arena's view, the shared regard for the market mechanism, which Eltis documents, is not sufficient to unite the two approaches.

It is with David Ricardo that the greatest controversy about the content of classical economics emerges. Did David Ricardo share the same model of price determination as Adam Smith and J. S. Mill, or was the relationship between market prices and prices of production fundamentally different in Ricardo's work? William Baumol contributes a fascinating chapter in which he questions the attribution to Marx and to Ricardo of any particular concern with the determination of the prices of individual commodities. Both, he claims, were addressing much larger questions. Pier Luigi Porta examines the significance of Piero Sraffa's magnificent edition of Ricardo's *Works and Correspondence*, the introduction (1951) of which led to a reading of David Ricardo quite different from that of Samuel Hollander.

André Lapidus and Nathalie Sigot reconsider the debate over the nature of Ricardian economics that raged during the 1970s, largely in response to

Hollander's work on Ricardo. Laurence Moss builds upon Samuel Hollander's reconstruction of Ricardo in order to uncover the significance of the inverse wage–profit relationship. That significance extends beyond the simple meaning of the inverse relationship. Instead, Moss locates the moment when "economic orthodoxy came of age" in the development of the wage–profit theorem.

Timothy Davis turns to Ricardo's macroeconomics, and considers the extent to which Say's Law characterized Ricardo's writing. He contends that, contrary to Keynes's assertion, Ricardo's analysis was more consistent with empirical evidence and more logically cogent than Malthus's argument. Ghislain Deleplace re-examines Ricardo's use of the quantity theory of money, and considers to what extent a heterodox component might be found in his writing. Thomas K. Rymes deconstructs Keynes's interpretation of Malthus in the light of Samuel Hollander's magisterial *The Economics of Thomas Robert Malthus*. He argues that the central assumptions of classical economics are the fixity of knowledge and natural agents (land), and considers the implications of relaxing the assumption of fixed knowledge. Rymes considers Keynes's true break with classical economics to be his introduction of uncertainty into the analysis, and concludes that Keynes's theory of effective demand is not present in Malthus, despite Keynes's claim to the contrary.

Sandra Peart turns her attention to a point of particular controversy, and examines the changes that took place in the classical canon between J. S. Mill and W. S. Jevons. She documents a narrowing of the boundaries of economic science attributable to Jevons's response to methodological challenges from the historical school. Jevons defended the substantially deductive method of Mill and called for increased subdivision within economics along the lines of subject matter and method. The consequence, she argues, is that theory, now believed to be universally applicable and invariant with respect to time and space, would be privileged over application and unwittingly insulated from challenges based on contrary evidence.

The last series of chapters examines the idea of canonicity more broadly, and reminds us of the essential ambiguity of the concept. Alessandro Roncaglia, Samuel Hollander's "best enemy," looks specifically at the debate over classical value theory, and asks to what extent Samuelson's canonical model is an adequate representation of classical economics.[1] He concludes that the idea of a canon is an interesting concept for historians of economic thought, but that it is essentially an ambiguous concept. In particular, he claims that it is possible to construct a "canonical" model that, unlike the narratives told by Samuelson and Hollander, demonstrates a sharp discontinuity between classical and marginalist approaches to economic theory. John Whitaker examines the use of "precursors" in economic debate, examining the various ways in which they are called upon by individual authors, by competing schools of thought, and by historians and methodologists of economics.

David Levy's essay considers the historical context in which the classical economists came to be considered "reactionaries." We became, he argues, the "dismal science" not, (as is still too commonly presumed) because of the assumption of fixed wages, but rather because of the role played by the classical economists in the abolition of slavery. Carlyle was the great defender of slavery, and the opposition he received from Harriet Martineau, J. S. Mill and others led him to apply the derogatory epithet to economics.

Robert Dimand develops the theme that the history of economic thought as the history of "great men" inevitably relegates many individuals to marginal status. This, he argues, accounts for the dearth of women in the canon. Women, he claims, are under-represented even when considered relative to their numbers in the population of contributing economists. Recovering the contributions of women economists will enrich the canon by reintroducing those themes that disproportionately attracted the attention of women economists, as well as by causing us to consider the role played by all past economists.

Finally, Warren Samuels examines canonical works and canonical interpretation in economics, and then considers the economics canon in a manner parallel to the general cultural or literary canon. How and why are certain ideas and certain works elevated to canonical status? How and why are some individuals remembered and associated with particular ideas, while others are forgotten?

Note

1 Roncaglia and Hollander, in the tradition of Malthus and Ricardo, have maintained a cordial and energetic debate about the reading of Ricardo for some two decades.

References

Hollander, S. (1973) *The Economics of Adam Smith*, Toronto: University of Toronto Press.
—— (1979) *The Economics of David Ricardo*, Toronto: University of Toronto Press.
—— (1985) *The Economics of John Stuart Mill*, Toronto: University of Toronto Press.
—— (1987) *Classical Economics*, London: Blackwell.
—— (1997a) *Ricardo – The New View. Collected Essays I*, London: Routledge.
—— (1997b) *The Economics of Thomas Robert Malthus*, Toronto: University of Toronto Press.
—— (1998) *The Literature of Political Economy. Collected Essays II*, London: Routledge.
—— (2000) *John Stuart Mill On Economic Theory and Method: Collected Essays III*, London: Routledge.
Samuelson, P. (1978) "On the Canonical Classical Model of Political Economy," *Journal of Economic Literature* 16: 1415–34.

2 "Classical economics"
A reification wrapped in an anachronism?

Samuel Hollander

Introduction

Classical economics is the economics to be found in Adam Smith's *The Wealth of Nations* ([first edition 1776] 1937), David Ricardo's *Principles of Political Economy* ([1817] 1951–73), Thomas Robert Malthus's *Principles* ([1820]) – and of course his *Essay on Population* ([1798]), and John Stuart Mill's *Principles of Political Economy* ([1848] 1965). Alternatively expressed, classical economics is orthodox British economics written during the century 1770 to 1870. Explicitly or implicitly, dozens of textbooks define "classical economics" in just this way, my own included. Of course I am being facetious. Though for some purposes I would wish to retain the brief "dictionary" sense of "classicism," to leave the matter there is to say everything and to say nothing. To extract a common core of doctrine from the massive tomes by Smith, Ricardo, Malthus and Mill proves in fact horrendously complex, a feature that might account for the intensity of the controversy engendered by some of my researches into the classics.

Let me start with a specific charge leveled against me a decade ago, that for some 2,200 pages I had been

> exploiting the term "classical" beyond acceptable limits, by reifying "Classical Political Economy", as though with its "classical method", and classical theories, it has some solid, independent existence apart from the variegated writings of an imprecisely defined group of writers. This reification is then wrapped in anachronism by attributing to "Classical Political Economy" ideas and definitions that were only formulated and widely used, much later, in the twentieth century.
>
> (Hutchison 1987: 121)

Those complaints appeared in a review of my book on *Mill*. I have since compounded the transgressions – if transgressions they are – by adding my *Malthus*, *Classical Economics* and *Ricardo – the New View*, thus raising the count to some 4,200 pages.

It is amusing to find the reviewer remarking only seven lines after his harsh strictures, oblivious to the self-contradiction involved: "It seems very difficult to deny that James Mill was a classical economist" (ibid.). But I accept the responsibility of dealing with his two charges, first that I have "reified" the term "classical economics," and second that I have imposed upon it a sense that could at best be meaningful only in the twentieth century. Quite simply, I deny that these charges are justified. The writing of separate volumes on each of the "classics" was forced on me by an early realization – some thirty years ago when I set out – that each of the major authors of the 1770–1870 period had to be considered in detail precisely in order to avoid "premature reification." As for the second complaint, I submit that my critic (like many others) has himself committed the sin of "sophisticated" anachronism (I owe the term to Paul Samuelson) by failing to recognize that many of what he believes to be concepts originating only in this century are merely restatements of much earlier formulations, albeit in different language.

I shall proceed by specifying what I believe to be the elements that constitute the "core" of classical doctrine, while at the same time keeping a close check on who amongst our authors maintains all, and who only maintains parts of the whole. In the course of this exercise I shall indicate the complexity that various contemporaries of the "classics," and even successors in the post-1870 period, who formally rejected the doctrine in whole or in part, prove from their texts to have been adherents. In the light of all this I shall raise the issue whether or not the classics can be referred to as a genuine "school." Finally, I allow for the policy dimension; for it distorts the perspective to focus solely on analytics.

I am, of course, aware of a variety of perspectives apart from my own: those preeminently of Marx, Sraffa (an offshoot of Marx), Jevons, and Keynes.[1] I submit however that these are either illegitimate – one's definition must have strong textual justification – or so narrow as to be distorting. My perspective on the classics is built up carefully from the texts and certainly cannot be charged with narrowness. Unfortunately, the time constraint obliges me to adopt more of an assertive tone than is ideally desirable, and to limit the coverage in various respects.[2]

The pure analytics

In considering the pure analytics of classicism I focus on growth, distribution and value theory, in effect the "real" dimension; and the theory of aggregate activity. These are, by and large, the issues that have most exercised protagonists in recent debate. Were I to widen the canvas and attend fully to monetary considerations it would be necessary to consider the great banking controversies and also allow conspicuously for the pre-Smithian contribution of David Hume, particularly the so-called specie flow mechanism. I imagine, to begin with, a representative classical author, "our author." Later on I attend to specific attributions. Where to start is somewhat arbitrary, considering the interdependencies involved in the fully-fledged renditions.

Elements of growth theory

The essence of our classicist's growth theory lies in its perception of the average real wage or, in the simplest models, the average corn wage, as a market-determined variable which, because of the land-scarcity constraint and in the absence of prudential population control (about which more when we come to policy), is subject (along with the profit (interest) rate) to downward secular pressure. The proximate cause of the falling real wage, it should be noted, is the deceleration in capital accumulation (and thus in aggregate labor demand) imposed by increasing land scarcity. The simultaneous decline in the returns to the variable factors, labor and capital, we shall call "the principle of the shared incidence of diminishing returns," referring to the falling marginal product of variable labor-cum-capital on fixed land. (Rent in this model is treated as a differential surplus, a position that implicitly assumes one-use land.) Whether or not the wage decline is steep or shallow, rapid or slow, the *essential* feature of the model is the necessarily simultaneous decline of the profit and wage rates. As for the celebrated "subsistence" wage, that rules in the stationary state alone – the end-point of the growth process – and is reached simultaneously with that profit rate corresponding to zero net capital accumulation.

How is it that if the corn wage is falling, the burden of diminishing returns cannot be entirely shifted on to labor, thus insulating the profit rate from decline? The explanation lies in the fact that the fall in the corn wage is *necessarily* smaller than that of the marginal product so that the wage share – proportionate wages – necessarily rises. And it is proportionate wages that govern the profit rate. This is an application of the inverse wage-profit relation.

The inverse wage–profit relation and the labor theory of value

I have spelled out the argument thus far in terms of corn, but our representative classical also translated into money values, and the inverse relation can be expressed in those terms. In the simple case where agricultural produce and money – let it be the manufactured commodity "gold" – are produced under the same technical conditions in the specific sense of the same factor intensities with respect to the ratios between "labor" and "capital" (or the *time* labor is invested), then a *labor* theory of value will be applicable, for in that case changes in the wage leave relative gold prices unaffected, since prices vary uniquely in proportion to labor embodiment; and if we further suppose the labor embodiment in gold to be constant while that in corn rises secularly with diminishing returns, then the gold value of a unit of corn rises precisely to reflect agricultural labor's reduced productivity. This in turn means that the gold value of the output of ten men's labor (or one man's labor or any unit of labor selected) is constant, the rise in the corn price compensating precisely for the fall in output. In brief, the money value of the output of a given unit of labor remains constant whatever the magnitude of the output might be.

Now in terms of such reasoning involving a "gold" measure of value – in effect a labor measure – our author restated the earlier proposition that the profit rate is inversely related to labor's proportionate share, and tends downwards during the course of growth despite the fall in the corn wage. For since the corn wage necessarily declines less steeply than the marginal product, the labor embodied in the corn basket paid to labor increases, an increase reflected in a higher *money* wage rate, money measuring labor embodied. But since the money value of the marginal output is constant, the residual (profits) is necessarily squeezed. In brief, in terms of labor-measuring "gold," the money wage reflects both labor embodied in the wage basket *and* proportionate wages. Notice that if we select as our minimum labor unit a day's work, we may restate the inverse wage–profit theorem thus: "the profit rate varies inversely with the fraction of the workday devoted to producing the laborer's own consumption goods," a familiar Marxian theorem.

The status of the labor theory I have outlined is to provide the simplest possible exposition of the inverse wage–profit relation in *value* rather than *physical* or *corn* terms. Our classical writer was much preoccupied with this issue, but was sensible enough to realize that everything could not be allowed to hinge on the satisfaction of the strong conditions required to obtain the results given above. For there were severe measurement problems, not least that commodities are not all produced by the same factor intensities. Yet notwithstanding, he stood by the inverse wage–profit relation, defending his position that the profit rate turns on the proportionate shares quite generally – assuming, that is, actual as distinct from "ideal" money, even assuming *fiat* rather than *commodity* money – and basing himself on the assurance of a constant general level of prices in the face of changing money wages, that is on a version of the quantity theory.

Cost-price and demand and supply analysis

The third element involves the theory of commodity pricing, and has been silently alluded to already in discussing labor values. For the labor theory is nothing more than a theory of long-run equilibrium price – cost price – under the special conditions of uniform factor intensities, as I shall explain.

"Cost of production" or "natural price" includes profits as well as wages each at its average or ordinary rate. Under conditions of uniform factor proportions, a state of general equilibrium such that prices reflect costs throughout the system, will be one satisfying both profit-rate uniformity and proportionality of price to *labor* inputs. More accurately, under the stated circumstances, uniformity of profit rates requires that proportionality. And it is the possibility of capital (and labor) movement between uses, or commodity-supply adjustment, which assures the tendency to cost price and proportionality to labor input.

In circumstances of *differential* factor ratios, the same assumption of factor mobility dictates a divergence of cost prices from labor inputs. However the entire notion of cost price presumes factors that have alternative uses; and whether or not costs are proportional to labor inputs, only those returns that reflect alternative opportunities are allowed for in costs. Embodiment of labor, or the pain cost attached to labor and abstinence, are of no relevance in price determination though they are in aggregative growth theory.

The principle of profit-rate equalization which provides the key to the analysis of resource allocation turns on standard demand–supply analysis. Since it is in response to profit-rate inequalities that capital transfers from one employment to another, an economy-wide change in labor productivity, or any other disturbance impinging equally on all commodities, has no differential effects on profitability at the initial long-run cost prices and therefore generates no changes in supply, leaving those prices unchanged. By contrast, a disturbance limited to a single industry, such as a change in input coefficients or a specific tax or subsidy, raises or lowers the industry return on capital and so will generate an increase or decrease in industry output and consequent alteration in price, to re-establish the original return in that industry. Applications of the distinction in question extend far and wide, one of the most important bearing upon the fundamental nature of trade. For a "cause" that raises the cost price of one or even a few manufactured commodities, would check their exportation; but if the same cause operates generally on all, the effect is merely nominal, and neither interferes with their relative cost values, nor in any degree diminishes the motive to trade.

Now the principle that cost prices reflect the absence of preferable alternative opportunities also provides the rationale for the *inverse wage–profit relation*. In the event of uniform factor proportions no price changes will occur when the general wage is raised; and since prices do not vary at all, general profits must be affected inversely. In the case of differential factor proportions between industries, the impact of a general wage increase is more substantial. At the initial prices the profit rate must decline across the board; but the decline will be sharper in "labor-intensive" than in "capital-intensive" industries and accordingly, consistent with the analysis of economic process just outlined, reallocation of resources between sectors will be set in motion in response to the disturbed structure of returns on capital. In the new equilibrium the prices of commodities produced by labor-intensive processes will have risen relative to those produced by capital-intensive processes – outputs contracting in the first category and expanding in the second – and the profit rate will again be equalized everywhere but at a lower level than in the initial equilibrium.

Two further details on allocation theory may conveniently be added here to our earlier discussion of the growth process. First, the downward pressure on the wage to which we there referred is motored proximately by the decelerating capital accumulation – and thus growth rate of aggregate labor demand – imposed by the land-scarcity constraint. Now labor-demand conditions turn, more specifically, not on total capital but on the so-called "circulating" as distinct from "fixed" component of capital. Thus they vary with technological change that plays on capital composition and also – and this is the point at issue now – by changes in the *pattern* of demand for final goods, in the event of non-uniform factor intensities in the affected industries. Final expenditure patterns matter for distribution. Conversely, changes in distribution can play upon final demand patterns. There is, in brief, a mutual relationship between distribution and pricing which complicates the simple growth pattern. Second, it should be noted that the margin of cultivation itself is an endogenous variable, with the long-run cost price of corn subject to the mutual conditioning of demand as well as supply, and satisfying the market-clearing requirement.

There is also a further extension. The logic of allocation economics emerges strikingly in the analysis of international trade where the assumption of factor mobility is abandoned. I refer to the celebrated theory of comparative advantage.

The "law of markets"

The notion that the money value of commodities supplied is identically equal to the money value of commodities demanded has been referred to as "Say's identity," and the very different notion that the two are equal only in conditions of equilibrium as "Say's equality," after the French economist J-B. Say (1767–1832). The former version may be interpreted to imply that money *per se* has no utility to recipients who, having no reason to hold it in the form of cash balances, attempt to disburse it immediately for goods. Under these conditions prices will be driven up to infinity given any positive money supply, which in fact implies the absence of money stocks, that is, a barter system wherein the price level has no relevance. This version of the law of markets is inconsistent with the "quantity theory," which implies a determinate level of prices for every given money supply.

The weaker version of the law of markets – it is the version to which our classicist adhered – avoids this inconsistency.[3] In *equilibrium* no attempt is made to add to money balances out of sales proceeds, but there may be temporary deviations of aggregate demand and supply. On this second view, a doubling of both the money supply and the price level will leave relative prices unchanged. Relative prices thus appear to be determined solely in the "real" sector of the economy, while the level of prices depends on the supply of money. In fact substitution of money for commodities and substitution between commodities occur in any transition between equilibrium states as just described; relative prices – and the interest rate – may well be affected (temporarily) by changes originating in the money market. On this second view too, while temporary deviations of aggregate demand and supply are recognized, there is nothing in the secular course of expansion to bring about such deviation. The only cause for profit-rate decline in the course of growth is the rising cost of wage goods as explained earlier; in the absence of such increase – reflecting increasing land scarcity – the system could expand without check.

Adherents to "classicism"

I have spoken thus far of a "representative" classical position. Let me come clean: I intended all along David Ricardo. The first three of the foregoing propositions will be found conspicuously in his works, usually in the mature *Principles* (Ricardo 1951–73), but confirmed in his correspondence and other informal contexts. There is though one qualification: the allocative rationale for the inverse wage–profit relation is implied by Ricardian logic but not spelled out by Ricardo; it is, however, explicitly formulated by J. R. McCulloch, Ricardo's "student" (Hollander 2000a). Ricardo's acceptance of Say's equality – though not the "real balance" rationale, for that is a post-classical rationale – is clear from various applications and policy recommendations.

Smith, Mill and Malthus, as we said at the outset, are all conventionally classed as "classical economists." Did they in fact though all maintain the full set of Ricardian propositions? We shall try to be very specific on this matter. Moreover, were there other – possibly unwitting – adherents? What can we also infer, in the light of this discussion, about the validity or usefulness of the term "classical school"?

Professor Samuelson (1978) finds in *The Wealth of Nations* a full-fledged "canonical," land-based, growth model. I accept that there are elements of the model in Smith's text: appreciation of increasing-cost industries and of differential rent, though not in the analysis of corn pricing; the impact of land-scarcity conditions in depressing the general profit rate to a minimum, though interspersed with the notion of increasing "competition of capitals" during the course of growth reflecting upward pressure on wages and downward pressure on final prices; in the context of economic development, the prediction of a fall in the agricultural relative to the manufacturing profit rate, as population growth generates increasing land-scarcity and a consequent rise in rents and fall in wages; and a downward wage path implicit in the notion of a minimum wage at which population growth ceases, that is, in the recognition of a stationary-state wage. However the growth analysis is incomplete: while high wages and high profits are said to characterize early states not yet subject to land-scarcity constraints – such as new colonies – the rationale for the downward course of wages in a deceleration of accumulation imposed by increasing land scarcity is not spelled out. Nor did Smith ask why, given scope for a decline in the real wage, there should be a necessary reduction in the profit rate, and thus did not reach the Ricardian position that the inverse wage–profit relation holds good in terms of proportionate shares, the falling secular wage entailing a necessary rise in labor's share in the declining "marginal" product. (There is also a celebrated but uncoordinated "increasing-returns" component of Smith's economics which treats innovation as an endogenous variable.) The growth model, it may be allowed, was "in the air" when Ricardo came on the scene, in so far as several of its elements are to be found in the *The Wealth of Nations*, but there is no fully-fledged Smithian version. Important too is the fact that the main contributors to the corn-law pamphlet literature of February 1815 (Ricardo, Malthus, Sir Edward West, Robert Torrens) did not find in Smith the principle of diminishing returns.

As mentioned, Smith lacked the inverse wage–profit relation as a proposition relating to proportions. This is *a fortiori* the case in a monetary system, since he maintained that any increase in the money wage can be passed on either to landlords or to consumers, in sharp contrast to the Ricardian position. Ricardo himself thought of his own analysis in these respects as making novel contributions to the science.

I turn to the law of markets issue. The famous Smithian doctrine of savings, which eulogized capital accumulation – Smith in one usage refers to labor in the capital-goods sector as "productive" labor – and maintained that the process of savings entails no leakages from the income stream, implies that no attempt is made to add to money balances from sales proceeds. Yet Smith did not explicitly formulate the proposition that there can (given tolerable security) be no general excess supply of commodities: the counterpart of the absence of net hoarding. Most significantly, we have referred to his increasing "competition of capitals" concept which implies a constraint on secular expansion wholly independent of increasing land scarcity thus reflecting a failure of markets to expand in proportion with aggregate output.

So, Smith in 1776 had not read Ricardo's *Principles* of 1817, but Ricardo certainly had studied Smith. What then did he take from the *The Wealth of Nations*? I would say primarily the general principle of cost price, or the analysis of pricing in the context of general equilibrium in the sense outlined earlier, whereby in equilibrium there are no further gains to be made by reallocation of resources between sectors; and also the relation between market-clearing short- and long-run prices which provides the process assuring a tendency to equilibrium. There is this difference, however: Smith included rent within cost price on grounds of multi-use land, and he undertook much of his allocative analysis in a developmental context involving an open economy subject to variations in factor proportions over time. On the other hand, there is the novel "Ricardian" application of price theory to the effect of a wage increase on relative prices in the case of non-uniform factor ratios. Standard partial-equilibrium analysis – the demand–supply analysis applied to a single industry – would be inappropriate for the analysis of the foregoing disturbance; for in the new equilibrium, while some prices will indeed be higher than originally, others will be lower, supply conditions having deteriorated in the former case but actually improved in the latter, "improved" in a *relative* sense as is meaningful only within a general-equilibrium framework.

In one other respect in a related context Ricardo corrected Smith. For Smith had asserted of agriculture that it was the most productive sector, having in mind a return to land (rent) in addition to the returns to capital (profit or, rather, interest) and labor (wages) which characterize the manufacturing sector, an easy error to make, reflecting a degree of agricultural bias perhaps absorbed from the French physiocrats. Ricardo pointed out that the payment of rent to the third factor reflected not only productivity but scarcity conditions, so that, first, were agricultural land to increase in supply, rents would fall to the benefit of workers and capitalists; and second, were natural forces to become scarce in manufacturing, a rent would have to be paid their owners at the expense of wage and profit earners. The deemed advantage of agriculture was an optical illusion. Here too there was analytical advance in 1817.

I turn next to Malthus, Ricardo's exact contemporary, basing myself on my recent researches into this most complex of writers (Hollander 1997). It would be an error to believe that because they spoke and wrote to each other, indeed liked each other, they understood each other. For Malthus labored under the misconception – endemic in his time and ever since – that Ricardo failed to apply demand–supply analysis to long-run cost pricing, working with what has recently been termed a "one-legged" theory allowing solely for supply conditions. Certainly Malthus strived to show that "the great law of demand and supply is called into action to determine what Adam Smith calls natural prices, as well as what he calls market prices," that "cost of production itself only influences prices of these commodities as the payment of this cost is the necessary condition of their continued supply . . . to the extent of the effectual demand for them." (Malthus 1836: 70–1) But this was precisely Ricardo's position too. Nothing Ricardo could say caused him to abandon his misinterpretation, including Ricardo's repeated insistence, first, that growth of population, and therefore of demand, must precede extensions of agriculture (the matter of the endogenous margin); and second, most generally, that he was arguing for the *primacy* of supply, not for supply as the sole consideration in pricing. There is little then to justify designating Malthus as a "subjective value" theorist in any sense that would not also apply to Ricardo. Indeed, in some important respects Ricardo's allocative orientation is more striking that Malthus's. For, unlike Ricardo, Malthus excluded long-run corn pricing from treatment in terms of demand and supply on the grounds that the demand and supply schedules are *interdependent* in that special case – having in mind the corn–population relation – whereas regular pricing analysis requires their *independence*. Malthus laid claim to a typical and non-Ricardian concern with the "short run"; but the corn-pricing analysis – which reflects in part his "physiocratic" heritage – is there to haunt him. Also to be noted is Malthus's acceptance of the erroneous Smithian notion of the superior productivity of agriculture, against which Ricardo remonstrated.

We turn now to Malthus on growth theory, specifically the shared-incidence principle. Splendid formulations will be found both in the *Essay on Population* (Malthus; fifth edition, 1817) and in the *Principles of Political Economy* (Malthus 1820, 1836) with explanations of the constraint on the fall in the real (corn) wage relative to the marginal product such that labor's *proportionate* share rises, thus depressing the profit rate. The precise incidence of diminishing returns between labor and capital is said to be market determined – an allusion to competition in the labor market – in criticism of Ricardo, though that was precisely Ricardo's position. We have to live, as I said, with this very human complexity. At least Malthus paid warm tribute to Ricardo for the general inverse wage–profit relation while at the same time he insisted on his own measure-of-value device to obtain the same result.

Lord Robbins opined that Malthus's role in building up the system of classical thought is "a matter likely to arouse much more controversy than the answer to a similar question in the case of the other great classical economists," though Robbins had little doubt of a profound contribution as far as regards "the central traditions of the theory of value and distribution," including here the theory of population in a land-scarcity context (Robbins 1970: 86, 89). There is indeed much common ground in this domain once we silence the noise emanating from the misunderstandings between himself and Ricardo and the exaggerated representation of his own procedures as substantively (and methodologically) distinct. At the same time, I would not ignore the physiocratic-based or Smithian agricultural-surplus construct which complicates the picture.[4]

The problem of placing Malthus in the "classical fold" is most troublesome regarding aggregate equilibrium. To my mind this problem does not pertain to his various allowances for unemployment and excess capacity, notwithstanding the impressive quality of his analysis of the post-Napoleonic depression, since Ricardo did not rule out short-term excess supply. It is in the secular realm that any notion of a common "classical system" seems to break down, considering Malthus's concern – it has Smithian pedigree – with the possibility of non-sustainable growth unrelated to land scarcity. Yet even here there are considerations that somewhat narrow the gap. First, the extensions made by Malthus to Smith's "competition of capitals" relate most specifically to the industrial sector; the law of markets he still applied to corn. Second, the problem of non-sustainable growth for Malthus entailed a danger of excessive accumulation: excessive because financed from reduced consumption rather than from increased profits; in so far as accumulation *is* motivated by the profit rate, as Malthus (taking the long view) believed was the case in advanced economies, there normally would *not* occur non-sustainable accumulation. We shall have more to say on all this in our later discussion of policy.

A word next on John Stuart Mill. Mill was profoundly Ricardian in nearly all respects and frequently came to Ricardo's defense against misrepresentation and miscomprehension on the issues raised in "The Pure Analytics." There is however this surprising exception, that while Mill himself adopted the falling real wage characterizing the canonical growth model, he apparently was unaware of Ricardo's true position, attributing to Ricardo a constant-wage model, and thus sowing much confusion. A second qualification – more positive – is in order. The canonical growth mechanism was combined by Mill with a new cyclical perspective, for an endogenous trade cycle, with phases merging into one another in semi-automatic fashion, was better developed by him than by any earlier writer. These fluctuations were envisaged as an outcome of the falling rate of profit due to land scarcity, the downward tendency during a period of "quiescence" engendering speculative moods, there being fewer safe investment opportunities available; conversely, capital losses associated with the cycle play back on the profit rate itself. And there are also Mill's brilliant elaborations of demand and supply theory and its application to international trade supplementing the comparative cost principle.

A widening of scope

Up until the present day there is commonly found reference to a Jevonian revolutionary break away from "classicism" in the early 1870s, on the theory of value, though with allowance for Malthus as embryonic precursor. Thus Schumpeter denied that cost prices were understood by Ricardo as reflecting equilibrium between demand and supply, or market-clearing prices, and maintained that Malthus went even beyond Say, "nicely indicat[ing] the locus of cost of production, which 'only determines the prices of commodities, as the payment of it is the necessary condition of their supply' – a turn of phrase that points far ahead toward Jevonian teaching" (Schumpeter 1954: 602). Jevons (who made the famous complaint against Ricardo that he "shunted the car of Economic science on to a wrong line – a line . . . on which it was further urged towards confusion by his equally able and wrong-headed admirer, John Stuart Mill") himself wrote warmly of Malthus:

> There were Economists such as Malthus and Senior, who had a far better comprehension of the true doctrines (though not free from the Ricardian errors), but they were driven out of the field by the unity and influence of the Ricardo-Mill school.
>
> (Jevons 1879: li–lii)

This same misapprehension regarding Ricardo, that he rejected the demand–

supply explanation of long-run price and excluded a subjectivist dimension, will also be found in Malthus himself (as we have shown) and numerous contemporaries; in early neo-classical writers in addition to Jevons, including Walras and Wicksell; in the modern literature (Arrow, Hicks, Samuelson); and – most conspicuously perhaps – in the Sraffian or "Cambridge" literature, though for Sraffian writers the alleged rejection is a matter for applause, not for blame. In reality, Malthus and Ricardo were at one – following Adam Smith – in maintaining a "two-legged" theory of long-run price. And to this extent "classicism" never died out, but was absorbed into modern doctrine *via* Marshall's great synthesis.

Much the same picture of a complex intellectual tableau emerges in the context of classical growth theory.[5] First, while nearly all the expert economists in the period 1815–75 (in addition to Ricardo, Malthus and J. S. Mill I would list West, Torrens, James Mill, Bailey, McCulloch, Chalmers, Senior, and Cairnes) adhered to the shared-incidence principle, they were, with some important exceptions (McCulloch, Senior and Cairnes), often unaware of Ricardo's own position, attributing to him some version or other of constant-wage growth. In brief, Ricardo did not fulfil the role of leader equivalent to Quesnay in eighteenth-century France; and the classical doctrine was upheld by, so to speak, an *invisible school* whose members in many cases made a living by *attacking* Ricardo. This observation applies specifically to the shared-incidence feature of the growth process, because warm tribute was widely paid to Ricardo for his inverse wage–profit relation as a general proposition regarding proportions. There was, that is to say, almost universal recognition of Ricardo's inverse wage–profit relation *given* productivity (the wage–profit frontier), but wide neglect of his elucidations of inward displacements of the frontier with increasing land scarcity such as assure a contemporaneous decline in the returns to both variable factors.

Second, I believe Paul Samuelson is quite correct when he argues that the canonical model was subscribed to by the late nineteenth-century "neo-classicals" and by moderns, who "all tell essentially the same classical story." For Samuelson justly denies that classical political economy offers an "alternative-paradigm" in Thomas Kuhn's sense "to modern mainstream economics" (Samuelson 1978: 1430n, 1415).

The position of W. S. Jevons is particularly striking in this regard. Jevons attributed to the British writers a *constant* wage-growth model and implied that he himself saw merit in shared incidence:

> It is the accepted opinion of the present day, that the rate of interest tends to fall because the soil does not yield proportionate returns as its cultivation is pushed. But I must hold that this decrease in the proportionate returns would chiefly fall upon the wages of the labourer.
> (Jevons [1862] 1866: 287)

Similarly, in a lecture of 1875 he objected to the subsistence-wage growth concept attributed to Ricardo and Malthus on the grounds that "every enlargement of our resources only tends to land us in a larger . . . but more straightened population" (Jevons 1977: vol. 6: 60). Jevons had no inkling that the position he was forwarding was precisely that of the "classical" orthodoxy from whose grip he sought to escape.

In the light of the foregoing discussion, and having in mind that the moderate classical position on the law of markets was retained in the post-1870 decades, we are left with the following generalizations. It may be helpful for some purposes to refer to the century 1770–1870 as the century of (British) "classical" thought, its commencement marking a major breakaway from mercantilist attitudes (I hasten to add that Smith was not literally the first in the field), and its close marking the transition to formal mathematical method. We must however be prepared to allow the following qualifications regarding substantive content. First, the various contributions of 1815 and 1817 constitute together an important transition stage towards maturity, with conspicuous reference to the implications of land scarcity. Second, adherence to Ricardian growth principles was so extensive as to include writers often considered (and in some cases who considered themselves) to be non-Ricardian, even anti-Ricardian, thus casting some doubt on the validity of the term "classical school," since a school usually has a recognized principal. That those Ricardian principles remained on the books long after the so-called "close" of the classical period carries the same implication.

There is one other matter alluded to at the outset. My position on classical analysis is based on firm textual evidence; I have been engaged in "historical" not "rational reconstruction," avoiding the anachronistic importation of modern "ideas and definitions." In fact, even algebraic or geometric renditions do not necessarily conflict with historical reconstruction.

Policy and application

The classical theory of economic policy entails a general presumption in favor of the competitive market in a private-property environment as means to maximize (per capita) national income – and thus the wherewithal for consumption and accumulation (see note 2 and the Section regarding "An alternative conception of classical economics") – though a role for government was allowed in cases of divergences between private and social returns.[6] I would like briefly to illustrate from some price-theoretic applications made by Ricardo, since so many of those engaged in Ricardo debate seem wholly unaware of this dimension, identifying it more with Smith and Mill.

There is first to note Ricardo's "subjectivist" welfare orientation in his discussion of the benefits flowing from international trade, namely the increase in "the mass of commodities, and therefore the sum of enjoyments":

> It is quite as important to the happiness of mankind that our enjoyments should be increased by the better distribution of labour, by each country producing those commodities for which by its situation, its climate, and its other natural or artificial advantages, it is adapted, and by their exchanging them for the commodities of other countries, as that they should be augmented by a rise in the rate of profit.
>
> (Ricardo 1951–73, vol. 1: 132)

Classical economics 19

International specialization – by the "pursuit of individual advantage" – "distributes labour most effectively and most economically: while, by increasing the general mass of productions, it diffuses general benefit" (ibid.: 133–4).

Given this orientation, it is scarcely surprising to find Ricardo insisting that corn-law abolition would entail much more than a mere transfer of wealth away from landlords; there would be assured a net social gain deriving from improved efficiency of resource allocation:

> The sole effect of high duties on the importation either of manufactures or of corn, or of a bounty on their exportation, is to divert a portion of capital to an employment, which it would not naturally seek. It causes a pernicious distribution of the general funds of the society – it bribes a manufacturer to commence or continue in a comparatively less profitable employment. It is the worst species of taxation, for it does not give to the foreign country all that it takes away from the home country, the balance of loss being made up by the less advantageous distribution of the general capital.
> (Ricardo 1951–73, vol. 4: 314)

The same logic underlies Ricardo's proposal for a countervailing duty on corn envisaged as an instance of legitimate intervention, the duty compensating for the differential burden on domestic agriculture imposed by the system of tithes:

> It must not be supposed . . . that . . . the importation of corn should be at all times allowed without the payment of any duty whatever. . . . [W]ith a view to the real interest of the consumer, in which the interests of the whole community are, and ever must be, included, whenever any peculiar tax falls on the produce of any one commodity, from the effects of which all other producers are exempted, a countervailing duty to that amount, but no more, should on every just principle be imposed on the importation of such commodity; and further, that a drawback should be allowed, to the same amount also on the exportation of the like commodity.
> (Ricardo 1951–73, vol. 4: 243)

By this means, runs the argument – again notice the consumer-directed orientation – "[t]he course of trade would be left precisely on the same footing as if we were wholly an untaxed country, and every person was at liberty to employ his capital and skill in the way he should think most beneficial to himself" (ibid.: 244).[7]

Policy considerations relating to the theory of growth are our next concern. I have made much in the discussions of classical analysis of diminishing agricultural returns as source of an increase in *proportionate* wages (wages as a share of the marginal product), and thus a fall in the profit rate, notwithstanding a secular decline in the real wage. Here I must emphasize that our major contributors – Ricardo, Malthus and John Stuart Mill – made no literal *prediction* of falling real wages such as is sometimes ascribed to them. To the contrary: the *raison d'être* of their analysis was to encourage the creation and development of institutional arrangements likely to assure against deterioration of standards, by altering labor-supply conditions in favor of prudential population control. Such efforts would, they fully realized, bring about a sharper rise in labor's proportionate share in the marginal product, and thus a sharper fall in the profit rate than in the absence of prudential population control and hasten the arrival of the stationary state; but it would be a tolerably comfortable state for the masses. Malthus, moreover, had most interesting things to say regarding the *endogenization* of population control. The classics, in brief, utilized their engine of analysis to indicate what might happen under alternative assumptions and what should, ideally, happen. Their models were *classificatory* devices used in the interest of social reform, not *predictive* devices.

Moreover, even the sharper fall in the profit rate that would result from successful population control might be avoided by the intervention of technical change. All the main contributors were aware of this fact, which in no way undermined the relevance of their model, as has been charged by some modern commentators blinded by the pseudo-scientific notion that literal historic prediction is the be-all and end-all of science. For whatever the pattern and rate of technical progress, living standards would be higher with, than without, population control.

Also to be emphasized here are striking new applications by John Stuart Mill of the Ricardian doctrine, which indicates its liveliness independently of the land-scarcity issue. Ricardo's was no "degenerating research programme." I shall give two examples: first, Mill's application of the inverse wage–profit theorem to the question of the responsibility of the emerging labor unions for price inflation; for in Ricardian theory any general wage increase has an impact on profits rather than on the general level of prices. Second are the implications drawn by Mill from his linkage of trend and cycle, particularly the potential for state investment in social amenity. Ricardian doctrine was alive and well at the time of Mill's death. It is regrettable that some of the economists of the 1870s sought to bury it along with Mill himself.

I wish to bring this part of my discussion to a close by reverting to Lord Robbins's observation that Malthus's place in the classical school is not easy to define. Regarding the theory of aggregate equilibrium this is so; and Robbins had this theme in mind largely. But the problem is less severe regarding monetary and fiscal policy, for it has been well remarked that so "classical" does Malthus appear at times in the *Principles* that he "is not so much an underconsumptionist as a supply sider" (Negishi 1989: 138–9). He refused to countenance government interference with the savings rate, viewing the profit motive as sacrosanct, the social index of the appropriate savings rate; similarly, he relied on "the interest of individual capitalists" with respect to the rate of adoption of machinery. Though he opposed debt repayment and the encouragement of increased saving during depression, his Friedmanesque "conservatism" regarding the gold standard, fear of inflation – he warned that inflationary note issues might ultimately end in depression once "failure of confidence" sets in – and muted perspective on counter-cyclical monetary policy can all be documented. The practical implications of his position are thus surprisingly "orthodox." Indeed, by his staunch defense of the gold standard he contributed to that near unanimity of opinion on policy that has been well described as "one of the most remarkable facets of nineteenth-century economic doctrine" (Laidler 1972: 169). Still we must not lose our balance. Ricardo, after all, stated his own clear preference to devaluation over severe deflation in making his case for a Return to Gold, which fact – had it been common knowledge – might have strengthened Keynes's case against Churchill in the 1925 episode. There is even evidence of Ricardo's support for a degree of discretionary monetary intervention, albeit modest by our standards (Hollander 1987: 293–7; Davis 1998). The "orthodox" position on these matters was scarcely as irresponsible as it is so often made out to have been.

In addition to a concern with "sustainable growth" unrelated to land-scarcity considerations, which sets Malthus apart, there is also his celebrated support for the 1815 protective Corn Laws. Possibly the finest tribute to Ricardo is the fact that, in the end, Malthus abandoned agricultural protectionism and much of its theoretical physiocratic underpinning, accepting the Ricardian vision of Britain's future as a mixed economy fueled by the industrial sector. With this step a common "classical" position on general policy was profoundly enhanced.

An alternative conception of classical economics

Piero Sraffa (1898–1983) and his followers adhere to a kind of sequence analysis, whereby given technology and the structure of production (output levels), knowledge of the wage rate – given by sociological considerations exogenous to the economic system – suffice for the determination of the profit rate and the set of relative prices satisfying the condition that the profit rate is uniform across all sectors. (Alternatively, the profit rate may be known initially, in which case we can solve for wages and relative prices.) There is no relationship of mutuality between final prices and distribution, in that either the wage or profit rate is given to the economic system prior to pricing. In fact, on certain more restrictive assumptions, the wage–profit relation is settled entirely in "physical" terms. Most strikingly, the machinery of demand–supply analysis, including the negatively sloped demand curve, plays no role, and equilibrium prices need not satisfy the equation of supply and demand.[8]

This general perspective on sound economics is attributed by Cambridge historians to a "classical" school said to extend back to Sir William Petty, Richard Cantillon and François Quesnay. In some versions Adam Smith is included, but pride of place is indubitably accorded Ricardo and Marx with particular reference to their alleged adoption of the real wage as *datum* in the analysis of the allocation of the social surplus across sectors. I illustrate this version by citations from the dean of Cambridge historians, Maurice Dobb:

> The nature of [Marx's] approach required him to start from the postulation of a certain rate of exploitation or of surplus-value (or profit–wage ratio in Ricardo's terms); since this was *prior* to the formation of exchange-values or prices and was not derived from them. In other words, this needed to be expressed in terms of production, *before* bringing in circulation or exchange.
>
> (Dobb 1973: 148; cf. 118–19)

> In the system of determination envisaged by Ricardo, and *a fortiori* and more explicitly as envisaged by Marx, there was a crucial sense in which distribution was *prior* to exchange: namely, that price-relations or exchange-values could only be arrived at *after* the principle affecting distribution of the total product had been postulated. The determinants of distribution, as we have seen, were sited in conditions of production (Ricardo's conditions of production of wage-goods; Marx's "social relations of production", introduced from outside the market, or as it were from a socio-historical fundament to phenomena of exchange).
>
> (Dobb 1973: 169)

> What is particularly striking (some might say revolutionary) about the Sraffa system viewed as a whole is its rehabilitation of the Ricardo-Marx approach to problems of value and distribution from the side of production; with the consequential result that the relative prices are independent of the pattern of consumption and demand.
>
> (Dobb 1973: 257)

> The fact that the level of wages has to be independently postulated as a *datum* in this mode of price-determination ("regarded as consisting of specified necessities determined by physiological or social conditions which are independent of prices or the rate of profits" (Sraffa 1960: 33) means that we are back at the methodology and approach of the (truly) classical system. No attempt is made to derive a theory of distribution from *within* the circle of exchange; and in the abandonment of this attempt we witness a reversion to the pre-Jevonian order or pattern of determination: prices are derived from (or in part dependent upon) conditions of distribution rather than distribution being derived from the structure of prices treated as being in turn a resultant of demand.
>
> (Dobb 1973: 261)

As for nineteenth-century trends, the main line is therefore said to run from Ricardo directly to Marx to be picked up again only in our century by Sraffa, in whose system – rather, in a sub-set of that system – the profit rate is yielded as a *physical ratio independent of relative prices*. Sraffa himself claims that his famous monograph was written from the "standpoint . . . of the old classical economists from Adam Smith to Ricardo [which] has been submerged and forgotten since the advent of the 'marginal method'" Sraffa 1960: v).

Now I do not maintain that the Sraffa-Dobb viewpoint on Ricardo is a figment of a fertile imagination.[9] But the textual evidence for it will be found in a select number of chapters in the *Principles* where Ricardo engages in highly simplified illustrative exercises yielding the Marx-like formula for the profit rate noted earlier. This constrained view neglects the much broader body of evidence pointing to Ricardo's elaboration of market determination of wages and prices and their interdependence. Though a given wage permits (*ceteris paribus*) a "forecast" of the average profit rate independently of prices and thus entails the priority of distribution, the wage is *not* in fact a datum, but is determined in the labor market and played upon both by the growth rate of capital (partly motivated by the return on capital) and the pattern of final demand, the latter itself partly governed by the (variable) income distribution. The breakdown between wages and profits is, for Ricardo, a variable determined within the market economy. The Sraffian view also sets at nought all of Ricardo's "allocative" applications to contemporary policy issues. Of course, Sraffa and the neo-Ricardians – and Marx for that matter – may have been inspired by the "truncated" Ricardo. There can be no objection to that. It is the view expressed of "what Ricardo really believed" – their alleged *historical* reconstructions – that troubles me.

There is a more specific consideration to note in this regard. Nothing that I have said disputes that the "classics", Ricardo included, were deeply concerned with matters relating to "surplus."[10] They focused particularly on the source of investible funds (and of tax capacity) in which context there was much discussion of the alternative savings patterns of the various classes. Indeed, that increased efficiency – via trade or technical change – expands the surplus available for accumulation and taxation, though not necessarily the profit rate, is a major theme for Ricardo. For example:

> Foreign trade . . . though highly beneficial to a country, as it increases the amount and variety of the objects on which revenue may be expended, and affords, by the abundance and cheapness of commodities, incentives to saving, and to the accumulation of capital, has no tendency to raise the profits of stock, unless the commodities imported be of that description on which the wages of labour are expended.
> (Ricardo 1951–73, vol. 1: 133)

> I have endeavoured to shew, that the ability to pay taxes, depends, not on the gross money value of the mass of commodities, nor on the net money value of the revenues of capitalists and landlords, but on the money value of each man's revenue, compared to the money value of the commodities which he usually consumes.
> (Ricardo 1951–73, vol. 1: 8)

Even the "source" of profits in surplus labor time is formally spelled out by John Stuart Mill (Mill [1857] 1965: 11, 411) and this before Marx, and is implicit in the Ricardian formula for the profit rate. At the same time, *pace* Marx, to isolate the source of profits (interest) in surplus labor time does not rule out the notion of interest as a necessary reward for saving such that "[t]he motive for accumulation will diminish with every diminution of profits" (Ricardo 1951–73, vol. 1: 111). Productivity conditions assure an excess over the output consumed by labor and are the basis for investment demand; while abstention from present consumption relates to capital-supply conditions. If however, as for Ricardo, the wage rate is a variable partly governed by capital-supply conditions, it follows that the "necessary" part of the work day is as much a consequence as a determinant of the "surplus" part. As Ricardo put the matter, there is a "natural equilibrium between profits and wages" (ibid.: 226).[11] Our classics inhabited a "Marshallian" not a "Marxian" universe.

Notes

This paper is printed with permission of the Center for Economic and Policy Education, Saint Vincent College, Latrobe, Penn.

1 The term, "classical," was used by Marx to cover a body of economics originating with Sir William Petty and concerned with "the real relations of production in bourgeois society, in contradistinction to vulgar economics, which deals with appearances only" (Marx [1867] 1965: 81n). See also Marx's representation of Petty as "the father of English political economy" (Marx [1859] 1970: 53).
2 For an illuminating account of "The French Foundations of the Classical Canon," see Eltis 1998. Eltis cites four fundamental propositions treated "comprehensively" in *The Wealth of Nations* but "originat[ing] previously in France":

> 1 Economies will function most efficiently where all markets are competitive, and where those who own property determine investment and production decisions. For these to be efficient, entrepreneurs must be confident that they will obtain the legal title to wealth they create.
> 2 Some economic activities are productive and have the potential to generate a net surplus. Others, and especially those organized by the state, are unproductive and can only be sustained from the surpluses of productive activities.
> 3 The growth of economies will depend on the reinvestment of surpluses from productive activities. If these are absorbed or more than absorbed by the unproductive, nothing will remain for investment, and a nation's output will stagnate or decline.
> 4 Population will expand indefinitely to match the demand for labor at a wage which maintains families at a standard of living where sufficient children survive.
>
> The classical school united to advocate free competition, the undiluted enforcement of capitalist property rights, the virtues of thrift over profligacy and the maintenance of low taxation and government expenditure.
>
> (Eltis, this volume: 185)

All this is acceptable, and implicitly taken for granted in my paper which focuses more on nineteenth-century British developments in analysis, but see "Policy and application," this chapter.
3 On this version, "supply creates its own demand" by means of changes in the price level. Thus, in the event of a reduction in the supply of money *ceteris paribus*, the resultant excess demand for money (and corresponding excess supply of commodities) will be corrected by way of a decline in the level of prices. The essence of the matter lies in the notion that the community wishes to hold a certain command over goods and services in the form of money balances; since the real value of any given stock varies with changes in general prices, the initial excess demand for money will be satisfied by a rise in the purchasing power of the (lower) money stock until a new equilibrium is achieved.
4 There is also evidence of a corn input-corn output approach to profit-rate determination in Malthus's post-1820 work. This matter is still, so to speak, *sub judice* (Hollander 2000b.)
5 I base these remarks on Hollander 1998.
6 It is also salutary in this day and age to remind free-marketeers of Adam Smith's championship of the contemporary usury laws, for a more striking instance of intervention than credit-market control can scarcely be envisaged (Hollander 1999).
7 The "efficiency" case is closely related to the question of surplus as source of savings.
8 See selections from Kurz and Salvadori 1998a, 1998b.
9 Here I base myself again on Hollander 2000a.

10 This dimension also figures large in the account given of eighteenth-century "foundations" in Eltis, chapter 10 this volume (note 2).
11 The context is taxation. The direct or the indirect effect of profit taxation is to reduce the rate of accumulation so that the burden is in fact shared between capital and labor:

> excepting in the immediate effects, I should think it of little importance whether the profits of stock, or the wages of labour, were taxed. By taxing the profits of stock, you would probably alter the rate at which the funds for the maintenance of labour increase, and wages would be disproportioned to the state of that fund, by being too high. By taxing wages, the reward paid to the labourer would also be disproportioned to the state of that fund, by being too low. In the one case by a fall, and in the other by a rise in money wages, the natural equilibrium between profits and wages would be restored.
> (Ricardo 1959–73, vol. 1: 226)

References

Davis, T. (1998) "David Ricardo's Macroeconomics: A Study in Historical Perspective," unpublished Ph.D. thesis, University of Toronto.
Dobb, M. (1973) *Theories of Value and Distribution since Adam Smith*, Cambridge: Cambridge University Press.
Hollander, S. (1987) *Classical Economics*, Toronto: University of Toronto Press.
—— (1997) *The Economics of Thomas Robert Malthus*, Toronto: University of Toronto Press.
—— (1998) "The Canonical Classical Growth Model: Content, Adherence and Priority", *Journal of the History of Economic Thought* 19 (Fall): 253–77.
—— (1999) "Jeremy Bentham and Adam Smith on the Usury Laws: A Smithian Reply to Bentham and a New Problem", *European Journal of the History of Economic Thought* 6(4) (Winter): 523–51.
—— (2000a) "Sraffa and the Interpretation of Ricardo: the Marxian Dimension," *History of Political Economy* 32(2): 1–46.
—— (2000b) "Malthus and the Corn Profit Model" and "Rejoinder to Professor Garegnani," in *Critical Essays on Piero Sraffa's Legacy in Economics*, ed. H. Kurz, Cambridge: Cambridge University Press.
Hutchison, T. W. (1987) Review (of S. Hollander, *Economics of John Stuart Mill*), *Journal of Economic Literature* 25(1): 120–2.
Jevons, W. S. [1862] (1866) "Brief Account of a General Mathematical Theory of Political Economy," *Journal of the Royal Statistical Society* 29(2): 282–7.
—— (1879) *Theory of Political Economy*, 2nd edn, London: Macmillan.
—— (1977) *Papers and Correspondence*, vol. 6: *Lectures on Political Economy 1875–1876*, ed. R. D. C. Black, London: Macmillan.
Kurz, H. D. and Salvadori, N. (1998a) *Understanding Classical Economics*, London: Routledge.
—— (1998b) *The Elgar Companion to Classical Economics*, 2 vols, Cheltenham: Elgar.
Laidler, D. (1972) "Thomas Tooke on Monetary Reform," in M. Peston and B. Corry (eds), *Essays in Honour of Lord Robbins*, London: Weidenfeld and Nicolson, 168–86.
Malthus, T. R. (1798) *An Essay on the Principle of Population*, 1st edn, London: J. Johnson.
—— (1817) *An Essay on the Principle of Population*, 5th edn, London: John Murray.
—— (1820) *Principles of Political Economy*, London: John Murray.
—— (1836) *Principles of Political Economy*, 2nd vol., London: William Pickering.
Marx, K. [1867] (1965) *Capital* vol. 1, Moscow: Progress.
—— [1859] (1970) *A Contribution to the Critique of Political Economy*, Moscow: Progress.

Mill, J. S. (1965) *Principles of Political Economy*, in *Collected Works*, vols 2 and 3, Toronto: University of Toronto Press.
Negishi, T. (1989) *History of Economic Theory*, Amsterdam: North Holland.
Ricardo, D. (1951–73) *Principles of Political Economy*, vol. 1 of *Works and Correspondence*, ed. P. Sraffa with M. H. Dobb, Cambridge: Cambridge University Press.
Robbins, L. C. (1970) *The Evolution of Modern Economic Theory*, London: Macmillan.
Samuelson, P. A. (1978) "The Canonical Classical Model of Political Economy," *Journal of Economic Literature* 16(4): 1415–34.
Schumpeter, J. A. (1954) *History of Economic Analysis*, New York: Oxford University Press.
Smith, A. [1776] (1937) *The Wealth of Nations*, ed. E. Cannan, New York: Modern Library.
Sraffa, P. (1960) *The Production of Commodities by Means of Commodities*, Cambridge: Cambridge University Press.

3 Notes towards an un-canonical pre-classical model of political oeconomy

A. M. C. Waterman

In the cultural history of our discipline, the great divide occurs in the first decade of the nineteenth-century. Before 1798 "economic thought" – and the nascent science of "political oeconomy" itself – is wholly compatible with, indeed almost a part of, Christian theology (Waterman 1998). After 1804 or thereabouts, political economy is hated and feared as "hostile to religion," and there suddenly appears what Donald Winch has lately described as "the schism, or fault-line, separating economists from the self-appointed spokesmen for human beings" (Winch 1996: 6, 402, 418).

Adam Smith lived and died on one side of this "fault-line"; Malthus, Ricardo, and J. S. Mill on the other. In a conference assembled to honor Samuel Hollander for his many distinguished contributions to the history of economic thought and in particular for his Herculean "Studies in Classical Political Economy," it seems appropriate to consider his work as a whole. Is Hollander's first volume the beginning of a series; or is it rather the prolegomenon to a significantly different enterprise that begins with the story of Malthus?

According to Paul Samuelson a single "canonical classical model of political economy" can be constructed which captures the most prominent analytical concerns of "Adam Smith, David Ricardo, Thomas Robert Malthus, and John Stuart Mill." "When the limitation of land and natural resources is added to the model of Karl Marx," he too "ends up with" the same theoretical scheme (Samuelson 1978: 1415). A one-sector, agricultural model with fixed land and diminishing returns to the variable "labor-*cum*-capital" variable input generates the "Ricardian" theory of rent, the (non-Marxian) falling rate of profit and the classical growth model leading to the stationary state.

In my opinion this is a powerful and fruitful reduction of Malthus, Ricardo and Mill. But a large historical question – one immediately raised by Hollander (1980) himself – is just how well it describes the analytical programme of *The Wealth of Nations* (*WN*) as a whole. Recognition of diminishing returns may be discovered in Smith's text as Hollander acknowledged. But Smith's immediate successors were quite unaware of it, believing they had discovered this key concept themselves. And so did everyone else at that time. The reason why a great gulf between economists and human beings opened up some time after 1800 is because of the theological "problem of evil" created by the dominance of scarcity in human affairs. That problem was stated for the first time in *An Essay on the Principle of Population* (Malthus 1798). As everyone – even Marx – agrees, the coherence (and cogency) of the *Essay* depends upon the implicit assumption of scarce land and diminishing returns. Before 1798 political oeconomy was a "chearful" and optimistic study of the nature and causes of the wealth of nations. After Southey's (1804) vitriolic review of the second *Essay*, it became a dismal science of scarcity and tragic choices. Before 1798, I wish to suggest, the chief constraint upon economic growth was supposed to be capital: after 1798 it was land, and whereas a capital constraint need only be temporary – for its cure is "parsimony" – there can be no lasting remedy for a land restraint.

It is therefore my purpose in this chapter to expose a bold conjecture to the ruthless refutation of other, better scholars. Broadly speaking – I shall postulate – most eighteenth-century authors before Malthus were chiefly concerned to investigate the development of a "market society" in which all production is demand-led, and in which a rural, agricultural sector, and an urban, manufacturing sector are mutually stimulating. If I am right, we might construct an "un-canonical", "pre-classical" model of political oeconomy which would capture all (or at any rate much) of what Mandeville, Hume, Cantillon, Quesnay, Steuart, Smith, Paley and others were attempting to analyze, and which differs sharply from the canonical classical model in treating land as a free good (to landlords though not to anyone else). Any such model is merely an observational instrument for viewing the economic literature of the past. In this chapter I shall describe my telescope and nothing more. Only if it survives the criticism of my colleagues may I later use it to behold the distant prospect of pre-Malthusian economic thought.

General characteristics of the model

Two sectors exist in an economy which may be closed or open: a rural, agricultural sector, A, and an urban, manufacturing sector, Q. Rural produce and urban manufactures are freely traded at competitive prices without transport costs or taxes. If the economy is open, A-sector goods are exported, Q-sector goods imported. Money is endogenous and is used in trade and for payment of wages, but plays no other part. Population, which is freely mobile between sectors, is always fully employed at the market-clearing real wage. Capital consists of one period's advance wages.

"Lords of the soil" employ a rural population N_A of "laborers" at an annual wage rate $w = (f + pq)$, measured in units of "the means of subsistence," conceived as a homogeneous "food." The component f is a *constant of nature* and is biologically determined by "the narrow capacity of the human stomach." The component q is measured in units of a homogeneous, manufactured "luxury" good and may vary. The price p is the rate of exchange between "food" and "luxuries" (discussed later). Lords employ some portion of N_A as a "productive" population/work-force N_a, to produce an annual output F of food, where $F = \alpha.N_a$. The technical parameter α may vary, and may be or become endogenous. All or part of the agricultural surplus $S = F - N_a w = (1 - w/\alpha)F$, is used by lords to employ the remainder of N_A in "unproductive" activity: services of various kinds, official, professional, artistic and menial.

Pre-classical model of political oeconomy 29

"Masters," who are the "owners of capital" in towns and cities, employ an urban population N_Q at the same, competitively determined wage rate, $w/p = (f/p + q)$, measured in units of the luxury good. Masters employ some portion of N_Q as a "productive" population/work-force N_q, to produce an annual output Q of luxuries, where $Q = \beta.N_q$. The technical parameter β may vary, may be an increasing function of scale, and may be or become endogenous. All or part of manufacturing profits, $P = Q - N_q w/p$, are used by masters to employ the remainder of N_Q in "unproductive" activity.

The food-price of luxuries, p, may be conceived *either* in terms of the labor theory of value, in which case $p = \alpha/\beta$; *or* as externally determined by international trade. In either case it can be treated as exogenous.

Lords and masters comprise a negligible proportion of total population, which is thus $N = N_A + N_Q = N_a + N_q + N_u$, where total unproductive population, $N_u = (N_A - N_a) + (N_Q - N_q)$. The food consumption of lords and masters may therefore be ignored. However there is no reason to assume that their consumption of luxuries is negligible.

At the end of any crop-year $(t-1)$ lords possess the total produce, F_{t-1}. They set aside a portion π_A of this to employ rural productive labor in period t, where the parameter π_A is the *degree of parsimony*. The remainder, $(1 - \pi_A)F_{t-1}$, may be spent in whole or in part on unproductive labor and – perhaps – in part on luxuries. Expenditure (measured in units of the F-good) by lords on luxuries in period t is thus $\lambda_A(1 - \pi_A)F_{t-1}$, and on unproductive labor is $(1-\lambda_A)(1 - \pi_A)F_{t-1}$, where the parameter λ_A is the *degree of luxury*. In the same manner, masters assign $\pi_Q.Q_{t-1}$ to the employment of urban productive labor in period t; and spend $\lambda_Q(1 - \pi_Q)Q_{t-1}$ on luxuries and $(1 - \lambda_Q)(1 - \pi_A)Q_{t-1}$ on unproductive labor. There is no reason to assume that the degrees of parsimony and luxury will be the same for lords as for masters.

The distribution of annual product in each sector is depicted in Figure 3.1.

Adjustment of output and population

Lords and masters determine production in response to "effectual demand." Demand for the output of each sector comes from lords and masters themselves (for investment in advance wages, and for luxury consumption), from the other sector, and – in the case of an open economy – from the rest of the world. Since $F_t = \alpha.N_a$, and since $N_a = \pi_A.F_{t-1}/w$, then current production is

$$F_t = (\alpha/w).\pi_A.F_{t-1} \tag{1}$$

and similarly

$$Q_t = (p\beta/w).\pi_Q.Q_{t-1} \tag{2}$$

When $\pi_A = w/\alpha$ and $\pi_Q = w/p\beta$, then $F_t = F_{t-1}$ and $Q_t = Q_{t-1}$, which is "simple reproduction," though not necessarily in steady state.

If demand changes, lords and masters must adjust supply in the current period by changing π appropriately. To meet an increase in demand for food

A-sector

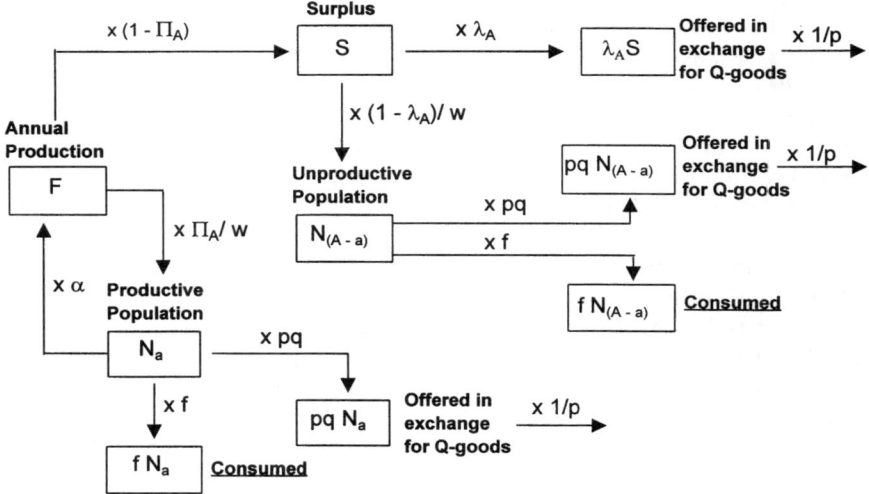

Q-sector

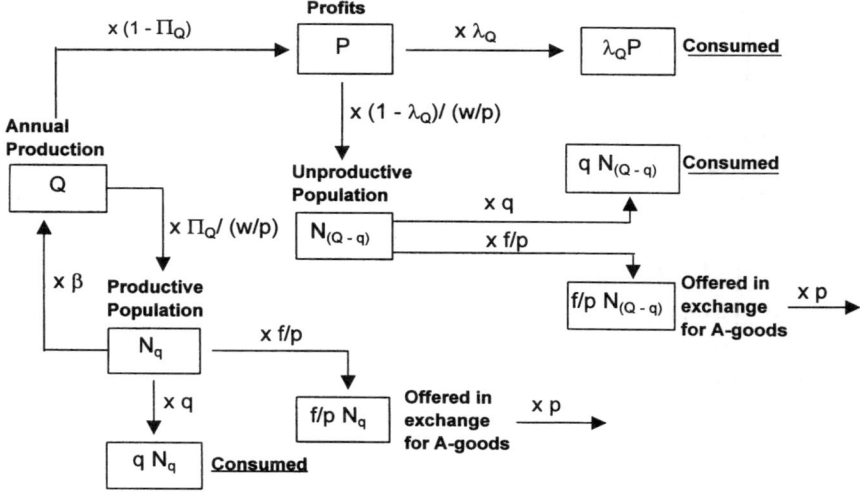

Figure 3.1 Distribution of product in each sector

for example, lords increase π_A, raising the proportion of last period's output devoted to employing productive labor. Current production increases, but current expenditure on unproductive labor and/or luxuries must decrease. Since the current wage-rate in the A sector must be the total portion of F_{t-1} assigned to employment divided by N_A, then

$$w_t = [1 - \pi_A(1 - \lambda_A)].F_{t-1}/N_A \tag{3}$$

and likewise, for the Q sector

$$w_t/p = [1 - \pi_Q(1 - \lambda_Q)].Q_{-1}/N_Q \qquad (4)$$

Since in the short period, when total population is given

$$N = N_A + N_Q \qquad (5)$$

(3), (4) and (5) form three simultaneous equations in w_t, N_A and N_Q. If π_A is increased in order to divert a larger proportion of the A-sector workforce into current production, F_t will increase by (1). But by (3), (4) and (5) w_t will also increase (though not by as much, proportionately, as π_A), and the A-sector will therefore gain population from the Q sector in order to equalize wages. Because growth of the A sector will increase demand for Q-goods, there will also be an induced increase in Q-sector output, in a manner to be analyzed in due course by means of the complete model.

If the wage-rate exceeds a socially-determined "subsistence" rate w^*, that is where $w > [w^* = (f + pq^*)]$, population will increase and vice versa. Thus for any value of the taste parameter q^* there exist unique, steady-state, simple-reproduction degrees of parsimony, $\pi_A^* = w^*/\alpha$ and $\pi_Q^* = w^*/p\beta$. If parsimony exceeds these values the resulting capital formation will raise both output and wages, and the latter will cause population to increase. Suppose therefore that there had been a once-for-all increase in demand for the F-sector, beginning from a position of steady-state simple reproduction. Initially $\pi_A > \pi_A^*$ causing output and wages to rise, and some population to move from the Q to the A sector. But total population would begin to grow in consequence of the wage-increase. As population grows with constant production at the new, higher level, wages begin to fall again. Now in order to keep production constant with a growing work-force employers must reduce the degree of parsimony. When $w = w^*$, $\pi_A = \pi_A^*$ and $\pi_Q = \pi_Q^*$, the process of adjustment is at an end. Population and production in each sector are higher, and the share of income assigned by lords and masters to unproductive labor and luxury consumption has returned to its original proportion.

It appears from this analysis that a model may be constructed of the "long-period" general equilibrium of A and Q sectors, when "long-period" is construed to mean, *when population is stationary at any particular w^**. Provided only that producers respond to once-for-all changes in demand in the manner outlined, the equilibrium degrees of parsimony, π_A^* and π_Q^*, are determined by the taste parameter q^* (the socially-determined component of the subsistence real wage devoted to the purchase of luxuries); and transitory, disequilibrium values of π may be ignored for purposes of comparative statics.

Construction of the two-sector model in population equilibrium

Demand for F-goods by the A sector alone, given that $F = \alpha.N_a$, may be conceived as the sum of S_0, the value of the agricultural surplus in a purely manorial (one-sector) economy – an "initial condition" or historical constant – and the wage-bill for productive labor:

$$F_A^D = S_0 + w^*N_a = S_0 + (w^*/\alpha).F \qquad (6)$$

Demand for F-goods by the Q sector is the food requirement of the total Q-sector population:

$$F_Q^D = fN_Q = fN_q + fN_{(Q-q)} \qquad (7)$$

In population equilibrium the unproductive Q-sector population, $N_{(Q-q)}$, must be equal to the Q-goods assigned to it, $(1 - \pi_Q^*)(1 - \lambda_Q).Q$ divided by the subsistence wage, w^*/p. Hence, given that $Q = \beta.N_q$,

$$F_Q^D = \{f/\beta + [fp(1 - \pi_Q^*)(1 - \lambda_Q)]/w^*\}.Q \qquad (8)$$

Let the net foreign demand for F-goods be X, then total demand for A-sector goods is

$$F^D = S_0 + (w^*/\alpha).F + f[1/\beta + (p/w^*)(1 - \pi_Q^*)(1 - \lambda_Q)].Q + X \qquad (9)$$

And at equilibrium of production, when $F = F^D$,

$$-a_1.F + a_2.Q = -(S_0 + X) \qquad (10)$$

where, when w^* is interpreted as $(f + pq^*)$ and π_Q^* as $(f + pq^*)/p\beta$, and when it is noted that $\alpha > w^*$ and $\beta > w^*/p$, $a_1 = [(\alpha - f - pq^*)/\alpha] > 0$, and $a_2 = \{[(f + pq^*)^{-1}.fp(1 - \lambda_Q)] + f\lambda_Q/\beta\} > 0$.

Demand for Q-goods by the A sector is the sum of the luxury-goods requirement of the A-sector population and the Q-goods value of the food that lords desire to exchange for luxury goods for their own consumption:

$$Q_A^D = q^*N_A + \lambda_A(1 - \pi_A^*).F/p \qquad (11)$$

Since by reasoning similar to that employed above in that case of N_Q above, it can be shown that $N_A = \{1/\alpha + [(1 - \pi_A^*)(1 - \lambda_A)]/w^*\}.F$, then

$$Q_A^D = [q^*/\alpha + (q^*/w^*)(1 - \pi_A^*)(1 - \lambda_A) + (\lambda_A/p)(1 - \pi_A^*)].F \qquad (12)$$

Demand for Q-goods by the Q sector is the sum of the luxury-goods requirement of the Q-sector population and the quantity of luxury goods that masters desire to consume themselves:

$$Q_Q^D = q^*N_Q + \lambda_Q(1 - \pi_Q^*).Q \qquad (13)$$

Given that $N_Q = [1/\beta + (p/w^*)(1 - \pi_Q^*)(1 - \lambda_Q)].Q$

$$Q_Q^D = [q^*/\beta + (pq^*/w^*)(1 - \pi_Q^*)(1 - \lambda_Q) + \lambda_Q(1 - \pi_Q^*)].Q \tag{14}$$

Thus from (12) for Q_A^D and (14) for Q_Q^D, total demand for Q-sector goods,

$$Q_D = [q^*/\alpha + (q^*/w^*)(1 - \pi_A^*)(1 - \lambda_A) + (\lambda_A/p)(1 - \pi_A^*)].F$$
$$+ [q^*/\beta + (pq^*/w^*)(1 - \pi_Q^*)(1 - \lambda_Q) + \lambda_Q(1 - \pi_Q^*)].Q \tag{15}$$

Let the import of Q-goods be M. Then at equilibrium of production, when $Q + M = Q^D$,

$$b_1 F - b_2 Q = M \tag{16}$$

where, when w^* is interpreted as $(f + pq^*)$, π_A^* as $(f + pq^*)/\alpha$ and π_Q^* as $(f + pq^*)/p\beta$, and when it is noted that $\alpha > w^*$ and $\beta > w^*/p$,

$b_1 = \{[p(f + pq^*)]^{-1}.(pq^* + f.\lambda_A)\} - (f.\lambda_A)/(\alpha p) > 0$, and

$b_2 = 1 - pq^*(1 - \lambda_Q)/(f + pq^*) - [1 - f/(p\beta)].\lambda_Q > 0$.

Equations (10) and (16) together produce the matrix equation

$$\begin{bmatrix} -a_1 & +a_2 \\ +b_1 & -b_2 \end{bmatrix} \bullet \begin{bmatrix} F \\ Q \end{bmatrix} = \begin{bmatrix} -(S_0 + X) \\ +M \end{bmatrix} \tag{17}$$

or more compactly,

$$J.V = C \tag{17A}$$

where $Det J = \Delta = (a_1 b_2 - a_2 b_1)$, and $Tr J = (-a_1 - b_2)$.

If we specify output adjustment in the usual Samuelsonian way as

$$dF/dt = h(F^D - F); h > 0 \text{ and} \tag{18}$$
$$dQ/dt = j(Q^D - Q); j > 0 \tag{19}$$

it can be shown that the out-of-equilibrium adjustment time-paths will be non-oscillatory; and that the system will be stable if $Det J > 0$ and $Tr J < 0$. Given the positivity of a_1, a_2, b_1 and b_2, the trace condition is apparent, but the determinant condition not so. Since, as will appear from Figure 3.2, the determinant stability condition is also necessary for existence of positive solutions, it will be assumed.

Comparative statics

Equation (17) affords solutions for the long-period equilibrium values of F and Q in the usual way:

$$F = \Delta^{-1} [b_2(S_0 + X) - a_2M] \text{ and} \tag{20}$$

$$Q = \Delta^{-1} [b_1(S_0 + X) - a_1M] \tag{21}$$

from which it is evident that both F and Q are positively related to X and negatively related to M, which is both intuitively obvious and trivial. The more interesting comparative-statics questions relate to changes in the behavioral parameters, for it is upon these that much of what is now regarded as "economic thought" in the eighteenth century may be seen to have turned. Mandeville, Hume, Tucker, Smith and Paley were deeply interested in the causal nexus between the spread of a taste for "luxury"– both among lords and masters and among the common people – and the economic development of a market society. Their thinking may be captured to a certain extent by comparative-statics exercises with (17), in particular by analysis of the effect of changes in the taste parameters λ_A, λ_Q and q^*. Because it is usual to suppose that masters were less interested in luxury than were lords (and because the qualitative effect of a change in λ_Q is the same as that of a change in λ_A) we need only consider λ_A.

The four coefficients are functions of q^*, and b_1 is also a function of λ_A.

$$a_1 = a_1(q^*): \quad \partial a_1/\partial q^* = -p/\alpha < 0$$

$$a_2 = a_2(q^*): \quad \partial a_2/\partial q^* = -fp^2/(w^*)^2 < 0$$

$$b_1 = b_1(q^*, \lambda_A): \quad \partial b_1/\partial q^* = f(1 - \lambda_A)/(w^*)^2 > 0$$

$$\partial b_1/\partial \lambda_A = f(\alpha - w^*)/(\alpha p w^*) > 0$$

$$b_2 = b_2(q^*): \quad \partial b_2/\partial q^* = -fp(1 - \lambda_Q)/(w^*)^2 < 0$$

Then by partial differentiation of (20) and (21) with respect to each of λ_A and q^* we obtain:

$$\partial F/\partial \lambda_A = -\Delta^{-2}[b_2(S_0 + X) - a_2M].\partial \Delta/\partial \lambda_A \tag{22}$$

$$\partial Q/\partial \lambda_A = -\Delta^{-2}\{\Delta(S_0 + X)\partial b_1/\partial \lambda_A - [b_1(S_0 + X) - a_1M].\partial \Delta/\partial \lambda_A\} \tag{23}$$

where $\partial \Delta/\partial \lambda_A = -a_2.\partial b_1/\partial \lambda_A < 0$. It is thus evident that in a closed economy [$X = M = 0$] (22) and (23) are unambiguously positive. They are also positive in an open economy upon the assumption that positive solutions exist for F and Q in (20) and (21). A once-for-all increase in the lords' degree of luxury brings about an increase in population and in production both of food and of luxuries, at long-period equilibrium. In the absence of any corresponding change in taste on the part of laborers, real wage is constant in population equilibrium, though it will have remained above w^* during the transition from one equilibrium to another.

By partial differentiation of (20) and (21) with respect to q^* we obtain:

$$\partial F/\partial q^* = \Delta^{-2}\{\Delta[(S_0 + X).\partial b_2/\partial q^* - M.\partial a_2/\partial q^*]$$

$$- [b_2(S_0 + X) - a_1M].\partial \Delta/\partial q^*\} \tag{24}$$

Pre-classical model of political oeconomy 35

and

$$\partial Q/\partial q^* = \Delta^{-2}\{\Delta[(S_0 + X).\partial b_1/\partial q^* - M.\partial a_1/\partial q^*]$$
$$- [b_1(S_0 + X) - a_1 M].\partial\Delta/\partial q^*\} \qquad (25)$$

where

$$\partial\Delta/\partial q^* = a_1.\partial b_2/\partial q^* + b_2.\partial a_1/\partial q^* - a_2.\partial b_1/\partial q^* - b_1.\partial a_2/\partial q^* \qquad (26)$$

The sign of (26) is seemingly ambiguous, as are those of (24) and (25). Equation (26) would be negative if

$$b_1.\partial a_2/\partial q^* < a_1.\partial b_2/\partial q^* + b_2.\partial a_1/\partial q^* + a_2.\partial b_1/\partial q^* \qquad (27)$$

which seems probable but is not necessarily the case. And when (26) < 0, then $\partial Q/\partial q^*$ is unambiguously positive. Even in that case though the sign of $\partial F/\partial q^*$ remains in doubt.

However it appears that the likelihood of positive signs for (24) and (25) is the greater the smaller is the value of q^*, and vice versa. In the extreme case where $q^* = 0$, (24) and (25) are positive, and (26) negative. The reason for these puzzling results is that at high levels of q^* a further increase, by raising the subsistence wage-rate w^*, would tend to inhibit that population growth which would otherwise take place during the period of transition when the market real wage is higher than w^*. It is conceivable that the depressing effect upon population of a rise in w^* could outweigh the effect upon population and production of an increased demand for luxuries. This was clearly recognized by Paley, who viewed population as an index of social welfare to be maximized.

> It appears, then, that luxury, considered with a view to population, acts by two opposite effects; and it seems probable that there exists a point in the scale, to which luxury may ascend . . . beyond which the prejudicial consequences begin to preponderate. The determination of this point [may] assume the form of an arithmetical problem.
> Paley ([1785] 1825, vol. 4: 486)

I have determined this "point" in a simple version of the present model (Waterman 1996). The conclusion of this analysis is therefore that a once-for-all increase in the taste for luxury of laborers would tend to increase production of food and luxuries, but that as q^* rises population would rise more slowly and might actually fall; in which case first F and then Q would pass their maxima and begin to decline.

Diagrammatical analysis

Much of the foregoing is easily illustrated by the means of the diagram in Figure 3.2. Let us re-write (10) and (16) as:

$$F = (a_1)^{-1}(S_0 + X) + \theta.Q \text{ and} \tag{10A}$$

$$Q = -(b_2)^{-1}M + \phi.F \tag{16B}$$

where $\theta = a_2/a_1$ and $\phi = b_1/b_2$. It is apparent that the geometrical requirement that $\phi^{-1} > \theta$ is satisfied by the determinant stability condition. The $F(Q)$ locus, of intercept $F_0 = S_0/a_1$ and slope θ, describes (closed-economy) production and population equilibrium in the A sector; the $Q(F)$ locus, of intercept zero and slope ϕ, describes (closed economy) production and population equilibrium in the Q sector. Their intersection in A determines the F,Q pair at which there is general equilibrium of population and production. If exports are made from the A-sector the intercept of $F(Q)$ is increased and the curve shifts upwards. If imports of Q-goods are made the intercept of $Q(F)$ is reduced and the curve shifts to the left.

If there is an increase in lords' degree of luxury the $F(Q)$ locus is unaffected. But because

$$\partial \phi / \partial \lambda_A = (b_2)^{-1}.(f/p).(\alpha - w^*)/\alpha w^* > 0 \tag{28}$$

(since α must exceed w^* for a surplus to exist), the $Q(F)$ locus will rotate clockwise illustrating the resulting increase in both Q and F.

If there is an increase in laborers' taste for luxury, the intercept of the $F(Q)$ will increase since a_1 decreases as q^*, and this shift captures the expansionary effect upon the A-sector of increased demand per capita.

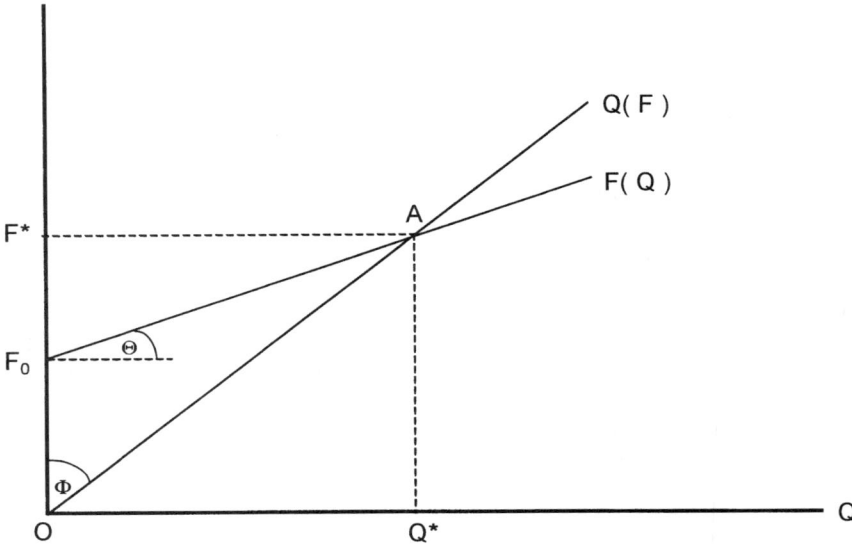

Figure 3.2 Interdependence of food and luxury production in population equilibrium

However since

$$\partial q/\partial q^* = (a_2)^{-1}.pf/(\alpha\beta w^{*2})[(w^{*2} - \alpha\beta p)\lambda_Q - \alpha\beta p] < 0 \qquad (29)$$

(because α must exceed w^* and β must exceed w^*/p, and therefore $\alpha\beta p$ must exceed w^{*2}) the $F(Q)$ locus will rotate clockwise; which captures the depressing effect on demand of the smaller equilibrium population associated with each equilibrium level of output. The $Q(F)$ locus will also rotate in a clockwise direction however, for

$$\partial\phi/\partial q^* = (b_2)^{-1}.f(1-\lambda_A)/w^{*2} + b_1/b_2^2.pf(1-\lambda_A)/w^{*2} > 0 \qquad (30)$$

Whether the new $F(Q)/Q(F)$ intersection occurs at higher levels of F or Q or both will depend upon the relative magnitudes of these three shifts.

However, if the taste for luxury were completely to disappear among both lords and laborers (in a closed economy) the $F(Q)$ intercept would become $(1-f/\alpha)^{-1}.S_0 = F$, and the slope of $Q(F)$, the angle $\phi = 0$. That is, the $Q(F)$ locus would rotate anti-clockwise until it became vertical, and the intercept of $F(Q)$ would decline to determine the equilibrium output of a subsistence manorial economy in which the surplus is employed only to maintain unproductive laborers. This is the message of Mandeville's *Fable* which I have analyzed in a simpler model (Waterman 1996).

Increasing returns to scale in the Q-sector

An important feature of *WN* at any rate is the emphasis upon specialization and the division of labor, with consequent increasing returns to scale in manufacturing. In terms of the model of (17) this effect can be represented by making β an increasing function of the output of Q:

$$\beta = \beta(Q); \beta(0) > 0, d\beta/dQ > 0 \qquad (31)$$

Since changes in β relative to α must normally affect the rate of exchange between A-goods and Q-goods, let us assume the labor theory of value and define $p = \alpha/\beta$. Thus when there are IRS in the Q-sector the food price of luxury goods will fall as the economy grows. Upon these assumptions the slope of the $F(Q)$ locus,

$$\theta = (a_1)^{-1} / [(\alpha.f(1-\lambda_Q)/w^*).\{\beta(Q)\}^{-1} + (f.\lambda_Q).\{\beta(Q)\}^{-1}] \qquad (32)$$

and its rate of change as Q varies,

$$\partial\theta/\partial Q = -(a_1)^{-1}.\beta^{-2}.[\alpha.f(1-\lambda_Q)/w^* + f.\lambda_Q] < 0 \qquad (33)$$

It is apparent from (32) that in the limit as Q increases to infinity the value of θ tends to zero.

The angle ϕ (reciprocal of the slope of $Q(F)$ in F,Q space) is

$$\phi = \{1 - \alpha(1 - \lambda_Q) q^*[w^*\beta(Q)]^{-1} - (1 - f/\alpha)\lambda_Q\}^{-1} \cdot$$
$$\{q^*/w^* + \alpha^{-2}.w^{*-1}.f.\beta(Q).(\alpha - w^*) \lambda_A\} \tag{34}$$

and

$$\partial\phi/\partial Q = (b_2)^{-2}\{b_2.f(\alpha - w^*)\lambda_A/(\alpha^2 w^*) - b_1\alpha(1 - \lambda_Q) q^*/(\beta^2 w^*)\}.d\beta/dQ \tag{35}$$

It is not obvious from (35) whether $\partial\phi/\partial Q$ is positive or negative. However when $Q = 0$, $\beta > 0$ and $0 < \phi < \theta$. And it may be seen from (34) that in the limit as Q approaches infinity the value of ϕ also tends to infinity. Since there are no relevant non-linearities in (35) these facts are sufficient to establish that $\partial\phi/\partial Q > 0$ so long as Q is non-negative.

The signs of (33) and (35) imply that an increase in β (and a decrease in p) as Q will have the effect of decreasing the slope of the $F(Q)$ locus, and of increasing the slope of the $Q(F)$ locus in Q,F space (that is, of decreasing it in F,Q space). These results are shown in Figure 3.3, where the $Q_c(F)$ and $F_c(Q)$ *loci* and their intersection in A illustrate the CRS case and are those of Figure 3.2. The $Q_i(F)$ and $F_i(Q)$ loci and their intersection in B illustrate the IRS case for the same set of all other parameters. It can be seen from Figure 3.3 that the effect of allowing IRS in the luxuries sector when all other things are equal, is to determine a general equilibrium of population and production at which Q is greater than in the CRS case. Though $F_i > F_c$ in Figure 3.3 it is not necessary that this should be so. In any case it is obvious that with IRS the ratio of Q-goods to F-goods in equilibrium must be greater than with CRS. This fact may explain why land scarcity does not figure to any significant extent as a constraint upon growth in *WN*. For with IRS the wealth of nations will be augmented chiefly by growth in the quantity of luxury goods available *per capita*. Relatively stationary food production (given the assumed constancy of f) implies relatively stationary population, so long as the taste for luxury goods grows *pari passu* with their availability.

"Competition of capitals" and the rate of profit

When capital is simply one period's advance wages and when $p = \alpha/\beta$, the rate of profit is

$$r_A = r_Q = \alpha/w - 1, \tag{36}$$

which is the most primitive form of the "inverse wage–profit theorem". If any single lord or master should increase π in order to employ a larger productive work-force, all other things remaining the same, his wage and profit rates would be unaffected. For any tendency of his action to bid up wages would be offset by an influx of labor from other "firms" (or "manors"). In effect, he would be able to increase his employment both of productive and unproductive labor proportionately, hence the decision to increase π would become self-reversing.

What might be the case for any single employer when all others remain passive cannot be so if all or most decide to act in the same way. For then increasing competition for productive employment with a constant work force must force up the wage-rate according to the argument of "Adjustment of output and population" earlier in this chapter. It is this "competition of capitals" which drives down the profit rate by (36).

It should be noted that the concept of a "competition of capitals" is only coherent when population/work-force is taken to be stationary, or at any rate to be growing more slowly than the demand for productive labor. It cannot be an explanation of any secular tendency for the rate of profit to decline and is thus incommensurable with the classical theory of a falling profit rate, which operates precisely through a decrease of marginal product in the A-sector (α) resulting from an increase in N.

Economic growth

It is necessary to distinguish "growth" from "development." By the latter I shall mean an occasional and intermittent enlargement of population and production brought about by changing tastes, as envisaged by many eighteenth-century authors and as described (or at any rate caricatured) earlier in "Comparative statics." By "growth" I shall mean a continuous expansion of population and production, with constant tastes, that is produced by a sustained attempt of masters (and/or lords) to keep $\pi > \pi^*$.

Suppose that with no change in tastes, masters expect and anticipate some increase in demand for luxuries. Suppose this causes them to increase their own demand for their own products over and above $\lambda_Q(1 - \pi_Q)Q$ in order to invest in stocks of salable goods. In order to increase production, π_Q must rise as described earlier in "Adjustment of output and population". Wages and population rise. If masters' initial expectations were correct, and if no further increase in demand is expected, the process will continue to a

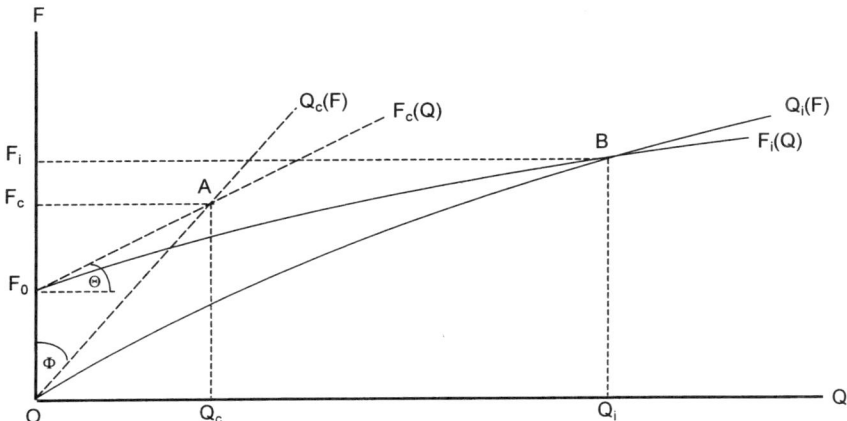

Figure 3.3 The Adam Smith modification

new population equilibrium as described in "Adjustment of output and population." The initial action by masters, however, will have been to some extent a self-fulfilling prophecy, for their accumulation of goods for sale will act like any other parametric increase in Q^D and induce further increases in both food and luxury production. Suppose in consequence that masters are led by this to continue to increase production for sale by permanently maintaining $\pi_Q > \pi_Q{}^*$. Wages would remain above w^* and output and population would grow continuously. Suitable assumptions about parameters and adjustment functions can thus produce a variety of "Adam Smith" growth models in which parsimony plays a central role.

It should be noted, however, that parsimony must be self-defeating unless masters' expectations of increased demand are fulfilled. Unsold stocks discourage production.

Relation between the un-canonical and canonical models

Aside from the relatively minor fact that the former is of a two-sector economy, the un-canonical, pre-classical model (UPM) differs from the canonical, classical model (CCM) in two important respects: first, diminishing returns; second, the accumulation growth-rule.

First, the hallmark of the CCM is diminishing returns in the A-sector.

$$F = F(N_a); F(0) = 0; F_N > 0; F_{NN} < 0 \tag{37}$$

The competitive wage-rate (strictly speaking the wage-rate plus the return to one *per-capita* unit of capital), $w = F_N$. So long as $F_N > w^*$ (capital and) population grow and F_N falls. When $F_N(N_a{}^*) = w^*$ there is a unique population equilibrium at

$$F^* = F(N_a{}^*) \tag{38}$$

Note that in a closed economy in stationary equilibrium (here assumed for simplicity of exposition), an amount of food equal to current production is consumed in the current period by the entire population. Hence

$$F = Nf, \text{ or } N = F/f \tag{39}$$

Total production of Q-goods will also be consumed, partly by the population/work-force, partly by lords and masters. Thus

$$Q = Nq + \lambda_A . S/p + \lambda_Q P \tag{40}$$

where $S = (1 - \pi_A)F$ and $P = (1 - \pi_Q)Q$. Thus

$$Q = Nq + \lambda_A(1 - \pi_A)F/p + \lambda_Q(1 - \pi_Q)Q \tag{41}$$

or in population equilibrium,

$Q^* = \psi.F$ (42)

where $\psi = [1 - \lambda_Q(1 - \pi_Q^*)]^{-1}.[q^*/f + \lambda_A(1 - \pi_A^*)/p]$.

Equations (38) and (42) determine the $F(Q)$ and $Q(F)$ loci respectively when plotted in the F,Q space used to depict the UPM in Figures 3.2 and 3.3. In Figure 3.4 the one-sector CCM is represented in the left-hand panel, showing the unique population and production equilibrium determined by tangency of a line of slope w^* to the locus of the $F(N_a)$ function. If there is a Q-goods sector, then $(N^* - N_A^*)$ on the horizontal axis of the left-hand panel measures N_Q^*; and Q^* is determined by the intersection of $Q(F)$ with the horizontal F^* line in the right-hand panel.

It is apparent that an increase in any of q^*, λ_A or λ_Q will increase ψ, rotate $Q(F)$ clockwise, and so (by itself) tend to increase Q^*. However, and this is the most striking difference between the CCM and the UPM, an increase in q^* will always reduce F^*. Hence the net effect upon Q^* is ambiguous.

$$\partial Q^*/\partial q^* = F/[f\{1 - \lambda_Q^*(1 - \pi_Q^*)\}] + \psi.p.F_N/F_{NN} \gtreqless 0 \quad (43)$$

From this standpoint at any rate, the CCM may be regarded as a degenerate case of the more general UPM.

Secondly, the other important difference between UPM and CCM lies in a quite different specification of the capital accumulation function. In the latter, the rate of accumulation is an increasing function of the rate of profit (Samuelson 1978: 1421 equation 6). But in the UPM the rate of accumulation is an increasing function of π. And as I have argued in "Competition of capitals and the rate of profit" earlier, an increase in p will reduce the rate of profit in the "short" period in which population and work-force is given. Since in steady state growth w must always exceed w^*, the rate of profit must be depressed

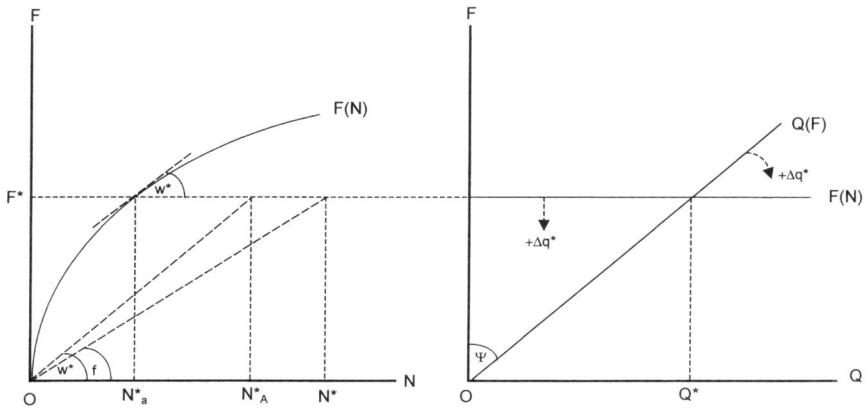

Figure 3.4 The canonical classical model in relation to the un-canonical, pre-classical model

below its stationary state value even in the "long" period when growth is occurring. To put the matter starkly: in the CCM the rate of accumulation is an increasing function of the rate of return; whereas in the UPM the rate of return is a decreasing function of the rate of accumulation.

Notes

Research for this paper was supported in part by a University of Manitoba/SSHRCC research grant and by a Visiting Research Fellowship in the Australian National University. Work-in-progress was presented to an economics seminar at that university in July 1998, and later at the University of Manitoba. The author wishes to thank Geoffrey Brennan, Samuel Hollander and Paul Samuelson for their valuable comments, criticism and encouragement.

References

Hollander, S. (1980) "On Professor Samuelson's Canonical Classical Model of Political Economy," *Journal of Economic Literature* 18.

Malthus, T. R. (1798) *An Essay on the Principle of Population*, 1st edn, London: J. Johnson.

Paley, W. [1785] (1825) *Principles of Moral and Political Philosophy*, in *The Works of William Paley, D.D.*, ed. E. Paley, vol. 4, London: Rivington.

Samuelson, P. A. (1978) "The Canonical Classical Model of Political Economy," *Journal of Economic Literature* 16.

Waterman, A. M. C. (1996) "Why William Paley was 'The First of the Cambridge Economists'," *Cambridge Journal of Economics* 20.

—— (1998) "The Beginning of Boundaries: The Sudden Separation of Economics from Christian Theology," Paper presented to ECHE 98, Antwerp, April 24 1998.

Winch, D. N. (1996) *Riches and Poverty: An Intellectual History of Political Economy in Britain, 1750–1834*, Cambridge: Cambridge University Press.

4 Bentham and the classical canon

Nathalie Sigot

Recently, Samuel Hollander returned to the canonical classical growth model, to point out both that it is shared by "nearly all the expert or properly-qualified economists" (Hollander 1997: 44) and that its priority must be given to Ricardo (ibid.: 5). Nevertheless, this priority does not rule out forerunners. Smith is particularly quoted: he was quoted before, in a previous article (Hollander 1980) about the same subject. However Hollander considers that the canonical model he defines "was in the air when Ricardo came on the scene" (Hollander 1997: 5; see also 1995: 267). Therefore he evokes another possible forerunner: Jeremy Bentham. This is a new reference: Bentham was not quoted in the 1980 article. Its justification lies in the recent discovery of a text which Hollander considers as the paper "on the effects on profits of cultivating successive qualities of land" that Piero Sraffa mentioned in *The Works and Correspondence of David Ricardo* (Ricardo 1951–73, vol. 10: 388n) and which he attributes possibly to Bentham (Hollander 1996, 1997: 8n13). (Editor's note: the references to Bentham as precursor do not appear in the published version of this paper (Hollander 1998).) In fact the evocation of Bentham as forerunner of the canonical classical growth model is not astonishing: he is generally considered as a minor economist (Mitchell 1934–5, vol. 1: 90; Singer 1953), but a classical one (Bonar 1922: 216, 218; Mitchell 1934–5, vol. 1: 90; Stark 1946: 583; Pribram 1983, ch. 10 ff.).

In contrast, this article aims at showing that Bentham's theory of growth has nothing to do with the canonical classical growth model defined by Hollander. As a result, if all classical economists share this model, we must conclude that Bentham can hardly be considered as classical. I shall use two types of argumentation to justify my position:

1   Negatively, first, I suggest that the principles on which, according to Hollander, are based the classical model are missing in Bentham's theory: in particular, neither decreasing returns nor "shared-incidence principle" are to be found in Bentham's theory. (See section I.)
2   Positively, then, I shall try to rebuild Bentham's growth model. Its originality comes from its overdetermination by political (instead of economic) factors: the wealth and progress of a country depend on its political situation – or, in Bentham's terms, on its degree of security (see section II).

I

According to Hollander the canonical classical growth model is characterized by "the shared incidence of diminishing agricultural returns between labour and capital" (Hollander 1997: 44). This implies the existence of decreasing returns and the adoption of the "shared-incidence principle," that is the *"necessarily simultaneous decline in wage and profit rates"* (ibid.: 2). However, these elements appear hard to find in Bentham's work.

Hollander acknowledges that "there are ... no formal statements to be found in Bentham's writings laying out the principle of diminishing returns" (ibid.: 8; see also Hollander 1996: 626). He adds, however that "it does not follow that [Bentham] denied to land scarcity a role in the growth process" (Hollander 1997: 8). The question of land scarcity does indeed need to be distinguished from that of the type of returns (Sigot 1999b). For Bentham, agricultural returns are either constant or increasing, depending on the conditions of applying capital to land:

> The application of capital to agriculture can not keep pace with the accumulation of the aggregate mass of capital. It is kept back by impediments that do not apply in equal degree, if in any degree, to manufactures. So much land as is in farms below a certain size stands excluded from the possibility of receiving improvement. [The occupier of such a small farm] set out with an insufficient capital. *The advantages attendant on operations conducted upon a large scale are prodigious not only in manufactures but (also) in agriculture.*
> (Bentham 1801: 299–300, my emphasis)

It is clear then that what matters is then the structure of ownership (which determines the surface area of lands), and not the global quantity of land available: on small-sized lands, technical progress can be implemented with difficulty; conversely, large surfaces of land yield increasing returns by enabling a greater division of labor (Bentham 1787: 300). When, in *Sur les prix*, Bentham mentions the possibility of a quicker increase in the volume of population than in its means of subsistence, it is not because he believes technical progress to have become more difficult.[1] He is speaking of a too-rapid population growth coupled with a state of war which has probably not enabled technical progress to advance quickly enough, thereby explaining the inadequacy of agricultural production.[2] This is why,

> though it be better to be in a situation of progressive prosperity than to be stationary or regressive, though it be more desirable to advance than to fall back, to rise than to descend, the slower our progress is in this career of success, the more it is in conformity with sound reason.
> (Bentham 1800–1: f. 52)

Bentham thus seems confident that agricultural production will increase via large-scale farming of the land. In "Population and Colonisation" for example, he sees this development as a plan concerning "the end of the terrestrial era" (ms. quoted by Poynter 1969: 123).

In fact, Bentham's position regarding the relationship between the volume of subsistence and the volume of population is a complex one, enough so to appear contradictory at first glance. One finds the assertion that population growth will come up against limits imposed by agricultural production, as well as that of an automatic population adjustment to the means of subsistence, which are likely to increase constantly. The optimism which appeared to dominate his initial writings may be compared with the somewhat Malthusian position of his later work: to my knowledge Bentham never mentions the possibility of underproduction before 1801, and it is in his post-1805 work that the idea becomes more apparent.[3] Nevertheless, such a statement is not of much use when it comes to understanding Bentham's economic theory. From a chronological stance first of all, if indeed the Malthusian position was the last he was to adopt, then it does not appear to have had a great influence on his theory, as his major economic writings were produced during the years 1790–1800 and he stopped writing on political economy in 1804. Second, from an analytical point of view, the only conclusion that might be drawn on this subject is that the author is inconsistent.

However, other arguments given by Bentham in his writings give glimpses of a different line of thought which would do away with the idea of incoherence altogether. Here a dual-sector economy in which total production (Q) is divided between agricultural (Q_1) and manufacturing (Q_2) productions needs to be envisaged.[4] The analysis of the links between these two sectors is essential: raw material from agricultural production is used for the manufacturing process (Bentham 1800–1: ff. 76, 79) while the latter is viewed as an "insurance against shortages" (Bentham 1802, vol. 2: 16) or a "security fund" (Bentham 1800–1: ff. 87–8). It is thus the relationship between these two sectors which will determine both the population growth rate and that of total and overall wealth.

II

The volume of agricultural production determines the population growth rate. This is a very general assertion which enables all the positions taken by Bentham regarding the relationship between agricultural production and the volume of population to be reconciled. However, the line of thought developed by Bentham does not presuppose perfect symmetry between situations where there is surplus in agricultural production when compared to the basic subsistence needs of the population, and those where it is insufficient. Indeed, Bentham supposes a sort of inertia lowering population levels. This inertia comes about through the relationship between the two sectors: when agricultural production is insufficient, manufacturing output is rationed, thereby taking on its role of insurance.

Two types of explanation may be put forward for this alteration in manufacturing production. The first consists in assuming that agricultural prices are flexible: the insufficient supply of agricultural goods results in a higher price for these products, which in turn leads to a decrease in demand for these goods as means of industrial production. However a "queuing" phenomenon may also be considered: the initial role of the supply of agricultural goods would be to satisfy the demand of individual consumers. It is only once this demand has been satisfied that industrial requirements will be taken into account. However, the way in which this priority can indeed come into effect must nevertheless be explained. Bentham's description of the adjustment mechanism prompts the retention of the first hypothesis implying the flexibility of agricultural prices. What is supposed here is a structural population adjustment which moves from the manufacturing to the agricultural sector. It is thus possible to believe that the fall in demand for agricultural goods from the manufacturing sector following a price increase brings about the redundancy of a large part of its labor force. Consequently, these people offer their services to the agricultural sector, thereby enabling output to be increased. Even if Bentham does not explicitly consider any price effect, the following quotation would appear to confirm our hypothesis:

> It may happen that in a particular bad year there shall be no superfluity of necessary good, or a less superfluity than the average amount. In such case there will be a proportionable addition of labor to that branch of agriculture, and a proportionable subtraction from other branches of agriculture and from the several branches of manufacture.
> (Mss. [17–61] in Bentham 1952–4, vol. 3: 502; see also Bentham 1800–1: ff. 87–8)

On the contrary, any agricultural surplus will bring about a rise in population. Despite this, the population growth rate will not be identical to that of the production of subsistence goods. Two arguments may be used to explain this phenomenon. The first concerns demography. Bentham indeed appears to suppose that an increase in the standard of living will give rise to a decrease in the birth rate: "agriculture without manufactures makes men more numerous, and less wealthy; agriculture with manufactures makes men more wealthy, and *consequently* less numerous" (Bentham 1787: 206). The second argument rests on the relationship between the two sectors of production. Any agricultural surplus will be matched by a rise in total population. This will certainly increase the need for agricultural goods but will also increase the demand for manufactured goods to a greater extent. The increase in the standard of living due to the agricultural surplus entails a change in the structure of consumption, as individuals devote a greater share of their budget to the purchase of manufactured goods:

> it is not in the nature of man to accumulate pure necessaries beyond his needs. When an Irish peasant has sown a sufficient quantity of potatoes for his yearly sustenance, will he take the useless trouble to sow more? Certainly not, unless he expects that, by the sale of that superfluous quantity, he will be enabled to procure himself other objects of desire which are not, for him, absolute necessaries.
> (Bentham 1800–1: f. 67bis)

The adjustment described by Bentham may thus be summarized in the following manner. The total active population (N) is divided into an agricultural population (N_1) producing agricultural goods (in value Q_1), and a manufacturing population (N_2) producing manufactured goods (in value Q_2):

$$N = N_1 + N_2 \tag{1}$$

$$Q = Q_1 + Q_2 \tag{1b}$$

The production of each sector is presumed to respond to the demand for it. Demand evolves in the same manner as the tastes of economic agents, given that the relative variation in demand for agricultural products ($\dot{Q}_1$) is always lower than the relative variation in manufactured goods ($\dot{Q}_2$), that is:

$$\dot{Q}_1 = b\dot{Q}_2 \quad (0<b<1)$$

or,

$$Q_1 = Q_2^b \tag{2}$$

To account for Bentham's idea of a certain inertia lowering the volume of population, we shall accept the existence of a value c of the agricultural product per head which guarantees that the population will remain stationary.

If Q_1/N is greater than c, the population will tend to rise; the "facility and disposition to marry" and to "produce" children "eating as they grow up" will increase, enabling this "terrible evil of a superabundance of provisions" (Bentham 1790: 216). On the contrary, should Q_1/N be less than c, total population will not vary, but population employed in agriculture will increase so that agricultural production per head will increase to c. Equation 3 describes the evolution of total population, depending on the difference between the ratio Q_1/N and c. Two situations must be distinguished: when this difference is positive, the population rises in a proportion depending on a coefficient k, which expresses the modification of the standard of living; on the contrary, when the difference is negative, the population does not rise, but cannot decrease thanks to its reallocation in favor of agriculture, which pushes Q_1/N to c. Thus, the evolution of total population is the maximum between $k(Q_1/N - c)$ and 0:

$$\dot{N} = sup \{k(Q_1/N - c), 0\} \quad (k > 0) \tag{3}$$

The adjustment mechanism described involves taking into consideration a second relationship which no longer concerns only the respective growth rates of population and agricultural production, but brings in the notion of wealth and its links with the structures of both population and production. Indeed, in Bentham's view, the scarcity of land is not a basic problem precisely because the population could be redistributed between the different production sectors. A quotation taken from the French translation of the *Manual of Political Economy* shows that Bentham is not preoccupied with limiting population growth in general, but only that of the inactive classes who create no wealth:

the growth of these purely consumer classes is of no advantage to the State nor to themselves. Their well-being is inversely proportional to their numbers . . . . It is in its own interest that the inactive class should not increase, indeed it should ideally decrease, either via celibacy or by moving into the working classes.[5]

(Bentham 1793–1801: 365)

Up to now Bentham has underlined the fact that a single section of the population produces the wealth to be shared among everyone. In other writings he clarifies his position by developing a sector-based reasoning. Not only does the activity rate of the population count, but also the way in which it is shared between the agricultural and manufacturing sectors, conditioning production structure and determining the level of wealth. It is now clear that the basic problem the author comes up against is that of the relationship between population and wealth.

Bentham is well aware of a possible antinomy between wealth and population. When he sets for the economy the double aim of obtaining "maximum of wealth" on the one hand and "maximum of population" on the other (Bentham 1801–4: 318), he leaves the practical solution of the problem to the legislator. The problem is simple: via its work the population is the creator of wealth, but for a given reserve of wealth the variation in opulence, described as "relative wealth" (that is, wealth per head) is inversely proportional to population volume (ibid.; see also Bentham 1800–1: ff. 67–67bis). Which variable should thus be maximized?

The ultimately optimistic position of Bentham, who believes that opulence and total wealth progress hand in hand "in the ordinary course of things" (Bentham 1795: 361), is understandable when one examines the factors which, according to the author, enable the economy to grow. Innovation and incentive to work are seen as decisive. However, these factors can only express themselves when certain political conditions prevail: this leads Bentham to insist on security, decisive in long-term economic growth.

Bentham regularly insists on the importance of the political regime by evoking this higher end of security (Bentham 1785–6: 307–11 in particular). Alas, a clear definition of it is not to be found in his writings; security is understood in its widest sense as it appears to designate the protection of property rights just as much as the individual (ibid.: 313).[6] It belongs to the field of legislation and it is up to the law to guarantee it. It is a higher objective to which all others should be subordinate. When Bentham defines the economy using two other intermediary aims – the economy targets the development of subsistence and abundance (Bentham 1802: vol 1: 344) – these two should always be sacrificed to law: "if industry creates, it is the law which preserves", states Bentham in *Traités de législation civile et pénale* (ibid.: 175). The argument is simple: neither subsistence nor abundance can be attained if individuals are not sure of being able to keep the property they have acquired. Security thus appears as a prerequisite for the development of wealth: "without law," says Bentham, "there is no security; consequently no abundance, nor even certain subsistence. And the only equality which can exist in such a condition, is the equality of misery" (Bentham 1785–6: 307). Security thus becomes "the seed of abundance" (Bentham 1801–4: 310). Aiming at security plays a decisive role in the growth process via two elements: innovation and the incentive to work.

Innovation was at the center of the argumentation that Bentham developed against Smith, favoring the abolition of the laws repressing usury. He countered Smith, who highlighted the dangers of a projector, with the courage of those few individuals who possess the "rare endowment of genius." Indeed, innovation is an engine of progress, contributing to the increase of wealth in society and consequently to happiness: "for the fabric of national opulence, that fabric of which you proclaim, with so generous an exultation, the continual increase," wrote Bentham when addressing Smith, "it required the reprobated hand of a projector to lay the first stone" (Bentham 1787: 177; see also Bentham 1793–4: 260–4). Even if a project finally turns out to be unprofitable and if the entrepreneur is ruined, society as a whole benefits in the sense that the experiment undertaken has given rise to technical progress (Bentham 1787: 180).

The incentive to innovate depends on potential profit: it rests on a calculation made by the innovator (Bentham 1793–4: 229, 261–4) which should in no way be different from that made by any individual regarding the pains and pleasures of any given action. Because "nature has placed mankind under the governance of two sovereign masters, *pain* and *pleasure*. [Because] it is for them to point out what we ought to do, as well as to determine what we shall do" (Bentham [1789] 1948: 1), the incentive to innovate could not develop if the property of patents were not protected by the law. This is why Bentham in his "proposals for an unburthensome augmentation of the revenue" especially quotes the "faculty of obtaining protection for the reputation of superior workmanship against counterfeits, by a man's registering his name and marks put upon his goods" (Mss. [72], in Bentham 1952–4, vol. 3: 542). Security comes into play here at two levels: on the one hand by guaranteeing the innovator can obtain immediate profit from his innovation, and on the other by allowing him to keep this profit and to experience the pleasure of his own property. Conversely, insecurity means an absence of innovation and the onset of poverty (Bentham 1793–4: 264–5).

The incentive to work obeys the same law: insecurity discourages individuals from using their "bodily energy" in production, as nothing guarantees they will be able to keep the fruits of their labor. Therefore they will do the minimum needed to ensure their subsistence. They will not seek to accumulate beyond their strict necessities: "Superfluity vanished little and little; absolute necessity must still be provided for, notwithstanding obstacles: man must live" (Bentham 1785–6: 311). Here again, it is human nature, via a calculation of pain and pleasure, which is proof of the need for security. Indeed, work means pain – "labour is too painful for idleness; it is too slow for impatience," explains Bentham (ibid.: 307) – a pain that the individual will only agree to bear on condition that the reward is of a higher value to him or her. This is why, in an insecure regime "Cunning and Injustice handedly conspire to appropriate its fruits [of labor]; Insolence and Audacity plot to seize [individuals] by open force" (ibid.). The nation consequently becomes poorer, "the torch of industry furnishes but a few dying sparks" (ibid.: 311).

On the contrary, wealth will develop by means of an accumulation of luxury goods made possible by the existence of a safe and stable regime. The statement "national wealth is not susceptible of considerable encrease otherwise than with regard to the stock of articles of fancy value, of luxury, or of superfluity" (Bentham 1800–1: ff. 67–67bis; also Bentham 1790: 216–7 and Bentham 1802 vol. 2: 15) is to be understood in this manner. When property is ensured, a surplus of agricultural goods may be produced, and this will be turned into luxury goods: "the more provisions a man raises over and above what is necessary for its own consumption, the more he has to give to others to induce them to provide him with whatever besides provision he choose to have" (Bentham 1790: 216–7).[7] Any surplus of agricultural goods thereby makes the raw materials available to be transformed into luxury goods (Bentham 1800–1: f. 67bis). Luxury goods produced by the manufacturing sector are thus an "insurance against shortages" (Bentham 1802 vol. 2: 16; see also Bentham 1801–4: 326–7). This is why Bentham states "agriculture without manufactures, contributes most to population: agriculture with manufactures to wealth" (Bentham 1787: 206).

The role played by these structural adjustments enables two outlines of economic evolution to be identified, according to whether the regime is secure or insecure. The security factor and its consequences can indeed be transferred to production in terms of returns.

For the sake of simplicity, agricultural returns are here supposed as being constant. We have seen that for Bentham, they cannot decrease:

$$Q_1 = aN_1 \quad (a > 0) \tag{4}$$

Conversely returns are variable in factories where:

$$Q_2 = F(N_2) \quad (F' > 0) \tag{5}$$

A greater or lesser degree of security acts upon the form of this production function. As a general guide, we will suppose that, in a secure regime, returns increase:

$$F'' > 0 \tag{5a}$$

whereas in an insecure regime they will decrease:

$$F'' < 0 \tag{5b}$$

These different equations are not claiming to represent the multiple aspects of Bentham's dynamics. But they have the advantage of highlighting the consequences of security on conditions in factory production and, through them, on the establishment of a stable state. Figures 4.1 and 4.2 aim at demonstrating this fact.

Production functions in agriculture (relation [4]) and in manufacturing (relations [5] – [5a] or [5] – [5b]) are respectively represented in Figures

4.1a, 4.2a and 4.1c, 4.2c. In Figures 4.1b and 4.2b, the segments denoting the distribution of the population between the two sectors have been added (relation [1]), then a straight line, passing through the origin, of which each point corresponds to a distribution of the overall population ensuring its stability. The equation of this straight line,

$$N_2 = (\frac{a}{c} - 1).N_1$$

can be deduced from relations [1], [4] and [3]. All the points under this line correspond to a structure of population producing an agricultural output per head higher than c, thereby provoking an increase in population.

The production structures matching the tastes of agents (relation [2]) are shown in Figures 4.1d and 4.2d. Each of the declining curves represents the production structures (Q_1, Q_2) using all the possible distributions of a given population N between the two sectors. But only one of these distributions is in stable equilibrium, enabling both a stable population and stable production to be attained. The position of these stationary situations is given by the rising curve $\dot{N} = 0$. Note that the slope of this curve decreases in Figure 4.1d and increases in Figure 4.2d – which would explain the different properties of the production functions of manufactured goods according to the security or insecurity of the regime.

When the $Q_1 = Q_2^b$ curve appears in the area above the $\dot{N} = 0$ curve, it may be interpreted as being a trajectory followed from left to right by the economy, after the increase in population.[8] In a secure regime (Figure 4.1d), it is possible (providing factory returns increase sufficiently in the face of the change in consumer tastes for manufactured goods) for economic growth to know no bounds. In an insecure regime, however (Figure 4.2d), where the economy reaches point S, the distribution between agricultural and manufactured goods perfectly reflects agents' tastes. Agricultural production is just sufficient to ensure the identical reproduction of the population. As long as the manufacturing production function does not change, no force will come to move the economy out of the stationary state into which it has fallen.

Now, one must be aware that for Bentham, there is only a difference of degree between security and insecurity: insecurity is not more than a low level of security. Thus, it is possible to distinguish different states of society depending on their lower or higher degree of security. The action of the legislator should be to increase the degree of security, that is, to allow society to switch from a state with low security to a state with a higher one. Formally this may be translated as a reduction in concavity – then as an increase in convexity – of the production function in factories (see Figure 4.3). The result of this, at the outset, will be an upward movement of point S on the $Q_1 = Q_2^b$ curve. The economy will therefore stop being in a stationary state as production and population increase simultaneously. Then, as soon as the convexity of the production function in factories has become sufficiently pronounced, the economy will have attained growth excluding any return to a stationary condition as long as security continues to exist.

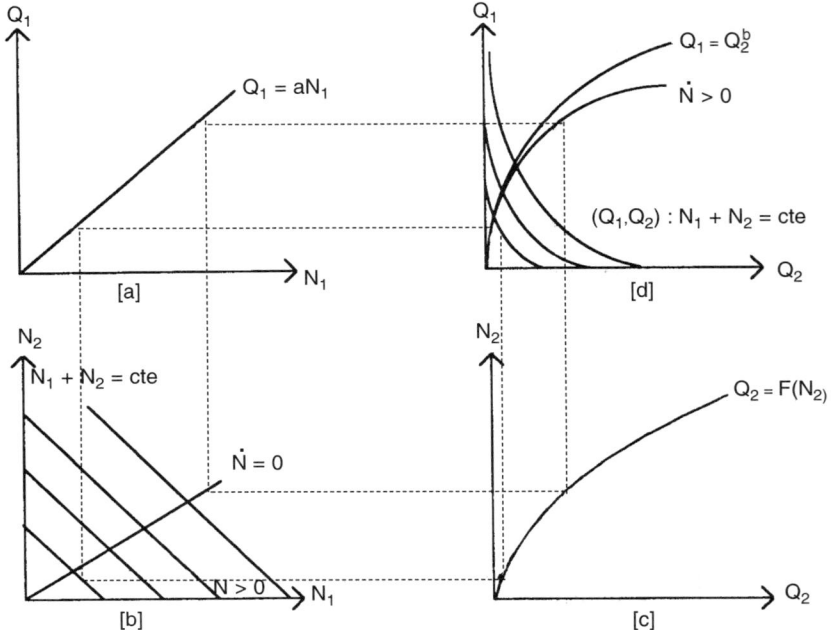

Figure 4.1 Secure regime

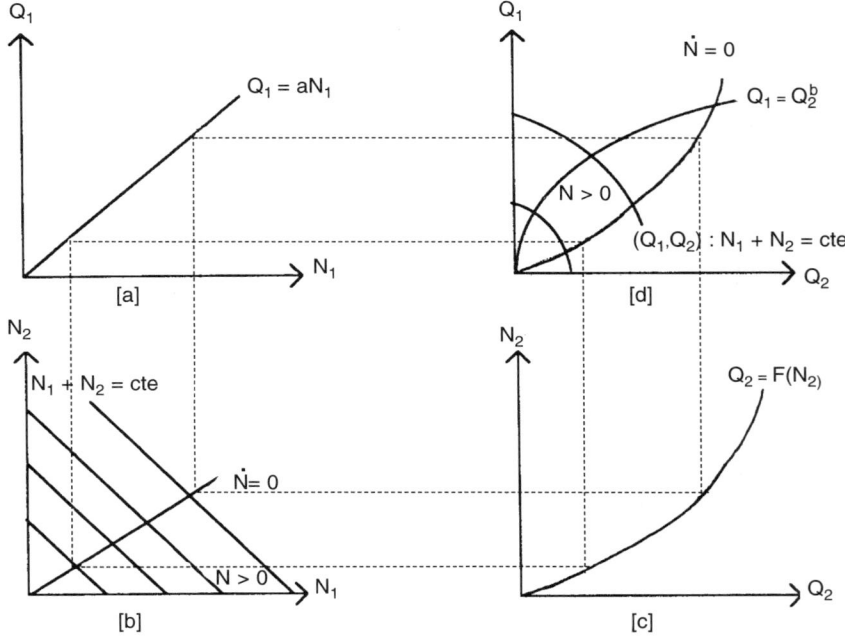

Figure 4.2 Insecure regime

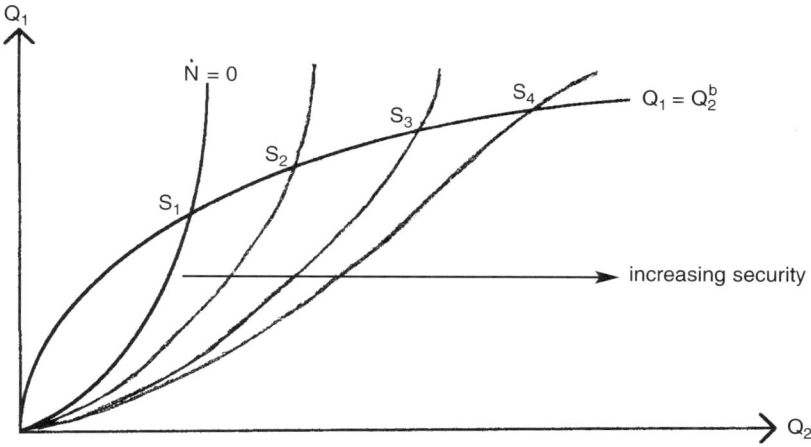

Figure 4.3 From insecurity to security

We thereby arrive at Bentham's conclusion according to which there is no brake to long term accumulation within a secure regime:

> where property is tolerably secure ... population goes on more or less encreasing, and wealth, the result of economy, at a still greater rate.
> (Bentham 1795: 361)

or:

> supposing the luxury of a country carried as far as it can be conceived in a sound civilization which gives security to property, the mass of national wealth must always go on encreasing.
> (Bentham 1800–1: f. 162)

On the contrary, in an insecure regime, luxury goods no longer play their part and one falls back on the stationary state which runs through the classical tradition but which cannot be attributed here to the existence of decreasing returns. It is because the legislator was not able to guarantee security that this stationary condition takes hold. Thus a country such as Turkey, explains Bentham, has a tendency to grow poorer day by day owing to "a political disease which arises from all the causes that render property uncertain" (Bentham 1800–1: f. 162; see also Bentham 1785–6: 310–11). Bentham's apparently contradictory statements concerning the link between population and subsistence can finally be seen to be consistent if one takes into account the context in which they are placed: a secure or an insecure regime. In the classical tradition as described by Hollander, the increase in the volume of subsistence necessary to cope with an increased population comes up against the barrier of decreasing returns following land scarcity. It is quite a different principle which may be found in Bentham: here the increase in subsistence is not ruled out and land scarcity is in no way a limiting factor.

Notes

I am indebted to Ghislain Deleplace, Richard Kleer and André Lapidus for helpful comments on successive drafts of this paper.

1 > If we consider further the rapid increase of population such as it has been even during the war, if we observe that it would soon, by its natural course, reach the point where it exceeds the means of subsistence which the two isles could produce, it will be recognized that the emigration of men and capital is a real good in the present state of Great Britain.
>
> (Bentham 1800–1: ff. 51–2)

It should be noted that when Bentham mentions the consequences of an increase in the accumulation of capital just a few lines earlier in this very book, he concludes that only the available amount of work represents a barrier to an increase in production:

> The effect of this stream of capital will be to further the production of real wealth as long as there remains a capacity for labor which can be put to work, and as rapidly as that capacity can be brought into action.
>
> (Bentham 1800–1: f. 51)

2 See also Bentham 1795: 361–2.
3 See L. Campos Boralevi (1983: 127–8): the quotes she gives, taken from an essay entitled "Paederasty" (1785), clearly show that Bentham believed in an automatic adjustment of the population to means of subsistence. See also *A General View of a Complete Code of Laws* (Bentham 1828–43, part 9: 170): "the population count is almost always equivalent to the means of subsistence."

Bentham's conversion to Malthusianism dates back to 1802 according to Stark (Bentham 1952–4, vol. 1: 57) or Poynter (1969: 142). Note that, to state his position, Hollander refers to two works prior to this date (*Defence of a Maximum*, 1801 and *The True Alarm*, English translation of the manuscript *Sur les prix*, 1801) and one partly posterior (*Institute of Political Economy*, 1801–4).

4 A justification for this two-sector approach has been suggested to me by Richard Kleer. It would allow one to capture one of Bentham's primary concerns: to defend the public utility of a manufacturing sector against criticisms from powerful landowners. It is nevertheless difficult to substantiate this interpretation because of the lack of references in Bentham's works to the economic role of landowners.

5 An extract from the *Pannomial Fragments* (Bentham 1831: 228) echoes this position: "sooner or later," writes Bentham, "the whole surface of the habitable globe cannot but be fully peopled, in such sort, that from no one to any other human creatures be transplanted in a living and about to live state." In fact, the discussion preceding this extract shows that Bentham here mentions (and criticizes), the then common practice whereby governments sent their poor to the colonies. Bentham on the contrary will always insist on the need to transform these poor who do no work and prefer public assistance into active people who produce wealth: this is the meaning of his suggestions in favor of a reform of the laws concerning the poor and of the creation of industry houses (see Sigot 1999a).

6 The protection of property rights "consists in an established expectation – in the persuasion of power to derive certain advantages from the object, according to the nature of the case" (Bentham 1785–6: 308).

7 This implies that wages are not defined in relation to the subsistence level. Bentham

certainly supposes the existence of such a minimum level but defined in a very particular manner: it is relative both in time and space and varies in accordance with the social status of he who receives it (Bentham 1787: 206–7; 1800–1: ff. 86–7). The position developed by Bentham regarding the link between wage level and social status is in *The Rationale of Reward* (Bentham 1782–7; see also Sigot 1996).

8 In the previous passage the possibility that the $Q_1 = Q_2^b$ curve may appear below the $N = 0$ curve has not been forgotten. This possibility is unlikely as it would mean that the agents are short of agricultural products and also that they prefer agricultural goods to manufactured goods. Bentham's idea of an asymmetrical answer to a surplus or a deficit per head brings out this improbability: should agricultural output be insufficient, population will not decrease but will redistribute itself between the sectors, thereby returning to the curve of stationary situations. Allowing for the very simplified hypotheses expressed here – especially the absence of any adjustment period of the population to the evolution in demand, expressed by relation (2) – the trajectory followed by the economy is found on the $Q_1 = Q_2^b$ equation curve, up to the point where the latter crosses the $N = 0$ curve at the upper portion.

References

Bentham, J. (1828–43) *The Works of Jeremy Bentham, Published Under the Superintendance of his Executer, John Bowring*, Edinburgh: Tait.
—— (1952–4) *Jeremy Bentham's Economic Writings*, ed. W. Stark, 3 vols, London: Allen and Unwin.
—— (1782–7) *The Rationale of Reward* (in Bentham 1828–43, vol. 7: 189–266).
—— (1785–6) *Principles of the Civil Code* (in Bentham 1828–43, vol. 2: 297–364).
—— (1787) *Defence of Usury* (in Bentham 1952–4, vol. 1: 121–207).
—— [1789] (1948) *An Introduction of the Principles of Morals and Legislation*, New York: Hafner.
—— (1790) *Colonies and Navy* (in Bentham 1952–4, vol. 1: 209–18).
—— (1793–4) *Manual of Political Economy* (in Bentham 1952–4, vol. 1: 219–73).
—— (1793–1804) *Manuel d'économie politique* in J. Bentham, *Théorie des peines et des recompenses* (1811), vol. 2, Paris: Bossange et Masson (2nd edn. 1818).
—— (1795) *Supply Without Burthen* (in Bentham 1952–4, vol. 1: 279–367).
—— (1797) *Observations on the Poor Bill* (in Bentham 1928–43, vol. 2: 440–61).
—— (1800) *Abstract or Compressed View of a Tract Intituled Circulating Annuities* (in Bentham 1952–4, vol. 2: 201–423).
—— (1800–1) *Sur les prix*, Manuscript Dumont 50, f. 30–440. Collection of the Bibliothèque Publique et Universitaire de la ville de Genève (English transcription by W. Stark: *The True Alarm*, in Bentham 1952–4, vol. 3: 61–216).
—— (1801) *Defence of a Maximum* (in Bentham 1952–4, vol. 3: 247–302).
—— (1801–4) *Institute of Political Economy* (in Bentham 1952–4, vol. 3: 303–80).
—— (1802) *Traités de législation civile et pénale*, ed. E. Dumont, 3 vols. Paris: Bassange, Masson et Besson.
—— [1813–5] (1984) *Chrestomathia*, Oxford: Clarendon Press.
—— (1831) *Pannomial Fragments* (in Bentham 1828–43, vol. 9: 211–30).
Bonar, J. [1893] (1922) *Philosophy and Political Economy in Some of their Historical Relations*, London: Allen and Unwin.
Campos Boralevi, L. (1983) "Jeremy Bentham's Writings on Sexual Non-Conformity: Utilitarianism, Neo-Malthusianism, and Sexual Liberty," *Topoi* 2(2) (December): 123–48.
Hollander, S. (1980) "On Professor Samuelson's Canonical Model of Political Economy," *Journal of Economic Literature* 18: 559–74.
—— (1990) "A Reply to Professor Stigler and Dr Peach," *Oxford Economic Papers*, in S.

Hollander (1995), *Ricardo: The New View*, London: Routledge: 265–7.
—— (1995) *Ricardo: The New View*. London: Routledge.
—— (1996) "Notes on a Possible Bentham Manuscript: A Mystery Unresolved," *Cambridge Journal of Economics* 20(5): 623–35.
—— (1997) "The Canonical Classical Growth Model: Content, Adherence and Priority," unpublished working paper.
—— (1998) "The Canonical Classical Growth Model: Content, Adherence and Priority", *Journal of the History of Economic Thought* 19 (Fall): 253–77.
Hutchison, T. W. (1956) "Bentham as an Economist," *Economic Journal* 66(262): 288–306.
Mitchell, W. C. [1934–5] (1949) *Lecture Notes on Types of Economic Theory*, 2 vols, New York: A. M. Kelley.
Poynter, J. R. (1969) *Society and Pauperism: English Ideas on Poor Relief, 1795–1834*, London: Routledge and Kegan Paul.
Pribram, K. (1983) *Les fondements de la pensée économique*, Paris: Economica.
Ricardo, D. (1951–73) *The Works and Correspondence of David Ricardo*, ed. P. Sraffa with M. H. Dobb, 11 vols, Cambridge: Cambridge University Press.
Sigot, N. (1995) "L'utilitarisme benthamien à la rencontre de l'économie classique", Ph.D. dissertation, Centre d'Histoire de la Pensée Economique, University of Paris I Panthéon-Sorbonne.
—— (1996) "Jeremy Bentham on Private and Public Wages and Employment: The Civil Servants, The Poor and the Indigent," in L. Moss (ed.), *Joseph A. Schumpeter, Historian of Economics*, London: Routledge: 196–218.
—— (1999a) "Bentham et les utilitaristes," in M. C. Révauger et P. Denizot (eds), *Pauvreté et assistance en Grande-Bretagne 1688–1834*, Paris: Publications de l'Université de Provence: 253–73.
—— (1999b) "A Note on Hollander's 'Notes on a Possible Bentham Manuscript: a Mystery Unresolved'," *Cambridge Journal of Economics* 23(3): 371–8.
Singer, K. (1953) "Bentham as Economist," *Economic Record* 29(57): 266–70.
Sraffa, P. (1955) "Biographical Miscellany," in *The Works and Correspondence of David Ricardo*, ed. P. Sraffa with M. H. Dobb, vol. 10, Cambridge: Cambridge University Press.
Stark, W. (1946) "Jeremy Bentham as an Economist II," *Economic Journal* 52(224): 583–608.
—— (1954) "Introduction" to *Jeremy Bentham's Economic Writings*, vol. I, London: Allen and Unwin: 11–78.

5 A new institutional perspective on the canonical model

The case of capital markets in *The Wealth of Nations*

Anthony Endres

Introduction: some historiographical reflections

It is now widely accepted that in terms of "pure logic and intellectual indebtedness," Paul Samuelson's canonical classical model of political economy may be a more faithful rendering of Ricardo's ideas (Hollander [1980] 1995: 360). The model incorporates the shared incidence proposition that labor and capital share the burden of diminishing agricultural returns, a proposition which is not patently obvious in *The Wealth of Nations* (hereafter: *WN*). What has made the canonical reconstruction plausible and interesting in its application to *WN* is its consistency with modern, formal equilibrium theorizing (Samuelson 1977, 1978).[1] The applicability of this reconstruction to *WN* has since been questioned in broader studies which attempt to recruit Smith into other economic frameworks or traditions, thereby producing alternative Smithian "canons."[2] For example, some see the presence of increasing returns deriving from endogenous technical change as central to Smith's model (for example, Kurdas 1988).

Whatever the historiographer's recruitment objective, it may be legitimate in this age of multicentered, pluralistic scholarship to allow for a diversity of objectives consistent with an attribution to Smith of more than one vision of the economic process (Brown 1997). Attempts to represent persistent lines of thought or "core" ideas in *WN* must at least satisfy enduring academic standards of persuasiveness, namely logical coherence and provision of ample textual evidence. In what follows we shall present evidence of a substantive institutional "core" in *WN* which can be reconstructed separately from, but does not compete with, Samuelson's neoclassical reconstruction.

Samuelson's canonical reconstruction provides a helpful point of departure for a variety of investigations concerning themes in *WN*. For instance, studies might assess different categories of exogenous variables in the canonical model (some of which are implicit). In this connection, it would be a misperception of the canonical model if we argued that it fails to take account of Smith's concern to study comparative economic performance given an observed set of heterogeneous factor endowments, technologies, tastes, attitudes, and general "non-economic" institutional conditions. Critics have lamented that these factors are interred as parameters in Samuelson's model. However Samuelson readily acknowledged that "dead-weight losses" may arise and could be rationalized if these assumed givens or constraining influences were configured unfavorably in particular circumstances (Samuelson 1988: 162).

The purpose of this paper is to pursue a line of inquiry on *WN* which begins with the canonical model and then purports to follow Smith's procedure faithfully by relaxing a pivotal assumption concerning the given, stable institutional "state of nature" (for example, the completeness of markets) upon which Samuelson's canon is constructed.[3] Special reference will be made to the problem of capital formation, arguably a preeminent issue in *WN*. It is significant that the canonical model relies implicitly on what we designate loosely as the complete or well-organized markets assumption of model Walrasian economics. Markets are complete if every agent is *able* to exchange every good either directly or indirectly with every other agent. Now are the enabling institutions in the right form in *WN*? Specifically, are the costs of arranging and enforcing contracts to create and use capital prohibitive?

For Smith, one of the main institutional prerequisites making capital formation possible turned on the matter of "security" created in well-organized markets. We contend that Smith's analysis of capital formation and allocation does not always employ the concepts of riskiness and insecurity as synonyms; this is consistent with what we would observe in disorganized capital markets where, for example, there might be contract enforcement problems or pathological institutions mitigating against capital formation. Beneath mere verbal similarities new meanings emerge through *WN*, particularly in respect of the concept of "security" and its significance for decisions to create capital. We will attend to the layers of meaning Smith attaches to that concept in various parts of *WN* compared with the presumptive treatment of risk in the canonical model.

Smith's analysis of profit: the canonical elements

Book I of *WN* (Smith 1976a) is perhaps the most well known and oft-quoted part of Smith's work from a purely economic, theoretic standpoint. Capital or "stock" has already been accumulated in the hands of its owners ("undertakers"); it consists in materials and subsistence, the excess of which over the undertaker's requirements provide the demand for labor. That portion of stock which employs productive laborers is, of course, vital to Smith's theory of economic growth (Bowley 1975: 368).

The stock of capital (as distinct from the flow) has a corresponding long-run "natural" rate of return indicated by the profit rate. Profit is described not as the wages of the undertaker, but as a compensation for "hazards" to which the undertaker is exposed when advancing materials and wages in the expectation of a surplus on the original amount invested (*WN* I vi 5). If capital is placed on loan its income is called interest; in this case interest is derived second-hand from the undertaker and is regarded as a part of profits (*WN* I vi 69–70). Later Smith adds agreeableness or "disagreeableness" as a separate determinant of profit (*WN* I xb 34); it may be "real or imaginary" (*WN* I xb 39). In any case it is a relatively uncommon factor specific to special investments.[4] Unlike the hazards which face the undertaker, disagreeableness makes "little or no difference in the far greater part of the different employments of stock" (*WN* I xb 34). Hazards are consonant with risks, and these are considered to be preeminent determinants of profit.

As Smith remarked when referring in general to the inequalities arising from different employments of labor and stock, risks pertain to "the probability or improbability of success" (*WN* I xb 1). At any one time this probability will vary between investments in different economic activities. The most hazardous trades may bring bankruptcy to "adventurers" (*WN* I xb 33), although normally the ordinary or natural rate of profit "varies more or less with the certainty or uncertainty of the return." Alternatively stated, the natural rate "always rises more or less with risk but not always in direct proportion to it" (*WN* I xb 34; also *WN* I ix 18, 22). Here Smith uses hazard, risk and uncertainty as synonyms pertaining to the "chance of a loss" (*WN* I xb 28).[5]

The chance of loss is normally constant in a natural, long-run or normal setting. That is, the expectation of success is on average not disappointed, or the divergence between actual and expected returns does not change. Smith did not assume away the difference between anticipations and realizations of profit; he merely presumes that there are no net surprises for undertakers, so that profit rates remain at their natural level and are equalized across different investments subject to normal risk levels (and to the minor consideration of "disagreeableness").[6] A profit rate in a particular sector would not exceed that in others, which is to say that it would be no lower than the risk premium associated with that sector. The rate of profit in an economy in which net saving falls to zero is defined as the "lowest ordinary rate of profit [which] must always be something more than what is sufficient to compensate the occasional losses to which every employment of stock is exposed. It is this surplus only which is neat or clear profit" (*WN* I ix 18). In an economy approaching general equilibrium or stationariness, the long-run natural or "neat" profit rate is a "surplus" proportional to the interest rate payable on loanable funds; it would be very low and tending toward zero at the end of the growth process.

So far our exposition is consistent with leading commentaries on Smith's analysis of profit (for example, Hollander 1973: 167–9). Samuelson provides a capsule summary on this matter, for all the classical economists including Smith for the stationary state case:

> The long-run profit rate might, in some theories, be zero (after, of course, all allowances for depreciation and replacement of principal have separately been allowed for; *after any needed actuarial premia for probable accidents and losses had been properly allowed for*; and after any wages of managing capital assets had been provided for).
>
> (Samuelson 1978: 1419, emphasis added)

For long-run, natural rate analysis Samuelson's canonical model is perfectly Smithian: capital supplied in the long run will be a *function* of a minimum profit rate after accounting for a normal risk premium. Smith's illustrations provisionally confirm the canonical reading.

The case of capital allocated to an insurance business forms an archetype from which comparison may be made with the riskiness of investments in other sectors in the long-run, natural state. According to Smith, in order to supply the product of insurance from "fire or sea-risk" the investor must ensure that "the common premium [is] sufficient to compensate the common losses, to pay the expense of management, and to afford such a profit as might be drawn from an equal capital employed in any common trade" (*WN* I xb 28).

In the business of fire and shipping insurance, trade is routinized so that risk is calculable or at least "reducible to strict rule and method" (*WN* V ie 32, 34). Therefore capital allocated to the insurance trade is attended by the greatest possible "security" (*WN* V ie 38) imaginable. The always "very modest profit of insurers" is the result of low risk or alternatively high security in that business. In addition, Smith asserts that low risk or security may be rendered to any trade or business from government-created protections or privileges (*WN* I xc 13).

In *WN*, risks attending capital allocation at the microeconomic level may be understood as the given, purely commercial or economic chance of loss ordinarily associated with a particular trade. This is what Smith refers to as the normally expected, "occasional losses to which every employment of stock is exposed" (*WN* I ix 18). When Smith uses the term "security" in Book I in relation to the circumstances affecting the natural profit rate on capital he expressly links it to risk. However, in this first book of *WN*, Smith treats risk in the long run: profits of stock are related to the "risk or security" with which that stock is associated, and where risk and security (for the latter read: risk minimization) are used as strictly converse categories (*WN* I xb 34). Otherwise, Smith's treatment of risk is progressively subsumed under security in *WN*, as security becomes an all-inclusive category applying in a process analysis of a growing economy undergoing a major regulatory and organizational transformation.

On the security of capital in a growing economy

As he proceeds in *WN* Smith adds further dimensions to the notion of security; he attaches a "risk-plus" connotation which is meant to apply in conditions of economic growth and development. Stock is employed for present consumption or for future profit, but there must be "tolerable security" at the macro or societal level before any stock is allocated to alternative future profit-making activities. Stock assumes the form of fixed and circulating capital. Rapid growth in annual produce is attributed to systemic increasing returns associated with investment in these types of capital in conditions of "tolerable security." Only "perfectly crazy" individuals would desist from employing their stock in one of these ways (*WN* II i 30), so full security ensures maximum utilization of the nation's capital and fullest possible exploitation of investment opportunities through time.[7]

Now in conditions where insufficient security is manifest, capital formation is compromised:

> In those unfortunate countries, indeed, where men are continually afraid of the violence of their superiors, they frequently bury and conceal a great part of their stock, in order to have it at hand to carry with them to some place of safety, in case of their being threatened with any of those disasters to which they consider themselves as at all times exposed.
>
> (*WN* II i 31)

Here the nature of portending "disasters" is of a different order from the riskiness of returns in the standard economic sense of a recognized, expected deviation from some natural or normal return. For, in normal secure times, a law of large numbers can be said to apply such that, while there is always risk in commercial affairs, by "dividing the whole circulation into a greater number of parts, the failure of any one company, an accident which, in the course of things, must happen, becomes of less consequence to the public" (*WN* II ii 106). The security conditions for capital formation are, by contrast, inestimable. Security is nevertheless consequential from the standpoint of society as a whole for both the employment of any capital and for actualizing its full potential. Capital may be threatened by insecurity which is indicated by an overwhelming feeling of investor unease.

In "secure" societies under changing economic conditions, money as a form of circulating capital plays an important role in controlling and transferring other components of capital (*WN* II ii 23). The profit rate may be demonstrably high, ordinarily running "between six and ten per cent" (*WN* II ii 69). The origination of fresh opportunities for investment by speculative projectors and adventurers continues apace. Smith locates supervision of the circulating function in the private banking system, but he is wary of accepting the view that financial capital markets could be left completely unregulated by governments.

While Edwin West (1990: 75–81) provides a modern treatment of Smith's analysis of money, banking and the rate of interest, he overlooks the place of security considerations in Smith's deliberations on interest rate regulation. First, West's interpretation follows Smith faithfully in recognizing the negative connotations placed on loans to prodigals in *WN*. Smith favored an interest rate ceiling in the loanable funds market, that is, a legal prohibition on high interest rates substantially above some normal rate. Such a prohibition would work to curtail consumption loans: loans which usually involve high risk for the lender. Second, speculative "projectors" may also have to be legally restrained: "where the legal rate of interest . . . is fixed but a very little above the lowest market rate, sober people are universally preferred, as borrowers, to prodigals and projectors" (*WN* II iv 15).[8] Credit rationing through an interest rate ceiling is required in situations where a commercial society is rendered insecure by a surfeit of prodigals and projectors directing and allocating capital relative to a smaller number of "sober people" who are similarly occupied. Indeed, Smith's concern for natural liberty and unregulated self interest in the commercial society was circumscribed by an awareness that there may be occasions when

> *a great part* of the capital of the country would . . . be kept out of the hands which were most likely to make a profitable and advantageous use of it, and thrown into those which were most likely to waste and destroy it.
> (*WN* II iv 15, emphasis added)

In the event, for Smith, intolerable security would loom larger at the societal level and, inevitably, economic advancement would be thwarted.

By contrast, the recommended interest rate regulation functioned to nurture the Smithian ideal of society-wide sobriety in commercial affairs, an attitude to investment which would bring regular and sustained growth rather than speculative boom and bust phenomena. A real-case boom and bust scenario is discussed disapprovingly, and the faults of certain bank lending practices are underscored. The British economy was at one point thrown into "clamour and distress" as a result, and the "real distress" of the country threatened not only the credit of projectors; more crucially, "the public credit" was placed in a parlous situation.[9]

As noted by the editors of the 1976 Glasgow edition of *WN*, the "sober" person is motivated by the virtue of prudence. Quoting the *Theory of Moral Sentiments* (*WN* VI i 6) they remark that "[s]ecurity is the first and principal object of prudence" (*WN* II iv 15 n 17). Prudence is not regarded as a strong extralegal moral force in *WN*, otherwise Smith would altogether have eschewed interest rate regulations.[10] At the early stage of economic development in the commercial society which is undergoing a major organizational transformation, moral conditions were not to be taken as ideal. Smith's underlying concern to contrive a modicum of societal security through specific government prohibitions, informs his judgement on credit rationing through interest rate regulation. In other words, the problem of security turns on non-economic considerations which were originally and fully enunciated in the *Theory of Moral Sentiments*, and these should not be passed over when reading *WN*.[11]

When Smith turns to discuss the "superior security of land" (*WN* II iv 17) over allocating capital to an interest-bearing loanable fund, he elaborates on another dimension of security. By security in this context Smith means much more than low economic risk, that is, liability to "accidents" in the process of investing capital in a specific activity (*WN* III i 3). The "other advantages" (*WN* II iv 17) of land ownership are explored later in *WN* Book III (ii). They are geographical proximity, tangibility of capital invested in land, and protection from institutional uncertainties which might prevail with other investments which may depend for their profitability on "elements of human folly and injustice . . . in distant countries [where there are people] . . . whose character and situation" are not fully understood. Moreover, another non-economic consideration figures prominently when assessing the security of land and agricultural investments:

> The beauty of the country besides, the pleasures of country life, the tranquillity of mind it promises, and . . . the independency which it really affords, have charms that more or less attract everybody.
>
> (*WN* III i 3)

When, allowing for ordinary risk premia, "equal or near equal profits" are in prospect from alternative investments, capital will be allocated toward land ownership and improvement rather than manufacturing or foreign trade. Security considerations clinch the decision in all cases provided the profit equalization condition is satisfied (*WN* III i 3, iv 19).

A strong physiocratic sentiment emerges at the end of *WN* Book III. After a long historical disquisition, Smith considers the physical presence and durability of land, and he concludes that capital is ultimately only fully secure when it is invested in the agricultural sector. Accordingly, capital "that is acquired to any country by commerce and manufacturers, is all a very precarious and uncertain possession, till some part of it has been secured and realized in the cultivation and improvement of its lands" (*WN* III iv 24). Smith is presumably interested in some socially optimal proportion of a nation's capital that must be allocated to agriculture, but he is not at all precise. Further, from the vantage point of a country as a whole, capital mobility is not perceived as a wholly desirable tendency, while the "lasting" nature of capital allocated to domestic agriculture is praised without exception.[12] Indeed, completely mobile capital in the hands of merchants (who are "not necessarily the citizen[s] of any particular country") implies insecurity for that country as a whole, and, as before, non-economic factors may be adduced to rationalize this view. For example, agricultural investments may be favored because of the tranquillity of rural pursuits and the semblance of solidity or permanence conferred on capital in agriculture (*WN* III iv 24 *passim*). Smith's predilection to downplay the purely economic, allocative advantages of freely mobile capital in the growth process therefore seems defensible if we give due regard to these factors.

The metaphor of the invisible hand is expressly used in *WN* Book *IV* (ii 9) to describe the optimal capital allocation in the process of economic development. Another dimension of the security concept adorns that metaphor, and it deserves elaboration because modern commentators have been remiss in neglecting it.[13] According to Smith:

> By preferring the support of domestic to that of foreign industry he [the investor] *intends only his own security*; and by directing that industry in such a manner as its produce may be of the greatest value, he intends only his own gain, and he is in this, as in many other cases, led by an invisible hand to promote an end which was no part of his intention.
>
> (*WN* IV ii 9, emphasis added)

This passage is underwritten by the doctrine of investment priorities which is first explained in *WN* Book *II* (v). Smith constructs an argument supporting a natural order of investments in dynamic conditions – "in every growing society" (*WN* II i 8). That order is headed by agriculture, followed by manufacturing, internal trade and foreign trade.

Ricardo, McCulloch and others contested and controverted Smith's argument.[14] Some recent rational reconstructions have defended and rehabilitated the Smithian doctrine of investment priorities (Hollander 1973: 277–304; Negishi 1985). If we survey uses of the term "security" in conjunction with Smith's statements on investment priorities, it becomes evident that the natural order of investments is determined by relative profit rates calculated with the conventional notion of risk in mind. However, there is also a security component informing investment decisions, which is unalloyed by degrees of risk on Smith's own terms, that is in terms of the "probability or improbability of success." First, matters of security relate to unanticipated, surprising capital losses or disasters; these have consequential negative effects on attitudes to investment. In practice, those attitudes were unlikely to have been well-informed in the first instance by rational calculations of actuarial risk.[15]

Market participants have limited rationality. Second, the security component implies that investment is historically contingent. Smith's sequence of sectoral investment priorities is logically arranged not only on the basis of expected profits adjusted for risk, but also historically. That is, as an historical generalization, Smith assigns agriculture a pivotal role as the sector of primitive capital accumulation.

The productivity of capital in different activities is approximated by the number of productive laborers employed (*WN* II v 19, 23).[16] As already adumbrated, in the early stages of economic development the positive association between economic progress and capital allocated to land or agriculture rests on those broader security considerations attaching to investment in land. Moreover, agriculture is preferred because manufacturing is exposed to uncertain variables on the demand side ("human folly"). Whereas an "artificer is the servant of his customers," an agriculturalist is more secure since he "cultivates his own land and derives his necessary subsistence from the labour of his own family [and] is really a master, and independent of all the world" (*WN* III i 3, 5). The role of security, for instance in determining the priority of investing in manufacturing for the home trade over foreign trade, is left mostly implicit.

Nevertheless, Smith argued as if security concerns were a necessary part of the investment decision. Most capital in foreign trade is allocated to transport. That is, more fixed capital is used in the "carrying trade" than is the case in manufacturing. Investments in the carrying trade were not very labor intensive and were based on significant unknowns, namely "the extent of the surplus produce of all the different countries of the world" (*WN* II v 30, 36). Excess capacity would often be experienced in the transportation of tradeable goods. The uncertainty or variability of geographically distant demands, and the temporal distance of returns on fixed capital employed in foreign commerce, count against the "safety" of investments in that sector (*WN* II ii 64; II v 28). By contrast, manufacturing for the home trade is geographically closer to its market, and demand uncertainties are of a different, lower order. The use of more labor-intensive methods in manufacturing relative to the foreign carrying trade means that the problem of the security of capital does not figure so prominently. Furthermore, relatively less fixed capital and more circulating capital in manufacturing means that initial capital investments in that sector will be more secure in the sense that cash flows will usually be more immediate (*WN* II v 10, 11).[17]

In the doctrine of investment priorities, geographical proximity, the physical presence of capital, demand uncertainties, and the speediness of returns must all be considered as dimensions of "security." While differential risk is a necessary element, it is not a sufficient condition for investment decisions. Investors' positive sense of security originates investment opportunities; it is always relevant to the willingness to create any capital whatsoever from society's investable surplus. As before, insecurity amounts to something more than assessable or calculable risk, especially in economies undergoing significant organizational reforms. To be sure, in both the economics of development and the comparative economic histories of growth and development outlined in *WN* Books II and III respectively, resource endowments, consumer demands, and risk premia are all factors influencing the return on capital and hence the pattern of investment decisions taken by individuals motivated by the profit motive (Hollander 1973: 302). However, the level or extent of investment is not guaranteed. Full resource utilization depends on the prevailing climate of security within which commerce is embedded; if satisfactory, it will shape the very nature of investment opportunities. We turn next to consider in more detail the institutional characteristics of security arrangements discussed in *WN*.

Security as an institutional constraint on investment

The vast collection of institutional material in *WN* was not arranged in an *ad hoc* fashion. As Ronald Coase maintained, there is a definite structure to that material: "one finds Adam Smith discussing the appropriate institutional framework for the working of a price system" (Coase (1977: 320). In respect of the concept of security for example, Smith systematically encapsulates all the institutional phenomena necessary and sufficient for capital formation in an "advancing" commercial society.

According to Douglas North, institutions are "the humanly devised constraints that structure human interaction. They are made up of formal constraints (such as, rules, laws, constitutions), informal constraints (such as, norms of behaviour, conventions, self-imposed codes of conduct), and their enforcement characteristics" (North 1994: 360). Smith's deliberations on the formal institutional constraints on long-term economic development were focussed on the appropriateness of the system of law and government in any country. The precise constituents of this system are formulated in *The Lectures on Jurisprudence* (Smith 1978) and *The Theory of Moral Sentiments* (Smith 1976b).[18] Nathan Rosenberg (1960) makes an early attempt to distil the specific institutional aspects of law and government required in the desired market form of economic organization proposed in *WN*. Rosenberg concentrates on institutions which had a direct impact on the behavior of individuals. That is, he explores the effects of extant incentive structures on individual or group behavior which Smith regards as deleterious to the development of opulence. He also outlines those structures which harness self-interest in commercial affairs to the general welfare. Rosenberg is led perforce to study specific aspects of the institutional framework analyzed by Smith at the micro-level which either thwart or are favorable to opulence.

Our attention in this paper is also avowedly on an institutional aspect of WN, but it is not one which Rosenberg fully investigates, perhaps because security for Smith often assumes the form of a macro-institutional problem. The attainment of security is frequently mentioned in *WN* as a fundamental social objective. This does not gainsay Smith's keen appreciation of the informal micro-behavioral consequences of reaching this objective – the desire for capital accumulation is indeed at the core of the matter. We have listed all those instances in which security is explicitly mentioned by Smith in conjunction with a summary of the context in Table 5.1.

At first glance, Smith's utterances on security might mistakenly be construed as an example of his entirely desultory use of a word which has minor significance in *WN* taken as a whole. Table 5.1 is constructed on the presumption that Smith's choice of terms should not be so deprecated; it demonstrates that security is not at all treated cursorily in *WN*. Each context in which the term is mentioned is classified thematically in the right-hand column according to whether Smith's predominant concern was with first, the absolute level of capital formation through the long-run development process or second, the pattern of capital allocation, that is, the capital structure at any point in time.[19] The separation of the first and the second is artificial and made only for heuristic purposes. In a growing economy the extent of capital accumulation and the capital structure are interdependent.

As for the level of capital formation in the growth process, Smith repudiates net hoarding: "What is annually saved is as regularly consumed as what is annually spent, and nearly in the same time too, but it is consumed by a different set of people" (*WN* II iii 18). Now this proposition is founded on the view that a system of natural liberty was enshrined in the constitution of society at the commercial stage of development. That is, net saving and net investment had substantial identity in countries where conditions of law and government supported natural liberty in commercial affairs. Specifically, as retrieved from Smith's early writings by Winch (1978), the concept of natural liberty is to be found in Smith's politics. It emphasizes the role of a strong government which protects personal and civil liberty. Liberty is protected in an impartially-administered system of natural justice based on rights such as the inviolability of private property and private contracts. (See also Werhane 1991.) These rights render security to individuals; they function "by securing to every man the fruits of his own industry" (*WN* IV vii c 54). Security is here used in the sense of a protection afforded to individuals by certain legal institutions (also *WN* V i b 1, 2). While capital formation depended on these fundamental legal institutions, the level of saving was determined by a complex of socio-cultural factors which in Smith's work are deeply rooted in history, and which prescribe virtuous behavior (Fitzgibbons 1995). In other words, saving depends on what Douglas North (1994: 360) calls "informal" institutions: on prudence and frugality; on the attitudes of people toward bettering their condition; in short, on habits and norms in any society. Moreover, savings decisions are not related directly to the prospect of some average rate of profit, although decisions to allocate savings to alternative investments will assuredly take relative profit rates as a guide.

In all the contexts in which level of capital formation is the principal referent for security in Table 5.1, it is notable that the formal macro-legal institutional framework in which investment decisions are made is uppermost in Smith's mind. For example, net investment is made if the "laws and institutions" in any country are favorable. Circumstances may be imagined where institutional arrangements are very different such that actual and potential capital formation diverge:

> The owners of "large capitals" may enjoy a good deal of security, the poor or the owners of small capitals enjoy scarce any, but are liable, under the pretence of justice, to be pillaged and plundered ... [T]he quantity of stock employed in all the different branches of business transactions [in

Table 5.1 Security and institutional factors in *The Wealth of Nations*

Explicit reference to security	Context	Predominant theme: Level of capital formation or the structure of capital allocations
I ix 15, 16	Owners of "large capitals" may be favored by legal and other institutional arrangements in any country to invest	Capital formation
I x c 13	Statutes of apprenticeship give no guarantee against poor workmanship and fraud	Allocative structure
I xi p 8	The consequences of inappropriate government policies are not well understood by indolent landlords whose investment decisions must accordingly be ill-informed	Allocative structure
II i 30, 31	Political instability reduces capital accumulation	Capital formation
III i 3	"Injustice of human laws" can "disturb" employment of capital in agriculture	Allocative structure
III ii 3	Landed estates and laws of primogeniture are institutions for the protection of capital	Allocative structure
III ii 6, 7	Legal institutions in Europe result in "great tracts of land" remaining uncultivated and thus lead to insufficient investment	Capital formation
III iii 12	"Order and good government" promotes "liberty and security"; it has resulted in high levels of investment in some European city states	Capital formation
IV vii c 43, 46	Commerce of Great Britain is rendered precarious by artificial constraints on utilization of capital, e.g. in the colony trade. Political "disorder and confusion" and misuse of capital ensues	Allocative structure
IV vii c 54	Both "liberty of trade" and "impartial administration of justice" give great encouragement to industry	Capital formation

68 Anthony Endres

Table 5.1 (continued)

Explicit reference to security	Context	Predominant theme: Level of capital formation or the structure of capital allocations
IV vii c 95	Monopoly affords protection for "a great profit"	Allocative structure
V i b 1, 2	Sovereign protects property rights and the individual from injustice. Civil magistrate protects individual from passions: envy, malice and resentment, and therefore encourages investment	Capital formation
V i b 12	Civil government protects property of the rich and thereby favors saving and investment	Capital formation
V i b 25 V i g 24	Capital investment and economic advancement depends on impartial administration of justice and civil government which protects the "liberty, reason and happiness of mankind"	Capital formation
V iii 7	Commerce flourishes with regular administration of justice, contract law and private property rights structure	Capital formation

such circumstances] . . . *can never be equal to what the nature and extent of that business might admit.*

(*WN* I ix 15, emphasis added)

The "science of the legislator" tradition of Adam Smith scholarship (Winch 1978, 1983, 1988; Haakonssen 1981) has appreciated the complexities in the relationship between commercial advance, as measured by the level of capital formation, and natural liberty. We should, in endorsing this reading, take the following statement from *WN* literally but not in isolation: "commerce and manufactures gradually introduced order and good government, and with them, the liberty and security of individuals" (*WN* III iv 4). The usual embroidery of carefully-selected quotations can make it appear, as in this passage, that the relationship between economy and political institutions, or between economic growth through what Smith called "commerce" and liberty, was unidirectional, when in fact *WN* frequently underscores their interdependencies.[20] As many of the illustrations in Table 5.1 demonstrate, a prerequisite for full utilization of a society's capital is a definite institutional order supporting personal and societal security, that is, some semblance, at least, of natural liberty (*WN* IV ii 42, *WN* VII c 54). Security connotes "confidence in the justice of government" (*WN* V iii 7).

At a more practical level, governance and enforcement of contractual relations and upholding property rights are necessary aspects of a government's administration of justice. And with confidence comes the growth of commerce and capital formation. Smith mentions the "risk and trouble" of employing capital (*WN* V ii f 2) as though such considerations were embedded in a broader framework of "security": risk and trouble pale into insignificance if societal security is threatened.

Institutional aspects of security in *WN* are elaborated as part of a theory of economic development. In the development process commerce had indeed been favorable to "liberty and security," but Smith hardly presumes that all is well with contemporary institutions within his purview; "liberty and security" could further be enhanced. As Winch (1983: 257) recognizes, commerce "had been favorable to liberty, but only under circumstances in which a political and legal order existed that was capable of being *consciously adapted and extended*" (emphasis added).

Table 5.1 reinforces Winch's reading. The mutual interdependencies between economic development and institutional adaptations having as their ultimate objective "liberty and security" are illustrated by the entries labeled "allocative structure" in Table 5.1. In many instances these entries refer to what Smith regards as capital misallocations arising from pernicious regulations of commerce: regulations which are in need of reform so as to be conducive to the prescribed market form of economic organization in *WN*. Some regulations produce personal security or security for a particular social class which conflicts with the best use of scarce capital, for example the statute of apprenticeships, laws affecting land tenure, and the colony trade. All these laws change the structure of incentives and disrupt the functioning of capital markets, such that the use of capital is delimited and driven into less productive activities. Such allocative constraints ultimately impact on the rate at which capital may be accumulated. If a system of natural liberty, however imperfect, is constitutionalized so that "order and good government" may be promoted, the disastrous economic consequences of capital misallocations can be minimized (*WN* III iii 12, iv 4).

All of Smith's references to security in the latter part of Book IV and V deal with the system of natural liberty. Smith locates the fundamental institutional aspects of security in general jurisprudential rules rather than in transitory, contemporary economic regulations. Smith's constitution-making agenda turns on the part played by general rules in establishing natural liberty (West 1976: 520–9). The point of constitutional economics in *WN* is to urge that even an approximation to natural liberty in a society's constitution would allow scope for economic progress despite the harmful effects of specific economic regulations. On one level of argument, security has various specific contextual referents in *WN*, that is at points when Smith recommends reforms of existing economic regulations affecting capital allocation. On another level, security has a general constitutional basis turning critically on the governance of contractual relations and property rights. The content of the security concept in this connection refers to protection of individuals from governments and from the force or fraud of other individuals. For those familiar with Smith's other writings this conclusion may be scarcely surprising; there are, for example, allusions to security wrought by constitutional rules in the *Theory of Moral Sentiments*.[21]

Conclusion

Adam Smith provides an institutional analysis of the allocation of a given volume of capital; he also extends that analysis to the forces determining the volume of capital itself. "Security" in *WN* becomes a multifaceted institutional factor to be distinguished from considerations regarding ordinary commercial risk. When insecurity is reduced to mere quantifiable risk in the canonical classical model, this underplays broader institutional aspects of capital markets which Adam Smith took seriously. Well-functioning capital markets may not exist; such markets require a complex set of institutional arrangements to avoid systemic market breakdown and large-scale capital underutilization. In the language of late twentieth-century institutional economics, institutions which produce security matter for macroeconomic performance and macroeconomic incentive alignment. They ultimately reduce the costliness of transactions involving the creation and allocation of capital (see North 1993, Williamson 1998).

Altogether, any treatment which explains Smith's analysis of capital formation, the capital structure and profit in terms of conventional risk and risk premia by-passes the problem of those very factors which give rise to security in an economy undergoing a major transformation in its organizational form. Smith is aware of the difficulties that follow from insecurity, its affects on long-run investment trends and on economic development. In *WN* there is a relationship between profit, capital supply and security, but it does not by any means have the equivalent content of a functional relationship (where interest plus risk is the independent variable and capital is the dependent variable) of the kind which the canonical model attributes to Smith's discussion of capital and risk in analyses of long-run equilibrium. Modern attributions of functional constructs to *WN* can be too limiting; they point us away from general reflections on moral and attitudinal factors, law, government, necessary regulatory adaptations, and constitution-making, which Smith regarded as vital factors influencing economic development.

Security is reflected in elements of an institutional character in dynamic circumstances, and these include various informal influences on capital formation: the common opinion as to the viability of exploiting known investment opportunities to the point of making the fullest possible use of a society's potential investable surplus; the extent to which attitudes to investment are dominated by prodigals as opposed to sober and prudent investors; and conventions about the physical propinquity of investments and immediacy of returns on capital in different activities. Other references to security in *WN*, as contrasted with these informal institutional aspects, are made in the context of reflections on the need to adapt the formal institutions of law and government. To promote security and thenceforth improve both the capital structure and the rate of capital formation, Smith makes two principal policy recommendations. First, he argues for reform of particular, contemporary economic regulations to alter incentives affecting the allocation of capital. Second, he recommends that general norms of natural justice be enshrined in the constitution of any society in the incipient commercial stage of economic development.

Adam Smith's discussion of capital offers much for both neo-classicalists and new institutionalists. For the former, Samuelson's ahistorical, canonical reconstruction allows for complete diffusion of institutional adaptations as capital is accumulated and profit opportunities are exploited. Decisions to create and allocate capital are optimal: risk and insecurity are substantially identical. For institutionalists, by contrast, institutional reforms matter for maximum capital accumulation, and they take time to effect. Institutional adaptations conducive to economic growth diffuse slowly. For Smith, the requisite constitutional arrangements must be established. The regulatory structure affecting incentives to allocate capital may need to be altered. Finally, the informal institutional setting, moral and attitudinal foundations must be appropriate to maintain a viable market organizational form. Security in Smithian capital markets obtains when all these institutional elements are configured favorably.

Notes

I am obliged to Ingrid Peters-Fransen for instructive comments on the development of the "security" concept in Smith's work; to my conference commentator, Arnold Heertje, and also to Christian Schmidt for specific comments on the earlier conference version of this paper. The usual disclaimer applies.

1 Notable is Samuelson's (1988: 162nl) point that the canonical model could be formulated "in pre-neoclassical or in Sraffa v. Neumann terms."
2 Winch (1997: 388, 396, 398) avers that "Smith was not trying very hard to be a general equilibrium theorist"; he fulminates against saddling Smith with a "comparative static allocation model based on full employment," concluding that Smith's "interest in equilibrium theorising was rarely sustained." Similar sentiments are expressed in Dow, Dow and Hutton (1997: 376–7).
3 The institutional dimension of *WN* originally received attention in Rosenberg 1960 and later Rosenberg 1990. See also Fitzgibbons (1995: 137–88).
4 For example:

> The keeper of an inn or tavern who is never master of his own house, and who is exposed to the brutality of every drunkard, exercises neither a very agreeable, nor a very creditable business. *But there is scarce a common trade* in which a small stock yields so great a profit.
>
> (*WN* I x b 4, emphasis added)

5 The term "hazard" was used in a similar sense by David Hume ([1755] 1955: 17), Richard Cantillon ([1755] 1931: 211) and Frances Hutcheson (1755: 73). That Smith generally favored the term "risk" is illustrated in his early lectures on justice (Smith 1896: 174–5). Cantillon's influence is noted there (ibid.: 174 n1). See also Knight (1921: 24, 1935: 254).
6 To be sure, Smith does not underestimate the difficulties in moving from this purely abstract conclusion to identifying profit rate equalization, let alone some average profit rate, in a real case. He admits that in reality "profit is so very fluctuating" (*WN* I ix 3,4).

7   Eltis (1984: 75) interprets Smith as arguing that a "country [must] maintain 'tolerable security' for creditors," but this view is too summary since even the investor who uses "his own" capital requires "tolerable security" (*WN* II i 30).
8   We should emphasize that Smith advocated restraint towards, rather than elimination of, projectors because he was not entirely hostile toward them. Projectors were inclined to plan their investments carefully, and this trait impressed Smith. For an elaboration of this point see Pesciarelli (1989: 524–7).
9   David Hume's comment on the situation as reported at this point in *WN* by the editors of the Glasgow Edition illustrates poignantly the nature of those broader societal security considerations which underwrote Smith's account of events: "We are here in a very melancholy situation: continual Bankruptcies, universal loss of credit, and endless suspicions . . . [E]ven the Bank of England is not entirely free from suspicion" (*WN* II ii 72 n 42).
10 Compare the theme maintained in Werhane (1991: 126), that constitutionalized commutative justice, combined with the purely extralegal forces of co-operation, frugality, a minimum level of public education, and prudence, would be sufficient to "regulate" private interests in Smith's commercial society, thus leaving natural liberty much scope to flourish. Also, the importance of prudence in Smith's conceptualization of entrepreneurship is lucidly brought out by Pesciarelli (1989: 533–6).
11 This example of the importance of this non-economic dimension of "security" in *WN* reinforces Winch (1983: 502) who concludes that "Smith's advice to the legislator depends on considerations that do not flow from *economic* reasoning alone" (emphasis in original). Smith's non-economic considerations are of no small consequence for his ideas in *WN*, and these are explored in general by Winch 1978 and 1988, and by Pesciarelli 1989 with particular reference to the concept of prudence as expounded in *The Theory of Moral Sentiments*.
12 See also *WN* II v 13–14 where, taking the stance of "any society" Smith looks unfavorably upon the capital of the merchant which "seems to have no fixed or necessary residence anywhere."
13 Streissler 1991: 388–9 is an exception. It hardly seems a coincidence that in the very paragraph where Smith mentions the invisible hand in *The Theory of Moral Sentiments* (Smith 1976b: IV i 10), he also refers to "security." For the invisible hand presupposes a complete set of supporting institutions which mitigate insecurity in capital markets.
14 Hollander 1973: 278–80 exposits the essence of the Ricardo-McCulloch critique.
15 Smith had already pointed out that investors are hardly careful or rational since they often tend to overestimate their own luck and the value of their opinions about the future. Thus, he reflects on the "over-weening conceit which the greater part of men have of their own abilities" and concludes that the "chance of gain is by every man more or less over valued, and the chance of loss is by most men undervalued" (*WN* I xb 26).
16 Bowley 1975: 374 outlines the obvious flaws in Smith's attempt to use productive employment as a measure of the value added by additional amounts of capital allocated to different sectors. See also Hollander 1973: 294 ff.
17 As foreshadowed in *WN* II ii 64, the "returns of the fixed capital are in almost all cases much slower than those of the circulating capital."
18 Furubotn and Richter 1997: 278 lament that the "set of formal and informal rules that steer individual behavior in a particular direction, was not much analyzed by economists after Adam Smith."
19 We set aside use of the term "security" when it refers directly to national security provided by defence forces (*WN* II iii 2, II v 30).
20 Compare Hirschman who takes Smith's idea in isolation and concludes that "Smith affirms here that economics can go it alone: within wide limits of tolerance, *political progress is not needed as a prerequisite* for, nor is it likely to be a consequence of, economic advance" (Hirschman 1978: 103–4, emphasis added).

21 Given a simple system of natural liberty, Smith maintains that in "ease of body and peace of mind, all the different ranks of life are nearly upon a level, and the beggar who suns himself by the side of the highway, possesses that security which kings are fighting for" (Smith 1976b: IV 1 10)

References

Bowley, M. (1975) "Some Aspects of the Treatment of Capital in Wealth of Nations," in *Essays on Adam Smith*, ed. A. S. Skinner and T. Wilson, Oxford: Clarendon Press.
Brown, V. (1997) "'Mere Inventions of the Imagination': A Survey of Recent Literature on Adam Smith," *Economics and Philosophy* 13(2): 281–312.
Cantillon, R. [1755] (1931) *Essai Sur la Nature du Commerce*, ed. H. Higgs, London: Macmillan.
Coase, R. H. (1977) "*Wealth of Nations*," *Economic Inquiry* 15: 309–25.
Dow, A., Dow, S. and Hutton, A. (1997), "The Scottish Political Economy Tradition and Modern Economics," *Scottish Journal of Political Economy* 44(4): 368–83.
Eltis, W. (1984) *The Classical Theory of Economic Growth*, London: Macmillan.
Endres, A. M. (1992) "Adam Smith's use of Historical Evidence as Illustrated from the Theory of Investment Priorities," *Journal of European Economic History* 21 (Fall): 257–71.
—— (1995) "Adam Smith's Advisory Style as Illustrated by his Trade Policy Prescriptions," *Journal of the History of Economic Thought* 17(1): 1–18.
Fitzgibbons, A. (1995) *Adam Smith's System of Liberty, Wealth and Virtue*, Oxford: Oxford University Press.
Furubotn, E. and Richter, R. (1997) *Institutions and Economic Theory*, Michigan: University of Michigan Press.
Haakonssen, K. (1981) *The Science of a Legislator: The Natural Jurisprudence of David Hume and Adam Smith*, Cambridge: Cambridge University Press.
Hirschman, A. (1978) *The Passions and the Interests: Political Arguments for Capitalism Before its Triumph*, Princeton: Princeton University Press.
Hollander, S. (1973) *The Economics of Adam Smith*, Toronto: University of Toronto Press.
—— (1980) "On Professor Samuelson's Canonical Classical Model of Political Economy," *Journal of Economic Literature* 18: 559–74. Reprinted in S. Hollander (1995), *Ricardo – The New View: Collected Essays I*, London: Routledge: ch. 20.
—— (1996) "The Canonical Classical Model of Growth: Content, Adherence and Priority," Paper given at an ECHE Conference, April 1997.
Hume, D. [1755] (1955) *Writings on Economics*, ed. W. Rotwein, London: Nelson.
Hutcheson, F. (1755) *A System of Moral Philosophy*, London: Millar and Longman.
Knight, F. H. (1921) *Risk, Uncertainty and Profit*, Boston: Houghton Mifflin.
—— (1935) *The Ethics of Competition and Other Essays*, London: Unwin.
Kurdas, C. (1988), "The 'Whig Historian' on Adam Smith: Paul Samuelson's Canonical Classical Model," *History of Economics Society Bulletin* 9(1): 13–23.
Negishi, T. (1985) *Economic Theories in a Non-Walrasian Tradition*, Cambridge: Cambridge University Press.
North, D. C. (1993) "Institutions and Economic Performance", in U. Mäki *et al.* (eds), *Rationality, Institutions and Economic Methodology*, London: Routledge.
—— (1994) "Economic Performance Through Time," *American Economic Review* 84(3): 359–68.
Pesciarelli, E. (1989) "Smith, Bentham, and the Development of Contrasting Ideas on Entrepreneurship," *History of Political Economy* 21(3): 521–36.
Rosenberg, N. (1960) "Some Institutional Aspects of Wealth of Nations," *Journal of Political Economy* 68: 557–70.

—— (1990) "Adam Smith and the Stock of Moral Capital," *History of Political Economy* 22(1): 1–17.
Samuelson, P. (1977) "A Modern Theorist's Vindication of Adam Smith," *American Economic Review* 67: 42–49.
—— (1978) "On the Canonical Classical Model of Political Economy," *Journal of Economic Literature* 16: 1415–34.
—— (1988) "Keeping Whig History Honest," *History of Economics Society Bulletin* 10(2): 161–7.
Smith, A. (1896) *Lectures on Justice, Police, Revenue and Arms*, ed. E. Cannan, Oxford: Oxford University Press.
—— (1976a) *An Inquiry into the Nature and Causes of Wealth of Nations*, ed. R. H. Campbell, A. S. Skinner and W. B. Todd, Oxford: Oxford University Press.
—— (1976b) *The Theory of Moral Sentiments*, ed. D. D. Raphael and A. L. Macfie, Oxford: Oxford University Press.
—— (1978) *Lectures on Jurisprudence*, ed. R. L. Meek, D. D. Raphael and P. G. Stein, Oxford: Oxford University Press.
Streissler, E. (1991) "'Genius or Engines': On Jürg Niehans' History of Economic Technique," *Journal of Institutional and Theoretical Economics* 147: 379–95.
Werhane, P. (1991) *Adam Smith and His Legacy for Modern Capitalism*, Oxford: Oxford University Press.
West, E. G. (1976) "Adam Smith's Economics of Politics," *History of Political Economy* 8 (4): 515–39.
—— (1990) *Adam Smith and Modern Economics*, Aldershot: Elgar.
Williamson, O. E. (1998) "The Institutions of Governance," *American Economic Review* 88(2): 75–79
Winch, D. M. (1978) *Adam Smith's Politics*, Cambridge: Cambridge University Press.
—— (1983) "Science and the Legislator: Adam Smith and After," *Economic Journal* 93: 501–20.
—— (1988) "Commentary," in *Classical Political Economy*, ed. W. Thweatt, Boston: Kluwer.
—— (1997) "Adam Smith's Problem and Ours," *Scottish Journal of Political Economy* 44(4): 384–402.

6 Beyond the canonical growth model

Knowledge and learning in classical economics, 1815–34

Masazumi Wakatabe

Introduction

> We used to think of the gap between developed and less-developed countries to be an object gap – the lack of capital. And we now realize that this is the gap in knowledge. And closing that gap is one of the most important strategies for development.
>
> (Joseph E. Stiglitz 1997)

Recently, Samuel Hollander has argued for the existence of a canonical classical growth model shared by most post-1815 classical economists, running from the four economists of February 1815 – Sir Edward West, Thomas Robert Malthus, David Ricardo, and Robert Torrens – to J. E. Cairnes (Hollander 1998b). According to the model, throughout the growth process both wage and profit rates decline simultaneously due to diminishing returns to capital, assuming that "knowledge" is given.[1] The purpose of this chapter is to examine the extent to which post-1815 classical economists committed to this assumption and attempted to construct a model in which knowledge changes. Knowledge in the broadest sense can influence the growth process in two ways: it can change productivity, and hence the capital accumulation rate; it can also change the "providence and forethought" of the population through education, and hence the population growth rate. This chapter deals mainly with the first channel, while it will touch upon the second where necessary.[2]

The status of knowledge in post-1815 classical economics has been discussed by Cannan (1929), Robbins (1968), Berg (1980), and Brewer (1991). Edwin Cannan (1929) criticizes "[t]he common neglect of knowledge" by the classical economists, pointing out three reasons. First, and "probably the principal," is that they knew the importance of knowledge, but did not emphasize it:

> economists have seldom been sufficiently alive to the fact that the most apparently obvious things are often the least noticed, and that it is consequently desirable for teachers to insist on them, even if they are liable to be told that "everyone knows that."
>
> (Cannan 1929: 122)

Second, Cannan traces the origin of such a neglect back to Adam Smith's unique formulation of knowledge, involving the division of labor:

> Adam Smith tucked away increase of knowledge under the wings of his exposition of the advantages of the division of labour, saying that division of labour encouraged the invention of machinery and promoted science by specialising particular persons to particular kinds of industry or research. Subsequent writers were often induced by this to forget that the progress of knowledge, though certainly enormously assisted by division of labour, is not wholly dependent on it.
>
> (Cannan 1929: 122–3)

Third, he points out the public-goods nature of knowledge: "most accumulated knowledge is free for the use of all in unlimited quantity, so that it has no value, and economists have generally been inclined to neglect things of no value, however important they may be" (ibid.: 122–3).

His arguments rest mainly on classical economists' tracts from around the 1840s; the prime example is the third edition of McCulloch's *Principles of Political Economy* (1843), including "no section for the accumulation or increase of knowledge, and it is scarcely referred to at all in the sections which exist." Senior, too, could only think of four "causes on which the productiveness of labour depends," and did not make knowledge one of the four in his *Outline* (Senior 1836). Though J. S. Mill is entitled to some credit for having broken this tradition, later writers were judged to have failed to develop the subject (ibid.: 123).

Robbins (1968) counters Cannan's assertions. After pointing out classical economists' attempts to propagate economic knowledge – James Mill's involvement in the Society for the Diffusion of Useful Knowledge and the works of popularizers such as Charles Knight, William Ellis, and Harriet Martineau, a rather different aspect of knowledge – he concedes that Cannan certainly made a point in that nineteenth-century classical economics as exemplified by Senior and McCulloch was not concerned with knowledge in its formal statements. However, he maintains that "[a]t the same time it must be said that other pronouncements by the two writers in question indicate without the possibility of contradiction a full awareness of this factor and its great importance" (Robbins 1968: 91), citing McCulloch's review of Babbage's *On the Economy of Machinery and Manufactures* (1st edn, 1832) in the *Edinburgh Review* (McCulloch 1833a) and Senior's lectures delivered at Oxford in 1848–9.[3] In addition to them, his main examples of classical economists concerned with knowledge consist of Charles Babbage, John Rae, and John Stuart Mill.[4]

In a full book-length study on post-1815 classical economists' conception of the "machinery" question, Berg (1980) argues strongly for their recognition of knowledge. She also maintains their growing interest in knowledge from the 1820s to the 1830s, with reference to John Rae among others. The book is wide-ranging, paying attention to economic history, various works of lesser economists, and "movements" such as the Mechanics Institute and the Society for the Diffusion of Useful Knowledge, so that it is closer to Robbins (1968), though it does not particularly refer to Cannan (1929) or Robbins (1968).

Brewer (1991) paints a similar picture of classical economics to Cannan (1929), with a major exception showing that John Rae was "genuinely original" in his conception of economic growth "wholly driven by invention." Admitting the impossibility of giving full consideration to all the significant writers of the period from 1776 to 1834, Brewer nonetheless claims that "Rae was substantially right in treating the whole classical school as faithful followers of Smith" (Brewer 1991: 9), that is, they neglected the role of knowledge creation.[5] His examination is focused on the four writers of February 1815, none of whom scored high in Brewer's evaluation. For West, "the trend of the profit rate is the net result of increasing returns in manufacturing (because of the division of labour) and decreasing returns in agriculture (because of land scarcity)," so "either might predominate, but because profit rates have actually fallen, diminishing returns must be the more important" (ibid.: 9; see also Brewer 1988). Torrens fared a little better because he dealt with technical change more thoroughly and more explicitly than any other classical writer of the time, but his analysis is then brushed aside as an "abstract exercise with no explanation of how it relates to observed growth" (ibid.: 10), with the overall framework of his theory remaining Ricardian. J. S. Mill and Senior are excepted from this generalization, because they wrote after Rae, and learned from him (ibid.: 11). As for Babbage, West questions the status of Babbage as an economist (ibid.: 11n).

Apart from certain ambiguities in the literature, two major issues are involved: whether or not classical economists appreciated the important role of knowledge in the growth process; and whether or not they constructed a "formal" presentation. In this chapter, I shall argue that most post-1815 classical economists recognized the role of knowledge; indeed the later generation more so than the earlier. However, concerning the modeling of knowledge in the context of growth, none took the extra step except John Rae.

The scope of this chapter is admittedly limited in terms of the coverage of people and works; the chapter is concerned with the two decades from 1815–34, so I do not discuss Senior's *Outline*, or John Stuart Mill's attempt to incorporate knowledge into the basic growth model in his monumental *Principles*, or Karl Marx, the keen observer of knowledge generation in the capitalist production system.[6] Furthermore, the concentration on the canonical classical growth model prevents us from examining many important writers such as Lord Lauderdale, Jeremy Bentham, J-B. Say, Samuel Read and George Poulett Scrope.[7] Unlike Robbins (1968) and Berg (1980), I shall not deal with dimensions other than their growth models, excluding the popularization and propagation of political economy of the day.

The chapter is organized as follows. "Reviewing the 'troops'" looks at the first generation Ricardians, the economists involved in the formulation of the land-based growth theory in February of 1815, and their immediate follower, James Mill. "The next generation Ricardians" examines perspectives on knowledge and growth of the newer generation Ricardians such as Nassau William Senior and John Ramsey McCulloch. The next section deals with an essentially microeconomic contribution of Babbage, and the final section is devoted to John Rae, the foremost knowledge-based growth theorist. The conclusion recapitulates and summarizes the main arguments.

Reviewing the "troops": the first generation Ricardians on knowledge

This section deals with perspective on knowledge of what I call the first generation Ricardians, the four "revolutionaries" of February 1815 and their immediate follower, James Mill.[8] Schumpeter (1954) calls them "pessimists," attributing their "vision" of economic growth, comprised of constant population pressure combined with diminishing returns, to "the complete lack of imagination," since they did not recognize ever-increasing opportunities for technological progress though they "lived at the threshold of the most spectacular economic developments ever witnessed" (Schumpeter 1954: 571).

Now we have to admit that there is some truth in this generalization, since their basic model did not explicitly incorporate knowledge creation. However, as for diminishing returns, a distinction as to empirical or theoretical character would be helpful to understand their "vision." While West and Malthus tended to hold an empirical notion of diminishing agricultural returns, Ricardo and Torrens held theoretical ones. Further, it is important to understand that they did not neglect ongoing technological change, and some of them, Torrens and Malthus in particular, began to discuss the role of knowledge in the economy over their career.

David Ricardo

Blaug's statement that the "core of [Ricardo's] argument abstracts from technical change" (Blaug 1997: 99), though not wrong, is misleading in several respects. First, Ricardo did analyze the effects of various types of improvements on secular movements of factor returns (compare Eltis 1984: 210–6). Also, mainly in his correspondence, Ricardo repeatedly emphasized the significance of an incessant flow of "improvements" even in the midst of the Napoleonic War. His letter to Malthus, 17 August 1813 reads:

> I have little doubt however that for a long period, during the interval you mention [the two decades 1793–1813], there has been an increased rate of profits, but it has been accompanied with such decided improvements of agriculture both here and abroad, – for the French revolution was exceedingly favourable to the increased production of food, that it is perfectly reconcileable to my theory. My conclusion is that there has been a rapid increase of Capital which has been prevented from shewing itself in a low rate of interest by new facilities in the production of food.
> (Ricardo 1951–73, vol. 6: 94–5)

It should be noted that Ricardo himself thought the presence of these "decided improvements of agriculture" as "perfectly reconcileable to [his] theory."[9]

Moreover, there is Ricardo's own reply to any assertion that he did not recognize the importance of technological improvements in his theory. Malthus (1820) charged that Ricardo had "never laid any *stress* upon the influence of permanent improvements in agriculture on the profits of stock, although it is one of the most important considerations in the whole compass of Political Economy." Ricardo replied:

> Once more I must say that I lay the very greatest stress upon the influence of permanent improvements in Agriculture. The passage quoted refers to a state of things when no improvements are taking place, and therefore the argument built upon it which supposes improvements has no foundation.
>
> (Ricardo 1951–73, vol. 2: 293)

Nonetheless Ricardo did not incorporate a theory of technological change into a "core" of his analysis. There are several possible answers to why Ricardo adopted an analytical framework incorporating the diminishing agricultural returns. First, he did it for the sake of simplicity, since his task at hand is to spell out the basic model as concisely as he can. Second, he did it because of the nature of the improvements he had in mind, since in Ricardo's *Essay on Profits* we can find that "since technological progress takes the form of random shocks it might be accorded secondary status compared to diminishing returns" (Hollander 1987: 337):

> The causes, which render the acquisition of an additional quantity of corn more difficult are, in progressive countries, in constant operation, whilst marked improvements in agriculture, or in the implements of husbandry are of less frequent occurrence. If these opposite causes acted with equal effect, corn would be subject only to accidental variation of price, arising from bad seasons, from greater or less real wages of labour, or from an alteration in the value of the precious metals, proceeding from their abundance or scarcity.
>
> (Ricardo 1951–73, vol. 4: 19n)

Third, Berg (1980, chap. 4) maintains that Ricardo presented his model based on diminishing agricultural returns precisely because he believed in large gains derived from technological improvements. Her explanation is consistent with Ricardo's "optimistic" evaluation of the growth prospect of the British economy, but does not really answer the question why Ricardo did not develop a theory of technological change.

A few words on Ricardo's famous chapter on machinery, his formal discussion of "improvements," are in order. As Ricardo himself was well aware, it is a very peculiar construction in several aspects: the introduction of machinery into the production process is treated as autonomous and sudden; and he assumed *constant* real wages throughout the analysis. No doubt he assumed them for the sake of simplicity of exposition, "to elucidate the principle," bearing in mind that he ended the chapter on machinery with an optimistic tone:

> To elucidate the principle, I have been supposing, that improved machinery is *suddenly* discovered, and extensively used; but the truth is,

that these discoveries are gradual, and rather operate in determining the employment of the capital which is saved and accumulated, than in diverting capital from its actual employment.

(Ricardo 1951, vol. 1: 395)[10]

Unfortunately this "gradual" operation of technological innovations, shared by most classical economists, was not developed into a formal analysis by Ricardo himself.

Thomas Robert Malthus

Malthus followed the pattern set by Ricardo; he did not neglect to discuss various types of improvements, but did not incorporate them into the model. The major difference, however, is that Malthus represented diminishing agricultural productivity as a strong *empirical* principle.[11] Diminishing returns prevail *in spite of* improvements in agriculture:

> With regard to improvements in agriculture, which in similar soils is the great cause which retards the advance of price compared with the advance of produce: although they are sometimes very powerful, they are rarely found sufficient to balance the necessity of applying to poorer land, or inferior machines. In this respect, raw produce is essentially different from manufactures.
>
> (Malthus 1815b: 7; 1986: 137)

On the other hand, the price of manufactures is supposed to decline, despite high wages due to high price of corn:

> the real price of manufactures, the quantity of labour and capital necessary to produce a given quantity of them, is almost constantly diminishing; while the quantity of labour and capital necessary to procure the last addition that has been made to the raw produce of a rich and advancing country, is almost constantly increasing. We see in consequence, that in spite of continued improvements in agriculture, the money price of corn is *ceteris paribus* the highest in the richest countries, while in spite of this high price of corn, and consequent high price of labour lower than in poor countries.
>
> (Malthus 1815: 7; 1986: 137)

"The continued improvements made in manufacturing machinery" were often mentioned as a factor to be taken into account in determining the duration of *temporary deviations* from the downward trend (Ricardo 1951–73, vol. 6: 88), yet his main model remained the canonical growth model.

Though Malthus did not develop a knowledge-based growth theory, he sometimes treated technical change as endogenous.[12] In *Principles of Political Economy*, Chapter 7, "On the immediate causes of the progress of wealth," Section V, "Of inventions to save labour, considered as a stimulus to the continued increase of wealth," labor-saving inventions are formally treated as *endogenous* to increasing land scarcity:

> Inventions to save labour seldom take place to any considerable extent, except when there is a decided demand for them. They are the natural products of improvement and civilization, and, in their most perfect forms, generally come in aid of the falling powers of production on the land. The fertility of the soil, being a gift of nature, exists whether it is wanted or not; and must often therefore exceed for many hundred years the power of fully using it. Inventions, which substitute machinery for mutual exertions, being the result of the ingenuity of man, and called forth by his wants, will, as might be expected, seldom greatly exceed those wants.
> (Malthus 1820: 401–2; 1836: 351)

Another stimulus to improvements is the higher profit rate due to an expanded demand for agricultural goods:

> Without however supposing capital to be taken from the land, the throwing of new objects of desire into the market will increase the value of the whole mass of commodities in the country, estimated either in money, or in corn and labour, and there will in consequence be a greater value of commodities to be exchanged for the raw produce. This increase in the value of raw produce must raise the profits of farming for a period of some duration; and it is in fact during these periods (with the exception of the first start as is America) that capital is most rapidly accumulated upon the land and the greatest improvements are made.
> (Ricardo 1951–73, vol. 6: 153)

But, as Hollander rightly emphasizes, "in what follows, innovation is effectively treated as if it were exogenous; there would otherwise be no rationale for the absolute cost reductions which are emphasized in the account" (Hollander 1997: 568).

Malthus's failure or indifference to incorporate "improvements" into the model does not necessarily mean his indifference to contemporary development marked by "improvements." He continued to revise his agricultural productivity estimates throughout his works, becoming more optimistic in his later works (see Hollander 1997, esp. 752–83). In line with the basic canonical growth model and empirical notion of diminishing returns, he estimated agricultural productivity as falling in 1815 despite new technology (Malthus 1815b: 7; 1986: 133–4). However, by 1817, Malthus had become quite optimistic about agricultural productivity; he even reevaluated his estimate of the war years. In his opinion, Britain was not approaching stationariness due to new technology and other disturbing causes:

> A country which, though fertile and populous, had been cultivated nearly to the utmost, would have no other means of increasing its population

than by admission of foreign corn. But the British isles shew at present no symptoms whatever of this species of exhaustion. The necessary accompaniments of a territory worked to the utmost are very low profits and extent [sic. Should read 'interest'], a very slack demand for labour, low wages, and a stationary population. . . . Instead, however, of such symptoms, we have seen in this country, during the twenty years previous to 1814, a high rate of profits and interest, a very great demand for labour, good wages, and an increase of population more rapid, perhaps, than during any period of our history. The capitals which have been laid out in bringing new land into cultivation, or improving the old, must necessarily have yielded good returns, or under the actual rate of general profits, they would not have been so employed: and although it is strictly true that, as a capital accumulates upon the land, its profits must ultimately diminish; yet owing to the increase of agricultural skill, and other causes . . . these two effects of progressive cultivation do not by any means always keep pace with each other. Though they may finally unite and terminate the career of their progress together, they are often, during the course of their progress, separated for a considerable time, and at a considerable distance.
(Malthus 1817, vol. 2: 491–3)

His optimism persisted throughout two editions of his *Principles* (1820; 1836), with the exception of the chapter on rent, but "[t]aking the *Principles* as a whole, we can discern no revision of the optimism expressed in the 1817 – and the 1826 – *Essay on Population* regarding prospective productivity increase" (Hollander 1997: 783).

Sir Edward West

West (1815) provided no consideration of growth paths other than the basic formulation precisely because of his *empirical* notion of diminishing returns; diminishing returns, "a fact acknowledged by all writers on political economy" based on "the history of agriculture" (West 1815: 8), must prevail notwithstanding counteracting force of knowledge generation due to the division of labor and new machinery. Though "the quantity of work which can be done by a given number of hands is increased in the progress of improvement, by means of the subdivision of labour and machinery even in agriculture"(ibid.: 12) and

[t]he division of labour and application of machinery render labour more and more productive in manufactures, in the progress of improvement; the same causes tend also to make labour more and more productive in agriculture, in the progress of improvement . . . another cause, namely, the necessity of having recourse to land inferior to that already in tillage, or of cultivating the same land more expensively, *tends* to make labour in agriculture less productive in the progress of improvement. And the latter cause more than counteracts the effects of machinery and the division of labour in agriculture; because, otherwise agricultural labour would either

become more productive, or remain equally productive, in the progress of improvement.

(West 1815: 25)

As a consequence,

> the profits of stock are always lower in a rich than in a poor country; and ... they gradually fall as a nation becomes more wealthy. This is evidenced as well by our own history as by that of every other country, in which the state and progress of commercial capital have been observed.
>
> (West 1815: 19)

West (1826) too maintained as "a matter of fact" this prevailing diminishing returns to capital despite various types of counteracting improvements:

> During that period [i.e., the period from 1793 to 1814], immense tracts of land were brought into cultivation; inferior soils, which had before afforded nothing but a scanty pasture, were forced at an immense cost to bear successive crops of corn; expensive improvements were made, and new modes of husbandry adopted; all of which augmented the annual produce in a very great degree. All this is matter of fact which cannot be disputed. But it can be as little disputed that this increasing produce, up to the year 1814, was not more than sufficient to feed the increasing population; that up to that period the demand had even outrun the supply.
>
> (West 1826: 12–3)

There is an interpretational issue involving the exact meaning of the "progress of improvement." Following Cannan (1917: 158–9), Brewer (1988: 506–7) maintains that West used the two concepts "work" (labor in efficiency units) and "hands" (the quantity of labor); the latter being converted into the former by a function exhibiting increasing returns, and "work" into (agricultural) products by another function exhibiting diminishing returns. Thus, "the increase in the 'work-hands' ratio in the process of improvement . . . is the result of increased scale, not of technical change arising from the passage of time."[13] Granted that at the time the distinction between a shift in the production function and a movement along the production function was not yet clear-cut, this interpretation seems a stretch. West (1826) came closer to grasping "improvements" as a shift in the production function, recognizing that the productivity increase is measured using the "same labour":

> In the first place . . . this usual law of the progress of a country [i.e., diminishing returns] is . . . liable to exceptions of considerable periods; as the effects of resorting to inferior soils may be counteracted by new subdivisions of labour, new inventions of machinery, and improved modes of husbandry, which may at one stage enable the *same labour* to raise as much from inferior soils as it could in a former stage from the better.
>
> (West 1826: 46, emphasis added)

Of course, it was not "the fact *generally* in England these last thirty years" (ibid.: 47), emphasizing once again the empirical character.

West did not discuss how improvements could be introduced, but distinguished two types of improvements:

> improvements in agriculture might . . . be distinguished into two kinds: those which enable the cultivator to save expense, or those which enable him to increase his produce without any increase of the rate of expense, and those which increase the produce but at an increased rate of expense. The former kind of improvement is always useful in every state of the market, the latter is called into action only under particular circumstances, and is not always applicable.
>
> (West 1826: 98–9)

Though West's concentration on the latter prevented him from developing any further analysis as to the former, the inducement of improvements in agriculture was specified as a reason for higher profit due to higher prices of agricultural products: "it will be remembered . . . that many of these new improvements of husbandry are applicable only to high prices, and that high price is actually necessary, and a condition precedent to their operation" (ibid.: 134, also 100–5).

Why did West consider diminishing returns as an empirical notion? A clue might be found in the surprisingly short-run orientation of West's work. Throughout his work, he was concerned very much with short-term cyclical fluctuations; the "subdivision of labour," the "chief cause of the increase of its productive powers" was said to have disadvantages since "it renders us more susceptible of the influence of fluctuation, of supply, and demand" (ibid.: 141). On the one hand, market participants, especially producers, are likely to misjudge market conditions:

> If human intelligence were perfect the supply would never exceed or fall short of the demand; and the further we recede from that point, the less perfect the intelligence and foresight of commerce, the more will the supply and demand vary from each other.
>
> (West 1826: 93–4)[14]

On the other hand, "improvements" take time: "The modern improvements made their way but slowly and gradually, and have never pervaded the whole country" (West 1826: 106–7). He summarized: "There is one circumstance indeed which may retard this rise of [corn] price, but I think it will merely retard, and not entirely prevent it. It is the gradual progress into all parts of the country of the improved modes of husbandry" (ibid.: 134).

Robert Torrens

Brewer (1991) claims that Torrens in *An Essay on the Production of Wealth* (1821) "deals with technical change more thoroughly and more explicitly than any other classical writers of the time" (Brown 1991: 10), though his analysis "is presented as an abstract exercise with no explanation of how it relates to observed growth."[15] However, it is misleading to characterize his analysis only as "abstract," and "with no explanation of how it relates to observed growth" (ibid.: 10), for Torrens must have believed in "the great importance of manufacturing industry" (Torrens 1821: 86) in human progress, "knowledge and improvement." He continued:

> though man must originally have lived by merely availing himself of nature's spontaneous gifts; yet the very first, or at most, the very second step towards knowledge and improvement must have led him to the attempt of superadding to these gifts some rude species of preparation.
> (Torrens 1821: 83–4)

Moreover his later work reveals a greater appreciation of knowledge.[16]

Manufacturing industry is important because without it, the variety of wealth would be limited to "that scanty supply of necessaries which nature presents in a state fit for immediate consumption" (ibid.: 85), and also because it provides the economy with "implements and machines" (ibid.: 86). It is capital upon which human labor acts: the "effective powers of manufacturing industry depend much more upon the skillful use of capital, than on the quantity of direct labour which may be employed ... almost all the grand results of manufacturing industry are brought about by means of capital" (ibid.: 89). Capital enters into other industries as a factor of production: "without [the manufacturing industry's] co-operation, no other branch of industry can be effectually carried on" (ibid.: 86).

Productivity increases characterize manufacturing industry: "the quantity of wrought goods which it required a hundred men to prepare in a rude, may be wrought by ten men in an advanced period of society" (ibid.: 90). The two main sources are those of the standard Smithian division of labor, invention and skill accumulation: "as men acquire experience and knowledge they are perpetually inventing improved machinery for the abridgement of labour," and

> as capital accumulates, the work to be done is divided and subdivided, until each individual acquires in his peculiar branch of the business a dexterity and skill unattainable in those small establishments where several operations must be performed by the same hand.
> (Torrens 1821: 90)

Noteworthy also is the fact that these improvement are considered consequent upon capital accumulation, since

> [a]s capital accumulates, and as labourers multiply, improvements take place in the application of machinery, and in the divisions of employment, and enable a smaller number of hands to work up the same quantity of material.
> (Torrens 1821: 96)

Because of these improvements, there is virtually no limit to growth in the manufacturing industry: "During the progress of improvement, and while capital continues to accumulate, and the number of labourers to increase, no limits can be assigned to the powers of manufacturing industry" (ibid.: 89–90). Yet, diminishing returns must eventually prevail in this industry, and thus in the economy as a whole, due to diminishing returns in agricultural industry:

> The additional portions of capital might still be capable of producing a higher proportional effect than those previously applied; yet as the productive powers of agriculture became stationary, it would be impossible that such additional portions should be attained ... Though manufacturing industry has not in itself any natural limits, yet it is affected by those which nature has assigned to agriculture.
> (Torrens 1821: 121)

This interdependence between agriculture and manufacturing, a major concern for Torrens, works in both directions. An improvement in agriculture can increase the productivity of manufacturing and vice versa:

> Improvements in agricultural science [for example, high farming], as throwing to a greater distance the point beyond which cultivation can be neither heightened nor extended, necessarily remove to a greater distance the point beyond which manufacturing capital can be no farther accumulated.
> (Torrens 1821: 128)

> As improvements in agriculture increase the quantity of capital which can be employed in manufactures; so improvements in manufactures remove to a greater distance the ultimate limits of agricultural prosperity, and admit of additional applications of capital to the soil.
> (Torrens 1821: 133)

He was fully aware of improvements in agriculture, whose effects are clearly spelled out:

> From the principles above stated, respecting the application of capital to land, it necessarily follows, that every improvement in agricultural science removes to a greater distance the point at which the spread of tillage and the amelioration of the soil must cease. Every thing which can with propriety be termed an improvement in agriculture, enables a given quantity of labour to raise a greater quantity of produce; or, what comes to the same thing, allows a given quantity of produce to be obtained by a less quantity of labour.
> (Torrens 1821: 122–3)

Various types of improvements in agriculture – a discovery of a better quality of seed and manure, invention of new machinery, and improvements in agricultural science – were considered, which increase not the gross, but the "surplus produce of the soil" (ibid.: 142).

Nonetheless, improvements in agriculture were not taken into account when he discussed the relative price movement of agricultural products (Brewer 1991: 10):

> As population increases, and it becomes necessary to take in new soils, or to cultivate the old in a more expensive manner, it constantly requires an augmenting quantity of capital to raise the same quantity of produce; while, on the contrary, the advance of a country in wealth and population, by giving occasion to improvements in machinery, and to more perfect divisions of employment, enables the same number of hands, and consequently the same expenditure for food, to work up a greater quantity of material. From the conjoint operation of these causes, the value of raw produce is, in the progress of society, perpetually increasing with respect to manufactured goods; or, to express the same thing in a different form, the value of manufactured goods is perpetually diminishing with respect to raw produce. But notwithstanding the operation of this two-fold cause, it is impossible that the period should ever arrive, when the manufacture shall be unable to do more than add to the raw material the value of the subsistence which he consumes while at work.
> (Torrens 1821: 144–5)

One justification for this neglect might be that improvements in agriculture always fall back to those in manufacturing, since improvements in manufacturing are due to the division of labor is constantly at work, while those in agriculture are irregular and sporadic, but Torrens was not clear on this point.

In the end, despite his analysis of technological change, or rather because of his analysis, Torrens did not see the end of growth as imminent, given there is no immediate limit for "agricultural resources" such as land (ibid.: 280–1). The real threat to growth comes not from wanting improvements in manufacturing, but from natural constraints of "agricultural resources." In this sense, he downplayed the important role of knowledge in the growth process.

In his later work, Torrens did not attend issues regarding the principles he set out in 1821, yet he showed a greater appreciation of knowledge in the growth process. In the appendix to the 1829 (fifth) edition of *An Essay on the External Corn Trade*, "the means of improving the condition of the labouring class" (also published as chapter 1 of *On Wages and Combination* (1834)), Torrens argued that "[t]here is no tendency in Population to increase faster than Capital, and thus to degrade Wages." Instead "we find that, in almost every society, the tendency is not to increase population faster than capital; but, on the contrary, to increase capital more rapidly than population" (Torrens 1929: 473, 474–5; 1834: 27, 29). The same point was made by Nassau Senior in his correspondence with Malthus, appended to *Two Lectures on Population* :[17]

> Were it true, as has been sometimes stated, that population has a tendency to increase more rapidly than capital [Torrens attributed this view to James Mill], all endeavours to improve the condition of the people would be

completely idle and abortive. The existence of such a tendency would fix the labouring class in a state, not only of hopeless, but of perpetually increasing misery, and would cause in each succeeding year a greater number to be cut off by famine, and by the epidemics it engenders. The fact, that the condition of the labouring classes has improved with the progress of wealth and civilization, demonstrates that population has not a tendency to increase faster than capital.

(Senior 1829: 27–8)

Citing Adam Smith,

at the present time, a common labourer, in England, is better off, with respect to food, clothing, and furniture, than were the chief men of the land in the days of the Saxon Heptarchy; and many an inhabitant of a work-house is better accommodated now than were the Kings of Britain at the period of the Roman invasion. These facts are totally inconsistent with the supposition, that a population has a tendency to increase faster than capital.

(Senior 1829: 28)

"New countries" such as North America were also characterized not only by rapid population growth, but also by rapid capital accumulation.

At this point, he did not analyze the causes of rapid capital accumulation growth, nor did he link his earlier analysis in 1821; his emphasis was more on the prudential check than capital accumulation:[18]

When the laws which give a bounty to over-population shall be repealed, and when prudence and precaution in entering upon the marriage state, and in limiting the numbers of families, instead of being objects of censure and dislike, receive from the approbation of an enlightened public voice, the reward to which their prevailing influence on human happiness entitles them, then will population be at all times so regulated, that the supply of labour will be duly apportioned to the quantity of fertile land, and to the amount of capital employed; and the labouring classes will emerge from their degradation, and will permanently enjoy independence and comfort, unaccompanied by the exhaustion of immoderate toil.

(Torrens 1829: 476; 1834: 31)

However, Torrens (1834) took capital accumulation into account, the growth rate of which depends on improvements, especially those in power source:

The funds for the maintenance of labour receive their greatest possible increase, when, in the working of machines, horse power is superseded. In this case, human subsistence is augmented, not only by the extension of tillage rendered practicable by the whole quantity of produce which the horses formerly consumed. This most important augmentation in the supply of human subsistence has now commenced. Already in this country steam is superseding horses, and it is scarcely possible to measure the extent to which this supplanting process may be carried. In a few years draught horses may disappear from all the great lines of traffic throughout England; and it seems not improbable, that at no distant period the plough and the harrow will be moved by steam, as well as the carriage and the waggon [*sic*]. Upon the funds for the maintenance of labour, the substitution of steam for cattle will have the same effect as that which would be produced by doubling the fertility of the soil. There will be an unprecedented increase in the demand for labour; doubling the number of people may be employed at the same wages, or the same number at double wages. . . . From this examination of the results of machinery, it appears that all inventions for abridging labour, and diminishing the cost of production . . . augment the funds for the maintenance of labour, and have the effect of increasing both maximum and actual wages.

(Torrens 1834: 43–4)

It is not entirely clear whether Torrens ever changed his mind regarding the prospects for growth. Short-run optimism is quite reconcilable with long-run pessimism about the ultimate end of growth at a far distant future. However, his optimism in this context is quite remarkable, though a further analysis regarding the economics of knowledge creation is still lacking.

James Mill

Despite his reputation as "the schoolmaster *par excellence*" (Winch 1966: 15) and his lifelong interest in knowledge and education, James Mill did not rank highly among his contemporary economists in the further development of the canonical growth model.[19] His *Elements of Political Economy* do not contain any substantial analysis of the growth process being driven by knowledge generation. Nonetheless, in his apparently mundane references to the division of labor as a source of improvements, a very familiar theme since Smith, he hinted at something which would be taken up later by Charles Babbage; namely, a concern with "the best division and distribution of labour." He contemplated the application of what he called analytical-synthetical operations:

> If the immense aggregate of the operations which are subservient to the complicated accommodations, required in an artificial and opulent state of society, were to be divided, under circumstances the best calculated for breaking it down into those small groupes [*sic*] of operations, which afforded the greatest aid to the productive powers of labour, the most perfect philosophical analysis of the subject would be the first operation be performed; the next would be an equally perfect philosophical synthesis.
> (Mill 1826: 215; see also Mill 1836)

However, he lamented "neither of these operations has as yet been performed, in order to obtain the best division and distribution of labour. It is equally certain that this division is still in a most imperfect state"(Mill 1826: 216), implying that Mill envisioned more scope for growth due to better organized improvements, though he did not spell out implications for growth.

In his *Elements*, Mill was more interested in the consequences of a reduced population growth rate than in those of increased productivity. Here he touched upon the class of people who would be responsible for knowledge generation in his discussion of policy measures to reduce the population growth rate:

> All the blessings, which flow from that grand and distinguishing attribute of our nature, its progressiveness, the power of advancing continually from one degree of knowledge, one degree of command over the means of happiness, to another, seems, in a great measure, to depend upon the existence of a class of men who have their time at their command; that is, who are rich enough to be freed from all solicitude with respect to the means of living in a certain state of enjoyment. It is by this class of men that knowledge is cultivated and enlarged; it is also by this class that it is diffused; it is this class of men whose children receive the best education, and are prepared for all the higher and more delicate functions of society, as legislators, judges, administrators, teachers, inventors in all the arts, and superintendents in all the more important works, by which the dominion of the human species is extended over the powers of nature.
> (Mill 1826: 241)

Supported by its "middling fortunes," the leisure time of this class is necessary for improvements: "they who are raised above solicitude for the means of subsistence and respectability, without being exposed to the vices and follies of great riches, the men of middling fortunes, in short, the men to whom society is generally indebted for its greatest improvements, are the men, who having their time at their own disposal, freed from the necessity of manual labour, subject to no man's authority, and engaged in the most delightful occupations, obtain, as a class, the greatest sum of human enjoyment." Though he believed in a high profit rate as a prerequisite to maintain this class, and thus that the rate of profit might affect inventive activity – an insight he could have developed – his discussion again returned to population issue:

> To enable a considerable portion of the community to enjoy the advantages of leisure, the return to capital must evidently be large. There is a certain density of population which is convenient, both for social intercourse, and for that combination of powers by which the produce of labour is increased.
> (Mill 1826: 242)

His much celebrated piece on "Education," a contribution to the supplement of *Encyclopaedia Britannica*, did link knowledge to progress in general terms. Referring to Hume, Mill said:

> Long ago it was observed by Hume, that knowledge and its accompaniments, morality and happiness, may not be strictly conjoined in every individual, but that they are infallibly so in every age, and in every country. The reason is plain; a natural cause may be hindered of its operation in one particular instance, though in a great variety of instances it is sure to prevail. Besides, there may be a good deal of knowledge in an individual, but not knowledge of the best things; this cannot easily happen in a whole people; neither the whole nor the greater part will miss the right objects of knowledge, when knowledge is generally diffused.
>
> (Mill 1828: 38)

In addition, there are two references to the linkage between education and productivity. Following Smith, the effect of the division of labor on the quality of the labor is mentioned: "That the quality of the labour, in which a man is employed, produces effects, favourable or unfavourable upon his mind, has long been confessed"(ibid.: 29). Moreover, Mill related education to labor productivity in his discussion of technical education, one of the four categories of education (the others being domestic, social and political):

> With a view to the *productive powers* of their very labour, it is desirable that the animal frame should not be devoted to it before a certain age, before it has approached the point of maturity. This holds in regard to the lower animals; a horse is less valuable, less, in regard to that very labour for which he is valuable at all, if he is forced upon it too soon. There is an actual loss, therefore, *even in productive powers*, even in good economy, and in the way of health and strength, if the young of the human species are bound close to labour before they are fifteen or sixteen years of age. But if those years are skilfully employed in the acquisition of knowledge, in rendering all those trains habitual on which intelligence depends, it may be easily shown that a very high degree of intellectual acquirements may be gained.
>
> (Mill 1828: 39–40, emphasis added)

However, there is no clear discussion of the implications of his analysis of education for the canonical growth model.

The next generation Ricardians: Nassau William Senior and John Ramsey McCulloch

This section deals with two of the most important classical political economists who started their career shortly after February 1815, Nassau William Senior and John Ramsey McCulloch. Their works are characterized by a more optimistic view of knowledge-driven growth than the first generation Ricardians.

Nassau William Senior

In many respects, Nassau William Senior, who started his career as a political economist by reviewing West (1815), symbolized a transformation of classical economics after the establishment of the canonical growth model, putting more emphasis on the role of knowledge in the growth process than any economist before.

In his unsigned review of West (1815) (Senior (1821)), Senior had not yet adopted the canonical growth model fully since he was not sure of West's rejection of the Smithian "competition of capital" argument (Senior 1821: 468).[20] Also he took for granted West's empirical notion of diminishing returns:

> that the net return [in agriculture] is diminished when additional capital is applied to land already in cultivation, *notwithstanding the improvement in skill and in division of labour with which it is applied,* appears from the mere fact that lands less fertile than the very best are cultivated.
>
> (Senior 1821: 468, emphasis added)

However, by the time he started lecturing as the first Drummond Professor of Political Economy at the University of Oxford, he had understood diminishing returns as one of the "general propositions" of the "theoretical branch of Political economy"· "That, *agricultural skill remaining the same,* additional labour employed on the land within a given district, produces a less proportionate return" (Senior 1827: 35, emphasis added).

Senior's correspondence with Malthus – an appendix to his *Two Lectures on Population* (1829) – exemplifies the difference in opinion on the empirical working of the population principle between the first generation and the second generation Ricardian economists. He maintained that there is a "natural tendency" that the growth rate of subsistence is greater the population growth rate:

> If it be conceded, that there exists in the human race a natural tendency to rise from barbarism to civilization, and that the means of subsistence are proportionally more abundant in a civilized than in a savage state, and neither of these propositions can be denied, it must follow that there is a natural tendency in subsistence to increase in a greater ratio than population.
>
> (Senior 1829: 49)

He further attributed this tendency to knowledge, among other factors, which, he conceived, can increase not only the "productiveness of labour" but also decrease the population growth rate:

> I will only say at present that *knowledge,* security of property, freedom of internal and external exchange, and equal admissibility to rank and power, are the principal causes which at the same time promote the increase of subsistence, and by elevating the character of the people, lead them to keep at a slower rate the increase of their numbers.
>
> (Senior 1829: 51, emphasis added)

The prosperity of America was also attributed to the knowledge which immigrants carried with them: "America, where the knowledge of an old people has, for a considerable time, been applied to a continent previously almost unoccupied" (ibid.: 57).

The debate with Malthus concerns more the relative importance of the effect of knowledge on the empirical working of population principle than the principle itself. For as Hollander (1997: 914) points out, Senior frankly admitted to having misread Malthus's *Essay on Population*, agreeing with Malthus in principle:

> I was misled by your use of the word "*tendency*." I supposed you to believe, that the desire of marriage, which tends to increase Population, is a stronger principle, or, in other words, a principle more efficacious in its results than the desire of bettering our condition, which tends to increase subsistence; and, consequently, that in an old country, with a people so fully supplied with necessaries as to make it possible for population to increase in a greater ratio than, such an increase would, in the absence of disturbing causes, be a more probable event than the opposite event; namely, than an increase of subsistence in a greater ratio than that of population.
>
> (Senior 1829: 56)

To which Malthus replied: "I was certainly not aware, that in saying that population had a tendency to increase faster than food, I should be considered as denying that it might practically at times increase slower" (Senior 1829: 60).

However, Senior's proposal to amend the principle further in the following manner initiated a debate. He wrote:

> In the absence of disturbing causes, food has a tendency to increase faster than population, because, in fact, it has generally done so, and because I consider the desire of bettering our condition as natural a wish as the desire of marriage.
>
> (Senior 1829: 58)

Malthus criticized this, and rejected Senior's proposal on both, empirical and theoretical grounds. Regarding empirical evidence, Malthus simply could not find it:

> I am compelled to say that both in your present impression of my doctrine, as given in your letter, and when you state as a fact, that food *has* generally increased faster than population, I am unable to go along with you.
>
> (Senior 1829: 65–6)

For example in America, though knowledge contributed to prosperity, population growth had been great too:

> America is by no means the only instance of the knowledge of an old state being applied to the comparatively unoccupied land of a new one. And in

all instances of this kind, where the food has once been abundant, an actual increase of population faster than food is not only probable, but absolutely certain.

(Senior 1829: 66–7)

Senior's other reason did not convince Malthus at all, since the laboring classes are "not the persons who accumulate farming capital, and employ it in agricultural improvements, and the increase of subsistence" (ibid.: 64). Rather they should be accountable for the population growth rate through prudential control: "Though they cannot much accelerate the increase of food, they are the only body of people who can essentially retard the increase of population." So Senior's optimistic prospect of growth must be qualified:

> though we may hope that they will become still more efficient as knowledge advances, yet as far as we can judge from history, there never has been a period of any considerable length, when premature mortality and vice, specifically arising from the pressure of population against food, has not prevailed to a considerable extent; nor, admitting the possibility, or even probability of these evils being diminished, is there any rational prospect of a near approach to their entire removal.
>
> (Senior 1829: 64–5)

Senior's rejoinder provides us with a better understanding of the length of period from which he derived the "general tendency":

> When I say that subsistence *has generally* increased in a greater ratio than population, I mean, that if we look back through the history of the whole world, and compare the state of each country at distinct periods of two hundred or three hundred years, the cases in which food has increased during the preceding period of two hundred or three hundred years, in a greater ratio than population, will be found to be more numerous than those in which population has increased during the preceding period in a greater ratio than food.
>
> (Senior 1829: 73–4)

It is noteworthy that despite his admission that progress is not steady, he believed in it nonetheless:

> Still I apprehend that, in the absence of disturbing causes, the retrogression would not be to the point at which food and population relatively stood, before the first improvement took place. I conceive the progress of human society to resemble the children's puzzle of a snail, which we are told every day crawled up the wall four feet and fell back three.
>
> (Senior 1829: 75)

where the general tendency is a progressive one, while

the poor laws to increase our numbers, the corn laws to prohibit, under ordinary circumstances, the importation of subsistence, and a commercial code by which the perverse ingenuity of centuries has laboured to fetter and misdirect our industry.

(Senior 1829: 75–6)

are considered "disturbing causes." Therefore, he understandably still expressed a positive opinion regarding the human capacity to overcome the population pressure, though on the second point, Senior conceded more to Malthus than he did on the first point (ibid.: 77).[21]

In his further reply, Malthus apparently concurred with Senior: "We do not essentially differ as to facts, when they are explained as you have explained them in your last letter" (ibid.: 82). But there is a certain contrast with Senior regarding the length of period, since Malthus seemed to think the period in which the growth rate of food is greater than the population growth rate as a short one:

> the period during which the pressure of population is lightened, *though it may not be of long duration*, is a period of comparative ease, and ought by no means to be thrown out of our consideration.
>
> (Senior 1829: 85, emphasis added)[22]

Though "Senior was really of the opinion that the progress of the human race was due to an inherent strain of ambition which, given reasonably favourable circumstances, was sufficient to maintain subsistence at least on a level with population" (Bowley 1937: 122), whether or not the difference between two economists is "fundamental" (ibid.: 120) depends on one's perspective. As Senior summarized, the debate is more about the relative emphasis one puts on two main components of the model than about the understanding of the model itself; they adhered to the canonical growth model, as is clearly shown in Senior's following statement, which probably took into account Malthus's above-mentioned criticism regarding the agent of improvements:

> No plan for social improvement can be complete, unless it embrace the means both of increasing production, and of preventing population from making a proportionate advance. The former is to be effected chiefly by the higher orders in society; the latter depends entirely on the lower. As a means of improvement, the latter is, on the whole, the more efficient. It may be acted upon, or neglected by very individual. But, in the present state of public opinion, and of our commercial and fiscal policy, perhaps more good is to be done by insisting on the former. The economist who neglects either, considers only a portion of his subject.
>
> (Senior 1829: 90)

Thus, the difference with Malthus is important in that it shows Senior emphasizing the role of knowledge, yet it is not as fundamental as Bowley wished it to be.[23]

John Ramsey McCulloch

One of McCulloch's earliest works on political economy was his review of Ricardo's *Principles* (McCulloch 1818). He "was extremely optimistic about the British economy. He believed it to have grown by an immense amount since 1760; and he saw virtually no limit to the continuation of this process" (O'Brien 1970: 271–2); the major source of growth was attributed to incessant improvements in technology.[24] From the beginning of his career, he was particularly impressed by inventions in the cotton industry:

> The discoveries, however, of Hargreaves, Arkwright, and other ingenious men, having, as has been lately computed, produced a saving of ninety-nine parts out of a hundred in the labour formerly necessary in this manufacture, the consumption of cotton goods has increased so prodigiously, that notwithstanding an immense fall in their prices, they are now manufactured to the value of THIRTY MILLIONS Sterling annually, and give employment to a vast body of people.
> (McCulloch 1817: 97)[25]

In 1827, he wrote that "[t]he rapid growth and prodigious magnitude of the cotton manufacture of Great Britain, are, beyond all question, the most extraordinary phenomena in the history of industry" (McCulloch 1827: 1) along with a detailed account of the history of inventions.

In his review of Thomas Chalmers's *On Political Economy* (McCulloch 1832b), he criticized Chalmers's claim that prudential control through education is the "*only*" means by which the condition of society can be improved." He wrote:

> The error of Dr Chalmers has arisen from his laying too much stress on the principle of population, as explained by Mr Malthus. Neither the repeal nor abolition of the most burdensome taxes or regulations, nor the discovery of new machines and processes for reducing the cost of production, can, in his estimation, be of any real service.
> (McCulloch 1832b: 54)

Instead he attributed the rising living standard between 1760 to 1832 to the growth of knowledge:[26] "The melioration has been *wholly* owing to extrinsic causes – to improvements in agriculture and the arts" (ibid.: 59, emphasis added).

Thus "the true reason why the national capital went on increasing, notwithstanding the prodigal expenditure of the last [Napoleonic] war" was that "[a]t its commencement the stupendous inventions and discoveries of Watt, Arkwright, and Wedgwood, were beginning to come into full play. The productive power of the country was, in consequence, immeasurably increased" (ibid.: 67). In 1833, he concluded that "[o]n the whole . . . there cannot be a doubt that, generally speaking, all the great branches of mercantile and manufacturing industry are in no ordinary degree prosperous" (McCulloch 1833: 58).

Cannan's (1929) claim that McCulloch did not deal with the increase in knowledge in his "formal presentation" is not quite valid, since concerning McCulloch there was a less clear distinction between "formal" and informal works; prolific as he was, he often used the same materials in many places (cf. McCulloch 1832a: 817–18; 1843: 289–90). In addition, even in his "formal presentation" the evidence does not support Cannan (1929). In his earlier formal works of political economy (McCulloch 1825a, 1825b), he seemed to be content with the basic canonical growth model, though he did discuss the machinery question. However, the second edition of *Principles of Political Economy* (McCulloch 1830) he added a section in Part I, Chapter II, characterizing the "Progressive nature of man": "It is the proud distinction of the human race, that their conduct is determined by reason, which, though limited and fallible, is susceptible of indefinite improvement." As such, this is a rephrasing of Adam Smith's "bettering one's condition" dictum, yet the indicated improvement is closely related to the human ability to learn:

> By slow degrees, partly by the aid of observation, and partly by contrivances of his own, he gradually learns to augment his powers, and to acquire an increased command over the necessaries, conveniences, and enjoyments of human life.
>
> (McCulloch 1830: 78)

It is the population principle, the "principle of increase," that presses people to invent and improve:

> The principle of increase implanted in the human race is so very powerful, that population never fails of speedily expanding to the limits of subsistence, how much soever they may be extended. Indeed, its natural tendency is to exceed these limits, or to increase the number of people faster than the supplies of food and other necessary accommodations provided for their support . . . despite [prudential control's] influence, the principle of increase is at all times, and under every variety of circumstances, so very strong as to call forth unceasing efforts to increase the means of subsistence. It forms, in fact, a constantly operating principle to rouse the activity and stimulate the industry of man. The most splendid inventions and discoveries do not enable him to intermit his efforts; – if he did, the increase of population would speedily change his condition for worse, and he would be compelled either to sink, or to atone for his indolence by renewed and more vigorous exertions.
>
> (McCulloch 1830: 80)[27]

It follows from the above mechanism that inventive activity is endogenously determined by population pressure, a rather Malthusian perspective. He wrote:

> The powers and capacities implanted in man seem capable of an almost indefinite improvement; but instinct did not direct him in their use . . .

> Pressed, on the one hand, by the strong hand of necessity, and stimulated, on the other, by a desire to rise in the world, our powers have been gradually developed according as observation or accident taught us the best method of effecting our ends. It is idle to suppose that men will be industrious without a motive, and though the desire of bettering our condition be a very powerful one, it is less so than the pressure of want, or the fear of falling to an inferior station. Want and ambition are the power springs that gave the first impulse of industry and invention, and which continually prompt to new undertakings.
>
> (McCulloch 1830: 224–5)

But, again like Malthus, innovations are treated as if they were exogenous.[28]

As a major contributor to the *Edinburgh Review*, McCulloch reviewed a great number of works, one of which was Babbage's *On the Economy of Machinery and Manufactures* (1832), to which we shall next turn.[29]

Toward a microeconomic analysis of innovation: Charles Babbage

Charles Babbage, inventor of the difference and analytical engines – precursors of the modern computer – and distinguished Lucasian Professor of Mathematics at the University of Cambridge, was immensely interested in the role of knowledge in human progress in general.[30] On this he wrote:

> The triumph of the industrial arts will advance the cause of civilization more rapidly than its warmest advocates could have hoped, and contribute to the permanent prosperity and strength of the country, far more than the most splendid victories of successful war. The influences thus engendered, the arts thus developed, will long continue to shed their beneficent effects over countries more extensive than those which the sceptre of England rules.
>
> (Babbage 1989, vol. 10: viii–ix)

Despite this knowledge-based growth perspective, in what follows, I shall argue that Babbage's contribution is essentially of a microeconomic nature, lacking an analysis of macroeconomic growth driven by knowledge generation. Therefore he did not fare well in the development of knowledge-based growth theory.

In his *On the Economy of Machinery and Manufactures*, Babbage conceived the central principle of economics differently from his contemporary economists, stating that "Perhaps the most important principle on which the economy of a manufacture depends, is the *division of labour* amongst the persons who perform the work" (Babbage 1835/1989: vol. 8, 169).[31] Indeed Babbage's major contribution arguably lies in his improvement on the Smithian division of labor.[32] Pursuing a direction suggested by James Mill (see earlier), he summarized the main advantage of the division of labor in the following manner, in what is called the "Babbage Principle":[33]

> It appears to me, that any explanation of the cheapness of manufactured articles, as consequent upon the division of labour, would be incomplete if the following principle were omitted to be stated. *That the master manufacturer, by dividing the work to be executed into different processes, each requiring different degrees of skill or of force, can purchase exactly that precise quantity of both which is necessary for each process; whereas, if the whole work were executed by one workman, that person must possess sufficient skill to perform the most difficult, and sufficient strength to execute the most laborious, of the operations into which the art is divided.*
>
> (Babbage [1835] 1989, vol. 8: 125)

Mainly using numerical illustrations, he showed that this judicious organization of workplace involved the reduction of costs, mainly wage costs:

> the effect of the *division of labour*, both in mechanical and in mental operations, is, that it enables us to purchase and apply to each process precisely that quantity of skill and knowledge which is required for it: we avoid employing any part of the time of a man who can get eight or ten shillings a day by his skill in tempering needles, in turning a wheel, which can be done for sixpence a day; and we equally avoid the loss arising from the employment of an accomplished mathematician in performing the lowest processes of arithmetic.
>
> (Babbage [1835] 1989, vol. 8: 141)

However, despite his discussion of the role of the wage rate in furthering the division of labor, Babbage failed to develop any further linkage between factor payments and the growth process.

His second major contribution to economics – his analysis of the determinants of the innovation process – is also firmly grounded in the division of labor, since "[a] central point for Babbage is that an extensive division of labor is itself an essential prerequisite to technical change" (Rosenberg 1994: 32). He wrote: "The arts of contriving, of drawing, and of executing [a new machinery], do not usually reside in their greatest perfection in one individual; and in this, as in other arts, the *division of labour* must be applied" (Babbage [1835] 1989, vol. 8: 186). It follows from these insights into the division of labor that the direction of technological improvement is determined as a response to the relative prices of factor inputs by a producer constantly looking for profitable opportunities:

> The great competition introduced by machinery, and the application of the principle of the subdivision of labour, render it necessary for each producer to be continually on the watch, to discover improved methods by which the cost of the article he manufactures may be reduced; and, with this view, it is of great importance to know the precise expense of every process, as well as of the wear and tear of machinery which is due to it.
>
> (Babbage [1835] 1989, vol. 8: 144)

And the investment in improvement is directly connected to the demand for the final product that the machines produce: "The inducement to contrive machines for any process of manufacture increases with the demand for the article"(ibid.: 151). He must have been implying the existence of a higher profit rate due to an increased demand as a stimulus to improvement, though his analysis lacked precision. Higher profit will not persist, however, since competition will eliminate it:

> [new machinery's] owner, in order to extend the sale of his produce, will be obliged to undersell his competitors; this will induce them also to introduce the new machine, and the effect of this competition will soon cause the article to fall, until the profits on capital, under the new system, shall be reduced to the same rate as under the old.
> (Babbage [1835] 1989, vol. 8: 231)

This very Smithian analysis might suggest the innovation process depended consequent entirely upon the size of capital. Indeed Babbage stated: "The division of labour cannot be successfully practised unless there exists a great demand for its produce; and it requires a large capital to be employed in those arts in which it is used" (ibid.: 143). Yet this is not the whole story; a large capital is a necessary condition, but not a sufficient condition.[34] First of all, he was quite aware of the practical difficulty in executing the above-mentioned "Babbage principle": "it is quite impossible, even with the best division of labour, to attend to it rigidly in practice" (ibid.: 151). He was also aware of difficulties in calculating exact costs:

> Whenever the new, or improved machine, is intended to become the basis of a manufacture, it is essentially requisite that the *whole* expense attending its operations should be fully considered before its construction is undertaken. It is almost always very difficult to make this estimate of the expense: the more complicated the mechanism, the less easy is the task; and in cases of great complexity and extent of machinery it is almost impossible.
> (Babbage [1835] 1989, vol. 8: 185)

Moreover, in chapter 27, "On contriving machinery," he made a distinction between successful invention-innovations and unsuccessful ones, analyzing further difficulties involved in the invention-innovation process. The process, according to Babbage, involves three interdependent stages, from drawings to preliminary experiments, to the execution of the machine. For example,

> [i]n conducting experiments upon machinery, it is quite a mistake to suppose that any imperfect mechanical work is good enough for such a purpose. If the experiment is worth making, it ought to be tried with all the advantages of which the state of mechanical art admits; for an imperfect trial may cause an idea to be given up, which better workmanship might have proved to be practical.
> (Babbage [1835] 1989, vol. 8: 184)

Beyond the canonical growth model 101

Thus the same invention-innovation might fail on one occasion, yet succeed on another:

> It is partly owing to the imperfection of the original trials, and partly to the gradual improvements in the art of making machinery, that many inventions which have been tried, and given up in one state of art, have at another period been eminently successful.
> (Babbage [1835] 1989, vol. 8: 184)

Even when an invention is successful, the innovation might fail for economic reasons:

> When the drawings of a machine have been properly made, and the parts have been well executed, and even when the work it produces possesses all the qualities which were anticipated, still the invention may fail; that is, it may fail of being brought into general practice. This will most frequently arise from the circumstance of its producing its work at a greater expense than that at which it can be made by other methods.
> (Babbage [1835] 1989, vol. 8: 185)

Furthermore, In Chapter 34, "On the exportation of machinery," Babbage stressed the difficulty associated with properly using machinery. He wrote:

> It is contended that by admitting the exportation of machinery, foreign manufactures will be supplied with machines equal to our own. The first answer which presents itself to this argument is supplied by almost the whole of the present volume; *That in order to succeed in a manufacture, it is necessary not merely to possess good machinery, but that the domestic economy of the factory should be more carefully regulated.*
> (Babbage [1835] 1989, vol. 8: 253)[35]

Though he recognized the difficulties associated with inventive-innovative activity, he did not extend his discussion to the motives of an individual facing constraints. His case for patents is essentially based on the division of mental labor, with scientists devoting their attention and time to one profession:

> the profit arising from the successful application to practice of theoretical principles, will, in most cases, amply reward, in a pecuniary sense, those by whom they are first employed; yet even here, what has been stated with respect to *patents*, will prove that there is room for considerable amendment in our legislative enactments: but the discovery of the great principles of nature demands a mind almost exclusively devoted to such investigations; and these, in the present state of science, frequently require costly apparatus, and exact an expense of time quite incompatible with professional avocations.
> (Babbage [1835] 1989, vol. 8: 261)[36]

We turn to the question of Babbage's classicism. Brewer (1991) argues against Robbins's (1968) inclusion of Babbage into classical economists on the ground that he was "hardly a mainstream economist" (Brewer 1991: 11n).[37] As is clear from this discussion, Babbage was intellectually a direct descendant of Smith regarding the division of labor, so that Babbage could be called a classical political economist in the same sense as Smith was. Regarding the canonical growth model however, Babbage's analysis is seriously wanting. Though his contribution to the microeconomic analysis of knowledge was quite impressive, his analysis was not clearly linked to a macroeconomic growth theory. There was no explicit reference to the Malthusian population principle, though it does not necessarily mean Babbage did not concur with Malthus on the issue.[38] Also lacking is an explicit analysis of land as a constraint on growth, though he discussed a possible exhaustion of power sources, one similar to the Jevonian "coal question":

> the discovery of the expansive power of steam, its condensation, and the doctrine of latent heat, has already added to the population of this small island, millions of hands. But the source of this power is not without limit, and the coal-mines of the world may ultimately be exhausted.
> (Babbage [1835] 1989, vol 8: 267)[39]

Without two major components of the canonical growth model, the advantages of manufacturing driven by knowledge generation are stated in quite general terms without any formal reference to diminishing returns to capital given knowledge. Also lacking is an analysis of the determination of factor returns, though he treated the innovation process, through the division of labor, as responding to factor returns. Therefore, concerning the canonical growth theory, we are in agreement with Brewer (1991), who questions Babbage's status as a classical economist.[40]

J. R. McCulloch reviewed Babbage's book favorably, though with some reservations. He lauded Babbage's contribution to the improvement on the Smithian division of labor, the so-called Babbage principle: "Mr Babbage has given an illustration of the influence of this division, which, though it had been observed before, was not noticed by Dr Smith, and has not attracted, at least in this country, the attention it deserves" (McCulloch 1833a: 322). Considering that "[t]he capacity to invent and contrive makes a part of the original constitution of man" (ibid.: 314; cf. Robbins 1968: 91–2), he found Babbage's following remarks on the invention-innovation process particularly valuable:

> The arts of contriving, of drawing, and of executing, do not usually reside in their greatest perfection in one individual; and in this, as in other arts, *the division of labour* must be applied ... The first step ... the ascertaining whether the contrivance has the merit of novelty, is most important; for it is a maxim equally just in all the arts, and in every science, that *the man who aspires to fortune or to fame by new discoveries, must be content to examine with care*

the knowledge of his contemporaries, or to exhaust his efforts in inventing again, what he will most probably find has been better executed before.

(Babbage [1832] 1986, vol 8: 186)

Yet McCulloch commented:

> This is sound and good, but it is far too general to be of much use. Mr Babbage, at least as it appears to us, would have done better had he illustrated his views by a sketch of the progress of invention; by examining in detail some of the more important operations of machinery, and showing, by practical instances, how inventors have been led to avail themselves of properties and combinations not previously taken advantage of.
>
> (McCulloch 1833: 326)

It is not clear what he meant by "of much use," but he must have had in mind a clear analysis of the effects of the invention-innovation process on "society." He spelled out the task at the outset:

> To produce a complete work on the economy of machinery and manufactures, would, we incline to think, require the combined efforts of various individuals; for it is, perhaps, too much to expect to find the requisite familiarity with the principles and processes on which the successful prosecution of manufactures depends, combined in the same person with a knowledge of the various historical, moral, and economical questions that must be examined in determining the influence of discoveries in machinery on society.
>
> (McCulloch 1833: 313)

This formidable challenge was in part taken by another inventor, John Rae.

Knowledge-based growth theorist *par excellence*: John Rae

> The phenomena incorporated in the new formal models, and neglected in many of the old ones, scarcely represent novel new insights or ideas. The basic notions –"technical change is largely endogenous"; "technology is at least somewhat proprietary"; "market structures supporting technical advance are not perfectly competitive"; "new technology often obsoletes old technology"; "growth fueled by technical advance involves externalities and economies of scale"; and "the investment rate may matter in the long run" scarcely smack of novelty.
>
> (Nelson 1997)

Against the background of the mainstream canonical growth theorists of the day, John Rae stood out as the foremost knowledge-based growth theorist: a crucial role is attributed to knowledge as the engine of growth. The economic analysis of knowledge creation is developed with special reference to the importance of the difference between private and social rates of return to knowledge creation, upon which policy proposals are based.

Rae's recognition of the important role of knowledge in economic growth is closely connected to the connecting principle of the economics of John Rae as a whole. According to Rae, what distinguishes man from other animals is his "provident forethought," "the capacity for perceiving, and retaining in his mind, the course of events and the connexion [sic] of one with another, that leads man to perceive what advancing futurity is to bring forth, and enables to provide for its wants" (Rae 1834: 81). Having viewed man as a foreseeing animal, he emphasized three things: the end–means relationship in human activity; the importance of the knowledge of such an end–means relationship; and the time element. As we have seen, McCulloch leaned toward this type of characterization of human beings as a basis for his economic theory, yet in Rae's case, this conception is pervasive throughout his work.

At the outset, Rae stated his concern; how to account for economic growth, as for example in the case of the English economy:

> The wealth of England is certainly ten times now what it was in the reign of Henry the VIII; we do not conceive, however, that it is formed by the multiplying tenfold such articles as constituted the sole riches of its inhabitants in that somewhat rude and barbarous age. We perceive here, that there is and must be, not only an *increase*, but a *change*.
> (Rae 1834: 18–19)

Without ignoring changes in the quality and variety of goods over time, he discerned that mere capital accumulation could not provide the explanation; the lever of riches must be "invention," his term for knowledge:

> What do we find to have been the most prominent accompaniment of this change? Any great diminution of the expenditure of a whole community [i.e., an increased saving, and hence capital accumulation], it will be found difficult to trace, but we shall always discover that invention has somehow or another been busy, either in improving agriculture and the other old arts, or in discovering new ones.
> (Rae 1834: 23; also 31)

Rae declared that "Invention is the only power on earth, that can be said to create. It enters as an essential element into the process of the increase of national wealth, because that process is a creation, not an acquisition" (ibid.: 15).

Why we need knowledge generation to prevent the economy from coming to a halt is the question Rae must answer theoretically. Rae's theory of economic growth required both the "accumulative principle," capital accumulation given knowledge, and the "inventive principle," capital accumulation with knowledge generation. We first deal with the former, though Rae never spelled out his full-fledged growth model given knowledge, since his concern was to explain the growth process by knowledge creation.

In Rae's model, the "quality and quantity of the materials owned" by a society plays an important role in generating theoretical diminishing returns to capital:

> The capacity which any people can communicate to the materials they possess, by forming them into instruments [i.e., capital], cannot be indefinitely increased, while their knowledge of the powers and qualities remains stationary, without moving the instruments formed continually onwards in the series ABC & c.: but, there is no assignable limit to the extent of capacity, which a people having attained considerable knowledge of the qualities and powers of the materials they possess, can communicate to them, without carrying them out of the series A B C & c., even if that knowledge remain stationary.
>
> (Rae 1834: 109)

The rate of return falls because of increased costs due to resource constraints regarding "materials":

> [A]s the stock of materials which any society possesses, is limited, its members, if we suppose them to acquire no additional knowledge of the powers of those materials, and yet to add continually to the amount of instruments they form out of them, must at length have recourse to such as are either operated on with greater difficulty, or being about desired events more sparingly or tardily. The efficiency of the instruments produced must therefore be generated by greater cost; that is, they must pass to orders of slower return.
>
> (Rae 1834: 113)

Rae always insisted on this particular assumption concerning "knowledge." It is the fixity or scarcity of "materials" that leads to diminishing returns to capital, which should be understood as a theoretical as opposed to an empirical notion. The process of capital accumulation depends on the interplay of capital productivity and time preference ("the effective desire of accumulation"), other factors held constant. Though his elaboration on this point is a theoretical high point, he argued that the effective desire of accumulation does not prevent economic growth from coming to a halt unless diminishing returns to capital are to overcome.

In his exposition of the "inventive principle," Rae offered the most comprehensive classification and treatment of various types of "knowledge," as can be found in his list of policies regarding the promotion of knowledge:

> In the following cases, it would at least seem not improbable, that the power of the legislator so directed, might be beneficial.
> I. In promoting the progress of science.
> II. In promoting the progress of art.
> 1. By encouraging the discovery of new arts.
> 2. By encouraging the discovery of improvements in the arts already practised in the country.

3. By encouraging the discovery of methods of adapting arts, already practised in other countries to the particular circumstances of the territory and community for which he legislates.

(Rae 1834: 15–6)

Though Rae clearly understood the distinction between science and technology ("arts") in the modern sense, the exact meaning of "invention" and "inventor" depends on the context (see Brewer 1998). Throughout the *New Principles*, he insisted that knowledge is inexhaustible since it does not depreciate. This constitutes the important contrast with the accumulative principle, that is, the diminishing returns to capital over the course of economic growth, given technology, and justifies his optimistic prospect for economic growth.

Rae's discussion is often described as being concerned with the psychology or sociology of innovation, with a slight implication of contempt (Niehans 1990: 85). In Rae's knowledge-based growth theory however, psychology or sociology do matter, because the motive governing what he called the "inventor" as to the production and application of knowledge is absolutely essential to his whole system of economic growth. The problem of the motives of the inventor was necessarily a riddle for him, because for Rae invention is not a usual activity for human beings: "Man is essentially imitative; his instincts impel him to amalgamate with the mass" (Rae 1834: 209). There is an incentive problem associated with knowledge because it has a positive externality and a public-goods character: "The fruits of the labors of genius. . . are the property of the whole human race"(ibid.: 222); the "successful efforts of the inventive faculty are not a gift to any particular artists, but to the whole community, and their benefits divided amongst its members" (ibid.: 259).

Rae's keen interest in the public-goods character of knowledge led him to differentiate invention-innovation and imitation ("mere transmitters of things already known"), though he did not distinguish between invention and innovation. "Real inventors" (inventor-innovators) encounter various kinds of obstacles in the process: "What is really new, has to encounter obstacles of two sorts" (ibid.: 215). Invention is simply not understood: "Whatever . . . is in any degree really new, being probably beyond these rules, is beyond their judgment"; and occasionally there is positive opposition: "Nor is this the worst; it is also very frequently in opposition to it; it disagreeably disturbs and jars the existing systems, by which men guide their feelings and reasoning." By contrast, the imitator does not confront such obstacles, because the inventor-innovator has already cleared up or weakened them: "they neither encounter similar difficulties, nor produce similar effects to the former. They neither oppose, nor direct the current" (ibid.: 213).

His recognition of the difficulties associated with invention-innovation creates a problem, since he insisted that there had been an incessant flow of new knowledge throughout history. How did he resolve this question? The answer turns on the motives of the inventor. The motive for invention is not what we usually consider as a market motive: "we in vain search for any sufficient motive exciting to this course of action, unless the good arising from communicating good, and the consequent desire to be a benefactor in the most extended manner" (Rae 1834: 210). Rae thus broadened his perspective to include non-market motives among the determinants of the inventive faculty. Real inventors are driven by other motives than are the mere transmitters:

> though, in the individual, manifestations of the inventive faculty imply a superiority in some of the intellectual powers, they rather imply, in the society, a preponderance of the social and benevolent affections. It is this general acuteness of moral sensation, and lively sympathy consequently with the pleasures arising to the individual, from the success of exertions for purposes of general good, that can alone excite, and nourish, the enthusiasm of genius
>
> (Rae 1834: 222)

where "general good" refers to a public-goods nature of their "fruits." Rae's solution – turning to non-market motives – should not be considered as his abandonment of economics; these are exactly the motives governing also the effective desire of accumulation: "the principles of our nature exciting to the advance of invention, would seem to be nearly identical with those giving activity to the effective desire of accumulation." Rae had a broader concept of economics around which he constructed his knowledge-based growth theory.[41]

Rae's discussion thus far has centered around the supply of knowledge generation, but knowledge creation is also dependent upon other factors, demand in particular. In his examination of "history of inventions," Rae analyzed the other factors which suggest that a scarcity of existent materials (natural resources) poses a necessity to discover new art (technology); also a change in materials presents an opportunity for invention (Rae 1834: 224–5).

Noteworthy in this context is his favorite example of the steam engine invented by James Watt. There is no significant distinction between invention and innovation in this example in that the invention of the steam engine was pursued by people whose purpose was its commercialization from the beginning. Rae listed conditions for this invention in which the real inventor is an economic agent making decisions regarding invention-innovation backed by capitalists. In fact, Rae's real inventor here is the closest thing to an entrepreneur (ibid.: 246–7).

According to Rae, there are four factors which affect invention. First, there has to be a potential demand for a particular invention, and it must be urgent:

> The urgent demand for some powerful agent, however rude and unwieldly in action. Had the operation to be performed, been in any degree complicated and nice in its nature, it would never probably have occurred to any one, that the expense and collapse of a vapor, shut up in iron vessels, could be brought to execute it.
>
> (Rae 1834: 246)

Rae admitted that in the beginning technology does not start in a perfect form, and he always emphasized the gradual progress of technology. Second, the conditions regarding materials matter, for the invention of the steam engine was in part due to the "materials, metal, coal, and water, being in these situations abundant." This factor would, again, link the inventive principle to materials. Third, the "previous improvement of machinery in general" matters. This reflects his idea of the continuous and cumulative nature of the generation of new knowledge: new knowledge does not come out of the blue. And finally, the role of the capitalist comes into the picture: "The want occurring to men of property, and of a class in general bold in enterprise, and accustomed to stake their funds freely" (ibid.: 246–7). Here Rae distinguished between two classes: capitalists and entrepreneurs. The latter class has to take risks attached with such an invention-innovation, a point always emphasized by Rae. For the realization of this invention-innovation could depend on the four conditions mentioned: "Had any of these been wanting, this extraordinary invention might yet have slumbered, veiled in the darkness which had covered it for so many thousands of years." It could be worse: "Perhaps it might have been stifled at its birth, for its first appearance gave but slight token of its inherent capabilities" (ibid.: 247).

Rae did not deal in any detail with category I – the promotion of basic scientific research – but chose to explore the last item of the list, technology transfer. He chose this item because of its relevance for his specific concern in the achievement of knowledge-based growth in an international context via protection, the so-called infant industry argument.[42] In the presence of transportation costs, the introduction of a manufacture – or of technology used in the manufacture – can be to a nation's advantage. It may be, however, "a matter of great difficulty" for private firms, the difficulty flowing from differences in the quality of the materials between prospective domestic and foreign countries, differences in climate, and differences in wage and profit rates (ibid.: 46). The essential problem faced by a potential manufacturer is how to acquire an accurate knowledge of such differences to assure a satisfactory outcome. Rae's description of this discovery process involving trial and error is worth quoting at length:

> When the discovery of that exact mode of procedure . . . has once been made, it may be found that they are on the whole more favorable, and such as will produce a better article, at less cost, in the country to which the manufacture is transported, than in that in which it was originally exercised. To make the discovery, however, of this exact procedure is always a matter of difficulty, and implies almost necessarily the previous commission of many errors and mistakes, and the incurring of much needless expense and loss. A single individual, whatever intelligence and application he may possess, can scarce hope to arrive at it; it requires the efforts of many individuals, continued through a considerable course of time.
>
> (Rae 1834: 339)

Unfortunately, "very few individuals have a thorough knowledge of every different part of any complicated manufacture" (ibid.: 47), a problem that aggravates the complexities of various aspects of management. For Rae, the success of a large manufacture depends on effective management skills, and such a manufacture is clearly conceived as a hierarchical entity with specialist managers attached to each department under the direction of one person. It is difficult, though, to find managers and workers who have the appropriate knowledge and skills.[43] Furthermore, the entrepreneur has to pay "exorbitant wages" in order to lure skilled workers from a foreign country.

Because of these difficulties,

> to transfer a manufacture from one country to another, must always be a very tedious and expensive operation, for any individual to perform. The consideration of his own profit . . . would never lead one, to engage in the enterprise of establishing a new manufacture in any country unless of such commodities as were of common consumption in it, and which he could therefore be sure to sell. The effecting this . . . would generally take more time and money, than any private individual can afford.
> (Rae 1834: 52)

The proposition that an individual cannot afford to transfer technology is strengthened further by taking the market competitive mechanism into consideration. Even

> granting that the funds of some private individuals could afford this requisite outlay . . . the more difficult question is, how is this great outlay to be reimbursed? A great part of an individual's capital has been expended. This expenditure can, evidently, be reimbursed to him only by his drawing proportionally larger profits, than he otherwise could, from what remains. To balance the extraordinary outlay, he must have extraordinary returns.
> (Rae 1834: 51–2)

Such extraordinary returns could not persist, though, because competition among entrepreneurs would reduce returns to the competitive level unless there is some entry barrier. Given that the technology transferred by the first firm was immediately imitated by the latecomers, an entrepreneur will never make the attempt unless he is "imprudent." Thus Rae concluded:

> It may, therefore, I think, be safely laid down as a principle, that, in all ordinary cases, a due regard to their own interests cannot be a motive sufficient to prompt individuals to such undertakings.
> (Rae 1834: 52)

On the other hand, the potential social gain from this transfer could be large: "the smallest present expenditure of the funds of the society which the project may occasion, may be more than repaid, by the large future revenue that it will bring in" (ibid.: 53). From this gap between the differential gain of society and that of the individual, Rae derived his central thesis:

> I hold, that it would be more just and judicious that the necessary first cost

of the scheme should be borne by the whole community: more just, as thus the burden necessary to be borne to procure a common benefit will be divided amongst all, instead of being sustained by one.

(Rae 1834: 53)[44]

Turning briefly to the secular movement of factor returns, as for the wage rate, Rae assumed "that the remuneration awarded the laborer, is, is in the same society always a fixed quantity"(ibid.: 97). However, it would be too hasty to concluded that Rae assumed a constant commodity wage throughout his model. That he did not consider the constant wage model as his whole story about the secular pattern of wage rate especially *when an economy is growing due to the inventive principle*, is absolutely clear:

> I may . . . observe that though, for the sake of simplicity of exposition, I have assumed, all along, that the wages of labor constitute an invariable quantity, yet I conceive that, *in a society making a steady and healthy progress, they should rather be continually increasing, the laborer as well as the capitalist, gaining something by the improvements which the progress of invention produces.*
>
> (Rae 1834: 327, emphasis added)

It should be noted that the constant wage assumption was explicitly said to be "for the sake of simplicity of exposition."

Concerning the rate of profits, the consequences of the working of the two principles – the accumulative and inventive – are unambiguously spelled out by Rae:

> 1. Accumulation of stock or capital, is the addition made to these, through the operation of the accumulative principle.
> 2. Augmentation of stock or capital, is the addition made to them, through the operation of the principle of invention.
> 3. Increase of stock or capital, is the addition made to them, by the conjoined operation of both principles. Accumulation of stock diminishes [the rate of] profits; augmentation of stock increases [the rate of] profits; increase of stock neither increases nor diminishes [the rate of] profits.
>
> (Rae 1834: 264)

He had in mind the special case in which the accumulative principle and the inventive principle work at the same strength so that the rate of profits remains constant. We must accordingly consider not one but three possible cases, depending on the relationship between the two principles generating falling, constant, or rising rates of profit. As for

> countries rising to riches, I conceive, that [the rate of] profits will commonly be high. They will be higher than where, the principle of accumulation having had time to work up all the materials within reach of its

strength, a stop is put to its farther advancing the stock of existing instruments, and the state of the society becomes stationary.

(Rae 1834: 264)

He gave as examples of such countries "most rapidly advancing to riches," North America and Russia, and there "[the rate of] profits and labor have been permanently high, from the unintermitting transfer to that continent of European arts, and from the generation of new arts in the country itself," confirming again a variable wage over time with the "inventive principle" working. Noteworthy is his clear recognition of the necessity of the incessant increase of knowledge to have rising profit and wage rates; otherwise, the accumulative principle will catch up and depress them.

Conclusion

> It is always depressing to go back to Adam Smith, especially on economic development, as one realizes how little we have learned in nearly 200 years. It is, however, perhaps worthy of notice that our father Adam saw very clearly that the learning process was the key to development, for if we examine his causes of the increase in the productive powers of labor, which is what we mean by economic development, we see that they all involve the knowledge process.
>
> (Kenneth E. Boulding 1966)

John Rae's preeminence among classical economists in his formulation of knowledge-based growth theory can be summarized as follows. For post-1815 classical economists, knowledge creation was important for an economy to grow; most recognized continual knowledge generation during their period, the later generation more than the earlier. For John Rae it was crucial.

More importantly, other classical economists often mentioned and discussed knowledge creation, while John Rae analyzed it. In the context of the machinery question, post-1815 classical economists did not deal with what prompts entrepreneurs to introduce new machinery; the introduction of machinery is treated as if exogenous. Many classical economists recognized the externality issue involved in knowledge generation. For instance, Malthus was aware of the difference between private and social rates of return on educational investment (Hollander 1997: 895):

> Much might be expected from a better and more general system of education. Everything that can be done in this way has indeed a very peculiar value; because education is one of those advantages, which not only all may share without interfering with each other, but the raising of one person may actually contribute to the raising of others. If, for instance, a man by education acquires that decent kind of pride, and those juster habits of thinking, which will prevent him from burdening society with a family of children which he cannot support, his conduct, as far as an individual instance can go, tends evidently to improve the condition of his

fellow labourers; and a contrary conduct from ignorance, would tend as evidently to depress it.

(Malthus [1803] 1986: 562–3)

Patents were justified on the externality ground too (see McCulloch 1832a: 817–8).

John Rae grounded his growth theory in the public-goods nature of knowledge. His insights into individual motives behind knowledge creation led him to recognize costs associated with knowledge generation due to the potential difference between private and public rates of return. Furthermore, in contrast to Babbage's essentially microeconomic contribution, Rae developed a macroeconomic growth theory based on his insights into the microeconomic considerations of knowledge creation. As for policy implications, though many classical economists understood the significance of knowledge-based growth policies such as patents, those ideas were not firmly incorporated into their theory. John Rae based his policy prescriptions on his growth theory.

There is another apparent difference between Rae and Babbage regarding the Smithian division of labor. Babbage claimed he followed Smith, while Rae attacked Smith quite fiercely; Babbage emphasized co-operation rather than competition among inventors and scientists (see earlier), while Rae tended to pay more attention to the competition side, the costs and difficulties of knowledge generation, and to outstanding individuals who can overcome such difficulties.

However, this difference is more rhetorical than substantial, and despite his strong words of criticism, John Rae in fact used the Smithian idea. Indeed, John Rae, a self-proclaimed critic of Smith, became closest to Smith when he criticized Smith most effectively. In his famous case for government intervention where knowledge creation matters, his version of the infant-industry argument, Rae criticized Smith for his failure to recognize the potential benefit of intervention, yet his criticism amounts to saying that Smith did not use his own idea of the supremacy of acquired advantage through learning as opposed to natural advantage in an international trade context.[45] As is clear from Rae's stress upon acquired advantage, Rae did not conceive of knowledge creation as solely carried out by outstanding individuals (see earlier), a point confirmed by Rae's gradual and cumulative view of technological change and economic growth and also shared by many classical economists such as Ricardo and West. Babbage, in turn, did not neglect the role of outstanding individuals:

> the power of inventing mechanical contrivances, and of combining machinery, does not appear, if we may judge from the frequency of its occurrence, to be a difficult or a rare gift. . . . It is however a curious circumstance, that although the power of combining machinery is so common, yet the more beautiful combinations are exceedingly rare. Those which command our admiration equally by the perfection of their effects and the simplicity of their means, are found only amongst the happiest productions of genius.
>
> (Babbage [1832] 1986: 182)

In the light of this analysis, we turn now to a comparison with the work of

Cannan and Robbins. Contrary to Cannan's (1929) assertion that classical economists neglected the role of knowledge in the growth process, in fact they paid growing attention to it, with a truly remarkable contribution by John Rae. Though the first-generation Ricardians were busy spelling out the basic model which holds "knowledge" as given, the second-generation Ricardians were more concerned with incorporating knowledge into the basic model. McCulloch's *Principles*, his most "formal representation," does contain a section on human progress and knowledge, and both McCulloch and Senior demonstrated their interest in knowledge as early as early 1830s. Rae's analysis based on the public-goods nature of knowledge thus defies Cannan's (1929) third point mentioned in the first part of this chapter. As far as Robbins (1968) is concerned, this chapter strengthens, yet modifies his position, treating the individual economists more carefully. Babbage's contribution, however important it may be, is not clearly linked to the canonical growth model, so that Robbins's inclusion is not justified.

In its emphasis on the post-1815 classical economists' recognition of knowledge, and on John Rae's important contribution, the chapter is in agreement with Berg (1980). Nonetheless, there are differences: using the canonical growth theory as a guide, we stress the role of knowledge in growth theory and how it is modeled; in light of this perspective, John Rae's importance is further strengthened compared to other economists' works. Furthermore, Rae's apparent indifference to the "machinery question" and to the justification of profit as a legitimate return for capital undermines Berg's (1980) main contention that the post-1815 classical political economists' attempts can be interpreted as ideological responses to the class issue.

Brewer (1991) is concerned with the way in which the role of knowledge in the growth process was modeled in the works of post-1815 classical economists. Though they were aware of the significance of knowledge, they did not go further to construct a knowledge-based growth model. In this respect John Rae stood out as the foremost knowledge-based growth theorist, as Brewer (1991) has rightly stressed. However, Brewer's (1991) review of post-1815 economists oversimplifies the picture since his concern was limited to a particular type of modeling strategy according to which knowledge has to be at the centre of the model, yet it is exogenously determined. This narrow construction of knowledge-based growth theory distorts the perspective; it leads us to neglect other modeling strategies used by post-1815 classical economists, such as the Malthusian one in which population pressure leads to improvements (Malthus, McCulloch and Alexander Hill Everett).[46]

It also drew attention from an important theoretical linkage between Smith and Rae, contrasting Smith and Rae too starkly. Eltis concludes his chapter on Smith:

> with the notable exception of Marx, increasing returns in industry played virtually no part in the thought of those who wrote about economics after Smith. Their books disregarded or discounted the significance of Smith's first three chapters with the result that a vital element in classical economics was lost.
>
> (Eltis 1984: 105)

114 *Masazumi Wakatabe*

If we mean knowledge creation is useful because it generates "increasing returns," it was John Rae, having wished to criticize Smith for his lack of a knowledge-based growth theory, who resurrected "a vital element." This was the very Smithian theme of constructing a knowledge-based growth theory within the canonical growth model framework.[47]

Notes

I would like to thank Nancy Churchman, Arnold Heertje and Andrew Tepperman for useful comments. Financial support from the Japan Society for the Promotion of Science (Grant-in-Aid for Encouragement of Young Scientists (A)), the Seimeikai Foundation, and Waseda University (Grant for Special Research Projects) are greatly appreciated. The section on John Rae is based on Wakatabe 1998b. The section on Malthus owes greatly to Hollander 1997.

1 On the formulation of the canonical growth model, see Samuelson 1978. For the textual evidence, see Hollander 1980 and Samuelson 1980. The treatment of knowledge has been the most contentious issue of the model, especially related to the inclusion of Smith into the model, since Smith's division of labor presumably entails the growth of knowledge throughout the growth path. West 1982 disagrees with the model in that

> Adam Smith was exceptional in that he *did* appreciate the effect and presence of continual innovation. In the canonical model the rightward progress down the curve DD' [representing diminishing marginal productivity] is caused by the accumulation of capital in the presence of diminishing returns *with technology assumed constant*. In Smith's work, in contrast, the accumulation of capital itself leads to more divisions of labour and *therefore to changing technology*.
> (West 1982: 317)

Smith's division of labor is the focus of the Kurdas(1988)–Samuelson (1988) exchange too. On the endogeneity of technological change in Smith's growth theory, see Berg 1980: 33–4, Eltis 1984: 69, Hollander 1987: 166–70, and Elmslie 1994.

2 Therefore I shall use the term "knowledge" rather comprehensively as anything which changes productivity, including invention, innovation, skill formation, technology transfer and so on, the usage corresponding more or less to classical economists' own usage of "improvements." On the subject of knowledge, classification for the sake of classification would not work, as Machlup's (1980–84) ambitious project did not succeed. A recent survey on learning and growth (Jovanovic 1997) emphasizes what he calls the "hybrid" growth model incorporating various types of knowledge.

3 As Robbins quickly points out, it is not fair to Cannan to quote from Senior's lectures which had not been available to Cannan. They were published in Levy 1928 for the first time.

4 Cannan knew Babbage and Rae and indeed he referred to them (Cannan 1929: 97), not in the context of the importance of knowledge but rather in Mill's quotation. Cannan 1917 did refer to Babbage, but not to Rae (Cannan 1917: 33, 89n).

5 Brewer understands Smith's growth theory as a capital accumulation-driven one in which knowledge generation is of a secondary status. For an examination of the relationship between Rae and Smith, see Wakatabe 1998a.

6 On Mill, see Hollander 1985: 226–7, 466–7. On Marx, see Rosenberg 1974, 1976.

7 See the following literature: Pesciarelli 1994 on Lauderdale; Pesciarelli 1989 and Hollander 1998b on Bentham; Koolman 1971 on Say; and Berg 1980 and Hollander 1977 on Read and Scrope.

8 Some might question the historical validity of calling them the "Ricardians." In this

paper, I shall use the label simply to denote the canonical growth theorists identified by Hollander (1998b). Hollander 1977 argues most of the post-1815 classical economists were substantially agreed on the theory of value and distribution.

9 True, there is a passage in *Essay on Profits* in which Ricardo sounded pessimistic:

> That great improvements have been made in agriculture, and that much capital has been expended on the land, it is not attempted to deny; but, with all those improvements, we have not overcome the natural impediments resulting from our increasing wealth and prosperity, which obliges us to cultivate at a disadvantage our poor lands, if the importation of corn is restricted or prohibited.
>
> (Ricardo 1951, vol. 4: 32)

However this is passing, not spelling out the implication for factor returns (see Hollander 1979: 606–7). On Ricardo's evaluation of the past and future performance of the British economy, see Hollander 1979, esp. 605–15.

10 Cf. Hollander 1979: 346–73; 1987: 188–91. For the most faithful formal presentation of Ricardo on Machinery, see Uchiyama 1997.

11 Malthus did not always interpret diminishing returns as an empirical notion. In the fifth edition of the *Essay on Population* (1817), technical change in agriculture is clearly distinguished from diminishing returns:

> [i]f new and superior modes of cultivation be invented, by which not only the land is better managed, but is worked with less labour, it is obvious that inferior land may be cultivated at higher profits than could be obtained from richer land before; and an improved system of culture, with the use of better instruments, may for a long period more than counterbalance the tendency of an extended cultivation and a great increase of capital to yield smaller proportionate returns.
>
> (Malthus 1817, vol. 2: 435–6)

Similarly in response to John Weyland's *Principles of Population and Production* (1816), Malthus kept diminishing returns and technological change separate. (Cf. Hollander 1997: 195–203.)

12 In the first edition of *Essay on Population* (1798), technical change is already represented as a part of the "normal" growth patterns: "Improvement in manufacturing machinery would of course take place," acting (together with the larger manufacturing workforce drawn from agriculture) to expand manufacturing output. But this occurs "without giving the labouring poor a greater command over the necessaries and conveniences of life," indeed even causing a net deterioration in well-being because of unhealthy conditions in the manufacturing centres and "the greater uncertainty of manufacturing labour" (Hollander 1997: 357n).

13 Also, cf. Stigler (1965): "The progress of improvement must be interpreted to mean the growth of output; West, like Malthus and Ricardo, gave little thought to technological improvements" (Stigler 1965: 175).

14 West did, though, point out the possibility of reducing fluctuations by a further extension of commerce which eliminates the risks involved in depending on few markets (West 1826: 142).

15 Indeed, Torrens took pride in analyzing the effects of improvement:

> The manner, and according to the different stages of improvement, the degree, in which manufacturing industry adds to the value of the material supplied by the other branches of industry, have not, as far as I recollect, been attended to by any preceding writer. This deficiency we shall now endeavour to supply; and the topics to be discussed will be found both novel and important.
>
> (Torrens 1821: 92)

16 He made his debut as a political economist arguing against the physiocratic notion of wealth and commerce of Spence and Cobbett in 1808 (see Torrens 1808). Torrens 1821 incorporated material from Torrens 1808, especially into his chapter on mercantile industry.
17 Torrens referred to Senior's *Three Lectures on the Rate of Wages* (1831) (Torrens 1834: 41), but, curiously enough, not to Senior 1829. Torrens might have been concerned about his "priority." According to Robbins, he "was definitely of the class of men who are touchy about priorities" (Robbins 1958: 10).
18 Torrens's references to education concern mainly the population principle as a promoter of the prudential restraint of laborers. (See Robbins 1958: 48–9, 150, 152.)
19 On the significance of education in the thought of James Mill, see Burston 1973 and Fenn (1987, chap 3). Though Mill's interest in knowledge is more political and propagandizing, rather dogmatically believing in political economy as a truth (see Mill 1836), his role in those functions should not be downplayed, as Robbins 1968 points out.
20 For the evidence of attribution to Senior, see Fetter 1958: 159n45. This article, often cited as Senior's dissent against the Ricardian rent theory, was in fact welcomed by Ricardo himself. See Ricardo's letter to Trower dated 11 December 1821 (Ricardo 1951–73: vol. 9, 122; also cf. Hollander 1977: 246.)
21 Adamant believer in human progress as he was, Senior did not neglect institutional considerations. For instance, his *Letter to Lord Horwick* (1832) took into account the influence of institutional structure on improvements, taking as an example the Irish tenure system as detrimental to improvements due to its adverse incentive effects (Senior 1832: 64, 70).
22 Still Malthus tended to maintain a rather extreme version of the population principle, arguing that free importation of corn would accelerate population growth quickly:

> if in any country means of doubling the quantity of food were suddenly discovered, population would increase *with extraordinary rapidity*, so as to overtake, or nearly to overtake, the food; and that the permanent condition of the labouring classes would not depend upon such discovery, but exclusively on the question of the final increase of moral restraint, or the moral condition of the population.
> In the same manner I must allow that it follows from my principles, that if by a free trade, corn were obtained much cheaper, and a labouring family could really command a much larger quantity of it, population would unquestionably increase with greater rapidity than before, so as to reduce the increased corn wages; and that the final condition of the labouring classes would not depend on this change which had taken place in the law, but upon the greater or less prevalence of the moral checks to population after the peculiar stimulus to its increase had subsided.
> (Senior 1829: 84–5, emphasis added).

However, this does not mean he was hostile to free trade, or social reform based on prudential control; in fact, he supported those initiatives. See Hollander 1997: 854, 905.

23 Senior confessed that "[i]t is possible, that in replying to those who appeared to me to exaggerate the probable effects of its powers, and to neglect the benefits to be derived from increased production, I may sometimes have undervalued the former, and overrated the latter" (Senior 1827: 89–90). He was persistent, maintaining the same view on the population principle throughout his career. For example, at the 5 February 1835 meeting of the Political Economy Club, Senior expressed the same opinion as in 1829 in answer to Tooke's question: "In the absence of disturbing causes, is it more likely that – in a given country – Population will increase more rapidly than Subsistence, or Subsistence more rapidly than Population, and would

either supposition be conveniently expressed by the word 'tendency'?" (Political Economy Club 1921, vol. 6: 42–3).
24 See O'Brien 1970, esp. ch. 12. Curiously O'Brien did not take issue with Cannan's assertions, though he referred to Cannan 1929.
25 He was to contribute an article on "Arkwright" (1853) to the eighth edition of *Encyclopaedia Britannica* (1853).
26 Chalmers actually insisted on a *falling* standard of living during the period, a point which McCulloch vigorously contested.
27 Influenced probably by Senior's view on population, McCulloch later came to realize that the growth rate of subsistence had been greater than the population growth rate. (Cf. O'Brien 1970: 316–9.)
28 Nonetheless, McCulloch came to clarify the difference between the theoretical notion of diminishing returns and knowledge generation counteracting it. In the Preface to third edition (1843), he referred to Senior's article on political economy in *Encyclopaedia Metropolitana* (1836), published as a book as Senior 1836:

> [Senior] lays it down, for example, as a general principle, or rather axiom, that, supposing agricultural skill to remain the same, additional labour employed on the land will, speaking generally, yield a less return. But though this proposition be undoubtedly true, it is at the same time quite as true that agricultural skill never remains the same for the smallest portion of time; and that increased agricultural skill may countervail, for any given period, the decreasing fertility of the soils to which recourse is necessarily had in the progress of civilisation.

(McCulloch 1843: xi–xii)

Improvements in agriculture can overcome diminishing returns for long time:

> the increasing sterility of the soil is sure, in the long run, to overmatch the improvements already made in machinery and agriculture, prices experiencing a corresponding rise, and profits a corresponding fall. Frequently, however, these improvements more than compensate, during lengthened periods, for the deterioration in the quality of the soils successively cultivated, and occasion a fall of prices and rise of profits; and when the increase of population has again forced the cultivation of still poorer lands, new improvements may again restore prices to their old level, or sink them to a lower.

(MuCulloch 1843: 498)

O'Brien interprets this passage as McCulloch's ultimate rejection of the Ricardian thesis, but he is mistaken in considering an empirically pessimistic statement as a Ricardian one; McCulloch's empirically optimistic position is Ricardo's. (See earlier; also cf. O'Brien 1970: 297–8.)
29 Along with his review of Andrew Ure's *Philosophy of Manufactures* (1835), McCulloch reviewed two most important tracts on industrial-technological commentary of the day. On Ure, see Berg 1980: 181 *et passim.*
30 For his life, see his autobiography *Passages from the Life of a Philosopher* (Babbage 1863; Babbage 1989: 11); and the excellent biography by Hyman (1982). On his economic ideas, see Romano 1982, Corsi 1991: 14–20, Stigler 1991, and especially Rosenberg 1994.
31 The book appeared in several forms and editions; it was first published in embryonic form as an article in the *Encyclopaedia Metropolitana* (1829), and subsequently as a book in four editions (1st and 2nd edn 1832; 3rd edn 1833; 4th edn 1835). The text used is the fourth edition since there are no significant alterations in the quoted passages.
32 Babbage [1832]1989, vol. 8: 175–6. He himself summarized the arguments, claiming the improvement on Smith as his contribution to political economy. (Cf.

Babbage [1863]1989: vol. 11: 327–8.) Most modern commentators concur: "Babbage's most distinctive contributions to the discipline of economics are generally regarded as his contributions to this subject [of the division of labor]" (Rosenberg 1994: 27; see also Stigler 1991: 1149–50).

33 Babbage did not refer to James Mill. In his *On the Economy of Machinery and Manufactures*, apart from Smith, Babbage referred to Malthus, Thomas Tooke, and Richard Jones, all of whom he knew as friends and members of the London Statistical Society which Babbage co-founded.

In J. S. Mill's words:

> The great advantage (next to the dexterity of workmen) derived from the minute division of labour ... is one not mentioned by Adam Smith, but to which attention has been drawn by Mr. Babbage; the more economical distribution of labour, by classing the workpeople according to their capacity.
> (Mill 1965–91, vol. 2: 128)

34 Despite his emphasis on the potential efficiency of larger-scale factories, he did not discuss a possible conflict between competition and increasing returns: "it is quite certain that no individual, nor in the case of pin-making could any five individuals, ever hope to compete with an extensive establishment" (Babbage [1835]1989, vol. 8: 151). See Romano 1982: 397–9 on Babbage's view on monopoly.

35 John Rae reached the same conclusion from an importer's point of view, pointing out the difficulties involved in technology transfer. See later. This is in a sharp contrast to classical writers' belief that "technological change, and scientific discoveries generally, tended to be diffused rather speedily and that no nation could expect for any length of time to keep new inventions secret" (Bloomfield 1994: 27).

36 In Chapter 1 of *Reflections on the Decline of Science in England*, "Of the inducements to individuals to cultivate science," he justified national need for the encouragement of science on externality grounds (Babbage 1830: 9–10).

37 O'Brien (1975) includes him among "fringe economists" along with G. R. Porter and J. W. Gilbart (O'Brien 1975: 14), not even mentioning him when he lists classical economists.

38 Stigler asserts that "[t]here is no evidence that he had a close relationship with any of the important economists of his age" (Stigler 1991: 1151). Yet he knew Malthus very well, with whom he founded the Statistical Section of the Royal Society; he supposedly sent drafts of his economic writings to Malthus for comments. (Cf. Romano 1982: 403n75.)

39 Babbage's optimism regarding the discovery of substitute energy sources in the future (for example, tidal power, volcanic power and so on) might imply his confidence in knowledge-based growth overcoming resource constraint, though he was not clear. (Cf. Rosenberg 1994: 40–1n24.) In contrast, as Peart (1996: ch. 2) has shown, Jevons's discussion of the coal question, must be interpreted in his growth theory context, which is lacking in Babbage's work.

40 Berg's summary holds:

> the general framework constructed by Babbage was foreign to the classical political economy of his time: contemporary classical economists, such as Ricardo, Malthus and others, were primarily concerned with macroeconomic issues such as value, income distribution and international trade. Going back to Smithian principles Babbage had analyzed industrial organization and the microeconomics of the manufacturing firm, never losing sight of technological constraints and opportunities
> (Berg 1989: 28)

However, this should not imply that Babbage exerted no influence on the development of classical growth theory; on the contrary, both John Stuart Mill and Karl

Marx owed an intellectual debt to him. George Poulett Scrope also learned from Babbage. Cf. Berg 1980: 127.
41 Stephan (1996) emphasizes these motives too in her search for the determinants of scientific activity.
42 Certainly he believed that technology transfer is very important at an early stage of economic development. A recent study (Baumol 1993: ch. 8) shows that even in developed countries, most technical change derives from transferred technology, confirming Rae's insight. Rae preferred a cautious and judicious manner of government intervention; in terms of the uncertainty involved in the generation of knowledge, this policy is probably the least uncertain.
43 The following is strongly reminiscent of Babbage's insight:

> In examining any large and successful manufacturing establishment, we commonly find that the various parts of it depend ... on the efforts of different individuals, who devote their whole attention to their own departments, and are no at all qualified to change places with each other; while the director of the whole has only such a general knowledge of each as enables him to say when it is properly conducted, not himself to point out the exact mode of best conducting it. It is his business to preserve the economy of the whole, and to search out the individuals best fitted for carrying on every part.
>
> (Rae 1834: 47)

There is no explicit reference to Babbage in Rae's work. Romano argues that Babbage was influenced by the Baconian method (Romano 1982: 390), which might suggest a certain linkage with Rae, a self-proclaimed Baconian. However, considering the elusive nature of such a method, we might be able to make a stronger case for a Baconian connection if we turn to the strong belief in the role of knowledge in progress – "knowledge is power" (cf. Robbins 1968: 83–5).
44 On John Rae's knowledge-based growth policy regarding education and immigration, see Wakatabe 1997.
45 On the relationship between Rae and Smith in terms of knowledge-based growth, see Wakatabe 1998a. For more similarities between John Rae and Adam Smith with respect to development policy and luxuries, see Hollander 1998a; with respect to international trade, see Dimand 1998.
46 In his review of Rae's *New Principles* (Everett 1835), Alexander Hill Everett, brother of the famous orator Edward Everett and influential member of the so-called Boston protectionists (who presumably supported the publication of Rae's book), criticized Rae's modeling strategy. He argued from the viewpoint of his Malthusian strategy of endogenizing technological change, maintaining that population pressure should lead to more improvements (Everett 1823. See Wakatabe 1997).
47 It is no easy matter to trace the influence of Rae either on Senior or on J. S. Mill. Yet O'Brien believes that "Mill was probably also influenced by Rae's treatment of invention – certainly he lays more stress than virtually any writer except McCulloch on this aspect of things" (O'Brien 1975: 220–1). Brewer (1991: 11) argues that Senior too learnt from Rae. To Cannan's (1929: 123) claim that "later writers have failed to develop the subject" [of knowledge in the economy], Robbins replies: "this is simply wrong. There are two excellent chapters on invention in [William Edward] Hearn's *Plutology* (1863), rightly praised by Sir Arnold Plant in his well-known article on Patents" (Robbins 1968: 93), referring to Plant 1934. Yet Hearn too might have learnt from Rae.

References

Babbage, C. (1830) *Reflections on the Decline of Science in England and Some of Its Causes*, London: B. Fellowes, reprinted in Babbage (1989), vol. 7.

—— (1832) *On the Economy of Machinery and Manufactures*, 1st edn, London: Charles Knight (2nd and 3rd edns also 1832; 4th edn 1835, reprinted in Babbage 1989, vol. 8).

—— (1851) *The Exposition of 1851; Or Views of the Industry, the Science, and the Government of England*, London: John Murray, in Babbage (1989), vol. 10.

—— (1863) *Passages from the Life of a Philosopher*, London: Longman, Green, Longman, Roberts and Green, in Babbage (1989), vol. 11.

—— (1989) *The Works of Charles Babbage*, ed. M. Campbell-Kelly, 11 vols, London: William Pickering.

Baumol, W. J. (1993) *Entrepreneurship, Management, and the Structure of Payoffs*, Cambridge, Mass.: MIT Press.

Berg, M. (1980) *The Machinery Question and the Making of Political Economy, 1815–48*, Cambridge: Cambridge University Press.

—— (1989) "Introduction" to *The Works of Charles Babbage*, ed. M. Campbell-Kelly, vol. 1, London: William Pickering.

Blaug, M. (1997) *Economic Theory in Retrospect*, 5th edn, Cambridge: Cambridge University Press.

Bloomfield, A. (1994) *Essays in the History of International Trade Theory*, Aldershot: Elgar.

Boulding, K. E. (1966) "The Economics of Knowledge and the Knowledge of Economics," *American Economic Review* 56(2): 1–13, 6.

Bowley, M. (1937) *Nassau Senior and Classical Economics*, London: Allen and Unwin.

Brewer, A. (1988) "Edward West and the Classical Theory of Distribution and Growth," *Economica* 55 (November): 505–15.

—— (1991) "Economic Growth and Technical Change: John Rae's Critique of Adam Smith," *History of Political Economy*, 23(1): 1–11.

—— (1998) "Invention" in O. F. Hamouda, C. Lee and D. Mair (eds), *The Economics of John Rae*, London and New York: Routledge : 129–43.

Burston, W. H. (1973) *James Mill on Philosophy and Education*, London: University of London/Athlone Press.

Cannan, E. (1917) *A History of the Theories of Production and Distribution in English Political Economy from 1776 to 1848*, 3rd edn, London: P. S. King.

—— (1929) *A Review of Economic Theory*, London: Frank Cass.

Corsi, M. (1991) *Division of Labour, Technical Change and Economic Growth*, Aldershot: Avebury.

Dimand. R. W. (1998) "Rae and International Trade," in O. F. Hamouda, C. Lee and D. Mair (eds), *The Economics of John Rae*, London and New York: Routledge: 177–84.

Elmslie, B. (1994). "The Endogenous Nature of Technological Progress and Transfer in Adam Smith's Thought," *History of Political Economy* 26(4): 650–63.

Eltis, W. (1984) *The Classical Theory of Economic Growth*, London: Macmillan.

Everett, A. H. (1823) *New Ideas on Population; with Remarks on the Theories of Malthus and Godwin*, 1st edn, Boston: Cummings, Hilliard; 2nd edn 1826.

—— (1835) "Rae's Political Economy," *North American Review* 40(Jan.): 122–41.

Fenn, R. A. (1987) *James Mill's Political Thought*, New York and London: Garland.

Fetter, F. W. (1958) "The Economic Articles in the *Quarterly Review* and their Authors, 1809–52," *Journal of Political Economy* 66(1): 47–64; 66(2):154–70.

Hamouda, O. F., Lee, C. and Mair, D. (eds.) (1998) *The Economics of John Rae*, London and New York: Routledge.

Hollander, S. (1977) "The Reception of Ricardian Economics," *Oxford Economic Papers* 29(2) (July): 221–57.

—— (1979) *The Economics of David Ricardo*, Toronto and Buffalo: University of Toronto Press.

—— (1980) "On Professor Samuelson's Canonical Classical Model," *Journal of Economic Literature* 18(2): 559–74.

—— (1985) *The Economics of John Stuart Mill*, 2 vols, Toronto: University of Toronto Press.
—— (1987) *Classical Economics*, Oxford: Blackwell.
—— (1997) *The Economics of Thomas Robert Malthus*, Toronto and Buffalo: University of Toronto Press.
—— (1998a) "John Rae and Adam Smith," in O. F. Hamouda, C. Lee and D. Mair (eds), *The Economics of John Rae*, London and New York: Routledge: 199–221.
—— (1998b) "The Canonical Classical Growth Model: Content, Adherence and Priority," *Journal of the History of Economic Thought* 20(3) (September): 253–77.
—— (1998c) "Jeremy Bentham and Adam Smith on the Usury Laws: A 'Smithian' Reply to Bentham and a New Problem," mimeo.
Hyman, A. (1982) *Charles Babbage: Pioneer of the Computer*, Oxford: Oxford University Press.
Jovanovic, B. (1997) "Learning and Growth," in D. M. Kreps and K. F. Wallis (eds), *Advances in Economics and Econometrics: Theory and Applications, Seventh World Congress*, Cambridge: Cambridge University Press, vol. 2: 318–39.
Koolman, G. (1971) "Say's Conception of the Role of the Entrepreneur," *Economica* 38(August): 269–86.
Kurdas, C. (1988) "The 'Whig Historian' Adam Smith: Paul Samuelson's Canonical Classical Model," *History of Economics Society Bulletin* 10(1): 13–23.
Levy, S. L. (ed.) (1928) *Industrial Efficiency and Social Economy by Nassau W. Senior*, New York: Henry Holt, 2 vols.
—— (1970) *Nassau W. Senior 1790–1864: Critical Essayist, Classical Economist, and Advisor of Governments*, Newton Abbot: David and Charles.
McCulloch, J. R. (1817) "On the Effects of the Employment in Manufacturing," *The Scotsman* 13 (April 19): 97.
—— (1818) "Ricardo's *Political Economy*," *Edinburgh Review* 30 (June): 59–87.
—— (1825a) *Syllabus of a Course of Lectures on Political Economy*, London: Hurst, Robinson.
—— (1825b) *The Principles of Political Economy: With Some Inquiries Respecting their Application, and a Sketch of the Rise and Progress of the Science*, 1st edn, Edinburgh: William Tait.
—— (1827) "Rise, Progress, Present State, and Prospects of the British Cotton Manufacture," *Edinburgh Review* 46 (June): 1–39.
—— (1830) *The Principles of Political Economy: With Some Inquiries Respecting their Application, and a Sketch of the Rise and Progress of the Science*, 2nd edn, Edinburgh: William Tait.
—— (1832a) *A Dictionary, Practical, Theoretical, and Historical, of Commerce and Commercial Navigation*, London: Longman, Rees, Orme, Brown, Green, and Longman.
—— (1832b) "Dr Chalmers on *Political Economy*," *Edinburgh Review* 56 (October): 52–72.
—— (1833a) "Babbage on *Machinery and Manufactures*," *Edinburgh Review* 56 (January): 313–32.
—— (1833b) "Present State of Manufactures, Trade, and Shipping," *Edinburgh Review* 58 (October): 40–64.
—— (1835) "Philosophy of Manufactures," *Edinburgh Review* 61(July): 453–72.
—— (1843) *The Principles of Political Economy: With Some Inquiries Respecting their Application, and a Sketch of the Rise and Progress of the Science*, 3rd edn, Edinburgh: William Tait.
—— (1853) "Arkwright," *Encyclopaedia Britannica*, 8th edn, Edinburgh: Adam and Charles Black, 3: 609–12.
Machlup, F. (1980–4) *Knowledge: Its Creation, Distribution, and Economic Significance*, 3 vols, Princeton, N.J.: Princeton University Press.

Malthus, T. R. (1803) *An Essay on the Principle of Population*, 2nd edn, 2 vols, London: John Murray, reprinted in Malthus (1986) vols. 2–3.

—— (1815a) *The Grounds of an Opinion on the Policy of Restricting the Importation of Foreign Corn*, London: John Murray, reprinted in Malthus (1986) vol. 7: 151–74.

—— (1815b) *An Inquiry into the Nature and Progress of Rent*, London: John Murray, reprinted in Malthus (1986) vol. 7: 115–45.

—— (1817) *An Essay on the Principle of Population*, 5th edn, 3 vols, London: John Murray.

—— (1820) *Principles of Political Economy*, 1st edn, London: John Murray, reprint ed. J. M. Pullen, 2 vols, Cambridge: Cambridge University Press (1989).

—— (1836) *Principles of Political Economy*, 2nd edn., London: William Pickering, reprinted in Malthus (1986) vols 5–6.

—— (1986) *The Works of Thomas Robert Malthus*, ed. E. A. Wrigley and D. Souden, 8 vols, London: William Pickering.

Mill, James (1826) *Elements of Political Economy*, 3rd edn, London: Baldwin, Cradock, and Joy, reprinted in Winch (1966): 203–366.

—— (1828) "Education" in *Supplement to the 4th, 5th, and 6th editions of the Encyclopaedia Britannica*, Edinburgh, 1824, 6 vols, reprinted in T. Ball (ed.), *James Mill: Political Writings*, Cambridge: Cambridge University Press (1992): 139–94.

—— (1836) "Whether Political Economy is Useful," *London Review* 2 (January): 553–71, reprinted in Winch (1966): 371–82.

Mill, John S. (1965–91) *The Collected Works of John Stuart Mill*, Toronto and Buffalo: University of Toronto Press, 33 vols.

Nelson, R. (1997) "How New is New Growth Theory," *Challenge* (September– October): 29–58, reproduced in *Journal of Economic Perspectives* 12(2) (Spring 1998): 235–6.

Niehans, J. (1990) *A History of Economic Theory*, Baltimore: Johns Hopkins University Press.

O'Brien, D. P. (1970) *J. R. McCulloch: A Study in Classical Economics*, London: Allen and Unwin.

—— (1975) *The Classical Economists*, Oxford: Clarendon Press.

Peart, S. (1996) *The Economics of W. S. Jevons*, London and New York: Routledge.

Pesciarelli, E. (1989) "Smith, Bentham, and the Development of Contrasting Ideas on Entrepreneurship," *History of Political Economy* 21(3): 521–36.

—— (1994) "Is there a Scottish Tradition in the Economics of Innovation?" in M. Albertone and A. Masoero (eds), *Political Economy and National Realities*, Torino: Fondazione Liuigi Einaudi: 269–87.

Plant, A. (1934) "The Economic Theory Concerning Patents for Inventions," *Economica* 1 (February): 30–51.

Political Economy Club (1921) *Centenary Volume*, London: Political Economy Club.

Rae, J. (1834) *Statement of Some New Principles on the Subject of Political Economy, Exposing the Fallacies of the System of Free Trade, and of Some Other Doctrines Maintained in the "Wealth of Nations,"* Boston: Hilliard, Gray, reprinted in R. W. James (ed.), *John Rae: Political Economist*, Toronto: University of Toronto Press, 2 vols (1965), vol. 2.

Ricardo, D. (1951–1973) *The Works and Correspondence of David Ricardo*, ed. P. Sraffa with M. H. Dobb, Cambridge: Cambridge University Press, 11 vols.

Robbins, L. (1958) *Robert Torrens and the Evolution of Classical Economics*, London: Macmillan.

—— (1968) *The Theory of Economic Development in the History of Economic Thought*, London: Macmillan.

Romano, R. M. (1982) "The Economic Ideas of Charles Babbage," *History of Political Economy* 14(3): 385–405.

Rosenberg, N. (1974) "Karl Marx on the Economic Role of Science," *Journal of Political Economy* 82(4): 713-28, reprinted in *The Emergence of Economic Ideas: Essays in the*

History of Economics, Aldershot: Edward Elgar (1994): 117–32.
—— (1976) "Marx as a Student of Technology," *Monthly Review* 28 (July–August): 56–77, reprinted in *Inside the Black Box: Technology and Economics*, Cambridge: Cambridge University Press (1982): 34–51.
—— (1994) "Charles Babbage: Pioneer Economist," in *Exploring the Black Box: Technology, Economics, and History*, Cambridge: Cambridge University Press: 24–46.
Samuelson, P. A. (1978) "The Canonical Classical Model of Political Economy," *Journal of Economic Literature* 16(4): 1415–34.
—— (1980) "Noise and Signal in Debates among Classical Economists: A Reply," *Journal of Economic Literature* 18(2): 575–8.
—— (1988) "Keeping Whig History Honest," *History of Economics Society Bulletin* 10(2): 161–7.
Schumpeter, J. A. (1954) *History of Economic Analysis*, ed. from ms by E. B. Schumpeter, New York: Oxford University Press.
Senior, N. W. (1821) "Report – On the State of Agriculture," *Quarterly Review* 25 (July): 466–504.
—— (1827) *An Introductory Lecture on Political Economy*, London: J. Mawman.
—— (1829) *Two Lectures on Population, delivered before the University of Oxford in Easter term, 1828, to which is added a Correspondence between the Author and the Rev. T. R. Malthus*, London: Saunders and Otley.
—— (1831) *Three Lectures on the Rate of Wages, with a Preface on the Causes and Remedies of the Present Disturbances*, 2nd edn, London: John Murray.
—— (1832) *A Letter to Lord Horwick, on a Legal Provision for the Irish Poor; Commutation of tithes, and a Provision for the Irish Roman Clergy, Third Edition with a Preface, Containing Suggestions as to the Measures to be Adopted in the Present Emergency*, London: John Murray (no change in the text throughout editions since 1st edn was published in 1831).
—— (1836) *An Outline of the Science of Political Economy*, London: W. Clowes (reprinted by Allen and Unwin 1938).
Stephan, P. (1996) "The Economics of Science," *Journal of Economic Literature* 34(3): 1199–1235.
Stigler, G. J. (1965) *Essays in the History of Economics*, Chicago and London: University of Chicago Press.
—— (1991) "Charles Babbage (1791+200=1991)," *Journal of Economic Literature* 29(3): 1149–52.
Stiglitz, J. E. (1997) Interview, *The Region* (Minneapolis Federal Reserve), September: 8–17, reproduced in *Journal of Economic Perspectives* 12(2) (Spring 1998): 239.
Torrens, R. (1808) *The Economists Refuted; or, an Inquiry into the Nature and Extent of the Advantages derived from Trade: with Observations on the Expediency of making Peace with France*, London: S. A. and H. Oddy.
—— (1821) *An Essay on the Production of Wealth with an Appendix in which the Principles of Political Economy are Applied to the Actual Circumstances of this Country*, London: Longman, Hurst, Rees, Orme, and Brown.
—— (1829) *An Essay on the External Corn Trade, A New Edition, with An Appendix on the Means of Improving the Condition of the Labouring Classes*, London: Longman, Rees, Orme, Brown, and Green.
—— (1834) *On Wages and Combination*, London: Longman, Rees, Orme, Brown, and Green.
Uchiyama, T. (1997) "Ricardo on Machinery: A Dynamic Analysis," mimeo.
Wakatabe, M. (1997) "'The Operations of the Legislator': The Role of Government in John Rae's Knowledge-Based Growth," mimeo.
—— (1998a) "John Rae and Adam Smith: Two Attempts at Theorizing Knowledge-

Based Growth," paper presented at History of Economics Society Annual Meetings, Montreal, Canada, June 26–28.
—— (1998b) "'The Creation of Wealth': John Rae's Knowledge-Based Growth Theory," *Journal of the History of Economic Thought* 20(3): 329–47.
West, Sir E. (1815) *Essay on the Application of Capital to Land, with Observations Shewing the Impolicy of the Importation of Corn, and that the Bounty of 1688 did not Lower the Price of it*, London: T. Underwood.
—— (1826) *Price of Corn and Wages of Labour, with Observations upon Dr. Smith, Mr. Ricardo, and Mr. Malthus's Doctrines upon those Subjects; and an Attempt at an Exposition of the Causes of the Fluctuation of the Price of Corn during the Last Thirty Years*, John Hatchard.
West, E. G. (1982) "Ricardo in Historical Perspective: A Review of S. Hollander, *The Economics of David Ricardo*," *Canadian Journal of Economics* 15(2): 308–26.
Winch, D. (ed.) (1966) *James Mill: Selected Economic Writings*, Edinburgh and London: Oliver and Boyd.

7 Reading *The Wealth of Nations* in context
Rethinking the canon of mid-eighteenth century British political economy

Richard A. Kleer

Introduction

In this chapter I consider the conference theme at one remove: the canon not of key works in the history of economic thought, but of contemporary writings considered relevant for interpreting *The Wealth of Nations* in context. Over the past two decades a canon of this second kind has taken definite shape. The purposes of this chapter are to establish its contours, examine the forces by which it has been shaped, and suggest modifications.

In "Recent contextual studies of *The Wealth of Nations*" I review those single-author books published in recent years which employ an intellectual-history approach to the study of the *Wealth of Nations*. For this purpose I accept Rorty's definition of the genre: "descriptions of what intellectuals were up to at a given time, and of their interaction with the rest of society" (Rorty 1984: 68). Into this category fall Muller (1993), Minowitz (1993), Brown (1994), Fitzgibbons (1995), Ross (1995), Winch (1996), Young (1997) and McNamara (1998).[1] The review, arranged in temporal order, will help set out the broad outlines of the canon of contemporary works and establish the several ways in which it has been deployed to make sense of Smith's system of political economy. In "Reflections on the canon of contemporary works" I examine the priorities guiding the choice of works for inclusion in the canon and the specific uses made of them. I argue that questions of the twentieth rather than the eighteenth century continue to provide the main point of orientation. Finally, in "An alternative model of intellectual history" I set out my own sense of the possibilities of intellectual history, propose an alternative focus for contextual interpretations of *The Wealth of Nations*, and derive the implications for the canon of contemporary works – it needs to be broadened considerably.

Recent contextual studies of *The Wealth of Nations*

It is best to begin with Muller, since his very catholic reconstruction of the contemporary setting for Smith's work conveniently summarizes the findings of several recent strands of interpretation among intellectual historians. First, there was the tradition, running from Plato and Aristotle through the Italian humanists to Enlightenment thinkers, according to which the goal of political philosophers was "to influence the holders of power or to occupy government posts themselves" (Muller 1993: 26). Fortunately, because "the patronage of men of extraordinary intellect by men of extraordinary wealth and power" was common in eighteenth-century Britain, Smith found himself in a position to offer advice to statesmen. Second, the country was then in the throes of revolutions in agriculture, finance, consumption and technology which together were pushing it headlong toward a materialist lifestyle. Finally, around the issue of growing commercialism a number of intellectual currents took shape. Christians and "civic republicans" were hostile to trade, upholding instead an ideal of virtuous dedication to a spiritual life or to the public good.

Scholars in the tradition of natural jurisprudence, writing under the shadow of the great religious wars of the seventeenth century, argued that the quest for an agreed code of public morality was itself part of the problem. They advocated instead concentrating on the rational design of a framework of laws capable of protecting individual liberty and keeping the peace. Renaissance humanists and their successors sought to secure virtue by means they considered more reliable than reason. Noting that virtuous behavior could be traced to fundamental egoistic drives, they "sought to analyze the passions in order to channel them into morally beneficial directions through social institutions," and writers such as Voltaire and Hume actively defended materialism (contemporaries called it "luxury"), arguing that it benefited the poor, enriched the state, and smoothed the rough edges of human nature.

Gerry Muller argues that Smith's central intellectual objective was to bridge the divide which civic humanists alleged existed between commerce and virtue. To this end Smith drew mainly upon the humanist tradition. "[H]is purpose was to make people more decent by designing social institutions which draw the passions toward socially and morally beneficial behavior" (Muller 1993: 6). Smith redefined the public good as the prosperity of the common person and sought to show that the most important institution by which this goal could be advanced was the market. "Self-interest . . . channeled by the market, leads to the division of labor and makes possible a society of universal opulence" (ibid.: 72). Increased wealth, widely distributed, was a great moral good in itself. The market also "promoted the development of co-operative modes of behavior and . . . made men more self-controlled and more likely to subordinate their asocial passions to the needs of others" (ibid.: 94). Smith recognized though that the market alone was not sufficient for generating fully moral human beings. He saw a need for other, supporting institutions, the proper design of which it was the business of intellectuals like himself to decide. There must be a strong government to prevent citizens from injuring one another and at the same time an impartial system of justice that protects citizens from the possible excesses of government. The nuclear family must be preserved (for instance by abolishing lax divorce laws), since according to Smith it is "society's most important moralizing institution" (ibid.: 127). Some kind of national defence is required to protect the nation's wealth (the fount of its superior morality) from foreign attack. Publicly-funded education (though with built-in market incentives) is needed to offset the stultifying effects of the division of labor. Churches should be independently funded; an established religion introduces a spiritual gap between the clergy and the lower orders, creating a moral vacuum that unscrupulous demagogues rush in to fill. And a small intellectual elite must be maintained to cultivate the "superior virtues" and "to influence men of power, to encourage their public spirit, and to provide them with concepts and information through which they could anticipate the probable consequences of government action" (ibid.: 174).

Peter Minowitz challenges recent trends in intellectual-history interpretations of Smith's work. In chapters two and three he draws on the text of Smith's two main works to question the view that Smith was at heart a political philosopher concerned with virtue and constitutional ideals. Smith did not consider political economy "a vehicle for deliberating about the proper ends of politics" (Minowitz 1993: 15); for he took its fundamental end as given: to increase national wealth. *The Wealth of Nations* is dominated by material concerns. Only in Book V does Smith move beyond the horizon of economics to broader issues of human nature; yet the title and general theme even of that book are "forthrightly pecuniary" (ibid.: 18). Never in *The Wealth of Nations* does he "endorse a particular ruling class[,] . . . extol a particular set of political institutions," or even try to categorize, let alone evaluate, the different forms of government (ibid.: 21). Even in the *Lectures on Jurisprudence* he was more concerned with "what we today would call public policy, than with the principles that would guide founders or constitution writers" (ibid.: 29). The praise bestowed in the *Theory of Moral Sentiments* upon the noble statesman was immediately offset by the succeeding criticism of the man of system. Smith clearly believed that government evolves naturally, without need for conscious human oversight (ibid.: 35–44).

While the *Theory of Moral Sentiments* is brimming with language meant to inspire virtue and nobility, the moral code that emerges requires "neither divine enlightenment, deep study, nor special talent"; it arises spontaneously from ordinary human behavior (ibid.: 47–8). Smith never bothered trying to justify political ideals like equality; "such philosophical and theological apparatus is superfluous because the necessary lessons are taught by nature directly, through the impartial spectator" (ibid.: 53). While references to wisdom and virtue may certainly be found in the *Theory of Moral Sentiments*, these are mere "vestiges" of more expansive classical ideals. The important point, as a famous passage in *The Wealth of Nations* makes clear, is that "Smith takes it for granted that society is glued together by the mercantile bond of utility rather than by love, gratitude, and friendship" (ibid.: 59).

Minowitz then sets out his own sense of the fundamental nature and achievements of Smith's intellectual project, one very much in keeping with the Straussian interpretation of Cropsey (1957). In Part VII of the *Theory of Moral Sentiments*, in a discussion of Plato's *Republic*, Smith identified two irrational faculties of the soul: *thymos* or spirit (politics: ambition, animosity, the love of honor, the desire for victory, superiority and revenge) and *epithymia* or appetite (economics: bodily urges, the love of ease and security). Smith's central concern in his two great works was to analyze and direct the interplay between these two passions. He traced the division of labor to the propensity to truck, barter and exchange, which derived in turn from the faculty of speech. In the *Theory of Moral Sentiments* he suggested that speech is itself rooted in ambition. The implications, Minowitz claims, are enormous. Smith was offering a new solution to an old problem of political philosophy. By liberating economic self-interest, the individual's drive for power – so destructive a force in Hobbes' account of politics – can be sublimated and transformed into a much more orderly, peaceful passion.

> Smith's books are permeated by his attempts to deflate human intoxication with various forms of 'dazzling' acquisition ... [He combats the usual admiration for violent rulers] by drawing attention to the 'sober lustre' that accompanies industry and frugality, virtues 'much less dazzling' than 'the more splendid actions of the hero, the statesman, or the legislator'.
> (Minowitz 1993: 81)

This is why Smith was so attracted to Stoic philosophy. The "bourgeois virtue" he was trying to inculcate demanded a long course of prudence, sustained by a sense of propriety. Since Stoicism encourages patience and self-denial, it "is especially useful as a counter to the Machiavellian longing for a sudden, bold, and violent stroke to change one's fortune" (ibid.: 90). It also accounts for Smith's atheism (several chapters are set aside to persuade the reader that, despite appearances to the contrary, Smith was in fact an atheist) and his very strong distaste for organized religions. He worried greatly about the influence and authority of the clergy over the minds of the common people. For of all kinds of spiritual ambition, "religious faction" is perhaps the worst

> because partisanship in the service of God cannot always be tempered by human concerns. The pursuit of salvation or piety, perhaps even more than the pursuit of glory, empire, or political hegemony, is poorly suited to the marginalism essential to the economic realm of marketplace bargaining and cost-benefit analysis.
> (Minowitz 1993: 183)

One might even say that Smith's chief concern was "reorienting politics from religion to economics" (ibid.: 184). In sum, "Smith wishes 'the great body of the people' to be absorbed in bettering their condition by lengthy, laborious industry and to be insulated from the intoxicating elixirs of politics" (ibid.: 185).

Vivienne Brown aggressively attacks interpretations like Muller's that use a context-based approach to show that Smith himself attached high moral worth to commercial societies. It is a mistake, she asserts, to make the eighteenth-century context the required point of departure for understanding Smith's work; for this supposes that the meaning of any text is governed by what its author was trying to say. Derrida, Foucault, Rorty and others have demonstrated that language has a peculiar fecundity which can impose itself upon authors and transcend their conscious intentions. Her interpretation builds rather from Smith's rhetoric and style of writing (Brown 1994: 2–3). This method reveals a fundamental discontinuity between *The Wealth of Nations* and the *Lectures on Jurisprudence* on the one hand and the *Theory of Moral Sentiments* on the other. The *Theory of Moral Sentiments* features many "voices" (humanity in general, the "we" of a moral agent and impartial spectator, a detached narrator, and so on) while *The Wealth of Nations* and *Lectures on Jurisprudence* are dominated by a single, authoritative voice. Now on Smith's own account, the practice of morality is "quintessentially dialogic" (ibid.: 33); truly moral behavior, that is, requires individuals to consult the views of others (the impartial spectator). So the "monologism" of the *Wealth* and *Lectures* must mean that "economic agents occupy a shadowy, twilight space in the moral universe, somewhat outside the site of moral discourse proper" (ibid.: 52). Prudence (the defining trait of successful economic agents) and justice are "lower-order virtues" or even "amoral." Still trying to prove that Smith distanced commerce from morality, Brown points to a distinction in Stoic philosophy between the moral excellence of the few and the merely acceptable behavior of the majority. The distinction found its way into the *Theory of Moral Sentiments*, she claims, through Cicero and Hutcheson. Hence the book's didactic voice, representing true virtue, speaks with "deep contempt" for things of which the mob usually approves: the moral and intellectual standards of statesmen, wealth and greatness, power and riches (ibid.: 87). True, other voices speak with admiration of prudence, a quality "attainable by persons of less elevated moral character." But it is anachronistic though to interpret this as an "endorsement of the morals, the behaviour, or the aspirations of what later came to be seen as the middle classes in an economic or entrepreneurial sense" (ibid.: 93); for by prudence Smith meant care of one's own person, not economic activity *per se* (ibid.: 97). Finally, Brown objects to the attempt of some intellectual historians to build a bridge between the *Theory of Moral Sentiments* (*TMS*) and *The Wealth of Nations* (*WN*) by construing Smith's intellectual project as the "science of a legislator". Citing Smith's own definition of political economy as a branch of that science (*WN* IV intro. 1), such scholars imagine that his major goal was to design a legal framework within which commercial activity could be placed on a firm moral basis. In this connection they lay great stress on the following passage from the *Theory of Moral Sentiments*:

> The leader of the successful party [in a civil war] . . . if he has authority enough to prevail upon his own friends to act with proper temper and moderation (which frequently he has not), may sometimes render to his country a service much more essential and important than the greatest victories and the most extensive [foreign] conquests. He may re-establish and improve the constitution, and from the very doubtful and ambiguous character of the leader of a party, he may assume the greatest and noblest of all characters, that of the reformer and legislator of a great state; and, by the wisdom of his institutions, secure the internal tranquillity and happiness of his fellow-citizens for many succeeding generations.
> (Smith, *Theory of Moral Sentiments* VI ii 2.14)

Such an interpretation is mistaken on two counts, alleges Brown. First, Smith did not consider his system of natural liberty to be part of any science of the legislator. For him "political œconomy" and the "legislator/statesman" were terms of disdain. He always used the former expression to refer to contrary systems of economic policy (mercantilism and physiocracy); in *The Wealth of Nations* the latter term was a symbol for the kind of active state management he opposed (Brown 1994: 128–34). Second, while certain predecessors rooted law in a Stoic moral code (the natural-law tradition of Grotius, Pufendorf and Barbeyrac) or in a concern for public virtue and active citizenship (the "civic humanism" of Machiavelli, Montesquieu and Rousseau), Smith decisively severed such links. For him jurisprudence was a matter of fixed rules, guiding behavior without need of that constitutive moment of true morality – individual recourse to an inner dialogue with the impartial spectator (ibid.: 102–22).

Fitzgibbons follows in an established line of interpretation that situates *The Wealth of Nations* within the natural-law tradition, though he turns it to a new purpose. Eighteenth-century Britain was facing a fundamental policy choice: should it "try to retain the close social bonds of an organic society, committed to medieval notions of Christianity and martial virtue, or should it evolve towards individualism and economic growth"? Smith set out to show "that there only appeared to be a conflict between morals and wealth, and that it was possible to synthesize the seeming contraries" (Fitzgibbons 1995: 14). To this end, he drew upon the tradition not of Renaissance humanism, as Muller maintains, but of natural jurisprudence. Smith did not think that people would become more moral by pursuing their economic self-interest within the market framework. In this regard he

> subscribed to that part of the Hobbesian philosophy which identified unrestrained human beings with wild animals, with an inclination 'to extort all they can from their inferiors' ([L]JA 23) and a 'love of dominion and authority over others' ([L]JA 187)".
>
> (Fitzgibbons 1995: 100)

Thus any regime that suffers from "valuelessness and lack of social commitment" (ibid.: 118) must ultimately self-destruct. In order for economic growth to set in and for a society to endure, morality must be built into its legal framework at the outset. For instance, on Smith's analysis, economic growth is caused by capital accumulation, which rests in turn on prudence or the propensity to save. In other words, "Smith believed that economic growth presupposed a compatible culture, and that this culture had to be rooted in moral notions" (ibid.: 145). Similarly, to stop the division of labor from alienating workers, the state needed to reform the institutions of education and religion. Christian casuistry had displaced the classical emphasis on the individual's moral excellence; a liberal education emphasizing "scientific morals" would correct this. And by paying stipends to priests, the state could stop the spread of fundamentalist Christianity, "which lacks any coherent notion of the Good" (ibid.: 158). Smith favored natural liberty not because it encouraged economic efficiency, but because the principles of commutative justice demanded it (ibid.: 173). He hated mercantilism because it was a perverse moral system, aiming at low wages when the only just aim of political economy was general prosperity, favoring the rich and powerful rather than the poor, and making trade a source of international dissension rather than co-operation (ibid.: 175). In tracing value to the labor cost of production, Smith showed that "there was a moral anchor beneath the tossing of the market" (ibid.: 180).

In sum, *The Wealth of Nations* was part of "a wider project to reform society by basing liberalism on ancient values, namely, the Stoic virtues" (ibid.: 187). This was to be achieved through the careful design of a system of laws, based on a scientific analysis of legal principles such as Smith intended to provide in his projected treatise on jurisprudence.

Ian Ross (1995), in the first full-scale biography of Smith since Rae 1895, has a great deal to say about the eighteenth-century context. We learn of the theological and political issues debated by the Scottish literati and are introduced to their major writings. The relationship of the ideas of Smith and Hume to those of prominent scholars and literary figures in England and on the continent is mapped out. There are short sketches of every major contemporary publication that Smith purchased for his library or that might have influenced his thinking on rhetoric, jurisprudence, moral philosophy or political economy. We discover that Smith read very widely in modern and classical literature and poetry, with discernment and well-defined tastes. The reader is kept abreast of major political and military events, especially the Jacobite Rising of 1745, the Seven Years' War, and the American and French revolutions. We learn too of the personalities and policy views of major English and French politicians, and of Smith's opinions about and personal interactions with some of them. There are long descriptions of specific developments in contemporary economic policy on which Smith had opinions or about which he was asked for advice: Scottish paper currency, conflicts of fiscal jurisdiction between the French crown and the *parlements*, taxation of the American colonies, the failure in 1772 of the Ayr bank, new fee structures for Scottish customs officers, Burke's attempts to reform the East India Company, the commercial treaty of 1786 with France, and so on.

Little of this however is brought directly to bear upon Ross' interpretation of Smith's two main published works. Nor does he make much use of the recent intellectual-history studies. True, in the closing paragraphs their main conclusion is echoed: Smith's central aims were to explain "how people in a relatively early phase of a commercial and manufacturing society might live with justice to themselves and others" (Ross 1995: 419) and to urge us "to aspire to virtue rather than wealth, and so become members of a truly civil society" (ibid.: 420). In the main body of the text however, the *Theory of Moral Sentiments* and *The Wealth of Nations* are treated largely in isolation from one another; there is no explicit attempt to bridge a perceived gap between economics and morals. Instead, Ross merely reiterates the older views of the editors of the Glasgow edition of Smith's works and correspondence. The *Theory of Moral Sentiments* was a "carefully considered and complex answer" (ibid.: 161) to the view of Hobbes, Mandeville and Rousseau that morals and law "were originally the inventions of the cunning and powerful, in order to maintain or acquire an unnatural and unjust superiority over the rest of their fellow creatures" (*Essays on Philosophical Subjects* (*EPS*): 251). Smith followed rather the natural-law tradition, which held that human beings are intrinsically sociable. To explain the specific process by which a moral code forms, he drew upon Hume's principle of sympathy. But he accepted Kames' criticism of Hume that more than sympathy must be at work; when an injury is done someone, our disapprobation derives not just from sympathy with the victim's resentment, but from an additional sense that the perpetrator ought not to have acted this way. To this end Smith added imagination and the impartial spectator to his moral theory (Ross 1995: 161–3). In *The Wealth of Nations*, Smith concentrated on theoretical analysis in Books I and II; Books III to V concerned history and the application of theory to questions of economic policy. In the analytic part he defined "the central problems of classical and neo-classical economics" (price determination, income distribution, profit-rate determination) and devised the method needed to attack them.

> If the economy is viewed as a machine governed by the price mechanism, involving a market for commodities and labour, then the outcomes though unintended will be amenable to law, and can be analyzed by the tools successfully employed in the natural sciences, especially physics.
> (Ross 1995: 238–9)

In constructing this "model", Smith drew on a wide array of sources, but mostly from Hume's teachings about specie-flow adjustments, interest rates, and the connection between commerce and civil liberty, as well as Hutcheson's ideas on the division of labor, the distinction between value in use and value in exchange, money as a medium of exchange and standard of value, and the role of supply and demand in determining prices (ibid.: 272). The applied part of the book gave Smith

> an opportunity to develop a polemic against mistaken and even mischievous attempts of government, chiefly inspired by 'mercantilism', to reorganize, redirect, and thwart economic activity against the tendencies of his 'simple system'.
> (Ross 1995: 280–1)

Smith was opposed in particular to mercantile principles like those of Sir James Steuart:

> the refusal to credit the economy of a modern commercial society with a self-correcting capacity when supply and demand are not in balance, and the tendency to promote the intervention of the 'statesman' to deal with market failure, also the belief that time 'necessarily' puts a stop to economic growth in a 'trading and industrious nations'.
> (Ross 1995: 243)

Two of the three Parts of Donald Winch (1996) concern Smith directly. In several decades of writing about him, Winch's intent has usually been negative: to disrupt received readings by telling us what Smith was *not* saying in *The Wealth of Nations*. This book continues the trend, though chapter 3 offers a new, positive statement of Smith's fundamental aims and achievements. For both purposes Winch employs a contextual approach. He has never much favored interpretations built around the themes of civic humanism or the Scottish Enlightenment (though he grants they have provided a "richer intellectual context"). His approach "treats Hume and Smith as being more responsive to European problems and audiences" (Winch 1996: 19). It has greater affinities therefore with studies emphasizing the tradition of natural jurisprudence. But neither does Winch tie himself down to that school; his perspective is consistently eclectic and unique. Though aware of post-modernist criticisms of contextual studies, he quickly brushes them aside.

> Many of the practitioners of alternative ways of writing intellectual history clearly feel they are engaged in resolving the weightier moral and political dilemmas of today, deploying sophisticated 'theory' and suitably technical apparatuses for the purpose. . . . [I am not convinced] that I am under any obligation to ape them when writing intellectual history. There are other, equally important things to do, and they rarely require the use of theories borrowed from other pursuits for the purpose of achieving historical understanding.
>
> (Winch 1996: 29–30)

On Winch's reading, Smith was not a dogmatic liberal, blindly supporting government quietism and a merely commutative view of justice. In Smith's "science of the legislator," it was the duty of the statesman "to protect 'every member of the society from the injustice and oppression of every other member of it'." This entailed more than just commutative justice; it also meant not giving favor to one social group at the expense of others, reforming institutions and policies that gave scope for combinations against the public interest, and – in a growing and changing commercial environment – assuming an increasingly prominent role to ensure that fair play still prevailed (ibid.: 98). Admittedly, in the *Theory of Moral Sentiments* Smith explicitly restricted justice to its commutative form.

> The main thrust of *The Wealth of Nations*, however, is in the opposite direction: it can be found in the statements on labour as the source of natural rights; on how the benefits of economic activity ought to improve the lives of those who do most of the work in society; in the defence of high wages; in the attacks on the effect of mercantile restrictions on wage-earners and consumers, and so on.
>
> (Winch 1996: 100)

Smith was not advocating a "system of political economy based solely on utilitarian calculations"; in fact it was the very "instrumental, utilitarian, individualistic, egalitarian, abstract, and rational" character of much mercantile writing on the subject that he disliked (ibid.: 103). Smith worked with a broader understanding of human nature; he knew that our sense of self-interest is "frequently faulty; that we suffer from over-weening conceit; that our behaviour, even in economic settings, is capable of being blown off course by other motives such as love of dominance and love of ease" (ibid.: 107). Smith did not "set legislative goals that were purely economic in character" or believe that "economic goals should take precedence over other legitimate public concerns" (ibid.: 114). He supported public education, for instance, not because it would make laborers more productive, but to protect and improve their moral character (ibid.: 119–20). Smith did not share the outlook of Godwin, Condorcet, Paine and Price, who favored remodeling political institutions "on the basis of rationalistic notions of right, without regard for existing interests." On this issue he was closer to Burke's conservatism (ibid.: 175). But Smith did not share Burke's views that competitive labor markets could be counted upon to deliver a fair and efficient wage (ibid.: 204), or that religious and economic corporations had useful, stabilizing roles to play in the social order (ibid.: 190, 212).

What then was Smith doing in the *Theory of Moral Sentiments* and *The Wealth of Nations*? Winch thinks he was forging a decisive new solution to a problem first formulated by Mandeville and Rousseau, and about which his contemporaries had been writing for decades. The common thrust of Mandeville's *Fable of the Bees* and Rousseau's *Discourse on Inequality* was that "'those laws of justice, which maintain the present inequality amongst mankind, were originally the inventions of the cunning and the powerful, in order to maintain or to acquire an unnatural and unjust superiority over the rest of their fellow creatures'" (Winch 1996: 67). This perspective reappeared in numerous contemporary jeremiads by Rousseau, Goldsmith, and others, on modern luxury; it was impoverishing the common people, depopulating the countryside, and depleting the supply of hardened and capable military leaders. Hume's moral philosophy offered one line of reply. Moral codes were

> the outcome of an unconscious process of social interaction between individuals, each acting on the basis of limited benevolence. ...This meant that law and government ... [were] more than a device by which élites transformed what would otherwise be obstacles to their desires into instruments.
>
> (Winch 1996: 68)

Hume also distinguished between innocent and blameable luxury and denied that the former was detrimental to modern states (ibid.: 75).

Obviously, Smith's moral philosophy led to similar conclusions. Johnson went about solving the problem in quite another way; he noted that by a "secret concatenation," the luxury of the rich ultimately redounded to the public good: it kept the masses employed and provided them with income (ibid.: 58). In drawing out this theme repeatedly in his own writings (recall the passages in the Early Draft and the *Lectures* contrasting the common day laborer and the African king, in the *Theory of Moral Sentiments* about the rich being led by an invisible hand to provide for the poor, and in *The Wealth of Nations* about how the rich and powerful were undone by their fascination for mere trinkets and baubles), Smith was obviously concerned with the same issues. But it was not until he came to write *The Wealth of Nations* that he unlocked Johnson's secret and provided the decisive solution to Mandeville's original paradox. First, by showing that the division of labor furnished a surplus above subsistence, he was able to argue that "the economic game is a positive one, with scope for both rich and poor to improve their position, however unequally the relative gains are distributed" (ibid.: 71). Second, and more importantly, he showed that though prodigality (luxury) might be widespread, in the normal course of human affairs frugality always prevailed. Thus in the long run capital would accumulate, productive laborers become more numerous than unproductive ones, and the society's annual produce steadily increase.

The evidence offered, in British jeremiads, of declining wealth and power was based on too short-term a perspective. "Only by taking the longer view of national wealth could the addition to capital and the slow rise in each year's annual produce be observed" (ibid.: 80). In sum, in *The Wealth of Nations*, "Smith had decisively altered the question by making continual increase rather than actual greatness of national wealth central" (ibid.: 87).

> In the context of the luxury debate . . . where others had seen only one aspect of the secret concatenation, the recirculation of wealth through consumption and employment, Smith moved beyond the static form of this argument which he had endorsed in the *Theory of Moral Sentiments* to see something else as well. Building on the foundations of an existing debate, Smith constructed the distinctive amalgam that constitutes the 'system of artificial plenty' in the *Wealth of Nations*. The desire for self-betterment expressed itself in abstention from present enjoyment rather than extravagance. When invested productively, the results of frugality showed that, contrary to Mandeville's vision, commercial society was constructed on more than mere whimsy and vanity, important though the latter might still be in explaining some aspects of human behaviour.
> (Winch 1996: 89)

Unlike many of the other works surveyed here, Jeffrey Young (1997) does not explicitly attempt to set Smith's writings against the backdrop of one or another contemporary intellectual tradition or to establish their central intent. Instead he proceeds directly to a close, internalist reading of certain key parts of *The Wealth of Nations*, connecting it for the most part only with Smith's two other main works. Nevertheless, Young's book is clearly informed by earlier intellectual-history studies of Smith's work and shares one of their leading concerns: to dispel the old myth that Smith posited an independent sphere of economic activity in which traditional concerns over morality and justice had no place. In the *Theory of Moral Sentiments* Smith argued that all societies gradually develop general rules of justice of universal validity. These rules provided a standard by which he himself judged contemporary social practices. On this basis he gave qualified approval to "self interest and the pursuit of material wealth. Within proper bounds there is nothing morally offensive about these motives and the behaviours they produce. Indeed, they are laudatory, approved, and conducive to promoting the common good" (Young 1997: 48). Despite the famous passage about the butcher, brewer and baker, Smith did preserve a role for morality in economic activity; in three main ways.

First, his whole schema of moral judgements "lie[s] in the background of certain key elements of the analysis of the division of labour, markets, prices, and distribution found in *WN*" (ibid.: 55). In his analysis of prices, for instance, Smith was heir to the Scholastic just-price tradition, as handed down to him through the natural-law writers, Grotius and Pufendorf. In its inception, barter was a form of mutual gift-giving that first developed among friends, in which partners to the exchange were motivated by gratitude to give the equal of what they had received. Granted, in modern markets, equality of exchange is no longer enforced by direct ties of friendship but by a much more impersonal mechanism. However, Smith showed that the end result is still perfectly consistent with commutative justice, even though individual traders do not consciously intend to be just in their own behavior. And for Young the important point is that equilibrium prices take shape around the morally-approved expectation of each individual to be fully compensated for their contribution to the production process (ibid.: 118–26). Similarly, the impartial spectator implicitly approves of the payment of rent and interest, for such payments derive from the right of property, and as Smith showed in the *Lectures on Jurisprudence*, the spectator approves of property in any thing which can be appropriated and is scarce (like land), or which (like capital) was acquired by prior labor.

Second, in his *critique* of contemporary economic policies, Smith paid considerable attention to distributive justice and left a fair amount of room for government intervention designed to enhance it. He was prompted by Rousseau's *Discourse on Inequality* to think a great deal on the issue. He continued to believe that some degree of inequality (the "distinction of ranks") was necessary to social stability, but he showed that in some larger sense this was consistent with distributive justice, for the invisible hand prompts the rich to distribute food supplies almost equally among all members of the society. He also considered inequality a stimulus to improvement in the arts, by which all would benefit and by which the power of landowners was gradually being reduced. While he generally condemned tariffs and bounties, this may only have been because they usually contributed to inequity. Thus he was opposed to the bounty on herring busses because of the fraudulent manner in which it was being used; but in his argument against it, he clearly allowed that if the bounty had lowered the price of food for the common people, it would have been a good thing. Likewise he was prepared to advocate subsidized education for teachers of the lower classes.

> We would suggest that these are examples of the sovereign commanding those acts of beneficence (giving to the poor) that on moral grounds alone would be left to individuals. . . .They are clear instances of marginal trade-offs of commutative justice for gains in distributive justice.
> (Young 1997: 148)

And as Hont and Ignatieff (1983) correctly point out, *The Wealth of Nations* was designed in part to afford a decisive new counter-argument to civic-humanist complaints of vast luxuries being afforded to the rich while most laborers toiled in extreme poverty. Specifically, Smith showed that over time, with economic growth, workers' real wages were bound to rise.

It was particularly Smith's introduction of economic growth and development into the moralists' debates that represented a revolutionary step, and the title of his *magnum opus* was well chosen to emphasize this innovation. This step greatly reduced the scope for the conflict between commutative and distributive criteria that the assumption of a static economy has fostered.

(Young 1997: 154)

Third, in Smith's scheme "both the individual and the government are under important moral obligations *vis-à-vis* the common good" (ibid.: 157). He valued the pursuit of public opulence for the most part only because he thought it would have morally uplifting effects and would advance the welfare of the laboring classes: the vast majority of the population. He maintained that all individuals have an important moral choice to make in their own conduct between frugality and prodigality. And he emphasized the invisible-hand mechanism in good measure because he believed its intellectual beauty might lure statesmen from their customary pursuit of their own gain and seduce them instead into a public-spirited concern for the common good (ibid.: ch. 8).

This last theme is central to Peter McNamara (1998), though he disagrees entirely with the broad thrust of studies like those of Winch and Young. He begins by rejecting the contextual approach to Smith. It is

> fatally flawed if it limits itself to asking, as Winch did, 'what it would be conceivable for Smith, or someone fairly like him, to maintain, rather than what later generations would like him to have maintained'. Historicity in this sense is a dogmatic, hermeneutical principle that tends to read out of Smith the universalistic, transhistorical, and epochal claims of both of his major works.
>
> (McNamara 1998: 14)

McNamara specifically objects to the natural-jurisprudence interpretations of Forbes (1975) and Haakonssen (1981), favoring instead Cropsey's (1957) emphasis on the timeless elements of Smith's thought. Cropsey attributed to Smith the view that economic progress spontaneously leads human beings to become more civilized, diminishing their desire for domination over others. This both increases liberty and reduces political contest; under capitalism, politics is destined to wither away. Forbes counters, and Haakonssen agrees, that Smith's vision of historical progress was less materialist and more open-ended than this, and that for him "there remains an independent role for politics and, sometimes, a decisive role for a legislator" (ibid.: 45). McNamara believes Cropsey's account is much closer to the truth than the revisionist one. From the *Theory of Moral Sentiments* we learn that there is a constant threat of conflict in human society; "private ambition, social station, and the order of nature conspire to perpetuate the potential for political and social turmoil" (ibid.: 21). Smith's grand objective was to find a solution to this enduring problem. He did not think it feasible, as Plato and Aristotle believed, to achieve order by educating the morals of the elite. Nor did he put any stock in Locke's proposals for constitutional reform. His solution, rather, was to appeal to the spirit of system "characteristic of [political] founders and leaders" – their "desire to imitate god – the architect and conductor of the universe." In the past, this spirit had acted only as a disrupting force, leading to a spiral of violence. "Leaders begin by pursuing a policy that is inherently violent, in that it attempts to force society out of its natural course. Furthermore, they realize that spectacular acts of violence prove to be useful for keeping followers in awe." Smith's fundamental contribution was to furnish statesmen with the idea of

> a system that avoids the dangers of systems. It teaches how the interests of the state can be achieved through moderate, though systematic, measures that satisfy [statesmen's] private ambitions of the highest order. First, Smith's political economy dispenses with the need for violent policy, because it is a system in harmony with the natural motions of society and individuals. Second, instead of requiring acts of spectacular violence to keep followers in awe, it proposes to occupy them with the systematic pursuit of wealth under the discipline of competition.
> (McNamara 1998: 32)

Thus Cropsey was right to suggest that Smith saw commerce as a progressive force in history. "The critical point is that economic progress establishes a framework of society that makes it possible for the peaceful desire to better one's condition to hold in check the desire to dominate others" (ibid.: 47). Liberty is a natural product of history itself, not of the statesman.

Recent scholars are also wrong, therefore, to have downplayed "Smith's commitment to what would today be called free-market economics" (McNamara 1998: 80). Their opinion is based on three main propositions: that Smith left a considerable role for the state in certain specific areas; that he thought free trade a utopian proposal, impossible of complete realization in a world still dominated by mercantilist policies; and that, believing in the superior productivity of agriculture, he actually counselled curtailing manufacturing and commerce. Certainly these historians are right, McNamara maintains, to have reminded us of the distance between Smith's political economy and the economic liberalism of the nineteenth and twentieth centuries. The exceptions Smith allowed to the principle of non-intervention however were not "so numerous or so grave as to call into question the validity of the general rule" (ibid.: 87). Though he granted the legitimacy of the Navigation Laws, for instance, he still thought many of its provisions "were unwise and stemmed largely from a misunderstanding of the principles of political economy" (ibid.: 88). The monopoly of colonial trade granted by the Navigation Act was a real burden to Britain; it had redirected capital flows to less productive sectors and slowed growth of the nation's commerce and shipping. While Smith admitted that retaliatory duties might be appropriate in response to discriminatory treatment from foreign countries, he felt this "may not be the wisest course of action." Unless it succeeded in removing the offending restrictions, "to retaliate is to respond to an injury by injuring oneself further" (ibid.: 89). Though he granted that free trade needed to be introduced slowly in industries and societies where it had never existed before (in justice to those with large investments and those who might be thrown out of work), he did not see this as a major obstacle. He recounted how, after the Seven Years' War, 100,000 former soldiers were readily absorbed into the workforce without "'convulsion or disorder'" (ibid.: 90). In sum, there is no gap between Smith and later free-market economics, as revisionist scholars claim.

> Smith's view of the role of the state surely differs from that of today's free-market economics. But this important fact should not distract us from Smith's central claim: the natural progress of opulence is the surest path to riches and power.
> (McNamara 1998: 91)

Reflections on the canon of contemporary works

From the foregoing review, it is apparent that recent intellectual histories of Smith's *The Wealth of Nations* are engaged in a submerged debate on certain fundamental questions of modern political economy: are market societies and modern property relations just? Are free markets consistent with the public good? What are the proper limits to state involvement in the economy? What forces lead the economic power of great nations to wax and wane? and so on. While it has successfully rescued Smith from the clutches of rabid *laissez-faire* liberals, the substantial new emphasis on the eighteenth-century context, it turns out, has served largely to link Smith's name with other, albeit more moderate, twentieth-century political programs. So for instance Winch tells us that "part of the background, if not motivation, for writing the essays in Part II" of his book is to challenge "the [late twentieth-century] belief that an harmonious relationship can be established between Smithian economic liberalism and Burkean conservatism."

> By combining the two positions one arrives at a spontaneous economic order that is the unintended outcome of individual choices, and a legal and governmental regime that respects custom and tradition while being protective of those 'little platoons' – the family, the Church, and other voluntary associations – that are thought to be essential to social cohesion and even nationhood. With little exaggeration one could say that this amalgam of Smith and Burke furnished the heady mixture of doctrines that fired the conviction politics of a recent British Prime Minister and her closest intellectual advisers.
> (Winch 1996: 11–12)

It turns out, Winch alleges, that Smith had little good to say about corporate institutions and preserved a significant public role for the statesman. It is much emphasized that he was fundamentally at peace with the existing order, thinking radical reforms unnecessary or even inadvisable.

The lessons of Smith's science of the legislator seem to be that commercial society is not precarious; that its defects can either be endured or minimised, that it is, in short, a viable basis for social existence, the full potentialities of which had yet to be attained.

(Winch 1996: 122–3)

While statements like this are all more or less accurate, we cannot help hearing in them Winch's own political preferences and fearing that the latter were allowed to set the interpretative agenda. In adapting the findings of contextual studies to his own purposes, Young's central aim is to further a project begun by Kenneth Boulding of re-integrating Christian morals with modern economic science. For Fitzgibbons, it seems a contextualized Smith teaches that a merely self-interested existence is inadequate, that the decay of once-great empires can be stopped by the reintroduction of firm moral standards into public life.

His message was that Britain did not have to revert to cultural backwardness and militarism, and that it could accept its economic opportunities, because a liberal political constitution would not lead to social disintegration. His message was not that Britain was locked into a predetermined future, but that one form of liberal constitution would allow British society to escape the historical wheel. Smith's theory of history indicated not an inevitable economic fate, but the need for a moral choice.

(Fitzgibbons 1995: 126)

If those further to the extremes of left and right object to a contextual approach, it is to turn Smith more readily into an inadvertent, almost unconscious critic of free-market capitalism (Brown 1994), or yet another representative of a modern disease: the deflection of political philosophy from politics – the quest for an ideal political regime conducive to the most lofty aspirations of humanity – to economics – the base somnolence of commercial societies (Minowitz 1993). Finally, McNamara plucks Smith out of his eighteenth-century context in order to let him serve as a clear symbol of an attitude to which he is strongly opposed: "Smith makes statesmanship subordinate to political economy, practice to theory." Hamilton, his American contemporary, is touted as a better guide to the business of economic policy decision-making. Hamilton knew economic-policy conflicts cannot be resolved by theory, since theory cannot grasp reality very well and theorists disagree among themselves or often work with ulterior political purposes. Hamilton looked instead to "enlightened statesmen and to the general policy of nations as guides for political practice" (McNamara 1998: 145–7). In all of this there are greater and lesser degrees of faithfulness to Smith's own position, but at base it is all political philosophy through the back door, not genuine intellectual history. As Muller himself puts it, "Smith needs to be rescued from those who claim him as their intellectual progenitor [or, we might add, antitype]" (Muller 1993: 7), regrettably a project which has yet to be carried out.

Historians' political preferences have also influenced the selection of contemporary works for inclusion in the canon. By viewing Smith as part of a Scottish Enlightenment reaction to the civic humanism of Machiavelli, Harrington and Andrew Fletcher of Saltoun, *The Wealth of Nations* can be made out as a commentary on a long-standing, almost timeless debate on the relationship between virtue and commercial societies. This opens the door to defending the moral status of modern capitalist societies or to disparaging their apparent lack of morals, as one chooses. Given its obvious importance in his own education and teaching, the European tradition of natural jurisprudence offers a much more promising avenue for approaching Smith's body of thought on its own terms. However in studies that have tried to make it the point of departure for interpreting *The Wealth of Nations*, we cannot help discerning a leading desire to claim Smith as a founding member of one or another favored variety of twentieth-century liberalism, or to invoke his authority for the proposition that modern market economies and property relations are fundamentally just. Winch's choice of the writings of Mandeville and Rousseau as the relevant point of entry into Smith's intellectual enterprise seems to have been dictated in large part by an aversion to modern neoclassical economics (specifically its purported separation of theoretical analysis from moral judgement) and the economic policy position with which it is typically associated. *The Wealth of Nations* was not the decisive first step in this divorce; for Smith, and Malthus as well, economic theory still fit hand-in-glove with the concerns of moral philosophy (Winch 1996: 409–21). Since it pays no twentieth-century political dividends to situate Smith's work in the context of numerous eighteenth-century British economic pamphlets and the larger studies of Dutot, Melon, Mirabeau, Turgot, Steuart, Tucker, and so on, those works receive little or no mention in recent studies (Ross 1995 is the honorable exception). Scholars' sense of the relevant context seems to have been defined and limited by the problems and perspectives of twentieth-century political philosophy.

This helps explain why the books under review are written as though the movement of ideas was from one great intellectual peak to another. They treat contemporary scholarly works as conversations among a small group of intellectuals on the cultural and political issues of the day; issues which turn out to bear a remarkable similarity to those exercising modern minds. They assume that to specify the relevant context for Smith's writings, one need merely restate the main scholarly propositions of his fellow intellectuals. We are frequently told, for instance, that in the *Fable of the Bees* Mandeville questioned the moral legitimacy of governments and systems of law. However, little or nothing is said of the social and political setting in which that book was written, the specific issues or practices to which it might have responding, the mind-set of the persons in Smith's day to whom it appealed, or the ideological uses commonly made of it in contemporary political debates. It is made to look as though Smith were responding simply to the ideas put forward there, to an intellectual position on one of the timeless questions of political philosophy. Without knowing something about the valleys of everyday politics and cultural strife in which the great intellectual peaks are situated, it is impossible to grasp their real significance, what their authors "were up to" in Rorty's sense.

Winch is certainly right when he notes that Smith's earlier interpreters treated him and contemporaries like Burke as mere emblems of modern political traditions like liberalism and conservatism (Winch 1996: 14). However, while Smith has begun to escape this kind of treatment, others of his fellow intellectuals have not been so fortunate. The names of Mandeville, Locke, Machiavelli, Grotius, Pufendorf, Shaftesbury, Hutcheson, Hume, Montesquieu, Rousseau, Ferguson and others are bandied about as markers for intellectual positions of whose contemporary ideological sway and pragmatic political associations we are not given the faintest idea. What matters for Smith scholars, it seems, is their modern symbolic resonance, the twentieth-century political categories with which their names have traditionally been associated or which, by a little reconfiguration, they can be made to represent: contractarianism, rationalism, corporatism, and so on. Putting Smith "in context" often has served just to change the modern category into which he can be slotted.

An alternative model of intellectual history

What might a properly contextual interpretation of *The Wealth of Nations* look like instead? To answer this question, I start with a larger one: what is the purpose of intellectual history?

Rorty (1984) thinks its main function is to clear the way for progress in the corresponding field of science. All scientists, he asserts, like to feel that there has been progress in their discipline; rational reconstructions, in which the ideas of a dead thinker are presented in modern terms, help persuade them of this. Historical reconstructions, which present a thinker's ideas in their contemporary context, serve to keep rational reconstructions honest. That is to say, they provide an accurate picture of what earlier thinkers actually thought, thereby ensuring a genuine measurement of subsequent progress. The business of what Rorty calls *Geistesgeschichte* is periodically to redefine the canon of a science by supplying a broad, sweeping sense of where it has been heading, pointing out the way for further real progress. Further, the canon thus constructed itself encourages progress by reminding present-day practitioners that there were great thinkers in the past who proved capable of it. The main function of intellectual history, finally, is to keep *Geistesgeschichte* honest, to correct the record of where the science has been and so the vision of where it is headed.

Whatever we might think of this model of intellectual history for Rorty's own discipline of philosophy, it seems inappropriate for economics. No one doubts that the science has progressed at a technical level; late twentieth-century economists, for instance, know a good deal more about the logical properties and behavioral implications of a Cobb-Douglas utility function than did Paul Douglas. But with regard to the really fundamental questions of economics, it is doubtful whether there exists a "right" answer and so any objective standard by which to measure progress. The Marshallian supply–demand framework, for instance, seeks to answer the question of how market prices are determined, but its way of conceiving the problem – there must be some general answer and it is mechanistic in nature – is far from being the only one possible.

Institutionalists might argue that every market price is the unique result of myriad specific historical, sociological and institutional factors which can only be grasped empirically, not by theoretical means of general application. Which approach is to be favored cannot be decided on criteria acceptable to both camps. So if we accepted Rorty's definition, an intellectual history of the discipline of economics would be pointless.

I suggest that in economics, intellectual history has other, more important roles to play. First, it can help free the mind from accumulated prejudices and so clear the way for fresh thinking. Human beings are no less creatures of habit in intellectual than in any other pursuits. Once a certain way of thinking about a given economic question has caught hold among recognized authorities, it can shape the minds of many subsequent generations, even though, in some broader sense, it might be misleading or counterproductive. Intellectual history lets us catch sight of a mind-set first taking hold, uncovering the circumstances that led intellectuals in that direction and closed off other promising avenues of thinking. Second, it can induce healthy scepticism about the reliability of reason as a guide to economic policy decision-making. It reveals that many of the great economic ideas were first forged in the context of some concrete dispute, serving to define or break a connection between the interests of one of the contestants and the alleged good of the general public. Opponents always had theories of their own, often equally plausible, yet with very different policy implications. Human reason seems very pliable, ever bending to the practical needs of the moment or the group, and it was only seldom, if ever, that statesmen chose a particular policy solution by thinking their way through competing theoretical analyses of what was best for the public. Finally, intellectual history can help alert us to the importance of traits other than rationality in determining how human beings think and act in matters of economic policy. It demonstrates that many economic theories first gained wide acceptance because they met certain deep-seated spiritual needs of their time, and it reveals that in one policy debate after another, the eventual victor was decided not by calm, analytical considerations but by a contest of ideologies or by the fit with the government's fiscal priorities and the political needs of the persons then in power.

For these purposes, serious intellectual histories of eighteenth-century British economics need to work from the fullest possible knowledge of the relevant context. We need to understand how key economic institutions worked; who the major political personalities were and what they were trying to achieve; which individuals, groups and corporations exercised political influence and for what specific causes they lobbied; what ideologies were available for politicians and legislative petitioners to make it seem that their proposals were in the public interest; in response to what particular issues each passing wave of pamphlet literature arose; and so forth. Intellectual historians must also learn to sound the deeper depths of intellectual life, discerning their spirit and tone: the strange fanaticism of Mirabeau's *L'ami des hommes*; the gleeful iconoclasm of Rousseau's *Confessions*; the dark and troubling cynicism pervading Mandeville's *Fable*; the hopes and grievances conveyed by the word "liberty" in the writings of Montesquieu or Paine; the fierce hatred of narrow pious minds for Hume's *Dialogues Concerning Natural Religion* or the suave urbanity of his essays on "Luxury" and "The Jealousy of Trade". Winch knows very well the kind of intellectual history I have in mind:

> The serious study of ideas in relation to practice, as opposed to the attribution of iconographic status to past thinkers, is best left to those prepared to work on the entire range of evidence, local and national, individual and corporate, required by any inquiry into administrative practices, legislative processes, and political alignments".
>
> (Winch 1996: 24)

No one has yet written an intellectual history of Smith's work along these lines, something comparable to what Ashcraft (1986) achieved in the field of Locke scholarship. The necessary components for it are being assembled however in numerous smaller studies, such as Rothschild (1992) and Fitzpatrick (1996); Ross (1995) will also be of great help.

Reading *The Wealth of Nations* with riches of this kind at our disposal, we would be less likely to stumble inadvertently into naïve, literal interpretations. In the studies reviewed earlier, it was asserted more than once, for instance, that Smith's advocacy of high wages shows he was a new kind of political economist: one who cared about the welfare of the great majority rather than of a small political and economic elite. However consider a little of the specific context in which he was writing. In the economic pamphlet literature of mid-eighteenth-century Britain, there were frequent complaints of the country's declining international competitiveness; markets once the sole preserve of British exporters were increasingly being lost to the Dutch or the French. The alleged problem was often traced to high wages, which were forcing domestic manufacturers to raise their prices to uncompetitive levels. On occasion this line of reasoning supported appeals to Parliament for legislation directly reducing wage rates or restricting worker "combinations." More often it was invoked by merchants petitioning for an export bounty or an import duty, allegedly to level the playing field with merchants from "low-wage" countries like France.[2] This suggests a very different interpretation of Smith's remarks on high wages. Very likely he was no more concerned for the common laborer's well-being than anyone else in the small circle of highly privileged intellectuals, merchants, landowners and politicians in which he moved and to whom his book was principally addressed.

No doubt it was increasingly fashionable among some segments of Britain's élite to profess such an outlook, and perhaps even genuinely to believe in it. However, the principle seldom translated into concrete changes in the way common folk were treated as a group, or in the comportment of individual members of the élite toward them as persons. Rather it was at base a required ingredient in a new ideological style useful to certain politicians and deeply satisfying to some of the bolder intellectuals. For Smith in particular, it offered a means of subverting a pattern of political lobbying by which a privileged few were able to advance their own narrow interests under cover of the alleged public good. Smith's advocacy of high wages was inspired first and foremost by a great spiritual quest for that most intangible eighteenth-century ideal: liberty from the perceived evil of arbitrary power and the outmoded superstitions by which it sustained itself.

A contextual reading of *The Wealth of Nations* of the sort I am proposing would also pay much more attention to its "economic" parts, largely ignored in recent studies. For anyone trying to construe the book as a commentary on the moral status of commercial societies, Smith's detailed comments on Scottish banking projects, the history of English coins, long-term trends in the value of silver, the best methods for funding the National Debt, the abuses of the herring bounty system, and so on, are of little interest or use. If they figure at all, it is only to illustrate his general principles on the proper role of government or his belief that market institutions are fundamentally just. However if we learn how to hear such passages the way contemporaries did, they might speak volumes more to us. Smith's remarks on funding the national debt, for instance, strike the untrained twentieth-century eye as dry, technical detail, but some of the greatest conflicts of contemporary British politics turned on the question of the national debt. Historically, it was an institution by which the Whig party had bought the support of a large, wealthy and powerful segment of the British merchant community. It continued to serve as a mainstay of successive administrations well into the nineteenth century, though at the same time it was an Achilles' heel on which opposition politicians, seeking the spoils of office, frequently concentrated their attack. The national debt, in other words, was an incredibly powerful political symbol. However innocuous Smith's remarks on the subject might seem to us, they would have been anathema to many and won vigorous applause from others. In short, they helped Smith to mark off a definite ideological territory, the boundaries of which we cannot even begin to make out unless we know a good deal about the world in which he wrote.

In an earlier study, Winch examined the concept of the national debt and brought out some of the resonance it had for contemporaries (Winch 1978: 121–45). But his account moves on the high ground of great principled and timeless ideals; it does not descend to the serpentine depths of party politics and court or parliamentary intrigue, where little is as it seems. Had Winch done so, his sense of what Smith was up to in this part of *The Wealth of Nations* would have been considerably deepened, and perhaps altogether transformed. And surely it must be possible to get beyond long-standing anachronisms, retailed once more in Ross (1995), about Smith's intent in the chapters on wages, profit and rent. Brown has made a good start on an interpretation that lets Smith speak on his own terms (Brown 1994: 165–79), but much more remains to be done.

Finally, for the kind of intellectual history I am recommending, the canon of contemporary works relevant for interpreting *The Wealth of Nations* in context would have to become much broader. There would no longer be an interest in enlisting Smith in one or another intellectual tradition and confining attention to its central writings. Too much is lost when scholars ignore or actively try to exclude whole subsets of contemporary thought. A great deal could be learned, for instance, from dusty political treatises long out of fashion, the relics of ethical systems and ideological programs that fell by the wayside as events passed them by. While they fail to move the modern mind, they bespeak mind-sets that enraged Enlightenment thinkers and gave substance to their perceptions of systemic intolerance and coercion.

Nor is it acceptable, whatever the pressures of scarce research time, to continue using key contemporary works as emblems. Too often it is supposed that the issues being addressed in a given "great" work, and so the meaning of the position it adopts, can be apprehended immediately, or at most after having read a few other contemporary books to which it might have been a reaction. The book's real significance, what its author was up to, can only be apprehended after having read extensively in the primary literature and acquired a good grasp of the concrete issues, personalities, institutions and cultural practices of the day.

Finally, if the goal is to understand how economic ideas were formed in eighteenth-century Britain, and what role they played in economic policy decision-making, it might be counter-productive to choose *The Wealth of Nations* as our point of departure. For modern historians of political economy it has become the undisputed center point of their canon of contemporary works. But this is largely the result of certain nineteenth- and twentieth-century political and economic trends. It is entirely possible that to understand eighteenth-century political economy, it would be better to start instead with a work like Steuart's *Inquiry into the Principles of Political Economy* (1767) or William Mildmay's *Laws and Policy of England Relating to Trade* (1765). At the very least, we must stop assuming that *The Wealth of Nations* was an investigation of the moral status of commercial societies, and learn to let the book tell us, on its own terms, by what questions Smith might have been exercised when he came to write it.

Notes

1 Rashid professes an interest in understanding Smith in context (Rashid 1998: 14). But he draws upon contemporary economic writings for the most part just to show that as an analytical economist, Smith was no better, maybe even worse, than his predecessors and contemporaries. Haakonssen 1996 certainly belongs in the category, but it devotes only one chapter expressly to Smith.
2 For a fuller discussion of this rhetorical strategy, see Kleer 1996.

References

Ashcraft, R. (1986) *Revolutionary Politics and Locke's* Two Treatises of Government, Princeton, N.J.: Princeton University Press.
Brown, V. (1994) *Adam Smith's Discourse: Canonicity, Commerce and Conscience*, London: Routledge.
Cropsey, J. (1957) *Polity and Economy: An Interpretation of the Principles of Adam Smith*, The Hague: Martinus Nijhoff.
Fitzgibbons, A. (1995) *Adam Smith's System of Liberty, Wealth and Virtue: The Moral and Political Foundations of* The Wealth of Nations, Oxford: Clarendon.
Fitzpatrick, M. (1996) 'The Enlightenment, Politics and Providence Some Scottish and English Comparisons," in K. Haakonssen (ed.), *Enlightenment and Religion: Rational Dissent in Eighteenth-Century Britain*, Cambridge: Cambridge University Press: 64–98.
Forbes, D. (1975) "Sceptical Whiggism, Commerce and Liberty," in A. S. Skinner and T.

Wilson (eds), *Essays on Adam Smith*, Oxford: Clarendon: 179–201.
Haakonssen, K. (1981) *The Science of a Legislator: The Natural Jurisprudence of David Hume and Adam Smith*, Cambridge: Cambridge University Press.
—— (1996) *Natural Law and Moral Philosophy: From Grotius to the Scottish Enlightenment*, Cambridge: Cambridge University Press.
Hont, I. and Ignatieff, M. (1983) "Introduction," to *Wealth and Virtue: The Shaping of Political Economy in the Scottish Enlightenment*, Cambridge: Cambridge University Press.
Kleer, R. A. (1996) "The Decay of Trade: The Politics of Economic Theory in Eighteenth-Century Britain," *Journal of the History of Economic Thought* 18: 319–46.
McNamara, P. (1998) *Political Economy and Statesmanship: Smith, Hamilton, and the Foundation of the Commercial Republic*, DeKalb: Northern Illinois University Press.
Minowitz, P. (1993) *Profits, Priests, and Princes: Adam Smith's Emancipation of Economics from Politics and Religion*, Stanford: Stanford University Press.
Muller, G. Z. (1993) *Adam Smith in his Time and Ours: Designing the Decent Society*, New York: Macmillan.
Rae, J. (1895) *Life of Adam Smith*, London: Macmillan.
Rashid, S. (1998) *The Myth of Adam Smith*, Cheltenham: Elgar.
Rothschild, E. (1992) "Adam Smith and Conservative Economics," *Economic History Review* 45: 74–96.
Rorty, R. (1984) "The Historiography of Philosophy: Four Genres," in R. Rorty, J. B. Schneewind and Q. Skinner (eds), *Philosophy in History: Essays on the Historiography of Philosophy*, Cambridge: Cambridge University Press: 49–75.
Ross, I. S. (1995) *Life of Adam Smith*, Oxford: Oxford University Press.
Smith, A. (1980) *Essays on Philosophical Subjects*, in W. P. D. Wightman and J. C. Bryce (eds), *Glasgow Edition on the Works and Correspondence of Adam Smith*, vol. 3, Oxford: Oxford University Press; facsimile reprint edn, Indianapolis: Liberty Classics (1982).
Winch, D. (1978) *Adam Smith's Politics: An Essay in Historiographic Revision*, Cambridge: Cambridge University Press.
—— (1996) *Riches and Poverty: An Intellectual History of Political Economy in Britain, 1750–1834*, Cambridge: Cambridge University Press.
Young, J. 1997. *Economics as a Moral Science: The Political Economy of Adam Smith*, Cheltenham: Elgar.

8 Justice versus expediency

The Wealth of Nations as an anti-political economy

Jeffrey T. Young

In reflecting on the canon in economics one must inevitably say something about Smith's great book. How do we situate the *Inquiry into the Nature* and *Causes of the Wealth of Nations* (*WN*) in the history of economic thought? Much, if not all, of the recent scholarship on Smith has been devoted in one way or another to debunking the canonical Smith, whoever he is. Thus, we are faced with the immediate dilemma that positioning Adam Smith in the history of economics takes us down two diverging roads: one representing the actual history of economics, the other the virtual path of the scholar representing Smith's intentions.[1] The canonical Smith is the one we read about in our history of economic thought texts, in introductory texts, or even occasionally in journal articles. We even run across him in the popular press. The scholar's Smith is a moral philosopher seeking to erect a general system of social science, of which what became the discipline of economics is only a non-autonomous part. The fact that Adam Smith was "the Adam and the Smith of systematic economics," as Boulding once quipped (Boulding 1969: 1), is a tribute to the success of *WN*, but it is one of the great ironies in the history of economics that it was not Smith's intention.

In this chapter I shall add my voice to the chorus of the debunkers and explore some issues dealing with Smith's intent in *WN* which cast further doubt on the validity of how economists have historically viewed the book, but first we must try to spot the canonical Smith. Vivienne Brown has recently offered the following description:

> Adam Smith's works have come to be seen as the classic statement of liberal capitalism. *The Wealth of Nations* is regarded by economists as a founding document in the canon of the history of economic thought from which modern economic analysis may trace its own descent. In providing a genealogy for modern economics, *WN* functions as a canonic text which supplies a history and a justification for present intellectual and political practices.
>
> (Brown 1994: 7)

She then closes her book with the observation that

> one of the great ironies is that Adam Smith's discourse ... has contributed centrally to the de-moralisation of economic and political categories and

to the construction of an economics canon in which moral debate has virtually no place."[2]

(ibid.: 220)

The canonical Smith is, therefore, credited with establishing economic science as an independent discipline, which eschewed as unfruitful any sort of moralistic discourse.

I have argued elsewhere at length (as have others) that this is a gross travesty of what Smith was trying to do, and that Boulding's notion of economics as a moral science is a more accurate depiction of Smith's work (Young 1997). I agree with Winch that Smith was attempting an integration of economics with moral philosophy, one which shows that Smith's notion of the science of political economy is a very different entity from what actually emerged under that name in the nineteenth century. However, I now contend that we have too hastily and uncritically accepted the view, going back at least to Dugald Stewart (Stewart 1980: 311), that *WN* is in fact a treatise in political economy.[3] On the contrary I shall argue in this paper that, as Smith understood the term, *WN* is more properly understood as an anti-political economy. His purpose may have been, as Winch argues, to position the science of wealth, or what the French writers at the time were calling simply "economic science" (Meek 1962: 213), within jurisprudence, the science of a legislator (Winch 1983). However, I now contend that he sought to eliminate the political economy branch of that science, placing economic science within the justice branch of jurisprudence.

The chapter is presented in four parts. The first two deal with Smith's definition of political economy in Book 4 of *WN* and his identification of the mercantile and agricultural as the two extant systems of political economy. I examine the approaches of Steuart and Quesnay to establish that they had in common a commitment to political economy as statecraft which entailed government stewardship over the nation's resources. The second part presents the core of my case that *WN* should be viewed as an attempt to end political economy, so understood, not to begin it as the canonical story has it. The argument depends, in part, on seeing justice, rather than utility, as the central normative premise of *WN*. Since the discourses in political economy are of a generally utilitarian character, this is a central part of the overall argument.

In the third part I address a problem which arises out of the fact that one cannot consistently draw a rigorous line between justice and utility in *WN* (or *Theory of Moral Sentiments (TMS)* for that matter). Here I confront this problem by first admitting that there are legitimate exceptions where government must infringe on justice for the general good and by pointing out that at least some of the utilitarian character of *WN* should be understood as a rhetorical device used to enhance the political effectiveness of the book. The fourth part offers a brief conclusion *vis-à-vis* the book's place in the history of economic thought.

Political economy and systems of political economy

Political economy is scarcely mentioned in *WN* outside of the fourth book which deals specifically with systems of political economy. It is never used to mean anything other than the definition Smith gives it in the introduction to Book 4, and nowhere is it used in reference to a system of policy other than either the mercantile system or the phyisocratic system. The definition in question is as follows:

> Political oeconomy, considered as a branch of the science of a statesman or legislator, proposes two distinct objects; first, to provide a plentiful revenue or subsistence for the people, or more properly to enable them to provide such a revenue or subsistence for themselves; and secondly, to supply the state or commonwealth with a revenue sufficient for the publick services. It proposes to enrich both the people and the sovereign.
>
> (*WN* Book 4: Introduction 1)

Smith then goes on to identify the mercantile and agricultural systems as the two systems of political economy which had emerged in the course of economic development.

This accords with what he had been telling his students in the jurisprudence part of his course in moral philosophy. After justice, the second branch of jurisprudence was police. Here

> the government will next be desirous of promoting the opulence of the state. This produces what we call police. Whatever regulations are made with respect to the trade, commerce, agriculture, manufactures of the country are considered as belonging to the police.
>
> (*LJ* (Smith 1978)(A) i. 2; see also *LJ* (B) 203)

In short, as Millar described it, the laws of police promoted expediency, not justice, and it was this consideration which separated the two branches of jurisprudence (Stewart 1980: 275).

Economic theory was incorporated into this part of Smith's course and, so the natural inclination was to assume that *WN* was exclusively concerned with police, or political economy. Smith's own statement in the Advertisement to the sixth edition of *TMS* seems to further confirm the identification of *WN* with the science of political economy:

> In the last paragraph of the first Edition of the present work, I said, that I should in another discourse endeavour to give an account of the general principles of law and government, and of the different revolutions which they had undergone in the different ages and periods of society; not only in what concerns justice, but in what concerns police, revenue, and arms, and whatever else is the object of law. In the Enquiry [*sic*] concerning the Nature and Causes of the Wealth of Nations, I have partly executed this promise; at least so far as concerns police, revenue, and arms.
>
> (*TMS*: Advertisement 2)

It is clear that "political economy" and "police" are synonymous, but is there any significance to the altered usage in *WN*? The terms are associated with the mercantilist pamphlet literature and the science of jurisprudence respectively, and it would appear that they refer to a form of statecraft, the use of the law to regulate economic activity. Since the bulk of Book 4 is devoted to the mercantile system, it is not, therefore, surprising that Smith would explicitly position it within the political economy discourse. Indeed, he may very well have had in mind Sir James Steuart's *Principles of Political Economy*, the only contemporary, English-language treatise which sought to offer a systematic account of that science.

Smith took pride in the fact that he nowhere mentions Steuart's book in *WN*, perhaps because he viewed it as his chief competition in his endeavor to influence British commercial policy. Consequently it is impossible to know the extent of its influence on Smith (either positive or negative). However, we do know from Smith's extant correspondence that his view of the book was largely negative. Writing to William Pulteney in 1772 Smith notes that "I have the same opinion of Sir James Stewarts Book that you have. Without once mentioning it, I flatter myself, that every false principle in it, will meet with a clear and distinct confutation in mine" (*Correspondence* (Smith 1977) 132: 164).

We also know that prior to the publication of *WN* Steuart was regarded as the leading expert on commercial policy in Britain (Skinner 1966: li), and so it would not be surprising if Smith took Steuart's *Principles* to be the definitive work on political economy at the time.[4] It will be instructive, then, to compare Steuart's definition of political economy to Smith's. Steuart begins the *Principles* stating that,

> Oeconomy, in general, is the art of providing for all the wants of a family, with prudence and frugality . . . The whole oeconomy must be directed by the head, who is both lord and steward of the family. It is however necessary, that these two offices be not confounded with one another. As lord, he establishes the laws of his oeconomy; as steward, he puts them in execution. . . . What oeconomy is in a family, political economy is in a state: with these essential differences, however, that in a state there are no servants, all are children, that a family may be formed when and how a man pleases, and he may there establish what plan of oeconomy he thinks fit; but states are found formed, and the oeconomy of these depends upon a thousand circumstances.
>
> (Steuart 1966: 15–16)

We see here some of the essential characteristics of Steuart's system, namely the supposition of a statesman implementing a plan of economic policy as the primary agent. This is made explicit when Steuart later comments that

> In treating every question of political economy, I constantly suppose a statesman at the head of government, systematically conducting every part of it, so as to prevent the vicissitudes of manners, and innovations, by their natural and immediate effects or consequences, from hurting any interest within the commonwealth.
>
> (Steuart 1966: 122)

Indeed, he praises Colbert, Law, and Walpole as outstanding examples of such statesmen, because "they were creators of new ideas, they found out new principles for the government of men, and led them by their interest to concur in the execution of their plan" (ibid.: 74). Steuart's statesman is activist in his economic policy to the point of practically taking over the entrepreneurial function. Steuart charges the statesman with taking over such functions as establishing the division of labor (ibid.: 40), new industries (ibid.: 64), and equilibrium prices (ibid.: 191) which Smith left to the invisible hand.

In addition, we also note that the statesman, while charged with implementing new plans, is constrained by the manners and customs of the people. Steuart's view is that plans of political economy are relative to time and place. Like Smith, his approach is historical, with the plan depending on the stage of historical development.

Smith, of course, does not speak of political economy as embodied in plans of statesmen in so many words. However, it is clear that he presupposes the agent of the statesman, and in speaking of systems of political economy he undoubtedly had in view a concept of central direction similar to Steuart's. Moreover, Steuart's assertion that, "The principal object of this science is to secure a certain fund of subsistence for all the inhabitants" (ibid.: 17) closely parallels Smith's definition. Smith's Book 4 definition of political economy is a truncated version of Steuart's more detailed definition. I do not think it is stretching the point to conclude that Smith intended to attach the same meaning to political economy as Steuart, and that he, therefore, viewed it as a form of statecraft which assigned a positive role of managing the economy to the government.

The test of this lies in the free trade system of the physiocrats. In advocating the dismantling of Colbert's system of preference to manufacturing and trade, they were apparently aligning themselves on the opposite side from Steuart, who, we have seen, was an admirer of Colbert. Smith considered physiocracy to be an alternative political economy, diametrically opposed on the specifics of policy, but a political economy nonetheless.

Ronald Meek has suggested that Quesnay viewed free trade as a means to promote agriculture, not as an end in itself. (Meek [1962] 1993: 27) More recently Samuel Hollander went farther than this, concluding that

> The Physiocrats, who have the reputation of being free trade reformers, were as much interventionist as the mercantilists. Had France been a net importer of corn they would not have recommended a free trade policy.
> (Hollander 1987: 51)

Indeed, Smith had already lumped Physiocracy together with mercantilism in the famous passage about natural liberty at the end of Book 4 as "systems either of preference or of restraint" (*WN* Book 4: ix 51). To see this we will consider Quesnay's view of political economy, since it is generally believed that he was the unstated source of most of Smith's chapter on the Physiocrats.

First we note that Quesnay believed that the economy required the direction of a government plan. In his article "Corn" Quesnay attacks the view that the damage government can do to the wealth of particular individuals is a matter of indifference because one person's loss is another's gain leaving the wealth of the nation unchanged.

> This idea is false and absurd; for the wealth of a state does not maintain itself on its own, but is maintained and increased only in so far as it is made to renew itself by *planning its employment intelligently*. If the cultivator is ruined by the financier, the revenue of the kingdom is wiped out; trade and industry languish; the worker is unemployed; the sovereign, the proprietors, and the clergy are deprived of revenue; expenditure and gains become non-existent; and wealth, locked up in the coffers of the financier, remains barren, or, if it is put out at interest, overburdens the state. Thus the government should take special care to maintain unimpaired, in the case of all productive occupations, the wealth which they require for the production and expansion of the kingdom's wealth.
> (Meek 1993: 82, emphasis added)

The idea of intelligent planning appears again in "Men" where we see that

> it is upon the employment of men and the increase of population that the maintenance and expansion of the successively regenerated wealth of nations depend. The state of the population and the employment of men is therefore the principal matter of concern in the economic government of states, for the fertility of the soil, the market value of products, and the proper employment of monetary wealth are the results of the labour and industry of men. These are the four sources of abundance, which co-operate in bringing about their own mutual expansion. But they can be maintained only through the proper management of the general administration of *men, goods, and products; a situation in which monetary wealth is valueless* is clear evidence of some unsoundness in government policy, of oppression, and of a nation's decline.
> (Meek 1993: 88, emphasis in original)

If we consider this in the light of a remark made in a different context that concern for a nation's population is "a leading and especially important branch of the speculations of political economy" (ibid.: 58), we may conclude that "economic government of states" refers to political economy.

A number of inferences follow from these two selections. First, we see that free markets cannot be allowed to operate in the financial sector, because financiers oppress the community. Their activity is wholly unproductive, even negatively productive. Second, this implies that the wisdom of government, guided by the truths of physiocracy, is alone capable of discerning productive from unproductive activities. The upshot is that "private interests do not lend themselves to an insight into the general welfare. Such advantages can be expected only as the result of the wisdom of the government" (ibid.: 97). Third, we find Steuart's notion of political economy as government direction of the economy, or stewardship over the resources of the state: men, soil, value, and money. Political economy in the hands of Quesnay is the same sort of enterprise, or branch of legislative science, as it is in those of Steuart.

Smith is, therefore, correct in treating Physiocracy as a system of political economy in precisely the same sense in which mercantilism is such a system. Thus, in the "General Maxims" we find the classic Quesnaysian statement of free trade:

> That complete freedom of trade should be maintained; for THE POLICY FOR INTERNAL AND EXTERNAL TRADE WHICH IS THE MOST SECURE, THE MOST CORRECT, AND THE MOST PROFITABLE FOR THE NATION AND THE STATE, CONSISTS IN FULL FREEDOM OF COMPETITION.
>
> (Meek 1993: 237, emphasis in original)

However, we also find, "That the nation should not suffer any loss in its mutual trade with foreign countries, even if this trade were profitable to the merchants who made gains out of their fellow-citizens on the sale of the commodities which were imported" (ibid.: 236), and, "That the prices of produce and commodities in the kingdom should never be made to fall; for then mutual foreign trade would become disadvantageous to the nation" (ibid.: 235).[5]

As with Steuart, Quesnay also supposes a statesman, but he frequently, and not surprisingly, resorts to medical analogies to make the point. He considers the Tableau Economique a tool, like medical knowledge, to diagnose sickness and health in the economy as the result of government policy (for example, see ibid.: 108). The significance of this analogy in the present context is the presupposition of the role of the physician (ibid.: 117) performing the same function Steuart ascribes to the statesman. The conclusion must be that Quesnay and Steuart maintain the same general view of the government, or statesman, as the lord and steward of the nation's resources following a plan of economic administration, and that Smith's definition is an accurate statement of what political economy meant in contemporary economic discourse. It is inextricably bound up with a conception of the paternalistic state.

The Wealth of Nations as an anti-political economy

Given the foregoing, it is not surprising that Mark Blaug once reacted to Smith's definition of political economy, noting that, "The introduction to Book 4 defines political economy as a branch of statecraft, a definition in violent opposition to the whole tenor of the *Wealth of Nations*" (Blaug 1978: 59).[6] Vivienne Brown expressed an even more radical sentiment in suggesting that Smith's definition is not intended to be a

> self-description of *WN* itself. But in this passage it is only the mercantile and agricultural system which are identified as systems of political economy; it is not stated that *WN* itself constitutes a distinct or third system of political economy.
>
> (Brown 1994: 128)

This, then, is part of a larger *critique* which argues that the "science of a legislator" view of *WN* is also unwarranted:

> Entrenched in the contemporary discourses pertaining both to the polity and the economy, the legislator/statesman symbolised so much of what Smith's writings and lectures were arguing against that it becomes implausible to identify Smith's own intellectual project as the "science of a legislator."
>
> (Brown 1994: 124)

I will argue that Brown is right that *WN* was not intended to be a treatise in political economy as defined in Book 4, but, since natural liberty is a system of justice (the first branch of the science of jurisprudence), it is not correct to go so far as to condemn Winch, Haakonssen, and many others, including myself, for treating *WN* as a treatise addressed to legislators (and the citizens which elect and/or influence them). Since jurisprudence has more than one branch, eliminating the political economy branch does not eliminate the science as a whole.

That *WN* is not a *Principles of Political Economy* is evident from the very title of the work. As we have seen earlier, Smith and his contemporaries viewed Steuart's book as his chief rival in the field. That he chose not to follow Steuart's lead in positioning his book as an inquiry into the principles of political economy is surely reflective of his desire to differentiate the product. His letter to Pulteney, quoted above, shows that he thought his product was both superior and really different. So his desire to differentiate was more than just a marketing maneuver; he really did have something different to offer. The central characteristic of this difference was reliance on spontaneous order-type explanations where Steuart relied on the visible hand of the government, a system of political economy. In distancing himself from Steuart, Smith was distancing himself from the very idea of political economy.

The famous passage at the end of Book 4 shows that natural liberty is a substitute for political economy, not an alternative system of political economy:

> All systems of preference or of restraint, therefore, being thus completely taken away, the obvious and simple system of natural liberty establishes itself of its own accord. Every man as long as he does not violate the laws of justice, is left perfectly free to pursue his own interest his own way, and to bring both his industry and capital into competition with those of any other man, or order of men. The sovereign is completely discharged from a duty, in the attempting to perform which he must always be exposed to innumerable delusions, and for the proper performance of which no human wisdom or knowledge could ever be sufficient; the duty of superintending the industry of private people, and of directing it towards the employments most suitable to the interest of the society.
>
> (*WN* Book 4: ix. 51)

Physiocracy and mercantilism are equally systems of preference or restraint, and they both impose upon the sovereign this duty of managing the industry of private individuals for the public benefit. As Millar described the police part of Smith's course, these are systems which are guided by expediency, the economic interest of society as a whole, not by justice. However, it would appear that this is not so for the system of natural liberty, where the laws of justice operate as the relevant constraint on individual behavior. I will return to this later.

Earlier in the same chapter Smith made the one statement in his extant writings which is usually read to establish that *WN* is indeed a treatise in political economy. The statement occurs when Smith is asserting that all of the Physiocrats follow very closely the ideas of Quesnay:

> This sect, in their works, which are vary numerous, and which treat not only of what is properly called Political Oeconomy, or of the nature and causes of the wealth of nations, but of every other branch of the system of civil government, all follow implicitly . . . the doctrine of Mr. Quesnai.
>
> (*WN* Book 4: ix. 38)

The fact that there is only one statement of this kind in Smith alone might suggest that it should not be taken seriously, especially in the context of the same chapter where he so clearly does not present natural liberty as a system of political economy. However, such a seemingly straightforward statement in contradiction of the argument must be taken seriously.

Vivienne Brown has already faced this problem, and she offers the following interpretation:

> Here the placing of the word "of" before "the nature and causes of the wealth of nations" suggests that the title of *WN* is to be differentiated from the area of "political economy"; though both descriptors may be applied to the agricultural system, the presence of the word "of" shows that they are not synonymous.
>
> (Brown 1994: 129)

I consider this an acceptable interpretation. The agricultural system entailed both a system of political economy and a science of wealth, but they are not the same thing. In fact, Smith thought the same applied to the mercantile system; it too relied on an implicit, though erroneous, view of wealth. Thus, while it may be impossible to have a system of political economy without an underlying science of wealth, it is very possible to have a science of wealth without having a system of political economy. Indeed, this is what Smith was proposing.

We can now see that Smith's title further distanced his work from political economy. Both systems of political economy rested on two different conceptions of wealth which Smith thought were fallacious. In Smith's mind there was a close connection between false principles and political economy in general. Thus, the first point which must be established in order to remove these systems was the true nature and causes of national wealth. A true view of wealth and its creation would obviate the need for any political economy. As a general rule the laws of justice would be sufficient to guide the economy.

Smith's arguments against both conceptions of wealth are well known. However, in placing agricultural investments in a privileged position *vis-à-vis* manufacturing and trade Smith does not fall into the erroneous view which was the basis upon which the physiocrats erected a "system of preference." Agriculture as sole producer of national wealth is a far cry from Smith's hierarchy of capital investments. Given the right circumstances, for example if free trade were to reduce the price of corn and thus reduce agricultural rents, the physiocratic system would not lead to a free trade policy. On the contrary, Smith's hierarchy implied that at the margin (given the inverse relation between capital accumulation and profit rates in each sector) in a rich country with free mobility of resources all investments would yield equal returns, and be equally productive. Thus, knowing that the superior productivity of agriculture naturally leads to its early development before manufacturing and trade, does not form the basis of an argument that government knows best how to manage the nation's resources, or that resource allocation decisions require central direction because of a divergence between private and public returns.

Smith's conception of wealth is central to his *critique* of both systems and to his advocacy of natural liberty. It is not surprising that he would choose a title which would immediately highlight this fact at the same time that it distanced him from the contemporary discourse of political economy in general and from Steuart's book in particular.

The famous passage at the end of Book 4 goes on to enumerate the duties of the sovereign:

> According to the system of natural liberty, the sovereign has only three duties to attend to; three duties of great importance, indeed, but plain and intelligible to common understandings: first, the duty of protecting the society from the violence and invasion of other independent societies; secondly, the duty of protecting, as far as possible, every member of the society from the injustice or oppression of every other member of it, or the duty of establishing an exact administration of justice; and thirdly, the duty of erecting and maintaining certain publick works and certain publick institutions which it can never be for the interest of any individual, or small number of individuals, to erect and maintain; because the profit could never repay the expence to any individual or small number of individuals, though it may frequently do much more than repay to a great society.
>
> (*WN* Book 4: ix. 51)

Where is political economy, or police, in this outline of the role of government "according to the system of natural liberty"? Compare this, for example, with "The four great objects of law are Justice, Police, Revenue, and Arms" (*LJ* (B): 5). Book 5 of *WN* deals with justice, revenue, and arms, but police cannot be found. We know from Smith's own description of *WN* that it did treat of police, but this is mainly in Book 4, not 5. In none of these three duties is the sovereign supposed to come up with a plan of national economic management. The third duty appears to stand in the place of police, and, indeed it is more clearly oriented toward expediency, and like police it entails wide-ranging government activity in the provision of education and social infrastructure. However, it cannot be construed as political economy. Policies aimed at and judged solely from the perspective of the maximization of national wealth are simply not on the table. It is an unintended consequence of the exact administration of justice, but it is not an explicit object of government action.

I have elsewhere argued that with the system of natural liberty Smith sought to replace the laws of police with the laws of justice, and that injustice was an important part of his attack on the mercantile system (Young 1997: 125). Here I want to suggest that the laws of justice differ from the laws of police in important ways and to briefly explore some aspects of the relation between justice and utility, or expediency, in *WN*.

There are two important differences between justice and police. First, although Smith realizes that the laws of any country at any given time are only an approximation to a system of natural jurisprudence (*TMS* Part 7: iv. 36), the laws of police are statute laws while the laws of justice have generally evolved through the common law. In the courts real judges confront real plaintiffs and defendants, causing the sympathetic interaction between the impartial spectator and the agents directly involved to operate in deciding the cases. Thus, Haakonssen observes that "judge-made law based on precedent has a better chance of approaching the principles of natural justice [than that] made by some authority other than a judge of concrete cases" (Haakonssen 1981: 151; also Cairns 1994). Second, we may note that justice is better served when its administration is removed from the executive branch of the government:

> When the judicial is united to the executive power, it is scarce possible that justice should not frequently be sacrificed to, what is vulgarly called, politics. The persons entrusted with the great interests of the state may, even without any corrupt views, sometimes imagine it necessary to sacrifice to those interests the rights of a private man. But upon the impartial administration of justice depends the liberty of every individual, the sense which he has of his own security. In order to make every individual feel himself perfectly secure in the possession of every right which belongs to him, it is not only necessary that the judicial should be separated from the executive power, but that it should be rendered as much as possible independent of that power.
>
> (*WN* Book 5: i. b. 25)

Police is a function of the executive and legislative branches of government. Not surprisingly Smith cites several instances of how police, even without corruption, leads to the sacrifice of personal rights for political purposes, but I shall take up the specifics of these in the next section of the chapter.

Turning now to the relation of justice to utility in *WN* we may note that, despite the foregoing on the importance of justice, expediency remains as a normative premise of *WN*. There is a decidedly utilitarian character to *WN* in that natural liberty maximizes national wealth, and this is a norm which *WN* appears to share with the discourse of political economy. We must address Smith's reasons for presenting in utilitarian garb a science of wealth based on justice. In the language of the *Lectures*, why use the standard of the police branch of jurisprudence when the goal is to replace the laws of police with the laws of justice?

A thorough investigation of the relation between justice and utility in Smith is beyond the scope of this paper, and ultimately not necessary. For the problem at hand I think there is actually a relatively simple answer. In the system of natural liberty the invisible hand leads self-interested individuals who are following the laws of justice to maximize social wealth. Expediency is an unintended, beneficial consequence of the laws of justice.

Smith was fascinated by such instances of spontaneous order and found them to be aesthetically pleasing (Rothschild 1994: 322). Their aesthetic appeal also contributed to their scientific validity, because they satisfied the criterion of theory choice he established in his "History of Astronomy":

> Philosophy is the science of the connecting principles of nature. Nature, after the largest experience that common observation can acquire, seems to abound with events which appear solitary and incoherent with all that go before them, which therefore disturb the easy movement of the imagination; which make its ideas succeed each other, if one may say so, by irregular starts and sallies; and which thus tend, in some measure, to introduce those confusions and distractions we formerly mentioned. Philosophy, by representing the invisible chains which bind together all these disjointed objects, endeavours to introduce order into the chaos of jarring and discordant appearance, to allay this tumult of the imagination, and to restore it, when it surveys the great revolutions of the universe, to that tone of tranquillity and composure which is both most agreeable in itself, and most suitable to its nature.
>
> (Astronomy 2 (Smith 1980: 12))

In short, invisible hand, or spontaneous order, explanations are uniquely capable of soothing the imagination by "representing the invisible chains."

In *TMS* Smith shows how such explanations which reveal the interconnections of a complex system can be politically useful. The context is a long paragraph in which he argues that it is the "love of system" which "frequently serves to recommend those institutions which promote the public welfare." (*TMS* Part 4: 1. 11) Thus, the utility (in the sense of fitness, or means utility) of the system of public policy, not sympathy for those who will benefit from good policy, is the motive behind the desire to establish good public policy. The goal of the system of policy, like all constitutions of government is to "promote the happiness of those who live under them. This is their sole use and end" (ibid.). Means and ends utility are here both involved in the evaluation of any system of policy, particularly those of political economy: "The perfection of police, the extension of trade and manufactures, are noble and magnificent objects" (ibid.). The paragraph concludes with the following observation:

> If you would implant public virtue in the breast of him who seems heedless of the interest of his country, it will often be to no purpose to tell him, what

160 *Jeffrey T. Young*

> superior advantages the subjects of a well-governed state enjoy; that they are better lodged, that they are better clothed, that they are better fed. These considerations will commonly make no impression. You will be more likely to persuade, if you describe the great system of public police which procures these advantages, if you explain the connexions and dependencies of its several parts, their mutual subordination to one another, and their general subserviency to the happiness of the society; if you show how this system might be introduced into his own country, what it is that hinders it from taking place there at present, how these obstructions might be removed, and all the several wheels of the machine of government be made to move with more harmony and smoothness, without grating upon one another, or mutually retarding one another's motions. It is scarce possible that a man should listen to a discourse of this kind, and not feel himself animated in some degree of public spirit.
>
> (Astronomy 2 (Smith 1980: 12))

The simple answer to the question, then, is that utilitarian explanations would appeal to the conscience "of him who seems heedless of the interest of his country." We can account for Smith's utilitarian approach to policy, then, at least in part as a rhetorical device to "arouse public spirit."

With respect to ends utility, it is true that *WN* shares with the political economy discourse the utilitarian value of the happiness of the people as the goal of national wealth. There is also a strong commitment to justice and equity, as Barry Gordon and I have argued elsewhere (Young 1986, 1997, Young and Gordon 1992, 1996). However, for Smith there is an essential difference, which again distances *WN* from political economy. In his view happiness arises as an unintended consequence of following the laws of justice, it is not the result of a plan of political economy, whether mercantile or agricultural.[7] In addition, political economy will much more readily sacrifice justice to achieve greater national wealth. Smith is extremely reluctant to do so, but this is the subject of the next section.

Sentinels and smugglers

In *TMS*, Smith had already confronted instances where justice and utility come into conflict. Recall that in the main utility is an unintended consequence of justice. It is from the feeling of resentment at the deed of a murderer, for example, that we want to inflict reciprocal harm on him or her. Furthermore, it is a concern for the feelings of others, their perception of the individual's character, which would prompt an individual to refrain from murdering. The result is that society is preserved, but this was not the original intention of the punishment. However, Smith notes

> Upon some occasions, indeed, we both punish and approve of punishment, merely from a view to the general interest of society, which, we imagine, cannot otherwise be secured. Of this kind are all punishments

inflicted for breaches of what is called either civil police, or military discipline.

(*TMS* Part 2: ii. 3. 11)

Consider first breaches of military discipline. In a case which actually occurred a sentinel was put to death for falling asleep on his watch (Raphael 1972–3: 95).

> A centinel, for example, who falls asleep upon his watch, suffers death by the laws of war, because such carelessness might endanger the whole army. This severity may, upon many occasions, appear necessary, and for that reason, just and proper. When the preservation of an individual is inconsistent with the safety of a multitude, nothing can be more just than that the many should be preferred to the one.
>
> (*TMS* Part 2: ii. 3. 11)[8]

As Raphael has shown, though, this is the exception which proves the rule, because the spectator feels differently about this case compared to the norm, even though he approves of the punishment (Raphael 1972–3: 95). As Smith explains:

> Yet this punishment, how necessary soever, always appears to be excessively severe. The natural atrocity of the crime seems to be so little, and the punishment so great, that it is with great difficulty that our heart can reconcile itself to it. Though such carelessness appears blamable, yet the thought of this crime does not naturally excite any such resentment, as would prompt us to take such dreadful revenge. A man of humanity must recollect himself, must make an effort, and exert his whole firmness and resolution, before he can bring himself either to inflict it, or to go along with it when it is inflicted by others.
>
> (*TMS* Part 2: ii. 3. 11)

Another such case, taken from the laws of police, is the case of wool smugglers. In the *Lectures*, Smith used it to prove his point about resentment versus utility.

> Wool in England was conceived to be the source of public opulence, and it was made a capital crime to export that commodity. Yet tho' wool was exported as formerly and men were convinced that the practice was pernicious, no injury, no evidence, could be got against the offenders. The exportation of wool is naturally no crime, and men could not be brought to consider it as punishable with death.
>
> (*LJ* [B] (Smith 1978: 182))

Consider this in the light of Smith's analysis of the corn trade in *WN*. As is well known he sides decisively with the rights of the farmers and dealers in grain. Regarding export prohibitions he argues that such restraints might be necessary in small states and Swiss cantons, but

> to hinder ... the farmer from sending his goods at all times to the best market, is evidently to sacrifice the ordinary laws of justice to an idea of publick utility, to a sort of reasons of state; an act of legislative authority which ought to be exercised only, which can be pardoned only in cases of the most urgent necessity.
>
> (*WN* Book 4: v. b. 39)

Several observations follow from these examples. First, utility may be the effect of justice, but it is not its cause.

Second, violations of police frequently entail no violation of justice; it is difficult to find a jury which will return a conviction for smuggling. The implication is the same in the corn case. However, here it is clearer that the prohibition, the police, is based on a false notion of the relation between the corn trade and public opulence. It is also an example of the abuses of power which Smith thought would be less likely when the administration of justice became independent from the executive function of government.

Third, placing the laws of justice above those of police will actually better serve public opulence. Part of the problem with the mercantile system was that a false conception of wealth fostered the notion that there was frequently a divergence between private and public costs and benefits. No one could be allowed, without the appropriate regulations of commerce, to act in the public interest. The system needlessly set private interest against the public interest, and the frequent result was harm to individuals.

However, the sentinel case reminds us that there will be a small residue of instances which do not fit the pattern, and there, indeed, are some such cases in *WN*. Smith recognized the existence of spillover effects and adverse selection in markets with asymmetric information. In the absence of the Coase theorem and of the wisdom of hindsight on how non-governmental institutions develop to cope with the lemons problem, Smith advocated government intervention on utilitarian grounds. Specifically he proposed constraints on the denomination of bank notes issued by private banks and legal ceilings on interest rates. In regard to bank notes he concluded that

> Such regulations may, no doubt, be considered as in some respect a violation of natural liberty. But those exertions of the natural liberty of a few individuals, which might endanger the security of the whole society, are, and ought to be, restrained by the laws of all governments; of the most free, as well as of the most despotical. The obligation of building party walls, in order to prevent the communication of fire, is a violation of natural liberty, exactly of the same kind with the regulations of the banking trade which are here proposed.
>
> (*WN* Book 2: ii. 94)

Here the threat to the public good is a real one, so the rights of the individual must be restrained. Modern economists have no difficulty recognizing this as a case of external costs driving a wedge between private and social costs. Unlike the sentinel case, however, the discrepancy between the seriousness of the individual's negligence and the resultant harm is much smaller, and so

Justice versus expediency   163

there would be less sympathy for the offender. Another difference is that there is no suggestion here that preserving the security of the whole society makes the law just; the distinction between justice and utility is preserved with utility receiving the higher priority.

Smith's acceptance of usury laws fall into a similar pattern. There are sound reasons of public utility which justify them, although individual rights are curtailed. His position is that the legal rate ought to be set above the lowest market rate.

> If the legal rate of interest in Great Britain, for example, was fixed so high as eight or ten per cent., the greater part of the money which was to be lent, would be lent to prodigals and projectors, who alone would be willing to give this high interest. Sober people, who will give for the use of money no more than a part of what they are likely to make by the use of it, would not venture into the competition. A great part of the capital of the country would thus be kept out of the hands which were the most likely to make a profitable and advantageous use of it, and thrown into those which were most likely to destroy it. Where the legal rate of interest, on the contrary, is fixed but a very little above the lowest market rate, sober people are universally preferred, as borrowers, to prodigals and projectors.
> (*WN* Book 1: iv. 15)

In the absence of institutions and procedures for screening, monitoring, and enforcing loan contracts, the problem of adverse selection will essentially ruin the market, as is the case in many third-world countries today. Since bad-risk borrowers are willing to pay more for a loan, in the absence of such institutions lenders have no way of knowing who is sober and who is prodigal. The result would be that prodigals outbid the sober for the money, do not repay, and banks fail producing a missing market. Smith's diagnosis of the problem was correct, although modern economists would be less likely to suggest that governments solve this problem with legal ceilings on interest rates.

The importance of these instances is that there are times when from a legitimate public concern the rights of individuals must be constrained. They would appear, therefore, to be counter-examples to the argument of this paper. I believe that fitting these into the overall structure of *WN* is difficult, and like the sentinel, constitute exceptions of which Smith was aware. However, while that case may be seen as the exception which proves the rule, I do not think a similar argument applies to bank notes and interest rates; public utility is clearly the basis for the approval of such laws and there is only slight indication that the spectator would sympathize with the individual whose liberty has been curtailed.

With a certain amount of trepidation I offer the following tentative suggestions. To repeat, the general presumption which runs throughout *TMS* and *WN* is that utility (in the sense of ends-utility) is the unintended consequence of justice. The laws of police have as their purpose the promotion of public utility, or national wealth, but this association is frequently erroneous. Thus, replacing the laws of police with the laws of justice will serve that end better, while better protecting individual rights. The regulations of bank note denomination and interest rates are exceptions, but they do not form the basis of an alternative system of political economy. The fact that Smith left out police when he explained the legitimate functions of government is at least circumstantial evidence that he did not believe that these cases constituted a new system of political economy.

I believe that it is also legitimate to conclude that Smith would be very circumspect in regulating private individuals. One would have to examine not only the economic justification, but also the source of political support for any new regulation:

> The proposal of any new law or regulation of commerce which comes from this order [employers], ought always to be listened to with great precaution, and ought never to be adopted till after having been long and carefully examined, not only with the most scrupulous, but with the most suspicious attention.
>
> (*WN* Book 1: xi. 10)

All new laws require scrupulous attention, but those supported by the employers of capital also require suspicious attention.

This, I contend, is Smith's considered view on how to approach constructing new regulations within the framework of natural liberty. That natural liberty is not a system of political economy, but one of justice stands. The fact that there are exceptions does not negate this conclusion. Smith, after all, was not a utopian.

Conclusion

If *WN* is not a treatise in political economy, or more accurately, if it is a treatise which sought to end political economy, understood as a form of statecraft designed to maximize national wealth, how do we situate it in the history of economic thought? By his own admission it is a treatise which treats of the same subject matter as political economy, but this does not negate the fact that he identified only two systems of political economy of which natural liberty was not one. Since natural liberty is a system of justice and political economy entailed utilitarian systems of expediency, Smith's failure to identify natural liberty as a new political economy and his failure to identify *WN* itself as principles of political economy must be intentional.

With regard to the economic analysis of *WN* contained in the first two books, I find the canonical view that *WN* marked the moment in time when analytical economics became an autonomous discipline unacceptable. Not only is it rooted in an Anglo-centric view of the history of economics, but also because natural liberty as a system of justice implies that *WN* was intended to be an integral part of his work taken as a whole. He certainly did not want to separate the discourse of scientific economics from that of moral philosophy and justice.

Winch's and Haakonssen's "science of the legislator" approach is, thus, vindicated against Brown's criticism. However, I conclude that instead of positioning *WN* generally, and the newly forming discourse of scientific economics specifically, within the police branch of the science (its location in the *Lectures*), Smith was positioning both in the justice branch.[9] The revenue and arms branches were the subject of Book 5, and what might be viewed as a residue of political economy remains both in Book 5 and in isolated exceptions to natural liberty found in the rest of the text. Since Smith never suggested that this "residue" consisted of a new political economy, the conclusion remains that *WN* is an anti-political economy.

Notes

1 The secondary literature on Smith is, of course, vast, as is the subset represented by what I have called the debunkers. I do not mean to imply that all who have taken issue with the canonical interpretation have reached an accord on the correct interpretation of Smith. However, I do believe that one can make a broad assertion that there is a decided movement away from the tendency to view the *WN* as a modern sort of text in economics in isolation from (or even in opposition to) the *Theory of Moral Sentiments* (*TMS*) and from what we know of his finished work on law and government from the *Lectures on Jurisprudence* (*LJ*). It is beyond the scope of this paper to enter into a survey of these contributions in order to assess their similarities and differences. Suffice it to say that I have in mind the writings of such scholars as Andrew Skinner, D. D. Raphael, Donald Winch, and Knud Haakonssen, to name a few of the most prominent and prolific of the modern interpreters of Smith.

2 Donald Winch, perhaps more than any other modern interpreter of Smith, has attempted to lay to rest the idea that the divorce of economics from moral philosophy was in any way a part of Smith's intentions (for examples see Winch 1978, 1983, 1992, and 1996). The following is typical of remarks which may be found in all of his work on Smith:

> While the success of a work such as the *Wealth of Nations* may have aided the process by which the science that became economics separated itself from politics and moral philosophy, *absorption* seems a more accurate brief description of what Smith himself was actually doing when he embarked on his ambitious attempt to provide the anatomy and physiology of commercial society, together with related excursions into its history and pathology.
>
> (Winch 1996: 22, emphasis in original)

3 For the view that the canonical view of Smith originated in the works of Dugald Stewart, see Rothschild 1992.

4 The fact that Smith viewed Steuart's work as full of errors is an indication that he viewed it not only as the definitive work of political economy, but also as the definitive statement of the specific form political economy took in the mercantile system. The usual judgment of historians has been that Steuart was a mercantilist, but some modern commentators have cast doubt on this, pointing among other things to the influence of both Hume and of the Physiocrats (Skinner 1966).

5 The ruling doctrine of the physiocrats that agriculture alone is capable of producing a net product making incomes earned in the sterile sector merely transfer payments does not logically entail a policy commitment to free trade. This is particularly evident in Malthus's position on the Corn Laws in the debates of 1815, where protectionism is argued partly on the physiocratic grounds that aggregate demand is a function of agricultural rent. For an in-depth discussion of Malthus's physiocratic leanings and his stance on the Corn Laws see Hollander's recently published monumental study of Malthus (Hollander 1997 and "Malthus as a Physiocrat" in Hollander 1998).

6 Blaug dropped the last clause of this sentence in subsequent editions, perhaps in response to Winch's argument that *WN* is best understood if Smith's definition is taken seriously as a description of Smith's intentions in WN (Blaug 1997: 56; Winch 1983: 501).
7 Smith makes a similar argument in *TMS* when he argues that although justice has utilitarian value in that it makes society possible, this is not the reason why people begin practicing the virtue of justice. Like all the moral sentiments, its origins lie in immediate sense and feeling, not utility. In this case the operative sentiment is the spectator's resentment toward the person perpetrating an injury upon another coupled with sympathy for the injured party. Thus, the utilitarian value of justice is an unintended consequence of those feelings which cause people to refrain from injuring each other. The *locus classicus* on the relation between justice and utility in Smith's moral philosophy is D. D. Raphael's "Hume and Adam Smith on Justice and Utility" (1972–3).
8 Raphael claims that in the sentinel case Smith concedes too much to Hume by asserting that the utility of the punishment makes it just (Raphael 1972–3: 96). The relation is more consistent and more in line with my argument in this paper in the case of the wool smuggler which I will consider presently.
9 This is the part of jurisprudence which housed economic analysis in Hutcheson's work, and Meek (1976) has argued that Smith also placed it here in his early Glasgow days. I do not know if there is any significance to his changing its location (if, in fact, he did so) in his course from the justice section to the police section, but it does suggest that there was substantial precedent for the idea that economic analysis could logically be taken up in the context of certain topics, such as property and contract, which belonged to justice, not police.

References

Blaug, M. (1978) *Economic Theory in Retrospect*, 3rd edn, Cambridge: Cambridge University Press.
—— (1997) *Economic Theory in Retrospect*, 5th edn, Cambridge: Cambridge University Press.
Boulding, K. E. (1969) "Economics as a Moral Science," *American Economic Review* 59(3) (June).
Brown, V. (1994) *Adam Smith's Discourse: Canonicity, Commerce and Conscience*, London: Routledge.
Cairns, J. W. (1994) "Adam Smith and the Role of the Courts in Securing Justice and Liberty," in J. Evensky and R. P. Malloy (eds), *Adam Smith and the Philosophy of Law and Economics*, Dordrecht: Kluwer Academic.
Haakonssen, K. (1981) *The Science of a Legislator: The Natural Jurisprudence of David Hume and Adam Smith*, Cambridge: Cambridge University Press.
Hollander, S. (1987) *Classical Economics*, Oxford: Blackwell.
—— (1997) *The Economics of Thomas Robert Malthus*, Toronto: University of Toronto Press.
—— (1998) "Malthus as Physiocrat: Surplus versus Scarcity," in *The Literature of Political Economy: Collected Essays II*, London: Routledge.
Meek, R. L. [1962] (1993) *The Economics of Physiocracy: Essays and Translations*, New York: Augustus M. Kelley.
—— (1976) "New Light on Adam Smith's Glasgow Lectures," *History of Political Economy* 8(4) (Winter).
Raphael, D. D. (1972–3) "Hume and Adam Smith on Justice and Utility," *Proceedings of the Aristotelian Society* n.s:. 73.
Rothschild, E. (1992) "Adam Smith and Conservative Economics," *Economic History Review* 45(1) (February).

—— (1994) "Adam Smith and the Invisible Hand," *American Economic Review* 84(2) (May).
Skinner, A. S. (1966) "Biographical Sketch" and "Analytical Introduction" to *Steuart's Inquiry into the Principles of Political Economy*, Chicago: University of Chicago Press.
Smith, A. (1976a) *The Theory of Moral Sentiments*, ed. D. D. Raphael and R. L. Meek, Oxford: Clarendon (*TMS*).
—— (1976) *An Inquiry into the Nature and Causes of the Wealth of Nations*, ed. A. S. Skinner and R. H. Campbell, Oxford: Clarendon (*WN*).
—— (1977) *The Correspondence of Adam Smith*, ed. E. C. Mossner and I. S. Ross, Oxford: Clarendon.
—— (1978) *Lectures on Jurisprudence*, ed. R. L. Meek, D. D. Raphael and P. G. Stein, Oxford: Clarendon (*LJ*).
—— (1980) *Essays on Philosophical Subjects*, ed. W. P. D. Wightman, Oxford: Clarendon (Astronomy, Stewart).
Steuart, Sir J. (1966) *Inquiry into the Principles of Political Economy*, ed. A. S. Skinner, Chicago: University of Chicago Press.
Stewart, D. (1980) "Account of the Life and Writings of Adam Smith, LL. D.", in A. Smith, *Essays on Philosophical Subjects*, ed. W. P. D. Wightman, Oxford: Clarendon.
Winch, D. (1978) *Adam Smith's Politics: An Essay in Historiographic Revision*, Cambridge: Cambridge University Press.
—— (1983) "Science and the Legislator: Adam Smith and After," *Economic Journal* 93 (September).
—— (1992) "Adam Smith: Scottish Philosopher as Political Economist," *Historical Journal* 35(1).
—— (1996) *Riches and Poverty: An Intellectual History of Political Economy in Britain, 1750–1834*, Cambridge: Cambridge University Press.
Young, J. T. (1986) "Natural Jurisprudence and the Impartial Spectator: A Reconsideration of Adam Smith's Theory of the Natural Price," *History of Political Economy* 18(3) (Fall).
—— (1997) *Economics as a Moral Science: The Political Economy of Adam Smith*, Aldershot: Elgar.
Young, J. T. and Gordon, B. (1992) "Economic Justice in the Schoolmen and the Natural Law Theorists," *Journal of the History of Economic Thought* 14(1) (Spring).
—— (1996) "Distributive Justice as a Normative Criterion in Adam Smith's Political Economy," *History of Political Economy* 28(1) (Spring).

9 The canon in the history of the Adam Smith problem

Ingrid Peters-Fransen

Introduction

Is the centrality of sympathy in *The Theory of Moral Sentiments* (*TMS*) consistent with the importance of self-interest in *The Wealth of Nations* (*WN*)? This question has been asked by the readers of Smith's works since the eighteenth-century. Some German scholars in the nineteenth century wondered how these two very different works could have been written by the same author. This problem of inconsistency, called *Das Adam Smith Problem*, continues to challenge commentators today; the response to the Adam Smith problem is intertwined with the approach to the canon.

Over the past two centuries in Smithian scholarship, the approach to the canon and the canon itself have changed. The "independent canons" approach of the nineteenth century views *TMS* as a 1759 statement of Smith's altruistic ethical theory and *WN* as a 1776 statement of Smith's egoistic economic theory. This approach treats the two books as different, but this difference can not be or does not have to be reconciled because the two are basically independent. Cannan's 1895 discovery of a set of student notes from Smith's *Lectures on Jurisprudence* (*LJ*) provided evidence of Smith's economic thought in the early 1760s. This change in the canon led to a re-evaluation of the approach to the canon. No longer were the two works treated as completely independent; they were parallel but not coincident. This "parallel canons" approach explains the differences and looks for similarities in the two books, but provides at best an argument for qualified consistency, or some might say qualified inconsistency. Another approach, that of the "evolving canon," focuses on the development of Smith's thought. This includes the development of Smith's ethical thought from the first edition of *TMS* in 1759 to the sixth in 1790, and the development of his economic thought from *LJ* to *WN*. More significantly, there has been a move away from the assumption that Smith's two books are different, and towards the assumption of consistency. Recently, the "evolving canon" approach has shifted away from the independent development of the ethical and economic canons, and considers how Smith's economic thought in 1776 incorporates his ethical theory, and how his ethical theory in 1790 incorporates his economics. Over the last century and a half, the approach to the canon has shifted from the independence to the interdependence of Smith's ethical and economic thought, and this shift has been accompanied by a move in arguments for the inconsistency to qualified consistency to the consistency of *TMS* and *WN*.

The "independent canons" approach

The most notable proponent of Adam Smith's inconsistency is Witold von Skarżyński. In his 1878 book entitled *Adam Smith als Moralphilosoph and Schoepfer der Nationaloekonomie*, he accredits Smith's ethical theory to the influence of Hutcheson and Hume and his economics to the influence of Helvetius and the physiocrats. In Skarżyński's assessment, Smith is a second-rate thinker whose feeble criticisms of Hutcheson and Hume reveal his lack of ability. Skarżyński acknowledges that Smith criticizes Hutcheson's treatment of self-interest (Skarżyński 1878: 39) but his basic agreement with Hutcheson is evident in his criticisms of Mandeville and Epicureanism (ibid.: 41). Similarly, Smith's section on propriety parallels Hume on utility (ibid.: 73), his section on merit echoes Hume on justice (ibid.: 74), and his section on utility distorts Hume's simple and natural idea into something odd and flat (ibid.: 74). Smith was clearly not an original thinker; he was a mere scribe reflecting the influences impinging on him at any given time and doing even this poorly. In Scotland, he was influenced by the Scottish sentimentalism of Hutcheson and Hume; in France, he was influenced by the egoism and materialism of Helvetius and physiocracy (ibid.: 95):

> Under Hutcheson's and Hume's influence Smith was an idealist, as long as he remained in England. After three years of exposure to the materialism that prevailed in France, he returned to England as a materialist. In this simple way the difference between *TMS* (1759) which was written before his trip to France and *WN* (1776) which was published after his return can be explained.
>
> (Skarżyński 1878: 183, translation mine)

Skarżyński attributes the difference between the two books to Smith's trip to France in 1764. There is no need to reconcile the two works because they are independent, written by an author who converted from altruism to egoism without a moment's hesitation. Skarżyński was so convinced of his explanation that he ignored or dismissed any evidence to the contrary: It is obvious that Smith knew nothing of economics *before* his trip to France (ibid.: 166) and Dugald Stewart's statement that the fundamental ideas of *WN* were evident in Smith's lectures before his trip to France is clearly suspect (ibid.: 100); similarly, there is no hint that Smith revised *TMS* after his trip to France.[1]

In Buckle's 1861 *History of Civilization in England*, the assessments of Smith's intellectual ability and consistency are quite different than Skarżyński's. Smith is "by far the greatest of all the Scotch thinkers" (Buckle 1878: 304), his mind is "capacious and insatiable" (ibid.: 314), "wide and organizing" (ibid.: 316): "He had in a most remarkable degree, that exuberance of thought, which is one of the highest forms of genius" (ibid.). Buckle and Skarżyński are agreed that Smith and Hume are not in the same league. For Skarżyński, Smith's inconsistency between his ethical and economic thought stands in stark contrast to the consistency of Hume's ethical and economic thought (Skarżyński 1878: 99), but for Buckle, Smith is the shining star: "Hume . . . had not the comprehensiveness of Adam Smith, nor had he that invaluable quality of imagination" (Buckle 1878: 331).

Given that Smith is such a brilliant thinker, how can his two books be explained? For Skarżyński, it is impossible to reconcile the two books because in essence two different authors wrote them; for Buckle, it is unnecessary to reconcile them because they were intended to answer completely different questions. Recognizing that people are motivated both by self-interest and by sympathy, Smith separates the problem into two parts: *TMS* describes the altruistic part of human behavior and *WN* the egoistic part:

> None of us are exclusively selfish, and none of us are exclusively sympathetic. But Adam Smith separates in speculation qualities which are inseparable in reality. In his *Moral Sentiments*, he ascribes our actions to sympathy; in his *Wealth of Nations*, he ascribes them to selfishness. A short view of these two works will prove the existence of this fundamental difference, and will enable us to perceive that each is supplementary to the other; so that, in order to understand either, it is necessary to study both.
> (Buckle 1878: 309)

In *TMS*, Smith recognizes the antagonism of sympathy and self-interest and concentrates on sympathy (ibid.: 313); *WN* is as equally one-sided as *TMS*, dealing with selfishness, rather than sympathy (ibid.: 314).[2] This division of motives was an intentional choice of tractability over realism (ibid.: 318). Although Smith's two works are independent of one another, both books are great books and both need to be read to appreciate his understanding of human nature. Buckle's claim for Smith's consistency is based on Dugald Stewart's statement that Smith's economic thought preceded the publication of his ethical theory: "But what shows that to their author both were part of a single scheme, is the notable circumstance, that, so early as 1753, he had laid down the principles which his later work contains" (ibid.: 314–5). Buckle and Skarżyński disagree about Smith's consistency but their approaches to *TMS* and *WN* are similar: both treat the two as independent works which are not to be reconciled.

The change in the canon and the "parallel canons" approach

Cannan's 1895 discovery of a set of student notes from Smith's lectures on jurisprudence in the early 1760s (*LJ*) substantiated Dugald Stewart's statement that Smith's economic thought preceded his trip to France and made Skarżyński's position that Smith's materialism was attributable to his trip to France untenable (Raphael and Macfie 1976: 23). Although this argument for inconsistency could be dismissed, it determined the question which would be asked: how could the ethical theory of *TMS* be reconciled with the economic theory of *WN*? Buckle's answer that Smith was addressing two different questions, and intentionally simplified his assumptions to make his analysis tractable, was not negated by the discovery of the lecture notes. Buckle had never assumed that Smith was inconsistent or that his economic thought had not predated the trip to France. Indeed he accepted Stewart's statement that Smith's lectures had included economic matters. His solution of total independence between the two works was not accepted, but his argument that *TMS* is about sympathy and *WN* is about self-interest is echoed by later commentators who choose, however, not to identify sympathy with benevolence directly. Buckle's idea that the two works addressed different questions was accepted in modified form, and the issue becomes the difference in interpersonal environment.

One commentator to recognize that the discovery of Smith's lecture notes on jurisprudence changes the reconciliation problem was Morrow:

> The problem is not to reconcile economic doctrines of 1776 with the ethical doctrines of 1759, but to reconcile the economic and ethical doctrines taught at the same period, the period of his professorship at Glasgow.
>
> (Morrow [1923] 1969: 5–6)

How can the difference between Smith's ethical and economic theories be explained? Morrow attributes the difference to different conceptions about social order (ibid.: 72). In *TMS*, human beings are first and foremost social beings whereas in *WN*, human beings are first and foremost individuals. This leads to an atomistic and utilitarian perspective in *WN* that is foreign to *TMS*:[3]

> But the moral world? How is it related to this order of economic individualism? We have seen from the *Moral Sentiments* that the moral experience cannot be interpreted in individual or utilitarian terms; hence the moral standpoint, though recognized, is never used in the *Wealth of Nations*. The moral judgment is excluded from scientific inquiry.
>
> (Morrow 1969: 82)

For Viner as well, the fundamental difference between *TMS* and *WN* is the difference in environment; the interpersonal environment in *TMS* where social sentiments such as sympathy have an important role is contrasted with the anonymous environment of *WN* where social sentiments have no role and people respond to rational self-interest (Viner 1960: 60). Macfie also comments on the change in interpersonal environment. In Smith's ethical theory, the sympathy of the impartial spectator is central but the impartial spectator of *TMS* is replaced by the impersonal market in *WN*:

> in the free markets that Smith advocated [in *The Wealth of Nations*], all the checks and controls which are relied on in the *Moral Sentiments* to govern the inevitable excesses and clashes of self-love (otherwise quite destructive) are simply not present in the economic markets of *The Wealth of Nations*. Especially, the controls of family affection and neighbourhood are absent . . . In the place of friends and neighbours you have an anonymous

multitude of units of demand and supply. Also, in the *Moral Sentiments* the impartial spectator mechanism is ascribed considerable power to control abuses. But this is again a personal activity. The impartial spectator in fact makes no appearance in *The Wealth of Nations*. He there becomes the impersonal market.

(Macfie 1967: 104)

Unlike *TMS* where sympathy and the impartial spectator have a role to play, *WN* deals with an anonymous and atomistic market environment.[4] The two canons are not independent; they are parallel and not coincident but are they consistent?

Is Smith's ethical theory at work in *WN* or is it at rest? The gist of the change in argument seems to be that sympathy and the impartial spectator no longer have roles to play in the market place. Is *WN* indeed an "amoral discourse" (Brown 1994: 46)? Are sympathy and the impartial spectator replaced by utilitarian considerations in *WN*? It certainly appears so. As was noted earlier, Morrow comments on the utilitarian perspective taken in *WN* which is foreign to *TMS*. Similarly, Viner states that in *WN*, Smith "valued [economic freedoms] from a utilitarian point of view, as giving maximum scope for incentives and to efficiency" (Viner 1968: 120). Macfie's position is difficult to discern. In his chapter "Adam Smith's *Theory of Moral Sentiments*," he argues that Smith is not a utilitarian in *TMS* (Macfie 1967: 45–8) but states that "utility is his inevitable starting point in *The Wealth of Nations*" (ibid.: 45); in "Adam Smith's *Moral Sentiments* as Foundation for his *Wealth of Nations*" written in the same year, Macfie declares:

> Today we should expect the link between a book on Ethics and one on Economics to be found in utility. But here this is not so. For in neither book does Utilitarianism or utility play an important part.
>
> (Macfie 1967: 59)

He goes on to say that the "economic man" in *WN* can be compared to the prudent man of *TMS* and that the doctrine of the prudent man in *TMS* does not reflect a "narrowly utilitarian" perspective (ibid.: 71). Despite the fact that the impartial spectator of *TMS* is replaced by the impersonal market in *WN* (ibid.: 104), the economic man of *WN* continues to be "under the sway of social sympathy and the impartial rulings of the informed spectator" (ibid.: 75). It is difficult to conclude whether sympathy and the impartial spectator are indeed absent from the pages of *WN* and whether they have been replaced by utility in Macfie's assessment. There does appear to be a shift towards utilitarianism in *WN* but not a full-fledged transformation. Others also are inclined to think that there is a shift between *TMS* and *WN*. Raphael recognizes that Smith was not a utilitarian in *TMS* but he states that the harmony in *WN* owes nothing to sympathy:

> Far from being a utilitarian, Adam Smith was a severe critic of utilitarianism in many parts of his ethics and jurisprudence. Of course he wrote in

The Wealth of Nations about a natural harmony of individual and social interests, but there he was abstracting economic activity from the whole of social life, and in any event that *harmony owed nothing to sympathy*. . . . In his final account of the matter [in *TMS*] Smith listed four grounds or "sources" of approval, and made a regard to utility the last and the least of these.

(Raphael 1975: 96, emphasis mine)

Does this imply that that *WN* is utilitarian? Thomson is somewhat more specific: "The goals of *The Wealth of Nations* seem *utilitarian*, and a rather materialistic concept of *utility* seems to replace the stoic ethic which underlies the *Theory of Moral Sentiments*" (Thomson 1965: 336). Witztum attributes the shift from sympathy in *TMS* to utility in *WN* to the self-interested nature of economic agents:

it is . . . self-interested people – the type of whom inhabit the *WN* – who are more likely than others to judge by the pleasure of utility than by the pleasure of sympathy. In that sense, *das Adam Smith Problem* has not really been resolved.

(Witztum 1998: 492)

The clearest statement of a change in Smith's ethical doctrine between his moral theory and his economic thought is made by Grampp:

The economic man of the *Lectures* is kept within the bounds of virtue by the prudent knowledge that honesty pays in the long run. His pecuniary interest is restrained not by the desire for moral renown but by a disinterested calculation of the returns to be expected from moral, as compared to immoral, conduct – a calculation which tips the scales in favor of virtue. By transferring the virtue from man's moral sentiments to his profit-and-loss statement, Smith worked an enormous change in ethical doctrine.

(Grampp 1948: 258)

This is an explicit statement describing the basis of the virtue of prudence in *LJ* as the utility of consequences for the individual and contrasting it with Smith's moral theory. Grampp, however, appears to change his mind. Three decades later, he states that *TMS* "is more clearly utilitarian" than *WN* because in *TMS*, Smith "said behavior was and should be judged by its consequences and not by its intentions" (Grampp 1979: 310). Grampp acknowledges in a footnote however that in *TMS* Smith "expressly denied that utility was the foundation of morals" (ibid.: 315 n.22). Despite Macfie's claim that Smith was not a utilitarian in *TMS* or in *WN* and Grampp's assertion that utilitarianism is evident in both books, the general view is that the change in interpersonal environment is accompanied by a shift towards utilitarianism.

The Adam Smith problem is the difficulty of reconciling the importance of sympathy in *TMS* with the importance of self-interest in *WN*. The problem of inconsistency that Skarżyński identified in the mid 1800s was that Smith's understanding of human nature had changed from altruism in *TMS* to egoism in *WN*. The "change in interpersonal environment" argument for consistency rejects a radical conversion in Smith's understanding of human nature but it does accept that Smith's justification for action changes from being based on sympathy in *TMS* to being based on utility in *WN*.

Another argument for consistency turns on the notion of virtue in *WN*. Virtue in *TMS* is associated with an appropriately regulated motive and "is threefold, consisting of prudence, justice, and benevolence" (Morrow 1969: 8). Each virtue is associated with one type of affection: prudence with the judicious pursuit of selfish affections, justice with the restraint of malevolent affections, and benevolence with the indulgence of benevolent affections. Expressed in economic terms, prudence is the virtue associated with self-regarding preferences: that is, self-interest as it relates to the individual with neither positive nor negative externalities; justice with the restraint of negative externalities; and benevolence with the indulgence of positive externalities. In *WN*, the virtue of benevolence is absent but the virtues of prudence and justice are present.[5]

How are the descriptions of justice and prudence in *WN* and *TMS* related? Are prudence and justice in *WN* defined in terms of utility? Are the virtues of prudence and justice described in *TMS*, which are understood in terms of the sympathy of the impartial spectator, consistent with a utilitarian interpretation?[6] Despite the absence of the impartial spectator in *WN*, Bitterman (1940) contends that the argument for justice in *both* works is basically utilitarian. Other commentators, however, maintain that the conception of justice does change. Grampp states that in *WN* "[j]ustice is no longer regarded as the special charge of a benevolent deity but as the particular care of government, which exists only for the very mundane reason of protecting property" (Grampp 1948: 262). Similarly, Viner contrasts justice as a moral sentiment in *TMS* with the need for coercive enforcement in *WN*.[7] In terms of justice, the need for government in *WN* displaces the roles of sympathy and the impartial spectator in *TMS* and the role of government is justified by utilitarian considerations.

Alternatively, Young and Gordon argue that Smith's treatment of justice is consistent in the two books. Young identifies three aspects of justice: first, commutative justice (or justice in exchange), second, distributive justice, and third, "general justice which deals with the obligations of the individual to the community" (Young and Gordon 1997: 110). Rather than pursuing the traditional argument that general justice is the link between the two books because it is a necessary precondition for exchange, Young and Gordon consider the aspects of commutative and distributive justice. Commutative justice is an outcome of, rather than a precondition for, exchange and Smith's natural price needs to be understood in terms of commutative justice (ibid.: 107–27). Also distinctive, as Young himself emphasizes, is their argument that the virtue of benevolence, defined as distributive justice (ibid.: 51), is evident in *WN* (ibid.: 129–55):

> Justice and beneficence are also intimately connected with political economy. That justice is so connected is well known and the subject of

some of the best of the recent secondary literature on Smith. The connection with beneficence is not well known, and, indeed, it is frequently denied that such a connection even exists.

(Young and Gordon 1997: 53)

Not only are commutative and distributive justice both evident in *WN* but "[t]he union between commutative and distributive justice is brought most closely to consummation in a developing market economy" (ibid.: 154).

Young, who does not focus on the virtue of prudence, states that "[t]he connection between prudence and the growth theory of *WN* is obvious and important" (ibid.: 53) but in the secondary literature, prudence apparently changes between the two books.[8] Prudence in *TMS* is self-interest restrained by the sympathy mechanism but in *WN*, prudence is self-interest restrained by rivalry or by justice. In contrast to *TMS* where "*self-interest* imparts the motion to society, and sympathy directs the motion within wholesome restraints" (Thomson 1965: 334), in *WN* self-interest imparts the motion and rivalry directs the motion within wholesome restraints. Morrow recognizes the importance of competition for social order in *WN*:

> It is self-interest *plus* competition which Adam Smith relies upon as the explanation of the economic mechanism. In other words, the really significant concept in the economic analysis is the concept of individuality, as inclusive of both self-interest and competition. Upon this conception the whole order rests.
>
> (Morrow 1969: 76)

Recktenwald expressly associates the impersonal environment with the need for rivalry to serve as a restraint on self-interest:

> The actual and potential pressure of rivalry permanently, immediately, and effectively restrains the egoistic conduct within due bounds. . . . Since fellow-feeling and beneficence as opposing forces diminish as the scale of 'society' increases from family, friends, and from parish up to nation and to world communities and the efficacy of other safeguards becomes weaker in this more impersonal atmosphere, competition becomes the most important restraint.
>
> (Recktenwald 1978: 264)

Franklin (1976: 472) similarly emphasizes the importance of competition as a harness for self-interest. For these commentators, rivalry in the impersonal marketplace replaces sympathy in the circle of friends as a control on the pursuit of self-interest. Commentators also interpret justice as a constraint on the pursuit of self-interest. Morrow, for example, states that "virtue is threefold, consisting of prudence, justice, and benevolence" and later modifies this statement by bringing prudence within the domain of justice: "virtue [Smith] regards as twofold, consisting of self-interest regulated by justice, and the higher virtue of benevolence" (Morrow 1969: 46). Morrow also mentions the "inferior virtues, that is, self-interest restrained by justice" (ibid.: 57). Brown says that prudence is approved of in *TMS*, in a limited way, only if it is "restrained by the laws of justice" (Brown 1994: 52), and Minowitz comments that in *WN*, "Smith's unleashing of self-interest is constrained or framed by justice" (Minowitz 1993: 35). Does rivalry in *WN* replace sympathy as a constraint on the pursuit of self-interest? Is prudence a virtue in its own right or is it defined by justice? According to Charlier, one problem plaguing scholars is the failure to define prudence:[9]

> If *prudence* constitutes a stumbling block for the scholar, its definition has not really been the focus of much attention. While the study of the moral qualities of the prudent man remains . . . neglected, the possible link between *The Theory of the Moral Sentiments* and *The Wealth of Nations* that this figure introduces is underlined.
>
> (Charlier 1996: 273)

The "parallel canons" approach that developed after the discovery of Smith's lecture notes on jurisprudence provides two arguments for consistency. The "change in environment" argument attempts to explain the difference in the two works, whereas the "virtue in *WN*" argument is based on linking the two books, albeit in a qualified manner. There is movement away from Buckle's explanation (Buckle 1878) that the two books are different to an explanation based on similarity but the underlying approach is still that the two works are parallel and not completely consistent. Justice and prudence are evident in both works but the change in environment affects how justice and prudence are interpreted.

The "evolving canon" approach

Two nineteenth-century commentators who recognized the continuity of Smith's ethical and economic thought over time were Zeyss and Oncken. Zeyss mentions both Stewart's statement that Smith's economic thought predates his trip to France (Zeyss 1889: 13–17) and changes to the sixth edition of *TMS* after the trip (ibid.: 19). Oncken also notes the continuity of Smith's ethics over time, the importance of Cannan's discovery of the lecture notes for his position that Smith's economic thought was consistent over time, and the consistency of his ethics and economics. The *Lectures on Jurisprudence* (*LJ*) which provided evidence of Smith's economic thought before the trip to France also led to questions about how Smith's economic theory developed and how it was influenced by the physiocrats and Turgot. Zeyss and Oncken were harbingers of the focus in the last several decades on the evolution of two canons, the one ethical and the other economic. The arguments for development or "evolution of thought" direct attention to the evolution of Smith's ethical thought from the early editions of *TMS* to the 1790 edition and on the evolution of Smith's economic thought from *LJ* to *WN*. Raphael and Macfie go further and suggest that the evolution is cross-disciplinary: *TMS* anticipates *WN* and *WN* anticipates the changes to *TMS*.

Raphael and Shinohara comment on the development of Smith's ethical thought from *TMS* (1759) to *TMS* (1790). Raphael (1992: 104–10) attributes the fairly extensive sixth edition revisions in 1790 to modification, clarification, and the addressing of omissions in previous editions. Smith had realized by the fourth (1774) edition that earlier versions of *TMS* had addressed only the second of two questions that he believed needed to be answered, first, the account of virtue and second, the principle of approbation.

According to Raphael, the subtitle in 1774, "or An Essay towards an Analysis of the Principles by which Men naturally judge concerning the Conduct and Character, first of their Neighbours, and afterwards of themselves," implied a recognition of the absence of an account of virtue from his moral philosophy. The sixth part that is added in 1790, "Of the Character of Virtue," corrected this omission. Shinohara's argument (Shinohara 1993: 27–33) is akin to Raphael's but he expresses the shift as one from a speculative theory of morals to a practical system of morals. Shinohara attributes Smith's recognition of the omission of a practical system of morals to Thomas Reid's book in 1788 entitled *Essays on the Active Powers of Man*. According to Shinohara, the added sixth part in the sixth edition of *TMS* is in response to Reid's distinction between a speculative theory and a practical system of morals. Both Raphael and Shinohara attribute the new sixth part in the 1790 edition to Smith's recognition that his speculative system of morals which had focused on the principle of approbation needed to be complemented by a practical system of morals which focused on the account of virtue.

Commentators have also identified changes in Smith's economic thought over time. Skarżyński (1878) correctly identified the physiocratic influence in *WN*, and modern commentators have highlighted this influence in the development of Smith's economic thought from *LJ* to *WN*. It is evident in the distinction between productive and unproductive labor which appears in *WN* (Spengler 1945: 329; Bowley 1975: 369–70) and in the increased emphasis in *WN* on capital accumulation (Meek 1951: 28; Bowley 1975: 361–2). Another issue that arises in the comparison of *LJ* and *WN* is the move from mercantilism towards economic liberalism:

> there is a significant shift in the basis of the economic argument from *LJ* to *WN*. While *LJ* are still constructed in terms of state regulationist discourse of "police", where the state's object is to secure cheapness and plenty, by the time of *WN*, 'police' is used to reflect the discourses of the mercantile system and the agricultural system of the Économistes, each of which proposes to favour one sector over the others.
>
> (Brown 1994: 6; see also 154)

Brown's position on this point, that *WN* reflects a change towards economic liberalism, contrasts with earlier positions such as Recktenwald's which emphasized continuity:

> Smith himself forcefully claimed, as we know, in a lost letter of 1755, to have discovered before 1748 "the obvious and simple system of natural

liberty'" meant as an analytic principle and a set of policy prescriptions, and he made it, we should add, objectively for the first time the pivot of an economic and social system.

(Recktenwald 1978: 271n59)

Smith was critical of mercantilism in *LJ* but the economic liberalism and the emphasis on economic growth in *WN* were influenced by physiocracy.

Another part of the evolution of Smith's thought that has captured the attention of commentators is the importance of *LJ* for understanding the relationship between *TMS* and *WN*. Winch (1978: 10–11) notes that *LJ* provides a bridge between *TMS* and *WN* in terms of Smith's treatment of justice. Lamb makes an even stronger statement about such a link:

> Smith's *Theory of Moral Sentiments* (1759) develops his views on ethical virtue; his *Lectures on Justice, Police, Revenue and Arms* (1763) develops his views on economics, law and justice; finally his *Wealth of Nations* (1776) integrated his theory of virtue with its exemplifications in economics, law and Justice.
>
> (Lamb 1987: 105)

This statement moves beyond the "virtue in *WN*" argument that the virtues of prudence and justice are found in both *TMS* and *WN* and asserts that the development from *LJ* to *WN* includes the integration of Smith's ethical theory into his economic thought in *WN*.

Raphael and Macfie's position on the "evolving canon" is evident in the following quote:

> Some of the content of the new material added to edition 6 of *TMS* clearly comes from the author of *WN*. No less clearly, a little of the content of edition 1 of *TMS* comes from the potential author of *WN*.
>
> (Raphael and Macfie 1976: 20)

It is not enough to look at the development of Smith's ethical and economic thought independently; his ethics inform his economics and his economics inform his ethics.[10] This leads Raphael and Macfie to conclude that there is no Adam Smith problem. Teichgraeber calls this dismissal of the problem a "surprisingly extreme position" (Teichgraeber 1981: 110). One of the difficulties with this position is that it has yet to be adequately argued. Brown states that it is more an assertion than an argument, "emanating from an untheorised reliance on the assumption of authorial unity" (Brown 1994: 26). Commentators "eager to establish the 'unified' nature of Smith's corpus of writing" (ibid.: 26) read back a moral dimension into *WN*.[11] Dickey's (1986) criticism is similar. He argues that Raphael and Macfie's approach is that of a "canon within a canon," rather than an "evolving canon." Dickey identifies three "motivating centers" in Smith's work: *TMS* (1759), *WN*, and *TMS* (1790). Viner uses *WN* as the "motivating center," or what I would call the "canon within the canon," and interprets *TMS* in light of *WN* (Dickey 1986: 586). 12 Raphael and Macfie, on the other hand, use *TMS* (1759) as the "motivating center" and interpret both *WN* and *TMS* (1790) in light of *TMS* (1759). Their continuity argument requires that "*WN* is conceptually assimilated back into the *TMS*" (Raphael and Macfie 1976: 584). Dickey's claim is that although Raphael and Macfie's position maintains that the canon evolves, it treats the canon rather statically by dealing with only "one [motivating center, i.e. *TMS* (1759)] within which the other two *must find their place*" (Dickey 1986: 589). There is some truth to Dickey's criticism that the continuity argument has been based on a "canon within the canon" approach while espousing an "evolving canon" approach. Raphael and Macfie are to be commended however for advocating an "evolving canon" approach, and Dickey is to be commended for realizing that only by coming to terms with the chronology of Smith's thought will commentators finally be able to put the Adam Smith problem to rest.

The earlier stages of the "evolving canon" looked at the ethical and economic canons independently by looking at the development of Smith's ethical theory from *TMS* (1759) to *TMS* (1790) and at the development of his economic thought from *LJ* to *WN*. In particular, the changes in his economic thought have been linked to the physiocratic influence in the intervening years without recognizing that the economic thought in *WN* reflects not only a distancing from that of *LJ* but also a shift towards the ethical theory of *TMS*, and the revisions of *TMS* in 1790 are interpreted as a response to Reid (Smith's replacement as Professor of Moral Philosophy at Glasgow) but these revisions are not explicitly linked to *WN*. Smith's "evolution of thought" must be interpreted not only in terms of changes due to contemporary influences, but also in terms of consistency reflecting his own process of integration. Dickey and Raphael and Macfie propose a new "evolving canon" approach which looks at the development and interdependence of Smith's ethical and economic thought from *TMS* (1759) to *WN* to *TMS* (1790). This approach neglects an important piece of the puzzle: *LJ*. The textual evidence allows for an "evolving canon" from *TMS* (1759) and *LJ* to *WN* to *TMS* (1790).

Conclusion

The approach to the canon over the last 150 years has influenced how the Adam Smith problem has been addressed. What approach to the canon proves the most promising? The "independent canons" approach of the nineteenth century assumes that *TMS* and *WN* portray different understandings of human nature, the one altruistic and the other egoistic. Whether this difference arises from Smith's inconsistency depends on how the difference is explained – as a result of a conversion from altruism to egoism or as a conscious decision to treat the altruistic and egoistic sides of human nature separately – but there is no need for reconciliation.

The "parallel canons" approach of the twentieth century argues for consistency by attributing the difference to a change in interpersonal environment between the two books. It provides only a qualified argument for consistency however because it assumes that the justification of action changes from being based on sympathy in *TMS* to being based on utility in *WN*. The "evolving canon" approach of the late twentieth century assumes that Smith's ethical and economic canons are interdependent, rather than independent. For dealing with someone whose works span three decades, this approach, which argues for Smith's consistency developing over time rather than arguing for static consistency, seems the best suited to addressing the Adam Smith problem.

Is the centrality of sympathy in *TMS* consistent with the importance of self-interest in *WN*? This question has been asked by the readers of Smith's two works since their appearance in the eighteenth century. For two of his contemporaries, Lord Kames and Thomas Reid, the answer was yes; these two works were consistent. Their argument was that Smith's ethical theory was based on self-interest. In his revisions for the third edition of *Essays on the Principles of Morality and Natural Religion,* Kames criticizes Smith's system of sympathy because the spectator's act of assuming the place of the sufferer involved self-satisfaction and because self-approbation could not be based on sympathy. In response to these criticisms, Reid writes to Kames in October 1778: "I have always thought Dr. Smith's System of Sympathy wrong. It is indeed onely a Refinement of the selfish System; and I think your Argument against it solid." The publication of *WN* would only have confirmed their suspicions. Winch also quotes from *The Times*: "[Smith] had converted the chair of Moral Philosophy into a professorship of trade and finance" (16 August 1790) (Winch 1993: 85). It is interesting that in the eighteenth century, Smith's ethical theory was viewed as self-interested (an allegation which Smith denied) and consistent with his economic thought, whereas in the nineteenth and twentieth centuries, Smith's ethical theory, unlike his economic thought, is not considered to be self-interested. Any satisfactory resolution to the nineteenth-century problem of inconsistency must also deal with the eighteenth-century claim of consistency.

The challenge for those who argue for consistency has been to identify the importance of self-interest in *TMS* and the importance of sympathy in *WN*. The importance of selfish affections in *TMS* "has been most clearly set forth in the excellent monograph of Zeyss, *Adam Smith und der Eigennutz,* which should once for all dispose of *Das Adam Smith Problem*" (Morrow: 8n12). This, however, only disposes of part of the problem. The contrast between sympathy and self-interest is no longer so stark but the question remains whether the sympathy of Smith's ethical theory is self-interested as his eighteenth-century contemporaries claimed and whether the sympathy of his ethical theory had any role to play in *WN*. Choi proposes that this second question remains unanswered: "I would like to suggest that we try something almost unthinkable, i.e., to look for sympathy in *WN*" (Choi 1990: 297).

The solution to the Adam Smith problem needs to address both how sympathy is at work in *WN* and what role self-interest plays in *TMS*. It additionally must deal with four documents: *TMS* (1759), *LJ, WN,* and *TMS* (1790). The answer to the Adam Smith problem will not be found by arguing for the qualified consistency of Smith's works or by asserting the unity of Smith's works; it needs to take into account the evolutionary transformation of Smith's thought, a transformation which led to the integration of his ethics into the economics of *WN* and a transformation which led to the integration of his economics into the ethics of *TMS* (1790). The "evolving canon" approach, which argues that Smith moved towards consistency over his lifetime, is the only approach which actually addresses the Adam Smith problem.

Notes

This paper borrows heavily from the introduction to my Ph.D. dissertation. I am grateful to Samuel Hollander for many helpful discussions and to Evelyn Forget, David Levy and Sandra Peart for their comments and encouragement.

1 Raphael and Macfie note Skarżyński's dismissal of Stewart's claim that Smith had lectured on economics before his trip to France. They also draw attention to his failure to appreciate "that lectures on economic matters were a recognized part of Moral Philosophy as taught in the Scottish Universities at that time" and to his use of the third, rather than the sixth, edition of *TMS* (Raphael and Macfie 1976: 24).
2 Buckle's argument does not hold water because he incorrectly equates sympathy and benevolence (Raphael and Macfie 1976: 20–1).
3 Although there clearly is a divergence between the two books in terms of interpersonal environment, Morrow concludes that the "theoretical doctrine of the relation of the individual to his social environment given in the *Moral Sentiments* is not to be regarded as abandoned" (Morrow [1923] 1969: 88).
4 Brown criticizes the argument that the market in *WN* is anonymous. The interpersonal relationships of the market are characterized by symmetry, not by anonymity (Brown 1994: 52–3). Despite this distinction, she agrees that there is a change in the moral environment: "indeed, moral agents are not present in *WN*, neither is the impartial spectator, and neither is a moral discussion of the virtues specific to the marketplace" (ibid.: 26). Fontaine also states that markets are not always impersonal or anonymous in *WN* which allows sympathy to play a small role: "Partial empathetic identification is assumed in *WN*, as is self-love" (Fontaine 1997: 271).
5 Bitterman 1940 and Grampp 1948 suggest that justice is the link between *WN* and *TMS*. Other commentators have stressed the importance of prudence in *WN* (Macfie, Gee, W. F. Campbell, Minowitz). Minowitz, in particular, defines bourgeois virtue as a "commitment to a long and steady course of industry and frugality" and notes that both of Smith's books approve of bourgeois virtue (Minowitz 1993: 79). Morrow and Brown recognize both the virtue of justice and the pursuit of self-interest in *TMS* and in *WN*. Both also distinguish the superior virtue of benevolence from the necessary virtue of justice and the pursuit of self-interest. According to Morrow, self-interest expressed in prudent conduct – not self-interest in general – is approved of in *TMS*, and self-interest is central to *WN*, but self-interest in *WN* does not appear to be specifically linked to the prudence of *TMS*. Morrow also notes the insignificance of benevolence and the importance of justice in the atomistic environment of the marketplace, for whereas the virtue of justice can exist in an individualistic environment, the virtue of benevolence is present only in a social and socialized environment where the doctrine of sympathy is at work.

Brown makes a similar remark regarding benevolence as one of the higher-order virtues, and associates the lower-order virtues, prudence as well as justice, with the market-place (Brown 1994: 5). Brown and Morrow are thus agreed that benevolence, a higher-order virtue, is not part of the market environment whereas justice, a lower-order virtue, is integral to the market place. Unlike Morrow, Brown allows that not only the pursuit of self-interest but the virtue of prudence itself is associated with the market place but she does not specify how Smith defines the virtue of prudence.
6 In Pack's assessment, the "virtue in *WN*" position that the virtues of prudence and justice are at work in *WN* "is only a partial resolution of 'the Adam Smith problem'" because differences in writing style and in the role of a deity remain (Pack 1997: 135–6); my argument is that the "virtue in *WN*" position is only a partial resolution because of the assumed changed justification of prudent and just behavior.
7 In a somewhat different vein, Campbell perceives a shift in focus from the justice of

interpersonal relations in *TMS* to the justice of intergroup relations in *WN* (Campbell 1967: 351).
8 This is in contrast to Fitzgibbons's statement that his "insistence that Smith had a moral theory of economic growth may be unfamiliar" (Fitzgibbons 1995: 147).
9 Similarly, Sen recognizes that to understand Smith's views, we need to "distinguish between prudence and the pursuit of selfishness and between the consequential usefulness of a motive and its being a virtue" (Sen 1986: 35).
10 Levy also considers how Smith's economics inform the ethics of the sixth edition of *TMS* (Levy 1995: 316–8). Evensky (1989) sees changes in Smith's writings over time, but the movement is from *TMS* (1759) to *WN* and *TMS* (1790), not from *TMS* (1759) to *WN* to *TMS* (1790). The civil jurisprudential language of Smith's earlier writings, which emphasized the perfection of positive law, changed to incorporate civic humanist language, which emphasized the duty of good citizenship. This change is evidenced by the language of *WN*, by additions to the third (1784) edition of *WN*, and by additions in the sixth edition of *TMS*.
11 Tribe also mentions "a recent trend to read Smith as critic, as a moral *instead of* an economic theorist. . . . reading *The Wealth of Nations* rather than *The Theory of Moral Sentiments* as a work of moral philosophy" (Tribe 1999: 629).

References

Anspach, R. (1972) "The Implications of *The Theory of Moral Sentiments* for Adam Smith's Economic Thought," *History of Political Economy* 9: 176–206.
Bitterman, H. J. (1940) "Adam Smith's Empiricism and the Law of Nature, Parts I–II," *Journal of Political Economy* 48: 487–520; 703–34, reprinted in J. Cunningham Wood (ed.) (1984), *Adam Smith: Critical Assessments*, vol. 1, London: Croom Helm: 190–235.
Bowley, M. (1975) "Some Aspects of the Treatment of Capital in *The Wealth of Nations*," in A. S. Skinner and T. Wilson (eds), *Essays on Adam Smith*, Oxford: Oxford University Press: 361–76.
Brown, V. (1994) *Adam Smith's Discourse: Canonicity, Commerce and Conscience*, London: Routledge.
Buckle, H. T. (1878) *History of Civilization in England*, 3 vols. vol. 3, new edn, Toronto: Rose-Belford.
Campbell, W. F. (1967) "Adam Smith's Theory of Justice, Prudence and Beneficence," *American Economic Review* 57: 571–7, reprinted in J. Cunningham Wood (ed.) (1984), *Adam Smith: Critical Assessments*, vol. 1, London: Croom Helm: 351–6.
Charlier, C. (1996) "The Notion of Prudence in Smith's *Theory of Moral Sentiments*," *History of Economic Ideas* 4: 271–97.
Choi, Y. B. (1990) "Smith's View on Human Nature: A Problem in the Interpretation of *The Wealth of Nations* and *The Theory of Moral Sentiments*," *Review of Social Economy* 48: 288–302.
Dickey, L. (1986) "Historicizing the 'Adam Smith Problem': Conceptual, Historiographical, and Textual Issues," *Journal of Modern History* 58: 579–609.
Evensky, J. (1989) "The Evolution of Adam Smith's Views on Political Economy," *History of Political Economy* 21: 123–45.
Fitzgibbons, A. (1995) *Adam Smith's System of Liberty, Wealth and Virtue: The Moral and Political Foundations of The Wealth of Nations*. Oxford: Clarendon.
Fontaine, P. (1997) "Identification and Economic Behavior: Sympathy and Empathy in Historical Perspective," *Economics and Philosophy* 13: 261–80.
Franklin, R. S. (1976) "Smithian Economics and its Pernicious Legacy," *Review of Social Economy* 34: 379–89, reprinted in J. Cunningham Wood (ed.) (1984), *Adam Smith: Critical Assessments*, vol. 3, London: Croom Helm: 470–8.
Gee, J. M. A. (1968) "Adam Smith's Social Welfare Function," *Scottish Journal of Political*

Economy 15: 283–99, reprinted in J. Cunningham Wood (ed.) (1984), *Adam Smith: Critical Assessments*, vol. 4, London: Croom Helm: 84–97.

Grampp, W. D. (1948) "Adam Smith and the Economic Man," *Journal of Political Economy* 56: 315–36, reprinted in J. Cunningham Wood (ed.) (1984), *Adam Smith: Critical Assessments*, vol. 1, London: Croom Helm: 250–72.

—— (1979) "Adam Smith and the American Revolutionists," *History of Political Economy*, 11: 179–91, reprinted in J. Cunningham Wood (ed.) (1984), *Adam Smith: Critical Assessments*, vol. 4, London: Croom Helm: 306–15.

Jones, P. and Skinner, A. S. (eds) (1992) *Adam Smith Reviewed*, Edinburgh: Edinburgh University Press.

Lamb, R. B. (1987) *Property Markets and the State in Adam Smith's System*, New York: Garland.

Levy, D. (1995) "The Partial Spectator in the Wealth of Nations: A Robust Utilitarianism," *European Journal of the History of Economic Thought* 2: 299–326.

Macfie, A. L. (1967) *The Individual in Society: Papers on Adam Smith*, London: Allen and Unwin.

Meek, R. L. (1951) "Physiocracy and Classicism in Britain," *Economic Journal* 26: 26–47.

Minowitz, P. (1993) *Profits, Priests, and Princes: Adam Smith's Emancipation of Economics from Politics and Religion*, Stanford: Stanford University Press.

Mizuta, H. and Sugiyama, C. (1993) *Adam Smith: International Perspectives* New York: St. Martin's Press.

Morrow, G. R. ([1923]1969) *The Ethical and Economic Theories of Adam Smith*, reprint edn, New York: Augustus M. Kelley.

Oncken, A. (1897) "The Consistency of Adam Smith," *Economic Journal* 7: 443–50, reprinted in J. Cunningham Wood (ed.) (1984), *Adam Smith: Critical Assessments*, vol. 1, London: Croom Helm: 1–6.

Pack, S. J. (1997) "Adam Smith on the Virtues: A Partial Resolution of the Adam Smith Problem," *Journal of the History of Economic Thought* 19: 127–140.

Raphael, D. D. (1975) "The Impartial Spectator," in A. S. Skinner and T. Wilson (eds), *Essays on Adam Smith* Oxford: Oxford University Press: 83–99.

—— (1992) "Adam Smith 1790: The Man Recalled; The Philosopher Revived," in P. Jones and A. S. Skinner (eds), *Adam Smith Reviewed*, Edinburgh: Edinburgh University Press.

Raphael, D. D. and Macfie, A. L. (1976) "Introduction" to A. Smith, *The Theory of Moral Sentiments*, Oxford: Oxford University Press.

Recktenwald, H. C. (1978) "An Adam Smith Renaissance *anno* 1976? The Bicentenary Output – A Reappraisal of his Scholarship," *Journal of Economic Literature* 16: 56–83, reprinted in J. Cunningham Wood (ed.) (1984), *Adam Smith: Critical Assessments*, vol. 4, London: Croom Helm: 249-77.

Sen, A. (1986) "Adam Smith's Prudence," in S. Lall and F. Stewart (eds), *Theory and Reality in Development: Essays in Honour of Paul Streeten*, London: Macmillan: 28–37.

Shinohara, H. (1993) "The Practical System of Morality in Adam Smith," in H. Mizuta and C. Sugiyama (eds), *Adam Smith: International Perspectives*, New York: St. Martin's Press.

Skarżyński, W. von (1878) *Adam Smith als Moralphilosoph und Schoepfer der Nationaloekonomie: Ein Beitrag zur Geschichte der Nationaloekonomie*, Berlin: Verlag von Theobald Grieben.

Skinner, A. and Wilson, T. S. (eds) (1975) *Essays on Adam Smith*, Oxford: Clarendon.

Spengler, J. J. (1945) "The Physiocrats and Say's Law of Markets," *Journal of Political Economy* 53: 193–211.

Teichgraeber III, R. F. (1981) "Rethinking *Das Adam Smith Problem*," *Journal of British Studies* 20: 106–23.

Thomson, H. F. (1965) "Adam Smith's Philosophy of Science," *Quarterly Journal of Economics* 79: 212–33, reprinted in J. Cunningham Wood (ed.) (1984), *Adam Smith: Critical Assessments*, vol. 1, London: Croom Helm: 323–41.

Tribe, K. (1999) "Adam Smith: Critical Theorist?" *Journal of Economic Literature* 37: 609–32.

Viner, J. (1960) "The Intellectual History of Laissez Faire," *Journal of Law and Economics* 3: 45–68.

—— (1968) "Adam Smith," in *International Encyclopaedia of the Social Sciences*, New York: Macmillan, reprinted in J. Cunningham Wood (ed.) (1984), *Adam Smith: Critical Assessments*, vol. I, London: Croom Helm: 111–21.

Winch, D. (1993) "Adam Smith: Scottish Moral Philosopher as Political Economist," in *Adam Smith: International Perspectives*, New York: St. Martin's Press.

—— (1978) *Adam Smith's Politics: An Essay in Historiographic Revision*, Cambridge: Cambridge University Press.

Witztum, A. (1998) "A Study into Smith's Conception of the Human Character: Das Adam Smith Problem Revisited," *History of Political Economy* 30: 489–514.

Wood, J. C. (1984) *Adam Smith: Critical Assessments*, 4 vols, London: Croom Helm.

Young, J. T. (1997) *Economics as a Moral Science: The Political Economy of Adam Smith*, Cheltenham: Elgar.

Young, J. T. and Gordon, B. (1997) "Natural Price and Commutative Justice: Adam Smith and the Just Price Traditions," in *Economics as a Moral Science*, Cheltenham: Elgar: 107–27.

—— (1997) "Distributive Justice," in *Economics as a Moral Science*, Cheltenham: Elgar: 129–55.

Zeyss, R. (1889) *Adam Smith und der Eigennutz: Eine Untersuchung über die philosophischen Grundlagen der älteren Nationalökonomie*, Tübingen: Verlag der H. Lauppschen Buchhandlung.

10 The French foundations of the classical canon

Walter Eltis

The classical school of economics evolved in the eighteenth-century. Adam Smith presented the first comprehensive account of its political economy in *The Wealth of Nations* in 1776, but several of his fundamental propositions originated previously in France. Smith discovered their importance during his visit to France in 1765–6: he met the leading physiocrats and their books subsequently found their way to his library. The classical canon, which he went on to establish, commandingly rests on five fundamental propositions:

1. Economies will function most efficiently where all markets are competitive, and where those who own property determine investment and production decisions. For these to be efficient, entrepreneurs must be confident that they will obtain the legal title to wealth they create.
2. Some economic activities are productive and have the potential to generate a net surplus. Others, and especially those organized by the state, are unproductive and can only be sustained from the surpluses of productive activities.
3. The growth of economies will depend on the re-investment of surpluses from productive activities. If these are absorbed or more than absorbed by the unproductive, nothing will remain for investment, and a nation's output will stagnate or decline.
4. Population will expand indefinitely to match the demand for labor at a real wage which maintains families at a standard of living where sufficient children survive.
5. Competitively determined market prices will converge on long-term costs of production which establish the basis for the value of output.

The classical school united to advocate free competition, the undiluted enforcement of capitalist property rights, the virtues of thrift over profligacy and the maintenance of low taxation and government expenditure.

The classical school's support for free competition in all markets superseded the *dirigiste* mercantilism which had dominated Europe's leading economies until the 1750s. The advocacy of universal free competition became possible after David Hume showed in 1752 how countries could generally achieve balance of payments equilibrium without any need to protect domestic agriculture, industry and commerce from more efficient foreign producers. The successful encouragement of domestic industry and commerce had previously been seen as the essence of statecraft. Hume showed that a country could realize its economic potential without such interference, which often involved the creation of monopolistic companies and political corruption. He was well known in France through his philosophical works and his residence in Paris on several occasions. His new economic essays were rapidly translated into French and absorbed into the corpus of French thought. Previous and subsequent French writers such as Claude-Jacques Herbert in his *Essai sur la police générale des grains* of 1755 wrote of the great potential advantages from the freeing of the grain trade; but it was Hume who showed definitively that this and other extensions to trade would not undermine the balance of payments. It therefore became possible to argue that the investment and production decisions of entrepreneurs acting in competition would prove superior to those even of such enlightened statesmen as Colbert or Cromwell.

It has always been understood that many statesmen place the wealth and power of their families above the welfare and prosperity of the kingdoms they govern. Until 1752 it nonetheless appeared that any country which sought industrial and commercial success required the support of ministers with the authority to preside over detailed policies to strengthen domestic powers of production and to supervise their protection from the competitive strengths of others. As soon as it became clear that competitive market forces, allowed to act freely, would create a structure of comparative international prices where exports were sufficiently competitive to pay for imports, it became possible to argue that the discretionary powers of statesmen had become redundant. They moreover lacked the collective knowledge of many thousand market participants, each free to exploit the opportunities they saw around them. This was powerfully noticed in the next decades on each side of the Channel. In Paris in 1775 the abbé de Condillac's advice to the future ruler of Parma was that:

> Governing an economy requires a comprehensive genius who knows everything, who weighs everything, and who directs all the resources of government in perfect harmony. It would be difficult, or rather impossible to find such a genius. The best intentioned and most skillful statesmen have made mistakes through ignorance or through over hasty action, for it is difficult to see all and bring all together without sometimes falling into error . . . statesmen never do more harm than when they wish to interfere in everything. It is wisest to confine oneself to preventing abuses and otherwise to pursue a policy of laissez-faire.
>
> (Condillac [1775] 1798, vol. 20: 488)

Almost coincidentally in 1776, Adam Smith wrote in precisely the same terms in *The Wealth of Nations*:

> The stateman, who should attempt to direct private people in what manner they ought to employ their capitals, would not only load himself with a most unnecessary attention, but assume an authority which could safely be trusted, not only to no single person, but to no council or senate whatever, and which would nowhere be so dangerous as in the hands of a

man who had folly and presumption enough to fancy himself fit to exercise it.

(Smith [1776] 1976: 456)

Before Hume, these would have appeared superficial approaches to economic policy, but by 1775–6 a preference for competition over statescraft had become a central element in enlightened political economy in both France and Britain.

After Hume, the conditions for the emergence of the classical school were in place.

The classical school's origin in France

The new competitive economics originated in Paris in the circle created by Jacques Vincent de Gournay, Intendant du Commerce from 1751–8. He himself published little, but the origins of the phrase "*laissez-faire et laissez-passer*" have been widely attributed to him. He arranged for the publication of important books, including notably Richard Cantillon's *Essai sur la nature du commerce*, and for the translation from English of Hume's essays and the work of other important British political economists. His circle included especially, Turgot, Forbonnais, Herbert and Plumart de Dangeul who each themselves wrote important and influential books (Hutchison 1988: 224–5).

Economic publication increased enormously in the 1750s. The number of books published on the economy doubled from 1745–9 to 1750–4, and doubled again between 1750–4 and 1755–9. (Théré 1998: 18) Four economic journals were founded in France in the 1750s and the 1760s, the *Journal Oeconomique* was published between 1751–72 (and in 1754 included a French translation of Hume's "Of the Balance of Trade"), the *Journal du Commerce* from 1759–62, the *Journal de l'Agriculture, du Commerce, et des Finances* from 1762–4, and what became the journal of the physiocrats, *Les éphémérides du Citoyen* from 1765–72 followed by the *Nouvelles Éphémérides* from 1774–6 (Hutchison 1988: 189). The first British and United States economic journals only emerged after 1880.[1] French economic journals therefore preceded the leading English language journals by more than a century.

French political economy is also notable for the social and political distinction of the authors of some of its leading contributions. As in Britain, every leading philosopher together with bankers and merchants published on political economy, but the early French writers also included Condorcet and the elder Mirabeau who held the rank of marquis, and Turgot who was briefly France's leading minister. The seventeenth and eighteenth-century British literature included nothing of significance from any member of the House of Lords or any member of a cabinet. Thirty-seven French ministers and intendants (heads of provincial government) published on economics between 1750 and 1789 (Théré 1998: 37). Some of the greatest French economists were close to the heart of government and utterly aware of immediate political developments.

As the Marquise de Pompadour's personal physician and the second doctor in ordinary to the king, François Quesnay lived at the heart of the court. Louis XV himself participated in the printing of the *Tableau*, and suggested the *pensée* (pansy) for Quesnay's coat of arms to symbolize that he was also a *penseur* of distinction (Hecht 1958: 244). The abbé de Condillac was director of studies to a grandson of Louis XV who was heir to the throne of Parma, the center of French influence in Italy. The closest that eighteenth-century British political economists came to government was Adam Smith's appointment as Commissioner for Customs for Scotland in 1778–80, after the publication of *The Wealth of Nations*.

In France in the 1750s, interest in economic issues became so great that Voltaire commented in his dictionary article, "*Bled ou blé*" that,

> Towards 1750, the French nation turned its attention away from tragedies, comedies, operas, novels, romantic histories, thoughts that were still more romantic and theological disputes . . . and set out to reason on corn. . . . Useful works were written on agriculture; everyone read them apart from the farmers.
>
> (Voltaire 1770–5: 37, 112)

Of Plumart de Dangeul's *Remarques sur les avantages et les desavantages de la France et de la Grande-Bretagne* of 1754, the Marquis of Argenson said in April of that year that "the king claimed to have read it, as did the rest of the court, and in the meantime they praised it without knowing what they were saying" (Argenson 1859–67: 8, 274).

The prime explanation for the exceptional interest in political economy in mid-eighteenth-century France was disappointment and puzzlement that while Paris was the intellectual capital of Europe, and France was Europe's leading power (which the rest of Europe several times had to contain), it was nonetheless unable to finance the elementary needs of government without debts which it repeatedly had to repudiate or renegotiate. The French state had to pay higher interest rates than the governments of Britain and Holland, and higher even than private borrowers in France had to pay, because of fear that escalating debt interest might once again become unfinanceable. The paradox of a rich country and a poor king repeatedly weakened France. Equally critically, the French towns and the countryside suffered repeated famines despite France's exceptional fertility. The resolution of these difficulties became the concern of every thinking Frenchman who cared for his country. Sir John Hicks has remarked on the tendency for fundamental advances in monetary economics to occur in times of crisis (Hicks 1977: 45–6). That is precisely why the attention of the greatest and the most creative in France was drawn to the paradox of French economic failure when France led Europe in many other ways. French economic weakness in comparison with Britain, France's principal competitor for European and world influence, also attracted particular attention.

François Quesnay's seminal contribution to the canon

The new excitement about the economy which induced so many to publish on this soon centered on the powerful and original contributions of François Quesnay, who in addition to his court appointments, was one of France's most distinguished scientists with honors which included Fellowship of the Royal Society of London. His first invitations to write on economics came from the editors of the *Encyclopédie,* the *philosophes* Denis Diderot (who himself published on economics) and Jean-le-Rond d'Alembert. The strength and influence of Quesnay's contribution however owed much to the coincidence of his principal policy proposals with those of Gournay's circle.

France's new economists agreed above all that the *police des grains* where corn, the principal food of the people, had to be sold through the state at prices which its agents determined, should be replaced by free competitive markets. Farmers should be free to sell corn for the best prices they could find, whether in France or overseas. France with regulated and highly administered grain markets suffered repeated famines, while in England, where farmers were free to sell corn for the best prices they could obtain at home or overseas, famine was unknown.

Quesnay discovered a coherent logical framework for the school of Gournay's new competitive economics. In the articles "Fermiers" and "Grains" which Diderot and D'Alembert published in the *Encyclopédie* in 1756–57, Quesnay showed in detail how modern capital-intensive farming (*la grande culture*) creates a surplus of 100 percent over current agricultural costs (*avances annuelles*), expressed as a money ratio of sales revenues over farmers' costs. Less efficient farming (*la petite culture*) yields a surplus of only about 35 percent, while peasants scratching a bare subsistence from the soil without significant farm capital produce no surplus at all (Eltis 1984: ch.1). The agricultural surplus or *produit net* as Quesnay described it was the crucial concept in his economics. It provided rents for landowners, tithes for the Church and taxes for the state. Adequate finance for the state required that *la grande culture* predominate because this yielded a *produit net* three times as great as that generated by less efficient farming. There had been previous statements about how agriculture creates the economy's principal economic surplus from Sir William Petty in London in 1662 and from Cantillon in 1755; but Quesnay set out its generation far more clearly and it became the core of his argument. He presented this through the *Tableau économique* which has been widely described as the first economic model. Here, the agricultural surplus is paid in money to the landowners, the Church and the state, who spend it to create the bulk of the economy's effective demand through a multiplier circulation process. Money circulates in the economy like blood in a human body.

In contrast to agriculture, industry and commerce which provide about half the economy's employment generate no taxable surplus, and depend for their market on the expenditure of the agricultural surplus. If agriculture creates a substantial *produit net*, industry and commerce, where half the income from the land is spent, will be large and prosperous. If agriculture produces only a small surplus, industry and commerce will suffer correspondingly. To underline the significance of this striking distinction, Quesnay controversially described agriculture as productive because it generated a *produit net*, while industry and commerce were sterile, because they generated no *produit net* and their prosperity depended on the success of agriculture.

The *Tableau* is complex and subtle, and there is a vast and growing literature on the intricacies of its interpretation.[2] Robert Eagly has described "the capital concept" as "the rich heritage of the Quesnaysian revolution" (Eagly 1974: 11), and Karl Marx described the *Tableau* as "an extremely brilliant conception, incontestably the most brilliant for which political economy had up to then been responsible" (Marx 1969–71, vol. 1: 344). Its creation will have given pleasure to the scientist and mathematician in Quesnay of a kind which Marmontel vividly portrays:

> In his *entresol*, Quesnay scribbled down his axioms and calculations about a rustic economy, as tranquilly indifferent to the movements of the court as if it had been a hundred leagues distant. Below us they were deliberating war and peace, the choice of generals, the dismissal of ministers; while in the entresol we discussed agriculture; we calculated the net product, or sometimes we dined gaily with Diderot, D'Alembert, Duclos, Helvétius, Turgot and Buffon; and Madame de Pompadour, unable to persuade this troupe of philosophers to descend to her salon, came up herself to see them at table and chat with them.
>
> (Marmontel 1972, vol. 1: 139)

Quesnay's complex calculations led to the publication of several *Tableaux* in disequilibrium in 1760 in a seventh additional Part to Mirabeau's *L'Ami des hommes* entitled "*Le tableau économique avec ses explications*" which show the circumstances in which the economy will grow or decline. Expanding agricultural investment is the key to growth because this creates an increasing *produit net*, growing effective demand and a continually improving market for the products of industry and commerce. Conversely, anything which causes agricultural investment to decline, will lead to the contraction of the finances of the state and of industry and commerce.

The disequilibrium *Tableaux* show how agriculture and therefore the economy, will contract if taxation is increased in any manner which reduces farmers' funds for investment. More controversially in the secondary literature where this conclusion has been widely questioned, Quesnay's calculations show that the economy will contract if demand switches away from agriculture (where production generates an economic surplus) and towards manufactures (where no *produit net* is generated).[3] There is his clear statement as early as the 1759 version of the *Tableau* that:

> It can be seen from the distribution delineated in the tableau that if the nation's expenditure went more to the sterile expenditure side than the productive expenditure side, the revenue would fall proportionately, and this fall would increase in the same progression from year to year successively. It follows that a high level of expenditure on *luxe de décoration* and on conspicuous consumption is ruinous. If on the other hand the nation's expenditure goes on the productive expenditure side the revenue will rise, and this rise will in the same way increase successively from year to year. Thus it is not true that the type of expenditure is a matter of indifference.
>
> (Quesnay [1758–9] 1972: 12)

This conclusion (which is unique to Quesnay) follows directly from his assumption that only agriculture generates a *produit net*. An economy where most economic activity is industrial and commercial will fail to generate an economic surplus sufficient to support the state and the Church. Quesnay maintains that commercial states such as Venice and Holland which apparently enjoy great wealth actually obtain much of this from primary producing colonies and from fishing. Thus the Dutch republic is not merely commercial, "It is also necessary to envisage it as proprietor of a territory which produces much: of colonies whose produce is extremely profitable to it, and of seas where it obtains a large product through fishing" (Quesnay [1768] 1958: 852). In the explanation to the 1759 *Tableau*, Quesnay nonetheless refers to "the small *produit net* which could be obtained from an external trade in manufactured commodities," but "free and unobstructed trade" will "happily" remove this (Quesnay [1758–9] 1972: 12).[4]

While excessive taxation, the wrong kind of taxation, and undue preferences for *luxe de décoration* which was pervasive in France were responsible for economic decline, growth would depend on whatever had the potential to raise the economic surplus. Quesnay's fullest account of a growth program for France is presented in a Memoir to a Society of Agriculture which is included in the physiocrat magnum opus, *Philosophie rurale,* which he and Mirabeau published together in 1763, and which according to Louis Salleron, the editor of the INED edition of Quesnay, provides "the most complete and authentic account of the physiocratic system considered as a whole" (INED: 687). Ronald Meek finds that "All the evidence, stylistic and otherwise, points to Quesnay as the author" (Meek 1962: 38) of this memoir which shows how the French economy can be expanded to a staggering extent in the nine years from 1761–70, which indicates that the memoir was written in 1758, 1759 or 1760.

The transformation of the French economy within a decade required three fundamental reforms.[5] The first was the creation of a free market for grain so that farmers could sell this for the best prices they could obtain at home or overseas, which would raise the price of grain 30 percent and more than double the *produit net* since farmers' costs would rise far less than 30 percent. The freeing of grain markets to bring this about was also the central policy proposal of Gournay's circle.

Quesnay's second policy reform, which further doubled the *produit net* so that it was quadrupled in all, was the removal of taxes which fell on farmers, and their replacement with taxes on agricultural rents to yield equivalent revenues. This concentration of all taxes on rents, the sole source of *produit net* is unique to the physiocrats. The initial quadrupling of the *produit net* as a consequence of these reforms, mostly remained with the farmers, until their leases came up for renewal at the end of the nine year term which French law required. The vast initial increases in farmers' incomes enabled them to transform agriculture from the less capital intensive *la petite culture* which yielded a *produit net* of only 35 percent to the more efficient *la grande culture* which yielded 100 percent.

As agricultural leases were gradually renegotiated at rents which reflected the vast increase in *produit net*, landlords would easily become able to pay the taxes which had been paid by farmers prior to the proposed reforms. Quesnay assumed that over the nine years from 1761 to 1770, farmers would invest the whole additional *produit net* which remained with them prior to the expiry of their leases, which would enable them to more than double agricultural advances and France's aggregate *produit net*.

Loïc Charles (1999 and 2000) has rediscovered a passage by Quesnay in Henri Pattullo's *Essai sur l'amélioration des terres* published in 1758 which includes an earlier account of this proposed transformation of the French economy. The relevant pages of Pattullo, which also include part of Quesnay's then unpublished essay, "*Hommes*" which he had written for the *Encyclopédie* in 1757 and subsequently withdrawn, are to be found in Quesnay's handwriting in the *Bibliothèque nationale*, and they were actually included as an unpublished note in the INED edition of Quesnay's works (INED: 53–4). It is Charles who has located their actual place and manner of publication, and he is the first to offer an account of their significance. Pattullo dedicated his book to Madame de Pompadour in words which moved her to tears, and by 1758 Quesnay was already beginning to publish his economics under pseudonyms and within the works of others: subsequently with Mirabeau in *l'Ami des hommes* and *Philosophie rurale*.

In this newly located statement of a growth program for France, Quesnay asserts that the freeing of grain markets will create 200 million *livres* of additional revenues, 100 million through additional exports and a further 100 million as a consequence of higher prices for grain within France. The investment of this 200 million in *la grande culture* with its implicit return of 100 percent will ensure that French agricultural output rises by 400 millions. A well-maintained farming family of four requires 800 *livres* a year, and the 400 million increase in agricultural incomes will suffice to support an additional 500,000 such families and therefore an increase in the agricultural population of 2,000,000.[6] This process will moreover be repeatable, year after year:

> But each year such an exportation of grain would procure a new increment of wealth of 100 millions, paid by the foreigner, and 100 million through the gain in price . . . these two portions would form annually an increase in wealth of 200 millions, which, employed in agriculture, would produce growth of a further 200 millions, to produce an annual increase of wealth of 400 millions.
>
> The annual increase of 400 millions would produce an annual increase of 2 million people who would be attracted by the gains procured through the annual expenditure of the increase of 400 millions, and these people would perpetuate the successive increases of wealth, through their consumption and their work.
>
> (Pattullo 1758: 240–1 [INED: 54])

Quesnay himself adds in the INED text that:

> One sees, by the rapidity of this progression, that a nation is able, through the freedom and ease of trading the foodstuffs it grows, to reach the highest degree of prosperity within a few years. But the vices of administration can obstruct this progress through badly understood regulations

which impinge on trade, through the intolerances . . . of religion, and through destructive wars which curtail the population, through ill-directed taxes which absorb or divert the wealth which ought to be employed in agriculture; because just as the successive growth of wealth can hasten the growth of revenues and of population, in the same way a continuing decrease in wealth can soon bring about a decline in population and revenues.

(INED: 54)

Quesnay clearly assumes that population is elastic with respect to income and wealth. Here he follows Cantillon who wrote that "Men multiply like mice in a barn if they have unlimited means of subsistence" (Cantillon [1755] 1997: 47), while according to Quesnay, "the growth of wealth increases the number of men in all remunerative occupations" (Quesnay [1757] 1958: 570).

More precisely, like the great British classical economists, Quesnay defined the wage at which the population is in equilibrium in terms of a specific quantity of corn, "The daily wage of a labourer is fixed on the basis of the price of corn, and amounts to a twentieth of the price of one *setier*" (Quesnay [1758–9] 1972: 10).

In the pages in Pattullo which immediately follow the passage in Quesnay's own handwriting, there is a remarkable account of the classical population supply mechanism. It is first suggested that the extraordinary progression of wealth and population just described has an earlier parallel in French history, precisely the one Quesnay reiterated in every edition of the *Tableau*:

> according to this progression, one ought at no point to be surprised by the rapid success of the economic government of M. de Sully. In thirteen years, this Minister paid off the debts of the Kingdom, reduced taxes and created a public treasure. The simple means of freedom to export was the principal resort he made use of. He said that without it, the subjects would have no money, and the King no revenue; he had no fear that freedom to trade in grain would cause famine; indeed after his wise reforms, France experienced no scarcity for sixty years.
>
> (Pattullo 1758: 242–3)

Either Quesnay himself or Pattullo then went on to show that the growth in population required to create the additional wealth enumerated in the progressions could actually be forthcoming:

> If it was necessary to prove through examples, the possibility and the reality of rapid progress in wealth and population, procured through the resources of agriculture and the ease of trade in its products; it would be enough to note the establishment of the English colonies in North America, which from their small beginnings in far distant countries, have been able in very little time to clear and populate immense deserts, to build great cities, to construct harbours, and to establish an extensive sea trade and shipping and commerce . . .
>
> It has been suggested that in countries whose people could live in

abundance, and would have the opportunity to marry and establish themselves while they are still young, the population could double every twenty or at most twenty-five years; and several English writers maintain that in their American colonies, its multiplication will follow this progression.

Besides the growth of population in a country is not limited to the effects of propagation; if the revenues and the expenditures of the landlords who live in the cities grow by one-quarter or double, men of all professions will arrive there from all quarters to share in the gains which this expenditure procures.

(Pattullo 1758: 243–8)

This reads with the boldness of Quesnay himself, but even if it is Pattullo, Quesnay will have read and approved a chapter which included forty pages which are unquestionably his, in a book dedicated to his patron, the Marquise de Pompadour, who secured the "permission of the King" [*privilège du Roi*] which permitted its uncensored publication.

After the publication of *L'Amélioration des terres* in which these powerful passages are to be found, Quesnay developed his theory and consequent calculations further. The *Tableau* evolved, with its zig-zags to describe inter-sectoral income flows, into a technical complexity which few could understand outside the circle of *les Économistes,* as his disciples soon came to be described. Quesnay was a brilliant dialectician and he took his followers through each detail of the argument in a regular weekly salon, which was attended during 1765–6 by Adam Smith, who was visiting Paris in a prolonged European tour as escort and tutor to the Duke of Buccleuch. Smith absorbed the new French economics, and in *The Wealth of Nations* he described Quesnay's system as "the nearest approximation to the truth that has yet been published on the subject of political economy" (Smith [1776] 1976: 678).

Intellectually Quesnay and his disciples had established a new approach to economics. Physiocrats were invited to advise monarchs in Germany and Russia. Quesnay had firmly established the economy's disposable surplus as the key to economic growth or decline, and this became one of the most significant elements in the classical canon. Quesnay's (and Cantillon's) account of population growth anticipated Malthus, and it is precisely the one that is central to the classical canon, including even the significance of corn in the definition of the natural wage.

The new French economics also emphasized the advantages of competitive markets. Food prices were not to be forced up artificially. The creation of free markets for food would raise the prices farmers received to the level the prosperity of France required. Two passages underline the classical nature of Quesnay's analysis which precisely foreshadows the free market economics of Adam Smith. In 1768, Quesnay wrote in *Physiocratie*:

You will come round again to the necessity of accepting the greatest possible freedom of competition in all branches of trade, in order to cut down as far as possible on the burdensome costs involved in them. As soon as you have calculated the effects of this general freedom prescribed by natural right, by virtue of which each person should have the legal power to render his situation as good as he possibly can, without infringing upon the rights of others, it will become self-evident to you that it is an essential condition of the growth of public and private wealth.

(Quesnay [1768] 1958: 911–12)

In 1776 Smith included an almost identical statement in *The Wealth of Nations*:

> All systems either of preference or of restraint, therefore, being thus completely taken away, the obvious and simple system of natural liberty establishes itself of its own accord. Every man, as long as he does not violate the laws of justice, is left perfectly free to pursue his own interest in his own way, and to bring both his industry and capital into competition with those of any other man, or order of men.
>
> (Smith [1776] 1976: 687)

One of Smith's most celebrated insights was that an 'invisible hand' would lead individuals, each of whom "intends only his own gain" to work together to promote the interests "of the society".(ibid.: 456). The equivalent statement from Quesnay and Mirabeau reads, "The whole magic of well-ordered society is that each man works for others, while believing that he is working for himself" (Quesnay [1764] 1972, vol. 1: 138).

The attempts to apply Quesnay's new competitive economics to France's financial problems for which it was created unfortunately failed.[7] Quesnay's technical physiocracy, and the more general conclusions of Gournay's circle coincided on the need to free agricultural markets. Louis XV played the role of the enlightened monarch which the establishment of physiocracy required, and appointed ministers who sought to free food markets in 1763, but the consequent price increases proved immensely unpopular, especially in Paris, and in 1768 the rigid regulation of the *police des grains* was restored. In 1774 the new monarch, Louis XVI, appointed the leading economist, Turgot, as controller-general of finances, to make another attempt to free food markets but this again resulted in higher food prices and riots. Turgot was replaced by a *dirigiste* only twenty months after his appointment. The attempts to use France's new economics to solve the financial problems of the *ançien régime* therefore failed; but they had a fundamental impact on Adam Smith and, principally through him, on the development of classical political economy.

Adam Smith's transformation of the French classical canon

Smith's understanding of the need for firmly established property rights, the importance of competition, and the potential gains from free trade were fully formed before his visit to Paris. These are all to be found in the lectures he gave in 1762–3 as a professor in Glasgow. But Smith's lectures lack any account of the creation of an economic surplus and its significance for whether the wealth of nations will grow or decline. This became the heart of Book 2 of *The Wealth of Nations* and it is evident that Smith discovered it in Paris, but he also transformed the argument and greatly improved it.[8]

Quesnay and the physiocrats identified the economic surplus wholly with agriculture, a restriction which was ridiculed by Voltaire in 1768 in *L'Homme aux quarante écus*. A peasant with a net income of forty *écus* (120 *livres*), about £6 sterling, rides with a wealthy merchant in his six-horse carriage. To the peasant's outrage and amazement the merchant is exempt from taxation on his income of 400,000 *livres* because profits from commerce are no part of the economy's net surplus, while the peasant has to pay half his 120 livres in taxes. Ten editions were published in 1768 alone, far more than of any book by the physiocrats.

Adam Smith corrected this error in *The Wealth of Nations* where manufacturers and not merely farmers generate an economic surplus:

> There is one sort of labour which adds to the value of the subject upon which it is bestowed: There is another which has no such effect. The former, as it produces a value, may be called productive; the latter, unproductive labour. Thus the labour of a manufacturer adds, generally, to the value of the materials which he works upon, that of his own maintenance, and of his master's profit. The labour of a menial servant, on the contrary, adds to the value of nothing ... A man grows rich by employing a multitude of manufacturers: He grows poor, by maintaining a multitude of menial servants.
>
> (Smith [1776] 1976: 330)

In Smith, anyone is productive who produces for sale goods or services which will finance his maintenance in the future, so merchants are also productive, and commerce is surplus-generating. The unproductive are those such as monarchs, soldiers, judges and servants of all kinds who rely on the incomes of others for the continuation of their employment.

In *The Wealth of Nations*, agriculture, industry and commerce each contribute to the value of a nation's output, while the unproductive make no contribution to this. According to Smith the best approximation to the value of a nation's output is the quantity of labor which can be purchased with, or commanded by, the aggregate output of agriculture, industry and commerce.

In contrast, Quesnay and the physiocrats confined their valuation of the economy's output to its total reproduction, the sales value of its annual output of food and raw materials, with normal harvests and food prices which covered fundamental costs. Quesnay always expressed the annual reproduction of the productive class as a quantity of money rather than as a quantity of corn or of agricultural labor. Manufacturers and merchants contributed nothing to the value of output. Worse still for the realism of physiocracy, the economy's *produit net* was generally located entirely in agriculture, while in *The Wealth of Nations*, the profits of industry and commerce also contribute to the investable and taxable surplus.

By 1867 when Marx published *Das Kapital*, industrial and commercial profits were 30 percent of Britain's national income while agricultural rents were 13 percent (Matthews *et al.* 1982: 164), so whatever the relative extent of profits and rents in the eighteenth century, the unique identification of the economy's surplus with agriculture was soon to become both a misconception and a growing statistical misunderstanding of the potential sources of tax revenues.

French economics could have made the same advance in 1776, for the abbé de Condillac published *Le Commerce et le Gouvernement* in the same year as Adam Smith. Here, "the work of artisans and merchants is as much a source of wealth . . . as the very work of the farmers", and he added that this "has been much obscured by some writers" (Condillac [1776] 1997: 105). The twentieth-century French Nobel prizewinner in economics, Maurice Allais, has described Condillac's book, which even anticipated the marginal revolution, as "definitely superior to Smith" (Allais 1992: 37), and in 1776, Louise d'Épinay described it to the abbé Galiani as "a classic work which makes the jargon of economics clearer than a mountain spring" (Galiani 1992–6: V, 69), but he was coldly received by the physiocrats so he made little impact on the development of economics in France. There the Économistes continued to defend the unique identification of the economic surplus with agriculture, while the analysis of the classical school was being simplified and generalized by Smith in Britain.

Smith echoes the French analysis that the economy will grow to the extent that the surplus of the productive exceeds the consumption of the unproductive, and in his account the latter mainly work for government:

> Great nations are never impoverished by private, though they sometimes are by publick prodigality and misconduct. The whole, or almost the whole publick revenue, is in most countries employed in maintaining unproductive hands . . . Such people, as they themselves produce nothing, are all maintained by the produce of other men's labour. When multiplied, therefore, to an unnecessary number, they may in a particular year consume so great a share of this produce, as not to leave a sufficiency for maintaining the productive labourers, who should reproduce it next year. The next year's produce, therefore, will be less than that of the foregoing, and if the same disorder should continue, that of the third year will be still less than that of the second.
>
> (Smith [1776] 1976: 342)

He shared the physiocrats' analysis that population would grow indefinitely at an adequate wage: "the demand for men, like that for any other commodity, necessarily regulates the production of men: quickens it when it goes on too slowly, and stops it when it advances too fast" (ibid.: 98). Like the physiocrats, he identified the wage at which the population will be sustained with a quantity of corn. Quesnay had described the equilibrium wage as equalling one twentieth of a setier of corn a day, while according to Smith, the money price of labor will always be such as "to enable the labourer to purchase a quantity of corn sufficient to maintain him and his family either in the liberal, moderate, or scanty manner in which the advancing, stationary or declining circumstances of the society oblige his employers to maintain him" (ibid.: 509).

The corn wage will be liberal if capital accumulates, so Smith attributes overwhelming significance to the virtues of thrift with striking phrases such as, "every prodigal appears to be a publick enemy, and every frugal man a publick benefactor" (ibid.: 340). Provided thrift predominates over extravagance, capital will grow, the wage will exceed what is required for a mere subsistence, population will expand, and there will be a great additional advantage. Long before Smith's visit to Paris, he had discovered the benefits for manufacturing industry from the division of labor which can be expected to produce ever-rising efficiency and these can only be enjoyed as capital accumulates. "As the accumulation of stock must, in the nature of things, be previous to the division of labour, so labour can be more and more subdivided in proportion only as stock is previously more and more accumulated" (ibid.: 277). The division of labor will continually cheapen manufactures and enable European workers to enjoy, as well as enough food for subsistence, woollen coats, linen shirts, shoes, knives and forks and kitchen utensils, earthenware plates and glass windows, with the result that their accommodation greatly exceeded that of "an African king" (ibid.: 23–4).

Smith's advocacy of a competitive approach to economics, the virtues of thrift, and his explanation of how agriculture, industry and commerce each contribute to the wealth of nations, marked out his contribution as the supreme achievement of the classical school. It was soon translated into French, and it immediately became the starting point for economic analysis on both sides of the Channel.

Say's extensions to the canon

After Smith, the principal developments of the classical canon occurred in Britain but there were two further significant developments in France. In 1803 Jean-Baptiste Say proposed his law of markets in the *Traité d'Économie Politique*. He insisted that the motivation for production is always the marketing of what is produced to obtain other commodities: "it is not so much an abundance of money which makes markets easy, as an abundance of other products in general. This is one of the most important truths in Political Economy" (Say 1803: 153). The proposition that supply creates its own demand, subsequently known as Say's law, became the element in classical economics which Keynes singled out for condemnation in *The General Theory of Employment, Interest and Money*.

Say's book was so important that Napoleon prevented the appearance of a second edition until 1814. After the apparent fall of the Emperor, Say dedicated his 1814 edition to Napoleon's leading conqueror, "His Majesty Alexandre I, Emperor of all the Russias." Napoleon had objected to Say's classical advocacy of the advantages of freedom for commerce, which was in sharp opposition to the Continental System which he had sought to establish.

Say shared the assumptions of the classical school and one of his notable contributions was a singling out of inventors as particular beneficiaries of mankind. He was even prepared to support state funding for research and development, since the advantages from new discoveries "being general advantages, it is not contrary to equity that the whole world should contribute to the price at which one obtains them" (ibid.: 146). Smith shared

French foundations of the classical canon 199

Say's willingness to countenance public investments which produced external benefits that market forces would not fully capture, such as expenditures to develop the infrastructure.

The canon in the nineteenth and twentieth centuries

This paper has focused especially on the French contribution to the classical canon. Samuel Hollander (1980 and 1997) has shown in conjunction with Paul Samuelson (1978) that from Adam Smith onwards, the great British political economists added a significant further element, the tendency for agricultural diminishing returns and/or capital saturation to produce a falling trend in the rate of profit, and a falling tendency in the wage towards a natural level at which population growth will cease. This element in the canon has received less emphasis in French political economy and it is of analytical rather than historical significance, for no nineteenth-century tendency for the rate of profit or the wage to fall has been observed in either Europe or North America.

A strong case can none the less be made for the practical significance of the Hollander-Samuelson element in the canon. By the 1840s British political economists were utterly convinced of the potential adverse impact of agricultural diminishing returns, and of how these would have a general tendency to diminish the rate of profit in both agriculture and industry until there was an eventual end to capital accumulation. John Stuart Mill's powerful account "Of the Tendency of Profits to a Minimum" (Mill 1848: Book IV, ch. 4) shows how this deepest and most perceptive of thinkers accepted this element of the canon.

But in the 1820s Ricardo had shown political economists a way out, which they all accepted. In 1820 he had written in his *Encyclopedia Britannica* article on "Funding Systems" which all will have read because of the importance of any question associated with Britain's national debt which had reached perhaps 275 percent of the national income at the conclusion of the Napoleonic wars:

> by the aid of foreign commerce . . . a country could go on for an indefinite time increasing in wealth and population, for the only obstacle to this increase would be the scarcity, and consequent high value, of food and other raw produce. Let these be supplied from abroad in exchange for manufactured goods, and it is difficult to say where the limit is at which you would cease to accumulate wealth and to derive profit from its employment.
> (Ricardo 1952–73, vol. 4: 179)

In May 1822 he told the House of Commons that with agricultural free trade:

> England would be the cheapest country in which a man could live; and it would rise to a state of prosperity, in regard to population and riches, of which, perhaps, the imaginations of honourable gentlemen could at present form no idea.
> (Ricardo 1951–73, vol. 5: 188)

After 1821 every political economist of significance together with ministers and members of parliament interested in economic questions became members of the Political Economy Club which Ricardo and Malthus founded. The first rules the members agreed to in 1821 (and they remain, virtually unchanged, in 1998), were:

> The Members of this Society will regard their own mutual instruction, and the diffusion amongst others of the just principles of Political Economy, as a real and important obligation.
>
> As the Press is the grand instrument for the diffusion of knowledge or of error, all the Members of this Society will regard it as incumbent upon them to watch carefully the proceedings of the Press, and to ascertain if any doctrines hostile to sound views on Political Economy have been propagated; to contribute whatever may be in their power to refute such erroneous doctrines and counteract their influence; and to avail themselves of every favourable opportunity for the publication of seasonable truths within the province of this science.
>
> (Political Economy Club 1921: 375)

Unanimity among economists is unknown in the late twentieth century, but in the 1830s and the 1840s they actually agreed that the removal of agricultural protection would prevent the fall in the rate of profit which would otherwise occur, and according to Hollander (1997) even Malthus had become an agricultural free trader by the 1830s (on the basis of conversations and letters but not his final publications). France had no equivalent to the Political Economy Club (after the influential Mirabeau-Quesnay Tuesdays of the 1760s), so those like Say, who supported free trade as much as Ricardo, had far less opportunity to influence official opinion and policy.

The triumph of the British political economists came in 1846 when the House of Commons (where most will have represented or benefited from landed interests), was persuaded to vote to repeal all agricultural protection [the Corn Laws], despite the adverse impact this would clearly have upon rents. The economists had few votes, as the Pope has no divisions, but their clear and unanimous opinion, reiterated over two decades, will have made an impact. Hence in 1846 Britain became the only country in Europe to introduce free trade in food. The result as Ricardo had predicted was a vast expansion of profits which greatly benefited industry and commerce. With unlimited food imports agricultural rents were held down, and the benefits from capital accumulation went entirely to profits to finance Britain's subsequent economic expansion. So it was precisely because the economically literate unanimously accepted the Hollander-Samuelson canon that its ill-effects were avoided. Its insignificance, *ex-post*, in the explanation of actual historical developments, is therefore a tribute to its *ex-ante* influence on a generation of political economists, whom it taught to understand the over-riding importance of policies to circumvent the developments it predicted.

Some of the elements of the canon which crossed the Channel from France also became obsolete in the course of the nineteenth century. The attribution of real wages to the influences which determine population growth failed to survive the marginal revolution. After the 1870s the iron law of wages was replaced in mainstream economics by the theory that these depend on the marginal productivity of labor. As capitalism progressed and technology advanced, the marginal productivity of labor rose, and the demand for labor and consequent living standards rose fastest in the economies such as the United States which benefited most from capital accumulation.

As workers' living standards rose, the classical attribution of saving and economic growth to surpluses which emerged mainly from profits and rents also became obsolete. With rising real wages, workers' saving for retirement became a considerable fraction of total saving, so the classical assumption that saving came predominantly from surpluses generated in production remained appropriate only to those centrally planned economies which disallowed the accumulation of private wealth. In market economies, workers' and salary earners' savings became much of the surplus on which investment and growth depended, so the element of the classical canon which regarded only some economic activities as surplus-generating became obsolete.

The element of the classical canon which has survived most strongly is belief in the benefits from competition and unrestricted trade. In the popular mind, this is still associated with the classical economics of Adam Smith, but it should be attributed equally to his French predecessors who created so much of the new economics in the decades before the publication of *The Wealth of Nations*.

Notes

I am grateful to Loïc Charles, Claude Jessua and Samuel Hollander for helpful comments on an earlier draft of this paper.

1 The Royal Economic Society's *Economic Journal* first appeared in 1890, while the first United States journal, the *Quarterly Journal of Economics* was founded in 1886. The *American Economic Review*, the official journal of the American Economic Association first appeared in 1910.
2 The classical interpretations especially include those by Meek (1962: 265–96) and Spengler 1945. More recent interpretations include Herlitz 1996, Pressman 1994, Vaggi 1987 and Eltis (1984 ch. 1).
3 Negishi (1989) has suggested that if demand in an agricultural kingdom shifts in favor of manufactures which, according to Quesnay, will reduce its *produit net*, it could continue to produce the same quantity of food, enjoy the same surplus, and use international markets to trade the food that has become superfluous to the kingdom's domestic requirements for the manufactures its population now desires. This solution however requires an unlimited potential to exchange food for manufactures in world markets at unchanged terms of trade, which is hardly appropriate to the eighteenth century.
4 Philippe Steiner (1998: 87) has rediscovered this statement which uniquely states that sterile manufacturing and commerce can apparently create a "small" *produit net*.
5 The Memoir is translated in full in Meek (1962: 138–49). It is explained in detail in Eltis (1996: 30–36).
6 Numbers differ in the near identical passages in INED: 53–4 and the subsequently

published Pattullo (1758: 237–41). The extra incomes from sales of grain supposedly generate twice the growth in population in the INED text which is earlier (the details are explained in Charles 1999). The less ambitious published numbers in Pattullo are quoted here.
7 Kaplan 1976 offers one of the fullest and most detailed historical accounts of the attempts to free French grain markets under the *ançien régime*.
8 See Skinner 1996 and 1999 for accounts of Quesnay's influence on Smith in Paris in 1765–6. Skinner finds Turgot superior to Quesnay, and his influence therefore more significant. Turgot does not receive an acknowledgement equivalent to Quesnay's in *The Wealth of Nations*, and the French account of capital accumulation and surplus-creation and their impact on economic growth which Smith absorbed into his own political economy after his visit to Paris, is far more fully developed in Quesnay.

References

Allais, M. (1992) "The General Theory of Surpluses as a Formalization of the Underlying Theoretical Thought of Adam Smith, his Predecessors and his Contemporaries", in M. Fry (ed.), *Adam Smith's Legacy*, London: Routledge.

Argenson, M. d' (1859-67) *Journal et Mémoires*, ed. E. J. B. Rathery, 9 vols, Paris.

Cantillon, R. [1755] (1952) *Essai sur la nature du commerce en général*, Paris: INED (2nd edn 1997).

Charles, L. (1999) "'Le masque et la plume': la contribution négligée de F. Quesnay à l'*Essai sur l'amelioration des terres*", *Économies et Sociétés* Série PE, 29: 29–59.

—— (2000) "*The Encyclopédie* to the *Tableau économique*: Quesnay on the freedom of grain trade and economic growth", *European Journal of the History of Economic Thought* 7(1) (Spring): 1–21.

Condillac, abbé de (1775) *Cours d'études pour l'instruction du Prince de Parme*, Paris, reprinted (1798) in *Oeuvres de Condillac*, Paris, vols 5–21.

—— (1776) *Le Commerce et le Gouvernement*, Paris, trans. as *Commerce and Government* (1997) ed. S. M. and W. Eltis, Aldershot: Elgar.

Dangeul, P. de (1754) *Remarques sur les avantages et les désavantages de la France et de la Grande-Bretagne* (supposedly translated from the English of John Nickolls), Paris.

Eagly, R. V. (1974) *The Structure of Classical Economic Theory*, New York: Oxford University Press.

Eltis, W. (1984) *The Classical Theory of Economic Growth*, Basingstoke: Macmillan.

—— (1996) "The Grand Tableau of François Quesnay's Economics," *European Journal of the History of Economic Thought* 3(1) (Spring): 21–43.

Galiani, abbé F. (1992–6) *Correspondence: Ferdinando Galiani with Louise d'Épinay*, ed. G. Dulac, 5 vols, Paris: Desjonquères.

Hecht, J. (1958) "La vie de François Quesnay," in *François Quesnay et la Physiocratie*, 2 vols, Paris: Institut National d'Études Démographiques (subsequently INED): 211–94.

Herbert, C.-J. (1755) *Essai sur la police générale des grains: sur leur prix & sur les effects de l'agriculture*, Paris.

Herlitz, L. (1996) "From Spending and Reproduction to Circuit Flow and Equilibrium: The Two Conceptions of Tableau Économique," *European Journal of the History of Economic Thought* 3(1) (Spring): 1–20.

Hicks, J. (1977) *Economic Perspectives: Further Essays on Money and Growth*, Oxford: Clarendon.

Hollander, S. (1973–97) *Studies in Classical Political Economy. I The Economics of Adam Smith* (1973); *II The Economics of David Ricardo* (1979); *III The Economics of John Stuart Mill*

(1985); *IV The Economics of Thomas Robert Malthus* (1997), Toronto: University Press.
—— (1980) "On Professor Samuelson's Canonical Model of Political Economy," *Journal of Economic Literature* 18: 559–74.
Hume, D. (1752) *Political Discourses*, Edinburgh, included in *Essays, Moral, Political and Literary*, Indianapolis: Liberty Fund (1985).
Hutchison, T. (1988) *Before Adam Smith: the Emergence of Political Economy 1662–76*, Oxford: Blackwell.
Kaplan, S. (1976) *Bread, Politics and Political Economy in the Reign of Louis XV*, 2 vols, The Hague: Martinus Nijhoff.
Marmontel, J. -F. (1972) *Mémoires*, Paris: Clermont-Ferrand.
Marx, K. (1969–71) *Theories of Surplus Value*, 3 vols, Moscow: Progress for Lawrence and Wishart.
Matthews, R. C. O., Feinstein, C. F. and Odling-Smee, J. C. (1982) *British Economic Growth, 1856–1973*, Oxford: Oxford University Press.
Meek, R. L. (1962) *The Economics of Physiocracy*, London: Allen and Unwin.
Mill, J. S. (1848) *Principles of Political Economy*, 2 vols, London.
Mirabeau, Marquis de and Quesnay, F. (1756–60) *L'Ami des hommes*, 8 parts, Avignon.
—— (1763) *Philosophie rurale*, Paris (2nd edn 1764, Scientia Verlag Aalen 1972).
Negishi, T. (1989) "Expenditure Patterns and International Trade in Quesnay's Tableau Économique," in *Developments in Japanese Economics*, Tokyo: Academic Press/ Harcourt Brace Jovanovich.
Pattullo, H. (1758) *Essai sur l'amélioration des terres*, Paris.
Petty, W. (1662) *A Treatise of Taxes and Contributions*, London, reprinted in 1899 in *The Economic Writings of Sir William Petty*, ed. C. H. Hull, 2 vols, Cambridge: Cambridge University Press: 2–97.
Political Economy Club (1921) *Centenary Volume*, London: Macmillan.
Pressman, S. (1994) *Quesnay's Tableau Économique*, Fairfield, N.J.: Kelley.
Quesnay, F. (1756), "Fermiers," INED: 427–58.
—— (1757) "Grains," INED: 459–510.
—— (1757) "Hommes," INED: 511–78.
—— (1758–9) *Tableau Économique.* republished 1972 as *Quesnay's Tableau Économique*, ed. M. Kuczynski and R. L. Meek, London: Macmillan.
—— (1768) *Physiocratie*, ed. S. Du Pont, Paris (Quesnay's articles in this are all included in INED).
Ricardo, D. (1820) "Funding System," Supplement to the 4th, 5th and 6th editions of the *Encylopedia Britannica*, reprinted in 1952–73 in *The Works and Correspondence of David Ricardo*, ed. P. Sraffa, 11 vols, Cambridge: Cambridge University Press, vol. 4: 149–200.
Samuelson, P. A. (1978) "The Canonical Classical Model of Political Economy," *Journal of Economic Literature* 16 (December): 1415–34.
Say, J-B. (1803) *Trait, d'économie politique*, Paris (2nd edn 1814, 3rd edn 1817, 4th edn 1819, 5th edn 1826, 6th edn 184).
Skinner, A. (1996) *A System of Social Science: Papers Relating to Adam Smith*, 2nd edn, Oxford: University Press.
—— (1999) "Adam Smith and Physiocracy", in R. E. Backhouse and J. Creedy (eds), *From Classical Economics to the Theory of the Firm: Essays in Honour of D. P. O'Brien*, Cheltenham UK and Northampton, Mass., USA: Elgar.
Smith, A. (1776) *An Inquiry into the Nature and Causes of the Wealth of Nations*, 2 vols, London (repr. Oxford University Press, 1976).
Spengler, J. J. (1945) "The Physiocrats and Say's Law of Markets," *Journal of Political Economy* 53 (September, December).
Steiner, P. (1998) *La "Science Nouvelle" de l'économie politique*, Paris: PUF.

Théré, C. (1988) "Economic Publishing and Authors, 1566–1789" in G. Faccarello (ed.), *Studies in the History of French Political Economy: from Bodin to Walras*, London: Routledge: 1–56.

Vaggi, G. (1987) *The Economics of François Quesnay*, London: Macmillan.

Voltaire, F-M. and Arouet, M. de (1768) *L'Homme aux Quarante Écus*, Paris.

—— (1770–5) "Bled ou blé," in "Questions sur l'encyclopédie distribuées en forme de dictionnaire par des amateurs," in *Collection complète des Oeuvres de Mr. de Voltaire: dernière édition*, 49 vols, Paris, vol. 37: 103–18.

11 J-B. Say and the French liberal school of the nineteenth century
Outside the canon?

Richard Arena

As Schumpeter (1954: 379–80) and Hicks (1983: 6–9) noticed, the period of time which elapsed from 1790–1870 is often associated with the "classical age." Both of them tried to define the analytical unity of this "age," through the description of the "classic scheme of the economic process" (Schumpeter 1954: 554–70) or of the " revolution" "which led to the establishment of 'classical' economics" (Hicks 1983: 6–9). If this analytical unity seems uncontroversial, it does not mean that it implied a degree of homogeneity comparable to a canonical knowledge. One of the empirical proofs of this assertion is provided by the mere existence of the French classical school of the nineteenth century. The period 1790–1870 is indeed, more or less, the period of birth and decline of this school and the investigation of its analytical nature will lead to an unquestionable conclusion.

Nineteenth-century French liberal contributions certainly belong to the classical approach but their significant differences with British (and, especially, Ricardian) political economy exhibit the outlines of a specific school which differs from both the so-called "classical" and "Walrasian" traditions. Therefore, it is impossible to characterize the French liberal school as a simple stage on the steady path from Ricardian towards the canon of Walrasian and, hence, modern economic theory.

Our contribution will include four steps. First, we shall consider the origin, birth and the constitution of the theoretical originality of the French liberal school. The name of Jean-Baptiste Say is obviously the crucial reference of this part. In the second and the third stages of our investigation, we shall analyze successively the originality of the methodological and the analytical approaches of the French classical school, especially in contrast with the British one. Finally, our fourth step will consist in the study of the deliberate strategy of diffusion and reinforcement of the liberal message privileged by the nineteenth-century French classical economists till the moment of their decline.

Origin and birth of French classical political economy

Jean-Baptiste Say is unquestionably the father of the French classical school. But his first project was not to found a new school but rather to contribute to the diffusion of Smith's school from *The Wealth of Nations* in Continental Europe. Say did not pretend to build a new analytical system. In the first edition of his *Traité d'Economie Politique* (Say 1803), he introduced his own contribution as a mere exposition of Smith's book, which he considered stimulating but also confusing:

> Smith's book is mainly a confused collection of the soundest principles of *political economy*, that are backed up with intelligent examples; a collection of the most curious body of *statistics* mixed in with instructive thoughts. But neither of these subjects is fully dealt with. His book is a vast chaos of right ideas and positive knowledge jumbled up.
>
> (Say 1803: iv)[1]

This is why Say only pretended to clarify some of Smith's issues:

> I would therefore be of great help to science by freeing it from the interference of discussions that prevent us from linking the different parts and understanding of the whole, even though I would not have made it stride forward.
>
> (Say 1803: xxvi)[2]

We know, however, that Ricardo and Malthus also asserted that their purpose was a mere extension of Smith's contribution. We also know that Say, Ricardo and Malthus actually offered three very different interpretations of *The Wealth of Nations* and that, therefore, they had to be considered as original thinkers. Moreover, Say's modesty progressively decreased with time. As soon as the second edition of the *Traité* was published, things changed. The reference to a mere exposition of *The Wealth of Nations* was omitted and Say stressed his own scientific discoveries (Say 1814). In the same period, he published his *Catéchisme d'Economie Politique*, the contents of which, according to the author, had been made original, that is, different from Smith's contribution. Refusing now, implicitly, to refer to *The Wealth of Nations*, he observed, "When you do not set out truths on behalf of a recognized authority, not only do you have to be right, but you also have to prove it" (Say 1821: 310).[3]

Say continued to stress his differences with Smith but this attitude was progressively and predominantly replaced by a reaction against the British heirs of Adam Smith. It was convincingly noticed that this "third stage" of the process of diffusion of Say's ideas began with his comments on Ricardo's *Principles* (Steiner 1986: 76). Say indeed reacted against the abstract method of British economists and, especially, of David Ricardo.

Ricardo was indeed blamed for his revival of Quesnay's deductivism and Say opposed to it a more inductive conception:

> Without referring to algebraic formulas that would obviously not apply to the political world, a couple of writers from the eighteenth century and from Quesnay's dogmatic school on the one hand, and some English econo-mists from David Ricardo's school on the other hand, wanted to introduce a kind of argumentation which I believe, as a general argument, to be inapplicable to political economy as to all sciences that acknowledge only experience as

#103 03-17-2011 9:43PM
      out to p10128931.

a foundation. By that I mean the argumentation that lies on abstract ideas. Condillac has rightly noticed that abstract reasoning is nothing but a calculation with different signs. But an argument does not provide, nor does an equation, the data that is essential, as far as experimental sciences are concerned, to get to the discovery of truth. Ricardo set it in a hypothesis that cannot be attacked because, based on observations that cannot be questioned, he imposes his reasoning until he draws the last consequences from it, but he does not compare its results with experience. Reasoning never wavers, but an often unnoticed and always unpredictable vital force diverts the facts from our calculation. Ricardo's followers ... considered real cases as exceptions and did not take them into account. Freed from the control of experience, they rushed into metaphysics deprived of applications; they have transformed political economy into a verbal and argumentative science. Trying to broaden it, they have only led it to its downfall.

(Say 1826: *Discours Préliminaire*)[4]

This dissent from Ricardo's method was considered by Say as a fundamental issue and this view was then adopted by most of Say's French liberal followers, forming therefore one of the crucial components of the liberal theoretical framework in France.

We shall come back to this theme later but, for the moment, its evocation is sufficient to exhibit Say's debt to British political economy. It is indeed clear that the reading of Smith by Say and the correspondence and exchanges between the author of the *Traité*, on one side, and Ricardo, Mill or Malthus, on the other side, strongly contributed to the formation of the French liberal school. However, other influences might also be mentioned which derived predominantly from the French economic tradition of the eighteenth century.

The first influence is certainly the direct influence of *Idéologie* since, during the French Revolution, Say himself had been the board editor of the *Décade Philosophique, Politique et Littéraire*, which he founded and in which he welcomed the *Idéologues* of the period. *Idéologie* was defined by his founder, Destutt de Tracy, as the "science of ideas." Based on Condillac's sensualism, this "science" was actually a philosophical system that considered sensations as the source of knowledge. The interaction of those sensations and the human mind created ideas that permitted a method of investigation of reality consisting in reducing it to simple and fundamental elements from which it was then possible to explain more complex phenomena.

The second influence is more diffuse. It is related to some of the concepts introduced by French economists or thinkers during the eighteenth century. Thus, the various debates on the notion of natural order (especially amongst physiocrats and "dissenters") strongly inspired French liberal economists who often distinguished efficient and inefficient institutions according to their adequacy within this order. The stress on the role of entrepreneurs within the French liberal representation of the economy is also due to Turgot's influence, for instance.

The last (but not least) influence certainly derives from Condillac's theory of value based on the concepts of utility and scarcity, especially, as it is exposed in *Le commerce et le gouvernement considérés relativement l'un à l'autre* (Condillac 1776).

These three influences combine to create a specific inspiration based on the French national tradition and distinct from the British one. They contributed, therefore, to the birth of a particular approach which Say built progressively and which differed from Smith's, Ricardo's as well as Malthus's theoretical constructions, even if their respective influences had been taken into account.

The methodological foundations of the French liberal school

As we already emphasized, Say did not share the Ricardian conception of scientific abstraction. According to him, economics was both a "*science de raisonnement*" and a "*science d'observation.*" He indeed accepted the deductive interpretation of economics in so far as it was "based on unwavering foundations, as far as the principles he uses as a basis are rigorous deductions of indisputable general facts" (Say 1803: *Discours Préliminaire*).[5]

However, this deductive dimension of political economy could not be stressed too much:

> Political economy, like exact sciences, consists of a few basic principles and a great many corollaries which are deduced from these principles ... But it would be hopeless to think that we could be more precise and give this science a definite procedure, using mathematics as the solution to the problem. Since minus and plus signs are used to quantify those values and quantities which the science deals with, it seems it might be included in the mathematical field. Yet these values and quantities are also influenced by possibilities, needs, and human will. It is true that we can predict how these actions are going to evolve, but we cannot rigorously witness their influence.
>
> (Say 1826: *Discours Préliminaire*)[6]

Economics is indeed also a "*science d'observation*":

> We must ... check every time we can, that the result we have been led to by reasoning is confirmed by reality. This is the way of sailors. They try to find where they are situated on the map, and correct their course every time they approach land with a known position from previous observations.
>
> Once applied to political economy, this method takes science away from the land of hypothesis, systematic and purely conjectural doctrines, to make it a positive science. Since its laws are no longer imaginary systems, but truths based on facts that anyone can witness, we are able to co-ordinate and develop them in such an order that they clarify one another. We have been able to make of it a solid body of doctrines that simplifies its study which will soon become common.
>
> Thus, political economy was wrongly considered as a science based on hypotheses rather than experience: it is indeed totally based on experience; but it needs people to take the nature of things observed into

account, along with experiences, to make sure that the phenomenon observed is truly the result of what we are looking at as its cause.

(Say 1843: 7)[7]

Say's methodological position is therefore well balanced and combines deduction and induction synthetically. However, compared to the typical British position – that is the Ricardian one – it appeared to be more inductive than deductive. This circumstance probably explains why most of Say's followers privileged the definition of economics as a "*science d'observation.*"

J. A. Blanqui and C. Dunoyer, who both belonged to the first generation of liberal economists, stressed the inductive aspect of economics. On one side, "political or moral sciences are no more arbitrary than physics or biology: in all of these sciences, we only learn through observation" (Dunoyer 1817: I; 163).[8] On the other side, in his *Histoire de l'économie politique en Europe*, Blanqui heavily criticized the physiocrats, the Ricardians and the mathematical economists because of their common advocacy of economic abstraction (Blanqui 1882; see also Arena 1991b: ch. 3).

L. Wolowski (1848), L. Reybaud (1862) and H. Baudrillart (1872), who might be included in the second generation of the French classical school shared the same hostility against deductive methodology and, even more, against the use of mathematics. L. Reybaud harshly criticized the Ricardians who wished "to feed principles with equations and give political economy a false air of algebra in order to impress minds who look for deep thinking" (Reybaud 1862: 301).[9] Finally, within the last generation of the school, P. Leroy-Beaulieu (1896), G. de Molinari (1887) and Y. Guyot (1881) again defended the conception of economics as a "*science d'observation*" or even a "*science expérimentale*" (Leroy-Beaulieu 1880: 9).

Only few authors resisted to this inductivistic tendency. P. Rossi, who was the most Ricardian of our authors and was also more Italian than French, defended the deductive approach:

> When starting with general data I came up with deductions. When I prove these truths that are so common today and yet were unknown for so long, does science not reveal truths *sui generis*, truths that can only be linked to the production of wealth and are true in every time and place? I therefore boldly came to the conclusion that the science of political economy, considered on a general and invariable point of view, is rather a science of reasoning than of observation.
>
> (Rossi 1854: I; 34)[10]

Induction could only modify these general and universal laws or rules but it could not change their substance. Fundamentally, theoretical economics was what Rossi calls a "pure science" or a "rational" science (ibid.: I: 36–7).

Rossi is unquestionably the only member of the school who privileged so strongly the deductive approach. J. Garnier took a more eclectic position, trying to preserve the methodological unity of liberal economists around the well-balanced position of J-B. Say (see Arena 1991a: 114–15; see, especially, Garnier 1858). This was also the position of J. C. Courcelle-Seneuil who tried to criticize both the Ricardian and the historical schools as respective examples of extreme and misleading deductivist and inductivist conceptions (Courcelle-Seneuil 1865; see also Marco 1991a: 150–1).

If the liberal school was not purely inductivist, it is nevertheless clear that it raised strong objections against the use of deduction and of mathematics in economics. This feature distinguished it from the British classical school that was not so hostile to abstraction. Therefore, it provided a first distinguishing characteristic – methodological – of the French liberal school: its anti-formalism and its prejudice in favor of induction.

The theoretical contents of the French liberal school

We now enter into the core of the liberal school, namely, its analytical contents. A part of these contents is unquestionably common to all members of the classical approach, either British or French. From this angle, we might refer, for instance, to the importance of the division of labor seen as the best means of increasing the amount of social wealth. This theme is present in British as well as in French classical political economy: it refers to what Hicks called "the study of the flow of wealth" and this author pointed out this study as the main purpose of the classical tradition (Hicks 1983: 7).

We could also mention the contents of the classical economic process of production and exchange. This process supposes the expense of advances in order to obtain a surplus-product that is the condition of economic reproduction and growth:

> In a highly populated and advanced society, almost the whole consumption process takes place after trade ... You have to sell what you produce to be able to buy what you want to consume ... For all social wealth, the goal of its output is consumption. The effect of saving and accruing is not to limit consumption, but to increase it. Savings are not taken away from consumption, they are only taken away from reproductive consumption. So, saving does not harm consumption, on the contrary, it increases it: while capital is being consumed by producing companies, it is restored by these companies to be consumed again, and so on, until it gets dissipated by a sterile economy.
>
> (Say 1835)[11]

This recursive conception of economic activity is obviously common to the majority of the classical economists, namely, Say but also Smith, Ricardo, Malthus and, even, Quesnay.

We might also refer to a third common feature of British and French classical economics, that is ... Say's law! This law was indeed rejected by some "dissenters," such as Malthus or Sismondi, but the major part of classical economists accepted it, so that it can be incorporated within the legacy of the classical tradition.

Other themes, however, concern the specific features of the French classical school. We shall now consider them successively.

Individual agents

The French liberal economists of the nineteenth century attributed a major role to individual agents in the working of economic activity. However, their conception of individual agents was very different from the one that Walras and the Lausanne school later popularized.

Say's individual agents are not isolated in the subjectivity of their preferences or their utility functions. In *Olbie ou Essai sur les Moyens de Réformer les Moeurs d'une Nation*, Say tries to show that two motives explain individual behaviors: self-interest, on one hand; but vanity also.[12] Now:

> Natural philosophers seem to believe that self-love or self-interest drives people's actions more than self-esteem or vanity. I would think it is the opposite. Vanity has generally more power over people than self-love has. We need only observe the number of times when men act proudly and go against their interests.
>
> (Say 1800: 121)[13]

If self-interest clearly fits with the Walrasian view of individual agents, vanity is however absent from the *Elements d'Economie Pure*. By contrast, according to Say's view, the realisation of general interest derives from the combination of self-interest and vanity, both seen as selfish motives. Vanity indeed helps individual agents to correct the possible excesses of self-interest. It makes them conscious of what could be considered as socially questionable in their behaviors. Therefore, in a way, they go beyond the limits of realm of their self-interest and take into account their social role within the normal working of the economic system, "Each and every one of us should know the place he occupies within the mechanics of society; one has to know if his wheel helps to make the machinery run" (Say 1803: xxxii, xxxiv.)[14] Self-interest then becomes "enlightened interest" and individuals can be characterized as enlightened agents.

This reference to enlightenment means that Say's agents are always socialized. They are not isolated as in a state of nature. They are supposed to have learned social rules through education, social interaction and access to social conscience (Say 1800: 71). Therefore, agents are social at once. They do not need to become social beings through their participation in exchange relations. This is why Say always refers to the concept of *l'homme en société*:

> In moral sciences, which are only the knowledge of laws according to which men's actions take place, the nature of things is mainly the nature of man. In other words, man as nature made him, with his powers, his envies, and his faults. It is obvious that his actions are the result of his determinations, and his determinations the result of his nature.
>
> If someone said that nature varies from one person to another and that

we need to study each person individually to know humankind as a whole, I would deny this assertion; I would answer that there is a certain number of qualities, some physical and moral properties that are innate to the nature of man which you cannot be exempted from when you are a human being. Have we stopped considering physiology or the study of the living human body as a science because some stomachs digest dairy food easily while others have trouble digesting solid food? Other people have opposite faculties; short-sighted eyes that cannot see far objects and far-sighted that cannot see near objects. Shall we stop studying *the moral man* [emphasis added/R. A.] because he has tendencies that differ? etc. . . .

But man does not only act as an individual. Nature made him live not only within a family, but also within society. Under the name of society the union of a certain number of families builds up a distinct moral being who has his own way of behaving passed on to him from his nature and the nature of other members, that is to say the nature of human beings of whom he is composed.

Therefore, we can say that political sciences exist just as moral sciences do. I use the word science in plural because *man within society* [emphasis added/R. A.} can be observed in many different ways.

(Say 1819: 92)[15]

Therefore, as Tiran (1995: 114) accurately noticed, Say's methodological individualism might be characterized as "a structural or an institutional individualism" (in the sense of F. Bourricaud (1977), for instance).

Social utility

If Say's individuals are enlightened, their economic needs must reflect the degree of civilization of the country in which they are living:

> The right valuation of things depends on judgement, intelligence, habits, and prejudices of the people who value it. Sane morals, precise notions about their interests, lead men to a right valuation of real goods. Political economy considers this valuation as a fact, and leaves science of the *moral man* and *man within society* [emphasis added/R. A.] take care of their enlightenment and direction on this point as on other acts of life.
>
> (Say 1803: 50)[16]

This relation between individual agents and social needs exerts a substantial influence on Say's conception of utility.

First, in Say's conception, utility cannot be assimilated to the subjective utility of marginal theory. Utility is defined by a social agent and not by a Walrasian individual. That means that the utility of goods must reflect social needs or the needs of the average civilized man (*l'homme en société*) and not strictly subjective ones related to one single person.

This is certainly why utility is defined by Say as a specific characteristic of goods, namely as one of their internal dimensions, "The ability of certain things to satisfy men's various needs, let me call it *utility*" (Say 1803: 51).[17] Say's utility, therefore, strongly differs from Paretian "ophelimity." It is very close to the notion of social use. This is why utility is generally defined by Say in relation with the distinction between the usual categories of social needs: food, clothing, housing, health, and so on:

> The value that men attach to things is first founded on the use they make of these things. Some are for food, others for clothing; some, like houses, protect us in harsh climate. Others, like adornments, embellish houses to satisfy our need for taste. Therefore, if people attach great value to something, it is because it is useful. They would not give anything for something that is good for nothing.
> (Say 1803: 50)[18]

This relation between utility and social use implies the existence of some hierarchy amongst social needs:

> Each individual or family . . . has to classify their needs to be able to satisfy the ones that are the most important to them, rather than the ones that are less significant. This classification has a great influence on the well being of families and humanity in general.
> (Say 1803: 320–1)[19]

Obviously, this classification strongly depends on both the geographical and the historical contexts (see Say 1821: 316) but this is a further indication of the differences between Say's social utility and Walras's subjective utility.

The social character of utility implies the concept of *valeur reconnue* (acknowledged value) (Say 1820: 299). In other words, in order to acquire this character, it is not sufficient that somebody attribute subjectively some utility to a given commodity. This attribution must be confirmed by society, namely by somebody else. Therefore, having in mind the fact that the price is the "measurement of the value of goods" and that "value is the measurement of the utility which was attributed to them" (Say 1803: 51) it is easier to understand why:

> As long as other individuals agree to give *something else* with its own value in order to get what we possess, then the value of what we possess is no longer arbitrary. It is equal to the value of what we are given in exchange.
> (Say 1819: 98)[20]

The preceding remarks help us to understand why value is the only means to measure utility. According to Say, utility cannot be measured with social objectivity if it is not "acknowledged," namely if it is not transformed in value. This view is defended by the followers of Say and, especially by Garnier who noted, "Utility can be evaluated by what needs are satisfied, but it can only really be measured by quantity (figures, weight and measures) or value" (Garnier 1880: 289).[21] It is easier then to understand the misunderstandings, which occurred between Walras and the French classical economists. One of the analytical reasons for which these classical economists refused Walras's theory of general economic equilibrium was indeed their objection to the measurement of utility. For the French liberals, Walras was wrong when he measured utility directly. The satisfaction of human beings could not be evaluated objectively without the help of value.

Garnier is a good example of the continuity amongst the liberal school from this angle. He describes utility as an intrinsic quality of objects, "whether it exists [in them] naturally or whether it has been created and put in them by the effort and work of men" (Garnier 1880: 8). This characterization of utility confirms that of Say and helps to explain why it is not easy to define individual utility within the theoretical framework of the French classical tradition.

Moreover, in Say as well as in Garnier or in the contributions of most of the French liberal economists, the notion of marginal utility and, *a fortiori*, the principle of decreasing marginal utility are clearly absent. This explains why the French classicals neglect or misinterpret the notion of scarcity. Garnier, as well as most of the members of the liberal school, claims that scarcity is also a cause of value. However, Garnier's definition of scarcity fundamentally differs from that of Walras. Scarcity is not characterized as the intensity of the last need satisfied and does not relate utility with the quantity of good. Scarcity is actually "an expression which is not very accurate" (Garnier 1880: 278), and which measures "the small quantity in its relation with abundance" and expresses "insufficiency whatever the quantity is, in relation with the need for the good" (ibid.: 272).

The French liberal economists never succeeded in formulating a consistent theory of value and prices since they did not clearly specify what meaning they attributed to the concepts of supply and demand, and since they never related accurately utility, scarcity, demand and prices. However, in spite of these inconsistencies, they had in their minds a conception of individual agents and of utility which completely discards the misleading view according to which, in the framework of value theory, *"J.B. Say se conduit en précurseur des marginalistes"* (J-B. Say acts as the precursor of the marginalists) (Reynaud quoted by Bourcier de Carbon 1971, I: 233).

The entrepreneur

As we know, the importance of entrepreneurs is also a major theme of the French classical school, strongly rooted in the tradition of the eighteenth century. Say characterized the entrepreneur as an agent who first demonstrated moral qualities:

> If you consider capacity only, more moral qualities compose the industrial world than is commonly considered. When we examined what kind of services the industrial entrepreneur contributes to production, we discovered what qualities, what talents he must possess to succeed in the kind of work he has taken up. Besides the knowledge of his trade, he needs good judgement, constancy, and a good understanding of people
> (Say 1843: 318)[22]

Moral qualities are however insufficient if they are not associated with a sufficient volume of capital. Finally, the entrepreneur must also be able to deal with the fundamental uncertainty that prevails in his activity (Say 1843: 329).

This characterization of entrepreneurs and the stress put on their importance provide a recurrent theme of the French liberal school. Blanqui strongly emphasized the role of entrepreneurs, considering them as the basis of the new liberal society to be built (Demier 1986: 108). Moreover, he strongly contributed to the fame and the development of the *Ecole Spéciale de Commerce* which was supposed to deliver the new message of liberalism and entrepreneurship to young students (again see Demier, 1986).

Dunoyer is another significant example of the emphasis of French liberal economists on the character of the entrepreneur. In 1827, Dunoyer even criticized Say for being too silent on this theme (Dunoyer 1827: 214–5). As Pénin (1991: 63–5) accurately observed, Dunoyer both analyses the essential functions devoted to entrepreneurs and the empirical consequences that these functions exert on concrete production decisions.

French liberal economists were not always apologetic for entrepreneurs. They also criticized their defects and tried to show how the French class of entrepreneurs could be improved by education (Garnier 1846). They also tried to find the main causes of business bankruptcies (Leroy-Beaulieu 1888).

The formation of the French liberal school

The history of the French liberal period may be divided in three main periods. The first consists in the progressive consolidation of the approach we just referred to. Say and, to a far less extent, Dunoyer, Bastiat and Rossi were the main builders of the French school. While constructing this school, French liberal economists also tried to diffuse their central message. During the first part of the nineteenth century (that is from 1800–48), this message was a progressive and, even, a revolutionary one. Thus, during the Restoration, Say was both supported by the most liberal and attacked by the most reactionary parts of the French political establishment. He used what possibilities he could to deliver and diffuse the message that the political revolution had more or less come to an end but had also to be completed by an economic revolution, consisting in the generalization of economic freedom. Blanqui and Dunoyer also defended the same views, and were convinced that this revolution would solve the problem of social poverty by permitting economic growth and industrial development.

However, Blanqui was constantly watched by the King's Police because of the contents of his lectures in *Ecole Spéciale de Commerce*, while Dunoyer was strongly attacked and then prosecuted because of his role in the review *Le Censeur Européen*. The liberal conceptions of Say, Blanqui and Dunoyer indeed strongly contrasted with the predominant message of Conservative Catholics. Villeneuve-Bargemont offers a significant instance of these anti-liberal views. In his *Economie Politique Chrétienne* (Villeneuve-Bargemont 1834), he violently condemned those who defended the new "despotic and oppressive" feodality of entrepreneurs.

After the Restoration, however, things changed drastically. The July

Monarchy clearly supported the French liberal tradition which was then consolidated until the 1848 Revolution. Thus, for instance, Dunoyer became Prefect of Allier and Somme, from 1833–7, while Blanqui became Deputy for Bordeaux from 1846–8.

After the 1848 Revolution, a new period began in which the monarchist conservatives had lost a large part of their influence but in which the opposition between liberals and socialists became predominant. During this period which corresponds to the peak of the French classical school, liberal economists tended to become the defenders of the existing social order and could no longer be considered as revolutionary thinkers. Some of them, like Garnier, Courcelle-Seneuil or Wolowski, had rather difficult relations with the Second Empire but most of them were satisfied with the political regimes which emerged after the Bourbon Restoration, from the July Monarchy to the Third Republic, passing through the Second Republic and the Second Empire. However, all of them dedicated an important part of their energy to attack the two schools they considered to be the main dangers: the protectionists and the socialists.

A third period began after 1870, during which the school gradually faded. On one side, the main figures of the French liberal school disappeared. On the other side, the liberals lost the battle of the creation of chairs of political economy within the Faculties of Law. In 1873, Paul Cauwès, a protectionist economist strongly opposed to the liberal school, was appointed to the first Faculty Chair created in Paris. In 1877, other chairs were created in France but only some of them were occupied by liberal economists, so that the dominance of the liberal school weakened.

Finally, in 1887, a new review (still existing today), the *Revue d'Economie Politique* was founded by a coalition of economists who had in common their opposition to the French liberal school. This journal which was supported by Charles Gide as well as by Paul Cauwès and Léon Walras, became a machine of war against the classical school.

These three periods in the history of the French liberal school show that its members were not pure theoreticians enclosed in their ivory tower. They tried to interact with their social environment and to establish an intellectual leadership devoted to the development of the influence of liberalism on the French society. This strategy was strongly helped by the familial links that homogenized the group of liberal economists. A first instance is given by the Say family. Thus, Horace, Jean-Baptiste Say's son, helped him to lecture to the audience of the *Conservatoire des Arts et Métiers* when he became ill, acting as a kind of assistant professor (Steiner 1986: 86). Louis, Jean-Baptiste's brother, was an entrepreneur in the sugar industry but he did not hesitate to dedicate a book to political economy in which he discussed the value theory of the *Traité* (Lutfalla 1991: 27–9). Léon, Jean-Baptiste's grandson, was a banker, then a politician and finally an academician, member of the *Académie des Sciences Morales et Politiques* (Lutfalla 1991a: 17). Charles Comte, one of the first French liberal economists, married Jean-Baptiste Say's daughter (Levan-Lesmesle 1986: 225).

Another instance, chosen in the second part of the nineteenth century, is offered by the Leroy-Beaulieu family. Thus, Paul Leroy-Beaulieu married

Michel Chevalier's daughter, while his brother, Anatole, became the manager of the *Ecole Libre des Sciences Politiques*. Pierre, Paul's son, was a member of the Parliament and strongly helped the liberals of the *Société d'Economie Politique* (Bourcier de Carbon 1971: I, 126–7). Those cases are only examples but they might be generalized: Joseph Garnier married Adolphe Blanqui's sister (Arena 1991a: 112); Léon Faucher was the brother-in-law of Louis Wolowski (Lutfalla 1991b: 186), who was himself ... the father-in-law of Louis Passy, Frederic's cousin (Lutfalla 1991: 187); and so on. The complete history of the familial relations amongst French liberals is certainly complex and is still to be done! These familial links undoubtedly reinforced the cohesion of the liberal group but this is only a dimension of what has to be described as a real strategy of intellectual, cultural and political penetration of the French society.

The social strategy of the French liberal school

This strategy was developed by liberal economists in three directions: educational institutions, scientific societies and economic journals. Liberal economists devoted a strong energy in order to control the educational institutions that played a major role in the process of diffusion of political economy. The first to be mentioned is certainly the *Athénée*, a private school, in which Say (from 1816–20), Dunoyer (from 1824–6), Blanqui (from 1827–9) and Garnier (from 1842–5) successively delivered conferences and lectures to a rather large audience (Steiner 1986: 79–84). The second one corresponds to another private school called *l'Ecole Spéciale de Commerce* and strongly supported by the Paris elite of banking and business. It knew a very substantial success amongst young entrepreneurs and strongly contributed to the diffusion of liberal political economy. Blanqui was the first lecturer of political economy at the *Ecole* from 1821 till 1848. Then, he became the manager of the institution and Garnier replaced him till the replacement of the school by the *Ecole Commerciale* in 1863 (Demier 1986; Arena 1991a).The third place to consider is the chair of political economy in the *Conservatoire des Arts et Métiers*. Created in 1819 and devoted to "industrial economics" (because the expression "political economy" frightened the Administration), this chair was successively occupied by Say (from 1820–32), Blanqui (from 1832–54) and Wolowski (from 1839–70).

The French Grandes Ecoles can help us to complete our list. The Ecole des Ponts et Chaussées also created a chair of political economy held by Garnier (from 1847–82), Baudrillart (from 1882–92) and Colson (from 1892–1932) who were all liberal. However, in 1908, Charles Gide was appointed for lecturing in the realm of social economics and this was certainly a sign of the decline of the liberal school. Obviously, we must also mention the chair of political economy of the Collège de France. Say was the first to lecture from March 1831 to November 1832, when he died. Rossi succeeded him till 1840, when Michel Chevalier began to lecture in his turn. Finally, in 1879, Paul Leroy-Beaulieu, who was the son-in-law of Chevalier was appointed to teach. Thus, most of the institutions or places in which political economy was taught were under the control of the French liberal school and its influence became, therefore, extremely high. The peak of this influence was reached when the liberals obtained the creation of the *Ecole Libre des Sciences Politiques* in 1871:

Anatole Dunoyer, son of Charles, taught economics while Emile Levasseur, another liberal economist, was appointed as a statistician. However, in 1877, the decline soon began with the creation of twelve Faculties of law that broadly escaped from the influence of the liberal school.

This influence was not limited to the educational institutions. It also appeared in the constitution of scientific societies. From this angle, two different dimensions have to be distinguished. On one side, in 1842, the liberal economists created the Société d'Economie Politique. As Levan-Lemesle noted, "this small society began modestly by informal dinners once a month of five friends, five defenders of the liberal political economy; but in 1858, it was necessary to limit the number of members to two hundred, which is an index of the number of militants of liberal political economy" (Levan-Lemesle 1986: 227). On the other side, the liberal economists always tried to control the Académie des Sciences Morales et Politiques. Founded in 1795, it was suppressed in 1803 because of its "revolutionary" positions. Guizot re-created it in 1832. From this period onwards, various liberal economists became members of this Academy: Dunoyer, Garnier, Wolowski, Chevalier, Leroy-Beaulieu, Courcelle-Seneuil and Léon Say were all academicians.

Finally, the liberal school also succeeded in controlling an important number of journals. Dunoyer was the manager of *Le Censeur*. Bastiat directed *Le Libre-Echange*. Leroy-Beaulieu founded *L'Economiste Français*. Chevalier was the manager of *Le Globe*. Molinari was the main editor of *Le Journal des Débats*. Guyot was the owner and director of *Le Siècle*. Amongst those journals, some specific room must however be afforded to the most important of them, *Le Journal des Economistes*, which was created in 1841 and continued to represent the French official liberal viewpoint till the beginning of the Second World War, when the review disappeared.

Finally, a special mention has also to be made to the Guillaumin Publishing House which strongly contributed to the diffusion of liberal ideas through its re-edition of the great classical authors, the books of the French liberals and the publication of two large dictionaries (*Dictionnaire du Commerce*, 1837 and *Dictionnaire de l'Economie Politique*, 1852–3).

Concluding remarks

We can now sum up the different dimensions of the French liberal school. On one side, this school indeed produced a self-contained approach associated with the founder of the tradition, Jean-Baptiste Say. Say did not only build the specifically analytical features, he also codified the characteristics of an original definition of political economy. Using this definition, Say labelled the production, the distribution and the consumption of wealth as the main issues of the discipline. This triad was accepted by most of the French liberal economists of the nineteenth century, who incorporated it in their various books. A kind of new economic knowledge based on a reproductive view of the economic system then emerged, which did not consider that market exchanges were the only or, even, the main concern of economics. The views were accepted by all the following generations of liberal economists, as if Say's work had offered a final and perfect version of political economy. Therefore, a common conception of economic reality emerged, which Garnier's Treatise expressed in its way (Garnier 1880).

French liberal economists, however, were jealous of the influence of their approach. Therefore, they built and implemented a strategy for the diffusion of this message. The liberal school thus formed a homogeneous group unified by familial links, friendship and participation in common Societies and Journals. This participation strongly contributed to the diffusion of the liberal central message. It was however decisively reinforced by the strategy of control of educational institutions. This control helped French liberal economists to diffuse their views and act as if they were the only ones who could be considered "economists," as such. Their cultural, political and social predominance was no longer questionable. Economists who did not accept the liberal views were proclaimed to be "heretics": they became "socialists" or "prohibitionists"; they actually lost their right of belonging to the realm of political economy.

The decline of French political economy began coincident with its rise. It was first related to the emergence of new educational institutions, the Faculties of law, and of a new journal, the *Revue d'Economie Politique*. These institutions and this journal then offered a machine of war to those who were the opponents of the liberal school. The destruction of the orthodox school went only in a second stage and its process took a rather long time: the message survived and only disappeared progressively. However the school died and, therefore, never participated in the construction of the canon.

Notes

I would like to thank all the participants to the Conference "Reflecting on the Canon" held in Toronto on September 26, 27 and 28 1998 and, especially, Evelyn Forget for her highly valuable help, Omar Hamouda and André Lapidus for their comments, critiques and suggestions. Usual caveats apply.

1 This and subsequent notes provide original French versions of extracts translated into English in the text.
   "L'ouvrage de Smith n'est qu'un assemblage confus des principes les plus sains de l'Economie Politique appuyés d'exemples lumineux; et des notions les plus curieuses de la statistique mêlées de réflexions instructives ; mais ce n'est un traité complet ni de l'une ni de l'autre. Son livre est un vaste chaos d'idées justes, pêle-mêle avec des connaissances positives" (Say 1803: iv).
2 "Ce serait donc déjà avoir rendu un service à la science, même quand je ne l'aurais pas fait avancer d'un seul pas, que de l'avoir dégagée des discussions parasites qui empêchent d'en saisir l'ensemble et d'en lier les parties" (Say 1803: xxvi).
3 "Lorsqu'on n'expose pas des vérités au nom d'une autorité reconnue, on est obligé non seulement d'avoir raison, mais de prouver qu'on a raison" (Say 1821: 310).
4 "Quelques écrivains du XVIIIème siècle et de l'école dogmatique de Quesnay d'une part et des économistes anglais de l'école de David Ricardo d'une autre part, sans employer les formules algébriques trop évidemment inapplicables à l'ensemble politique, ont voulu y introduire un genre d'argumentation auquel je crois, en thèse générale, qu'elle se refuse, de même que toutes les sciences qui ne reconnaissent pour fondement que l'expérience: je veux dire l'argumentation qui repose sur des abstractions. Condillac a judicieusement remarqué qu'un raisonnement abstrait n'est qu'un calcul avec d'autres signes. Mais un argument ne fournit, pas plus qu'une équation, les données qui, dans les sciences expérimentales, sont indispensables

pour parvenir à la découverte de la vérité ... Une fois placée dans une hypothèse qu'on ne peut attaquer, parce qu'elle est fondée sur des observations non contestées, Ricardo pousse ses raisonnements jusqu'à leurs dernières conséquences, sans comparer leurs résultats avec ceux de l'expérience. ... Le raisonnement marche en ligne droite; mais une force vitale, souvent inaperçue et toujours incalculable fait dévier les faits loin de nos calculs ... Les partisans de Ricardo ... ont regardé les cas réels comme des exceptions et n'en ont pas tenu compte. Affranchis du contrôle de l'expérience, ils se sont jetés dans une métaphysique sans application; ils ont transformé l'économie politique en une science de mots et d'arguments; sous prétexte de l'étendre, ils l'ont poussée dans le vide" (Say 1826: *Discours Préliminaire*).

5 "établie sur des fondements inébranlables, du moment que les principes qui lui servent de base sont des déductions rigoureuses de faits généraux incontestables" (Say 1803: *Discours Préliminaire*).

6 "L'économie politique, de même que les sciences exactes, se compose d'un petit nombre de principes fondamentaux et d'un grand nombre de corollaires, ou déductions de ces principes ... Mais ce serait vainement qu'on s'imaginerait donner plus de précision et une marche sûre à cette science, en appliquant les mathématiques à la solution de ses problèmes. Les valeurs et les quantités dont elle s'occupe, étant susceptibles de plus ou de moins, sembleraient devoir entrer dans le domaine des mathématiques; mais elles sont en même temps soumises à l'influence des facultés, des besoins, des volontés des hommes; or on peut bien savoir dans quel sens agissent ces actions diverses, mais on ne peut pas apprécier rigoureusement leur influence" (Say 1826: *Discours Préliminaire*).

7 "On doit ... chaque fois qu'on le peut, vérifier si le résultat où l'on a été conduit par le raisonnement est confirmé par la réalité. C'est ainsi qu'agissent les marins. Ils cherchent, par l'estime, à connaître le point de la carte où ils se trouvent, et rectifient leur route chaque fois qu'ils touchent une terre dont la position leur est connue par des observations antérieures

Cette méthode ... une fois qu'elle a été appliquée à l'économie politique, l'a tirée de la région des hypothèses, des doctrines systématiques et purement conjecturales; elle en a fait une science positive. Ses lois n'étant plus des systèmes imaginaires, mais des vérités fondées sur des faits que tout le monde peut constater, il a été possible de les coordonner, de les développer dans un ordre qui les éclaircit les unes par les autres; on a pu en faire un corps complet de doctrine qui en facilite l'étude et la rendra bientôt générale. ...

C'est donc à tort qu'on a dit que l'économie politique était une science fondée sur les hypothèses et non sur l'expérience: elle est au contraire toute entière fondée sur l'expérience; mais elle veut que dans les jugements que l'on porte, on tienne compte de la nature des choses observées, aussi bien que des expériences, afin d'avoir la certitude que le phénomène observé est bien véritablement le résultat de celui qu'on regarde comme sa cause" (Say [1843]1968: 7).

8 "les sciences morales et politiques ne sont pas plus arbitraires que les sciences physiques ou naturelles: dans les unes comme dans les autres on ne s'instruit que par l'observation" (Dunoyer 1817: I; 163).

9 "mettre les principes au régime des équations et donner à l'économie politique un faux air d'algèbre, bien propre à en imposer aux esprits qui visent à la profondeur" (Reybaud 1862: 301).

10 "Quand, en partant des données générales, j'arrive à ces déductions; quand je démontre ces vérités aujourd'hui si triviales, mais qui ont été ignorées si longtemps, la science ne révèle-t-elle pas des vérités sui generis, qui ne se rapportent qu'à la production de la richesse et qui sont vraies en tout temps et en tout lieu? D'où je conclus hardiment que la science de l'économie politique, envisagée ainsi dans ce qu'elle a de général et d'invariable, est plutôt une science de raisonnement qu'une science d'observation" (Rossi 1854: I; 34).

11 "Dans une société nombreuse et avancée, la presque totalité des consommations ne

s'opère qu'à la suite d'un échange . . . Il faut vendre ce qu'on produit pour acheter ce que l'on veut consommer . . . Le terme de toute richesse sociale, le but de sa production est la consommation . . . L'effet de l'épargne et de l'accumulation n'est pas de restreindre cette consommation mais de l'augmenter. Les valeurs épargnées ne sont pas soustraites à toute consommation; elles sont seulement soustraites à la consommation reproductive. Loin donc que l'épargne nuise à la consommation, elle la redouble: en même temps que le capital est consommé par les producteurs, il est rétabli par eux pour être consommé de nouveau et ainsi de suite jusqu'à ce qu'il soit dissipé par une consommation stérile" (Say 1835).

12 We translated "amour-propre" or "vanité" as "vanity," but this does not mean that we assimilate Smith's and Say's respective roles of "vanity" in their constructions.

13 "Les philosophes naturalistes paraissent croire que l'amour de soi, l'intérêt dirigent les actions des hommes plus que ne le fait l'amour-propre, la vanité. Je serai tenté de croire le contraire, que la vanité exerce sur eux plus d'emprise généralement parlant que l'amour de soi. Il suffit d'observer dans combien de cas les hommes agissent par vanité d'une manière opposée à leurs intérêts" (Say 1800: 121).

14 "Il est bon que chacun connaisse la place qu'il occupe dans le mécanisme social, qu'il sache si son rouage est utile au jeu de la machine" (Say 1803: xxxii, xxxiv).

15 "Dans les sciences morales qui ne sont autres choses que la connaissance des lois suivant lesquelles arrivent les actions des hommes, la nature des choses est principalement la nature de l'homme, en d'autres mots, l'homme tel que la nature l'a fait avec ses facultés, ses appétits, ses défauts. Il est clair que ses actions sont le résultat de ses déterminations, et ses déterminations le résultat de sa nature.

Que si l'on disait que la nature varie d'un individu à l'autre et qu'il faudrait étudier chaque personne en particulier pour connaître l'humanité en général, je nierais cette assertion; je répondrais qu'il y a un certain nombre de qualités, de propriétés physiques et morales qui tiennent à la nature de l'homme et dont on ne saurait être exempt du moment qu'on est homme. A-t-on cessé de considérer la physiologie, ou l'étude du corps humain vivant comme une science pour la raison qu'il y a des estomacs qui digèrent difficilement les laitages et facilement les aliments solides, et d'autres qui ont des facultés contraires; parce qu'il y a des yeux myopes qui ne voient nettement que les objets qui sont proches et des yeux presbites qui ne distinguent bien que les objets éloignés? De même faut-il cesser d'étudier *l'homme moral* [emphasis added] parce qu'il y a des penchants qui diffèrent beaucoup les uns des autres ? etc.

. . . Mais l'homme n'a pas seulement une conduite individuelle; la nature a voulu non seulement qu'il vécut en famille ; mais qu'il vécut en société; et la réunion d'un certain nombre de familles forme sous le nom de société un certain être moral composé, qui a sa manière d'être aussi qu'il tient de sa nature et de la nature des membres, c'est-à-dire des êtres humains qui le compose.

Il y a donc des sciences politiques aussi bien que des sciences morales; je dis des sciences au pluriel, car *l'homme en société* [emphasis added] peut être observé sous plusieurs rapports" (Say 1819: 92).

16 "La juste appréciation des choses dépend du jugement, des lumières, des habitudes, des préjugés de ceux qui les apprécient. Une saine morale, des notions précises sur leurs véritables intérêts, conduisent les hommes à une juste appréciation des vrais biens. L'économie politique considère cette appréciation comme un fait, et laisse à la science de *l'homme moral* et de *l'homme en société* [emphasis added] le soin de les éclairer et de les diriger sur ce point comme dans les autres actes de la vie" (Say 1803: 50).

17 "Cette faculté qu'ont certains choses de pouvoir satisfaire aux divers besoins des hommes, qu'on me permette de la nommer utilité" (Say 1803: 51).

18 "La valeur que les hommes attachent aux choses a son premier fondement dans l'usage qu'ils en peuvent faire. Les unes servent d'aliments, les autres de vêtements; d'autres nous défendent de la rigueur du climat, comme les maisons; d'autres, telles que les ornements, les embellissements, satisfont des goûts qui sont une espèce de

besoin. Toujours est-il vrai que si les hommes attachent de la valeur à une chose, c'est en raison de ses usages: ce qui n'est bon à rien, ils n'y mettent aucun prix" (Say 1803: 50).

19 "Chaque individu, ou chaque famille . . . sont obligés de faire une sorte de classement de leurs besoins pour satisfaire ceux auxquels ils attachent le plus d'importance, préférablement à ceux auxquels ils en attachent moins. Ce classement exerce une fort grande influence sur le bonheur des familles et de l'humanité en général" (Say 1803: 320–1).

20 "du moment que d'autres particuliers consentent à donner pour avoir la chose que nous possédons, *une autre chose* qui de son côté a sa valeur, oh ! alors la valeur de celle que nous possédons n'est plus arbitraire. Elle est égale à la valeur de la chose que l'on consent à nous donner en échange" (Say 1819: 98).

21 "L'utilité s'apprécie par les besoins satisfaits mais elle n'est réellement commensurable que par la quantité (en nombres, en poids et mesures) ou par la valeur" (Garnier 1880: 289).

22 "A ne considérer que la capacité seulement, l'industrie se compose de plus de qualités morales qu'on ne le suppose communément. Lorsque nous avons cherché par quelle espèce de services un entrepreneur d'industrie concourt à la production, nous avons vu quelles qualités, quels talents il faut qu'il possède pour réussir dans l'espèce de travail qu'il a embrassé. Outre la connaissance de son art, il lui faut du jugement, de la constance, une certaine connaissance des hommes" (Say 1843: 318).

References

Arena, R. (1991a) "Joseph Garnier, libéral orthodoxe et théoricien éclectique," in Y. Breton and M. Lutfalla (eds), *L'économie politique en France au XIXe siècle*, Paris: Economica.
—— (1991b) "Adolphe-Jérôme Blanqui, un historien de l'économie aux préoccupations sociales," in Y. Breton and M. Lutfalla (eds), *L'économie politique en France au XIXe siècle*, Paris: Economica.
Baudrillart, H. (1872) *Manuel d'Economie Politique*, Paris: Guillaumin.
Blanqui, J. A. (1882) *Histoire de l'économie politique en Europe depuis les anciens jusqu'à nos jours*, 5th edn, Paris: Guillaumin.
Bourcier de Carbon, L. (1971) *Essai sur l'histoire de la pensée et des doctrines économiques*, Paris: editions Montchrestien.
Bourricaud, F. (1977) *L'individualisme institutionnel. Essai sur la sociologie de Talcott Parsons*, Paris: PUF.
Breton, Y. and Lutfalla, M. (eds) (1991a) *L'économie politique en France au XIXe siècle*, Paris: Economica.
—— (1991b) "Conclusion Générale," in Y. Breton and M. Lutfalla (eds), *L'économie politique en France au XIXe siècle*, Paris: Economica.
Condillac, E. de. (1776) *Le commerce et le gouvernement considérés relativement l'un à l'autre*, Amsterdam/Paris: Jombert et Cellot.
Coquelin, C. and Guillaumin, G. (1852–3) *Dictionnaire de l'Economie Politique*, Paris: Guillaumin.
Courcelle-Seneuil, J. G. (1865) *Traité sommaire d'économie politique*, Paris: Guillaumin.
Demier, F. (1986) "Avant-gardes économiques et diffusion de l'économie politique en France de 1815 à 1914," *Economies et Sociétés*, Oeconomia n°6.
Dictionnaire du Commerce (1837) Paris: Guillaumin.
Dunoyer, C. (1817) "Editorial", *Le Censeur*, vol. I.
—— (1827) *Revue Encyclopédique*, Paris: Guillaumin.
—— (1845) *De la liberté du travail*, 3 vols, Paris: Guillaumin.
Garnier, J. (1846) "But et limites de l'économie politique," in *Eléments de Finance*, Paris: Guillaumin.

—— (1858) *Traité théorique et pratique d'économie politique*, Paris: Guillaumin.
—— (1880) *Traité d'économie politique, sociale ou industrielle, exposé didactique des principes et des applications de cette science*, 8th ed., Paris: Guillaumin.
Guyot, Y. (1881) *La science économique, ses lois inductives*, Paris: Guillaumin.
Hicks, J. (1983) "Revolutions in economics," in *Classics and Moderns,* vol. 3 of *Collected Essays on Economic Theory,* Cambridge, Mass.: Harvard University Press.
Hollander, S. (1985) "On the Substantive Identity of the Ricardian and Neoclassical Conceptions of Economic Organization: the French Connection in British Classicism," in G. Caravale (ed.), *The Legacy of Ricardo,* Oxford: Blackwell.
Leroy-Beaulieu, P. (1888) *Précis d'Écomomie Politique*, Paris: Guillaumin.
—— (1896) *Traité théorique et pratique d'économie politique*, Paris: Guillaumin.
Levan-Lemesle, L. (1986) "De la Société d'Economie Politique aux Facultés de Droit," *Economies et Sociétés, Oeconomia* n°6.
—— (1991) "L'institutionalisation de l'économie politique en France," in Y. Breton and M. Lutfalla (eds), *L'économie politique en France au XIXe siècle*, Paris: Economica.
Lutfalla, M. (1991a) "Jean-Baptiste Say, 1767-1832, le fondateur," in Y. Breton and M. Lutfalla (eds), *L'économie politique en France au XIXe siècle*, Paris: Economica.
—— (1991b) "Louis Wolowski ou le libéralisme positif," in Y. Breton and M. Lutfalla (eds), *L'économie politique en France au XIXe siècle*, Paris: Economica.
Marco, L. (1991a) "Jean Gustave Courcelle-Seneuil, 1813–1892, L'orthodoxe intransigeant," in Y. Breton and M. Lutfalla (eds), *L'économie politique en France au XIXe siècle*, Paris: Economica.
—— (1991b) "Les agents dans pensée économique française," in Y. Breton and M. Lutfalla (eds), *L'économie politique en France au XIXe siècle*, Paris: Economica.
Molinari, G. de (1887) *Les lois naturelles de l'économie politique*, Paris: Guillaumin.
Penin, M. (1991) "Charles Dunoyer, l'échec d'un libéralisme," in Y. Breton and M. Lutfalla (eds), *L'économie politique en France au XIXe siècle*, Paris: Economica.
Reybaud, L. (1862) *Les économistes modernes*, Paris: Guillaumin.
Rossi, P. (1854) *Cours d'Economie Politique professé au Collège de France*, vol. 1, Paris: Guillaumin.
Say, J. -B. (1800) *Olbie ou Essai sur les Moyens de réformer les moeurs d'une nation*, reissued ed. J. P. Frick, Nancy: Presses Universitaires de Nancy.
—— (1803) *Traité d'Economie Politique*, 1st edn, Paris, Crapelet.
—— (1814) *Traité d'Economie Politique*, 2nd edn, Paris: Renouard.
—— [1819] (1996) "Cours à l'Athénée," in *Cours d'Economie Politique et autres essais*, ed. P. Steiner, Paris: Garnier Flammarion.
—— [1820] (1996) "Lettres à M. Malthus," in *Cours d'Economie Politique et autres essais*, ed. P. Steiner, Paris: Garnier Flammarion.
—— [1821] (1996) "Catéchisme d'Economie Politique," in *Cours d'Economie Politique et autres essais*, ed. P. Steiner, Paris: Garnier Flammarion.
—— [1826] (1971) *Traité d'Economie Politique*, 5th edn, Paris, Calmann-Levy.
—— (1835) "Economie Politique," in *Répertoire des connaissances usuelles*, vol. 23, Paris.
—— [1843] (1968) *Cours complet d'Economie Politique Pratique*, Rome: editions bizzari.
—— [1841] (1972) *Traité d'Economie Politique*, 6th edn, reprinted and ed. G. Tapinos, Paris, Calmann-Levy.
Schumpeter, J. (1954) *History of Economic Analysis*, New York: Oxford University Press.
Steiner, P. (1986) "J.B. Say et l'enseignement de l'économie politique en France," *Economies et Sociétés, Oeconomia,* n°6.
Tiran, A. (1995) "J. B. Say (1767–1832) "Essai biographique," in J-B. Say, "Manuscrits sur la monnaie, la banque et la finance," *Cahiers Monnaie et Financement*, University of Lyon II.
Villeneuve-Bargemont, A. de (1834) *Economie Politique Chrétienne*, Paris.
Wolowski, L. (1848) *Etudes d'économie politique et de statistique*, Paris: Guillaumin.

12 Priceless value (or almost so)
Misunderstood concerns of Marx and Ricardo

William J. Baumol

> When I use a word . . . it means just what I choose it to mean.
> (Humpty Dumpty)

> my training did instil in me a respect for the texts, particularly an appreciation of the necessity to read *in context*. It is disrespect for the texts that is the source of much of the myth-making that bedevils the history of economics.
> (Samuel Hollander 1998: 23)

Neither Marx nor Ricardo ever advocated a labor theory of pricing. In other words, their labor theory of value, though related to pricing, had at best an imperfect connection with the latter, so that values and prices were not used by either as perfectly synonymous. Indeed, a little thought about the matter should suggest strongly (and correctly) that for neither author was an explanation of the determination of the prices of individual commodities a matter of central concern.

These assertions, that differ so markedly from the standard representation of the ideas of these two authors, are not deduced by guesswork on my part. For both of them have left clear statements about the role of value theory in their writings, and at least Marx explicitly, repeatedly and more than a bit intemperately, rejected the common depiction of what he was about. In short, the story offered here should not be interpreted as a piece of revisionism. On the contrary, if I am right, it is the standard portrayal that constitutes revisionism, and it is my goal to reverse the process by going back to what those authors actually said.

Unfortunately, many writers on the subject apparently have not followed Sam Hollander's example of meticulous scholarship, and in writing about Marx and Ricardo they have chosen instead to report what they believe these authors "ought" to have said or what they should be suspected of having intended, rather that confining themselves to what their subjects actually put into writing. This is an instance of a disease not uncommon among those who write on the history of ideas, and not only in economics. The discussion therefore assumes an importance well beyond the immediate subject of this paper. Rather, *pace* Viner, it is a modest appeal for modesty in the craft of scholarship, urging those who labor in the field to attribute unto others only what those other authors had actually said for themselves. This is not meant to rule out indirect evidence where explicit assertions are scarce or lacking altogether. Where no more than indirect evidence is available however, this should surely be made clear, and both the evidence and its shortcomings laid out fully.

Summary of the contentions

Specifically, it will be argued here that neither Ricardo nor Marx had any special interest in explaining the determination of the prices of individual commodities. Marx's concern was, of course, to promote the introduction of a socialist society and to explain both the deficiencies of capitalism and its historical role as a step toward the communist economy. Ricardo's interests were less radical, but the canvas on which he painted was also large, for his value theory was clearly brandished as a weapon in the Corn Law debate, on behalf of freedom of trade and its contribution to the growth of the economy, to prolongation of the economy's "progressive state."[1] To use Lerner's example, why on earth should either of them have devoted his energies to devising a complex analysis whose purpose was to explain the process that determines the price of peanuts?

I will argue, following Henderson's conclusion, that Ricardo's objective was not to explain individual prices, but was rather to provide a firmer foundation for his analysis of income distribution with its crucial role in his macro model of the growth process, the "canonical model," as termed by Samuelson and Hollander.

It is ironic that the legends about Marxian economics more readily give credence to the idea that he (perhaps more than Ricardo) was primarily concerned with income distribution, allegedly denouncing capitalism for its exploitation of workers, and the inadequate compensation of their labor through the extraction of surplus value, under the rule of the "iron law of wages." That tale is ironic since its claims already aroused Marx's anger during his lifetime, leading him to denounce them repeatedly and in tones that were far from dulcet. Rather, as the subtitle of Volume I of *Capital* tells us, his concern was production, not distribution.

There is one final and overriding irony. As I hope to demonstrate, neither Ricardo nor Marx advocated a labor theory of pricing. Ricardo, from the first edition of the *Principles* and in his correspondence, recognized the role of cost of capital in the pricing process and always described prices as being determined by cost of production, including the cost of capital, and certainly not by the payment to labor alone. Indeed, a central point of his argument, as we will see, is that wages either cannot affect prices, or can only affect prices very little. Marx, too, adopted a cost-of-production pricing model. He explicitly allied himself with Adam Smith on the theory of pricing, which is a labor theory only for societies studied by anthropologists. That is, it bases itself on labor alone only for "the early and rude state of society" in which neither capital nor land have been appropriated and used by owners as remunerated inputs for the production process. For the capitalist economies, for Marx as for Smith, prices are determined by cost of production and never by labor alone.

True, labor values and prices are not unrelated, even in Marxian doctrine, but they are far from being the same thing. That, after all, is what the transformation problem is about.[2] Thus, it is perfectly consistent for Marx to have held to a labor theory of what he called "value," a subject that interested him profoundly, and yet to subscribe to a cost-of-production model of pricing, a subject that concerned him very little.

Ricardo's analytic problem and the role of the 93 percent labor theory of value

Those of Ricardo's economic writings that did not focus on money and inflation were certainly connected with the Corn Law debate and were arguably stimulated by that debate. His contribution to the discussion was the contention that facilitation of the import of grain would permit England to forgo the use of less productive grain-growing land, thereby reducing the resources needed to grow corn on marginal land. That would cut the market value of the subsistence wage, incidentally reduce the income of landowners, but directly raise the rate of return to capital. The crucial result would be a stimulus to accumulation and economic growth that could be expected to continue until expanding population stimulated by higher real wages (contributed in turn by the enlarged supply of capital) required recourse to inferior lands. This would eventually reduce the return to capital to a point where accumulation would cease, until the stationary state was attained.[3]

To support these observations Ricardo constructed as the centerpiece of his theory a coherent dynamic model in which distribution, production and population growth were the key components. In particular, it proceeded by laying out a model of long-run wage determination and then deducing the behavior of profits from what he proposed as their relationship to wages. It is to confirm the postulated inverse relationship between wages and profits that he felt himself driven to formulate a theory of price. This theory of value however then took what appears to be a very peculiar form, because it was designed to deal primarily with the wage–profit relationship rather than with the pricing of individual commodities.

That the theory of value was of secondary importance to Ricardo, at least as a theory of price of particular commodities, becomes clear when we recall that the *Principles* (first edition, 1817) was initially intended as an elaboration of his pamphlet, the *Essay on Profits* (24 February 1815).[4] The *Essay* had focussed on issues related to income distribution, as the title implies, and had provided no systematic or formal theory of value. By the time Ricardo undertook the writing of the *Principles*,

> Ricardo had come to the realization that his theory of the interconnection between rent, profit and wages was dependent upon a theory of value and price. This theoretical innovation was what differentiated his argument in the *Essay* from his *Principles*. . . . 'Before my readers can understand the proof I mean to offer, they must understand the theory of currency and price.'
> (Ricardo 1951–73, vol. 6: 348–9, Ricardo to Mill, December 30 1815)
> (Henderson and Davis 1997: 340)

Specifically, Ricardo's problem was this: he asserted that profits were determined residually, by the level of wages, so that if diminishing returns made subsistence more costly and the normal level of wages consequently rose, then profits would have to decline correspondingly. "The significance of this point to Ricardo's central thesis lay in the fact that Malthus had claimed that if wages rise the resulting price effect would more than compensate for the adverse effects upon profits" (Henderson and Davis 1997: 440). To deal with this claim, Ricardo was forced to provide a theory that could serve as a general theory of value, seeking to show that real commodity prices could not rise in response to an increase in wages, or, at most, could rise by a negligible amount. It is here, as we will see, that the labor theory, or at least the "93 percent labor theory," came into play. I will argue presently that this is a clear purpose of Chapter 1 of the *Principles*, dictating its peculiar form that has proven so puzzling to many readers. That is, the chapter is expressed as a necessary prologue to the theory of distribution rather than as a theory of price determination. Despite the fact that it is the first chapter of the book, it is best understood as an afterthought, as a step in laying the foundation for the dynamic distribution model that was really the author's central focus.

Ricardo's solution of his problem and the role of his value theory

Ricardo's discussion of value devotes considerable space (three of the seven sections of Chapter 1) to the modifications in relative values of commodities with fixed ratio of their labor content that can be expected to result from differences in the quantities and durability of the capital employed in making those commodities. If he had been concerned primarily with the relative prices of such commodities then one would have expected his discussion to proceed in a way very different from the path that it actually takes. Elsewhere, in his discussion with Malthus, he subscribes to a cost of production interpretation of price setting, emphasizing that this cost must include the profit on capital.[5] Thus, in algebraic terms, one would have expected him to consider an expression such as

$$V = [wL + K(1+r)]/[wL^* + K^*(1+r)] \qquad (1)$$

where V is the relative value of the two goods in question, w is wage rate, r is rate of return on capital, L and K are, respectively, the quantities of labor and capital used to produce the one good, and L^* and K^* represent the corresponding magnitudes for the other good. If his main goal had been to provide a theory of pricing one should then have expected him to inquire about the effect on V of changes in the absolute or relative magnitudes of L, L^*, K and K^*. But Ricardo does not do that. Instead, he consistently investigates the effect on V of a change in w.

Ricardo starts out by noting that if the labor theory were strictly accurate as an explanation of V, that is, if $K = K^* = 0$ (in Adam Smith's "early and rude state of society"), then the w in the numerator and in the denominator cancel and we must clearly have $dV/dw = 0$.

> No alteration in the wages of labour could produce any alteration in the relative value of these commodities [game and fish]; for suppose them to rise, no greater quantity of labour would be required in any of these occupations, but it would be paid for at a higher price.
> (Ricardo 1951–73, vol. I, sect. 3: 28)

This then can be interpreted as a sort of test of the accuracy of the labor theory as an explanation of pricing. That is, the larger is the absolute value of dV/dw the more imperfect we can deem the labor theory to be as an explanation of price determination.

But, as we will see next, the significance of this derivative is more than that. For Ricardo uses this reasoning to argue that if wages do not affect relative good prices " it must at once be seen, that profits would be high or low, exactly in proportion as wages were low or high" (Ricardo 1951–73, vol. I: Section III, 27). He goes on at once to bring in the pertinence of his analysis to the valuation of gold:

> and the same reasons which should make the hunter and the fisherman endeavour to raise the value of their game and fish, would cause the owner of the mine to raise the value of his gold . . . the relative value of game, fish, and gold would continue unaltered.
> (Ricardo 1951–73, vol. I, sect. 3: 28)

The price of gold is critical here because the direct challenge of Malthus was not in terms of *relative* values. In arguing about the responsiveness of final product prices to changes in wages, it is absolute (real) price that matters, and Ricardo was able to show that this price, too, cannot change in the wake of a rise in wages, so long as values satisfy the rules of the labor theory. For the absolute price of commodity X is the amount of money a unit of X is able to command in the market place. However, if money consists exclusively of gold that is supplied commercially under competitive conditions, then it must also be governed by the pricing rules of the labor theory, as Ricardo pointed out in the passage just quoted. If so, a rise in wages cannot possibly affect the relative values of good X and gold, but that relative value of X and gold is just another name for the absolute price of X. In sum, in such a world, there is no way that the absolute price of X can change in the wake of a rise in wages. Thus, the assumption that gold is supplied by competitive private enterprise, and is therefore also governed by the labor theory of value, constitutes the core of a solution to the Malthusian challenge.

Ricardo also has a fallback position here. Even if his assumption about the position of gold in the economy fails, he points out several times that when wages rise, with relative goods prices unchanged, it might still be possible for the prices of all goods to rise in proportion. But then the value of money would, by definition, fall proportionately, so that capitalists would have obtained no real gains from the price increases (see later for such a quotation from the chapter on profits).

Ricardo then argues that the use of capital in production does not automatically require modification of his analysis. Thus, he notes that if capital is employed but the quantity used in each good is strictly the same proportion to the quantity of labor it employs, then by (1) we continue to have $dV/dw = 0$.

> A rise of wages would not raise [a commodity's value] . . . relatively to any other commodities, the production of which required no additional quantity of labour, which employed the same proportion of fixed and circulating capital, and fixed capital of the same durability.
> (Ricardo 1951–73, vol. I, sect. 3: 29)

Matters are, however, different when the proportions of capital to labor vary from good to good. Then wage movements will affect relative values. But he goes on at once to argue that the effect must be relatively small.

> The degree of alteration in the relative value of goods, on account of a rise or fall of labour, would depend on the proportion which the fixed capital bore to the whole capital employed. All commodities which are produced by very valuable machinery, or in very valuable buildings, or which require a great length of time before they can be brought to market, would fall in relative value, while all those which were chiefly produced by labour, or which would be speedily brought to market, would rise in relative value.
>
> The reader, however, should remark, that this cause of the variation of commodities is comparatively slight in its effects. With such a rise of wages as should occasion a fall of one percent. in profits, goods produced under the circumstances I have supposed, vary in relative value only one percent. . . . The greatest effects which could be produced on the relative prices of these goods from a rise of wages, could not exceed 6 or 7 percent.; for profits could not, probably, under any circumstances, admit of a greater general and permanent depression than to that amount.
> (Ricardo 1951–73, vol. I, sect. 4: 35–6)[6]

Ricardo's argument in the last paragraph, incidentally, can be translated as follows. Ricardo is considering a case in which investment consists entirely of expended wages. In one product they are invested for two years while in the other they are invested for only one year. Then we have $V= wL(1+r)^2/wL^*(1+r)$ or, writing $R = L/L^*$, $V = R(1+r)$. Hence, if r were to fall from 10 to as little as 3 percent V would fall by the proportion *[R(1.1 – 1.03)/ 1.1R] = 1.07/1.1*, or less than 7 percent.

Ricardo goes on to point out that variability in the durability of the capital used to produce different goods will also permit a change in wage rate to affect relative values:

> Every rise of wages, therefore, or, which is the same thing, every fall of profits, would lower the relative value of those commodities which were

produced with a capital of a durable nature, and would proportionally elevate those which were produced with capital more perishable. A fall of wages would have precisely the contrary effect.

(Ricardo 1951–73, vol. I, sect. 5: 39–40)

All of this means that capitalists may be able to raise final-good prices when wages rise if gold is produced with a relatively low labor-capital ratio, so that the exchange value of the good at issue, in terms of gold, that is, the money price of the good, would then increase. However the price could vary only modestly:

If, for example, [gold] were produced under the same circumstances as we have supposed necessary to produce cloth and cotton goods, it would be a perfect measure of value for those things, but not so for corn, for coals, and other commodities produced with either a less or a greater proportion of fixed capital, because, as we have shown, every alteration in the permanent rate of profits would have some effect on the relative value of all these goods, independently of any alteration in the quantity of labour employed on their production. . . . but I have already remarked, that the effect on the relative prices of things, from a variation in profits, is comparatively slight.

(Ricardo 1951–73, vol. I, sect. 6: 45)

This, then, brings Ricardo, in his chapter on wages, to the bottom line of his argument, the inverse relationship between wages and profits:

It appears, then, that the rise of wages will not raise the prices of commodities, whether the metal from which money is made be produced at home or in a foreign country. All commodities cannot rise at the same time without an addition to the quantity of money. This addition could not be obtained at home, as we have already shown; nor could it be imported from abroad. To purchase any additional quantity of gold from abroad, commodities at home must be cheap, not dear.

(Ricardo 1951–73, vol. I, ch. 5: 105)

Recognizing, however, that the nation's money supply is not composed exclusively of precious metals, Ricardo ends the discussion at this point by adding:

The extensive use of paper money does not alter this question, for paper money conforms, or ought to conform, to the value of gold, and therefore its value is influenced by such causes only as influence the value of that metal.

(Ricardo 1951–73, vol. I, ch. 5: 105)

This argument is again summarized in Ricardo's chapter on profits:

In the Chapter on Wages, we have endeavoured to show that the money price of commodities would not be raised by a rise of wages, either on the

supposition that gold, the standard of money, was the produce of this country, or that it was imported from abroad. . . . Thus then I have endeavoured to show, first, that a rise of wages would not raise the price of commodities, but would invariably lower profits; and secondly, that if the prices of all commodities could be raised, still the effect on profits would be the same; and that in fact the value of the medium only in which prices and profits are estimated would be lowered.
(Ricardo 1951–73, vol. I, ch. 6: 126–7)

Thus, he ends the story by noting that, given the (approximate) validity of the labor theory of value, even a monetary system not tied to precious metals does not undermine his conclusions on distribution.

Marx and the morality of capitalist income distribution

Once we recall Marx's commitment to the idea that ways of thinking and, in particular, standards of ethical conduct are determined by historical circumstances, it should be obvious that he would not have subscribed to the notion that wage setting in the capitalist economy is "immoral." Even less could he be expected to argue that this is a primary justification for replacement of the capitalist society by socialism. Indeed, Marx and Engels leave us in no doubt on this score.

Early in *Capital*, just after the discussion of the value of labor power, Marx tells us unequivocally, "It is a very cheap sort of sentimentality which declares this method of determining the value of labour-power, a method prescribed by the very nature of the case, to be a brutal method" (Marx 1906, vol. 1: 102). As early as the *Grundrisse* he asserted that the wage level "determined . . . by the specific state of society . . . [is] economically just" (Marx 1973: 426 ff). Much later, in the *Critique of the Gotha Programme* he reiterated "is [the present-day distribution] not, in fact, the only 'fair' distribution on the basis of the present day mode of distribution?" (Marx 1875: 14). Probably his last piece on economics, *Marginal Notes on Adolph Wagner*, reiterates this position even more unequivocally:

> The obscurantist [Wagner] foists on me the idea that 'the *surplus-value* produced by the labourers *alone improperly* remains with the capitalist entrepreneurs' (114n3). In fact, I say the direct opposite . . . that according to the *law of value* governing [capitalist commodity production] the 'surplus-value' is properly the capitalist's and not the labourers'
> (Marx 1879–80: 61, Marx's italics)

Engels unequivocally endorsed this interpretation of Marx on the ethics of capitalist distribution.

> According to the laws of bourgeois economics, the greatest part of the product does not belong to the workers who have produced it. If we now say: that is unjust, that ought not to be so, then that has nothing

immediately to do with economics. We are merely saying that this economic fact is in contradiction to our moral sentiment. Marx, therefore, never based his communist demands upon this ... he says only that surplus value consists of unpaid labour, which is a simple fact.

(Marx 1846–7: Preface to the first German edition, 10–11)

Not only did Marx reject the claim that he believed capitalist distribution to be immoral. He also denied, repeatedly and emphatically, that capitalism condemned workers to anything like a subsistence wage. The "iron law of wages," an invention of Ferdinand Lassalle whom Marx detested, always elicited his rage. Calling it "this so-called law," Marx went on to indicate why he considered it a weapon of the reactionaries:

> Basing themselves directly on this, the economists have been proving for fifty years and more that socialism cannot abolish poverty *which has its basis in nature*, but can only make it *general*, distribute it simultaneously over the whole surface of society!
>
> (Marx [1875] 1937: 22, Marx's italics)

The point here is that the "iron law" rested on the Malthusian population model that in Marx's view was "a libel on the human race," for it envisioned a human race incapable of ever raising wages above the level of subsistence because it was helplessly in the grip of its sexual urges.

Thus, on the one hand, the doctrine was dangerous because it could be used to deny that socialism offered any hope of elimination of poverty. On the other hand, it was mired in indefensible middle-class morality that trivialized the revolutionary struggle:

> Vulgar socialism ... has taken over from the bourgeois economists the ... treatment of distribution as independent of the mode of production and hence the presentation of socialism as turning principally on distribution ... It is as if ... slaves who have at last got behind the secret of slavery and broken out in rebellion ... were to inscribe on the programme of the rebellion: Slavery must be abolished because the feeding of slaves in the system of slavery cannot exceed a certain low maximum!
>
> (Marx [1875] 1937: 18, 23)

Marxian values and price determination

Value in the Marxian writings is emphatically not a magnitude determined by market forces or any other form of direct human interaction except to the degree that the state of technology and, hence, each commodity's labor content, is determined by economic forces. Rather, as careful reading of Volume I of *Capital* will confirm, it is merely the redefinitional adoption of a word to denote the amount of labor that must be used to make some particular good. Marx was in the habit of employing words to mean something different from what others meant by them. For example, "commodity," "productive labour," and even the word "contradiction," can be shown to have been used by him to mean things quite different from their common connotation. The term "value" is a prime example. Marx explicitly indicated that his use of the term entailed tautology:

> Since the exchange value of commodities is, in fact, nothing but a mutual relation of the labours of individuals . . . it is a tautology to say that labour is the only source of exchange value and consequently of wealth, insofar as the latter consists of exchange values. Similarly, it is a tautology to say that matter in its natural state has no exchange value because it does not contain any labour.
>
> (Marx 1906: 31–2, Marx's italics)

Price, to Marx, was something quite different, and something Smith had already explained correctly.

> Price regulated in this way [that is, in a manner consistent with the solution of the transformation problem] = the expenses of capital + average profit . . . is what Smith calls the *natural price, cost price, etc.*
>
> (Marx 1909, vol. 3, ch. 9: 160, Marx's italics)

Note that this is a cost of production, not a labor, theory of price, with price equal to the amount the capitalist must lay out on all inputs required for a commodity, plus the normal profit on this expenditure. He recognizes that this is the result of the competitive process under which ". . . every part of the capital yields uniformly the same profit. . . .(ibid., vol. 3, ch. 9: 200).

As already noted, there is, according to Marx, a relation between prices and his values. The determination of this relationship is a key part of the transformation problem. However, while I will presently return briefly to that problem, I shall leave the subject at this point because it is not part of our concern here. For my current purpose it is enough to have shown that value theory in Marx was not primarily a matter of analysis of the price determination process. While value was, patently, one of his primary concerns, pricing, emphatically, was not. Otherwise, how would one explain his postponement of any systematic discussion of price setting until Volume III of *Capital* and, even there, why is it a matter very subsidiary to the relation between surplus values and the sum of profits, interest and rent, as a careful reading will confirm?

What was Marx really after?

Having argued that there were two things, price setting and the ethics of income distribution, that emphatically were not primary concerns for Marx, the natural question is, what, then, was his actual focus? This is rather more difficult to answer, because the Marxian writings offer us no unambiguous answer. Though at several points we are provided with what appear to be such assertions, it must be admitted that there remains something Delphicly mysterious about them. This section, and those that follow directly, therefore, unlike the remainder of this chapter, cannot avoid reasoning by conjecture.

It seems plain that his real aim must have had some relation to the demise of capitalism and the desirability or inevitability of a socialistic substitute for the capitalist regime, and Engels tells us something of the sort. The passage previously quoted in which he asserts that an allegation that the capitalistic determination of wages is "unjust . . . has nothing immediately to do with economics [and is merely an expression of] our moral sentiments" goes on to assert that "Marx, therefore, never based his communist demands upon this. . . ." Rather, Marx based those demands "upon the inevitable collapse of the capitalist mode of production which is daily taking place before our eyes" (Engels [1878] 1934: 11).[7] Yet Marx seems never to have described any mechanism that would lead to the collapse of the capitalist economy. Instead we are provided with passages that are poetic rather than analytical:

> Along with the constantly diminishing number of magnates of capital, who usurp and monopolize all advantages, grows the mass of misery, oppression, slavery, degradation, exploitation; but with this too grows the revolt of the working class, a class always increasing in numbers, and disciplined, united, organized by the very mechanism of capitalist production itself. The monopoly of capital becomes a fetter upon the mode of production which has sprung up and flourished along with, and under it. Centralization of means of production and socialization of labour at last reach a point where they become incompatible with their capitalist integument. This integument is burst asunder. The knell of capitalist private property sounds. The expropriators are expropriated.
> (Marx 1906, part 8, ch. 32: 836–7)

Clearly, there is little of Marxian value theory here.

Other assertions by Marx perhaps give us a better clue. I have already noted that, in Marx's view, Volume I of *Capital* is devoted to production, as its subtitle indicates, and this view can be corroborated by other quotations. However that takes us only one step, for it is not quite clear what he meant when he referred to his analysis of production. Certainly, there is no explicit production function, no analysis of substitution, complementarity (though there are some references to economies of scale), that is, there is little of what today's economist would consider a theory of production. Rather, Marx's discussion can be conjectured to deal with two issues: first, the unprecedented productivity of the capitalist economy and what he took to be the inevitability of its subsequent decline; second, the role in the productive process to which the laborer was condemned by the very nature of the capitalist mechanism.

These are both conjectures, but they are not entirely devoid of evidence. On the first, we have already had our hint from Engels when he told us that "Marx . . . based his communist demands . . . upon the inevitable collapse of the capitalist mode of production . . ." while the second explanation is suggested by the quote from the *Critique of the Gotha Programme* in which he decries a battle against slavery driven by a protest against the slave's low wages. Rather, he implies, success requires the slaves to "get behind the secret of slavery," that is, their recognition that the system of production assigns them a key role, but a role no different from that played by the domesticated animals that the slave holder also employs in the process.

Marx and the productivity of capitalism

So far as I am aware, no economist has ever outdone Marx's unstinting praise of the productive accomplishments of capitalism.

> The Bourgeoisie [that is, capitalism] cannot exist without constantly revolutionizing the instruments of production. . . . Conservation of the old modes of production in unaltered form was, on the contrary, the first condition of existence for all earlier industrial classes. . . . The bourgeoisie, during its rule of scarce one hundred years has created more massive and more colossal productive forces than have all preceding generations together.
> (Marx and Engels 1848, *Manifesto of the Communist Party*)

Thus, the historic role of capitalism was to unleash the vast but latent productive powers of humanity which were constrained by "the most slothful indolence" of the Middle Ages, and to produce an abundance that is necessary to make socialist society possible:

> Fanatically bent on making value expand itself, [the capitalist] ruthlessly forces the human race to produce for production's sake; *he thus forces the development of the productive powers of society, and creates those material conditions, which alone can form the real basis of a higher form of society in which the full and free development of every individual forms the ruling principle.*
> (Marx 1906, ch. 24, sect. 3: 649, my italics)

Note the significance of the italicized passage, saying clearly that a necessary condition for the socialism Marx envisaged is the abundance that the capitalist system of production alone made possible.[8] The point is that abolition of division of labor that Marx welcomed must surely handicap productivity. Perhaps, to make this possible, in the view of Marx and Engels the historically unprecedented abundance provided by capitalist production is indispensable.

This much is clear enough. But why the productive powers of capitalism are, according to Marx, condemned to erosion, is never fully explained. The nearest thing to a direct answer seems to be provided in Volume 3 of *Capital*, in the relatively brief (for Marx) discussion of the declining rate of profit.[9] This material remains pertinent to our subject despite the well known logical error in his argument.[10] The consequences that Marx deduced from his falling profit principle included falling real wages, increased concentration of industry, and reduced rates of accumulation (investment).

The reduced real wages (and the accompanying lengthening of the working day) are discussed only very briefly (in six lines: vol. 3: ch. 14, sect. 2). It is described as one of the ways that businesspeople tend to offset the declining profit rate, through increases in the rate of surplus value.

Concentration of industry is discussed somewhat more explicitly:

> with the development of the capitalist mode of production, there is an increase in the minimum amount of individual capital necessary to carry on a business under its normal conditions. The smaller capitals, therefore, crowd into spheres of production which Modern Industry has only sporadically or incompletely got hold of. Here competition rages in direct proportion to the number, and in inverse proportion to the magnitudes, of the antagonistic capitals. It always ends in the ruin of many small capitalists, whose capitals partly pass into the hand of their conquerors, partly vanish.
> (Marx 1906, ch. 25, sect. 2: 686–7. See also Marx 1909, vol. 3, chs 13 and 15: 257, 294)

Finally, declining profits lead to decreased accumulation, and undercut the vigor of the capitalist economy and pave the way to its extinction:

> The rate of profit, that is, the relative increment of capital, is above all important for all new offshoots of capital seeking an independent location. And as soon as the formation of capitals were to fall into the hands of a few established great capitals, which are compensated by the mass of profits for the loss though a fall in the rate of profits, the vital fire of production would be extinguished. It would fall into a dormant state. The rate of profit is the compelling power of capitalist production, and only such things are produced as yield a profit. Hence the fright of the English economists over the decline of the rate of profit. . . . What worries Ricardo is the fact that the rate of profit, the stimulating principle of capitalist production, the fundamental premise and the driving force of accumulation, should be endangered by the development of production itself. . . . It is demonstrated in a purely economic way, that is, from a bourgeois point of view, within the confines of capitalist understanding, from the standpoint of capitalist production itself, that it has a barrier, that it is relative, that it is not an absolute, but only a historical mode of production.
> (Marx 1909, vol. 3, part 2: 304)

It should be noted how fundamental the value theory is to this argument. With the value of labor power, call it W (the labor time necessary to produce wages) fixed, and the length of the working day, H, set by the market and the mobility of labor (Marx 1909: vol. 3, ch. 10: 206) the rate of surplus value $[(H-W)/H] = s$ is also determined. Since according to Marx only "variable capital" – the investment in labor – yields surplus value, let V, measured in days of labor, represent that value, and let K represent the value of "constant capital" – the remaining investment in production. The (Marxian) rate of profit (neglecting interest and rent) becomes, in value terms, $sV/(V + K)$. This obviously declines as the ratio of K to V increases, if everything else remains equal. That, essentially, is Marx's analysis of the allegedly declining rate of profits, and it is, arguably, one of the reasons for Marx's interest in the theory of value, as he defines it.

Alienation and the mode of production

A second reason that, I suspect, underlay Marx's concern with value theory encompasses the mode of production, accumulation of surplus value and alienation. Alienation is a concept that occurs early in the Marxian writings and it has been suggested that it was a passing notion of the younger Marx that soon disappeared from his thought. Yet it has a significant role in the *Grundrisse* of 1858, completed just as he was about to begin the drafting of *Capital*. Many pages in his writings were devoted to the subject of alienation, but none of them seems to have been published during his lifetime. It was only in the middle of the twentieth century when Marx's notes and previously unpublished manuscripts began to be printed in the Soviet Union that the concept was widely recognized among Marxian scholars. Even then, the idea seems to have been more attractive to sociologists and political scientists than to economists.

I will argue that there are two sides to the concept, and that the variant that is most pertinent to us here is the one that has elicited less attention than the other. The relationship that appears to be discussed most frequently relates to division of labor and its implications for the psychological state of the worker. By replacement of artisanship with repetitious and exceedingly specialized tasks, a wall is placed between the worker and the quality of the product as a whole. By treating the worker or, rather, his labor power, as a mere commodity bought and sold in the pursuit of profit the worker loses any sense of satisfaction in his work and identification with his product. He becomes alienated as the medieval artisan was not.

> The direct relationship between the worker and production . . . replaces labour by machines, but it throws one section of the workers back to a barbarous type of labour and it turns the other into a machine. It produces intelligence – but for the worker, stupidity, cretinism. . . . what . . . constitutes the alienation of labour? First . . . that in his work . . . he . . . does not feel content but unhappy, does not develop freely his physical and mental energy but mortifies his body and ruins his mind.
> (*Economic and Philosophical Manuscripts* (1843) (*Collected Works* vol. 3: 273–4))

This view of alienation, the circumstances dramatized by Charlie Chaplin in his film *Modern Times*, is presumably what underlies Marx's and Engels' persistent and passionate denunciation of the division of labor that has already been noted here (see note 8).

It is however the second form of alienation that is more closely associated with what Marx called "the laws of motion of capitalism." It relates to the control of the means of production that emerge from the accumulation of the capitalist. The essence of the matter is that the worker finds himself controlled by the very machines that he himself has created. Thus, after he produces the means of production the worker is confronted with these objects a second time. This time though they encounter the worker as domineering alienated objects. The items that the worker has created with his own hands have become foreign objects, without which he cannot gainfully employ his labor, and that the capitalist uses to control him:

> the objective conditions of labor assume an ever more colossal independence . . . that social wealth confronts labour in more powerful portions as an alien and dominant power. The emphasis comes to be placed on the state of being alienated, dispossessed, sold; on the condition that the monstrous objective power which social labor erected opposite itself . . . belongs not to the worker, but to the personified conditions of production, that is, to capital.
>
> (Marx 1973: 831)

Thus, under capitalism the control of labor through a slave relationship is replaced by control through the machine that the worker himself has created and that has been alienated from him. As in the passage quoted earlier from *Critique of the Gotha Programme*, where it is noted that the objectionable feature of slavery is not underpayment of the slaves, here, the issue is not unethical distribution of the income from production, but the subservient position into which the worker is placed by the very nature of the capitalist production process, a position that deprives him of control of his existence. It is a form of alienation that is automatically exacerbated with the passage of time, that grows progressively more severe as accumulation progresses, so that the amount of capital required for the worker's employment grows ever larger, and opportunities for self-employment are ever narrowed.

What has all this to do though with Marxian value theory? A little consideration makes the answer clear. The identification of value with labor content is a formalization of the assertion that the plant and equipment are among the products that the worker himself has created. Moreover, surplus value becomes the instrument by which the producers' goods are alienated from the worker and fall into the hands of the capitalist. The value theory becomes for Marx the organizing principle with whose aid he believes he can analyze the dynamics of the production process, with its key components – creation of products by the worker, alienation through surplus value, accumulation that raises productivity and at the same time tightens control over the worker, and the allegedly declining rate of profits that reduces the ranks of the capitalist class and undermines the very accumulation that fuels the capitalist productive process.

Concluding comment

It must be emphasized once again that the assertions of the preceding sections cannot be documented, chapter and verse. We know enough about Marx's thought to be confident that he believed most if not all of the things I have ascribed to him. Yet I have not been able to find any grand summation by him that tells us precisely what he was after and exactly what the role of the value theory was in his greater scheme. We can be sure of two things, both in his case and that of Ricardo: neither of them studied the theory of value primarily as a means to explain the pricing of individual commodities, and neither of them advocated a pure labor theory of pricing.

Notes

I am grateful to the C. V. Starr Center for Applied Economics, New York University, for its support of this research.

1. On the relation of the historic pamphlets of 1815 to the Corn Law debate, and the earlier discussions of such matters as the role of diminishing returns, see Hollander 1998: 194–6.
2. Though it emphasizes even more the relation between surplus value and the sum of profit, interest and rent. On this see my article (Baumol 1974: 56–7).
3. This is not to say that Ricardo was a pessimist about the future. There is evidence that he hoped innovation (as well as other influences) could postpone the stationary state indefinitely. On this see Hollander 1998: 232. See also various examples of Ricardo's views on the subject in his speeches in Parliament, as described in Gordon 1976.
4. Henderson and Davis (see for example 1977: 465, 496–9) come to a similar conclusion, one I had reached independently long before their work appeared.
5. "Mr. Malthus appears to think that it is part of my doctrine, that the cost and value of a thing should be the same;– it is, if he means by cost, 'cost of production' including profits" (Ricardo 1951–73, vol. 1: 47).
6. This passage is what led Stigler to conclude that Ricardo held to a "93 percent theory of value." If we interpret this passage to refer to the use of the effect of wages on relative values as Ricardo's test of the accuracy of the labor theory, Stigler's conclusion follows. I am arguing here however that this relationship was not intended as such a test, but rather as a basis for the conclusion that wages and profits must vary inversely.
7. It is interesting that by the time he wrote this (1884, two years after the death of Marx) Engels apparently was no longer so sure that capitalism would collapse abruptly in a great debacle. "The period of general prosperity preceding the crisis still fails to appear. If it should fail altogether, then chronic stagnation would necessarily become the normal condition of modern industry, with only insignificant fluctuations" (Engels 1934: 18n).
8. Why socialism could not function without this abundance seems never to have been made clear. Here, too, I have a conjecture. The one feature of socialism that Marx and Engels stressed throughout their careers was abolition of all division of labor! (See for example, Marx, *The German Ideology* (1845): 1 (*Collected Works*, vol. 5: 47). See also Engels, *Anti Duhring*, ch. 6: 221 (1st edn 1878, 3rd edn 1894).) Marx reviewed and contributed to the first edition shortly before his death:

    > in time to come there will no longer be any professional porters or architects, and that man who has for half an hour given instructions as an architect will also push a barrow for a period, until his activity as an architect is once again required. It is a fine sort of socialism which perpetuates the professional porter!

9. Marx, incidentally, was well aware of his prolixity, which he adopted deliberately: "I am stretching out this volume [*Capital*, vol. I] since those German dogs estimate the value of books by their cubic contents" (Marx to Engels, June 18 1862).
10. Such slips in logic are rare in the Marxian writings. The source of the problem here is that Marx sought to divorce his "law" from that of the classical theorists and its basis in Malthusian population theory. Instead, Marx argued that competition forces businesspeople to increase constantly their investment in "constant capital,"

such as plant, machinery and so on, thereby raising the ratio of constant to "variable capital" (labor power). With labor the source of all value, this reduces the ratio of surplus value (total value produced minus the value of labor power) to total capital and therefore leads to a downward trend in rate of profit. The error, of course, is that money profits are not the same as surplus values. Moreover, the added constant capital should reduce the labor time necessary to produce wage goods and should therefore automatically lower the value of labor power. This can cut the wage bill without reducing real wages, and offset any fall in profit rate that might otherwise take place. Marxists such as Paul Sweezy (1942) have recognized this error.

References

Baumol, W. J. (1974) "The Transformation of Values: What Marx 'Really' Meant," *Journal of Economic Literature* 12 (March): 51–62.

Engels, F. ([1878] 1934) *Anti Duhring*, London: Lawrence and Wishart.

Gordon, B. (1976) *Political Economy in Parliament 1819–1823*, London: Macmillan.

Henderson, J. P. and Davis, J. B. (1997) *The Life and Economics of David Ricardo*, Boston: Kluwer Academic.

Hollander, S. (1979) *The Economics of David Ricardo*, Toronto: University of Toronto Press.

—— (1998) *The Literature of Classical Political Economy*, London and New York: Routledge.

Marx, K. (1904) *A Contribution to the Critique of Political Economy*, Chicago: Charles H. Kerr.

—— (1906) *Capital. A Critique of Political Economy*, vol. I, Chicago: Charles H. Kerr.

—— (1909) *Capital. A Critique of Political Economy*, vols II and III, Chicago: Charles H. Kerr.

—— [1875] (1937) *Critique of the Gotha Programme*, Moscow: Progress.

—— (1973) *Grundrisse*, ed. and trans. Martin Nicolaus, Harmondsworth: Penguin.

—— [1879–80] (1972) "*Marginal Notes on Adolph Wagner's 'Lehrbuch der politischen Ökonomie'*," translated by Althar Hussain, Theoretical Practice, 5 (Spring).

—— [1846–7] The Poverty of the Philosophy, London: Martin Lawrence, n.d.

Marx, K. and Engels, F. (vars dates) *Collected Works*, Moscow: Progress.

—— (1848) *Manifesto of the Communist Party* (477–519 in *Collected Works*, vol. 6, Moscow: Progress).

Ricardo, D. (1951–73) *The Works and Correspondence of David Ricardo*, ed. P. Sraffa with M. H. Dobb, 11 vols, Cambridge: Cambridge University Press.

Stigler, G. (1958) "Ricardo and the 93% Labor Theory of Value," *American Economic Review* 48 (June): 357–67.

Sweezy, P. M. (1942) *The Theory of Capitalist Development*, New York: Oxford University Press.

13 Sraffa's Ricardo after fifty years
A preliminary estimate

Pier Luigi Porta

Introduction

Among significant issues in the history of economic thought is Piero Sraffa's scientific work, and particularly Sraffa as an interpreter of classical economics. Nobody will deny, I think, that a major contribution to the critical reappraisal of classical economics during the twentieth century has come precisely from the scientific and intellectual work of Sraffa. Sraffa's own conceptions on the nature and on the internal development of classical economics, which for some time became extremely popular worldwide, remain issues to be faced by economists and historians of economics alike even today, when the idea of classical economics is again under transformation and is likely to take a new shape.

As is well known, the Sraffian notion of classical economics is deeply connected with Sraffa's interpretation of Ricardo; and on that vital connection it is only proper to recall here Samuel Hollander's epoch-making discussions, particularly his 1979 book on the economics of David Ricardo as well as his other books and a number of his articles, some of which we mention later. Samuel Hollander's contributions have shaped my generation's changing views about the canon on classical economics.

Sraffa's work as David Ricardo's editor is the subject of this chapter. This is a tribute to Sraffa as one of the greatest scholars of the twentieth century. Moreover, not only was the work on Ricardo, and particularly on the Ricardo edition, almost Piero Sraffa's lifelong work (1930–73), but a special character associated with Sraffa's contribution lies in a peculiar interaction between theory and interpretation on one side, and interpretation, text and context on the other.[1] Although it is a difficult philosophical problem to establish which comes first, theory or text, within the limits of our subject and in the case under investigation, it will be a contention of this chapter that theory comes first: Sraffa, indeed, provides a strong case in point. A tribute to Sraffa thus implies a tribute to the history of economic analysis, in Schumpeter's sense.[2]

The defense of Schumpeter's methodological canon seems particularly timely today as that canon is largely and unduly suffering: most economists and historians of economics alike seem to agree – in the footsteps of both Menger and Schmoller in their time – that the historians of a discipline are usually *not* its greatest theoreticians. It should be noted that, from this perspective, in the example discussed in this chapter the editorial work on Ricardo becomes the clue to understanding *Sraffa*.[3] The same idea seems to be conveyed by the obituary of Sraffa in the *Economic Journal*, by Bertram Schefold, published in 1996. It was, Schefold writes, as he summarizes Piero Sraffa's scientific curriculum,

> above all, his magnificent edition of the works of David Ricardo which was recognised in the whole world as a landmark of scholarship and which, on account of the editorial introduction, provided a link between classical economic theory and the post war discussions on growth and distribution.
> (Schefold 1996)

It is the purpose of this chapter to put Sraffa's Ricardo in a historical perspective. After fifty years this appears to be timely on two grounds. First, as I recall later, Sraffa has been singularly enshrined and made into a bloodless entity for a considerable time; only today it becomes possible to revive his image in flesh and blood and it seems proper to do so. Second, the Sraffa archives at Trinity College have now been made accessible and it is expected that permission can be granted to make use of the extant documents for the purpose.

Sraffa's Ricardo: from the definitive edition to the "definitive interpretation"

While the semicentennial of Sraffa's work on the Introduction to Ricardo's *Principles* is rapidly approaching, a curious reflection comes to mind. This particular work of Sraffa's, though celebrated in many ways, has surprisingly never been read in itself, at least to the extent to which such an exercise is legitimately conceivable. Its fate has been the singular one of being read, in time, following two opposed extreme canons, as are in fact hinted in Schefold's statement, namely the "landmark of scholarship" on one side and the link of past and present theory on the other – call them respectively pure transparency and pure theory – neither of which is entirely satisfactory and fully suited to do justice to the work itself. Especially to those scholars who are well acquainted with Sraffa's personality and work and with the wealth of Sraffian literature which flourished for a considerable while, this opening statement may seem purely provocative. I will argue in this chapter that this is not so.

A few years ago I ventured to face a similar problem, in a paper entitled "Piero Sraffa, 'Superb Editor'" (Porta 1992), presented at the Lausanne conference on editing economists and economists as editors. That paper of mine has certainly profited from being included in an otherwise very attractive volume. Further to that my "Superb Editor" paper has gained some reputation within the inner circle through the good offices of Giancarlo de Vivo. In a comment (de Vivo: 1996; my rejoinder 1996), de Vivo has taken issue with me on the title of the paper; he points the finger at the fact that the words "Superb Editor" are in inverted commas. Those inverted commas make him uneasy, as they appear to him as a form of mockery or at least irony concerning Sraffa. Of course this is not so in the least, and this in fact turns out to be a case where an extremely sensitive reader can be driven to a complete misunderstanding.

My inverted commas in fact quite simply contain a quotation from an article by Kenneth Arrow on "Ricardo's Work as Viewed by Later Economists" that appeared in the Spring 1991 issue of the *Journal of the History of Economic Thought*. I had chosen at the time to quote Arrow because he was then providing one of the latest and clearest instances of an unending series of appreciations of a similar kind concerning Sraffa. What is interesting and makes it worth going back to that paper by Arrow, is that Arrow – although he certainly does not rule out other perspectives – evidently appears to imply that his judgement of excellence must be understood mainly on *philological* grounds. Sraffa was, Arrow wrote, the "diligent and very slow" editor of Ricardo. Of course, he noted, both Sraffa and his sponsor Keynes each had his own intellectual agenda, where (as Arrow was probably right to take for granted) the points of difference greatly outnumber those of contact. It must, however, be ascribed to Keynes' merit that he "did not confuse an antiquarian interest in seeing Sraffa produce a good edition of Ricardo with any excessive respect for an obstacle to what he saw as correct thinking." Thereby he "correctly foresaw that Piero Sraffa would be a superb editor." The task is one that requires, Arrow observed, "leisure," with which of course Sraffa was abundantly provided, having given up lecturing in 1930 precisely in coincidence with the assignment of the Ricardo enterprise in February of that year. This observation about leisure is evidently designed to describe an ideal condition for work of an editorial kind, and it would certainly not be made in the same fashion in the case of analytical work in any branch of economic research. Arrow aptly summarized the ingredients of the legendary figure of the "Superb Editor," besides recalling how that characteristic image of Sraffa came to take shape with its aureola of academic laziness.

One of the best pictures we have of Sraffa was once sketched by his professor and mentor Luigi Einaudi, who had known the young Sraffa as a student and as a scholar, and had been otherwise intimate with his familial and social *milieu* since the turn of the century. In a famous review article of the Ricardo volumes, which appeared in the *Giornale degli economisti* for 1951, under the title "From the legend to the monument," Einaudi delivered unmixed praise of the edition. Comparing Sraffa's achievement with Cannan's enterprise on Adam Smith, Einaudi concluded that "Sraffa emulates Cannan and overrides him." Einaudi's celebration of the edition focuses on its philological and aesthetic qualities. He had himself in a paper published sixteen years earlier, in 1935 – prompted by the then recent edition of Francesco Ferrara's *Lectures* – established and discussed at some considerable length a few fundamental canons for the editing of economic classics. Among other things Einaudi had emphasized that editorial introductions and notes should never intrude. Their function – Einaudi explained – is to supply missing references or soberly illustrate a view; "never to correct, integrate or criticize." He also added: "An editor does not give evidence of sound taste when he seizes the occasion and prefaces the texts with an exposition of his own." The examples of Cannan, Ashley and Hollander were then mentioned approvingly. Sixteen years later, in 1951, Sraffa appears to Einaudi to have fully and satisfactorily fulfilled all the requirements of the model editor. Unspoilt crystal transparency appears to be the substance of which Sraffa's "monument" is made.

Perhaps the clearest comment on the Sraffa edition at the time of its first appearance came from Sir Austin Robinson. It is interesting that Robinson's comments, in his review of the edition for the *Economic Journal*, were directly concerned with the now famous Introduction to Volume I, although of course the remarks of the reviewer did extend to the style and character of the edition as a whole:

> Mr. Sraffa's preface is a model of what such a preface should be. He is concerned wholly and exclusively with Ricardo, with Ricardo's own controversies with his contemporaries, and with anything in Ricardo's own letters and writings which can contribute to our ability to understand what Ricardo was trying to say. He is *not* concerned to provide us with ready-made judgements as to whether it was Ricardo, or Jevons, or neither, who "shunted the car of Economic Science on to a wrong line." He does *not* provide us with a "Ricardo in modern dress", with Ricardo's ideas translated into the terminology in which most of us can more readily think to-day. But just so far as he can help Ricardo to speak to us for himself, and in his own language, he gives us every possible assistance. That I believe is as it should be. We are given all help in going back to Ricardo himself. But Mr. Sraffa firmly refuses to stand between Ricardo and his reader as an intermediary and interpreter, creating, as such interpreters so often do, a host of new misconceptions and misunderstandings.
>
> (Robinson 1951: 850)

Particularly after Keynes' death, Austin Robinson had experienced very directly the effects of the labors of a superb editor. It is not improper to conjecture that he must have written the above words with that sense of liberation and satisfaction which accompanies a great achievement. However, perhaps more significantly, these plain unequivocal words are, in a sense, the tip of an iceberg; they express at best a very common sentiment toward the Ricardo edition at the time of publication and a sentiment that would then be dominant throughout the 1950s. That is a very simple common opinion: for any question that may arise on Ricardo, it will be enough to turn to Sraffa. That is the service of the edition.

In the same vein Blaug himself (Blaug 1958) – setting out in his early days to ask once again "what Ricardo really meant" – declared that nothing could have justified another forced march over such well-worn terrain were it not that the recent edition of the complete *Works and Correspondence of David Ricardo* had thrown new light on almost every aspect of Ricardo's writings.

Let us now turn to the latter half of the title of this section. The "monument" of the superb editor is, in actual reality, a powerful rhetorical construct deserving wonder and admiration. It was, in fact, Sraffa's supreme ability to replace the foundations of the edifice of Ricardian economics without any one of the onlookers taking the slightest notice of what was going on for a considerable time.[4] After the publication of *Production of Commodities by Means of Commodities* in 1960, the Introduction to Ricardo's *Principles* came to be seen in a different light. In the heyday of Sraffian economics in Cambridge I remember a number of jokes about neoclassical economics. One such joke depicted the representative neoclassical economist as a rather dull person totally unable to understand the message from Sraffa's Introduction. Sraffa felt then obliged to deliver his book to the benefit of the neoclassicals. Of course the story gained currency as the benefit had turned into scorn. However that may be, there is a grain of truth in Paul Samuelson's 1987 dictum that no scholar had so great an impact on economic science as Sraffa did; further, the impact increased with Sraffa's age and also, in his view, with the passage of time.[5]

Now I would like to put my readers to test. Take the following statement:

> Sraffa's edition of the *Works and Correspondence of David Ricardo* proved to be more than a great scholarly achievement. For in his Introduction to the *Principles of Political Economy and Taxation* Sraffa presented an entirely new interpretation of Ricardo's theory of value and distribution. Sraffa's interpretation established a new, theoretically consistent version of the surplus approach to the analysis of distribution in the Essay on Profits. Further, he demonstrated that this approach was sustained in the *Principles* by Ricardo's use of the labour theory of value.

Suppose now you are in a wine-tasting contest and are asked to guess which vintage (pre- or post-1960) this particular wine belongs to. I do not want to anticipate your answer at this stage, as I am pretty sure that any careful reader will have no difficulty in putting forward the right reaction.[6]

In spite of the grain of truth in Samuelson's dictum (just quoted), it is a fact of life that some of you may well prefer the young wine to the old in many cases. In our present instance the meaning and impact of Sraffa's work seems, indeed, to have become stronger and clearer as time goes on (that is, after 1960); but, what actually happened was that the reception and the image of Sraffa's work on Ricardo *changed in nature*. As a consequence of inertia, however, little wonder that the new image did show a marked tendency to get squeezed, as it were, into the old one, thus giving rise to the "definitive interpretation" of Ricardo. The *definitive edition*, inadvertently and almost automatically, became the *definitive interpretation*. For a number of years nobody noticed the curious transformation; more particularly, the circumstance that, while the former phrase makes perfect sense, the latter is an insult to science went completely unnoticed.

An echo of that transformation seems to surface even today in the opening sentences of the *Economic Journal* Obituary (Schefold 1996):

> But it was, above all, his magnificent edition of the works of David Ricardo which was recognised in the whole world as a landmark of scholarship and which, on account of the editorial introduction, provided a link between classical economic theory and the post war discussions on growth and distribution. His *definitive* work, *Production of Commodities by Means of Commodities*, a slender volume, caused two controversies, one on the validity of neoclassical theory, the other on the revival of classical thought.
>
> (Schefold 1996, emphasis added)

In what sense, it may be asked, can *Production of Commodities* be described as a "definitive work"? This is far from clear, unless perhaps it is thought to be the work which renders definitive the "link between classical economic theory and the postwar discussions on growth and distribution" provided by the Introduction to Ricardo. That this means travelling long distances in some logical dimension still (2000) seems to remain totally unadverted.

Back to the text: philology and interpretation in the work of the greatest economist-editor

The curious deplorable fate met by Sraffa's Introduction to Ricardo's *Principles* seems to create a moral obligation on the part of any scholar who has acquired full consciousness of the facts to go back humbly to the text itself. Some may find the idea awkward to start from scratch and read Sraffa's Introduction, simply and directly, "for the first time", as it were. Years ago, as one participant to a colloquium appeared to offer rather naïve remarks and commonplace quotes, a friend, sitting by me, somewhat disparagingly observed: "You cannot just read Ricardo and Sraffa." "Be careful!" – I whispered back to him – "You may end up very close to saying that it not necessary at all, even dangerous, to read!" Such things do indeed happen. After (almost) fifty years we can, at last perhaps, be confident that we can actually *read*, unintruded on and probably unobserved.

To be fair, back in the 1950s, at least one of the top commentators, George Stigler, in his review of the Ricardo edition in the *American Economic Review*, 1953, had made some qualification in his appreciation for the "pure transparency" qualities of the edition. "*Aside from the introduction to vol. 1,*" Stigler wrote (emphasis added),

> Sraffa's editorial prefaces and notes serve an informative, rather than an interpretative, function. This severe self-abnegation was wise; the facts are relatively timeless but even the best analysis of a predecessor will change with the interests and knowledge of the science.
> (Stigler 1953; reprinted in Stigler 1965: 304)

In what follows I shall propose a reading of Sraffa's Introduction, by focussing upon those elements which appear to go beyond pure philology and discussing the links of those elements with Ricardo's own texts and with the Ricardian literature. Next I will discuss Sraffa's sources and trace whatever evidence exists on the construction of Sraffa's interpretation of Ricardo.[7] Finally I shall draw some conclusions on Sraffa's Ricardo in historical perspective.

The 'corn model'

The passage on the 'rational foundation' in Sraffa's Introduction to the *Principles* is too famous. Even the humble readers that we are here and now can dispense with the quotation. Precisely on this issue Samuel Hollander started to challenge the consensus on the "definitive interpretation" in his 1973

Economica paper. The effectiveness of Sraffa's exposition here takes advantage from the beauty, simplicity and robustness of the corn-ratio principle and from the suggestion that the principle itself must have been formulated by him in his (as Sraffa wrote: cf. Ricardo 1951–73, vol. 1: xxxi) "'lost' papers on the profits of Capital' of March 1814 or in conversation, since Malthus opposes him in . . . terms which are no doubt an echo of Ricardo's own formulation." The charisma of the economist-editor, whose expert eye has evidently acquired an unparalleled knowledge of the original documents as well as of the primary literature, is indeed very great; due to that charisma, that the principle was "never explicitly stated by Ricardo" (ibid.) becomes an advantage. Wouldn't it be flatly obvious, were the principle to be found in plain words just stated by Ricardo? It would be disappointing indeed. The way the principle is actually carved out of Ricardo's frame of mind makes it a precious discovery.

All of this, in turn, makes it just plain sailing for Sraffa to proceed like this:

> The advantage of *Ricardo's method of approach* is that, at the cost of considerable simplification, it makes possible an understanding of how the rate of profit is determined without the need of a method for reducing to a common standard a heterogeneous collection of commodities.
> (Ricardo 1951–73, vol. 1: xxxii, emphasis added)

The result is that a number of treatments on Ricardian economics deal with *Ricardo's* corn-ratio theory of profits.[8] Of course this is not the desirable outcome of the work and influence of an editor, who is necessarily at the same time an interpreter; this is, rather, the product of a peculiar conflation of philology and interpretation, the result of which is the monster of the "definitive interpretation."

"Adding up" theory of price

The phrase has become the common expression to designate Smith's theory of price. Here too the belief is widespread among scholars that the phrase itself belongs to Adam Smith. This is hardly the case. The adding up theory of price, in fact, is an original contribution of Sraffa, who appears to have been first to coin the English term and who made use of that in his Introduction to Ricardo's *Principles*.[9]

Sraffa's Introduction calls attention to the fact that the development of Ricardo's thought on income distribution was bound to call into question "the generally accepted view that a rise in corn prices, through its effects upon wages, would be followed by a rise of all other prices," thus leading Ricardo to establish the proposition "that a rise of wages does not raise prices." Ricardo soon discovered the important principle – which would later occupy the first section-heading in the chapter "On Value" of his *Principles* – that (in Sraffa's words: Ricardo 1951–73, vol. 1: xxxv) "the value of a thing was regulated by the quantity of labour required for its production, and not by the remuneration of that labour." These two statements should be read carefully: although they are appear almost side by side in Sraffa's text, they are *not* equivalent, the latter statement including, as it does, Ricardo's value theory on which the former says nothing. More important here, there is another difference between the two statements, and that is that the former statement implies that wages and prices move in the same direction, while the latter only criticizes the existence of a relationship between wages and prices, whatever its sign may be. For example in the *Principles*, Chapter 22 ("Bounties on exportation") Ricardo resorts to the former of the two arguments and criticizes Smith for considering (Ricardo's words) "a rise in the price of commodities as a necessary consequence of a rise in the price of corn"; but in the opening section of Chapter1 ("On value"), Smith is criticized for adopting the labor command standard of value, using the latter of these two arguments.[10] The implication of Ricardo's text in this case actually concerns an *inverse* relationship between wages and prices, because higher wages imply a lower command of labor and therefore a lower value of commodities. This is the same criticism Ricardo will level against Malthus (Ricardo 1992: *Notes on Malthus*: n.11): "What we want is a standard measure of value which shall be itself invariable. . . . And on what does Mr. Malthus fix as an approximation to this standard? The value of labour." Pages of sharp controversy follow in the *Notes on Malthus* at this point, as this is precisely the greatest conceivable mistake in Ricardo's eye, namely making the measure of value depend on a value: a vicious circle and therefore vicious reasoning.

On this point Sraffa intervenes with an interpretation of his own. Sraffa's interpretation reads *any* proposition on the relation of wages to prices in the additive sense, which is in fact only one of two possibilities *both utilized* by Ricardo. That Ricardo thus appears to be a critic of the wage–price relationship in the additive sense only paves the way to his being turned into the critic of the *adding up theory* as a perfectly natural consequence of "Ricardo's approach." Let us read Sraffa:

> The importance which Ricardo came to attach to the principle that the value of a thing was regulated by the quantity of labour required for its production, and not by the remuneration of that labour, reflected his recognition that what his new theory was opposed to was not merely the popular view of the effect of wages on prices but another and more general theory of Adam Smith (of which that effect came to appear as a particular case) – what Ricardo referred to Mill as Adam Smith's original error respecting value". This latter theory, in brief, was that "as soon as stock has accumulated in the hands of particular persons" and "as soon as the land of any country has all become private property", the price of commodities is arrived at by a process of *adding up* the wages, profit and rent: "in every improved society, all the three enter more or less, as component parts, into the price of the far greater part of commodities." In other words, "wages, profit, and rent, are the three original sources . . . of all exchangeable value." Adam Smith speaks also of the natural price varying "with the natural rate of each of its component parts, of wages, profit, and rent". (Sraffa's footnotes in this passage refer the reader to *The Wealth of Nations*: bk. 1 ch. vi; Cannan edn, vol. 1, 50–2, 54, 65).
>
> (Ricardo 1951–73, vol. 1: xxxv–vi)

This is the passage which has created the ongoing misperception on the nature of Adam Smith's theory. Again: Sraffa's procedure is perfectly legitimate once you realize that it is *one* interpretation.[11] The question then becomes not so much of seeing through the "true" Ricardo; rather it is a matter of understanding what Sraffa is doing. Let me offer, as a consolation to the reader, Cannan's opinion on the point. Speaking of Smith's Book 1, Chapter 6, Edwin Cannan wrote: "It is not very clear what exactly is supposed to happen – whether products acquire an *addition* to their labour-value for profit and rent or not"; at any rate "the equality of the wages, profits and rents with the price is no proof that the price is caused by the wages, profits and rents: it may be the other way round"(Cannan 1929: 168, 171, emphasis added).

The standard of value

In his analysis of the standard of value Ricardo was concerned with the requirement of invariability of the standard itself. The standard, in fact, must be invariable with respect to difficulty of production *and* with respect to changes in the distribution of income. These two aspects are naturally linked together in Ricardo's system, where diminishing returns in agriculture and the labor theory of value are the building blocks of the theory of production and distribution. In the course of his investigation of the problem of the standard of value, Ricardo became gradually convinced that a satisfactory standard, that is, one possessing invariability, could not be found. He therefore discussed a number of cases in order to reach the conclusion that a perfect standard was unattainable. In so doing, Ricardo discussed in detail the effects of changes in the distribution of income on the relative value of commodities produced under different circumstances, without extending the analysis to include the fact that the conditions of production themselves are subject to change with changes in the income distribution. Typical is his discussion of Malthus's position. Malthus had argued in favor of a labor-commanded principle and had introduced the example of a commodity obtained by labor alone, "without any advances above the food of a day," a standard in terms of which "no rise in the price of labour could take place" (See *Principles of Political Economy*, in Ricardo 1951–73, vol. 2: 81).

Ricardo, who had initially addressed to Malthus the same criticism of arbitrariness and lack of invariability already levelled against Smith, was later led to argue that Malthus's case provided yet another special case of conditions of production of a standard – indeed an extreme case – which made it no more liable to objection than any other standard that can be imagined. That fact is – Ricardo concluded in his last letter to Mill (Ricardo 1951–73, vol. 9: 387) – that "there is not in nature any correct measure of value nor can any ingenuity suggest one, for what constitutes a correct measure for some things is a reason why it cannot be a correct one for others."

All these Ricardian discussions on the standard of value are dominated by the *negative* purpose of a proof of impossibility; as a matter of fact, only going through a number of examples (and indeed *counter*-examples), Ricardo was able to reach the general negative conclusion just reported from his last letter to James Mill.[12]

It is against that background that we are left to read the interpretation given by Sraffa on Ricardo's continuing preoccupation with the effects of changes in wages.

> This preoccupation with the effect of a change in wages arose from his approach to the problem of value, which, as we have seen, was dominated by his theory of profits.... Thus the problem of value which interested Ricardo was how to find a measure of value which would be invariant to changes in the division of the product; for, if a rise or fall of wages by itself brought about a change in the magnitude of the social product, it would be hard to determine accurately the effect on profits. (This was, of course, the same problem as has been mentioned earlier in connection with Ricardo's corn-ratio theory of profits.)
> (Ricardo 1951–73, vol. 1: xlviii–xlix)

The sources of Sraffa's analysis

My argument in this chapter is that Sraffa's analysis is largely inspired, on the constructive side, by Marx's *Theorien über den Mehrwert*, together with a pervasive need – on the negative and destructive side – to counter the Marshallian synthesis in economics.[13] For a considerable time, as hinted earlier in this paper, any attempt to put Sraffa in a historical perspective was generally found unacceptable and sometimes even publicly condemned. The absurdity of turning Sraffa into an absolute was, however, bound to finish, although it is only at present that it is giving way to the buds of a new Sraffian historiography.[14] The core of the new historiography, in my view, should be developed through simple-minded exercises going back to the actual reading of Sraffa's own text (as exemplified earlier), undoubtedly supplemented with what has not been done earlier, that is, bringing in the relevant texts by Ricardo and Marx for proper comparison. This corresponds roughly to the former of the two grounds (see the introductory section to this chapter) for the present inquiry. It is contended that only this approach can possibly do justice to Sraffa as one of the great scholars of the twentieth century.

The latter ground remains to be dealt with. It is necessary, in other words, to trace the actual development of Sraffa's thought and consider whatever evidence exists on the sources of Sraffa's analysis also in the light of the archival materials and literary remains of Sraffa around the world. It is the purpose of this section to introduce a first discussion on the extant documents and evidence with particular reference to the papers left, by Sraffa's own will, to Trinity College, Cambridge, and kept there at the Wren Library. In this chapter, I shall actually confine myself to a few documents dating from the late 1920s, that is, those drafted during the period when Sraffa's thought indeed appeared to pass from the criticisms on the Marshallian system to the reconstruction of the classical approach to economic theory. We shall see presently that my conjecture on the Marxian inspiration of Sraffa as an interpreter of the classical economists is entirely brought out by the documents, which prove essential to adding a number of original aspects and perspectives.

This research has taken advantage of access to the archives of the Wren Library at Trinity College, Cambridge. Early attempts of a catalogue of Sraffa's literary remains, during Sraffa's own lifetime, were made by John Eatwell and Alessandro Roncaglia. Work was resumed, after Sraffa's death, by the late Krishna Bharadwaj and by Pierangelo Garegnani, Sraffa's literary executor. Sraffa's papers have now been catalogued by Jonathan Smith, archivist and manuscript cataloguer at Trinity.[15] In what follows I shall discuss sundry items among Sraffa's literary remains of the late 1920s.

Notes and jottings from the Sraffa papers

Sraffa's legacy at Trinity includes a number of items, such as, for example, his own magnificent library. As far as Sraffa's papers are concerned, they have been classified under ten headings, including, for example, career, family, diaries, correspondence, notes and lectures. The section heading of interest in the present context is section D ("Notes, Lectures and Publications"), from which I shall quote below.

A folder, marked "Notes/London, Summer 1927/(Physical Real Costs etc.)" in Sraffa's hand, makes up a rather nice set, now catalogue item D3/12/3 on Physical Real Costs, of 71 (as numbered by Sraffa) ruled exercise-book sheets mostly written one side in ink in Sraffa's hand. This is in fact a set of coherent notes, sometimes in the form of quickly sketched sentences sometimes written down in more expository style. They come under the title (cf. p.1) of "General Scheme/The adventures of the T.V. The problems which were prominent in the mind of the older economists" etc.

We find here a telling sketch for a possible history of economic analysis centered upon "T.V." (which in those times of course meant "Theory of Value"):

> [p.1] It is with Ricardo that T.V. becomes the central doctrine of P.E., and from him that schools and controversies originate. . . . But then taken up by Marx, and used as weapon for workers . . .[p. 2] Immediate (?) simultaneous success of utility with Jevons, Menger, Walras. It always happens with discoveries: and, as always, it is later found that unsuccessful predecessors had already discovered the whole thing. Reason to be found in anti-socialism . . . It should not be thought that theories devised (or accepted generally) for partisan purposes have no scientific value: they contain element of truth, which is of scientific value, and is added to knowledge and seldom is lost again. How thus theory goes on improving. Work of Marshall is combining results of two schools: "causes" of value, notion of equilibrium, fundamental, whatever we think of Marshall's particular applications. Curious misunderstanding as to Marshall and Ricardo's relation to Marx's surplus value: acceptance of Marshall due to belief that it combined classical with orthodox school, and did not lend itself, like the former did, to Socialistic interpretation. Nonsense: Marx's surplus value does not depend upon labour being the only cause, [p. 3] or even one cause of value, but to its being proportional to value: explain in detail difference of the two notions.

Ludicrous belief that Marx says "labour is the only cause of value, therefore all value must go to labour."

(Sraffa 1927: D3/12/3)

Two ideas should be singled out from this passage which are very important to illustrate Sraffa's intellectual development: first, the ideological sources of the success of utility, and second, the tendency of value theory, with the ideological reaction based on utility, to focus on causes rather than measures of value. These points are hinted in the pages just quoted and we have to turn to other documents to reconstruct the two ideas more fully.

Let me now consider a set of notes dated, from a pencil annotation in Sraffa's hand, "End of November 1927." These are catalogued D3/12/4 and can be considered as preparations for the Lectures 1928–31: the latter are the best and most interesting manuscript in this section of his papers.[16] Here Sraffa presents a summary sketch of the historical inquiry he has in mind. In the fourth set of sheets, item 10, we read:

<u>Classical Political Economy</u> (the age of Ricardo) or A. Smith?
from Petty to Ricardo. |
    Right conception (fundamental assumptions) primitive, rudimentary technique
(A. Smith had strong "vulgar" tendencies: he can truly be said to be the "founder of modern economics"!)
<u>Vulgar Political Economy</u> (the age of Mill)
from Malthus to Stuart Mill |
    All wrong here: they have the wrong conceptions of modern economics and the rudimentary technique of the classical
Period dominated by Mill: Marx stands here towering as the last of the classical amongst the vulgar, just as Smith stood isolated among the classicals, being the first of the vulgars.
<u>Economics</u> (the age of Marshall) since Jevons & Co, and Marshall |
    Highly refined technique, rotten conceptions and fundam. assumptions.
But techniques so highly perfected that sometimes compels them unconsciously to modify their conscious assumptions (justly contradicting themselves) and thus reaching partially true conclusions
<u>Note</u> that at the end of the classics developed primitive socialism (Owen, Hodgskin) and <u>caused</u> Vulgar P.E. At the end of vulgar period came Marx and <u>caused</u> economics.

(Sraffa 1927: D3/12/4)

I dwell on the issues and first examine the full force of the ideological element in Sraffa's image of the historical progression from political economy to economics. A premise of all this is given by the importance Sraffa attributes to the historico-analytic approach. In a set of papers (D3/12/11) again dated November 1927 he speaks of the approach to be adopted in a prospective book. The only way (he notes writing in Italian cf. the original text in note 17) is in going through history in reverse, that is: from the present state of economics and how that came to be reached, showing the difference and the superiority of the old theories, and then expounding the theory. If a chronological order is followed: Petty, the physiocrats, Ricardo, Marx, Jevons, Marshall (Sraffa continues) then it is necessary to give as a premise to all that a statement of my own theory in order to explain where we drive at; which means expounding first *all* of the theory. Then there is however the danger of ending up like Marx, who started publishing his *Capital* and later was unable to complete the *History of Doctrines*, and what is worse is that he has been unable to make himself understood without the historical explanation. My plan is (Sraffa concludes): first, treat the history which is what is really essential and second, make myself understood, which requires me to proceed from the known to the unknown, from Marshall to Marx, from disutility to material cost.[17]

Sraffa's ambitions are very clear. The lectures he has been appointed to deliver at Cambridge are to be made the occasion for a book in which the historico-analytic method is adopted for an eminently theoretical purpose. Marx, but *not* Marx in general, Marx the historian of analysis *manqué*, must provide the guide both in method and in contents, as also the list of past authors indicates. Marshall, of course, that is, the present, is the starting point.

What follows is a rather lengthy quote of the same period. It is not my purpose here to be exhaustive, as the amount of notes and documents is very large and, at any rate in the present context, it would be impossible to follow all nuances and variations on the themes proposed. Therefore, let me turn to what looks like a lucid typical statement of that stage in the development of Piero Sraffa's thought. In a note entitled "Metaphisics," again November 1927, Sraffa further wrote:

> In this theory it will be thought that the important part is the analytical and constructive. The significance of the historical side will be missed. And yet, this is truly important, that which gives us a real insight into the mystery of human mind and understanding, into the deep unknown relations of individuals between themselves and between individual and society, (the social, or rather the class mind).
>
> It is terrific to contemplate the abysmal gulf of incomprehension that has opened itself between us and the classical economists. Only one century separates us from them: how can we imagine to understand the Greeks and the Romans? The classical economists said things which were perfectly true, even according to our standards of truth: they expressed them very clearly, in terse and unambiguous language, as is proved by the fact that they perfectly understood each other. We dont understand a word of what they said: has their language been lost? Obviously not, as the English of Adam Smith is what people talk to-day in this country. What happened then?
>
> I foresee that the ultimate result will be a restatement of Marx, by substituting to his Hegelian metaphysics and terminology our own modern metaphysics and terminology: by metaphysics here I mean, I suppose, the emotions that are associated with our terminology and frames (schemi mentali) – that is, what is absolutely necessary to make the theory living (lebendig), capable of assimilation and at all intelligible. If this is true, it is

an exceptional example of how far a difference in metaphysics can make to us absolutely unintelligible an otherwise perfectly sound theory. This would be simply a translation of Marx into English, from the forms of Hegelian metaphysics to the forms of Hume's metaphysics (Keynes today, 26.XI.27, has clearly outlined the divorce between English and Continental thought: the first descending from Descartes and Hobbes, two original geniuses, to Locke, Hutcheson and ultimately Hume; the second from Spinoza (did he say that of S.?) from Kant to Hegel: they always remained foreign to one another).

If this is true it also shows (or is it an exceptional case? in Physics it doesnt seem to be indifferent) how little our metaphysics affects the truth of our conclusions, and how the same truths can be expressed in two widely divergent forms. Our metaphysics is in fact embodied in our technique; the danger lies in this, that when we have succeeded in thoroughly mastering a technique, we are very liable to be mastered *by* her.

The typical case of Marx's metaphysics is his statement that "only human labour produces (causes) values," "values are embodied human energy (crystallized)": there is no doubt that he attached to it some metaphysical meaning.

The extraordinary thing is that the same metaphysical notion is held by such an anti-Marxian as Cannan (Theories: 380).

The metaphysics of the modern economist is that "a commodity . . . is the embodiment of measurable efforts and sacrifices" (Marshall, Memorials, 126); on the same plane as Marx's "crystallized labour." And much more Clark's notion that marginal distribution being equal to product of each is "just." Clark's metaphysics is much more grossolana than Marx's: it is equal to Proudhon's, Hodgskin etc. who believed (<u>against</u> Marx) that since labour produces the whole it must get the whole.

All the inquiry about value has always been (and still is and probably always will be) a purely metaphysical quest. When the old economists asked for the "causes" or the "measure" of value, they really were looking – as in fact we are, under the illusion of our equations "determining" value – for the "nature" of value (It is not by accident, as Cannan, elsewhere, says that the word is in A. Smith's title) in the same metaphysical sense in which we look for the nature of "matter" or of "mind." In fact, we want to "explain" in terms of familiar words, or notions (i.e. to which we are used) the "new" thing that we meet: but when we have got used to them (as now economists have with prices) we take them for granted and require no further explanation. The explanation has simply to be "satisfactory" that is to provide the accommodation suited for our mental habits, and prove restful to the mind – cool down the fever of quest and satiate the thirst for explanation.

Still more terrific. In the middle of the 19th century a man succeeds, either by accident of by superhuman effort, in getting again hold of the classical theory: he improves it, and draws its practical consequences from it.[18]

(Sraffa November 1927: D3/12/4; 14–17)

The manuscript, unfortunately, breaks off at this point. Who that man could be remains to be guessed, although it does not seem too difficult.

History, to Sraffa, means a sort of entropy of the theory of value. We are in the presence of a degenerating ("rotten conceptions") research program. The great fears aroused by the advent of socialism have made economic theory respond on the same degenerate theoretical plane on which the vulgar had argued: in that way the entire body of economic theory is affected by the illness, and the soundness of the classical approach is lost. This is a crude reconstruction of what was in Sraffa's mind at the time, and it seems particularly useful to the understanding of Sraffa as editor of Ricardo and his sources. The basic point is that Marx himself is at risk of being confused with the vulgar, while in truth it is the contrary ("stands towering"). It becomes imperative to go back to the classical approach to value theory, which to Sraffa must be the right approach to cost and value to be highlighted in the lectures. However before turning to the lectures, let us examine another example of the description of the process of degeneration itself, November 1927:

> Degeneration of cost & value
> A. Smith, Ricardo and Marx indeed began to corrupt the old idea of cost, – from food to labour. But their notion was still near enough to be in many cases equivalent.
>
> The decomposition went on at a terrific speed from 1820 to 1870: Senior's abstinence and Mill's mess of the whole thing. Cairnes brought it to the final stage "sacrifice" (did Marshall take it from Cairnes? see his Princ. note p. 339; seems not)[.] Simultaneously a much bigger step was taken in the process of shifting the basis of value from physical to psychical processes: Jevons, Menger, Walras.
>
> This was an enormous breach with the tradition of Pol. E.; in fact, this has meant the destruction of the classical P.E. and the substitution for it, under the old name, of the Calculus of Pleasure and Pain (Hedonistic). V. Retro.
>
> When the Jevonsians turned back to write their own history, they found with pride (it ought to have been with dismay) that they had no forerunners amongst P.E.; their forerunners were mainly two or three cranks, an engineer Dupuit, a mathem. Cournot, a prussian Civil Servant Gossen, who had only cultivated P.E. as a Hobby. V. Retro. They had not the slightest knowledge of the works of the Classical economists. They drew it out of their fancy. In fact, no competent P. Emist, with a conscience of his tradition, would have degnato to entertain those views.
>
> (Sraffa November 1927: D3/12/4 item 2)

The two retros read:

> I do not mean by this that cranks can never find new theories: on the contrary, when a big breach with tradition is required, their intervention is usually necessary. What I meant to prove is that there has actually been a breach with tradition, and the intervention of the cranks is an element of the evidence; and that Marshall's attempt to bridge over

the cleavage and establish a continuity in the tradition is futile and misguided.

(ibid.: 1927)

It is unfortunate that so much time has been taken to change the name of P.E. into Economics: but it is appropriate: it marks the cleavage, or rather the abyss, between the two.

(ibid.: 1927)

The main text of these notes continues thus (on a new sheet numbered "2" by Sraffa, still belonging to item 2 of the same set):

What had happened in the meantime, to change so much the mind of the economists, and induce them to scrap all that had been done up to that time? (It was in fact scrapping the whole: Jevons, Preface, and Cannan, Theories, 379–83, "must be visited with almost unqualified condemnation" are right from the point of view of *Economics*).

Socialism has been the cause of all this. In fact, classical P.E., with its surplus to be arbitrarily divided, leads straight to Socialism. When after the death of Ricardo the first timid attempts of using socialistically his theory of value were made (Hodgskin, Thompson: they were misguided if (?) they used the moral argument that labour produces everything as Proudhon, but not Marx did), Senior and Mill and Cairnes rallied to the defence by making cost psychological.

But when the mass attack of Marx, and the threat of the rampant International and the Paris Commune came, a much more drastic defence was called for: not only sacrifice, but utility, – and simultaneously J. M. W. and their success. The classical economy was becoming too dangerous as a whole, it had to be scrapped bodily. It was a burning house which threatened to set to fire the whole structure and foundations of the capitalist society – it was forthwith removed.

(ibid.: 1927)

A pencilled remark is added at the bottom of the page and completes it: "(Mention Rae, Ferrara, Carey? Schuling cost of reproduction as a link between disutility and utility, to justify the passing from one to the other."

Here significantly comes a sheet (D3/12/4, item 3) with the most famous quote from Petty ("The Method I take . . . Angles of Incidence and Reflection," from the preface to *Political Arithmatick*). Carefully written down, it shows the significance this has for Sraffa, to whom it epitomizes the *correct classical* conception of cost of production. Compare with the following vivid highlight from the following sheet (item 4 of the same set):

Evolution of concept of cost.

It was only Petty and the Physiocrats who had the right notion of cost as "the loaf of bread." Then somebody started measuring in labour, as every day's labour requires the same amount of food.

Then they proceeded to regard cost as actually an amount of labour. The[n] A. Smith interpreted labour as "the toil and trouble" which is the "real cost" (Ricardo: 10, 15 n) and the "hardship."

Then this was by Ricardo brought back to labour, but not far back enough, and Marx went only as back as Ricardo.

Then Senior invented Abstinence. And Cairnes unified all the costs (work, abstinence and risk) as sacrifice.

Now Davenport, Cassell, Henderson, have carried it a step further, the last step in the wrong direction.

(Sraffa November 1927: D3/12/4 item 4)

In his published articles of the mid-1920s, as is well known, Sraffa had chosen to criticize "the wrong direction," though approaching the subject from a different starting point. However, behind the scenes, the ambition was much larger. The Lectures, and a *fortiori* the notes and documents, are indeed behind the scenes. We are now in a position to appreciate that, despite the long delay, the Ricardo edition is probably the place where Sraffa (helped by Dobb) comes closest to committing his entire ambitions to the printed page. Marx, of course, is the pivot of the 'new' theory born from the resurrection of classicism, suitably dressed this time in an impeccable positivist-empiricist 'metaphysics'. If Smith continues to play the herald of the vulgar, Ricardo must be defended: only by misinterpreting him can we put him among the degenerate, as we shall see next. An example in that sense is afforded by Hollander and that makes Sraffa literally furious. Again in November 1927, he wrote:

Hollander, Ricardo,/p. 126 "Perversions of R. by Marx" / "... Ricardo regarded embodied labour as merely one of a series of possible units of value measurement but he was very far from asserting its unique efficacy, and indeed ultimately arrived at ... agnosticism ... He wrote to McCulloch ... we have a choice only among imperfect measures ..." / Idiot! It is sufficient to see Ricardo's Works, p. 11 / Cp. p. 68 n.3. R. "unwilling to concede" that command over labour instead of labour embodied is the foundation of value!!!

(Sraffa 1927: D3/12/11; 105)

Here are the remote sources of Sraffa's pervasive harshness on Hollander throughout the Ricardo edition.

Sraffa's lectures on value, 1928–31

I now to turn to Sraffa's notion of cost, developed at that time. Here, again, my analysis is not supposed to be exhaustive, but it is limited to the essential points. It is proper to turn to the Lectures, mentioned earlier and listed under D2/4, with D3/12/4, discussed earlier, in mind.

Although I do not mean to discuss here the whole development of Sraffa's argument in the Lectures, it is worth going back through that particular text to the theory of value: the issue of value not only was in fact the main subject of the lectures, but logically does provide the necessary background to the classical notion of cost, which it is among Sraffa's main objects to emphasize.

The theory of value – Sraffa argues – is no purely logical exercise. It is influenced by "practical problems", which makes room for history (see note 2). Sraffa's compelling reasons are for a historico-analytic approach:

> There is also another reason for the necessity of the knowledge of the history of their origin in order to understand economic theories. Every economist finds that the public to whom he addresses himself has already found for himself an explanation, whether right or wrong, of economic phenomena; and therefore a large part of his work is directed to correct popular opinions and to dispel widespread prejudices. Thus every economist tends to frame his theories in such a way that certain elements acquire in them an importance which is entirely out of proportion of the part they play in real life, but reflects the necessity in which the economist has been of opposing obsolete theories or popular prejudices. And when the theory has crystallised and we have forgotten the way in which it has grown, we are often inclined to over-estimate the importance of certain elements simply because for long forgotten historical reasons they play a very large part in accepted economic theory.
>
> A further disturbing element is that in the background of every theory of value there is a theory of distribution. The real problem to be solved by a theory of value, that is "Why is a commodity exchanged with another in a given ratio?" is constantly transformed into the entirely different one: "How is the price received for the product distributed between the factors of production?"
>
> (Sraffa 1928–9: 3, 4)

Thus:

> Ricardo's theory of value, whatever may have been in the back of his mind, or in his footnotes and in his private letters to Malthus and McCulloch, was understood by everybody in his time to mean that quantity of labour was the only cause of value, and this is what in practice mattered.
>
> (Sraffa 1928–9: 11)

Now, as the social conflict from one between landlords and manufacturers turns historically into one between labor and capital, Ricardo's theory of value "obviously becomes a strong argument in favour of labour. / A Socialist school arose in the twenties and thirties of last century which seized this opportunity." That "caused a good deal of confusion amongst the orthodox Ricardian economists, who saw their doctrines used in such an unexpected way"; the Ricardians in this country (Torrens, McCulloch, Malthus) were still at work to understand Ricardo's exceptions to the labor value rule. The turning point, though, (ibid.: 14) is the early 1970s with the publication of *Das Kapital* by Marx (ibid.: 14–15) "in which his critique of capitalism is entirely based upon

Ricardo's theory of value, although of course he interpreted it in an entirely different way from the early Utopian socialists" on one side and the rise of marginalism on the other. Concerning the latter point, after a brief discussion of the issue, "I rather prefer" – Sraffa wrote (ibid.: 16–17) – "to accept Prof. Fetter's and Sir W. Ashley's view, that there is a close relation between the emerging of Marxism and the extraordinarily ready acceptance of the theory of marginal utility amongst orthodox economists."

At this point (ibid.: 17) Sraffa first makes clear the main purpose of the historical reconstruction, which leads to the central role of the notion of cost and to the imperative of a return to the classical conception of it:

> The point I wish to make, is the independence in the development of the two opposite conceptions, of cost and of utility. In Marshall's theory they appear as closely connected, in fact they are for him two quantities of the same nature, one positive and the other negative; they can be added or subtracted and balanced against one another. But this unification, and therefore the statement of the symmetry between cost and utility, and through them of supply and demand, has been to a large extent the result of Marshall's work – not of the historical development of the theory of value. Their origin has to be traced to entirely distinct sources, and their development has been quite independent of one another. Then Marshall has brought them together and has made an attempt to conciliate the two opposite views, which I shall refer to as of Ricardo and of Jevons, each of whom thought that it was possible to group all causes of value under one single notion at the exclusion of the other[.] / [18] What is important to realize however is that the notion of cost of production, as understood by the classical economists, would not have allowed such a unification; to make this possible it had itself to pass through a series of small changes which gradually brought it to its present position.
>
> (Sraffa 1928–9: 17–8)

We come now to the classical conception of cost.

> Marshall regards the "real cost of production" of a commodity as the sum of "efforts and sacrifices" involved in the abstinences or waitings and in the labour of all kinds that is directly or indirectly required for the production of a commodity. Real cost therefore is an aggregate of the unpleasant feelings of various sorts felt by the individuals connected with production./ For Petty and the Physiocrats cost i.e. what in their theory plays the role of cost is nothing so subjective; on the contrary, it is a stock of material, that is required for the production of a commodity; this material being of course mainly food for the workers. But Petty wants to make it quite clear that his notion of cost has nothing to do with the pleasant or unpleasant feelings of men, and he defines "the common measure of value" as "the days food of an adult Man, at a Medium, and not the days labour." / This cost is therefore something concrete, tangible, and visible, that can be measured in tons or gallons. It stands therefore at the opposite extreme of Marshall's cost, which

is absolutely private to each individual, and can only be measured (if at all) by means of the monetary inducement required to call forth the exertion.
(Sraffa 1928–9: 20–1)

H. Kurz has recently published a paper on the Sraffa manuscripts that he had presented at the Caravale Memorial Conference in Rome (June 1988). In a yet unpublished comment read at the conference, Giorgio Rodano captured a message from Kurz's paper (Kurz 1998: esp. sec. 4: 447) in the fact that it is maintained that there is no evidence that Sraffa aimed at re-establishing the labor theory of value. While this is no doubt true, it would be unwarranted to infer that Sraffa had little contact, even little knowledge, of Marx's thought at an early stage, and that his starting point was Marshall's theory. Rodano's comment, indeed, went as far as taking the latter view, which does not fit with the evidence. If we connect the published articles with the lectures and finally with his personal notes, the emerging picture of Sraffa is one of an ambitious reconstruction of economic theory centered upon Marx. Marx, in other words, is to Sraffa far from being a synonym of the labor theory of value. In this way he undoubtedly also relied on the lesser-known parts of Marx's analysis and he did not even need to mention Marx too often, although his intellectual background comes out quite clearly from the personal notes. Sraffa's quotations from Petty, for example, had been, without significant exception, accurately sieved by Marx himself.[19]

Similar remarks do apply to the view, Sraffa conveys to his students, on the Physiocratic system, which, he argues:

> turns upon the conception of cost which I have outlined. . . . Measuring both the product and the cost in physical amount it is obvious that in agriculture, say in a corn farm, the amount of corn produced is greater than the amount used for seed and for subsistence of the workers. . . . [N]o doubt . . . in agriculture, owing to the identity in the quality of the product and of the materials used up in production, the comparison for the calculation of the surplus is possible to some extent without introducing the disturbing element of price for measuring the quantities.
> (Sraffa 1928–9: 25–6)

All this also heeds Marx's *Mehrwert* analysis quite closely.[20] This is far from being the end of the analysis that can be done on Sraffa's sources: but, at least, is it not clear enough where the "corn model" comes from? It is both useful to learn and natural to conclude that the surplus approach (and together with it, incidentally, the notion of fixed capital, although we are not discussing the latter at this stage) both originate from that particular period during the 1920s.

Another unmistakable Marxian element is the attribution to Smith of the usual ambiguous role. "It is A. Smith" – Sraffa noted in 1927 – "that shunted the car on the wrong track. In fact we have ceased to understand value from the moment the economic science was found."[21] In the Lectures Sraffa wrote:

> A. Smith adopted this notion of surplus, and with it the idea of cost of the

Physiocrats. But he has also a different idea of cost – and it is in a sense true that the Wealth of N. as a whole represents the connecting link between the eighteen[th] century economics and the modern one. Thus he conceives of labour as an amount of "toil and trouble": although he uses this expression only incidentally, Marshall has thought it so important and significant as to say that "the point of view . . . from which a commodity is regarded as the embodiment of measurable efforts and sacrifices" "was conquered for us by A. Smith" (Mem[orials,] 126).

(Sraffa 1928–9: 27)

Of course this sets in the transformation or degeneration of the conception of cost, eventually leading us to conceive, with Marshall, of "wages, interest and profits . . . simply [as] shares in the product; they are coordinate quantities, that can be regarded as acting upon the value of the product in the same way" (ibid.: 22). Is it not clear that Sraffa's adding up conception belongs, much as it is for Marx's *Zusammenaddierung*, to the 'degenerative' process? Ricardo was different; of course he had his own doubts; he "reduces cost to a single element, labour, with some doubts as to whether to include the services of capital in addition to the labour that has produced the capital goods" (ibid.: 36).

A passage from a letter to McCulloch, on the "by two causes instead of by one" question, is given (ibid.: 39); that letter is the one of June 1820, very wellknown to Ricardian scholars, which appears in the 1951 Introduction (pp. xxxix–xl), and the interpretation of which was entirely subverted by the Introduction itself.

In sum: the causal degeneration of the theory of value starts with Ricardian socialism and continues with marginalism, which is fully-fledged 'vulgar' political economy. Sraffa's reaction is to rectify the historico-analytic interpretation of Ricardo and Marx via eliminating the metaphysics on value and via the return to the Classical conception of cost.

A few cautionary remarks are made explicit in the conclusions; earlier remarks, as already hinted, are only meant to offer a few highlights of the work that needs to be done on Sraffa's sources. That work is necessary for an adequate discussion on the classical school in economics; it allows us to acquire the proper historical perspective on the interpretation of Ricardo. In the domain of Ricardian scholars Sraffa is likely to emerge, perhaps not immediately but probably into the new millennium, as an extreme case.

Sraffa's Ricardo in historical perspective

Sraffa's interpretation of Ricardo largely occupies the center of the stage in the literature on Ricardo and on the classical economists down to the present day. Sraffa produced the most fascinating bold endeavor to implement the Marxian program, whereby the surplus perspective becomes the unifying element for a number of systems constituting 'classical political economy' in Marx's sense.

The Sraffian reading of Ricardo – too often misrepresented either as a "definitive" reading (as if that could be thought of) or as a preferred target for criticism – needs to be reconsidered in a comparative perspective with respect to its own inspiring sources, as well as with regard to parallel or different readings. Once the necessary critical reconsideration has been completed, the following problems will presumably emerge.

First, Sraffa's interpretation shares with some of the neoclassical interpretations the strong tendency to involve Ricardian analysis with disputes about the origin and the moral justification of the distributive rates, and thereby with problems on which Ricardo had little to say.

Second, each party claims Ricardo as a predecessor. While a number of neoclassical authors focus on Ricardo in a continuistic perspective, Sraffa's interest lies in making room for the dichotomy of a classical versus a neoclassical school in a fashion which resembles the contribution given by Jevons or, more directly, Marx's analysis on the dissolution of the Ricardian school and the advent of the *Vulgärökonomie*. This Marxian factor is the decisive force pushing Ricardo into the front line of the divide.

Third, Sraffa's perspective should also be judged within the context of the postwar revival of Marxian economics and of Marxian studies more generally. The criticisms levelled against Sraffa from the Marxian camp have now been silenced but were far from unfounded. In particular giving up the labor theory of value implies that the core concept of exploitation becomes problematic.

The analysis developed in this chapter has demonstrated – under the conditions discussed and with the proviso that no definitive judgement exists in economics – that the editorial work of Sraffa has shown conclusively that the implementation of the Marxian program on classical economics has failed to establish the new orthodoxy or mainstream interpretation. Canon ambitions are at present probably to some extent misplaced, which incidentally, besides being a historical fact, also provides a methodological guideline worth considering. The notion of classical school in economics no longer appears centered on Ricardo to the same extent. Although it remains true that economics is based upon different paradigms, Ricardo plays a lesser role in the distinction.

In recent papers, Samuel Hollander (Hollander 1998 and 2000) partly disputes the present historical perspective on Sraffa's work. It is now proper briefly to dwell on Hollander's view.[22]

"In an ongoing investigation," Hollander writes (Hollander 1998: 432–3), "I approach the general position of Bronfenbrenner and Porta as an hypothesis: can the 'Sraffian' reading of Ricardo only be rationalized in 'post-Marxian' terms ?" He goes on to argue that an investigation must be made, which is in fact one object of the paper, on "how in *actuality* did Sraffa arrive at his reading." In brief, the upshot of the exercise is a demonstration that "to take the 'Sraffian' view requires that one limits the reading of Ricardo to parts of select chapters in the *Principles* – specifically chapters 1 and 6 – involving highly simplified illustrative exercises." Therefore – Hollander concludes – as

> an appropriately 'truncated' view of Ricardo yields the Sraffian attributions, Professor Porta's objections to the Sraffa reading prove to be too

severe. Nonetheless, the hypothesis that this perspective might reflect a reading through Marx's spectacles cannot be dismissed out of hand.

(Hollander 1998: 433)

However, in spite of a number of concessions, in the final instance Hollander's view of Sraffa's Ricardo seems to be one of selective reading. Hollander's approach on this point is indeed parallel to the approach adopted by Heinz Kurz and Neri Salvadori, in their paper on "The 'Standard Commodity' and Ricardo's 'Invariable Measure'" in the recent Pasinetti *Festschriften* volume. Limiting themselves to the search for the invariable measure of value, Kurz and Salvadori observe that Sraffa's 1951 Introduction

> focussed attention on those aspects of Ricardo's search for an invariable measure of value which concerned the theory of value and distribution with a given technological environment, whereas the intertemporal and interspatial aspect of Ricardo's problem is neglected.
>
> (Kurz and Salvadori 1993: 107)

In the light of the evidence examined in this chapter, it is maintained here that the Marxian perspective provides the most powerful and convincing assumption on the development of Sraffa's thought, and particularly on the formative process of his interpretation of Ricardo. In his attempt to avoid this conclusion Hollander ends up with the following statement: we cannot exclude "a possible inclination towards the 'narrow' [i.e. the selective reading] view of Ricardo for additional, independent, reasons" (Hollander 1998: 435). When it comes to spelling out those "reasons," the suggestion, advanced by Hollander, is Sraffa's "hostility ... towards subjectivist economics," the Marshallian synthesis included. My section "The sources of Sraffa's analysis" has shown that that is not in fact to be rated an independent reason; therefore, in my view, the Marxian connection must be retained as the only viable hypothesis in the reconstruction of the development of Sraffa's thought, and particularly in the reconstruction of his interpretation of Ricardo. That the close of Hollander's 1998 article refers to "a powerful Marxian undercurrent" seems to suggest at least some acknowledgement on his part of the substantial validity of my argument in this chapter.

I am far, on the other hand, from any temptation of toying with deconstructionist opinions. It seems appropriate to conclude the present inquiry with a note of caution. This chapter is in fact aiming at a preliminary estimate in an ongoing investigation. The greatest attention has been given to avoid all possible confusion between Sraffa's own positions and the positions of the various interpreters of Sraffa as they emerge from the literature. This of course is more difficult than at first it appears to be. Much as the young researcher in David Lodge's popular romance *Small World* surprised his mentors when he proposed to write a thesis on the influence of T. S. Eliot on William Shakespeare, we are ourselves concerned, in a sense, with Sraffa's influence on Ricardo rather than the other way round; and the same, of course, can apply to Sraffa himself.[23] Hermeneutic sophistry has caused the saga of "what so and so *really* said" to lose much of its appeal.

We try, as much as possible, to argue on the basis of Sraffa's own words, and that is important for a reconstruction based on due identification and recognition of subsequent intellectual influences. No doubt the choice of the words contains a subjective element; B. Schefold, for example, shows that (see note 8) Sraffa was careful "to avoid concepts that did not appear explicitly in Ricardo's text": yet, as we have seen, he is no less of an interpreter of Ricardo. One related question deserving emphasis is that our argument implies an assumption of continuity and "time consistency" in the development of Sraffa's own research program. I think this is a sensible assumption to adopt, although it is important to be alert to the fact that there may be some who consider that standpoint to imply an unwarranted concession to the common image of Sraffa as the man of few immutable lifelong relentlessly pursued questions.

What seems important at the present stage is to undertake an investigation, as systematic as possible, on the basis of the available evidence. The question of the sources of Sraffa's economic analysis is still a very open question. As examples of further directions in the investigation, we can mention the fact that we are still unable to go beyond very conventional statements on the actual influence, if any, of Russian-German Marxism on Sraffa. Another rather surprising fact is that we are totally at a loss to find any trace whatever of the actual elaboration of the Introduction to Ricardo. Given Sraffa's method of work such as can be inferred from the state of his literary remains, that is very surprising indeed.

However these are mere examples in a continuing investigation: the reconstruction of Sraffa's scientific personality is the real object of an inquiry which seems now happily starting. Achieving that will certainly vindicate Samuelson's dictum (note 5) that Sraffian studies lead to new intellectual discoveries.[24]

Notes

I am grateful to Ross Emmett, Augusto Graziani, Gary Mongiovi, Samuel Hollander, Nerio Naldi, Luigi Pasinetti and Paul Samuelson for appreciations, discussions and criticisms through the formative stages of this paper. The usual disclaimer applies. I have certainly not been able to take full advantage of their valuable suggestions in the present draft.

A special obligation must be recorded to Pierangelo Garegnani for granting permission to quote from Piero Sraffa's unpublished writings.

An acknowledgement is due to the Librarian of Trinity College, Cambridge for granting access to their manuscript collection. I have a special obligation to the staff of the Wren Library at Trinity, particularly to Jonathan Smith and Diana Chardin, for help and assistance on innumerable occasions.

1 One could well argue that the period should extend to reach 1992, nine years after Sraffa's death, when David Ricardo's *Notes on Malthus's "Measure of Value"* were published. The publication of the *Notes*, encouraged by Sraffa himself, virtually belongs to his own feat.

2 Sraffa was himself sympathetic to an *ante-litteram* Schumpeterian approach. Theories – he wrote in his yet unpublished lectures, (1928–29: 2–3) – arise from practical problems; "once they have arisen in this way, theories transform and develop in a way which to some extent is independent from the practical interests from which they have originated."

Sraffa added, however, that "this is not the end of the story." For it is precisely "by reason of this independence and of the prestige [theory] derives from it, [that] its effectiveness for supporting or opposing a particular policy is again increased, and thus inevitably the theory again becomes the object of controversies of a practical character." This is an essential qualification to the Schumpeterian view, implying that the historico-analytic perspectives are never definitive, as I argue in the course of this chapter.

3 The above – *mutatis mutandis*, but very little indeed needs to be altered – applies to Samuel Hollander as well, although in the comparison the latter's style undoubtedly is more openly provocative ("There is no sharp distinction between Ricardo and Walras," Hollander 1979: 683, for example) compared to Sraffa's. It is hardly necessary to recall that, from that methodological standpoint, Sraffa and Hollander move on one and the same ground. That their respective conclusions are wide apart still seems to excite interest rather than create doubts.

4 This was of course the very same indictment Sraffa had issued against Marshall in the 1920s (Sraffa 1998: 347).

This instance is an example of an important psychological mechanism: we are never so able to expose a behavioral or mental process in our fellows as is the case when we are unconsciously pursuing the very same process to a much higher degree.

The following well-known passage in the Gospel according to Luke provides a striking illustration of the mechanism.

> And why beholdest thou the mote that is in thy brother's eye, but considerest not the beam that is in thine own eye? Or canst thou say to thy brother, Brother, let me cast out the mote that is in thine eye, when thou thyself beholdest not the beam that is in thine own eye? Thou hypocrite, cast out first the beam out of thine own eye, and then shalt thou see clearly to cast out the mote that is in thy brother's eye."
>
> (Luke VI, 41–2)

Parenetic overtones aside, this is an admirable description of a psychological process of which Sraffa himself may well have been entirely unaware.

5 See the close of the entry on "Sraffian economics" by Paul A. Samuelson in the *New Palgrave*. "Piero Sraffa" – Samuelson concluded – "was much respected and much loved. With each passing year, economists perceive new grounds for admiring his genius."

6 You are welcome to check the details on the source of the passage in the text in note 24 at the end of this chapter.

7 This preliminary estimate still is necessarily incomplete as far as these extensions of the analysis are concerned.

8 Schefold 1998 affirms that the entry "Corn-ratio theory of profits" in Sraffa's index to the Ricardo edition "is almost unique in taking up an economic concept used not by Ricardo but by his editor." On the other hand – he goes on to observe – "Ricardo was not very good at naming concepts which he had created," whereas, he adds, Sraffa was equally good both at naming new concepts and at creating them.

Whose creation actually was the corn-ratio idea remains mysterious. (see, however, p260). In my essay on Ricardo (in Becattini 1990: 113) I put forward the view that the corn model, if it ever came across Ricardo's mind at all, did so as a "strong case," i.e. a counter-example to refute Malthus's theory of profits. I surmise I did argue that way in the same logic, leading Sam Hollander to write:

> Ricardo's emphasis upon corn in the wage basket has its source in . . . the very strong objection Ricardo took to Malthus's view that the profit rate is affected by events which do not work their way through changes in the cost of producing wage goods at all
>
> (Hollander 1979: 146).

Curiously enough (but this is perhaps a special by-product of their friendship) *if* the idea of a corn model ever was at all present to Ricardo's mind, that came through

Malthus himself, who on the other hand only mentioned perfect homogeneity of inputs and outputs in order to emphasize that it ought to be excluded. (Cf. also Hollander 1997: 455 ff.; Porta 1985.)

9 No less an authority than Samuel Hollander lists Adam Smith's adding up theory of price in the index to his volume on Smith. On the issue, see my own 1988 paper.

10 This is what Ricardo had called, in a letter to Mill a few months before, Smith's "original error respecting value." (See Ricardo 1951–73, vol. VII: 100 and cf. ibid.: 105.)

11 It may be usefully added that the term "adding up" is the English translation of Marx's *Zusammenaddierung* and *Zusammensetzung*, used in his *Theorien über den Mehrwert* in the context of a discussion on Smith's concept of natural price (see Marx 1862–63, MEW, Bd. XXVI. I. 3. 7: "*Seine Ansicht vom 'natürlichen Preis' als Summe von Arbeitslohn, Profit und Rente*"). According to Marx, Smith had initially (and correctly) established that the value of a commodity regulates wages, profit and rent. However he later came to adopt the opposite procedure (closer to empirical appearance and current opinion), whereby natural price comes to be determined through the adding up (*Zusammenaddierung, Zusammensetzung*) of the natural prices of wages, profit and rent. It is Ricardo's main merit – Marx goes on to observe – to have put an end to such a confusion.

Sraffa's index does refer, albeit indirectly, to the adding up theory as "Adam Smith's original error." Cf. the entries "Price" and "Smith, Adam," containing a reference to pp. xxxv–vi of the Introduction to vol. I, where Smith's "original error" is in fact equated to the adding up theory.

12 Cf. Porta 1990, 1992.

13 To a lesser extent, but certainly no less important to Sraffa, is the need to respond to Jacob Hollander's centenary estimate of Ricardo's work.

Luigi Pasinetti – in a contribution read at the Sraffa Conference at the Fondazione Einaudi, Turin, October 1998 on continuity and change in Sraffa's thought (Pasinetti forthcoming) – argues that it is possible to discern a fundamental continuity in Sraffa's transition from the criticism of Marshall's theory to the reconstruction of the classical approach on cost and value. He appeared to differ from Pierangelo Garegnani (who presented a paper at the same conference on Sraffa's interpretation of the classical economists through the late 1920s) on several points.

I look forward to reading both contributions in a written form. In particular I found Pasinetti's continuity argument extremely robust and appealing. As far as the late 1920s are concerned, Sraffa's Lectures, 1928–29, seem to me to provide compelling evidence on continuity.

May I mention on the issue, in passing, a significant recent addition to the Sraffian literature: the English translation of Sraffa's 1925 article "Sulle relazioni fra costo e quantità prodotta," in Pasinetti 1998: 323–63.

14 Hollander 1998 and 1999; Kurz 1998.

I had been pleading for a new historiography in the above sense since 1979, when I circulated a first draft of my introduction to the Italian Utet edition of Ricardo. At the time I was able to call in support of my argument, by Sraffa's own permission, a few passages from his unpublished lectures on the advanced theory of value (cf. note 16).

I am pleased to recall that in 1979 I did have Sam Hollander, then on leave in Israel, as one of my readers. At least fifteen papers of mine have later developed the subject through the years, a story I am summarizing in my forthcoming book on *The Classical School in Political Economy*. I am now relieved that the buds of the new historiography have at last started to develop and bear the names of outstanding scholars of Sraffa.

15 As hinted in the text, besides the *Piero Sraffa Papers*, Trinity have in their possession and have catalogued the *Piero Sraffa Collection*, which includes printed books and peri-

odicals together with a number of manuscripts acquired by Piero Sraffa. The whole constitutes an extraordinary and invaluable fund. It should be further mentioned that certainly a significant amount of manuscripts, notably letters, by Sraffa are in the possession of other institutions and individuals particularly in Britain, Italy, the USA and elsewhere in the world. A systematic inquiry appears to be needed.

16 Sraffa's Lectures are a beautiful ms. of well over a hundred foolscap sheets, largely in Sraffa's hand. I was deeply impressed when, over twenty years ago, I first had the privilege of studying the ms. under the supervision of Sraffa himself in his own room at the Marshall Library. It bears the inscription in Sraffa's hand "16 Lectures in Michaelmas Term 1928–29 'Advanced Theory of Value' e 1929–30 e Lent 1931." It is now classified D2/4.

17 Here is the full wording of what is paraphrased in English in this page of the present text.

> Impostazione del libro/L'unico sistema è di far la storia a ritroso, e cioè: stato attuale dell'ec.; come vi si è giunti, mostrando le differenze e la superiorità delle vecchie teorie. Poi, esporre la teoria./Se si va in ordine cronol., Petty, Fisiocr., Ric., Marx, Jevons, Marsh., bisogna farlo precedere da uno statement della mia teoria per spiegare dove si 'drive at': il che significa esporre prima *tutta* la teoria. E allora c'è il pericolo di finire come Marx, che ha pubbl. prima il Cap., e poi non è riuscito a finire l'Histoire des Doct. E il peggio si è che non è riuscito a farsi capire, senza la spiegaz. storica./Il mio scopo è: I esporre la storia, che è veramente l'essenziale / II farmi capire: per il che si richiede che io vada dal noto all'ignoto, da Marshall a Marx, dalla disutilità al costo materiale.
> Cf. Sraffa papers, D3/12/11, item 55 (Nov. 1927)

18 I have omitted three footnotes to the two initial paragraphs of this passage.

19 The flavor of Sraffa's classicism as far as cost theory is concerned can be captured in the following (fully Ricardian) explanatory note among his Nov. 1927 slips:

> When I say that the value of a product is 'determined' by the physical volume of commodities used up in its production, it should not be understood that it is determined by the value of those commodities. This would be a vicious circle, because – by what then is determined their value? Besides it would be wrong because the value of the product is equal to the value of the factors *plus* the surplus produced.
> What I say is simply that the numerical proportions between amount of factors and amount of product is, by definition, the absolute value of the product.
> (Sraffa November 1927: D3/12/11, item 101)

20 In a note from his reading of Marx's *Histoire des Doctrines Economiques*, Sraffa wrote:

> Marx, Hist, I, 44-45/ Physiocrats, why they saw surplus value in agriculture and not in industry: because in agriculture the labour produces and consumes the same thing (seed & food) and the difference between outlay & produce is easily perceived, it requires only a subtraction. In industry the process is more intricate.
> (Sraffa November 1927: Cp. D3/12/11 item 100)

Let me mention further that the point, among a few others, is the object of a pencilled annotation in Sraffa's hand ("Physiocrates: pourquoi ils ont vu la plus value en agriculture et non en industrie 44-45") on the inside back cover of his own copy of the Molitor translation of the Kautsky edn. of Marx's *Theorien* published in Paris in 1924.

21 See Sraffa papers, D3/12/11, item 64. This is a slip on "History of cost."

22 The draft of Hollander's 2000 paper I am using here bears the title "Sraffa and the

Interpretation of Ricardo: the Marxian Dimension" and is dated 1 October 1998.
23 Think as a possible example of the influence of Garegnani on Sraffa.
24 The passage quoted (note 6) belongs to the article "Sraffa Piero" in the *New Palgrave: A Dictionary of Economics* (1987), London: Macmillan, vol. 4: 449.

References

Arrow, K. J. (1991) "Ricardo's Work as Viewed by Later Economists," *Journal of the History of Economic Thought* 13(1) (Spring): 70–7.
Becattini, G. (ed.) (1990) *Il pensiero economico: temi, problemi e scuole*, Biblioteca dell'economista, serie VIII, sec. iii, vol. 3, Torino: Utet.
Blaug, M. (1958) *Ricardian Economics*, New Haven: Yale University Press.
Cannan, E. (1929) *A Review of Economic Theory*, London: King.
Caravale, G. A. (ed.) (1985) *The Legacy of Ricardo*, Oxford: Blackwell.
—— (ed.) (1991) *Marx and Modern Economic Analysis*, 2 vols, Cheltenham: Elgar.
Caravale, G. A. and Tosato, D. (1980) *Ricardo and the Theory of Value, Distribution and Growth*, London: Routledge.
de Vivo, G. (1996) "Piero Sraffa and the Mill-Ricardo Papers: A Comment," *Cambridge Journal of Economics* 20(5) (September).
Einaudi, L. (1951) "Dalla leggenda al monumento," in *Giornale degli economisti e annali di economia*, n.s.; also in *Saggi bibliografici e storici intorno alle dottrine economiche* (1953), Roma.
Hollander, J. H. (1910) *David Ricardo: A Centenary Estimate*, Baltimore: Johns Hopkins University Press.
Hollander, S. (1973) *The Economics of Adam Smith*, Toronto: University of Toronto Press.
—— (1973) "Ricardo's Analysis of the Profit Rate, 1813–15," *Economica* 40 (August).
—— (1979) *The Economics of David Ricardo*, Toronto: University of Toronto Press.
—— (1997) *The Economics of Thomas Robert Malthus*, Toronto: University of Toronto Press.
—— (1998) "Sraffa in Historiographical Perspective: A Provisional Statement," *European Journal of the History of Economic Thought* 5 (Autumn).
—— (2000) "Sraffa and the Interpretation of Ricardo: The Marxian Dimension," *History of Political Economy* (July).
Kurz, H. D. (1998) "Against the Current: Sraffa's Unpublished MSS and the History of Economic Thought," *European Journal of the History of Economic Thought* 5 (Autumn).
Kurz, H. D. and Salvadori, N. (1993) "The 'Standard Commodity' and Ricardo's 'Invariable Measure'," in M. Baranzini and G. Harcourt (eds), *The Dynamics of the Wealth of Nations: Essays in Honour of Luigi Pasinetti*, London: Macmillan.
Marx, K. H. (1862–3) *Theorien über den Mehrwert* (Vierter Band des 'Kapitals'), in K. Marx and F. Engels, *Collected Works*, vol. 36 (1965–68) Berlin: Dietz.
New Palgrave (1987) *A Dictionary of Economics*, 4 vols, ed. J. Eatwell, M. Milgate and P. Newman, London: Macmillan (article "Sraffa, Piero").
Pasinetti, L. L. (ed.) (1998) *Italian Economic Papers*, vol. 3, Bologna/Oxford: il Mulino/Oxford University Press.
—— (forthcoming) "Piero Sraffa: from youth to maturity. Some notes on the evolution of his attitudes and thought," paper presented at the centenary conference on Pierro Sraffa, Turin: Fondatione Luigi Einaudi, October 15 1998.
Porta, P. L. (1985) "The Debate on Ricardo: Old Results in New Frameworks," in G. A. Caravale (ed.), *The Legacy of Ricardo*, Oxford: Blackwell.
—— (1988) "The Classical Theory of Price: A Note on the Sraffian Interpretation," *Economies et Sociétés*, série Œconomia, Octobre.
—— (1990) "David Ricardo: la sistemazione teorica della concorrenza e del mercato,"

in G. Becattini (ed.), *Il pensiero economico: temi, problemi e scuole*, Biblioteca dell'economista, serie VIII, sec. iii, vol. 3, Torino: Utet.
—— (1992,)"Piero Sraffa, 'Superb Editor'," *Revue Européenne des Sciences Sociales* 30(92): 25–34.
—— (1996) "Piero Sraffa and the Mill-Ricardo Papers: a Rejoinder," *Cambridge Journal of Economics* 20(5) (September).
Ricardo, D. (1951–73) *Works and Correspondence*, ed. Piero Sraffa with M. H. Dobb, 11 vols, Cambridge: Cambridge University Press.
—— (1992) *Notes on Mr. Malthus's 'Measure of Value'*, ed. P. L. Porta, Cambridge: Cambridge University Press.
Robinson, Sir A. (1951) Review of "The Works and Correspondence of David Ricardo," *Economic Journal* 61.
Schefold, B. (1996) "Piero Sraffa 1898–1983," *Economic Journal* 106 (September): 1314–25.
—— (1998) "Reading Sraffa's Indices – A Note," *European Journal of the History of Economic Thought* 5 (Autumn).
Sraffa, P. (1927) "Notes/London, summer 1927/(Physical Real Costs etc.)," unpublished ms.
—— (1928–29) *Advanced Theory of Value*, sixteen lectures in Michaelmas Term 1928–29, unpublished ms.
—— (1960) *Production of Commodities by Means of Commodities*, Cambridge: Cambridge University Press.
—— (1998) "On the Relations between Cost and Quantity Produced," in L. L. Pasinetti (ed.), *Italian Economic Papers*, vol. 3, Bologna/Oxford: il Mulino/Oxford University Press: 323–63 (original Italian article published 1925).
Stigler, G. J. (1953) "Sraffa's *Ricardo*," *American Economic Review* 43 (September); also in *Essays in the History of Economics*, Chicago (1965).

14 David Ricardo's contribution to the constitution of the canon of Ricardian economics
A reconsideration of 1970s interpretations of the 1815 debate

André Lapidus and Nathalie Sigot

In the mid-twelfth century, Gratian collected the wide range of "discordant canons" coming from the various decisions of the Popes and Councils, thus giving birth, in the *Decretum*, to an apparently homogeneous body of doctrine known as the "canon law": the law of the Church. Very much later, in 1973–5, a short exchange appeared in *Economica* between Samuel Hollander and John Eatwell. This concerned David Ricardo's early theory of profits, such as it emerged from his writings of the period 1813–15, dominated by the publication of the *Essay on the Influence of a Low Price of Corn on the Profits of Stock* (hereafter *Essay*) in February 1815, the same month when Thomas Malthus's *Inquiry into the Nature and Progress of Rent* and Edward West's *Essay on the Application of Capital to Land* were published. The articles by Hollander and Eatwell bear witness to the coexistence of two different "canons" of Ricardian economics, to which Ricardo himself might have contributed in different ways. Now, unlike the medieval case, the Ricardian canons remained uncompromisingly conflicting. This chapter aims precisely at explaining the intellectual process which led to such a coexistence.

The starting point of this process is Piero Sraffa's publication of the first volume of the edition of the *Works and Correspondence of David Ricardo*. This edition had matured for twenty years, and needed at this time twenty more years before being completed.[1] Sraffa's general introduction to this volume (Sraffa 1951) renewed the admitted view on Ricardo's intellectual plan, and granted utmost importance to the *Essay*.[2] Reading this last, Sraffa thought that it might be interpreted as a description of a two-sector economy, agriculture and manufacturing. The alleged particularity of agriculture was that corn is produced with corn, either directly as seed, or indirectly through the food provided to the cattle and to the workers (Sraffa 1951: xxxi). On the contrary, in manufacturing, goods are produced by means of themselves and of corn. A significant consequence results from this technological difference. From the point of view of the economy as a whole, the rate of profit appears as a ratio between the values of heterogeneous quantities: the physical surplus and the advanced capital. Henceforth, it depends on the relative prices of agricultural and manufactured products.

Now – and this was the main analytical innovation involved in the Sraffian interpretation of the *Essay* – the particular case of agriculture, within the economy, deserves our attention: the physical homogeneity between agricultural products and means of production makes the agricultural profit rate independent of the structure of relative prices. If one accepts the idea that competition between capitalists generates a uniform profit rate, it follows that this agricultural profit rate should also be the overall profit rate. The formal structure that Sraffa perceives in the *Essay* – the corn-profit model – makes it possible to view the identification of the profit rate as an operation logically prior to the identification of relative prices.

Ten years later, the same Sraffa published *Production of Commodities by Means of Commodities*. As is well known, an interesting feature of this book is that it describes a "standard system," derived from the initial production system through a modification of the proportions of the different branches, so that its product and means of production might appear as different quantities of the same composite commodity (the "standard commodity").[3] By expressing the wage rate in terms of this standard commodity, Sraffa succeeded in measuring the profit rate independently of the system of relative prices. The analogy with David Ricardo's *Essay* is striking, and the author did not hesitate to invoke his classical inspirations: the standard system indeed appeared as a generalization of agriculture in the corn-profit model, in which a composite commodity produced by means of itself would come to replace corn.[4] However, Sraffa's 1960 contribution did not only make possible a formalization of the "Introduction" of 1951, it also allowed us to reconsider the constitution of the canon of Ricardian economics. From this perspective, Ricardo's *Principles* appeared as a detour from the direct route leading from Ricardo's *Essay* straight to Sraffa's *Production of Commodities*.

The following thirteen years were punctuated by Sraffa's edition of the eleven volumes of Ricardo's works and correspondence. Simultaneously, *Production of Commodities* was to play a central part in the development of what has been known as the "Cambridge controversies."[5] Thirteen years: resting both on historical (the "Introduction" of 1951) and on analytical *(Production of Commodities)* grounds, the Sraffian influence was presumably at its culminating point. It was in this context that Samuel Hollander published an article challenging Sraffa's interpretation of the *Essay* (Hollander 1973). Drawing on the *Essay* itself, as well as on Ricardo's correspondence, Hollander did not find any textual evidence favoring the assumption of physical homogeneity between product and means of production in agriculture (ibid.: 265–7). Nevertheless, this last was not completely dismissed from Hollander's understanding of Ricardo's plan, but rather reconsidered as a highly disputable rhetorical argument, which left room for the repeated idea that the rate of profit is determined by the money wage rate.

The controversy that followed, between Eatwell and Hollander (Eatwell 1975, Hollander 1975), made it obvious that these conflicting interpretations of Ricardo's *Essay on Profits* rested on methodological and analytical divergences. Whereas the Sraffa-Eatwell interpretation aimed at a rational reconstruction favoring comparative statics, the Hollander interpretation tended to an historical reconstruction, giving the first place to dynamics. The consequences of such a divergence are analyzed through Eatwell's opposition to Hollander's assertion that, according to Ricardo, an increase in the price of corn followed from a decrease in agricultural productivity, in order to prevent the profit rate from falling, with this latter diminishing afterwards, as a result of the increase in the money wage rate. In the context of a simple linear model assuming input–output physical homogeneity in agriculture, it is then shown that even if the rate of profit can be determined independently of prices from a comparative statics point of view (Eatwell's position), this is no longer true within a dynamic framework, since the variations of the money wages and prices explain the process of adjustment (Hollander's position).

The consequence is obvious. A solvable debate between the two interpretations of the *Essay* would require a sufficient intersection between the protagonists' analytical and methodological positions. Such was not – and is still not – the case. As far as the interpretations of the *Essay* concerned two conflicting legitimacies – we mean: two legitimate analytical and methodological approaches – which cannot be indisputably settled, the controversy became, from a scientific point of view, a non-debate. Both interpretations are thus condemned to coexist in an endless conflict: the Ricardian canons remain irreconcilable.

The neo-Ricardian foundations of Ricardian economics

Ricardo, over Sraffa's shoulder: the "Introduction" of 1951

Still today, in spite of the distance which separates us from the publication of the first volumes of Ricardo's *Works* and in spite of the emergence of the theory of prices of production within contemporary economic knowledge, the thesis of the "Introduction" of 1951 remains brilliant. The pages devoted to the *Essay* favor a comparative statics perspective rather than an approach in terms of dynamics. Now, when following this comparative statics approach, Sraffa shows himself more a paleontologist than an historian: from Ricardo's writings, such as we know them, he draws carefully a Ricardian theory, such as it might have been. The most significant trace of this theory would be the well-known "Table" of the *Essay*, "which shows the effects of an increase of capital, both capital and the 'neat product' are expressed in corn, *and thus the profit percent is calculated without need to mention price*" (Sraffa 1951: xxxii; our italics). In particular, the second part of the "Table," which recapitulates the results established in the first, shows the existence of an inverse relation between profit and rent, without the knowledge of prices being apparently required.

Still like the paleontologist who infers general morphological regularities from anatomical particularities, Sraffa does not provide any definite textual evidence that, according to Ricardo, the

> rational foundation of the principle of the determining role of the profits of agriculture ... is that in agriculture the same commodity, namely corn, forms both the capital ... and the product; so that ... the determination

of the ratio of this profit to the capital, is done directly between quantities of corn without any question of valuation.

(Sraffa 1951: xxxi)

Of course, this may lead one to look for more convincing anatomical particularities in Ricardo's works. On the other hand though, it raises the question of knowing why it was so necessary, a century and a half after the writing of the *Essay*, to disclose in Ricardo's writings some explicit statement of the "rational foundation." Obviously, if Sraffa's intention was only to determine a rational foundation, the compatibility of this statement with the propositions to which it relates would have been conclusive, even against Ricardo's explicit aim. That is, there is no clear necessity for the rational foundation to have an historical foundation. Assuming that this rational foundation also takes place within the works of Ricardo – that is, it is also an historical foundation – it would only strengthen the Sraffian interpretation of the *Essay*. Ricardo would appear more convincingly as the result of our rational reconstruction if we could establish that it is also a faithful description of what Ricardo intended to do. The search for an historical foundation of the Sraffian interpretation thus appears as the search for a lateral argument, which would neither seriously confirm, nor invalidate, the main thesis.

It is outside the *Essay* that Sraffa extends his investigation, in order to find such an historical foundation. Two elements are selected from Ricardo's correspondence.[6] The first consists of an extract from a letter to Malthus, dated June 26 1814, in which Ricardo explains that "[t]he rate of profits and of interest must depend on the proportion of production to the consumption necessary to such production" (Ricardo 1951–73, vol. 6: 108). The second element is only an indirect index since it concerns a letter sent to Ricardo by Malthus on August 5 1814, in which the latter refutes the idea of a rate of return expressed in physical terms.[7] Following Sraffa, this would suggest that Ricardo had indeed supported the rejected thesis, either in lost "papers on the profits of Capital," or on the occasion of a private conversation.

Of course, such material is a little bit too flimsy to persuade a skeptical reader. From this point of view, the rational reconstruction of what the Ricardian theory might have been – independently of what Ricardo actually said – is far more convincing. Not only does the assumption that in agriculture the means of production and the product consist of the same commodity create a consistent explanation of the leading role of agricultural profits, but it also makes consistent Ricardo's intellectual itinerary, from the *Essay* up to the successive editions of the *Principles* as from 1817, and to "Absolute Value and Exchange Value," written just before his death in 1823. Still, according to Sraffa, who inserted his interpretation of the *Essay* in the section of his "Introduction" devoted to the chapter on value of the first edition of the *Principles*, Ricardo created his analysis of value during the gestation period of his major work, "out of the fragmentary elements of such a theory which are to be found in the *Essay*" (Sraffa 1951: xxx). As from the 1817 edition, indeed, Ricardo would have developed a theory of value allowing him to give up the "considerable simplification" of the *Essay* – corn produced exclusively with corn – so that the agricultural rate of profit would have been deprived of its determining role in the economy. As attested by the successive transformations of the chapter "On value" of the *Principles*, the operation was not so simple. However the new theory of value would have made it possible, for Ricardo, to conceive a derived form of homogeneity between capital and product, "the rate of profits [being determined] by the ratio of the total labour of the country to the labour required to produce the necessaries for that labour" (ibid.: xxxii).

From the *Essay* to the *Principles*, Ricardo's objective would then have remained the same: as stated in the "Preface" of this last work, the "principal problem in Political Economy" was of determining the laws which regulate distribution (Ricardo 1951–73, vol. 1: 5). From this perspective, the issue of value – accessory in the *Essay*, essential in the *Principles* – is subordinated to that of distribution: as Sraffa states it, "The problem of value which interested Ricardo was how to find a measure of value which would be invariant to changes in the division of the product" (Sraffa 1951: xlviii). The question was raised, but it remained open: at least until 1960, when Sraffa provided it with its missing answer.

Production of commodities: *a child's guide*

The publication, in 1960, of *Production of Commodities* made it clear that the stake of the Sraffian interpretation of the *Essay* did concern the whole Ricardian system. The effect of the 1951 "Introduction" was to contrast a preliminary – simplified, but consistent – version of Ricardian economics to a more general but unfinished version of the *Principles*. By contrast, the 1960 book revealed that the simplification of the preliminary version might be given up without any counterpart, so that this early work was a carrier, in an embryonic form, of what the general version did not successfully achieve.

Before the appearance of *Production of Commodities*, the Ricardian tradition was primarily expressed in the framework of models of accumulation and distribution, sometimes with one single agricultural sector (Kaldor 1955–6), sometimes with two or more sectors (corn and gold, respectively necessary and luxury goods in Pasinetti, 1959–60), in which first, labor was the only factor of production, second, wages (made up of corn) constituted the only advance of capital, and third, decreasing returns prevailed in agriculture and constant returns in other activities. Such contributions already emphasized the place of surplus in neo-Ricardian economics, and highlighted the main features of the dynamics of capitalism described by Ricardo: increase of rent and decrease of the profit rate, independence of distribution *vis-à-vis* relative values, and the determining role of necessary goods. Garegnani's book (1960), drawn from his Ph.D. dissertation, systematized the critical dimension of an economic reflection based on classical thought reconstructed by means of Sraffa's 1951 "Introduction."[8] However, before the publication of *Production of Commodities*, it was probably impossible to anticipate that the theory of prices of production developed in this last book would allow neo-Ricardian economics to enjoy such an expansion, so that it could pretend to inherit the Ricardian legacy.

David Ricardo's contribution 275

The theory of prices of production, in the elementary case of "simple production with surplus" presented by Sraffa in his 1960 book, has now become quite familiar. The price system $p = [p_i] \geq 0$ $(i = 1, \ldots n)$, the wage rate w and the profit rate r are solutions of the equation:[9]

$$(1+r)Ap + 1w = p \qquad (1)$$

where $A = [a_{i,j}] \geq 0$ $(i, j = 1, \ldots n)$ is the matrix of production in which a_{ij} represents the quantity of commodity j required as mean of production of one unit of commodity i, and where $1 = [l_i] > 0 (i = 1, \ldots n)$ is the vector of direct labor used in the production of each commodity i.[10] It should be noted that wages, like profits, are withdrawn from the net product, and not advanced at the beginning of the period. The unit of account for prices and wages is derived from the construction of the "standard system" – this latter being simply a linear transformation of the initial production system, obtained by applying to each branch i a coefficient $q_i \geq 0$, so that:

$$qA = \lambda q \qquad \text{(where } q \text{ is normalized by } q1 = 1\text{)}$$

$\lambda \geq 0$ and $q = [q_i] \geq 0$ are respectively the dominant eigen-value of the matrix A and its associated left-hand eigen-vector. As a result, qA and q might be interpreted as the means of production and the product, physically homogeneous, of a composite "standard commodity." The prices and the rate of wages are then normalized on the basis of the net product of the standard system, i.e.:

$$q(I-A)p = 1$$

Denoting $R = (1/\lambda)-1$ the physical rate of return of the standard system, the rate of profit which, in equation (1), seemed to depend on relative prices, now appears as independent of the price system, in what is known as "Sraffa's relation":

$$r = R(1-w) \qquad (2)$$

The procedure used to construct the standard system shows an interesting property. If A is irreducible, it cannot be re-written as

$$A = \begin{bmatrix} A_{11} & 0 \\ A_{21} & A_{22} \end{bmatrix} \quad (A_{11} \text{ being itself an irreducible square matrix})$$

q is strictly positive, which implies that each commodity enters into the composition of the standard commodity. On the contrary, if A is reducible and $\lambda(A_{11}) > \lambda(A_{22})$, $q = [q_1, q_2]$ is such that $q_1 > 0$ and $q_2 = 0$.[11] Therefore, "basic commodities" only – that is, commodities which are both products and means of production in the sub-system A_{11} – are parts of the standard commodity, and all other ("non-basic") commodities are excluded.[12]

A neo-Ricardian interpretation of Ricardo's writings

Without referring explicitly to the *Essay*, Sraffa however pointed out, in Appendix D to *Production of Commodities*, the similarity between his own approach and the one that he ascribed to Ricardo. Henceforth, the same elementary formalization makes it possible to represent the thesis of the *Essay* simply, such as it is understood by Sraffa. However there is a second step in this process of extension of the formalization of *Production of Commodities*, where the *Principles* are also concerned. Not in the same way as the *Essay*: if the reader is persuaded that the corn-profit model did constitute the analytical core of the *Essay*, he is also persuaded that, for want of mathematical skill, Ricardo missed the point in the *Principles*. From 1960 onwards, it became evident that remaining faithful to the question raised by Ricardo required that one stood aloof from the kind of answer provided in the successive editions of the *Principles*. Indeed, the Sraffian theory of prices of production showed that the assumption of the *Essay* on homogeneity in agriculture was not as drastic as it seemed to be. This assumption could be given up without implying the tedious working-out of the different versions of the first chapter on value in the *Principles*, without preventing the profit rate from remaining a ratio of homogeneous quantities, independent of the price system.[13]

The corn-profit model as a model

The corn-profit model has now become some kind of common knowledge. It might be represented as follows.[14]

Assume that the productive combination of branch $i = 1$ is that of the land which pays no rent, that prices are expressed in terms of corn ($p_1 = 1$), and that w now denotes a real wage rate, exclusively made up of corn. In order to elude the problems raised by the coexistence of fixed and circulating capital in the Ricardian system, it is also assumed that wages are part of the circulating capital – advanced at the beginning of the period – and that there is no fixed capital properly speaking. Natural prices p hence appear as solutions of:

$$(1+r)(Ap+1w) = p$$

or writing $A^*(w)$ the matrix the elements of which are $a^*_{i1} = a_{i1} + l_i w$, and $a^*_{ij} = a_{ij}$ for all $j \neq 1$:

$$(1 + r)A^*(w)p = p \qquad (1a)$$

At first glance, just like in the ordinary model of prices of production, the determination of the profit rate r does not seem independent from that of the natural prices p. Nonetheless, the Sraffian hypothesis of homogeneity in agriculture being expressed by $a_{11} > 0$ and $a_{1j} = 0$ for all $j \neq 1$, corn appears as the only basic commodity in the sense defined above. It follows that the rate of profit r is determined in agriculture only (the standard system, reduced to a single-commodity economy), without any reference to other prices:

$$r = \frac{1 - (a_{11} + l_1 w)}{a_{11} + l_1 w} \tag{2a}$$

The fundamental principle that Sraffa believed he had found in Ricardo's *Essay* hence finds an analytical expression.[15] Obviously, the weight of this analytical expression should not be overestimated: it only bears witness to the consistency of Sraffa's intuition from 1951. But the advantage of this quite elementary formalization is that it helps focus on the fact that further orientation of the Ricardian system, such as perceived by Sraffa, is related to first, the permanent will to establish the logical priority of distribution to prices and second, the relaxation of the assumption of physical homogeneity in agriculture.

What could have been found in the Principles, *had Ricardo been Sraffian*

It should be clear for the modern reader that this double requirement, even in the more complex context of the *Principles*, did not necessitate all the subtleties of the chapter on value. Rewriting the *Principles* in the light of *Production of Commodities* is therefore a much different exercise from that of rewriting the *Essay*. The outcome is not an alleged analytical core of the *Principles*, but a consequence of the analytical core of the *Essay*.

The only difference introduced by the generalization of the corn-profit model to the *Principles* is that the physical wage rate, instead of being made up exclusively of corn, from now on appears as a basket of goods $w = [w_i]$ ($i = 1, \ldots n$) and that the elements a_{ij} of matrix A are no longer necessarily equal to zero when $j \neq 1$. The matrix $A^*(w)$ in equation (1a) is thus redefined as $a^*_{ij} = a_{ij} + l_i w_j$ ($i,j = 1, \ldots n$). And the system of natural prices can be written as follows:

$$(1 + r) A^*(w) p = p \tag{1b}$$

The same procedure as that used in the construction of the standard system can thus be employed. If, as previously, q represents the left-hand eigen-vector of $A^*(w)$, associated to its dominant eigen-value λ, it is observed that:

$$rqA^*(w) = q(I - A^*(w)) \tag{2b}$$

So that, even within the general framework of the *Principles*, the rate of profit may appear as a ratio, independent of the price system, between homogeneous quantities. Here again, the distinction between basic and non-basic commodities – which echoes the Ricardian distinction between necessary and luxury goods – makes it clear that only basic commodities enter the construction of the standard system and, like corn in the model of the *Essay*, in the quantitative ratio from which the profit rate is derived.

The analogy between the formal structures of equations (1) – (2), (1a) – (2a), and (1b) – (2b) highlights the new dimension of the stake of the Sraffian interpretation of the *Essay*, after the publication of *Production of Commodities*. For the reader who agreed with Sraffa's interpretation ten years earlier, the *Essay* displayed a correct but oversimplified theory, whereas the *Principles* were general enough, but somewhat confusing. Now, from 1960 onwards, the *Principles* clearly appeared as misleading. Equations (1b) – (2b) should now represent the solution – technically out of reach for David Ricardo at the time he was writing the *Principles* – to the obstacles raised by the relaxation of the *Essay* hypothesis of physical homogeneity in agriculture. Therefore, (1b) – (2b) would now occupy an intermediary position, between the pioneering construction of the *Essay* given by equations (1a) – (2a), and the modern formulation of a theory of prices of production in equations (1) – (2). The joint effect of Sraffa's 1951 and 1960 contributions is hence to revise the place usually granted to Ricardo in the history of economics: a – presumably major – contributor to Ricardian economics.

From paleontology to speleology: Hollander's challenge, 1973–5

One had to wait until the 1970s to for an actual challenge of the Sraffian interpretation of the *Essay*. This occurred through an article by Sam Hollander published in *Economica* (Hollander [1973]), followed by a short controversy with John Eatwell in the same journal (Eatwell 1975, Hollander 1975).

Ricardo, over Hollander's shoulder: strong and weak propositions in the Essay on Profits

The originality of Hollander's historiographic approach was to identify in Ricardo's writings a strategy of argumentation which develops throughout the period 1813–15. The principle of the strategy leads one to distinguish between: first, the "essence of the *Essay*" (Hollander 1973: 282) – unfortunately referred to by the phrase "weak proposition" (ibid.: 275) – which constitutes the core of Ricardo's message, according to which the general profit rate is determined by the money wage rate, itself influenced (non-exclusively) by the price of corn, which depends on the productivity in agriculture; and second the over-simplified argument which at least makes the discussion easier – the "strong proposition," as Hollander (ibid.: 269–70) calls it – synthesized in the well-known statement that the overall profit rate is regulated by the agricultural profit rate.[16]

Hollander detects the presence of the weak proposition in Ricardo's correspondence with Malthus from the middle of 1813. His numerous references to the determinant role of agriculture express the fact that, via the price of subsistence goods, the fall in agricultural productivity is reflected in the wage level and consequently affects the general profit rate. The very same materials which were the main basis for Sraffa's interpretation are thereby called upon to support quite a different theory.

On rereading Ricardo's letter of June 26 1814 to Malthus in which he explained the profit rate by the "proportion of production to the consumption necessary to such production" (Ricardo 1951–73, vol. 6: 108) and where Sraffa identified two physically homogeneous magnitudes, Samuel Hollander (1973: 262) finds textual evidence that, according to Ricardo, this ratio "depends upon the cheapness of provisions, which is after all . . . the great regulator of the wages of labour" (Ricardo 1951–73, vol. 6: 108).

In the same way, Hollander (1973: 265–6) sees in Malthus's objection when corresponding with Ricardo that "[i]n no case of production, is the produce exactly of the same nature as the capital advanced" (letter of 5 August 1814, Ricardo 1951–73, vol. 6: 117) not the echo of any past conversation or of lost notes, but very probably of a letter written by Ricardo several days beforehand in which he wrote that

> [t]he capitalist "who may find it necessary to employ a hundred days labour instead of fifty in order to produce a certain quantity of corn" cannot retain the same share for himself unless the labourers who are employed for a hundred says will be satisfied with the same quantity of corn for their subsistence that the labourers employed for fifty had before.
> (letter to Malthus of July 25 1814, Ricardo 1951–73, vol. 6: 114–15)

At first glance, this extract appears to confirm Sraffa's interpretation. Hollander however mentions two letters written in the same period, which contextualize the previous one and reflect the permanent position of Ricardo – the weak proposition favoring the effect of variations in money wages on profits – a position which was to strengthen despite the circumstantial wording adopted in his letter of July 25.[17]

Therefore, not only should the text of the *Essay* be reappraised in the light of its author's correspondence, but it is, in Hollander's opinion, far from providing the textual arguments that Sraffa believed he would discover within it. The "Table," which was its centerpiece, in no way illustrated a reasoning within which the product and the means of production would be physically homogeneous. Ricardo no doubt introduced a capital estimated in corn; but in no way assumed a capital composed of corn (Hollander 1973: 274).[18] The latter, Hollander claims, is no more than a unit of account, an interpretation which seems confirmed by Ricardo's own commentaries on the "Table" and neglected by the Sraffian interpretation. It thus becomes easier to understand Ricardo's assertion in the *Essay*, that he only aimed at "proving that the profits on agricultural capital cannot materially vary, without occasioning a similar variation in the profits on capital, employed on manufactures and commerce" (Ricardo 1951–73, vol. 4: 12n.), not as an argument in favor of the strong proposition, but as the expression of the impossibility of agricultural and industrial profit rates diverging in the long run (Hollander 1973: 275–6). It thus appears, according to Hollander's interpretation, that whereas the weak proposition – rooted in the 1813–14 correspondence – would imply the theoretical results of the *Essay*, Ricardo happened to reinforce it rhetorically by an ambiguous use of the strong proposition – the determining role of the agricultural profit rate – this last ultimately referring to the somewhat different assertion that competition equalizes the profit rates.

Historiographical divergence, analytical divergence

Despite the apparent strength of the textual counter-arguments, Hollander's refutation of Sraffa's interpretation of the *Essay* remained surprisingly qualified. Indeed his aim was not to confirm that the hypothesis of a corn-profit model – the strong proposition – is lacking in Ricardo's presentation, but rather to discuss its place within it. In the same way, he seems to have no serious quarrel with the importance, today, of a determination of the profit rate independently of prices in the theory of prices of production. Symmetrically, the position defended by Sraffa in the 1951 "Introduction" obviously leads to the conclusion that variations in wage rate and variations in the overall profit rate are opposite. At the outset, the divergence is thus seen to be historiographic: whereas Sraffa attempts to reconstruct some sort of objectivity regarding Ricardo's message – an objectivity which may emerge without Ricardo himself being aware of it – Hollander endeavors to reveal a Ricardian rhetoric, a strategy of argumentation which appears in the absence of conclusive demonstration. Now, on the one hand, objectivity does not become more apparent by means of explicit words, except to consider as equivalent what Ricardo said, what he meant and what the theorist understands by it today. On the other hand, rhetoric is not given for what it is, except to compromise what enables its existence: the private information of the author concerning the distance between what he says and what he means.

Sraffa's palaeontology, which reconstructs what may have existed, finds a counterpart in Hollander's speleology seeking what was intended to remain hidden. In a symptomatic manner, Sraffa speaks of "rational foundation" (Sraffa 1951: xxxi), Eatwell talks of a "presumably indisputable" formal basis (Eatwell 1975: 185), whereas Hollander seeks to find what Ricardo had – or did not have – "in mind" (Hollander 1973: 381; 1975: 190). With an ingenuity which was, perhaps, real, Hollander acknowledged the irreducibility of these two approaches in his reply to Eatwell's reaction to his article:

> my interpretation in no way touches upon the 'usefulness' of the corn profit model as an analytical structure. It is the historical question of whether we can legitimately attribute such a structure to Ricardo which is the subject matter of my article.
>
> (Hollander 1975: 201)

This observation does not put a definite end to the debate however, by opposing its protagonists: it is simply an incentive to remind us that methodological divergences can give rise, on the one hand, to an agreement on wider conclusions; but, on the other hand, to much narrower possibilities for debate than those which were initially imagined.

However, these possibilities for debate between Sraffa's interpretation and Hollander's are still reduced, drastically, as the change in the historiographical perspective is coupled with a change in analytical perspective. As already noted, the pages Sraffa devotes to the theory of profit in the *Essay* come under comparative statics. Now, from this point of view, the leading effect of the agricultural profit rate laid down by the strong proposition reflects not a temporal causality expressed via an adjustment mechanism, but a structural independence of agriculture compared to the structural dependence of industry. In the same way, the weak proposition within the Sraffian context would suggest that the effect of money wages on the profit rate could only be seen via the succession of states of equilibrium which goes hand in hand with the cultivation of less and less fertile land. By contrast, Hollander's article aims at highlighting the interactions between adjustment dynamics, outlined by Ricardo in the *Essay* and in his correspondence during the period 1813–15. Although this perspective does not discredit the meaning, from a Sraffian point of view, of the strong and weak propositions, it does encourage a different interpretation of them. Thus, the strong proposition, understood this time as being in a dynamic perspective, not only supposes the structural independence of agriculture as in the case of comparative statics; but it also signifies that first, the mechanisms determining the rate of agricultural profit have no direct action upon the industrial profit rate, and second, the variation in the agricultural profit rate generates an adjustment mechanism of the industrial profit rate, bringing the second into line with the first. At the same time, the weak proposition means that first, the factors influencing the money wage rate have no direct influence on the general profit rate; and second, the variations in money wages give rise to an adjustment in both the agricultural and industrial profit rates.

The non-debate issue

Hollander, over Eatwell's shoulder

John Eatwell's (1975) answer to Samuel Hollander illustrates perfectly this quasi-suppression of the possibilities of debate, originating from this double change in perspective. For want of a sufficiently wide intersection between the respective contributions of Sraffa and Hollander, Eatwell seems reduced merely to recalling Sraffa's argument. On the one hand he insists upon the specificity of Sraffa's historical approach, by underlining with some acrimony that "[e]vidently, Hollander has not understood the logic of the role which the standard of value plays in Ricardo's theory of distribution, and the puzzle that Ricardo was trying to solve in the *Essay on Profits*" (Eatwell 1975: 183). It is quite natural that here, the "puzzle" is the one Sraffa lends Ricardo, and that in Sraffa's attempt to solve it, while he mentions the deliberate will of the author of the *Essay*, it remains of secondary importance. And when this will is unambiguously expressed, for both Eatwell and Sraffa, it is to break, in the *Principles*, with the problematic *Essay* by introducing a value theory, perhaps sketched out, but assuredly superfluous in the text of 1815. It is thus understandable that in his reply to Eatwell, Hollander (1975: 188) – for whom the permanence of the weak proposition and the need for an outline of a theory of value in 1815 reflect the continuity of the Ricardian plan from the *Essay* to the *Principles* – sees his opponent's position as "based upon a preconceived notion of the nature and content of Ricardian profit theory and of Ricardo's place in the history of economic thought": the "preconceived notion," from the point of view of an author careful to underline a strategy of argumentation in Ricardo's work, is hardly an affable way to highlight the attempt at the rational reconstruction of an objectivity which is not apparent at first glance.

On the other hand, the evaluation given by Eatwell regarding Hollander's contribution is even harsher, given that, placed within the Sraffian context of comparative statics, he agrees there is "*no* incompatibility" (Eatwell 1975: 183) between the decisive role of money wages on profits (the weak proposition) and the argument of Sraffa (strong proposition). A remarkable sign of the narrowness of the intersection between the interpretations of the *Essay* in terms of comparative statics and of dynamics is to be seen through the brief exchange concerning the equalization of profit rates. Hollander (1973: 276–7) highlighted an error in the reasoning of Ricardo – an error that other passages from the *Essay* managed to correct – when he imputed the fall in the agricultural profit rate to the decrease in productivity in this sector, and the fall in industrial profit to the increase in money wages. Quite the contrary, explains Hollander, the

> increase in the price of corn reflects the fall in agricultural productivity and *to this extent* any fall in agricultural profits is *prevented*. Profits decline in agriculture for precisely the same reason that they decline in manufacturing, namely as a consequence of rising money wages.
> (Hollander 1973: 277)

Eatwell's reply, in a simple footnote, seemed unanswerable: "This is nonsensical in the case of the Table in the *Essay* in which input and output are the same commodity, and hence no change in price can alter the rate of profit in agriculture" (Eatwell 1975: 185n.).

Obviously, Eatwell's assertion is supported by the consequences, from the point of view of comparative statics, of the hypothesis of physical homogeneity in agriculture. In a more formal manner and to simplify the presentation, it will be supposed, using the above notations, that the economy is divided into two sectors: agriculture producing corn, and factories producing gold. Let p_1 and s be the money price of corn and the money wage rate – that is, expressed in gold, whose conditions of production do not vary. The technologies on the marginal land at dates t_0 and t_1 are respectively (a_{11}^0, l_1^0) and (a_{11}^1, l_1^1), so that $a_{11}^0 \leq a_{11}^1$ and $l_1^0 < l_1^1$ – which expresses the fall in agricultural productivity between these two dates. Initially, the profit rate r^0, prices p^0 and the monetary wage rate s^0 are such that:

$$(a_{11}^0 p_1^0 + l_1^0 s^0)(1 + r^0) = p_1^0 \tag{3a}$$

$$(a_{21} p_1^0 + l_2 s^0)(1 + r^0) = 1 \tag{3b}$$

$$s^0 = w p_1^0 \tag{3c}$$

When agricultural productivity has fallen, the same profit rate, price and wage rate, r^1, p^1 and s^1 are the solutions to:

$$(a_{11}^1 p_1^1 + l_1^1 s^1)(1 + r^1) = p_1^1 \tag{4a}$$

$$(a_{21} p_1^1 + l_2 s^1)(1 + r^1) = 1 \tag{4b}$$

$$s^1 = w p_1^1 \tag{4c}$$

The equations (3a) – (3c) and (4a) – (4c) evidently confirm Eatwell's point concerning the absence of any effect of the variation in the price of corn on the agricultural profit rate, since r^0 and r^1 can be calculated independently from price. It is also to be noted that the real wage rate being given, prices are determined by the relative production conditions of corn and gold. Eatwell's concession to Hollander is thus founded, as the increase in the price of corn ($p_1^1 > p_0^0$) goes hand in hand with an increase in money wages ($s^1 > s^0$) and with a fall in the profit rate ($r^1 < r^0$).

Hollander's mechanism

Despite this, Hollander's argument was of a different nature. Its implications, even in the apparently most unfavorable case, when the hypothesis of structural independence of agriculture has been accepted (the strong proposition from the point of view of comparative statics), is not without interest. Let us keep the point of departure given by the equations (3a), (3b) and (3c). As with Eatwell, profit rates are determined independently of price. However, the adjustment suggested by Hollander supposes that the effects of the shock caused by the fall in agricultural productivity are not immediately shown by equation (4a), but by an increase in the price of corn from p_1^0 to $\tilde{p}_1^0$ which would keep the profit rate at the same level $\tilde{r}^0$ in both agriculture and industry, whereas money wages would remain constant:

$$(a_{11}^1 \tilde{p}_1^0 + l_1^1 s^0)(1 + \tilde{r}^0) = \tilde{p}_1^0 \tag{5a}$$

$$(a_{21} \tilde{p}_1^0 + l_2 s^0)(1 + \tilde{r}^0) = 1 \tag{5b}$$

The resulting fall in the real wage rate should thus give rise to a dynamic adjustment in the money wage rate, which Hollander noticed in Ricardo's writings from the correspondence with Malthus in the years 1813–14, concerning the effects of a restriction of corn imports (Hollander 1973: 260–5).[19] This adjustment could take the form:

$$\dot{s}^t = k(w\tilde{p}_1^t - s^t) \quad (k > 0) \tag{6}$$

where w is the real wage rate in corn at t_0, now different from the real wage rate at t,

$$c^t = \frac{s^t}{\tilde{p}_1^t}$$

At date t, prices $\tilde{p}^t$ and the profit rate $\tilde{r}^t$ are as such that:

$$(a_{11}^1 \tilde{p}_1^t + l_1^1 s^t)(1 + \tilde{r}^t) = \tilde{p}_1^t \tag{7a}$$

$$(a_{21}\tilde{p}\,_1^t + l_2 s^t)(1 + \tilde{r}^t) = 1 \tag{7b}$$

Beginning from the situation given by equations (5a)–(5b), process (6), (7a)–(7b) converges toward the state of the economy represented by equations (4a), (4b) and (4c), where prices and profit rates are p^I and r^I respectively.[20] Throughout this process, the profit rate decreases as much as a consequence of an increase in wages (6), as of the change in the price of corn, which is likely to either fall or rise but in the latter case, more slowly than the money wage rate. The agricultural profit rate as such has had no decisive part in this.[21] However, once the process is over, the agricultural profit rate is indeed determined independently from prices and imposes itself, via the price of corn, on the entire economy. It is thus possible both to accept the strong proposition in a context of comparative statics and to reject it in a dynamic framework.

The non-debate situation

From a scientific point of view, the debate could have ended up this way in 1975, after *Economica* let Samuel Hollander have the final word in the controversy setting him against John Eatwell and, through him, against the Sraffian interpretation of the *Essay*. Not that this debate was won outright by one or the other of the parties. Indeed, there were neither winner nor loser: merely a clarification of the conditions likely to entitle each position to be maintained.

It could thus be considered that Sraffa's interpretation was likely to escape any objections raised against it provided that:

1 it was limited to the search for an objectivity of Ricardo's message, even if this were to be regardless of Ricardo's explicit words
2 comparative statics was confirmed as being the essential – if not exclusive – theoretical stake, so that the weak proposition might appear as a consequence of the strong proposition.

Contrary to this, Hollander's interpretation was acceptable provided that:

1 it aimed at determining the objective sought by a strategy of argumentation; possibly to the detriment of the accessory analytical constructions generated by this strategy
2 Ricardian dynamics were favored, which (as we have noted), should exclude the strong proposition, even if its existence would have been readily granted within the context of comparative statics.

Certainly it remained feasible to reproach Hollander with having neglected Ricardian objectivity and comparative statics, Sraffa or Eatwell with having neglected Ricardian rhetoric and dynamics. This double negligence was, however, deliberate and could not, even today, be settled. Both on methodological and on analytical grounds, Sraffa-Eatwell's and Hollander's interpretations have too little in common to give rise to an actual debate likely,

David Ricardo's contribution 285

at least in principle, to give rise to a solution.[22] They depict two alternative views on the way Ricardo contributed to the constitution of the canon of Ricardian economics. They therefore enter in conflict – and this one should be ranged among the most merciless – just because they exist, not because they intersect. The debate has ceased since there is no room for it. However there is still no reason for the conflict to die.

Appendix – Hollander's case: behavior of (6), (7a) and (7b)

Let (6), (7a) and (7b) be rewritten as follows, omitting the superscripts on the variables:[23]

$$\dot{s} = k(w\tilde{p}_1 - s) \quad (k > 0) \tag{6}$$

$$(a_{11}\tilde{p}_1 + l_1 s)(1 + \tilde{r}) = \tilde{p}_1 \tag{7a}$$

$$(a_{21}\tilde{p}_1 + l_2 s)(1 + \tilde{r}) = 1 \tag{7b}$$

Relation between the variation of the money wage rate ds *and the variation of the profit rate* d$\tilde{r}$:

$$(7a) \Rightarrow d\tilde{p}_1 = (1 + \tilde{r}) a_{11} d\tilde{p}_1 + (1 + \tilde{r}) l_1 ds + (a_{11}\tilde{p}_1 + l_1 s) d\tilde{r}$$

$$(7b) \Rightarrow 0 = (1 + \tilde{r}) a_{21} d\tilde{p}_1 + (1 + \tilde{r}) l_2 ds + (a_{21}\tilde{p}_1 + l_2 s) d\tilde{r}$$

Eliminating $d\tilde{p}_1$:

$$\left(\frac{(1+\tilde{r})l_1}{1 - (1+\tilde{r})a_{11}} + \frac{(1+\tilde{r})l_2}{(1+\tilde{r})a_{21}} \right) ds + \left(\frac{a_{11}\tilde{p}_1 + l_1 s}{1 - (1+\tilde{r})a_{11}} + \frac{a_{21}\tilde{p}_1 + l_2 s}{(1+\tilde{r})a_{21}} \right) d\tilde{r} = 0$$

or,

$$\alpha ds + \beta d\tilde{r} = 0$$

Let R – which may be interpreted as the physical rate of reproduction of corn – be the solution of $(1+R)a_{11} = 1$. Assume that $R > 0$, which means that the agricultural sector produces a surplus in corn. Now, if $0 < \tilde{r} < R$, it is obvious that $1 - (1+\tilde{r})a_{11} > 0$ and, consequently, that $\alpha, \beta > 0$. It follows that the signs of the variation of the profit rate $d\tilde{r}$ and of the variation of the money wage rate ds are the same.

Relation between the variation of the variation of the real wage rate dc *and the variation of the profit rate* d$\tilde{r}$:

Recalling that $c = s/\tilde{p}_1$, (7a) and (7b) can be written under matrix form as follows:

$$\begin{bmatrix} a_{11} + l_1 c & 0 \\ a_{21} + l_2 c & 0 \end{bmatrix} \begin{bmatrix} \tilde{p}_1 \\ 1 \end{bmatrix} = \frac{1}{1+\tilde{r}} \begin{bmatrix} \tilde{p}_1 \\ 1 \end{bmatrix}$$

Now, since $1/(1 + \tilde{r})$ is the dominant eigen-value of the matrix in the left-hand member of the above equation, it is a non-decreasing function of the elements of this matrix and, more precisely, an increasing function of c. This means that the sign of the variation of the profit rate $d\tilde{r}$ is the opposite of the sign of dc, the variation of the purchasing power, in terms of corn, of the money wage rate.

Convergence of the real wage rate c to the normal real wage rate w

From the definition of c, it is obvious that (6) can be presented in an equivalent form:

$$\dot{s} = k(w - c)\tilde{p}_1 \quad (k > 0) \tag{6'}$$

After the initial shock in agriculture at t_1, when a less fertile land had to be cultivated, the real wage was such that $c < w$. According to (6'), $ds > 0$. $d\tilde{r}$ is thus negative and dc positive. The real wage rate c will therefore increase until it becomes equal to the normal wage rate w which prevailed at t_0. This means that the price of corn, the real wage rate and the rate of profit in the process described by equations (6), (7a) and (7b) converge to a limit (where $\dot{s} = 0$) defined by the equilibrium values of prices and distribution in equations (4a) and (4b):

$$(a_{11}^1 p_1^1 + l_1^1 s^1)(1 + r^1) = p_1^1 \tag{4a}$$

$$(a_{21} p_1^1 + l_2 s^1)(1 + r^1) = 1 \tag{4b}$$

Notes

1 About Sraffa's intellectual evolution between 1930, when H. Foxwell, President of the Royal Economic Society, entrusted him, on the suggestion of Keynes, with the responsibility of the edition of the works of Ricardo, and the publication of *Production of Commodities* in 1960, see Potier 1987 and Pasinetti 1990.
2 This renewal should nonetheless be qualified. In a general context in which the interest in the *Essay* was in an inverse proportion to that for the *Principles*, two contributions emphasized the place of the 1815 text in Ricardo's work. The first one was H. Biaujeaud's Ph.D. dissertation (Biaujeaud 1933), which was praised by Sraffa himself (Sraffa 1951: xxxviiin.) for its "unusual view" on the evolution of Ricardo's theory of value, but which did not actually interpret the *Essay* as a corn-profit model. Anyway, Biaujeaud's work was to remain largely unknown. However, the second contribution might have had a far greater influence: W. Mitchell's lectures were published two years before Sraffa's "Introduction," and clearly expressed – to our knowledge, for the first time – that the discussion of

agriculture in the *Essay* was based on the idea that capital and output were the same commodity (Mitchell 1949: 141).
3 The procedure of construction of the standard system and of the standard commodity, in the elementary case of simple production with surplus, is presented by Sraffa in chapters 4 and 5 of his book.
4 See Sraffa 1960: Appendix D.
5 According to the title of G. Harcourt's book in 1972: *Some Cambridge Controversies in the Theory of Capital.*
6 Other textual arguments, supporting Sraffa's interpretation, were to be added progressively. For example, the footnote in the *Essay* (Ricardo 1951–73, vol. 4: 12), where Ricardo specifies his plan, explaining that he was only "desirous of proving that the profits on agricultural capital cannot materially vary, without occasioning a similar variation in the profits on capital, employed on manufactures and commerce," came into the debate (see, for instance, Hollander 1973: 275, who nonetheless rejects Sraffa's interpretation).
7 See Sraffa 1951: xxxi–xxxii, who quotes Malthus's objection according to which "[i]n no case of production, is the produce exactly of the same nature as the capital advanced. Consequently, we can never properly refer to a material rate of produce" (Ricardo 1951–73, vol. 6: 117).
8 The hypothesis of a physical homogeneity in agriculture in the context of the *Essay* is hence considered as granted by Garegnani, and it plays the same role as for Sraffa to understand Ricardo's evolution from the *Essay* to the *Principles.* (Garegnani [1960] 1980: 20–3).
9 One is indebted to P. Newman (1962) for the first formalization of Sraffa's "simple production with surplus," using notations and results from the methodology of linear models.
10 In accordance with Sraffa's own interpretation (Sraffa 1960: v), it is not necessary to assume constant returns: it is indeed sufficient to normalize quantities a_{ij} on the basis of the total production of each branch $i.$
11 This assumption allows us to eliminate the "freak case" imagined by Sraffa (1960: 90–1), in which the rate of reproduction of a non-basic good used in its own reproduction is so low as to be lower than that of the standard system.
12 This introduction of Sraffa's model of simple production remains quite elementary. For a more thorough discussion of the formal properties of the model, see for instance, among many other references, Pasinetti [1975] 1977: 77–121, Abraham-Frois and Berrebi 1976, Bidard 1991, Kurz and Salvadori 1995: 94–118.
13 A similar position, following Sraffa's own remarks (Sraffa 1960: Appendix D) was supported by various commentators in the years which followed the publication of *Production of Commodities.* See, for example, Napoleoni 1961, Robinson 1961 or Meldolesi 1966.
14 See note 12. This presentation deliberately leaves aside the way historical and analytical investigations were related in the course of Sraffa's career; on this question, see Lapidus 1996: 883–9.
15 This expression goes, however, beyond Ricardo's explicit intention, since the variations of r generated by the variations of w usually come with an adjustment of the prices of non-basic goods, whereas in the *Essay,* Ricardo changed his previous opinion and assumed that industrial prices remain constant when their conditions of production do not vary (see Sraffa 1951: xxxiv).
16 Typically, this position is expressed in Ricardo's letter to H. Trower of March 8 1814: "It is the profits of the farmer which regulate the profits of all other trades" (Ricardo 1951–73, vol. 6: 104).
17 Letters of June 26 and August 11 1814; Ricardo 1951–73, vol. 6: 108, 119–20.
18 Hollander (1973: 274n) mentions, for example, the title of the first column of the Table in the *Essay*: "Capital estimated in quarters of corn" (Ricardo 1951–73, vol. 4: 17).

19 Hollander seems to have admitted that the profit rate remains unchanged at r^0. But this can only be so either in the – after all, not so – particular case where $a_{21} = 0$ (no corn is directly used in the production of gold), or if it is accepted that the industrial rate of profit alone falls temporarily under the agricultural rate. On the contrary, it is assumed here that the price of corn has increased only to the extent that the industrial profit rate remains at the level of the agricultural profit rate. As a result, whereas the increase of the price of corn is a response to the fall of agricultural productivity, aiming at thwarting the threat of a decrease in profitability, this rise is limited by the conditions of production in the industrial sector.
20 See Appendix.
21 One might object that it is still possible to rewrite (7a) as

$$(a_{11}^l \tilde{p}_1^t + l_1^l c^t \tilde{p}_1^t)(1 + \tilde{r}^t) = \tilde{p}_1^t$$

In such a case, the agricultural profit rate might seem independent from prices. However, contrary to w, the purchasing power of wages in terms of corn, c^t, is not given, but calculated on the basis of the money wage rate and of the price of corn. As a result, the agricultural profit rate can still not be considered independent from prices.
22 Such would not be the case, of course, for a controversy between authors whose methodological and analytical approaches share common ground. An interesting example is given by Peach 1993, who both adheres to Sam Hollander's rejection of the corn-profit interpretation of the *Essay*, and nonetheless challenges his historical reconstruction.
23 The notation and equations of the appendix are the same as for the body of the chapter.

References

Sources referenced in this bibliography deliberately do not concern the continuation of the controversy on the interpretation of Ricardo's *Essay on Profits* beyond Hollander's and Eatwell's exchange in 1975. This is the reason why most references on this subject are not later than this date.

Abraham-Frois, G. and Berrebi, E. (1976) *Théorie de la Valeur, des Prix et de l'Accumulation*, Paris: Economica.
Biaujeaud, H. [1933] (1988) *Essai sur la Théorie Ricardienne de la Valeur*, Paris: Economica.
Bidard, C. (1991) *Prix, Reproduction, Rareté*, Paris: Economica.
Eatwell, J. (1975) "The Interpretation of Ricardo's *Essay on Profits*," *Economica* 42 (May): 182–7.
Garegnani, P. [1960] (1980) *Le Capital dans les Théories de la Répartition*, Paris: Presses Universitaires de Grenoble/Maspéro.
Harcourt, G. C.(1972) *Some Cambridge Controversies in the Theory of Capital*, Cambridge: Cambridge University Press.
Hollander, S. (1973) "Ricardo's Analysis of the Profit Rate, 1813–15," *Economica* 40 (August): 260–82.
—— (1975) "Ricardo and the Corn Profit Model: Reply to Eatwell," *Economica* 42 (May): 188–202.
Kaldor, N. (1955–6) "Alternative Theories of Distribution," *Review of Economic Studies* 83–100.
Kurz, H. and Salvadori, N. (1995) *Theory of Production – A Long Period Analysis*, Cambridge: Cambridge University Press.

Lapidus, A. (1996) "Introduction à une Histoire de la pensée économique qui ne verra jamais le jour," *Revue Economique* 47(4) (July).
Meldolesi, L. (1966) "La Derivazione Ricardiana di 'Produzione di Merci a Mezzo di Merci' di Piero Sraffa," *Economia Internazionale*,19(4): 612–38.
Mitchell, W. C. (1949) *Lecture Notes on Types of Economic Theory*, New York: A. M. Kelley.
Napoleoni, C. (1961) "Sulla Teoria della Produzione come Processo Circulare," *Giornale degli Economisti e Annali di Economia* (January–February): 101–17.
Newman, P. (1962), "Production of Commodities by Means of Commodities," *Schweizerische Zeitschrift für Volkswirtschaft und Statistik* 98.
Pasinetti, L. (1959–60), "A Mathematical Formulation of the Ricardian System," *Review of Economic Studies* 78–98.
—— [1975] (1977) *Lectures on the Theory of Production*, London: Macmillan.
—— (1990), "A la Mémoire de Piero Sraffa, Economiste Italien à Cambridge," in R. Arena and J. Ravix (eds), *Sraffa, Trente Ans Après*, Paris: Presses Universitaires de France.
Peach, T. (1993) *Interpreting Ricardo*, Cambridge: Cambridge University Press.
Potier, J-P. (1987) *Un Economiste Non Conformiste, Piero Sraffa (1898–1983) – Essai Biographique*, Lyon: Presses Universitaires de Lyon.
Ricardo, D. (1951–1973) *The Works and Correspondence of David Ricardo* (11 vols), ed. P. Sraffa with M. H. Dobb, Cambridge: Cambridge University Press.
—— [1817] (1951) *Principles of Political Economy and Taxation* [1821, 3rd edn], in *The Works and Correspondence of David Ricardo*, vol. 1.
—— [1815] (1966) *An Essay on the Influence of a Low Price of Corn on the Profit of Stock* in *The Works and Correspondence of David Ricardo*, vol. 4: *Pamphlets and Papers – 1815–23*: 9–41.
Ricardo, D. (1952) *The Works and Correspondence of David Ricardo*, vol. 6: *Letters – 1810–1815*.
Robinson, J. (1961) "Prelude to a Critique of Economic Theory", *Oxford Economics Papers* 13: 53–8.
Sraffa, P. (1951) "Introduction" in D. Ricardo, *The Works and Correspondence of David Ricardo* (11 vols), ed. P. Sraffa with M. H. Dobb, Cambridge: Cambridge University Press, vol. 1: xiii–lxiv.
—— (1960) *Production of Commodities by Means of Commodities*, Cambridge: Cambridge University Press.
—— (1962) "Note on 'Essay on Profits'" in D. Ricardo, *The Works and Correspondence of David Ricardo* (11 vols), ed. P. Sraffa with M. H. Dobb, Cambridge: Cambridge University Press, vol. 4: 3–8.

15 Ricardian economics

Reasoning about counter-intuitive tendencies when system constraints are present

Laurence S. Moss

Introduction

I do not think that science is "refined common sense." I especially do not think economic science is so organized because many of its patterns of thought are counterintuitive. David Ricardo's formulation of several organizing principles in our discipline appears to be especially counterintuitive. Indeed, the purpose of this chapter is to highlight one of these organizing principles, namely, the inverse wage–profit theorem. This idea, in one form or another, dominated British economic thought after Adam Smith.[1] Despite its presence in the writings of David Ricardo, James Mill, Thomas Malthus, Mountifort Longfield, John E. Cairnes, and John Stuart Mill, the theorem never seeped out of the halls of academia to penetrate the popular mind. Down to this day, public opinion has it that anything that raises the cost of labor in a region ratchets up prices: "cost-plus-pricing" is what people believe, because it is apparently consistent with everyday experience in the marketplace.[2]

After reviewing, in the second section, the evidence about the persistence of the inverse wage–profit theorem, especially in the writings of David Ricardo and John Stuart Mill, in the third and fourth sections, I document that this theoretical approach was not well known outside of the Ricardian literature during most of the nineteenth century. As to why the idea did not stick in the public's mind, I agree with Paul Krugman's suggestion: most non-economists find it difficult, if not virtually impossible, to imagine how a huge prosperous currency area such as the USA can be hemmed in by system constraints and governed by potent negative feedback mechanisms.

Trained economists, especially those trained in what I shall call "the orthodox tradition," have an easier time conceptualizing the economy in these terms, and do so especially when passing on the principles of the discipline from one generation of university students to the next.[3] Intelligent observers, such as business leaders and heads of state, find orthodox patterns of thought arcane, obscure, and terribly difficult to understand. The development of economics as a scientific discipline is marked by the recognition that the social world is characterized by tendencies constrained by negative feedback effects. Large parts of neoclassical economics consist of ideas and analyses most properly rooted in the inverse wage–profit theorem of Ricardian economics.

The inverse wage–profit theorem holds that an economy-wide increase in wages tends to lower overall profits and not raise the price level. This inverse wage–profit theorem is so important to the structure of the Ricardian framework of analysis that it is a more than likely candidate for the status of what Samuel Hollander has declared "the central doctrine" of Ricardian political economy (Hollander 1977: 221–57).

Neither Adam Smith nor ordinary citizens would ever think to invoke such a peculiar theorem. It is simpler to generalize from the microeconomic idea that long-run selling prices tend to gravitate toward money costs of production. Therefore, inflation must be caused by a generalized rise in the money costs of production. What could be easier to understand? What could make better sense? But prices are not one-dimensional magnitudes. Prices are "ratios," and a set of ratios can not rise without the money commodity itself increasing or circulating more rapidly. Ricardo was certainly not the first economist to realize this basic fact about the structure of prices in the macroeconomy.[4] These insights informed all of Ricardo's subsequent scientific work.

Ricardo's basic claim was that increases in the general level of wages create a tendency throughout the economy for profits to fall. Unless the quantity of money, or specie, in the economy just happened to expand to validate the required higher level of income (or the "velocity" of money rose by exactly the right amount), there would be no obvious way a higher wage level could coexist with a higher price level. The demonstration of this claim involved an appeal to David Hume's specie-flow mechanism and the macroeconomics of what has come to be known as the "currency school" approach (Schwartz 1991: 182–6). That mechanism showed that a higher price level in response to a rise in nominal wages could not persist in a particular currency area without upsetting the region's "external" trade balance. Under the gold-exchange system, the loss of specie through the balance of payments mechanism would drive the higher price level back down again toward its original level. In the end, the higher nominal wage level would be financed by a reduction of investor profits. This inverse wage–profit theorem is as surprising and counterintuitive as the specie-flow mechanism on which it is based. These ideas in tandem constituted part of the core of Ricardian economic reasoning and constitute the orthodox tradition in modern macroeconomics.[5]

Consider for a moment the counterintuitive features of Hume's remarkable specie-flow mechanism. According to Hume, while it made sense to try to keep specie or money flowing into a region because it activated the "spirit of industry in the nation" (Hume [1742] 1985: 288), in the long run it would prove quite impossible to sustain that specie inflow. The inflow of liquid assets would raise prices and discourage exports. The trade deficit would be matched by a reverse flow of precious metals. After the new specie had sparked industry and changed certain habits in a region, such as the tastes of consumers for imported fabrics, exotic spices, and so on, the specie subsequently would flow out of that region to other regions of the world as if to stimulate business appetites there (Moss 1997: 313–14). This outflow of money and other financial assets must have an inflationary price impact abroad. Altogether, Hume's specie-flow mechanism identified genuine negative feedback effects that operate independently of the rhetoric of businessmen, politicians, and moralists.

Hume has been widely credited for his understanding of the "self-reversing" specie-flow mechanism. Eventually, Hume believed, the money specie of the world would be marvelously reallocated among the trading regions of the world so as to enable all of those regions to participate in a lively international trade. These institutional mechanisms are self-regulating and have moral implications as well. In Hume's words, the process constitutes a

> happy concurrence of causes in human affairs, which checks the growth of trade and riches, and hinders them from being confined entirely to one people ... [when one region gains specie and experiences higher commodity prices this sets in motion a reverse process via the balance of payments mechanism, and this] sets bounds to it in every country, by [eventually] enabling the poorer states to undersel[l] the richer in all foreign markets
>
> (Hume [1742] 1985: 283–4)

Decades later, Ricardo welded Hume's specie-flow mechanism on to his general analysis of the pricing mechanism, as I shall explain later. This combination gave birth to Ricardo's inverse wage–profit mechanism and one central organizing principle of neoclassical economics. In a nutshell, high wages do not and cannot bring about inflation unless the imagined higher price level is grounded in reality by the presence of a larger money supply.[6]

On Samuel Hollander's most illuminating reading of the writings of the classical school, the "higher wages cause higher prices" fallacy – the contrary doctrine – was quite basic to Adam Smith's reasoning in *An Inquiry into the Nature and Causes of the Wealth of Nations* ([1776] 1976). One after another, starting with Ricardo and continuing in the writings of James Mill, James McCulloch, Nassau Senior, Mountifort Longfield, John Stuart Mill, Thomas Malthus, and John E. Cairnes – that is in the British economic literature from the first decades to the end of the nineteenth century – refutation of the Smith "high wages cause high prices" mechanism became the hallmark of the new science of political economy (especially according to the Ricardian wing of the classical school). Ignorance of the principle, no matter how innocent and well-meaning, became the mark of amateurism in the new discipline and a badge of opposition to neoclassical orthodoxy.

Some economists ignorant of the frustrations of their predecessors a whole century earlier still experience the same frustrations with the popular mind. Consider Paul Krugman's 1996 response to the army of highly intelligent business leaders that teamed up with the Clinton administration to get the US economy "back on track."[7] Krugman's main point was that policy makers must understand that the economy is a closed system that faces negative feedback effects. Unfortunately, this is not something business leaders can easily comprehend. Practical corporate leaders are most effective when they think in terms of open systems and positive feedback effects. Unable to think in terms of closed systems and negative feedback effects, such business leaders remain poor policy-makers and do more harm than good.

Ricardo's writings and the generation of British writers influenced by Ricardo's approach might have generated the orthodox monetary tradition and its image of the economy as an integrated but closed system. If my dating is correct and holds up under critical scrutiny, then the Ricardian-wing of the classical school becomes a veritable crossroads in the history of economic reasoning. This is when professional economic reasoning departed quite sharply from casual commonsense. Economics became less a "dismal" and much more an arcane or esoteric science.

The subsequent critics of classical and later neoclassical economics have picked away at its supposedly rigid deductive framework initiated by Ricardo and his school. They complained that the Ricardians lack appreciation for historically-rooted institutions and for how they vary from one society to the next. These criticisms are about the generality claimed by the Ricardian analysis but not the analysis itself. Still, as criticisms they pale in comparison to the real significance of the Ricardian wing of the classical school, which is its novel pattern of thought. My view is that what made the new economics of Ricardo and his followers so maddeningly difficult to master was that it required thinking about the economy as a closed system disciplined by negative feedback mechanisms. I go beyond Krugman, who restricted his criticisms to the high-powered CEOs of the world. Not only business leaders have difficulty with modern economics: most non-economists have precisely the same trouble. It may be said that the neoclassical tradition in economics departed from the simple commonsense of household management when the insights associated with closed systems and negative feedback loops became part of how economists viewed the world and interpreted public policy.

The origins of the inverse wage–profit mechanism

According to Hollander, the most

> outstanding relationship in the entire [*Principles of Political Economy* by David Ricardo in 1817], can only be evaluated, and accordingly Ricardo's place in the development of economic thought identified, if full attention is paid to the instigating force behind the investigations. The relevant consideration in this regard is Ricardo's objection to received doctrine based upon the Smithian analysis.
>
> (Hollander 1979: 269)

Smith's analysis of the "wage–price–trade mechanism"

What Hollander termed "the received doctrine" of Smithian economics is presented at various locations in both Books 4 and 5 of his *The Wealth of Nations*. In Book 4, we are told that the "real effect" of a bounty on corn is to lower the purchasing power of money (that is, raise all prices and lower the purchasing power of silver and gold; the two money commodities). According to Smith, a bounty or corn-subsidy raises the price of corn in the home market above what "it otherwise would be in that state [of the economy]" (Smith [1776] 1976, Book 4: 514). Why is this so? Surely by subsidizing the exporter and promising to pay out of the public coffers so many coins for each unit of corn exported, it would seem that the nominal price of corn (now stabilized) should be greeted by a huge increase in the amount of land and effort devoted to corn production. Ordinarily, supply and demand principles would drive us to a greater volume of corn to be traded but at a lower market clearing price as a result of the bounty or corn-subsidy. This, however, was not Smith's conclusion.

Smith rejected the conclusion because he refused to treat issues involving food as a simple exercise in what we today call "partial equilibrium analysis." Smith understood that subsidies and taxes, when imposed on special commodities such as food and necessities, must have far-reaching macro-equilibrium consequences. According to Smith, there was something mysteriously special about the money price of corn. It "regulates that of all other homemade commodities" (Smith [1776] 1976, Book 4: 509). Smith held that the bounty on corn had the effect of raising the prices of almost all commodities (that is, lowering the value of silver and gold).[8] This central modeling idea constitutes one of the organizing features of Smithian economics.

As I read Smith, the export bounty raises the nominal price of corn and by this route affects the domestic wages of the laboring poor. The corn bounty encourages food exports, leaving less annual production at home and available for sale. Higher food prices are the bane of poverty-stricken workers who suffer a decline in real income.[9] Some of the workers react to higher food prices by finding it impossible adequately to "educate and bring up their children." As a result, marriages are delayed and the population of the country is restrained (Smith [1776] 1976, Book 4: 508). With nominal wages enhanced by the decline in laborers coming of age and entering the labor force, the real purchasing power of the worker's wage is restored. Now, with the higher nominal wage bill, factory owners raise their selling prices to cover their higher labor costs. The general rise of local selling prices, originally caused by the corn bounties but now operating indirectly through labor market mechanisms and boosting all prices, diminishes the purchasing power of the currency unit. In Smith's terminology, the real value of silver is "degraded" (ibid.: 509).

In modern terminology, the corn-subsidy has thrown this nation's price level out of line with those of its major trading partners. The bounty produces a vicious cheapness in the local value of the metals gold and silver. Foreigners react to the higher prices in the food-subsidized nation by switching to other sources of supply for their manufactured goods, and the corn-export-bounty nation suffers a dreaded loss of overall trade advantage. Aside from food exports, most other lines of exporting decline. There is a deterioration in the balance of trade and a tendency for specie to flow out of the nation. Miraculously, specie is kept from flowing out only because of the bounty on corn, and it is this subsidized corn that itself gets exported to pay for the nation's import imbalance. Smith goes on to analogize the stock-flow problem described here to a dam that holds back a certain amount of water; the corn bounty, like a dam, holds back specie and keeps it from flowing out of the region. This redundant coinage in the region sustains a price level higher than international conditions truly warrant (ibid.: 512).

Now let us move away from the corn subsidy debate and consider a tax on necessities, meaning the grains and related food products that ordinary working people consume. Let us suppose these commodities are taxed. The tax will raise the nominal wage of the workers to "cover them" for the tax-augmented cost of production of the necessities. The manufacturers will cover themselves for the higher nominal wages by hiking up the price of the manufactured commodities that they sell. Silver and gold will be degraded in the nation (that is, the purchasing power of the currency unit will decline) and the balance of trade will worsen. Specie flows out of this food-taxing region to pay for the merchandise deficit on the trade account. Smith's "received doctrine" about the similar effects of bounties and taxes when they are imposed on food is important to our understanding of Ricardian economics.[10]

There was something special about the food producing sector of the economy. The "whole body of the people are purchasers of corn" (Smith [1776] 1976, Book 4: 508) and that is why the conditions surrounding corn production and its pricing really become macroeconomic problems affecting the overall structure of the market system. The bounty-subsidy on corn exports operates exactly like a tax on necessities, and subjects the entire community, and especially the vast majority of the day-laborers in the fields and in the factories, to necessarily pay more for their food. This is a "heavy tax upon the first necessary of life" (ibid.). The foremost necessity of life is food. The consequence for the laboring poor is either that the wage of labor falls reducing the "subsistence of the labouring poor" (ibid.), or more humanely, it will augment "their pecuniary wages, proportionable to that in the pecuniary price of their subsistence" keeping the real wage intact (ibid.). In the short run, living standards fall; in the long run by way of the population–wage mechanism, the real wage is restored.[11]

Finally, in Book 5 of *The Wealth of Nations*, Smith devoted "Article III" to the topic of "Taxes upon the Wages of Labour" (Smith [1776] 1976, Book 5: 864–7). Smith maintained that a tax on the wages of common direct labor will always raise the nominal wages of labor.[12] If the taxed worker were employed in the agricultural sector of the economy, then the farmer would finance the higher wage bill by reducing the rents paid to the landlord "in the long run." If the taxed worker were employed in manufacturing then the

> master manufacturer . . . would both be entitled and obliged to charge it, with a profit [since the higher wages are advanced to the worker and there command interest], upon the price of his goods [that is, the manufacturer would raise the selling prices of his goods to cover the higher wages and need for more working capital].
> (Smith [1776] 1976, book 5: 864–5)

Smith's conclusion is that "in all cases, a direct tax upon the wages of labour must, in the long run, occasion both a greater reduction in the rent of land, and a greater rise in the price of manufactured goods, than would have followed from the proper assessment of a sum equal to the produce of the tax, partly upon the rent of land, and partly upon consumable commodities" (ibid.: 865).

Smith repeated this same analysis elsewhere in *The Wealth of Nations* and concluded that "whatever might be the state to which a tax of this kind reduced the demand for labour, it must always raise wages higher than they otherwise would be in that state, and the final payment of this enhancement of wages must in all cases fall upon the superior ranks of people" (ibid.: 888). In other places, we have seen, Smith stated that the enhanced wages must cause a deterioration in the purchasing power of the money commodity and a trade imbalance. This was the "received doctrine" at the dawn of the Ricardian school in 1817. The received doctrine is Smith's claim that whatever raises the nominal wages of an area raises the price level as well and discourages commerce and trade mostly through an adverse balance of trade mechanism. Let us now turn to the Ricardian response to the Smithian wage–price–trade mechanism.

Ricardo's response to Smith's wage–price–trade mechanism

Ricardo's *On the Principles of Political Economy and Taxation* (Ricardo [1817] 1951) set out to establish the most general principles that can be stated about an economy in which landowners lease land to capitalist farmers, manufacturers invest their capital in competitive settings, and workers display a tendency to have large families whenever economic conditions turn favorable. Later on in the nineteenth century, John Stuart Mill explained how these same general principles can be successfully modified to apply to other societies in other vastly different institutional settings, such as those in which land arrangements differ or workers are motivated to be more prudent in their family planning. With Ricardo at one end of the period (1817) and John Stuart Mill (1871) at the other, it makes sense to write of a genuine Ricardian school of thought in the history of economic thought. There is little disagreement among intellectual historians that such a tradition existed (Blaug 1958, Hollander 1977). The disagreement stems more from identifying the central organizing principles of the Ricardian conversation. This section sets them out in some detail.

I agree with Hollander that the inverse wage–profit theorem might well be the central organizing principle of the Ricardian school of economics.[13] What was that theorem and in what context did it appear? The best place to start is with Ricardo's own words. According to Ricardo:

> It has been my endeavour to shew throughout this work [his *Principles*], that the rate of profits can never be increased but by a fall in wages, and that there can be no permanent fall of wages but in consequence of a fall of the necessities on which wages are expended. If, therefore, by the extension of foreign trade, or by improvements in machinery, the food and necessities of the labourer can be brought to market at a reduced price, profits will rise.
>
> (Ricardo [1817] 1951, vol. 1: 132)

Ricardo opposed Smith's corn-bounty analysis because it implied that the rate of return in agriculture would not be increased in a bounty system. Smith insisted that the rise in the price of necessities (that is, corn prices) would be followed by a rise in wages, thereby keeping profit margins constant. Instead, Ricardo insisted that the corn-bounty would increase returns in agriculture and thereby shift capital investments out of manufacturing toward agriculture.

The profit rate differential in favor of agriculture would quickly disappear as capital was attracted from the manufacturing sector into the agricultural sector. The extra flow of new corn production would lower corn prices, and the net effect of the bounty or subsidy system would be to change the composition of sectoral output and increase the relative share of corn. At this point in his analysis of Smith's corn-bounty, Ricardo insisted that

> whether or not money wages rise during the process of adjustment to the disturbance [brought about by the bounty offer to the farmers], a profit differential would be created in favour of agriculture by the rise in the market price of corn and accordingly resources would be attracted from manufacturing.
>
> (Hollander 1979: 295)

Ricardo's non-Smithian analysis of the corn-bounty program was designed to demonstrate to the world that the rate of return among the sectors of the economy was not much affected by shifts in the relative demand for final output. The relative increase in returns to corn production facilitated by the bounty system would be neutralized quickly by way of a reshuffling of resources. When equilibrium was once again restored, the bounty on corn would increase the size and level of investments in the corn production sector, but all rates of return would once again return to their competitive levels. A general fall in the rate of wages could permanently increase the rate of return in corn production. Unfortunately, in this corn-bounty example, wages threatened to increase by way of the wage–population mechanism, and if that occurred, then profit rates throughout the economy would indeed fall. Smith did not grasp the subtle operation of the inverse wage–profit mechanism. It is to that mechanism that we now turn our attention.

The long Chapter 16 of Ricardo's *On the Principles of Political Economy and Taxation* (Ricardo [1817] 1951: 215–42) is devoted entirely to another of Smith's policy analysis problems. Can a tax on wages be passed on entirely to consumers by way of higher commodity prices? Ricardo had serious doubts about the Smithian wage–price–trade mechanism, especially when it is applied to the prices of wage-goods: those goods consumed by the vast majority of the workers. We have already seen how Smith relied on this mechanism in his analysis of the effects of a bounty on corn production.

Ricardo's position was that always and inevitably "taxes on wages will raise wages, and therefore will diminish the rate of the profits of stock" (ibid.: 215). Contrary to Smith's claim that the tax on wages will be passed on to all consumers in the form of higher commodity prices, Ricardo insisted that neither the workers as consumers nor the landlords as consumers would bear the incidence of such a tax. There was only one group left on whom the incidence of the tax on wages could fall: the manufacturers and other investors. There is a short-cut to Ricardo's conclusion, but first, I shall summarize the full mechanism.

According to the classical theory of land rent, the rental share of the national dividend paid to the landlord is determined by scarcity of land and the fact that land exists with different degrees of fertility. All land produces one uniform commodity – food – and, with competitive markets, food must sell everywhere at a uniform price. According to Ricardo, that single price of corn is determined by the costs of producing corn on the worst or least fertile land under cultivation. Because the productivity of land varies, the flows of revenue from the sale of the corn will vary from one farm to the next. Farmers competing to lease the most fertile lands will offer landowners the highest rents. Less fertile land generates lower rents. In long run equilibrium, land rents vary from farm to farm, with the practical effect of yielding a single rate or return on investment on all farms regardless of whether the farm is very fertile or not so fertile.

From this, Ricardo concluded that unless a tax changes the costs of producing the marginal bushel of corn, the implementation of the tax will not affect the rent paid to the landlords. A direct tax on rents will indeed lower rents (although the landlords will devise strategies speedily to avoid the tax). The only tax falling on rent, is a tax directly imposed on rents. Some taxes fall on profits. Any tax that has the effect of increasing wages – such as a direct tax on wages – will ultimately be "paid by a diminution of profits, and, therefore . . . a tax on wages is in fact a tax on profits" (Ricardo [1817] 1951: 226). This claim was so important to Ricardo that it might be called his signature theoretical argument. The inverse wage–profit theorem has become for Hollander and other writers the leading test of a Ricardian economist (Hollander 1977: 221–57).[14]

Because of the importance of the inverse wage–profit theorem, let me say something more about how it works. Suppose a sales tax were imposed on corn. The initial impact of the tax will be to increase corn prices as farmers try to ratchet up their selling prices to pass that tax on to their customers, thereby preserving their profit margins. This is the common sense analysis of the impact of a tax on supply; most noneconomists find it reasonable that the sellers, trying to sustain profits, will simply pass the tax on to their buyers. An increase in corn prices will cause the nominal wage paid to the worker to lose purchasing power; that is, the real wage of the worker must decline. As a practical matter though, the working class is "never able to bear any considerable proportion of taxation" (Ricardo [1817] 1951: 159). Unable to subsist on these lowered real wages, the number of workers will gradually decline and their relative scarcity will reverse the tendency for wages to decline. The wages of the workers will then increase again. Without any increase in the quantity of money in the economy (and without a rise in velocity), the higher nominal wages paid to the workers must be financed out of profits. The tax on wages will be paid out of the profits of stock.

Now for the short-cut version of the same theorem.

Under the customary interpretation of Ricardian economics – what we call "crude Ricardianism" – the real wage of labor is fixed by social habits and customs, and is not affected in the long run by market forces. This means that the tax on wages cannot be financed out of the real wages of the workers. Because the landlords do not pay the tax, and the workers do not pay the tax, there is only one functional class left in society to pay the wage tax, and that is the investors or owners of stock who now obtain smaller profits. Although this simple crude model gets us to the right conclusion about Ricardo's claim about the incidence of the wages tax falling entirely on profits, the approach omits the more subtle aspects of Ricardo's analysis.

Let us take a look at one pattern of his argument as set out especially in Chapters 9 and 16 of Ricardo's *Principles*. Assume, for the sake of argument, that a tax on wages cannot, even in small part, come out of current nominal wages. In this case and in the context of Ricardo's simple model, there are only two choices. The wage tax is paid by the consumers of the product in the form of higher commodity prices resulting from higher manufacturing costs, or the tax is paid out of the profits that ordinarily are paid to the owners of the capital goods. In the first case, in which the employers of labor are faced with higher nominal wages and try to mark up their commodities' prices, the international value of the currency unit will be lowered. Whenever the value of money is lowered (in the absence of government prohibitions on gold exports), the region is subject to Hume's specie-flow mechanism. In losing money, the area experiences decreasing incomes and depressing prices. Prices fall, and the tax comes to be paid out of the profits otherwise accruing to the capitalist. The net effect of the rise of wages is to change relative commodity prices and the allocation of investments in the economy – the return on capital changes as well – but *the price level will remain unchanged*.[15] In a nutshell, the macroeconomic consequences of a rise (or fall) in nominal wages throughout the economy affect the long-run accumulation process by way of their effect on profits.

Ricardo's inverse wage–profit theorem

Ricardo's arguments in support of the inverse wage–profit theorem included his theory of comparative advantage.[16] This theory ingeniously sets forth the claim that it is comparative costs and not absolute costs that govern the pattern of international trade. With the introduction of international trade, we may have what economists popularly call an "open economy."[17] The expression "open economy" must not be understood to imply that the process governing the circulation of goods and incomes is without any system constraints. Indeed, it was Ricardo's lasting contribution to point out, in painstaking detail, what those constraints were. Ricardo succeeded in extending the Hume specie-flow mechanism to the analysis of trading patterns based on comparative advantage. This synthesis is consistently presented in his published works and throughout his correspondence with Malthus and other writers. It was Ricardo's clever linking of the inverse wage–profit mechanism to the other mechanisms governing international trade that constitutes the basic framework of Ricardo's analysis.

Ricardo's idea about international trade and exchange is related to his criticisms of Smith's cost-price mechanism. Suppose now in an open economy the wages of the laborers are taxed either directly or indirectly through a tax on the necessities the workers consume. The resulting increase in the nominal wages of the workers will not, in turn, increase the price level. Suppose by way of a thought experiment all prices did in fact increase (in accordance with Smith's analysis and also common sense). Will not export prices increase also? It might seem at first that with higher export prices the foreigners will pay some part of the tax. The tax on necessities will be passed on to the foreign buyers of the region's products. In other words, a Smithian perspective might indicate that with higher export prices, the incidence of the tax, or some part of the incidence of the tax, falls on the foreign importers of the first nation's production. According to the Hume specie-flow-mechanism this partial effect is not likely to occur.

The increase in all prices means a dramatic lowering of the purchasing power of money, along with its international or external value. Local citizens will try to import more goods rather than purchase them from local suppliers, and foreigners will refrain from consuming imported goods because they are too expensive. The trade balance will turn negative, and specie or commodity money will flow out of the high-price currency area. According to Ricardo, commodity money (gold and silver) will continue to leave the area until local prices have fallen once again to reveal the very basis for trade in the comparative advantages of each respective trading area. Ricardo said,

> I hope, I have satisfactorily proved, that a comparatively low price of the precious metals, in consequence of taxation, or, in other words, a generally high price of commodities, would be of no disadvantage to a State, as part of the metals would be exported, which, by raising their value, would again lower the price of commodities [that is, the higher price level brought about by the tax on necessities will not stick].
> (Ricardo [1817] 1951: 232)

Indeed, this is just a special application of the general principle first advanced by Hume that

> gold and silver having been chosen for the general medium of circulation, they are, by the competition of commerce, distributed in such proportions amongst the different countries of the world, as to accommodate themselves to the natural traffic which would take place if no such metals existed, and the trade between countries were purely a trade of barter.
> (Ricardo [1817] 1951: 137)

This is the source of John Stuart Mill's and others' view that money is only a veil that needs to be stripped away if one wishes to understand the fundamentals of international trade and exchange based on comparative advantage.

The Ricardian wing of the classical school held that the tax on wages could not by itself alter the pattern of international trade or even the level of trade. That is because the pattern of international trade depends on relative prices and not absolute prices. Still, it had to be admitted that in cases in which capital-intensive production is used, an increase in wages would narrow profit margins by less than it would in more labor-intensive methods of production. This would lead to a reshuffling of resources among industrial sectors until the rate of profit were equal again in all lines of endeavor. Indeed, the tax would change relative commodity prices but not the general level of prices. Any tendency for the general level of prices to move up (or down) as a result of some form of taxation would be checked rapidly and most effectively by the international financial mechanism, especially in the version appropriate to a commodity standard system. The international financial mechanism would completely neutralize Smith's notorious wage–price–trade mechanism. Indeed, this result could be demonstrated more precisely if all prices were measured in terms of Ricardo's theoretical ideal money, but the details of this search had better be left for another time and place.[18]

Qualifications

There are several qualifications to this line of argument that must be pointed out. First, if the tax were not imposed on necessities but on luxury goods only, then working-class money wages would not rise. In this case, the overall profit rate would not fall, and the incidence of the tax would fall entirely on the consumers of these luxury products (that is, non-necessities), and this includes foreign consumers. Thus, a tax on English pewter plate service would be paid by the consumers of the pewter plate service with due allowance for the fact that, faced with higher prices, they may buy smaller amounts of it. It is only when a tax is imposed on the commodity or bundle of commodities that constitutes the complete wage basket consumed by the great mass of the working man and working woman that the incidence of that tax sets in motion the macroeconomic mechanisms of Hume's specie-flow mechanism and by implication the Ricardian inverse profit–wage theorem. Smith and Ricardo, as well as subsequent Ricardian writers, accepted and developed this important analytic distinction between a disturbance that affects only particular markets to which a partial supply and demand style analysis is relevant, and a disturbance that has an impact on the entire level of prices, and by implication the international exchange rate itself.

A second important qualification concerns the internal consistency of Ricardo's *Principles* and by implication the entire Ricardian school. As Mountifort Longfield – a self-proclaimed critic of Ricardian economics – was one of the first to realize in 1834, Ricardo's ideas about the accumulation process allowed for the possibility that the workers' nominal wage could be substantially above the minimum subsistence level set by the habits and customs of the workforce. This high real wage could persist for significant periods of time. Indeed, Ricardo had admitted as much in his *Principles* and in other places as well (Hollander 1979). That would explain how it was possible for the size of the population to expand. It would expand because the workers' wage rate was significantly above subsistence. With such an assumption about wages, the incidence of diminishing agricultural returns is always "shared" during the accumulation process by both the capitalists and the workers. Both capitalists and workers experience a decline in their distributive shares. Hollander, Paul Samuelson, David Levy, and J. R. Hicks attest to the prevalence of the Ricardian "shared incidence theorem," which is based on the claim that the worker's wage has, at any moment along the accumulation trajectory, a significant amount of "slack" before the population–wage mechanism is triggered (Hicks and Hollander 1977).

One important implication of this shared-incidence theorem is that taxes on necessities can indeed come out of wages without diminishing population size. If they are paid out of wages then the general wage rate need not increase. If the nominal wage rate does not increase, then profits will not fall. All this is despite the fact that the real wage has fallen due to this tax. This conclusion does not contradict the inverse wage–profit mechanism: rather, it renders it inoperative.

Once we admit that the burden of any wage tax or tax on the necessities of the working class could, in principle, fall directly on the wages of the working class who simply pay the tax without suffering severe impoverishment, then it follows that (net real) wages fall and profits do not necessarily decrease. Profits do not decrease because despite the tax on necessities, nominal wages have not risen. Such a scenario is both a logical possibility and one that interferes with the inevitable or at least general application of the fundamental theorem of Ricardian economics: that is, the inverse wage–profit mechanism. The fundamental inverse wage–profit theorem of Ricardian economics, when juxtaposed alongside the shared incidence theorem, is apparently subject to serious exceptions. It remained for Ricardo's successors, and especially John Stuart Mill, to offer a more qualified version of Ricardo's inverse wage–profit theorem, although the result is not without some interpretive difficulties, as I shall now demonstrate.

John Stuart Mill's version of the inverse wage–profit mechanism

I agree with Hollander's assessment that on most counts, John Stuart Mill offered a series of improvements on the economics of Ricardo and not an entirely different economics (Hollander 1985: 245). This is especially the case with the inverse wage–profit mechanism that appears in different places in his written work.

In Book 3 of *Principles of Political Economy with Some Applications to Social Philosophy*, Mill presented the general principles of the theory of exchange. Mill explained that in popular mind, "high wages make high values. . . . But this is a contradiction in terms" (Mill [1848] 1965, Book 3: 479). High wages must fall on profits. In Mill's words,

> there is no mode in which capitalists can compensate themselves for a high cost of labour, through any action on values or prices. [The high wages] cannot be prevented from taking its effect on low profits. If the labourers really get more, that is, get the produce of more labour, a smaller percentage must remain for profit. From this Law of Distribution, resting as it does on a law of arithmetic, there is no escape. The mechanism of Exchange and Price may hide it from us, but is quite powerless to alter it.
> (Mill [1848] 1965, Book 3: 480)

Mill's so-called law of distribution is nothing more than the inverse wage–profit theorem.

In Book 5 of his *Principles* (ibid.: 799–872), Mill dealt with the influence of the government intervention and its effects on the economy. Here we have a large variety of issues involving taxation and the ultimate incidence of the taxes. In Book 5, Chapter 4, Mill wastes no time in exploding the Smithian fallacy. An across-the-board increase in nominal wages will not increase all prices in the economy because the money commodity also has its price, and all prices cannot go up absolutely. This outright rejection of Smith's mechanism once again signals Mill's affection for the larger analytic tradition Ricardo established in which the inverse wage–profit mechanism plays a central organizing role. According to Mill,

> when the cost of production is increased . . . by a tax, the effect is the same as when it is increased by natural causes. If only one or a few commodities are affected, their value and price rise, so as to compensate the producer or dealer for the peculiar burthen: but if there were a tax on all commodities, exactly proportional to their value, no such compensation would be obtained: there would neither be a general rise of values, which is an absurdity, nor of prices [the price level], which depend on causes entirely different.
> (Mill [1848] 1965: 838)

After emphasizing the important analytic distinction (also found in Ricardo) between causes that affect all prices and causes that affect particular prices, Mill considered the effect of a "taxes on necessaries" (ibid.: 840). According to Mill,

> taxes on necessaries must thus have one of two effects. Either they lower the condition of the [working] classes; or they exact from the owners of capital, in addition to the amount due to the state on their own necessaries, the amount due on those consumed by the labourers. In the last case, the tax on necessaries, like a tax on wages, is equivalent to a peculiar tax on profits; which is, like all other partial taxation, unjust, and is specially prejudicial to the increase of the national wealth.
> (Mill [1848] 1965: 841)

This analysis is entirely consistent with Ricardo's analysis and at the same time allows for the possibility (already explained by Longfield) that when the market wage is far larger than the meager sum that would provide the workers and their families with a subsistence minimum, a tax on wages or necessaries, in principle, could be paid out of wages and therefore would not have any lowering effect on profits. In this case, nominal wages would not increase and the inverse wage–price mechanism would not come into play. Mill's qualified statement of the inverse wage–profit mechanism significantly improves on Ricardo's formulation by removing one of the apparent inconsistencies that I noted earlier. In Mill, the inverse wage–price mechanism and the shared-incidence theorem coexist quite peacefully.

In other ways as well, Mill provided a qualified analysis of the inverse wage–profit mechanism. First, Mill makes the important distinction between a tax that has only partial effects on the economy and one that has a generalized impact throughout the entire economy. A tax that affects one firm or one industry or even one sector of the economy will have different macroeconomic effects on relative prices than will a tax that has generalized effects in all industries throughout the economy. Even in adhering to a tax such as a tax on food that all the economists of the day assume would have a generalized impact throughout the economy, we must once again distinguish two cases. The first case is when such a tax falls completely on the worker who bears the incidence of that tax out of his or her relatively abundant wages, in settings where capital is being rapidly accumulated. The second case is when the tax succeeds in raising wages (perhaps via the Smith–Ricardo wage–price mechanism). In this second case, the higher wages come out of profits. In both cases, the incidence of the tax is entirely local and has no effect on the international value of the currency.

However, what market mechanisms in Mill's work explain these causal sequences, and does Mill offer a market process account of the adjustment process? Let us review the sequence of events that is clearly set out in Ricardo's account of a tax on wage goods. The sequence of events was as follows: first, money wages are taxed; second, the cost of production of labor (that is the nominal wage rate) rises by virtue of the population–wage mechanism; third, commodity selling prices rise throughout the economy including the wage of labor; and fourth, the Hume specie-flow mechanism brings the level of prices down again. In the end, profits fall because wages have increased.

Surprisingly, Mill does not present an account of this sequence of events where it most obviously belongs, that is, in Book 5 of his *Principles* where he goes into great detail about the incidence of taxes. The Hume specie-flow mechanism is indeed expressly set out in Book 3, Chapter 21 (Mill [1848] 1965: 630–46), but the two discussions are separated by more than a hundred pages. It is revealing that in order to connect Mill's thinking more closely with Ricardo's, Hollander is forced to reach outside the *Principles* text and refer his readers to Mill's *Fortnightly Review* article entitled "Thornton on Labour and its Claims," which appeared late in Mill's career in 1869 (Mill [1869] 1967: 633–68). In that essay, virtually the whole Ricardian presentation is nicely laid out. At one place, the analysis parallels the finest passages in Ricardo's *Principles*. Consider this passage:

> There cannot be a general rise in prices unless there is more money expended. But the rise of wages does not cause more money to be expended. [All a rise in wages does is] take from incomes of the masters and adds to those of the workmen; the former have less to spend, the latter have more [to spend]; but the general sum of the money incomes of the community remains what it was, and it is upon that sum that money prices depend. There cannot be more money expended on everything, when there is not more money to be expended altogether.
> (Mill [1869] 1967: 661)

Now (mirroring Ricardo), Mill immediately considers the hypothetical situation where, for whatever reason, the general level of prices does somehow increase after an increase in nominal wages. This surge in prices will have dramatic international implications and therefore not be self-sustaining. Mill explained:

In the second place, even if there did happen a rise in all prices, the only effect would be that money, having become of less value in the particular country, while it remained of its former value everywhere else, would be exported until prices were brought down to nearly ... their former level.

(Mill [1869] 1967: 661)

Here we have a clear and unequivocal appeal to the Hume specie-flow-mechanism, again harking back to a market process account of how equilibrium is reestablished in the face of a disturbance. From these theoretical considerations, Mill concludes that "a real rise of general wages cannot be thrown on the consumer" (Mill [1869] 1967: 661). Let me now return to Mill's *Principles* text.

In his *Principles* (Book 5, Chapter 4), in the chapter entitled "Of Taxes on Commodities," Mill does not discuss the market process by which the international monetary mechanism operates to prevent all prices from rising in response to a rise in nominal wages. Instead, Mill rules out the possibility of all values rising as a "[logical] absurdity." It is absurd to suppose that all prices can increase because increases and falls always must be relative to some baseline. It makes no sense to say that all values can rise at once: they cannot. Surprisingly, Mill makes no reference to the Hume specie-flow mechanism that was to be explained so eloquently in his 1869 *Fortnightly Review* article. The specie-flow mechanism can be found in other places in the *Principles* (Mill [1848] 1965: 630–46), but it is not invoked here. Logical absurdities do not require elaborate market process refutations and that is, no doubt, the reason Mill did not provide one in Book 5 of his *Principles*. Thus, if John Stuart Mill's presentation represents an advanced phase in the development of the Ricardian analysis, we see a certain hardening of the Ricardian position about the impact of a general increase in wages on prices: it cannot happen. Case closed.

After distinguishing (as Ricardo had done before) between taxes that shift the margin of cultivation in agriculture and those that do not, Mill makes a second important distinction between a tax on necessaries and a tax on luxuries. The taxes on necessaries or "[raw] produce ... do not affect rent [and therefore] fall on the consumer; profits, however, generally bearing either the whole or the greatest part of the [tax] which is levied on the consumption of the labouring classes" (Mill [1848] 1965: 843). Commodity taxes, which are paid out of profits, discourage accumulation and "in the ultimate result, the minimum of profits will be reached with a smaller capital and population, and a lower rental, than if the course of things had not been disturbed by the imposition of the tax" (ibid.: 844). This is clearly and unequivocally the inverse wage–profit theorem, but the fuller account of how that relationship is established in the market place through the negative feedback mechanisms of the specie-flow mechanism is notoriously absent.

The incidence of a specific tax on some particular necessities will fall at least in part on the final purchasers of the product. Mill cited large passages from his early essay written sometime between 1829 and 1830, "Of the Laws of Interchange Between Nations; and the Distribution of the

Gains of Commerce Among the Countries of the Commercial World" (Mill [1844] 1967: 232–61). Because the final terms of trade in the simple case of two-country, two-commodity trade fall somewhere between the limits set by the comparative production costs in the two regions, it is logically possible for a particular tax to fall on the international consumers of the product that is taxed. The final outcome, Mill explains, depended on the intensity of the reciprocal demands on the part of any two trading partners. The new (equilibrium) commodity terms of trade that would emerge after the imposition of a tax on traded goods would be brought about and maintained by the same balance of trade mechanisms on which Ricardo also relied, and they would be between the limits established by the comparative production costs in the two trading regions. This analysis of the international payments mechanism is tacked on to Book 5, but the application is to a tax that has partial effects only, such as a tax on a particular industry or sector of the larger economy. The analysis of a tax on wages is not explored any further in Book 5. I now turn to another major interpretive issue that has relevance to my claim about the central logical impact of the inverse wage–profit mechanism.

Relevance of the wage fund debate

A large literature exists on the subject of the "wage fund" and whether, in his 1869 *Fortnightly Review* analysis of Thornton's book, Mill recanted his position on the issue of whether or not the wage fund was "fixed" in some meaningful sense of the term "fixed." The idea behind the analysis is simply that production processes are time-consuming. A worker gets paid months before the materials on which he worked have taken shape and are finally sold in the market. The savings of the factory owners provide the implicit fund out of which wages are paid and consumption takes place. Apparently, some economists claimed that this wage fund was relatively fixed in real terms, at least over short periods of time. Should certain workers contrive through trade union activity to have their real wages increased and thereby grab a larger share of the wage fund, there would be less left for the other workers whose real wages would necessarily decline. The conventional wisdom among contemporary historians is that in 1869 Mill boldly recanted the wage-fund doctrine, thereby claiming that trade union activity could increase the real income of union members without one group of lucky workers grabbing another group's share of the wage fund.[19]

Regardless of what Mill specifically admitted or confessed to in his 1869 review of Thornton's book, it appeared that the fundamental theorem of Ricardian economics – the inverse wage–profit mechanism – permitted a simultaneous increase in both the nominal and the real wage share. A consistent advocate of the inverse wage–profit theory would be hard put to deny this possibility. Indeed, the whole point of the inverse wage–profit theorem is that a general increase in the wages of the great mass of the working people will not cause inflation, but be financed out of the share of the gross domestic product that might otherwise have gone to the investors in the form of profits. The fundamental Ricardian theorem implies that the aggregate capital of society that is available to pay workers is definitely not a fixed amount. If the wage fund theory asserts the opposite (according to Hollander's account there is a "primitive version of the wage fund" doctrine that meets this specification [Hollander 1985: 419]), then this is the particular version of the wage fund theory that Mill denied. His denial of that version is consistent with the fundamental theorem of Ricardian economics and with the central importance of the inverse wage–profit theorem to the entire enterprise of Ricardian economic analysis.

The basic architecture of Mill's *Principles* contained the fundamental theorem from 1848 when it was first published until its last edition in 1871, and this is especially obvious if we tack together the discussion of the Hume specie-flow mechanism in Book 3 with what we find about tax incidence in Book 5. This means that Mill was not obligated to recant anything in particular about the formation of wages in market settings as presented in his main theoretical work on economics. I agree completely with Hollander on this point. The wage fund doctrine in this primitive form was neither part of Mill's *Principles* nor a logical part of the Ricardian tradition.[20]

The endurance of the Smithian wage–price–trade mechanism

So we have followed Hollander and identified a distinctive and in many ways robust body of analysis centering about the inverse wage–profit mechanism. This body of analysis is embedded in a certain macroeconomic modeling approach that characterizes the Ricardian wing of the classical school. It may indeed have been the badge of a skilled economist to analyze that basic mechanism and explain its relevance to the major policy debates of the day. One major policy debate of the day that continued well into Mill's was whether or not high money wages make it unprofitable for one region of the world to trade with another region of the world. Surely, it seemed to many onlookers that high domestic wages must operate to keep domestic prices high and discourage export sales. Government tolerance of trade union activity also might be short-sighted because it could lead to a loss of export sales. Government policies that artificially elevated money wages were against the public interest. High wages meant high prices, and high prices meant dwindling foreign sales and depressed trade. What could be clearer to common sense and what could be more easily understood? Indeed, it was the popular economic idea of its time and perhaps of all times. It was the "conventional wisdom," to borrow John K. Galbraith's felicitous expression. The Ricardian school argued that any situation in which wages were too high to encourage exports would set in motion self-correcting tendencies by way of Hume's specie-flow mechanism.

Trade unions can raise wages

The anti-Ricardian idea (part of Smith's discussion) that high wages cause a nation permanently to lose its competitive advantage was firmly ingrained in the public mind in Mill's day as it is in ours. Mill himself complained about the conventional wisdom in a private letter to George Adcroft on June 21 1870. Mill disagreed with Adcroft's statement about the abilities of the trade unions to increase wages. Most significantly, he disagreed with Adcroft's claim that a "general rise of wages would be of no use to the working classes because it would produce a general rise in prices." Mill explained the logic of the fundamental Ricardian theorem as follows:

> A general rise of prices, of anything like a permanent character, can only take place through a general increase of the money incomes of the purchasing community. Now a general rise of wages would not increase the aggregate money incomes, nor consequently the aggregate purchasing power of the community; it would only transfer part of that purchasing power from the employers to the labourers. Consequently a general rise of wages would not raise prices but would be taken out of the profits of the employers; always supposing that those profits were sufficient to bear the reduction.
> (Mill 1972: 1734–5)

Had Adcroft been more familiar with the contents of Mill's *Principles* he would have learned that he had unknowingly uttered what Mill identified in Book 3 to be one of those annoying "propositions which may and do become, and long remain, accredited doctrines of popular political economy" (Mill [1848] 1965, Book 3: 479). Those who hold the "high wages cause high prices" doctrine are bearers of an "amazing folly" that no doubt originated in the writings of the earliest mercantilists and even crept in to the architecture of Smith's *The Wealth of Nations*. Despite the cleansing efforts of Ricardo, Mill, and others, the doctrine congealed in Smith's wage–price–trade mechanism is now firmly rooted in popular culture.

Indeed, the evidence suggests that between *The Wealth of Nations* and the last edition of Mill's *Principles* in 1871 – a period spanning nearly a whole century – the popular prejudice was that high wages paid to the general factory laborers are bad for international export sales.

The corn law debate after 1838

The policy dispute was whether Britain should continue to place a duty of any kind on imported grains. Alternatively, perhaps all duties on imports should be repealed completely and English protectionism abandoned once and for all. Curiously, enormous political agitation grew in response, especially after 1838 and especially after the formation of the Anti-Corn Law League in 1839, and the mass agitation for the repeal of all tariffs on food became a central event in the history of the democratic movement in Britain. The agitation for repeal was mainly centered in the cities of Manchester and London. Manchester in particular was the home of the English export trade, and the repeal of protectionism was thought by many business leaders to be good for business. After all, by lowering food prices, wages, and money costs of production, export prices must decrease and international sales expand. What could be plainer and more consistent with common sense?

Prime Minister Disraeli christened the collection of politicians, businessmen, journalists, and others "the Manchester School." It was a school in name only. There was no central body of academic analysis handed down from teacher to student. Indeed, according to William D. Grampp, "none of the well-known economists appear in the register to the Manchester School" (Grampp 1960: 17). The Manchester School did not even have a "consistent and comprehensive doctrine" (ibid.: 15). It is clear that the business community thought that the removal of all restrictions or taxes on necessaries such as food would lower prices and expand British international trade. But what about import prices, and would not corn prices fall in the domestic markets once the foreign imports were no longer taxed? Would not the farmers and landlords suffer? And according to the familiar Ricardian wage–population mechanism, how about money wages? Following Smith, would not nominal wages follow corn prices downwards?

The great orator and advocate of repeal, Richard Cobden, refused to admit that money wages would (or should) fall after repeal (ibid.: 111). If a tax on necessities were removed, then nominal wages had to fall and profits increase; this was a central principle of Ricardian economics! In fact the antagonists in the political debate did not turn to the fledgling science of political economy for answers, although discussions of these issues did take place at the Political Economy Club of London, and at their meetings Ricardian theory may have had some influence on the legislators who attended (Blaug 1958: 44, 130).

The repeal movement did occasionally mention the name of David Ricardo. Cobden credited Ricardo with having explained to him that "free trade is the way to peace," and Cobden used this idea again and again in his speeches and writings (Grampp 1960: 7). As for the inverse wage–profit theorem or any of the logical foundations on which it was based, there was not even a mention.[21] Surely, Ricardo's sophisticated efficiency arguments against protectionism established a valuable baseline from which all subsequent discussion of free trade could begin (Hollander 1979: 632–7). However such conceptual discussions never did begin. At any rate, "unilateral free trade" – which is what repeal amounted to – remained controversial among economists (Robbins 1958: 182–231). With the exception of Malthus who supported protectionism (especially in his early writings), the ideal of free trade in grain was generally something the Ricardian group supported (Mill [1848] 1965, book 2: 231).

Mill supported the work of the Anti-Corn Law League (Mill 1963: 463), but he remained relatively silent about the repeal movement and its achievements in his main economic writing, his *Principles*. This was despite the fact that his *Principles* was written while the agitation for repeal was a major local event and published only two years after the corn laws had in fact been repealed. Apparently, Mill never complained publicly (as we noted he had complained to Adcroft in private correspondence) about the low level of economic understanding and "folly" that surrounded this most sensational of debates in English history.

The slow diffusion of orthodox economic reasoning

There may be deeper and more interesting reasons that the propositions of scientific economics made so little headway in the practical debates of the day. Reasoning about policy matters in the manner of an economist requires a certain "style of thinking . . . very different from that which leads to success in business" (Krugman 1996b: 41). Krugman's assessment of why economic reasoning is so difficult for contemporary business people to master may go part of the way toward explaining why Ricardo's way of thinking about the relationship between wages and prices made so little headway in his time and for a half-century after. Let me summarize Krugman's findings with regard to contemporary business leaders' thinking, then return to the implications of Krugman's diagnosis for appreciating the novel elements in the variant of classical economics largely derived from the work of Ricardo.

In a curious and characteristically playful article entitled "A Country is Not a Company," published in the *Harvard Business Review* (Krugman 1996b), Krugman asks why business leaders who, on the average, seem to have superior intelligence over economists, almost always misunderstand economic policy and advocate impossible policy. The problem is that they think that what is good for their particular company also must be good for the entire nation. This is specious reasoning because a company is not a country.

Size and complexity obviously distinguish a modern economy from even the largest of the large companies. According to Krugman, business leaders consistently are ignorant of these relative magnitudes (Krugman 1996b: 44). Indeed, the problem goes much deeper than this. An economy, and especially a large complex economy, is a "closed system," whereas a corporation is mostly an "open system" (ibid.: 48). Closed systems often, if not invariably, produce negative feedback mechanisms, and today's modern business leaders can successfully ignore whatever negative feedback mechanisms might imperil their companies because these mechanisms "are often weak and almost always uncertain" (ibid.: 50). According to Krugman, these mechanisms are strong and unforgiving for an economy like the USA.

Economists know that with the central bank keeping all those able and willing to work employed and inflation down to a modest level, increasing exports will not create new jobs. It will transfer workers out of domestic production and into jobs catering to the wants of foreign buyers. This reallocation of resources may be from more valued to less valued types of output and consumption. To an economist, working to help foreigners live better is not a clear net improvement in domestic social welfare.[22] Business leaders dismiss these concerns because they do not think of exports in terms of lost consumption opportunities, as do economists starting with Ricardo and continuing down to our day. The executives think of exports as revenues tied to increased world market share. Because a company's increasing market share is often identified with managerial success, why should the same not hold true for an entire economic system?

It is not that executives are consistently wrong on this point, because the issue is not so simple. Rather, executives, like most untutored commentators, cannot think clearly about the issues involved. An economist knows that with flexible exchange rates it is impossible to have a "surplus" on the capital account and at the same time, or over the same period of time to maintain a true sustained "surplus" on the trade account. The impossibility stems from the underlying barter structure of mutually-advantageous trades. A region cannot on balance continuously sell its assets (including its local money deposits) without purchasing on net more than is sold of current production. Business leaders have something of an aversion to closed systems, and they are shy to admit that negative feedback mechanisms discipline their aggregate business behavior. Unlike economists, business leaders appeal to common sense. Those habits of mind that make them successful business leaders also blind them to a deeper economic understanding about the way the world works. Krugman's insights about the difficulty executives have in learning economics comes as no surprise because "a financial wizard makes a fortune not by enumerating general principles of financial markets, but by perceiving particular, highly specific opportunities a bit faster than anyone else" (Krugman 1996b: 43).

Krugman's discussion about patterns of thinking that are difficult to understand especially by business leaders bears a striking resemblance to the main lines of reasoning among the Ricardian wing of the classical school. In fact, Ricardians were not simply organizing common sense about everyday matters of earning a living, managing a business, or managing a household. The Ricardian analysis broke new ground by conceptualizing the economy as a closed system and relating Hume's specie-flow mechanism to the study of relative distributive shares. Ricardo linked together the micro with the macro and pioneered a new style of reasoning that was as difficult for lay people to grasp in his time as it is in our time.

The idea that the fledgling discipline of political economy contains insights that escape the understanding of the common individual dates far back in the history of the discipline. Surely, it is Mill's judgment that those fallacious "doctrines of popular political economy," such as the high-wages-cause-high-prices theorem are nothing more than "amazing foll[ies]" (Mill [1848] 1965, Book 3: 479). But in demonstrating the folly implied by the claim, Mill implied and Ricardo invoked the Humean specie-flow mechanism. Ironically, Hume presented his theorem as part of a refutation of a certain "fallacy," often part of "common conversation," that nation-states are weak when they are short of money (Hume [1742] 1985: 293–4). In refuting these errors of everyday understanding, Hume, Ricardo, Mill, and two centuries of orthodox economic reasoning that followed relied on and employed the twin analytic devices of closed systems and negative feedback mechanisms.

Conclusion

Clearly, Ricardo and the classical school pioneered a certain approach of understanding the international economy that is still not well known today. They thought of the economy as a closed system subject to negative feedback mechanisms. The negative feedback mechanisms restrain and force substitutions, and sometimes make the triumph of the personal will impossible. We have seen that the inverse wage–profit mechanism was not just another theorem to come out of economics; it personified a sophisticated and disciplined manner of thinking about how things really fit together. Nor was it common sense. Indeed, the claim that higher costs of production do not easily translate into higher selling prices and falling currency values is counter-intuitive.

With Ricardo and the Ricardian wing of the classical school we have the triumph of a way of thinking about the economy. The macroeconomic dimensions of the economy reflect features that were not evident when we studied the individual parts and components that together made up the economy. The whole economy contains features that differ qualitatively from the sum of its parts, and that is something worth knowing. The effort to overturn the Smithian wage–prices–trade mechanism was more than simply one scientific theory pitted against another. The inverse wage–profit theorem came out of a different and more challenging conceptual framework about the market system and how it works; this sort of economic reasoning is not just refined common sense.

If Ricardo's approach seems amazingly modern, it is not because we have dextrously read the twentieth century back in Ricardo's texts, as the textbook writers often do when they write about the history of economics. What I have written here is more than a rational reconstruction of distant texts. I think (with Krugman's help) I have put my finger on what I believe to be the moment economic orthodoxy came of age. Ricardo and his followers established the methods and subtleties of research that are still part of the orthodox framework today, and that makes this older literature seem so modern and relevant. The inverse wage–profit theorem is just one thread, but it is a thread that we understand to pull together a new and ruthlessly logical method of thinking about the economy that still guides us today. With that theorem and perhaps others like it, economic discourse lost its reputation as refined common sense and became an academic subject.

Notes

1 George Stigler casually refers to "Ricardo's basic theorem on distribution" but erroneously insists that it is thus strictly dependent on his measure of value" (Stigler [1952] 1965: 190–1). Blaug expands on Stigler's point (Blaug 1958: 22–9). Hollander established that the inverse wage–profit theorem is one of the organizing principles of Ricardian economics (Hollander 1979).
2 See Alchian and Allen 1972: 95–7.
3 I use the expression "orthodox tradition" in a loose impressionistic way to distinguish the Ricardian-style tradition, which spawns the hard money school of economics, from all the other traditions including the many variants of the heterodox tradition. (On the many varieties of the heterodox tradition, see Arestis and Sawyer 1992). The orthodox tradition, as I understand it, insists on the importance of a monetary framework or constitution as precondition for a prospering market system. There is a bias toward one or more versions of the gold-exchange system as a device to discipline misbehaving monetary authorities who unless constrained will pander to short-run oriented politicians. One of my teachers, Joseph Dorfman, also used such a simple distinction when illuminating the history of economic ideas in North America (Dorfman 1959).
4 This distinction is basic to Adam Smith's *The Wealth of Nations* (Hollander 1973: 127). I have no idea who the first was, but Samuel Bailey's presentation of this idea ([1825] 1967: 1–36) is worth noting, even though it appeared eight years after the first edition of Ricardo's *Principles*.
5 Cf. Alchian and Allen 1972: 703–4. When a single merchant's costs go up, he (or she) sometimes passes on that increase to the customers, especially when there is good reason to believe that the cost increase is a general market-wide phenomenon.

It is common sense to reason that a rise in wages or food prices will raise the price level and lower the purchasing power of money. It is much more subtle to understand why this might not happen.
6 Of course, we are implicitly assuming that the transactions structure of the economy is not undergoing change. According to the Fisherian equation we are holding the velocity of money constant.
7 See for example Paul Krugman 1994 and 1996a.
8 If we jump ahead in time and recall the post-Napoleonic controversy about to ensue about the presence of "diminishing returns" in corn production, the extension of the corn cultivation might push the community to harvest less fertile land and the (marginal) cost of production rises, raising the supply price of corn. The rising (supply) price of corn overtakes the favorable price effects of the subsidy. This however was not Smith's approach. Smith did not resort to the diminishing-returns argument, at least not in the context of his analysis of the corn bounty. Smith stated that "it is not the real, but [only] the nominal price of corn [that] can in any considerable degree be affected by the bounty" (Smith [1776] 1976, Book 4: 509). The bounty on corn exportation will bring about a tragic sequence of events involving international monetary flows that one after another will retard the "the ability of the employers of the [laboring] poor to employ so great a number as they otherwise might do" (ibid.: 508). The subsidy on corn exportation has the unintended effect of diminishing the international demand for home-country exports and, as a consequence, causing domestic unemployment, and discouraging trade, industry, and commerce.
9 In John Stuart Mill's day – almost a century later – the laborers were still quite poor and considered as such by the Ricardian writers as we shall see later. According to Phyllis Deane, the English worker's living standards exceeded those of other workers on the Continent, but still "many of them [were] living in overcrowded unsanitary urban conditions, whose real standard of life was much less desirable than that currently enjoyed by their North American or Australian contemporaries with somewhat lower money wages" (Deane 1979: 289).
10 In summary, the Smithian cost-push doctrine is as follows. High corn prices lead to high nominal wages. High local prices cause trade imbalances (balance of trade "deficits"), and deficits ultimately discourage employment, trade, and commerce. According to Hollander, even those writers who opposed Smith's free-trade policies, such as Thomas R. Malthus, the Earl of Lauderdale, and William Jacob, "accepted the fundamental notion that higher corn prices will be reflected (although to a limited extent) by way of the money-wage rate in the higher prices of manufactured goods" (Hollander 1979: 54–5).
11 This is part of the core reasoning in Smith's *The Wealth of Nations*. The purchasing power of money sinks whenever the nominal price of corn increases because the "money price of corn regulates [the prices] of all other home-made commodities" (Smith [1776] 1976, Book 4: 509). The nominal price of corn especially

> regulates the money price of labour, which must always be such as to enable the labourer to purchase a quantity of corn sufficient to maintain him and his family either in the liberal, moderate, or scanty manner in which the advancing, stationary or declining circumstances of the society oblige his employers to maintain him.
>
> (Smith [1776] 1976, Book 4: 509)

12 Furthermore, Smith mentioned, it is a quantitative anomaly that the amount by which the wages of labor is raised is always greater than the magnitude of the tax itself. That is, a 20 percent tax on wages will raise his wages by a full 25 percent so that after the tax is computed and paid the worker will still net precisely the same nominal amount he received before the raise. A numerical example might best illustrate what Smith had in mind. Suppose the worker is receiving 100 units of

money (coins) per week before the tax is imposed. Now it is ordered that each worker turn over to the state 20 percent or 1/5 of his nominal wage. If the worker's wage remain unchanged then the worker will net only 80 coins rather than 100. Clearly, if the worker's wage were to rise to 125 coins per week and this higher nominal wage were taxed at 20 percent, the worker would net exactly 100 coins, the same as before. Notice, however, that for the worker's net wage to remain constant the actual increase in the nominal wage has to be 25 percent even though a 20 percent tax has been implemented.

13 In 1979, I argued that there was a consensus view in economics, especially about the significance of Ricardian economics. The consensus view held that the agricultural theory of profit is the key to Ricardo's entire theoretical system. This consensus view necessarily held that the inverse wage–profit theorem was of secondary importance (Moss 1979). Hollander replied to the effect that the agricultural theory of profit was not the key to the *Principles*, and that those who thought it was, misinterpreted Ricardo and perhaps classical economics (Hollander 1982). In my reply I insisted that Hollander's best argument is that the agricultural theory of profit is incomplete, not inappropriate (Moss 1982). In 1997, Hollander admitted that the agricultural theory of profit was in Malthus's *Principles* but not Ricardo's! According to Hollander, Malthus "develop[ed] a corn-profit model for the agricultural profit rate" (Hollander 1997: 498). From this I conclude that Hollander now believes that the corn model and the agricultural profit rate theory are essential to one part of the classical school but not to Ricardian economics. It follows that the Ricardian economic tradition, which included nearly every British economist, may now have to be defined to exclude Malthus. Malthus and his corn model represent either an anti-Ricardian or simply alternative-to-Ricardian tradition. If in the alternative we include Malthus in the Ricardian tradition, then my reply to Hollander seems coherent and needs to be renewed. The agricultural theory of profit was "a key" to Ricardian economics.

14 The list of classical school economists who accepted this doctrine includes nearly every major commentator and writer. In addition to Ricardo's polemicists and friends, James Mill and J. R. McCulloch, fellow travelers, Mountifort Longfield, John Stuart Mill, and John E. Cairnes approved of versions of that theorem (although not always in the same contexts); see Hollander 1977.

15 This is one of the main points Hollander succeeds in making in his valuable reading of Ricardo (Hollander 1979).

16 The contrary view has been advanced by Murray Rothbard (1995). Rothbard held that "except for the three passages on comparative advantage [contained in Ricardo's *Principles*, Ricardo] displays no interest in [the theory of comparative advantage]" (Rothbard 1995: 97). Rothbard goes on to argue that it was James Mill who probably tacked the argument on to the *Principles*. Furthermore, James Mill is the inventor of the whole idea and was the one who "prodded Ricardo on including a discussion of comparative cost ratios" (Rothbard 1995: 98). Rothbard bases his claims on an earlier study by William O. Thweatt (1976).

17 Please do not confuse the term "open economy" with "open system." An open economy means that one regional economy trades with one or more other regional economies, making it possible for the first economy to "live above its means" by running a current account deficit financed by the net asset purchases of foreigners (a surplus on the capital account of the balance of payments). An open system analysis abstracts from the disciplinary regimen of budget constraints and fixed amount of money and credit. In a nutshell, the open economy is often conceptualized as a closed system with negative feedback mechanisms. This is the heart of the orthodox approach to monetary economics.

18 The fact that capital labor ratios are different throughout the economy from one sector to another, from one industry to another, and even from one firm to another, makes the simple empirical observation that wages and profits vary inversely, impos-

sible to detect. We have here a "tendency" that may or may not manifest itself in a historical process. Still, it is possible to imagine circumstances under which relative market prices would reveal the underlying economic law: the inverse wage–profit mechanism. Those circumstances involve the measuring of all relative prices in terms of a specially-contrived numeraire commodity that was produced with the average capital labor ratio resulting from the actual capital labor ratios characterizing each firm in the economy. Ricardo's quest for the ideal numeraire measuring rod is a wonderful topic, but one that I pass over here. See however, Hollander 1979.
19 According to R. B. Ekelund Jr. and R. F. Hébert (1990: 190), "in an 1869 issue of the *Fortnightly Review* a curious event took place within the classical orthodoxy of Great Britain that shook the foundations of the classical theoretical system. John Stuart Mill recanted the wage-fund doctrine."
20 What then did Mill do in 1869? Essentially, he repudiated a vulgar primitive doctrine about the existence of some fixed sum of real goods and (therefore) affirmed that the workers could, through trade union activity, "force a real increase of wages at the expense of profits, with no loss of employment" (Hollander 1985, Book 1: 419). Since the vulgar primitive doctrine was not part of the Ricardian school it is factually incorrect to assert (as some texts do assert) that Mill's supposed recantation is "indicative of a collapse of confidence in the central features of the classical doctrine" (ibid.). Indeed, the evidence indicates that the core conceptual apparatus of the Ricardian system of analysis remained the dominant and most excellent contribution of analytic economic thought throughout the nineteenth century. To paraphrase the modern period, the Ricardian school with sophisticated understanding of the market process did indeed dominate English economic reasoning throughout most of the nineteenth century.
21 Grampp's claim that it is "one of the ironies of the free-trade movement that it had to combat what at first thought was its natural ally: classical economics" seems to be an overstatement (Grampp 1960: 17).
22 Generally, foreign nationals are implicitly ignored by most so-called "welfare economists" who weave a theory of utility maximization deeply rooted in nationalist politics. In the end, the welfare embodied in modern economics (if it exists at all) is cosmopolitan in both word and deed, since neoclassical economics is about exchange and its implications.

References

Alchian, A. A. and Allen, W. R. (1972) *University Economics: Elements of Inquiry*, Belmont, California: Wadsworth.
Arestis, P. and Sawyer, M. (1992) *A Biographical Dictionary of Dissenting Economists*, Aldershot: Elgar.
Bailey, S. [1825] (1967) *A Critical Dissertation on the Nature, Measure and Causes of Value*, New York: A. M. Kelley.
Blaug, M. (1958) *Ricardian Economics: A Historical Study*, New Haven: Yale University Press.
Deane, P. (1979) *The First Industrial Revolution*, Cambridge: Cambridge University Press.
Dorfman, J. (1959) *The Economic Mind in American Civilization*, 5 vols, New York: Viking.
Ekelund, R. B. and Hébert, R. F. (1990) *A History of Economic Theory and Method*, New York: McGraw Hill.
Grampp, W. D. (1960) *The Manchester School of Economics*, London: Oxford University Press.
Hicks, [Sir] J. and Hollander, S. (1977) "Mr. Ricardo and the Moderns," *Quarterly Journal of Economics* 91 (August): 351–9.
Hollander, S. (1973) *The Economics of Adam Smith*, Toronto: University of Toronto Press.

—— (1977) "The Reception of Ricardian Economics", *Oxford Economic Papers* 20 (July): 221–57. (In S. Hollander, *Ricardo – The New View: Collected Essays [of Samuel Hollander]*, London: Routledge 1995: 283–322.)

—— (1979) *The Economics of David Ricardo*, Toronto: University of Toronto Press.

—— (1982) "'Professor Hollander and Ricardian Economics': A Reply to Professor Moss," *Eastern Economic Journal* 8 (July): 237–42.

—— (1984) "The Wage Path in Classical Growth Models." *Oxford Economic Papers* 36: 200–12. (In S. Hollander, *Ricardo – The New View: Collected Essays [of Samuel Hollander]*, London: Routledge 1995: 226–40.)

—— (1985) *The Economics of John Stuart Mill*, 2 vols, Toronto: University of Toronto Press.

—— (1997) *The Economics of Thomas Robert Malthus*, Toronto: University of Toronto Press.

Hume, D. [1742] (1985) "Of Money" *Essays Moral, Political, and Literary*, ed. E. F. Miller, Indianapolis: Liberty Classics: 281–94.

Krugman, P. (1994) *Peddling Prosperity: Economic Sense and Nonsense in the Age of Diminished Expectations*, New York: Norton.

—— (1996a) *Pop Internationalism*, New York: MIT Press.

—— (1996b) "A Country is not a Company," *Harvard Business Review* (January–February): 40–51.

Levy, David (1976) "Ricardo and the Iron Law: A Correction of the Record," *History of Political Economy* 7 (Summer): 235–52.

Longfield, M. [1834] (1971) *Lectures on Political Economy*, Dublin: Richard Milliken. (In *The Economic Writings of Mountifort Longfield*, ed. R. D. Collison Black, New York: A. M. Kelley.)

Mill, J. S. (1963) *The Earlier Letters of John Stuart Mill 1812–1848*, ed. F. E. Mineka and D. N. Lindley, in *Collected Works of John Stuart Mill*, vol. 13, Toronto: University of Toronto Press.

—— [1848] (1965) *Principles of Political Economy with Some Applications to Social Philosophy*, in *Collected Works of John Stuart Mill*, ed. J. M. Robson, vols 2–3, Toronto: University of Toronto Press.

—— [1844] (1967) "Of the Laws of Interchange Between Nations; And the Distribution of the Gains of Commerce among the Countries of the Commercial World," in *Essays on Economics and Society*, 2 vols. (In Collected *Works of John Stuart Mill*, ed. J. M. Robson, vol. 4, Toronto: University of Toronto Press: 232–61.

—— [1869] (1967) "Thornton on Labour and Its Claims," *Fortnightly Review* 5 (May): 505–18; 5 (June): 680–700. (In *Collected Works of John Stuart Mill*, ed. J. M. Robson, vol. 5, Toronto: University of Toronto Press: 631–68.

—— (1972) *The Later Letters of John Stuart Mill 1849–1873*, in *Collected Works of John Stuart Mill*, ed. F. E. Mineka and D. N. Lindley, vol. 17, Toronto: University of Toronto Press.

Moss, L. S. (1979) "Professor Hollander and Ricardian Economics," *Eastern Economic Journal* 5 (December): 501–12.

—— (1982) "Reply to Hollander." *Eastern Economic Journal.* 8 (July): 243–5.

—— (1997) "David Hume (1711–1776)," in David Glasner (ed.), *Business Cycles and Depressions: An Encyclopedia.* New York: 313–4.

Political Economy Club (1921) *Minutes and Proceedings of the Political Economy Club*, vol. 6, London: Political Economy Club.

Ricardo, D. [1817] (1951) *On the Principles of Political Economy and Taxation.* In *The Works and Correspondence of David Ricardo* (11 vols), ed. P. Sraffa with the collaboration of M. H. Dobb, Cambridge: Cambridge University Press.

Robbins, L. (1958) *Robert Torrens and the Evolution of Classical Economics*, London: Macmillan.

Rothbard, M. (1995) *Classical Economics: An Austrian Perspective on the History of Economic Thought*, Brookfield, Vt.: Elgar.
Samuelson, P. (1978) "The Canonical Classical Model of Political Economy," *Journal of Economic Literature*, 16 (December): 1415–34.
Schwartz, A. J. (1991) "Banking School, Currency School, Free Banking School," *The New Palgrave: A Dictionary of Economics*, 4 vols, New York: Macmillan: 82–186.
Smith, A. [1776] (1976) *An Inquiry Into the Nature and Causes of the Wealth of Nations*, ed. R. H. Cambell and A. S. Skinner, 2 vols, Indianapolis: Liberty Classics.
Stigler, G. [1952] (1965) "The Ricardian Theory of Value and Distribution," in *Essays in the History of Economics*, Chicago: University of Chicago Press: 156–97.
Thweatt, W. O. (1976) "James Mill and the Early Development of Comparative Advantage," *History of Political Economy* 8 (Summer): 207–34.

16 Ricardo's use of Say's law

The case of the post-Napoleonic war depression

Timothy Davis

Introduction

By virtue of his central place in the classical tradition and because of strong statements in his writings, David Ricardo is closely associated with the law of markets, being rivalled only by James Mill and – in introductory textbooks – by J-B. Say.[1] This chapter examines part of the evidence on which this view of Ricardo is based, specifically, excerpts from his debate with Malthus on the causes of Britain's economic troubles after the Napoleonic Wars.[2] By comparing Ricardo's writings with the historical record, I demonstrate that he did not, when assessing postwar economic conditions, employ Say's identity. To the contrary, his analysis, including his argument about misallocated capital, reflects actual events. Malthus does not fare as well in my view. He lacked Ricardo's depth of knowledge. He also never managed more than a tenuous link between macroeconomic theory and Britain's postwar experience.

Authors who question Ricardo's analysis of postwar events do so on the basis of a stylized account (explained later) of the economic history of the period. That account, often implicit in the secondary literature, is a subtle yet crucial element of the critics' arguments, for anyone who accepts it must cede either that Ricardo was ignorant of contemporary events or that he employed Say's identity in the face of overwhelmingly contradictory evidence. Moreover, anyone who accepts the account can reasonably commend Malthus for the empirical aspects of his work and for his prescience of the revelations that would unfold in the *General Theory*. Keynes himself reached these conclusions, and it is to him that I credit their wide acceptance.[3] In his *Essays in Biography* Keynes states:

> Ricardo was the abstract and *a priori* theorist, Malthus the inductive and intuitive investigator.... The almost total obliteration of Malthus's line of approach and the complete domination of Ricardo's for a period of a hundred years has been a disaster to the progress of economics.
>
> (Keynes 1933: 95, 98)

In contrast, Keynes (1933: 101) praised Malthus for his facility with practical economic problems, even describing Chapter 7 of Malthus' *Principles* as "the best economic analysis ever written of the events of 1815–20."

These criticisms of Ricardo have not been answered, even by authors favorable to him, and here I refer to Professor Hollander, who, though he argues that Ricardo did not adhere to a strict version of the law of markets, provides little defense of Ricardo on the postwar depression:

> Ricardo, despite his occasional strong statements (and despite his criticism of Say on the need for "counter-commodities") adhered to that version of the law of markets labelled "Say's Equality," which allows for temporary deviations between the money values of commodities supplied and demanded, that is, for temporary excess demand for money. We are not, however, yet out of the woods. For as we shall now see, in his analysis of the post-war depression Ricardo failed to recognize the relevance of temporary excess money demand.
> (Hollander 1979: 512–13)

Indeed, we are a long way from *terra deserta*, for the criticism cannot be answered by anyone who accepts, as Hollander implicitly does, the stylized account of the postwar period. According to this account, all industries in Britain were stagnant from 1815–22 (or 1823), unsold commodities glutted markets, and laborers suffered persistent unemployment. The depression, it is assumed, resulted from a persistent lack of effectual demand by British consumers, a problem later compounded by an ill-advised contraction of the money supply after Parliament approved the 1819 Resumption Act.[4]

In actual fact, the "postwar depression" did not continue for almost a decade, but was limited to two periods: the immediate postwar crisis, lasting from the fall of 1815 to the spring of 1817; and a subsequent crisis, arising from a sudden decrease in the demand for British exports, that began in early 1819 and continued through the spring of 1820. In addition to these two periods of general depression, there were two intervals of low agricultural prices: from late 1813 through early 1816 and from the harvest of 1820 through the end of 1822.

The following summarizes Malthus' analysis of the postwar period, then turns to Ricardo's position. The comparison reveals that Ricardo's analysis has greater empirical merit than Malthus' and also shows that Ricardo was not using a simplistic version of the law of markets to explain economic conditions incompatible with that theory.

Malthus's account of "the" postwar depression

Malthus did not distinguish between the two postwar depressions, but treated the entire period from 1815 to 1823 as one protracted crisis.[5] The depression began, in his view, when agricultural prices collapsed during the fall of 1813, causing "a severe shock to the cultivation of the country and a great loss of agricultural capital" (Malthus 1815: 139), and forcing "a great number of agricultural labourers out of employment" (ibid.: 155). Malthus believed that with the fall in the incomes of landlords and farmers there occurred "an actual diminution of home demand" (ibid.: 161).[6] In his analysis, the consequent glut of manufactured goods in the home market prompted merchants to export excessively, leading to a collapse in the prices of British goods in foreign markets that eroded the purchasing power of merchants. Malthus thought that reductions in the money supply aggravated the crisis. He attributed monetary contraction to, first of all, "the great failures which have taken place among country banks" (ibid.: 143), and later to the Resumption Act (July 16 1821) (Ricardo 1951–73, vol. 9: 22). His position is summarized in the *Principles*:

> It [the stagnation of effectual demand] commenced certainly with the extraordinary fall in the value of the raw produce of the land, to the amount, it has been supposed of nearly one third. When this fall had diminished the capitals of the farmers, and still more the revenues both of landlords and farmers, and of all those who were otherwise connected with the land, their power of purchasing manufactures and foreign products was of necessity greatly diminished. The failure of home demand filled the warehouses of the manufacturers with unsold goods, which urged them to export more largely at all risks. But this excessive exportation glutted all the foreign markets, and prevented the merchants from receiving adequate returns . . . [The crisis was] aggravated by a sudden and extraordinary contraction of the currency.
>
> (Malthus 1820: 493–4)

The cessation of wartime government expenditures was, for Malthus, an additional cause of diminished aggregate demand, since he did not believe that the loss had been countered by a corresponding increase in private expenditures:

> The returned taxes, and the excess of individual gains above expenditure, which were so largely used as revenue during the war, are now in part, and probably in no inconsiderable part, saved. . . . [This] contributes to explain the cause of the diminished demand for commodities, compared with their supply since the war. If some of the principal governments concerned spent the taxes which they raised in a manner to create a greater and more certain demand for labour and commodities, particularly the former, than the present owners of them, and if this difference of expenditure be of a nature to last some time, we cannot be surprised at the duration of the effects arising from the transition from war to peace.
>
> (Malthus 1820: 499–500)

The central problem of the postwar depression, as perceived by Malthus, was thus a decrease in aggregate demand relative to a stable supply.[7] While he also accepted the view that "over-saving" – the term refers to too rapid an investment program, not to hoarding – could, in theory, cause an increase in production without a corresponding increase in aggregate demand, this does not seem to have been part of his explanation of the postwar depression.[8]

Ricardo's response to Malthus

Low corn prices had not caused a general depression

Ricardo denied the central premise of Malthus's analysis: that a decline in the incomes of the landed interests caused a reduction in aggregate demand, leading to a general depression. His response was not based on blind adherence to the law of markets, but derived from his observation that the sudden fall in corn prices and agricultural incomes in 1813 did not prevent aggregate economic activity – as measured by tax data – from expanding.

In response to a letter from Malthus which claimed that low corn prices had caused a depression, Ricardo stated:

> It is dangerous to listen to reports respecting briskness or slackness of trade. It is I believe certain that the revenue has been uncommonly productive the last quarter which is no indication of diminished trade . . . you appear to me to attribute effects much too great to the fall of raw produce which has lately taken place.
> (Ricardo 1951–73 [October 17 1815], vol. 6: 304)[9]

Ricardo's answer indicates nothing of the naive overconfidence in abstract theory – especially in the law of markets – of which he has been accused, for he answered Malthus' concerns about the economy on the factual grounds that "the revenue has been uncommonly productive the last quarter," referring to the Treasury report on quarterly government tax receipts that appeared on July 11 1815 (*Journal of the House of Commons* 1814–15: 726).[10] He rightly cited the report of July 11 because it indicated that both customs and excise revenues increased from the third quarter of 1813 – the same quarter when agricultural prices began to decline – through the second quarter of 1815, the most recent quarter for which returns were available.[11] Ricardo understood that without a change in tax rates – and there had been no change – an increase in customs and excise revenues as revealed by the Treasury report could not have occurred unless preceded by an increase in economic activity. Given the coincidence of low corn prices and a robust general economy from the harvest of 1813 through the second quarter of 1815, Malthus's conclusion – that low corn prices caused a reduction in aggregate activity – seemed inadequate.

The postwar relocation of capital

Though Ricardo had refuted Malthus's analysis of the 1813–16 agricultural depression, there remained for him the challenge of explaining the general depression that began the third quarter of 1815, immediately after hostilities ended. The account he proposed centered on the difficulties of switching from wartime to peacetime production.[12] The chapter "On sudden changes in the channels of trade" in the *Principles* (1817) provides a thorough statement of his analysis, which, in short, is that fixed capital cannot easily be transferred between employments – and might even be rendered useless by a change in the pattern of final demand – and that laborers are likely to be unemployed while capitalists "are removing their capitals and the labour which they can command from one employment to another" (Ricardo 1951–73, vol. 1: 263).

> The commencement of war after a long peace, or of peace after a long war, generally produces considerable distress in trade. It changes in a great degree the nature of the employments to which the respective capitals of countries were before devoted; and during the interval while they are settling in the situations which new circumstances have made the most beneficial, much fixed capital is unemployed, perhaps wholly lost, and labourers are without full employment. The duration of this distress will be longer or shorter according to the strength of that disinclination, which most men feel to abandon that employment of their capital to which they have long been accustomed. It is often protracted too by the restrictions and prohibitions to which the absurd jealousies which prevail between the different States of the commercial commonwealth give rise.
>
> When, however, such distress immediately accompanies a change from war to peace, our knowledge of the existence of such a cause will make it reasonable to believe that the funds for the maintenance of labour have rather been diverted from their usual channel, than materially impaired, and that after temporary suffering, the nation will again advance in prosperity.
>
> (Ricardo 1951–73, vol. 1: 265)

Ricardo thought that British industry was particularly liable to this type of distress because of its relatively high capital intensity.

> In rich and powerful countries, where large capitals are invested in machinery, more distress will be experienced from a revulsion in trade, than in poorer countries where there is proportionally a much smaller amount of fixed and a much larger amount of circulating capital . . . It is not so difficult to withdraw a circulating as a fixed capital, from any employment in which it may be engaged. It is often impossible to divert the machinery which may have been erected for one manufacture to the purposes of another.
>
> (Ricardo 1951–73, vol. 1: 266)

In this regard, his account has generally been viewed favorably (Schumpeter 1954: 693, 740; Sowell 1972: 29, 30; Jonsson 1997: 203) because of the extent to which Britain's economy had to be realigned after the war.[13]

Ricardo's explanation of subsequent events

Historians of thought have been less inclined to accept Ricardo's explanations of later crises – meaning the 1819–20 general depression and the 1820–22 agricultural depression – in terms of misallocated capital (Blaug 1958: 77; Tucker 1960: 125-6; Hollander 1979: 518). Their comments echo those of Malthus, who in September 1820 wrote to Ricardo:

The present state of things indeed in England America Holland and Hamburgh still more than in France does appear in the most marked manner to contradict both his [Say's] and your theory. The fall in the interest of money and the difficulty of finding employment for capital are universally acknowledged and this fact, none of your friends have ever accounted for in any tolerably satisfactory manner; but what confidence can be placed in a theory as the foundation of future measures which is absolutely inconsistent with the past and the present state of things.

(Ricardo 1951–73, vol. 8: 260)

Malthus was critical of Ricardo's argument about misallocated capital because he understood Ricardo to mean that Britain's economy was still adjusting from wartime to peacetime production. This is clear from oft-quoted passages in his *Principles* where he asks:

Where is there any considerable trade that is confessedly understocked, and where high profits have been long pleading in vain for additional capital? The war has now been at an end above four years; and though the removal of capital generally occasions some partial loss, yet it is seldom long in taking place.

(Malthus 1820: 333–4)

I cannot bring myself to believe that this transfer can require so much time as has now elapsed since the war; and again ask, where are the understocked employments, which, according to this theory, ought to be numerous and fully capable of absorbing all the redundant capital.

(ibid.: 498–9)

On the basis of these passages, Hollander describes Ricardo's misallocated capital explanation as "incompatible with the evidence, particularly with the pervasiveness of the depression and the absence of those potentially profitable industries presumed to exist in that account." In the same vein, Peach (1993: 139, 140) alludes to Malthus' letter of September 25 1820 (quoted earlier) and to Ricardo's response as proof that Ricardo "believed passionately in the practical relevance of his doctrine [the law of markets] to such an extent that he blamed reality for not conforming to the 'model,' not *vice versa.*"

I question the conclusions of Hollander and Peach on two grounds. First, Ricardo's statements about "misallocated capital" after 1819 do not refer to an ongoing transfer of capital from wartime to peacetime manufacturing. Rather, he was describing the miscalculations in foreign trade and domestic manufacturing that began in late 1818 and continued into 1820; certain of his comments also refer to overinvestment in agricultural production and the need to withdraw capital from farming to manufacturing. Contrary to the interpretations offered by Peach and Hollander, at no time after 1819 do his remarks suggest that he believed the earlier, wartime-to-peacetime transition was continuing. My second reason for questioning the critical interpretations of Ricardo's position is that there actually were profitable industries in 1819,

1820 and thereafter, so that, far from being "incompatible with the evidence," Ricardo's analysis is empirically valid.

Miscalculations in foreign trade and domestic manufacturing

That Ricardo was aware of the depression in foreign trade and domestic manufacturing in 1819 and 1820 cannot be doubted. His correspondence with Thomas Smith in April 1819 contains a full account of the crisis:

> You will find the politicians of this country in a very gloomy mood. Commerce is languishing – merchants and manufactures are failing – overtrading has become general and all our markets are glutted with goods. Cotton and many other articles are lower in price here than they can be grown for in the countries where they are produced. Pauperism is increasing and employment cannot be found for the industrious. To crown the whole we are labouring under great financial difficulties, our revenue being insufficient to meet our expenditure.
> (quoted in Heertje and Weatherall 1978: 570)[14]

His remark about excessive imports – "cotton and many other articles" – reflects an understanding that there had been miscalculations in foreign trade.[15] It is likely that he also appreciated the extent to which foreign markets were then glutted with British goods.[16] In praise of a speech by William Grenville in the House of Lords on November 30 1819, he wrote:

> I hope your Lordship will not think I take too great a liberty, in expressing my satisfaction at finding that my opinions on the causes of the present distresses, concur with those which your Lordship has so ably stated in the pamphlet before me. The distress which proceeds from the misapplication of capital, and the miscalculation of demand by our manufacturers may, it is to be hoped, be slowly removed, but that which arises from the disproportion between capital and population will necessarily be of a more permanent description.
> (Letter dated January 10 1820, quoted in Heertje 1991: 523–4)[17]

Ricardo's references to "the misapplication of capital" and the "miscalculation of demand by our manufacturers" allude to Grenville's assertions that the demand for British manufacturers had fallen due to the "distresses of foreign nations," and that the crisis had been worsened by "hazardous and groundless speculations" in trade (Parliamentary Debates, *Hansard* 2s, 41: 452–3).

The 1820–22 agricultural depression

Concerning the 1820–22 agricultural depression, Ricardo attributed the fall in corn to excess domestic production, itself caused by overinvestment in land and farm machinery. He argued that if British agriculture was to become profitable, large tracts of marginal land would have to be withdrawn from cultivation:

He agreed with an observation of a Noble Person [Lord Liverpool] in another place, that part of the distress was owing to too much corn being produced, and agriculture must lessen its produce so as to suit the demand.... It had been said that importation would throw the whole of the lands out of cultivation. But this was assuming that the remunerating price was for every grower the same; whereas, corn was raised in some lands at 40s. and in others at not less than 70s.

(Ricardo 1951–73 [March 7 1821], vol. 5: 84, 85)[18]

His analysis has considerable merit. The Board of Agriculture determined (*Report of the Commons Committee on the Corn Laws* 1814: 80–83) that, as the margins of cultivation extended, the costs to farm 100 acres of arable land in Britain increased from £411 in 1790 to £547 in 1803 and again to £771 in 1813: a rise of almost 90 percent. Poorer farms, it is true, were abandoned in the agricultural depression of 1813 to 1816 and marginal production costs must have fallen accordingly. However as corn prices increased – and eventually surpassed 100s. per quarter in 1817 – these farms were again brought into cultivation. Ricardo was well informed of the investments both in land and farm machinery made from 1817 through 1819, for these were documented by the 1821 Agricultural Committee on which he served.[19] In fact, he repeatedly referred to the causes of the agricultural depression in his correspondence (Ricardo 1951–73 [1821], vol 8: 369; [1822], vol. 9: 157), during Parliamentary debates (ibid. [1821], vol. 5: 94; [1821], vol. 5: 108; [1822], vol. 5: 125; [1822], vol. 5: 151) and in *Protection to Agriculture* (ibid. [1822], vol. 4: 259–61).

The existence of profitable industries

As to the existence of profitable industries in Britain after the Napoleonic Wars, conditions were generally prosperous in 1817 and 1818, with both high corn prices and an expanding foreign trade.[20] Corn prices remained high through 1819; the ports were open to all grains except wheat until August, and investment in land and farm machinery was ongoing. Exports, which had been very strong in 1818, declined in 1819, causing distress in trade and manufacturing. However by September 1820 – the date of Malthus's letter cited earlier – the demand for British exports had returned to normal levels. Tax returns show an increase in aggregate activity beginning the third quarter of 1820; commercial reports indicate that manufactures were returning to profitability and to full production at the same time.

For the year 1820, total exports increased by £5.5 million and imports were also higher. Britain's foreign trade continued to expand in 1821 – the official value of exports increased by £2.5 million – and this contributed to the ongoing improvement of the textile manufactures, as described by the *Annual Register*:

> The improvement which had begun in the course of the preceding year, to show itself in the state of our manufactures, still continued. In Yorkshire and Lancashire, the seats of the woollen and cotton manufactures, the

working classes found regular employment, and received a liberal remuneration for their services.

(*Annual Register* 1821: 69)

General progress continued through 1822. Castlereagh said that "at no period in the history of the country had they [the manufacturing and commercial interests] been in a condition of more healthful, though temperate prosperity" ([February 15 1822] Parliamentary Debates, *Hansard* 2s, 6: 354). And in June 1822 Robert Peel, the Home Secretary, provided a thorough description of the continued rise of exports, leading to an increase in manufacturing production – even at the ironworks – and consequently to full employment at good wages (ibid., 7: 1014–5).

Conclusion

I began this article describing how critical authors attribute an extreme version of the law of markets to Ricardo on three grounds: a few isolated statements in his *Principles*; his general aversion to public spending; and his analysis of economic conditions in Britain after the Napoleonic Wars. The third of these arguments essentially is that since the postwar depression affected all industries and lasted about ten years, Ricardo's references to misallocated capital and profitable industries show that either he was unaware of Britain's economic state, or though informed of business conditions, he ignored the implications of a chronic depression for the extreme version of the law of markets which he cherished.

I have shown the weakness of this argument by establishing that his analysis of the postwar period is essentially correct and far better, in fact, than the assessment provided by Malthus. Beginning with the depression of 1815–17, we have seen that the crisis was not caused by a fall in corn prices after the harvest of 1813 as Malthus claimed. Rather, it was not until the third quarter of 1815, after foreign demand collapsed and hostilities against France ended, that the general economy became depressed. With respect to later crises – the reversals in trade and manufacturing in 1819 and the 1820–22 agricultural depression – Ricardo's analysis was correct on key points: British merchants did miscalculate foreign demand in 1819 and early 1820; and the margins of cultivation in agricultural had been extended to the point that farmers were losing money when corn dropped below famine prices in 1820.

Regarding the claim that there were profitable industries in Britain after the War, Ricardo's arguments again are reasonable. Farming became very lucrative with the high corn prices of 1816–19, and during this period much investment occurred in land and machinery. Similarly, domestic manufactures – even the ironworks – prospered in 1817 and 1818. Manufacturers and foreign merchants suffered a temporary setback when the demand for exports declined in 1819, but foreign trade recovered by the third quarter of 1820, and with it manufacturers returned to full employment. These facts all coincide with Ricardo's explanation of events. In contrast, Malthus questioned whether there were profitable industries, and continued to suggest that Britain's economic troubles stemmed from a chronic deficiency of effectual demand. On this final point, it is worth noting that the consumption of basic commodities by British consumers – as measured by excise returns – increased steadily from 1817 through 1824, except for a drop of less than 1 percent from 1818–19.

In summary, Ricardo's analysis of postwar economic conditions suggests that he was a practical theorist, well-informed about contemporary events. The claim that he adhered to an extreme version of the law of markets must stand, if it stands at all, on grounds separate from his treatment of the postwar period. Malthus has not fared as well. His account of contemporary events seems less empirical than Ricardo's. And though his recognition of the possibility of deficient aggregate demand, leading to a general glut of commodities, can be seen as anticipating modern macroeconomic theory, he did not effectively relate this insight to postwar conditions.

Notes

1 Various meanings have been attached to the expression, "the law of markets" (see Baumol 1977 and Thweatt 1980), but in this study I limit my attention to an extreme version termed Say's identity, which is the idea that the incomes generated by production are fully spent as they are received, thus leaving no possibility for a deficiency of aggregate demand and a general glut of commodities.
2 Ricardo's critics cite three categories of textual evidence to show that he employed Say's law in an extreme form. There are, first of all, statements in his *Principles of Political Economy* (1817) that seem to employ Say's identity. Second, there is Ricardo's aversion to public spending, which some interpret as anticipating the "orthodox Treasury dogma" and as implying his acceptance of Say's identity (Hutchison 1952: 75, 76; Paglin 1961: 101). Finally, authors associate Ricardo with Say's identity because he rejected Malthus's argument that Britain's troubles after the Napoleonic Wars resulted from a lack of effectual demand in the home market.
3 Ahiakpor (1997: 71) explains how Keynes's interpretation of classical economics was propagated by Hicks, Robinson, Kahn, and others.
4 The 1819 Resumption Act required the Bank of England to return, over a three-year period, to a position where it would redeem its notes in gold on demand at the Ancient Mint price of £3 17s 10½d. Because the currency was gradually revalued, the money supply, consisting of bank notes and coin, remained stable from 1819 through 1822, and contrary to the fears of inflationists in Parliament, the Act did not instigate a period of monetary deflation.
5 Link (1959: 63) has noted Malthus's confusion on the timing of the postwar depressions: "Malthus dated the postwar slump from 1813 or 1815, and again there seems to have been little recognition that there were shorter fluctuations. Judging by his review of Tooke, Malthus treated the whole period from the end of the war to 1822 or 1823 as a unit, marked by contraction and then by stagnation."
6 He implicitly assumed that the reduction in expenditures by agriculturalists, owing to their loss of income, was not counterbalanced by an increase in consumption by the remaining two-thirds of the populace, whose real incomes increased with the fall in corn prices.
7 Malthus also believed that the distress experienced by the laboring poor in consequence of the decrease in the derived demand for labor had been aggravated by an increase in the population during the War: "The powerful stimulus which had been given to population during the war continued to pour in fresh supplies

of labour, and, aided by the disbanded soldiers and sailors and the failure of demand arising from the losses of the farmers and merchants, reduced generally the wages of labour, and left the country with a generally diminished capital and revenue" (1820: 494). Notwithstanding this observation, Malthus believed that the supply of capital was still excessive relative to the demand for it (see Hollander 1997: 596).

8 Hollander 1997 devotes an entire chapter to Malthus' views on sustainable growth, see especially pages 514–26.
9 Malthus had written to Ricardo: "Is it possible for above half the national income to fall very greatly in price, without affecting the demand and the other half. I confess I feel no doubt that the main cause of the present slackness of trade is the diminished incomes of the landlords and farmers" ([16 October 1815] 6: 303).
10 Hollander 1997: 146 has interpreted the quote critically, saying: "Ricardo went so far in his reply as to deny the putative facts of excess aggregate supply."
11 Excise revenues actually increased through the third quarter of 1815.
12 Ricardo first mentioned his theory about capital adjustment – at least as it related to the 1815–17 depression – in a letter to Trower of December 25 1815 (d, 6: 345): "In every change from peace to war and from war to peace there must be great changes in the distribution of capital and much individual distress." He remained optimistic about the return to prosperity ([July 15 1816] Ricardo 1951–73, vol. 7: 49), even when the transition process proved more difficult than expected ([8 September 1816] ibid.: 67).
13 In the years 1815 to 1817 Government spending declined by £53.3 millions, creating havoc in war-related industries (*Edinburgh Review* (June 1816): 262). The reduction in Government spending accounted for almost 18 percent of aggregate demand as compared with estimates of nominal British national product during census years: £232 million in 1801; £301 million in 1811; and £291 million in 1821 (Dean and Cole 1967: 166).
14 When writing to Smith, Ricardo could have seen two quarterly tax reports for 1819 – the first appeared on 4 February, the second on 6 April. The February report showed an increase in total tax revenues over the previous quarter, though customs returns were down; the April report showed a decline in customs, excise and total tax revenues.
15 Cotton and wool were two commodities associated with heavy losses for importers, losses estimated at not less than £3 million (*Blackwood's* February 1819: 630).
16 Grenville responded the following day: "I am unaffectedly gratified by knowing that the general view which I take of the causes of the present distress is sanctioned by your high authority" ((11 January 1820) Ricardo 1951–73, vol. 8: 150).
17 Malthus, Ricardo and those of their circle divided economic problems into two categories: short-term crises – reversals in trade, or in modern parlance, downturns in the business cycle – and long-term troubles owing to a low capital–labor ratio. I do not address long-term issues in this article; though central to the doctrine of the wages fund, they do not pertain to Ricardo's use of the law of markets.
18 He made similar remarks on other occasions ((9 October 1820) Ricardo 1951–73, vol. 8: 277; (December 1820) ibid.: 334n).
19 Key witnesses, including Mathias Attwood and David Hodgson, attested to the increase of cultivation since 1816. (245, 265, 276)
20 Monthly commercial reports clearly indicate a revival in trade. The following excerpt, for example, appeared in *Blackwood's* in January 1819:

> The agricultural interests of this country are recovered from their severe depression. . . . All our manufactures are in full activity. . . . The extension of our trade from the additional and increasing arrivals and departures from every port is truly great and cheering.
>
> (*Blackwoods*: 497)

References

Ahiakpor, J. (1997) "Full Employment: A Classical Assumption or Keynes's Rhetorical Device?" *Southern Economic Journal* 64(1): 56–74.
Annual Register, London.
Baumol, W. (1977) "Say's (at Least) Eight Laws, or What Say and James Mill May Really Have Meant, " *Economica* 44(174): 145–62.
Blackwood's Edinburgh Magazine.
Blaug, M. (1958) *Ricardian Economics*, New Haven: Yale University Press.
Buer, M. C. (1921) "The Trade Depression Following the Napoleonic Wars," *Economica* 1(2): 159–79.
Bulletins of State Intelligence, London.
Cannan, E. [1894] (1953) *History of the Theories of Production and Distribution*, London: Staples.
Dean, P. and Cole, W. A. (1967) *British Economic Growth, 1688–1959*, 2nd edn, Cambridge: Cambridge University Press.
Digest of All the Accounts...Diffused Through More than 600 Volumes of Journals, Reports, and Papers, Presented to Parliament during the last Thirty-five Years (1833) compiled by J. Marshall, London: J. Haddon.
Dunbar, C. (1887) "Ricardo's Use of Facts, " *Quarterly Journal of Economics* 1(4): 474–6.
Edinburgh Magazine.
Edinburgh Review.
Gayer, A. D., Rostow, W. W. and Schwartz, A. J. (1953) *The Growth and Fluctuation of the British Economy*, vol. 1., Oxford: Clarendon.
Great Britain *Journals of the House of Commons.*
Great Britain *Parliamentary Debates,* published under the superintendence of T. C. Hansard: London.
Great Britain *House of Commons Parliamentary Papers.*
Hawtrey, R. G. (1934) *Currency and Credit*, London: Longman.
Heertje, A. (1991) "Three Unpublished Letters by David Ricardo," *History of Political Economy* 23(3): 519–26.
Heertje, A. and Weatherall, D. (1978) "An Unpublished Letter of David Ricardo to Thomas Smith of Easton Grey," *Economic Journal* 88(351): 569–71. (Reprinted in J. Wood (ed.), *David Ricardo: Critical Assessments* (1985) vol.4: 152–55, London: Croom Helm.)
Hilton, B. (1977) *Corn, Cash, Commerce*, Oxford: Oxford University Press.
Hollander, S. (1979) *The Economics of David Ricardo*, Toronto: University of Toronto Press.
—— (1997) *The Economics of Thomas Robert Malthus*, Toronto: University of Toronto Press.
Hutchison, T. W. (1952) "Some Questions about Ricardo," *Economica* 19: 415–32. (Reprinted in J. Wood (ed.), *David Ricardo: Critical Assessments* (1985) vol. 1, London: Croom Helm: 86–95.)
Jenks, L. [1927] (1963) *The Migration of British Capital to 1875*, Toronto: Nelson.
Jonsson, P. (1997) "On Gluts, Effective Demand and the True Meaning of Say's Law," *Eastern Economic Journal* 23(2): 203–18.
Keynes, J. M. [1933] (1972) *Essays in Biography.* (Reprinted in *The Collected Writings of John Maynard Keynes*, vol. 10, Cambridge: Cambridge University Press.)
Link, R. (1959) *English Theories of Economic Fluctuations*, New York: Columbia University Press.
Maital, S. and Haswell, P. (1977) "Why Did Ricardo (Not) Change His Mind? On Money and Machinery, " *Economica* 44(176): 359–68.
Malthus, T. R. [1815] (1970) *The Grounds of an Opinion on the Policy of Restricting the*

Importation of Foreign Corn; Intended as an Appendix to "Observations on the Corn Laws", New York: A. M. Kelley.

—— (1820) *The Principles of Political Economy*, London: Murray.

New Monthly Magazine.

Paglin, M. (1961) *Malthus and Lauderdale: The Anti-Ricardian Tradition*, New York: A. M. Kelley.

Peach, T. (1993) *Interpreting Ricardo*, Cambridge: Cambridge University Press.

Ricardo, D. (1951–73) *The Works and Correspondence of David Ricardo*, 11 vols, ed. P. Sraffa with M. H. Dobb, Cambridge: Cambridge University Press.

Robbins, L. (1976) *Political Economy: Past and Present*, London: Macmillan.

Rostow, W. W. (1942) "Adjustments and Maladjustments after the Napoleonic Wars," *American Economic Review* 32(1), Supplement part 2: 13–23.

Schumpeter, J. A. (1954) *History of Economic Analysis*, New York: Oxford University Press.

Scots Magazine.

Smart, W. [1910–17] (1964) *Economic Annals of the Nineteenth Century*, 2 vols, New York: A. M. Kelley.

Sowell, T. (1972) *Say's Law: An Historical Analysis*, Princeton: Princeton University Press.

Thweatt, W. (1980) "Baumol and James Mill on Say's Law of Markets," *Economica* 47(188): 467–9.

Tooke, T. (1838) *A History of Prices*, vols 1 and 2, London: Longman.

Tucker, G. S. L. (1960) *Progress and Profits in British Economic Thought*, Cambridge: Cambridge University Press.

17 Does Ricardo's theory of money belong to the classical canon?

Ghislain Deleplace

I would like first to warn the reader that I shall here understand the word "canon" as a synonym for "orthodoxy." The concept of "classical canon," as used by Samuelson (1978) and Hollander (1980), refers to a growth model in which money plays no part. Hence any confusion generated by this terminological substitution should be avoided. Now Ricardo is generally considered as the champion of classical monetary orthodoxy, based principally on his defence of the quantity theory of money. For example, Schumpeter (1954: 703) attributes to Ricardo this theory "in [a] strict sense," and Blaug (1995: 31) insists that Ricardo was "espousing a hard-line version" of it. Samuel Hollander is more cautious: observing that Ricardo made "repeated applications of the 'quantity theory' of money during the course of the bullion debate" he shows that "the precise characteristics of the Ricardian formulation of the theory" (Hollander 1979: 474) are more complex.

In a paradoxical way, the most virulent critic of the Ricardian macroeconomic theory, Keynes, praises some of Ricardo's monetary positions in his *Treatise on Money*: "If Ricardo had had his way with his ingot proposals, commodity money would never have been restored, and a pure managed money would have come into force in England in 1819" (Keynes 1930: 14). It is worthwhile to notice that Keynes mentions the "ingot proposals," that is Ricardo's plan for establishing an "economical and secure currency" in 1816.

The purpose of this chapter is less to discuss the orthodoxy in Ricardo's theory of money than to look for a possible heterodox component in this plan, which is of particular importance because it was defended as early as 1811, quoted in the second edition of *On the Principles of Political Economy and Taxation* (Ricardo 1819), and submitted by its author to Parliament the same year. The chapter is organized in the following way. The first section considers the relation between the quantity of money and its value, in the context of a mixed monetary regime with convertibility of notes into specie. The second section focuses on the changes introduced by the "ingot plan," where convertibility is in bullion. The third section examines the role of the international adjustment process following a premium on bullion, on the basis of the understanding of it given by Hollander (1979).

The relation between the quantity and the value of money

This relation is obviously central to Ricardo's theory of money throughout his works, and constitutes what may be called the orthodox component of this theory. The role of the standard in the stabilization of the value of money is here derived from this relation:

> The only use of a standard is to regulate the quantity, and by the quantity the value of the currency . . . without a standard it would be exposed to all the fluctuations to which the ignorance or the interests of the issuers might subject it.
>
> (Ricardo 1816: 59)

Then the question arises of *why* the regulation of the quantity of money is necessary to regulate its value. The answer is provided in the first pages of Chapter 27 of *On the Principles of Political Economy and Taxation* ("On Currency and Banks"). If the monetary standard is gold, it has, like every commodity produced in competitive conditions, a market price regulated by its natural price, itself determined by the difficulty of its production. This price (augmented by the seignorage if one exists) determines the value of circulating coins according to the quantity of pure metal which they contain. In a mixed regime where both specie and bank notes circulate, the stability of the value of money requires that the current value of notes equals the value of the coins of same denomination. In other words, a £1 note should not be depreciated in circulation as compared with the £1 coin. If it is, this depreciation manifests itself in a rise in the market price of bullion (purchased with notes) above the legal value of the same weight of gold in coins.

However a difficulty appears. In contrast with the gold coin, the note has no "intrinsic value," since its face value bears no relation with the difficulty of production of the paper. Its value only results from the confrontation between the quantity of notes issued and the needs of the circulation for it:

> There is no point more important in issuing paper money, than to be fully impressed with the effects which follow from the principle of limitation of quantity.
>
> (Ricardo 1817: 353)

The needs of circulation being given by the aggregate level of transactions implemented with notes, the only way to ensure monetary stability is to regulate the quantity of notes issued so that their value remains equal to that of the coin.

This analysis may be summarized in the following way. Let x_G be the quantity (measured in ounces) of fine gold contained in a newly issued £1 coin; $\overline{P}_c$ the legal price (measured in £) of an ounce of coined gold; P_G the market price (measured in £) of an ounce of gold bullion paid in notes, $\overline{V}_c$ and V_c the legal and current value of the £1 coin, V_B the current value of the £1 note (if deprived of legal tender, the note has only a current value). Gold being the monetary standard, these values are measured in gold weight (ounces). By definition:

$$\overline{V}_c = x_G \tag{1}$$

$$\overline{P}_c = 1 / x_G \tag{2}$$

These equations simply state that the £ is legally defined by the weight of fine gold contained in the £1 coin.

The current value of a coin is the gold weight which it really contains. If all the circulating coins have the legal weight, $V_c = \overline{V}_c = x_G$. The note being deprived of intrinsic value, its current value is indirectly measured by its purchasing power in the market of the monetary standard, that is, gold. As a consequence:

$$V_B = 1 / P_G \tag{3}$$

The equilibrium condition of a mixed monetary regime where coins and notes circulate side by side, that is, the equality between the current values of notes and coins, reads :

$$V_B = \overline{V}_c = x_G \tag{4}$$

From equations (3) and (4) it follows that:

$$x_G P_G = 1 \tag{5}$$

This condition may also be written, following (2):

$$P_G = \overline{P}_c \tag{6}$$

This means (equation 5) that the gold weight contained in the coin is paid for in notes in the bullion market at a price of £1, or (equation 6) that the market price of an ounce of gold in bullion paid for in notes is equal to the legal price of an ounce of coined gold. Every rise in the market price of bullion over the mint price (then £3.17.10½) is then a proof of the depreciation of the note in respect to the coin.

The problem is now to determine V_B. One may define the circulation period as the time during which every note is used once to make a payment. If Q_i is the quantity of i (with i from 1 to n) exchanged for notes during this period, and P_i is its money price (measured in £), the aggregate gold-value of the transactions during the period is equal to:

$$\sum_{i=1}^{i=n} Q_i P_i \overline{V}_c$$

This value is necessarily equal to the gold-value $Q_B V_B$ of the quantity Q_B of notes in circulation, so that:

$$V_B = (1 / Q_B) \sum_{i=1}^{i=n} Q_i P_i \overline{V}_c \tag{7}$$

The quantities Q_i and the gold-prices $P_i\overline{V_c}$ being given, the current value of the note depends on its quantity. Then the working of a mixed monetary regime requires the regulation of the issuing of notes, which guarantees the equalization of the current value of the paper to the legal value of the coin of same denomination.

It should be observed that no equation requires the convertibility of notes into coins. This is stressed by Ricardo:

> On these principles, it will be seen that it is not necessary that paper money should be payable in specie to secure its value ; it is only necessary that its quantity should be regulated according to the value of the metal which is declared to be the standard.
>
> (Ricardo 1817: 354)

One should now inquire what advantages may be derived from a regime with convertibility into bullion. This is the purpose of the "ingot plan."

The "ingot plan"

The idea of the convertibility of notes against bullion was exposed for the first time by Ricardo in the *Appendix* (1811) to the fourth edition of his pamphlet *The High Price of Bullion, A Proof of the Depreciation of Bank Notes* (first edition 1810). The "benefits to the public" of this idea, Ricardo contended, were that "the same security against the depreciation of the currency can be obtained by more gentle means" than through convertibility into specie (Ricardo 1811: 124). This idea was recast and expanded in Ricardo's *Proposals for an Economical and Secure Currency* (1816), and defended by him in 1819 during the depositions before the Committees of the Houses of Commons and of Lords on the Resumption of Cash Payments.

The "ingot plan" – as it is called in the literature – was considered by Ricardo as a permanent monetary regime, designed to substitute for the post-1797 inconvertibility *and* the pre-1797 convertibility ones, and not (as it would be eventually adopted by Parliament in 1819) as a temporary arrangement, designed to facilitate the resumption of cash payments. As exposed in 1816, this plan exhibits two main principles:

1 The quantity of banknotes issued should be regulated according to the observed market price of bullion, instead of being left to the discretion of the Bank, as before. This constitutes a "judicious management of the quantity" of paper money (Ricardo 1816: 57). Hence I shall call this aspect of the plan the "management principle."
2 The banknotes should be convertible in bullion, instead of specie as before 1797. This I shall call the "ingot principle."

The orthodox tradition has put a great emphasis on the first principle, which is consistent with the repeated warning by Ricardo against the evils of an "excess of paper." But there is no doubt that, for Ricardo, the "uniformity in the value of money" (that is, its stability through time at the official level) comes not only from this principle, but also from the second one. In other words, in the title of the pamphlet (*Proposals for an Economical and Secure Currency*), the "security" does not come only from the first principle, the "economy" being left to the second one (in the Smithian tradition). The convertibility in bullion is supposed to bring more stability to the value of money, whatever the principle adopted to regulate the issue of paper. This observation is based on the great emphasis put by Ricardo on the relationship between his proposed system for the Bank of England and the banks of Amsterdam and Hamburg, which he praises for their security:

> The plan here proposed appears to me to unite all the advantages of every system of banking which has been hitherto adopted in Europe. It is in some features similar to the banks of deposit of Amsterdam and Hamburgh. In those establishments bullion is always to be purchased from the Bank at a fixed invariable price. The same thing is proposed for the Bank of England . . . . The currency could neither be clipped nor deteriorated, and would possess a value as invariable as gold itself, the great object which the Dutch had in view, and which they most successfully accomplished by a system very like that which is here recommended.[1]
>
> (Ricardo 1811: 126–7)

This opinion is also to be found in the *Notes on Bentham's "Sur les Prix"* (1810–11):

> The Bank of England is certainly not *quite* so secure as a bank of deposit such as Amsterdam and Hamburgh. . . . In Holland and Hamburgh the advantages of the Banks is 1° in the use of paper instead of metals which has been admirably described by the author [Bentham], and 2° in having a uniform measure of value subject to no debasement or deterioration.
>
> (Ricardo 1810–11: 288)

The Bank of England has one advantage over the other two: she "is infinitely more useful in making the whole capital of the country available" (ibid.), because notes may be issued by discounting commercial paper, while in Amsterdam and Hamburg they can only be obtained against precious metals, so that "[the banks] have actually in their coffers, as much bullion, as there are credits for bank money in their books; accordingly there is an inactive capital as great as the whole amount of the commercial circulation" (ibid.: 126). However this advantage has a counterpart: notes may be issued in excess, hence the necessity to regulate their issue. Nevertheless the Amsterdam and Hamburg system embodies in itself a principle of security which, according to Ricardo, may be borrowed through the convertibility of notes in bullion.[2]

How may the second principle contribute to "the uniformity in the value of money" more than convertibility into specie? This question may be divided in two. First, how may it reduce the risks for the market price of bullion to depart from the official price of the metal chosen as standard? And second, how may it improve the adjustment process, allowing the market price of bullion to return to its official price when it departs from it?

The answer to the first question lies in the understanding of the fact that what is at stake in the adoption of the "ingot plan" as a permanent regime is the demonetization of gold in the domestic circulation. Ricardo is not advocating a mixed regime of coins and paper convertible in bullion, but a pure regime of convertible paper. Under such a regime, the issuing of currency would no longer be shared by the Mint and the Bank, but would be performed by the Bank alone. There would still be a metallic standard, but it would no longer circulate domestically. Of course, this did not mean *immediately* either decrying the coins remaining in circulation, or abolishing the minting of specie. However it was clear for Ricardo that, if the Bank stopped contributing to the circulation of specie, because she would stop providing it in exchange for notes, and on the contrary absorbed progressively the coins in circulation by being compelled to purchase gold at a price high enough to compensate for the loss of interest during the fabrication of the coins at the Mint, the circulation of specie would progressively vanish and a pure regime of convertible notes would smoothly be implemented.[3]

The model outlined must be modified in order to encompass such a regime. The definition of the unit of account, the £, is no longer stated by a weight of gold coined in the £1 coin, but by a weight of uncoined gold (y_G). In other words, the official price (maintained at £3.17.10½) no longer refers to an ounce of gold coined in guineas, but to an ounce of bullion, kept in the vaults of the Bank of England in the form of ingots. If one calls $\bar{V}_L$ the legal value (measured in fraction of an ounce) of the £ in bullion, and $\bar{P}_L$ the legal price (measured in £) of an ounce of gold in bullion, by definition:

$$\bar{V}_L = y_G \tag{8}$$

$$\bar{P}_L = 1/y_G \tag{9}$$

Equation (3) giving the current value of the note is unchanged:

$$V_B = 1/P_G \tag{3}$$

Equation (4) which gives the equilibrium condition of the monetary regime becomes :

$$V_B = \bar{V}_L = y_G \tag{10}$$

Thanks to equation (3), this condition may be rewritten:

$$y_G P_G = 1 \tag{11}$$

or:

$$P_G = \bar{P}_L \tag{12}$$

This means (equation 11) that the weight of gold legally defining the £ is paid in notes in the market at the price of £1, or (equation 12) that the legal and market prices of an ounce of bullion are equal. In the quantity relation (7), the derivation of the gold-value of commodity i from its money price P_i is no longer made with the value of the pound $\bar{V}_c$ but $\bar{V}_L$. This equation becomes:

$$V_B = (1/Q_B) \sum_{i=1}^{i=n} Q_i P_i \bar{V}_L \tag{13}$$

The "management principle" of Q_B is supposed to allow the stabilization of V_B, hence the fulfilment of the equilibrium condition (12). But another way exists to stabilize *directly* P_G: it is the arbitrage made by the buyers and sellers of bullion between the market and the Bank. This stabilization of the market price for bullion requires that the Bank be able to provide all the bullion demanded for her notes at the legal price $\bar{P}_L$, and that she be compelled to purchase all the bullion offered for her notes at a fixed price $\bar{P}_L'$, called "Bank buying price."$\bar{P}_L'$ would be fixed below $\bar{P}_L$, and as close to $\bar{P}_L$ as might seem desirable:

$$\bar{P}_L' = \bar{P}_L (1 - b) \tag{14}$$

If the two above conditions are fulfilled, one gets:

$$\bar{P}_L \geq P_G \geq \bar{P}_L (1 - b) \tag{15}$$

which means that the margin of variation of P_G – hence of V_B – is reduced to b. Then the purpose of the "ingot plan" is :

> To prevent the value of money from varying from the value of bullion more than the trifling difference between the prices at which the bank should buy and sell, and which would be an approximation to that uniformity in its value which is aknowledged to be so desirable.
> (Ricardo 1816: 67)

Now two complementary answers may be offered to the first question. First, as observed by Ricardo in the list quotation from the *Notes on Bentham*, the elimination of the circulation of the standard would provide the same advantage as in Amsterdam or Hamburg, of "having a uniform measure of value subject to no debasement or deterioration." As is well known, this problem had long been central to the debates on the defects of precious metals in performing the function of standard of money.[4] The proposed plan allowed the suppression of these defects without the need to renounce the existence of a metallic standard.

Second, in a regime of convertibility into specie, two reasons may lead holders of notes to demand the conversion of their notes: the belief that they will be unable to retain the same purchasing power as coins in domestic circulation, and the desire to obtain gold to hoard or export it. As, according to Ricardo, no regime may protect against a panic resulting in hoarding, one should concentrate on circulation and export only. In the first case, coined metal is looked for, because of its supposed better quality as means of circulation; this leads to an "internal drain" of Bank reserves. In the second case, uncoined metal is looked for, and specie is only demanded to be melted and exported as bullion; this leads to an "external drain" of Bank reserves.

Now, with the "ingot plan," the internal drain disappears, since the abolition of specie eliminates any possible demand for convertibility aimed at replacing the notes in domestic circulation. The domestic circulation (of notes) and the international circulation (of bullion) are separated, the only link being the convertibility of notes into bullion. Of course, a drain of Bank reserves may still occur, but it may only be external. This advantage has been clearly seen by Keynes, who attributes to Ricardo the paternity of the "gold exchange standard."[5] This aspect may be linked to the attribution by Keynes to Ricardo of another idea: that of "managed money" (cf. the earlier quotation from *A Treatise on Money*, 1930). In a monetary regime with a non-circulating standard, the management of the currency (first principle of the "ingot plan") allows the maintenance of the "objective" character of the standard, by making money conform to it. Hence the link between the two discoveries of Ricardo. Keynes only pushes the argument a little further: if, although objective, the standard does not circulate, it may be anything. If it is gold, that is, the internationally accepted means of payment, the management of money aims at the external stability of the value of money. If it is a basket of goods significant for domestic purposes, whatever it is, it will aim at the internal stability of the value of money, which, in Keynes's view, is preferable.[6]

Let us now turn to the second question of the adjustment process. What happens if the market price for bullion departs from its official price? If it is from below, an arbitrage occurs when P_G falls to the Bank buying price $\bar{P}_L'$: holders of bullion will prefer to sell it to the Bank than in the market. The Bank simply replaces the Mint in the function of absorbing the undervalued gold, until the market price of bullion returns to its official level. During this process, the quantity of notes increases, but it is not necessary to assume that this increase is the cause of a decline in their current value V_B, hence of the increase in the market price of bullion P_G. The adjustment is simply the consequence of arbitrage between the market for bullion and the Bank.

One should observe that the new obligation imposed on the Bank to purchase bullion at a fixed price (again in imitation of Hamburg) is not an additional principle; it is contained in the "ingot principle." In a pure metallic monetary regime, the standard is the only commodity which may be sold (at the Mint, with the cost of the seignorage) and purchased (in circulation, with the cost of melting and possibly of fraud) at a fixed (administered) price. In a mixed regime with notes convertible into specie, it is also possible to purchase it at the same fixed price. In a pure regime of notes convertible in bullion, the standard might still be purchased at a fixed price, but not sold. Then no limit would exist to the decline in the market price of bullion. The obligation imposed on the Bank to purchase it at a fixed price is nothing other than the way to ensure that the standard keeps the same specificity in regard to other commodities as in a regime with specie. The consequence of this obligation is for the Bank a reduction of her profits in such circumstances, since she is forced to issue notes against bullion, which provides no revenue, instead of discounting commercial paper, which provides one. However this loss is compensated by the cost she evades in the opposite case of a demand for conversion of notes, as compared with convertibility in specie, since she does not have to bear the loss of interest during the time of fabrication of the coins at the Mint.

What now happens precisely in this latter case, when the market price P_G increases above its official price $\overline{P_L}$? It seems that the only adjustment process will rely on the first principle of the "ingot plan," that is, the regulation of the quantity. However, if it is so, there exists no advantage of the convertibility in bullion instead of specie: the management of the currency may be performed in the same way (i.e. according to the market price of bullion, which induces here a limitation of the emission) in both regimes. It cannot even be said that it would be performed at a lower cost for the Bank or society. On the contrary, the level of the market price of bullion which starts the demand for conversion is now lower than in the old convertibility regime (because there is no longer any cost of melting and fraud), and this might be viewed as increasing the volatility of Bank reserves, hence as an argument against the convertibility in bullion.

This argument may be compensated by another one: the demonetization of gold in circulation structurally increases Bank reserves, because holders of coins sell them to the Bank when the increased supply of metal drives down its market price to the Bank buying price. Of course, the quantity of circulating notes increases in proportion, but we have seen that this is not the same as the case of the potential demand for convertibility: the holders of notes for domestic circulation are not a source of drain. Bank reserves then increase while the risk of conversion does not.

Then the superiority of the convertibility in bullion, as far as the adjustment process in case of depreciation of the currency is concerned, is not clear-cut, and one should look for the possibility of another adjustment process than the regulation of the quantity of notes. The international one seems to be a good candidate, since we have seen that one characteristic of a pure regime of notes convertible in bullion is to limit the role of the standard as means of payment to external transactions only.

The international adjustment process in the case of a premium on bullion

As is well known, a recurrent idea in Ricardo's pamphlets during the bullion controversy is that, when a redundancy of money pushes the market price of bullion above its mint price – thus indicating a depreciation of the currency – the excess is exported and this restores the value of the currency, bringing back the price of bullion to its official level. Then, in case of a premium on bullion, for whatever reason, its export should be considered as an adjustment process alternative to the limitation of the emission.[7]

In his celebrated book *The Economics of David Ricardo* (1979), Samuel Hollander has focused attention on the logical conditions of such an international adjustment process and offered an illuminating interpretation of Ricardo's position in the Bullion debate (Hollander 1979: 435–42). He first studies "the important case," from the empirical perspective, of a "*mixed circulation comprising inconvertible paper as well as coin,* the clearest account of which was first given in the *Reply to Bosanquet*" (ibid.: 437, SH's italics). In short, the process goes as follows. A money supply increase (for example through an additional emission of notes) above its equilibrium level leads to a depreciation of the currency, which manifests itself in increased money prices of commodities, including gold bullion. The premium on bullion over the mint price offers a possibility of profit for holders of coins ready to melt them (even fraudulently) and supply the metal in the market for bullion. This has two consequences: the reduction in the quantity of currency increases the value of money and thus reduces the money prices of all commodities; but the increased supply of bullion drives down its money price further than that of commodities, so that the relative price of bullion in terms of commodities falls. If the initial situation was an equality between the purchasing powers of bullion over commodities in the country and abroad, this fall leads to an export of bullion and a corresponding import of goods. The conclusion is rather impressive: "The import of the discussion is that a corrective process is at work even in the inconvertible case provided that coin constitutes part of the initial circulation" (Hollander 1979: 438–9), which was the situation of England in 1799–1802 but no longer in 1809–10. At the time of Ricardo's involvement in the bullion controversy, then, no "corrective process" of this kind still existed.

I shall not discuss here this model for the case analyzed, but ask whether it applies to the two convertible regimes under consideration, and, if so, what differences appear between them. Hollander mentions two cases of convertibility. The first one is "*a mixed currency of coin and notes,* convertible into specie on demand, and freedom of metallic exportation" (ibid.: 439, SH's italics): that is, the pre-1797 regime, amended for freedom of melting and export. Again the coins driven out of circulation are melted, the supply of metal is increased and export takes place when its relative price in terms of goods has declined. The second one is "*the case where (convertible) notes alone circulate*" (ibid.: 440, SH's italics), with also convertibility in specie. This latter case, for which no reference to Ricardo is given, is rather strange, because it is unclear why convertibility would be in specie if coins are deprived of legal tender. One may understand it as a variation on the "ingot plan" (to which Hollander does not refer), the important point being that bullion obtained directly from the Bank or through the melting of non-circulating coins is supplied in the market, which drives its relative price down, leading to its export. The conclusion of Hollander is clear:

> As far as concerns the mechanism of bullion movement, *the two cases of convertibility are analytically identical with the inconvertible case where a mixed currency circulates,* for in this case too an addition to the note issue will generate corrective outflows.
> (Hollander 1979: 440, SH's italics)

This generalization does not seem to me to be acceptable. There is an obvious difference between the inconvertibility case and the convertibility ones: if agents may obtain gold (in whatever form) from the Bank at a fixed price and without limit, they will not drive it out of circulation, either because coins are banished from circulation (regime with exclusive circulation of notes) or because there is a cost to gather them (mixed regime). Because the Bank is then the sole source of gold supply, convertibility of notes introduces a special effect, which prevents the money price of bullion from falling as a consequence of an increased supply, and hence prevents the "corrective process" from being set into motion. This effect is mentioned by Ricardo in *The High Price of Bullion* in the case of convertibility of notes into specie:

> If to supply the deficiency of their [the Bank's] stock of gold they were to purchase gold bullion at the advanced price, and have it coined into guineas, this would not remedy the evil, guineas would still be demanded, but instead of being exported would be melted and sold to the Bank as bullion at the advanced price.
> (Ricardo 1810: 58)

Ricardo mentions on this point Adam Smith for an "analogous case," which concerns the Mint and not the Bank, although Ricardo replaces one by the other in his quotation: "'The operations of the Bank,' observed Dr. Smith, alluding to an analogous case, 'were upon this account somewhat like the web of Penelope, the work that was done in the day was undone in the night'" (ibid.). He also mentions Thornton (1802) and concludes:

> The Bank would be obliged therefore ultimately to adopt the only remedy in their power to put a stop to the demand for guineas. They would withdraw part of their notes from circulation, till they should have increased the value of the remainder to that of gold bullion.
> (Ricardo 1810: 59)

This "Penelope effect" comes from the fact that, rather than exporting bullion, their holders prefer to sell it back to the Bank who has to demand it to replenish her reserves; the profit is higher than in the export, because no transportation cost has to be incurred. In Hollander's terms, bullion is *not* exported, since its relative price in terms of commodities does *not* fall; and it is so because the depressive effect on the money price of bullion of an additional supply is always counteracted by an increased demand for bullion from the Bank. On the contrary, in the mixed regime with coins and inconvertible notes, one is sure that the increased supply of bullion drives down its market price, since there is no demand for it originating anywhere else in the economy, until a demand for export appears, that is, precisely until, according to Hollander, the market price for bullion has declined far enough to depress its relative price in terms of goods by a margin allowing its export to become profitable.

It seems to me, then, that the international adjustment process described by Hollander cannot apply to a monetary regime with convertibility of notes. It is discarded by Ricardo himself in the case of convertibility in specie. But the same line of argument applies to the "ingot plan" regime with convertibility in bullion: the "Penelope effect" is set into motion even quicker and with a larger profit, since no melting cost is incurred.

If this international adjustment process through exports of bullion does not work in the "ingot plan" (no less but no more than with convertibility in specie), does it mean that the only possibility of adjustment must come from the internal management principle of notes? I do not think so, because of another consequence of the "ingot plan," which, as far as I know, has been overlooked by the literature. If the monetary regime is deprived of a Mint and of a circulation of specie, that is, of possibilities of arbitrage with the market for the sale and the purchase of the metal, and if the Bank purchases and sells bullion at fixed prices as close as would appear desirable, this means that the Bank of England becomes the regulator of the London market for gold, and in the circumstances of the time, the centrepiece of the world market for gold.[8]

Now let us go back to the initial situation considered. A premium on bullion, whatever its cause, means that, when this premium exceeds the cost of transportation of bullion, there is an inducement to *import* it, because, at the ruling exchange rate, the price in sterling of bullion in London (after deduction of transportation cost) is higher than abroad. Note that, if this premium on gold is just enough to start imports of that commodity (allowing for the profit required in this business), and even if the money price of the commodities increases in London by the same proportion (which means that this general price increase has a monetary origin), this will *not* start imports of commodities from abroad, because divergence between domestic and foreign prices must be higher for commodities than it is for gold, which is, according to Ricardo, "the cheapest exportable commodity" (Ricardo 1810: 63).[9] Then the transitory situation is characterized by an addition to the supply of gold in the London market, which may actually correct its market price downwards.

This adjustment process is independent of any type of convertibility: it is simply the consequence of arbitrage between the bill of exchange markets and the gold markets in London and abroad. However, when the London market is centered on the Bank (that is, in the case of the "ingot plan"), this import of bullion by international arbitrage allows the Bank to resist the pressure put upon her by the demands for conversion of her notes, and constitutes an obstacle to the "Penelope effect" because the Bank may postpone her purchase of gold in the market.

Of course, this international adjustment process only works if the premium over gold is great enough to induce gold imports, but small enough (when it is accompanied by a similar increase in commodity prices) not to induce imports of goods. If it is larger, other imports will occur, some of them by British importers preferring to buy cheaper abroad than at home. I said earlier that the standard is the only commodity which may be purchased domestically at a fixed price. This means that any private agent, even if not looking for enrichment through the "Penelope effect" but needing gold for industrial purposes, may escape at home (that is, without having to import it) the consequence of an increased market price of gold. For all other commodities, this is not true: the only way is through import. The consequence will be an increased demand of bills of exchange denominated in foreign currencies, and therefore a decline in the exchange rate. When this decline is great enough to make export of bullion profitable, a reversal of international bullion flows occurs, which puts an external drain on the Bank.[10] From now on, the orthodox Ricardo may come again: there is no other way, in Ricardo's perspective, than a limitation of the note issue.[11] The "management principle" of the "ingot plan" comes again into force, and the "ingot principle" has no longer any advantage above the old-fashioned convertibility in specie.

Nevertheless, even in Ricardo's perspective, the convertibility of notes in bullion is a better regime for a fine-tuning of the value of money. In other words, the general property of a monetary standard is to stabilize the value of money, but the particular property of a non-circulating monetary standard (in the "ingot plan," a gold exchange standard) is twofold: apart from unavoidable situations of panic, it reduces the risk of drain on the reserves of the Bank to the external one, and, in circumstances of small variations in the money price of the standard (for whatever cause), it allows an automatic stabilization of the value of money.

One should observe that both advantages are independent of *any* relation between the quantity of money and its value. In the earlier model, inequalities (15) are ensured independently of equation (13) – i.e. of the "management principle" – through arbitrage between the bullion market and the Bank: when P_G falls to $\bar{P}_L{}'$, the supply of bullion in its market stops, which prevents P_G from falling more, and when P_G increases above $\bar{P}_L$, the supply of bullion in its market increases through import, and P_G is driven back to it. Not only is the "ingot principle" independent of the "management principle," but it guarantees by itself the stability of the currency in normal conditions, making redundant the regulation of the quantity of paper, except in situations of open crisis.

In short, the "ingot plan" does not assume any equilibrium quantity of money, which would determine its equilibrium value. There exists a legal value of money, the reciprocal of the legal price of bullion, and a current value of money, the reciprocal of the market price of bullion. If, thanks to the convertibility in bullion, the market price of bullion is stabilized as desirably as it may seem at the level of its legal price, the current value of money will be stabilized at the level of its legal value as well. Then the stabilization of the value of money does not rely on the regulation of its quantity. It is the variation of the quantity of gold in its market which stabilizes its price, hence the value of money, and not the variation of the quantity of money in circulation which stabilizes its value, hence the market price of gold. This interpretation pictures Ricardo on money in a rather unusual way, but makes sense of his opposition to the convertibility in specie and of his fierce defence of the "ingot principle," which would be ignored by monetary orthodoxy during more than a century after his death.[12] There lies, it seems to me, the heterodox component in Ricardo's theory of money.

Notes

I thank for their comments Marie-Thérèse Boyer-Xambeu, Nancy Churchman, Timothy Davis, Gilles Dostaler, Lucien Gillard, Emmanuel Masset-Denevre, Jean-Nicolas Rieucau, Michel Rosier, Mehrdad Vahabi.

1. This relationship between Ricardo's plan and the Bank of Hamburg is also aknowledged by the banker Alexander Baring in his deposition before the Committee of the House of Commons on March 11 and 12, 1819: "The plan in question is, in fact, no other than that of the bank of Hamburgh, only substituting a currency of paper in lieu of a transfer of book debt; and the bank of Hamburgh has always been found, from long experience, the best institution for preserving the standard of value; the payments of the bank of Hamburgh are solely in silver bullion" (in Ricardo 1951–73, vol. 5: 358).
2. Ricardo observes that "in one occasion the Bank of Hamburgh was obliged to suspend its payments in consequence of having made too great advances on gold bullion." This occurred in 1766–7. Cf. *Reply to Bosanquet*, in Ricardo 1951–73, vol. 3: 175–6n.
3. This explains the variations of his position between 1811, 1816, and 1819 on some technicalities of his plan, such as the choice offered or not to the Bank to pay in bullion or specie, and the responsibility given to the Mint or the Bank to stamp the ingots. See Sraffa's introduction to the debates of 1819 in Ricardo 1951–73, vol. 5: 350–70.
4. For example, see Steuart 1767.
5. In *Indian Currency and Finance* (1913), Keynes mentions this paternity in a discussion of the Indian system of currency. See Keynes 1971–89, vol. 1: 22, 51; vol. 15: 70.
6. It follows that if the market price for gold in Ricardo is interpreted as a proxy for a general price index, the link between Ricardo and the Keynes of the *Treatise* becomes still closer. The only difference remains as whether the stability of this index should be pursued for internal or external reasons. However, if Ricardo is also considered as the father of the Purchasing Power Parity theorem, as Keynes viewed him in his *Tract on Monetary Reform* (1923), both views are reconciled in a strictly orthodox fashion.
7. One should observe that I consider here the international adjustment process in response to a premium on bullion, and not to a decline in the exchange rate, which is a different question and does not really concern Ricardo.
8. One of the two major bullion brokers in London at the time, N. M. Rothschild, seems to have understood the danger, since he strongly opposed Ricardo's plan in his deposition before the Commons' Committee on March 8 1819. The reasons invoked are the consequences for the Bank of a panic in case of war, and the possibility of disguising silver bars as gold bars (see Ricardo 1951–73, vol. 5: 357). One may think that these dangers, in Rothschild's view, could be avoided thanks to the expertise of a competent bullion broker . . .
9. On this notion, see Marcuzzo and Rosselli 1991: 128–9.
10. This explanation of the export of bullion, based on direct international comparisons of money prices (through the exchange rate), may be preferred to the model offered by Hollander, based on international comparisons of relative prices, even in Ricardo's perspective. One should observe that, according to this explanation, imports of goods occur before the export of bullion – and not as a consequence of it – and that this export is not the consequence of a fall in the relative price of gold in terms of commodities, but results from a decline in the exchange rate.
11. From another perspective, illustrated by the line of reasoning Thornton–Tooke–Goschen, there exists another way of escape: an increase in the discount rate, which attracts short-term capital and restores the exchange, in such a way that gold may flow in again.

12 Until the Gold Standard Act of 1925. Such an interpretation also tends to deprive Ricardo of any paternity in the Bank Charter Act of 1844, which imposed a quantity rationing of note issue through a 100 percent backing of its increase by additional metallic reserves of the Bank, and questions the analytical continuity between Ricardo and the Currency School.

References

Blaug, M. (1995) "Why is the Quantity Theory of Money the Oldest Surviving Theory in Economics?" in M. Blaug *et al.*, *The Quantity Theory of Money. From Locke to Keynes and Friedman*, Aldershot: Edward Elgar: 27–49.
Deleplace, G. (1996) "Does Circulation Need a Monetary Standard?" in G. Deleplace and E. J. Nell (eds), *Money in Motion. The Post Keynesian and Circulation Approaches*, London: Macmillan: 305–29.
Hollander, S. (1979) *The Economics of David Ricardo*, London: Heinemann.
—— (1980) "On Professor Samuelson's Canonical Model of Political Economy," *Journal of Economic Literature* 18 (June): 559–74.
Keynes, J. M. (1930) *A Treatise on Money. The Pure Theory of Money*, in *Collected Writings*, vol. 5, London: Macmillan.
—— (1971–89) *Collected Writings*, 30 vols, London: Macmillan.
Laidler, D. (1987) "Bullionist Controversy," in J. Eatwell, M. Milgate, and P. Newman (eds), *The New Palgrave: A Dictionary of Economics*, London: Macmillan, vol. 1: 289–94.
Marcuzzo, M. C. and Rosselli, A. (1991) *Ricardo and the Gold Standard. The Foundations of the International Monetary Order*, London: Macmillan.
Ricardo, D. (1810) *The High Price of Bullion, a Proof of the Depreciation of Bank Notes*, in *Works and Correspondence*, vol. 3, Cambridge: Cambridge University Press.
—— (1810–11) *Notes on Bentham's "Sur les prix"*, in *Works and Correspondence*, vol. 3, Cambridge: Cambridge University Press.
—— (1811) *Appendix to the Fourth Edition of "The High Price of Bullion"*, in *Works and Correspondence*, vol. 3, Cambridge: Cambridge University Press.
—— (1816) *Proposals for an Economical and Secure Currency*, in *Works and Correspondence*, vol. 3, Cambridge: Cambridge University Press.
—— (1817) *On the Principles of Political Economy and Taxation*, in *Works and Correspondence*, vol. 1, Cambridge: Cambridge University Press.
—— (1951–73) *Works and Correspondence*, ed. P. Sraffa with the collaboration of M. Dobb, 11 vols, Cambridge: Cambridge University Press.
Samuelson, P. A. (1978) "The Canonical Classical Model of Political Economy," *Journal of Economic Literature* 16 (December): 1415–34.
Schumpeter, J. A. (1954) *History of Economic Analysis*, New York: Oxford University Press.
Steuart, J. [1767] (1967) *An Inquiry into the Principles of Political Economy*, New York: A. M. Kelley.
Thornton, H. [1802] (1991) *An Enquiry into the Nature and Effects of the Paper Credit of Great Britain*, New York: A. M. Kelley.

18 On Hollander's and Keynes's "canonical" interpretations of Malthus

Thomas K. Rymes

Prologue

I was honored to present a paper at the Conference "Reflecting on the Canon" to celebrate Professor Samuel Hollander. Years ago, he came up to Carleton to address my History of Economic Thought students on what was then his new view of Ricardo. Professor Hollander elevated their study to a new level of exacting scholarship and my account of classical economics to one of excitement and immediacy of relevance. What a lasting impact Professor Hollander made on those fortunate students!

Introduction

Two attributes characterize classical economics. (The content of one of Professor Hollander's works so titled explains what I mean by such a phrase.) The first, a matter of prediction, is that populations and capitals grow relative to land, that land is exogenous and independent of the growth process. The second, a more normative characteristic, is that money should also be exogenous. Now, stocks of money, if metallic, do grow relative to land, as metals are ripped from the land, even if under conditions of diminishing returns. So, the "canonical" classical growth model would say that commodity or real wage rates and net real rates of return to capital will fall (or maybe initially rise as initial knowledge and returns to scale are realized, but then approach stationary levels) as population growth and capital accumulation come to their respective standstills. (See Hollander 1998.) One would say, in Marshallian terms, that the prices of working and waiting would equilibrate at levels such that the flow of working and waiting would be just sufficient to maintain stocks of population and capital. The classical stationary state would eventually prevail.

If the stock of monetary metals grew apace with capital, then commodity prices in money terms, that is, for example, the gold prices of (say) consumption goods, would on average remain unchanged. If the stock of metals did not grow apace, because of diminishing returns, then one would predict that the gold price of commodities would fall.[1] The growing scarcity of land is a natural phenomenon, provided the passion between the sexes keeps the classical canonical growth model fueled.[2] The scarcity of fiat money, which replaces metallic money, is, however, not a natural phenomenon: it is contrived. Classical monetary theory and policy argued that the contrivance of money should be treated as if it were land, treated, that is, as if it were strictly exogenous. The money supply should itself be governed by natural laws, so that the long-run price of gold in terms of commodities should be governed by its cost of production. If a fiat or conventional money is in existence, then the money price of gold should be fixed. It should not be an unconstrained, nor even a constrained, private or public contrivance. It should not be unconstrained for fear of inflation. Even constrained private or public contrivances such as central banks with inflation targets are not advisable, since such constraints are so costly to enforce.

A related theme in classical economics, if I may neglect the full equilibrium effects of discoveries of monetary metals and the effects of steady inflation or deflation, is that money is neutral. Real wage rates, real net rates of returns and real prices of land are given independent of stocks of nominal or fiat monies (though not of monetary metals).

The two canons of classical economics are first, the growth model implying declining real wage rates and net rates of return to capital, and second, the neutrality of money.[3] They are based on the natural exogeneity of land and the maintained exogeneity of money. Both are critically based on the assumption of an unchanging given stock of knowledge.

The first canon and technical advance

John Rae's attack on classical economics is based on his perception that classical (or Smithian) economics had failed to account for the interaction between technical progress and capital accumulation.[4] If technical progress is exogenous then we have the Solow version of the classical growth model. If technical progress is a function of the rate of accumulation, then we have one aspect of the theory of endogenous growth. Certainly, Smith had increasing returns to scale, the crucial fact however being that as the economy expanded, different machines would sequentially come into play with the whole problem of measuring capital and the Cambridge capital controversy thus coming to the fore. I cannot find any reference in Malthus to the effect that with increasing returns or continuous endogenous technical progress undermining the scarcity of land, real wages might continually rise with growing stocks of capital and constant rates of profit, which means workers and capitalists together continually gain from growth. Certainly there are passages, as Professor Hollander points out in his *The Economics of Thomas Robert Malthus* (1997), where Malthus stresses that the approach to unchanging real wages and unchanging real stocks of capital and unchanging real stock prices of land might take a long time, and necessity may be the mother of invention.[5] That is, however, not the same thing as postulating exogenous or endogenous technical progress so that steady state growth in real wages and real prices of land with constant profit rates could be conceived. Thus, I do not subscribe to Professor Eltis's interpretation of Malthus as having, in his theory of capital accumulation, a constant rate of exogenous technical progress and a rate of endogenous technical progress that is positively related to rates of return to capital above some minimum rate of return.[6]

It is hard for me to see where Malthus spells out the steady state characteristics that I have outlined of such assumptions about advances in knowledge. To assume advances in knowledge, some of which are produced by the economic system, which must constantly undermine the scarcity of land and the natural laws so characteristic of classical economics, and at the same time not find in Malthus a preeminent awareness of such far-reaching implications, suggests that the assumption of unchanging stocks of knowledge remains a classical and Malthusian preoccupation. Rae's critique of classical economics stands and the limitations of the first canon are clearly understood.

Yet in Malthus, increased savings, particularly reduction in expenditure of rents on luxuries, involved a problem of the transfer of resources from the consumption goods to investment goods sectors. Keynes in *The General Theory* refers to Malthus's argument that excessive savings, by depressing profit rates, might dampen accumulation, whereas a proportionate balance of expansion in unproductive consumption would not impair motives to production and thus prematurely check the progress of wealth.[7]

Malthus did not assume that saving out of (say) rents was automatically invested; rather, it depressed profits (and savings?) and consequently accumulation.[8] The distress of 1815–20, Keynes stresses, was interpreted by Malthus as requiring for its solution increased public works and increased consumption by "landlords and persons of property" to offset the unfavorable effects on profits and accumulation stemming from the reduction in collective consumptive military expenditures.

Yet if increased frugality, private or collective, did reduce the net rate of return to capital or profit rate, why did not both investment and consumption increase to resolve the glut problem?

As Professor Hollander has written, if "savings are positively stimulated by the return to capital, $s = f(r)$, reflecting both the motive and ability to save" (Hollander 1997: 177), then an increase in savings would lower the rate of return and, as capital increased relative to land, would lead to even more capital-intensive techniques of production being employed and lower rates of saving. Was there in Malthus's analysis the canonical classical capital model, where lower real rates of return are supposedly associated with more capital intensive techniques? It is not easy to say, but the Malthusian equilibrium to which his system was tending certainly entailed more capital and lower rates of return. If so, the problem of the glut as stated by Malthus must be a short-run problem of adjustment of the labor force between consumption and investment goods trades. No doubt such problems could exist, but this is not what Keynes was dealing with in *The General Theory*.

In his biographical essay, after restating Malthus's argument that to encourage the greatest increase in wealth there had to be some balance between investment and consumption, since excess saving would damage motives to capital accumulation and production, Keynes goes on to say:

> Surely, it was a great fault in Ricardo to fail entirely to see any significance in (Malthus's) line of thought. But Malthus's defect lay in his overlooking entirely the part played by the rate of interest. Twenty years ago I should have retorted to Malthus that the state of affairs he envisages could not

occur unless the rate of interest had first fallen to zero. Malthus perceived, as others, what was true; but it is essential to a complete comprehension of why it is true, to explain how an excess of frugality does not bring with it a decline to zero in the rate of interest.

(Keynes 1971–89, vol. 10: 102)

The question Keynes poses is difficult for a classical economist to answer in any other way than to say that, abstracting from any Marshall-Fisher effects in different real and nominal rates of interest, rates of interest must be determined by real net rates of return to capital, allowing that some trades are riskier than others, a fact well recognized in classical economics. Then the rate of profit must adjust to ensure that a glut is but temporary.[9] If a general glut did exist, then prices must fall. What prices? Money prices!

The counter to Malthus, if what is contemplated is a general glut, is that all money prices must fall, including wage rates and nominal rentals on capital goods and land, through a fall in the stock prices of capital goods and lands. This must, by the operation of any metallic standard, free up the money metals so that the excess savings come to an end, or the banking system eventually becomes so replete with resources that interest rates fall and again the excess savings are eliminated.[10] For one country on (say) the gold standard, the balance of trade would improve to counterbalance the advance effects of the increased savings on the "motive to production." One does not, I think, have to rely on "real balance" effects to offset supposed classical dichotomies, to see that if a general glut should set in motion a general fall in prices, the operation of metallic standards, with banking systems seeking to expand loans and deposits as the real value of their reserves grows, or by improvements in the balance of trade, the general glut would eventually be eliminated.

As Hollander points out (1997: ch. 13), Malthus did argue that any expansion in the money supply would do little to raise economic activity if (say) new notes were put in the hands of the entrepreneurs, with an expansion of real capital occurring via a forced saving process, because under a convertible system, the ability of the banks to expand their note issue would be sharply restrained, and any expansion with a rise in prices would be offset by balance-of-trade effects. The equilibrating process under a convertible system works in the other direction. If notes were extracted from entrepreneurs by saving and were returned by savers to the banks, the banks would find re-issue immediately profitable and/or any fall in prices would be offset by balance-of-trade effects. It was the possibility of inconvertibility that was a bane to Malthus. Why? While it is believed that inconvertibility would unleash the demons of inflation, the theoretical problem, which it is doubtful Malthus understood, is that inconvertibility with fiat money means price-level indeterminacy and the failure of the preceding equilibrating arguments to hold.

The second canon and technical advance

What is involved with technical progress or advances in knowledge, however, is the realization that efficiency gains exist, resulting from moving to a system of inconvertibility. That is, it is both privately and socially profitable to switch to fiat money without a base. What is involved (as Edgeworth (1888) and following him, Wicksell ([1898] 1936) pointed out) is that banking develops, via clearing arrangements, to a point where reserves have shrunk to zero and a pure credit economy emerges. What to Wicksell was a theoretical possibility became to Keynes in *A Treatise on Money* V and VI a possible state of affairs to which our world today of reserve-less central banking attests. No matter how small, if monetary metals play some reserve role and bank notes (and deposits) are redeemable at any unchanged prices, then the monetary canon of classical orthodoxy holds. (Of course the empirical reality of the canon, like all "real" balance effects, becomes truly monastic.)

Unemployment *equilibrium* is an impossibility in classical economics, which is surely the outcome of the Malthus–Ricardo debate. It was Malthus's failure, as Keynes notes, to deal with the monetary aspects which separates Malthus from Keynes.[11] Once it is realized, as I claim Keynes did (Rymes 1998b), that the existence of base money is otiose, then the money prices of commodities must be determined in an endogenous or discretionary way. What really is the base of the monetary system is not gold or central bank notes but rather the conduct of monetary policy by the Central Bank. All this was in the *Treatise*.[12]

In Keynes's version of a competitive pure credit economy, that is, "the banana plantation parable," it is real events which determine the price level which essentially from a monetary viewpoint is indeterminate. I attach greater significance to the plantation parable than does Professor Rutherford, because it is Keynes's monetary theory in its purest form. The Central Bank operates on the price level by affecting the supply of central bank liquidity services – not money – operating on the bank rate. What this entails, however, is the Keynesian theoretical innovation, namely that the rate of interest, and therefore the real rate of return to capital, cannot be determined independently of the supply of liquidity services by the Central Bank, as is required in a world of Keynesian uncertainty. The second of the canons of classical economics falls to the ground, in the sense that the information or technical knowledge which is pertinent to a monetary economy is incompletable and endogenous, a fact partly but importantly calling for the existence of a Central Bank.

Conclusion

The two canons of classical economics which were embraced by Malthus are first, that commodity wage rates and real net rates of return to capital run up against the inelasticity in the supply of natural agents with given stocks of knowledge, and second, that money prices are set by money stocks, which in a gold-standard system are a given natural agent. (If the money stock is bank notes, they are set exogenously by adherence of Central Banks to gold-standard rules so that these values are also determined indirectly by the natural agents.) The central canon in classical economics was the fixity of nature and knowledge. Thrift and capital accumulation undermined natural scarcity, but given the assumptions about knowledge could not undermine it in a perpetual way. Bank notes might be over-issued, but if convertibility applied Hume's "poverty, beggary and sloth" would be avoided. Money rates of interest could be lowered, but inflation would only result in the long run if such rates lay below real net rates of return to capital. (In our day, we say monetary policy cannot affect real rates of interest, a direct contradiction to the theory Keynes offered in his *Treatise* and *General Theory*.)

Like Professor Hollander, I think Kates (1996) overstates his claim that Keynes's theory of effective demand is to be found in Malthus, because as Keynes himself states, the problem is about money rates of interest and satisfactory theorizing about them is simply not found in Malthus. Fundamentally, Keynesian uncertainty, the disjointing effects of which are soothed but never resolved by the supply of liquidity services by Central Banks, is continually in existence in the short run and the long run (Rogers 1997). Malthus's emphasis, in Keynes's interpretation, on the short run is consistent with Keynes's views on knowledge.[13] There can be no doubt, however, that Malthus and Ricardo adhered to long-run economic analysis where the turbulent uncertainty associated with the ever-changing facets of incompletable knowledge was set aside. It would not be possible to understand Keynes's criticism of Malthus – that he does not have a theory of the money rate of interest necessary to maintain effective demand and to offset a permanent general glut – without basing it on Keynes's abandonment of the fundamental canon of classical economics, that knowledge is given and incompletable. Keynes broke with classical economics by dealing with uncertainty. This is Keynes's canonical break with classical economics, and is why Keynes's emphasis on money and monetary institutions is so pre-eminent compared with classical economics. It is certainly wrong to attribute this break to Malthus as well. Keynes did not, I think, make this mistake.

Conjectural postscript

If landowners (actual or potential) should save in an endeavor to hold land (rather than capital) for liquidity purposes, then Keynes may have thought about providing a land-"monetary" theoretic basis for Malthus's theory of general gluts. Keynes says (in *The General Theory*):

> There is, clearly, no absolute standard of "liquidity" but merely a scale of liquidity – a varying premium of which account has to be taken, in addition to the yield of use and the carrying-costs, in estimating the comparative attractions of holding different forms of wealth. The conception of what contributes to "liquidity" is a partly vague one, changing from time to time and depending on social practices and institutions. The order of preference in the minds of owners of wealth in which at any given time they express their feelings about liquidity is, however, definite and is all we require for our analysis of the behavior of the economic system.
>
> It may be that in certain historic environments the possession of land has been characterized by a high liquidity-premium in the minds of owners of wealth; and since land resembles money in that its elasticities of production and substitution may be very low, it is conceivable that there have been occasions in history in which the desire to hold land has played the same role in keeping up the rate of interest at too high a level which money has played in recent times. It is difficult to trace this influence

quantitatively owing to the absence of a forward price for land in terms of itself which is strictly comparable with the rate of interest on a money debt. We have, however, something which has, at times, been closely analogous, in the shape of high rates of interest on mortgages. The high rates of interest from mortgages on land, often exceeding the probable net yield from cultivating the land, have been a familiar feature of many agricultural economies. Usury laws have been directed primarily against encumbrances of this character. And rightly so. For in earlier social organization where long-term bonds in the modern sense were non-existent, the competition of a high interest-rate on mortgages may well have had the same effect in retarding the growth of wealth from current investment in newly produced capital-assets, as high interest rates on long-term debts have had in more recent times.

That the world after several millennia of steady individual saving, is so poor as it is in accumulated capital-assets, is to be explained, in my opinion, neither by the improvident propensities of mankind, nor even by the destruction of war, but by the high liquidity-premiums formerly attaching to the ownership of land and now attaching to money. I differ in this from the older view as expressed by Marshall with an unusual dogmatic force in his *Principles of Economics*, p. 581:

"Everyone is aware that the accumulation of wealth is held in check, and the rate of interest so far sustained, by the preference which the great mass of humanity for present over deferred gratifications, or, in other words, by their unwillingness to 'wait'".

(Keynes 1971–89, vol. 7: 240–2)

Yet, as Lerner (1953) pointed out, an increased demand for land for liquidity purposes should drive up the consumption-good price of land until the real rate of return on land, adjusted for the liquidity premium, equals the real rate of return on capital, so that, if saving were maintained capital accumulation would be maintained.

(Of course, the same argument would seem to apply to gold or fiat money. An increased demand to hold money would lower money prices of consumption goods and increase "real" money balances until the liquidity-premium-adjusted rate of return on money equals the real rate of return on capital, so again maintaining capital accumulation. In the two cases, if land-wealth or money-wealth becomes high enough, savings will be reduced and consumption increased. The Malthusian glut problem and the Keynesian unemployment equilibrium problem vanish.)

One can argue, as Robinson did, that there may be times when lending to impecunious landlords by erstwhile owners of capital may be less risky than investment, a phenomenon which may limit capital accumulation. She did not, I think, attach much significance to this argument and, in general, argued that when Keynes was writing Chapter 17, he was "... groping for ideas that were new to him, and I do not think that he ever quite succeeded in seizing them"(Robinson 1965: 138).[14]

It is meaningless to attempt to rescue Keynes's conjecture in a world where, with the assumption of unchanging technology or steadily-maintained land augmenting technical progress, land is held as wealth across overlapping generations with positive time preference. Samuelson carefully demonstrates in such a world that an increase in the supply of land, if it lowers the marginal product of land and leads entrepreneurs to hire proportionately more of it, so creating an increase in the "demand" for land per person, will raise the rate of interest if the desired supply of land per person for wealth-holding purposes does not behave perversely with respect to the rate of interest (Samuelson 1979).

Yet in Samuelson's own analysis, which is concerned with the effects on the rate of interest of the supply of land, an increased desire to hold land for wealth purposes (again neglecting perversities) will lead to a lower rate of interest, contrary to Keynes's result.

Once liquidity preference is expressed over land, gold or even fiat money, the Lerner-Robinson structures against Keynes's conjecture hold. Keynesian support for the Malthusian glut stems not from the holding of land, gold or fiat money for liquidity needs, but from the fact that the sources of liquidity are not so much attached to money as produced by the services of private financial intermediaries, and the central banks under whose control the private intermediaries operate. The general level of prices is not determined fundamentally by the stock of money. Nor is it that money is endogenous, which would seem to undermine the second classical canon embraced by Malthus. It is rather that the services of liquidity, essential in a world of uncertainty but undefined in the classical world, are produced privately and collectively through banks and central banks, with such services always playing a role in the maintenance of effective demand. It is not surprising that, since he could see no role for central banks, Malthus was, as Professor Hollander notes (1997: 676), led to advocate the abolition of the Bank of England in favor of a more *laissez-faire* banking system, such as the American one based strictly on convertibility.

Notes

A draft of this paper was given at a conference "Reflecting on the Canon" given in honor of Professor Samuel Hollander, Toronto, Ontario, September 27 1998. I thank Professors M. Wakatabe and W. Eltis for their critical comments. I thank especially my colleague, Professor Nancy Churchman, for spotting errors and ambiguities in a second draft. The responsibility for all errors and misinterpretations remains mine.

1 For the case for a falling price level in a growing economy as something to be arranged rather than just as a classical prediction, see Selgin 1997.
2 One would also predict that the monetary metallic price of land would be rising until it reached the classical equilibrium level, since with real rates of return to capital constant or falling, a rising price of land is necessary for rentals not to be falling relative to wages and profits.
3 *The Shorter Oxford English Dictionary on Historical Principles* (1973) (Oxford: Clarendon) offers a number of definitions of "canon." The one I like best, with tongue in cheek, is "A book of the rules of a monastic order"!
4 I have attempted an understanding of Rae's growth theory in Rymes 1998a.
5 See T. R. Malthus's *Principles of Political Economy* [1820] 1998, in particular Chapter 7, Section 5: "On inventions to save labour, considered as a stimulus to the continued increase of wealth."

6 See Eltis 1984, in particular equation 5.7 on p. 169. I am uncertain of Professor Waterman's views on this point: see Waterman 1998.
7 Keynes, *The General Theory* (Keynes 1971–89, vol. 7: 362ff.), taken from ibid., vol. 10: letters from Malthus to Ricardo, July 1821.
8 Because I have eliminated steady growth with technical progress from this paper, I cannot say that an increase in savings will lower real rates of return and as a consequence capital accumulation and growth. I cannot attribute therefore to Malthus problems with what Joan Robinson calls the Keynesian paradox thrown into the long run, namely that increased thriftiness lowers the real net rate of return, the rate of accumulation, technical progress and growth. (See Robinson 1962: 48.) Robinson sets out the crucial problem in endogenous growth theory, the co-determination of rates of growth and rates of return to capital, independent of the overall capital intensity conditions: independent, that is, of the Cambridge capital controversy and the Sraffian interpretation of one commodity models.
9 If saving takes the form of capital accumulation, then excess savings in Malthus's sense must mean excessive capital accumulation so that rates of return would be driven down. Is there some minimum rate of return below which the motive to accumulation would fail? Why? One could argue there would be some minimum rate savers would require, but then would not the excess saving correct itself? Is there any evidence in classical and Malthusian economics that investment and savings would equilibrate at negative rates of interest? If not, the general glut must be a temporary thing, a problem of adjustment. Again, this has little if anything to do with Keynes.
10 Sometimes called the "Keynes effect."
11 This is, as I understand him, the final conclusion of Kates on the Malthus-Keynes connection. See the Symposium, "Say's Law Revisited" organized by Steven Kates, (1997), though the importance of money is not stressed in his "Keynes, Say's Law and the Theory of the Business Cycle" (Kates 1996). Nor is the importance of money stressed by Waterman: see Waterman 1998.
12 Though I take a different slant, Rutherford's claim (Rutherford 1987) that it was the Keynes of the *Treatise* who is relevant in a comparison of him and Malthus is well founded.
13 Good accounts of Keynes's views of incompletable knowledge are in Bateman 1996 and Dow and Hillard 1995.
14 I think Robinson believed that Keynes's conception of liquidity preference as part of the explanation of the level of the rate of interest pertained only to short-period considerations.

References

Bateman, B. W. (1996) *Keynes's Uncertain Revolution*, Ann Arbor: University of Michigan Press.
Dow, S. and Hillard, J. (eds) (1995) *Keynes, Knowledge and Uncertainty*, Aldershot: Elgar.
Edgeworth, F. Y. (1888) "The Mathematical Theory of Banking," *Journal of the Royal Statistical Society* 51: 113–27.
Eltis, W. (1984) *The Classical Theory of Economic Growth*, London: Macmillan.
Hollander, S. (1997) *The Economics of Thomas Robert Malthus*, Toronto: University of Toronto Press.
—— (1998) "The Canonical Classical Growth Model: Content, Adherence and Priority," *Journal of the History of Economic Thought* 20(3): 253–78.
Kates, S. (1996) "Keynes, Say's Law and the Theory of the Business Cycle", *History of Economics Review* 25(1–2): 119–26.
—— (ed.) (1997) "Say's Law Revisited", Symposium, *Eastern Economic Journal* 23 (Spring): 191–239.

Keynes, J. M. (1971–89) *Collected Writings*, 30 vols, London: Macmillan.
Lerner, A. P. (1953) "The Essential Properties of Interest and Money," *Quarterly Journal of Economics* (reprinted in *Essays In Economic Analysis*, London: Macmillan (1953)).
Malthus, T. R. (1820) *Principles Of Political Economy Considered with a View to their Practical Application,* London: John Murray (reprinted in the Variorum Edition ed. J. Pullen (1998) Cambridge: Cambridge University Press).
Robinson, J. (1962) *Essays in the Theory of Economic Growth*, London: Macmillan.
—— (1965) "Own Rates of Interest", *Collected Economic Papers 3*, Oxford: Blackwell.
Rogers, C. (1997) "Existence of a Monetary Long-Period Unemployment Equilibrium," in G. C. Harcourt and P. A. Riach (eds), *A "Second Edition" of the General Theory,* London: Routledge.
Rutherford, R. P. (1987) "Malthus and Keynes," *Oxford Economic Papers* 39 (March): 175–89.
Rymes, T .K. (1998a) "On Rae and Capital and Growth," in O. F. Hamouda, C. Lee and D. Mair (eds), *The Economics of John Rae*, London: Routledge.
—— (1998b) "Keynes and Anchorless Banking," *Journal of the History of Economic Thought* 20: 71–82.
Samuelson, P. A. (1979) "Land and the Rate of Interest," in H. I. Greenfield *et al.* (eds), *Theory for Economic Efficiency: Essays In The Honor Of Abba P. Lerner*, Cambridge, Mass.: MIT Press.
Selgin, G. (1997) *Less Than Zero*, IEA Hobart Paper no. 132, Institute for Economic Affairs.
Waterman, A. M. C. (1998) "Malthus, Mathematics, and the Mythology of Coherence," *History of Political Economy* 30(4): 571–600.
—— (1998) "Reappraisal of 'Malthus the Economist', 1933–97," *History of Political Economy* 30(3): 293–334.
Wicksell, K. [1898] (1936) *Interest and Prices*, trans. R. F. Kahn, London: Macmillan.

19 Theory, application and the canon

The case of Mill and Jevons

Sandra Peart

> Boundary questions, it has been well said, are always perplexing.
> (*Economist* 1882: 845)

Introduction

Whatever disputes remain about the nature and content of the "canon" of economics, it is widely accepted that the boundary of economic science was narrowed throughout the nineteenth century (Winch 1972). This chapter offers a partial explanation for that narrowing in the methodological developments that occurred during the second half of the century. For reasons of practicality in the face of pronounced "multiplicity of cause," John Stuart Mill called, in his 1836 Essay *On the Definition of Political Economy; and on the Method of Investigation Proper to It*, and again in his 1843 *Logic*, for a separate and specialized science of political economy. The problem of multiple cause implied that the science should be substantially deductive in nature. Yet Mill accorded a role to induction, in the establishment of the basic causal framework, and to the process of verifying the accuracy of the theoretical analysis. Revision of the theory in the light of such verification established a key link between theory, and application.

In the 1870s this method was strenuously resisted by the British Historicists, notably John Kells Ingram and T. E. Cliffe Leslie.[1] Contemporary critics of economic method feared that the deductive method, abstracting as it did from the full array of causes that influenced economic phenomena, would lead to unjustifiable neglect of relevant causes. By contrast, Ingram and Leslie called for empirical studies, upon which they envisaged the theory of economics (and the broader sociological study they favored) could be constructed.

William Stanley Jevons's response to the critics of economic method served to narrow the canon while at the same time yielding a place for empirical studies within the discipline. He called for subdivision within economics, along both subject matter and methodological lines (Black 1972, Peart 1996). He defended the substantially deductive method outlined by Mill for economic theory, and then called for "subdivision" of the discipline as a remedy to its "chaotic" state. Historical studies would, consequently, become a specialization within the discipline alongside "empirical," "applied," and "theoretical" studies. As such, the historical and empirical study of economics would not supplant but would instead complement the theoretical basis for the discipline. Jevons never clearly spelled out the relationships among the separate specializations of economics, yet two features of his calls for subdivision will become clear. First, the role of historical and empirical study is said to be limited to verifying the truth of the theory in widely different settings. Second, an implicit hierarchy was envisaged, in which theory, with its mathematical precision, logical consistency and universally relevant status, is granted an elevated status, above applications.

Such calls for increased subdivision served, perhaps unwittingly, to insulate theory – a theory now said to be universally applicable – from evidence, and to facilitate the development of empirical studies that were not necessarily well linked to theory. For a mechanism was furnished whereby the theory was separated from application, and while the theory was presumed invariant to time and space, variations were presumed to occur in application. Most significantly, what such variation implies for theory is never spelled out. However, if the canon as it is usually defined consists of theoretical principles that are central to the discipline, then questionable, refuted or otherwise doubtful principles can be relegated to subdivisions – to what Jevons called "applied" or "historical" economics – and do not call the canon itself into question.

Mill's case for specialization

The debate on method of the late nineteenth century was intimately linked with that on Ireland, in which Mill was an active participant.[2] The Irish question in fact constituted a catalyst for the issue of whether the axioms of political economy might be considered universally relevant, or of limited temporal and spatial applicability. Mill's proposal for widespread land reform in Ireland and his review essay, *Leslie and the Land Question*, are methodologically revealing. For his position, like that of the historicists, is that institutional and cultural differences in Ireland may render the conclusions of political economy invalid there: Mill was keenly aware of the limited relevance of conclusions developed in the context of the English institutional and cultural arrangements. It is no coincidence that while Jevons rarely objects to Mill's policy recommendations, Ireland constitutes one instance where he finds Mill's position – advocating broad land reform – questionable.[3] Jevons wrote little directly on Ireland. His objections to Mill's reform proposals appear in an 1880 *Contemporary Review* article, "Experimental Legislation and the Drink Traffic," where he argued that Mill's reform proposal was too wide-ranging. In its stead, Jevons favored peasant proprietorship on a small – and presumably voluntary – scale (Jevons 1882: 274). Here, as in his *Theory of Political Economy*, he thus moved ever so slightly towards removing economic analysis from institutional concerns.

Perhaps more than any economist of his time or since, Mill was a synthesizer. However, for reasons of practicality in the face of multiple causation, he called for specialization in the social sciences. The argument for specialization presumed that to discover how humans behave under the influence of all circumstances, one should first isolate causes and study the resulting effects separately. This is precisely the argument that Jevons was later to use. Both also presumed that the process was generally additive, and thus that the separate effects of causes, once known, could be added to yield a total.

Mill maintained that economists faced great difficulties as a result of the "composition of causes" that characterizes the phenomena they study. Since "every attribute of the social body is influenced by innumerable causes," social phenomena, for Mill, were characterized by a pronounced multiplicity of cause:

> the phenomena of society do not depend, in essentials, on some one agency or law of human nature, with only inconsiderable modifications from others. The whole of the qualities of human nature influence those phenomena, and there is not one, the removal or any great alteration of which would not materially affect the whole aspect of society, and change more or less the sequences of social phenomena generally.
> (Mill [1843] 1973, vol. 8: 894)

Recognition of this problem underscores all of Mill's writing on method. Two major implications resulted from this preoccupation. First, in the face of such complexity, Mill argued strongly in favor of a deductive method modeled after physics, that compounds the effects of various causes considered separately:

> The Social Science, therefore (which, by a convenient barbarism, has been termed Sociology), is a deductive science; not, indeed, after the model of geometry, but after that of the more complex physical sciences. It infers the law of each effect from the laws of causation on which that effect depends; not, however, from the law merely of one cause, as in the geometrical method, but by considering all the causes which conjunctly influence the effect, and compounding their laws with one another. Its method, in short, is the Concrete Deductive Method: that of which astronomy furnishes the most perfect, natural philosophy a somewhat less perfect, example, and the employment of which, with the adaptations and precautions required by the subject, is beginning to regenerate physiology.
> (Mill [1843] 1973, vol. 8: 895)

Multiplicity of cause implied that induction was insufficient to establish causality: "the causes on which any class of phenomena depend are so imperfectly accessible to our observation that we cannot ascertain, by a proper induction, their numerical laws" (ibid., vol. 7: 620). Because possibilities for experimentation were so limited, and since theoretical specification of effects in the face of pronounced multiple cause was impossible, using the "laws of quantity" to "calculate forward to an effect," (what Jevons would call "inductive quantification"), was inappropriate in social science (ibid., vol. 7: 620–1). (For a demonstration of the difference between Jevons and Mill in this respect, see Peart 1993.) In such instances:

> specific experience affords nothing amounting to empirical laws. This is particularly the case where the object is to determine the effect of any one

social cause among a great number acting simultaneously; the effect, for example of corn laws, or of a prohibitive commercial system generally.
(Mill [1843] 1973, vol. 8: 908; cf. vol. 4: 332)[4]

Such complications meant that great caution was in order. Yet while limited experimental possibilities rendered it impossible to infer laws of causation through observation, the basic causal structure was accessible through observation and introspection (Mill [1836] 1967, vol. 4: 329; Hausman 1992).

Second, and perhaps more importantly given the theme of this chapter, the complexity of economic phenomena rendered it impossible to specify all the causal factors at work in all cases. Consequently, Mill urged that scientists select the main (or "general") causes in action, and reason based on those selections. This formed the methodological basis for limited specialization within social science:

> By reasoning from that one law of human nature, and from the principal outward circumstances (whether universal or confined to particular states of society) which operate upon the human mind through that law, we may be enabled to explain and predict this portion of the phenomena of society, so far as they depend on that class of circumstances only.... A department of science may thus be constructed which has received the name of Political Economy.
> (Mill [1843] 1973, vol. 8: 901)

The outcome of such a procedure is "hypothetical," correct only to the extent that no additional causes interfere with it:

> All the general propositions which can be framed by the deductive science, are therefore, in the strictest sense of the word, hypothetical. They are grounded on some suppositious set of circumstances, and declare how some given cause would operate in those circumstances, supposing that no others were combined with them. If the set of circumstances supposed have been copied from those of any existing society, the conclusions will be true of that society, provided, and in as far as, the effect of those circumstances shall not be modified by others which have not been taken into account.
> (Mill [1843] 1973, vol. 8: 900)[5]

In his 1836 *Essay*, Mill's language was somewhat stronger in pointing to the hypothetical character of economic reasoning: political economy, he writes there,

> does not treat of the whole of man's nature as modified by the social state, nor of the whole conduct of man in society. It is concerned with him solely as a being who desires to possess wealth, and who is capable of judging of the comparative efficacy of means for obtaining that end. It predicts only such of the phenomena of the social state as take place in consequence of

the pursuit of wealth. It makes entire abstraction of every other human passion or motive; except those which may be regarded as perpetually antagonizing principles to the desire of wealth, namely, aversion to labour, and desire of the present enjoyment of costly indulgences.
(Mill [1836] 1967, vol. 4: 321)

Thus, in this context Mill argued that one abstracts from the multitude of desires and motivations that prompt a being to act in a social context, and reasons based on the premise that economic actions are mainly influenced by self-interest.[6]

Recognition of the inadequate causal basis of analysis necessarily meant that such reasoning was based on an explicitly-recognized incomplete set of causes: economists' deductive conclusions were derived from a set of causes that abstracted from, (or held constant), additional causes known to affect the phenomena in question. The resulting reasoning would therefore provide an adequate representation of reality only if all of the general causes influencing the phenomena have been taken into account by the theorist (ibid.: 329; see Hausman 1992). Even in these circumstances, however, partial or disturbing causes were bound also to influence the phenomena on occasion, so that the conclusions of the theory were never borne out completely by observation. As a consequence of this recognition, Mill insisted on an additional methodological step, of verification. The deductive conclusions of political economy, he urged, were to be checked constantly against specific experience. The importance of combining the a priori method with verification increased as the "composition of causes" became more pronounced; "[a]t every step," Mill urged scientists

> to assure ourselves that no other law of nature has superseded, or intermingled its operation with, those which are the premises of the reasoning; and how can this be done by merely looking at the words? We must not only be constantly thinking of the phenomena themselves, but we must be constantly studying them; making ourselves acquainted with the peculiarities of every case to which we attempt to apply our general principles.
> (Mill [1843] 1973, vol. 7: 710)

Verification was the means to assessing the effects of "partial" or "disturbing" causes, which, once determined, might be added to or subtracted from the effects of general causes (Mill [1836] 1967, vol. 4: 330). Disturbing causes (which "have their laws, as the causes which are thereby disturbed have theirs") might be "brought within the pale of the abstract science if it were worthwhile" (ibid.: 331), "inserting among its hypotheses a fresh and still more complex combination of circumstances, and so adding *pro hâc vice* a supplementary chapter or appendix, or at least a supplementary theory, to the abstract science" (ibid.). However the role of verification was not limited to this; it might also reveal

> errors in thought, still more serious than what can with any propriety be termed a disturbing cause. It often reveals to us that the basis itself of our

whole argument is insufficient; that the data, from which we had reasoned, comprise only a part, and not always the most important part, of the circumstances by which the result is really determined.

(Mill [1836] 1967, vol. 4: 332)

Two types of revisions of the theory thus result from the process of verification. A set of general causes, A, B, and C is used to predict the outcome E. E* is observed, leading the scientist to revise the causal framework by adding D to the model. Alternatively, the procedure of verification might reveal that the axioms have been inferred from an incomplete set of circumstances. In this instance observation of E* leads the scientist to revise A, B and C to A*, B* and C* (Peart 1993). Mill never clarified, however, how one is to distinguish between these two problems.

A key consequence of the recognized inadequacy of the reasoning was the limited predictive capacity of the science:

> Sociology, considered as a system of deductions *a priori*, can not be a science of positive predictions, but only of tendencies. We may be able to conclude, from the laws of human nature applied to the circumstances of a given state of society, that a particular cause will operate in a certain manner unless counteracted; but we can never be assured to what extent or amount it will so operate, or affirm with certainty that it will not be counteracted; because we can seldom know, even approximately, all the agencies which may co-exist with it, and still less calculate the collective result of so many combined elements.
>
> (Mill [1843] 1973, vol. 8: 898)[7]

The conclusions of political economy were consequently of limited relevance, either because they were true only to the extent that additional causes did not interfere with those specified in the reasoning, or because additional causes whose effects were presumed constant had in fact varied.[8]

The significance of Mill's emphasis on verification for the theory–practice distinction (and the nature and flexibility of the canon of economics), is that it provides a loosely-defined but nonetheless significant mechanism whereby the basic causal structure can be modified, as a result of close empirical scrutiny, in order better to describe "real world" phenomena. One telling instance of such modification involves the basic self-interest motivation.[9] Here Mill altered the theoretical model in order to incorporate the influence of "custom." The analysis entails an attempt to account theoretically for observations of contemporary market structures. It is a matter of circumstance how custom is to be classified; in some instances the influence of custom is so strong and pervasive that it must be treated as the general cause, relegating to competition the role of disturbance:

> hitherto it is only in the great centres of business that retail transactions have been chiefly, or even much, determined, by competition. Elsewhere it rather acts, when it acts at all, as an occasional disturbing influence; the

> habitual regulator is custom, modified from time to time by notions existing in the minds of purchasers and sellers, of some kind of equity or justice.
>
> (Mill [1836] 1967, vol. 4: 243)

Methodological challenges

In the latter half of the century, and especially during the 1870s, several attacks on the nature and scope of Economics were mounted by, among others, J. K. Ingram, and Cliffe Leslie.[10] These attacks focused first and foremost on the relative roles of induction and deduction in economics, and on the legitimacy of studying economic phenomena separately from social phenomena.[11] So successful were they that in 1876 Sir Francis Galton attempted to have economics removed from Section F of the British Association for the Advancement of Science, and the following year the Adam Smith Centennial Dinner of the Political Economy Club broke into an acrimonious discussion of the nature of economics. Following the dinner, the *Pall Mall Gazette* reported that "the natural philosophers have been frightened out of their wits by the ladies who flock to the Section of 'Economic Science and Statistics' and who insist on reading papers and starting discussions which are not only not scientific but which savour of the singular antipathy to science for its own sake common to all the feminine movements of the day" (Jevons 1972–81, vol. 4: 272–3).

Ingram's Presidential Address to Section F (Economic Science and Statistics) of the British Association at the 1878 Dublin meeting consisted of "an exhaustive argument in vindication of the right of Political Economy and Statistics to citizenship in the commonwealth of science" (*The Times*, August 17 1878, p. 10). Relying squarely on the authority of Comte (whose influence on Ingram is very strong), Mill and Spencer, Ingram defended the scientific status of the study of "economic facts." But the question that followed was in what sense economics was scientific. Ingram strongly objected to the method advocated by Mill, which attempted to specify a limited set of causal factors and study them in depth:

> the pretension of the economist to isolate the special phenomena they study, the economic phenomena of society, from all the rest – its material aspect from its intellectual, moral, and political aspects, and to constitute an independent science, dealing with the former alone, to the exclusion of the latter.
>
> (Ingram 1878: 608)

In opposition to that procedure, Ingram urged that the mutual relationship between economics and "the general body of human knowledge" constituted "the most radical and vital" question of economic studies, one on which the future of political economy depended (ibid.).[12]

Ingram reiterated these arguments in his popular textbook, *History of Political Economy*: "Economics must be constantly regarded as forming only one department of the larger science of Sociology, in vital connection with its other departments, and with the moral synthesis which is the crown of the whole intellectual system" (Ingram [1888] 1967: 296). Social phenomena, he argued there, were not independent one from another as was commonly presumed, but were instead mutually determining. As a result, isolated consideration of one set of causes necessarily neglected key determining influences; most importantly, also, such procedures neglected the "high moral issues" to which, Ingram contended, political economy is "subservient" (ibid.: 297).

Ingram allowed that, for Mill, the method of political economy entailed a key role for verification. Yet Mill is said to "halt" between the correct method of the scientific study of sociological phenomena – the method revealed to him by Comte – *a posteriori*, and the deductive method of "his youth" (Ingram [1888] 1967: 150). Ingram was consequently critical of Mill's reliance on abstraction: Mill's hypothetical "economic man" comes in for particularly harsh criticism as an unrealistic and thus unscientific construct (ibid.: 151–2). Cairnes receives harsh criticism as well; his logical method of political economy is said to constitute "a retrogression in methodology" because, unlike Mill, Cairnes concludes that verification is unnecessary in political economy (ibid.: 150–1). Ingram attributes the "larger and more philosophical spirit in which Mill dealt with social subjects" to the influence of Comte (ibid.: 146).

In a series of articles written in the 1870s, the Irish political economist, Cliffe Leslie similarly challenged the claim to distinctness by political economy, and argued in favor of developing a historical method:

> The truth is, that the whole economy of every nation, as regards the occupations and pursuits of both sexes, the nature, amount, distribution and consumption of wealth, is the result of a long evolution in which there has been both continuity and change, and of which the economical side is only a particular aspect or phase. And the laws of which it is the result must be sought in history and the general laws of society and social evolution.
> (Leslie 1876: 227)[15]

Little had been accomplished, however, in the discovery of such laws of evolution, and Leslie warned that such important work would soon be taken over by sociologists, if political economists continued their neglect (ibid.: 241). He blamed political economists – and particularly the formalization of economic theory – for such lack of progress: "The bane of political economy has been the haste of its students to possess themselves of a complete and symmetrical system, solving all the problems before it with mathematical certainty and exactness" (ibid.: 241).

Leslie's criticism focused on what he regarded as overly abstract methods used by political economists. He allowed that Mill possessed some historical sensibilities, but argued that Mill's training in the Ricardian school and methods caused him to neglect or suppress such sensibilities (ibid.: 221). Consequently, Millian-style analysis overly simplified the causal structure underlying economic phenomena:

> The real defect of the treatment by economists of these other principles is, that it is superficial and unphilosophical; that no attempt has been made even to enumerate them adequately, much less to measure their relative force in different states of society; and that they are employed simply to prop up rude generalizations for which the authority of 'laws' is claimed. They serve, along with other conditions, to give some sort of support to saving clauses, – such as 'allowing for differences in the nature of different employments,' 'caeteris paribus,' 'in the absence of disturbing causes,' 'making allowance for friction' – by which the 'law' that wages and profits tend to equality eludes scrutiny. Had the actual operation of the motives in question been investigated, it would have been seen to vary widely in different states of society, and under different conditions.
>
> (Leslie 1876: 226)

In opposition to Mill (and, as we will see later, to Jevons) Leslie tended to focus on just those causes the economists downplayed:

> Had Mr. Mill looked to actual life, he must have at once perceived that among the strongest desires confounded in the abstract 'desire for wealth,' are desires for the present enjoyment of luxuries; and that the aversion to labour itself has been one of the principal causes of inventions and improvements which abridge it.
>
> (Leslie 1876: 225)

In fairness to both Leslie and Mill, however, one might note that Leslie's criticisms were generally aimed not so much at Mill as at the simplistic and narrow so-called "followers" of classical economists' methods. In particular, politicians who based poorly designed policy measures loosely on arguments of classical economists, come in for harsh criticism.

Like Ingram, Leslie was also critical of calls for the development of a separate science of political economy. He allowed that the science might select a "special class of social phenomena for special investigation," but he insisted that it must nonetheless "investigate all the forces and laws by which they are governed" (Leslie 1879a: 404).

Leslie also objected to any claim that the maximization axiom was universally relevant:

> Mr. Jevons, though favourably disposed by philosophical culture and tastes towards historical investigation in economics, has urged on behalf of deduction from the acquisitive principle, that even the lower animals act from a similar motive.
>
> (Leslie 1879a: 389)

While the limited capacity of the human mind rendered the pragmatic separate study of economic phenomena a necessary evil, Leslie cautioned against paying insufficient attention to "all the causes" affecting such phenomena. Thus, he argued, it is legitimate to make economic phenomena, the division of labour, the nature, amount, and distribution of national riches, the subject of particular examination; provided that all the causes affecting them be taken into account. To isolate a single force, even if a real force and not a mere abstraction, and to call deductions from it alone the laws of wealth, can lead only to error, and is radically unscientific

(Leslie 1879a: 404)

The problem was all the more serious because economists "more often still have jumped to the laws without heed to the phenomena" (ibid.: 378).

In contrast to the substantially deductive method of political economists, Leslie urged that a combination of methods be used in economics.[13] Specifically, he advocated the "formal incorporation of economic science with statistics," a combination which would tend to correct the tendency of one-sided reliance on theory on the part of economists, and on facts, on the part of statisticians (Leslie 1873a: 377; cf. 378).

In a telling indictment of the state of political economy late in the decade, the Oxford professor Bonamy Price questioned the limited achievements of the discipline as well as its very scientific nature (Price 1879: 182).[14] Price objected to the treatment of political economy as an exact science, a treatment encouraged by Ricardo (though Price suggested that Ricardo did not actually regard economics as an exact science) and, to some extent, J. S. Mill (ibid.: 198). In the case of Mill, however, Price argued that

His whole temper and disposition rendered him incapable of being restrained by bounds inapplicable to the subject, even when they had been prescribed by himself. Consequently, throughout his whole work, he boldly deserts, whenever it suits him, the endeavour to write scientifically; and the best parts of his work are when he does so

(Price 1879: 198)[15]

It is, in fact, this attention to detail as well as the fuzzy boundary to the subject matter that Price admired in Mill, and the lack of which he objected to in Jevons (ibid.: 200–1).

Jevons's response to the challenge

Jevons's defense of economics in the face of such challenges was spelled out in an 1876 lecture delivered at University College, "The Future of Political Economy," as well as the 1879 'Preface' and 'Introduction' to his *Theory of Political Economy*. Having recognized in the lecture that "the state of the science" was "almost chaotic" (Jevons [1905] 1965: 191), his response to the critics was two-sided. First, Jevons called for further subdivision within the discipline, now in fact proceeding a step beyond Mill, advocating a permanent separation of economic from sociological studies, and subdivided "historical," "empirical," "theoretical," and "concrete," or applied, studies within economics. For the theoretical study of economics, Jevons's methodological recommendation was very much in line with that of Mill. Where he differed from Mill was in his insistence on further specialization within the discipline.

In addition, and somewhat paradoxically, Jevons also favored the use of statistical methods in economics, and he conducted some pioneering statistical studies himself. Not surprisingly, this won him some support from the dissenters above, most notably Cliffe Leslie. Leslie remained troubled, however, by Jevons's inattention to the full potential array of causal factors influencing the specific phenomena under investigation.

In his 1876 lecture, Jevons recognized the "absolutely essential" nature of the type of historically based empirical study advocated by Leslie (Jevons [1905] 1965: 196). Yet he held fast, in opposition to Leslie and other Historicists, to the argument that historical studies would neither "destroy" nor "replace" "abstract theory." He opposed the historicists' argument outlined earlier concerning the limited relevance of the conclusions of political economy, arguing instead that the laws of political economy – including the "most fundamental" law "that human wants are limited in extent" – "are so simple in their foundation that they would apply, more or less completely, to all human beings of whom we have any knowledge" (ibid.: 196). Jevons concluded, "They seem to be in a very rudimentary state among the Eskimo. ... Nevertheless we can trace in [the] transaction of the borrowed boat the simple principles which are at the basis of economy" (ibid.: 196), and he speculated that "I should not despair of tracing the action of the postulates of political economy among some of the more intelligent classes of animals. Dogs certainly have strong though perhaps limited ideas of property" (ibid.: 197).

As a consequence of his conviction that "the first principles of political economy are so widely true and applicable that they may be considered universally true as regards human nature," Jevons argued that the role of historical political economy would necessarily be limited to "exhibiting" and "verifying" the "long-continued action of its laws in most widely different states of society" (ibid.: 197).[16] In sharp contrast with the historicists, then, Jevons carved a specialization within economics (theory) in which individual – rather than social – phenomena were placed squarely at the centre of the analysis.[17]

However, Jevons allowed that Leslie's calls for historical studies of economic phenomena should not go unheeded. He called for subdivision within the discipline, and argued that historical studies should constitute one of the subdivisions within the discipline. "The fact is," Jevons maintained, "it will no longer be possible to treat political economy as if it were a single undivided and indivisible science."[18] He enumerated several ways in which such subdivision should occur – along both the lines of subject matter, as well as methods. Thus, he argued first:

> There is, firstly, the old distinction of the laws of the science, according as they treat of the production, exchange, distribution, or consumption of wealth. In this respect economy may be regarded as an aggregate of two or more different sciences, there being, in fact, little connection between the principles which should guide us in production and those which apply in distribution or consumption.
>
> (Jevons [1905] 1965: 197–8)

In addition, a division should occur according to whether the subject matter were theoretical, or applied.[19] Here, Jevons insisted again on the "generality" of the theoretical laws, while allowing that variation might occur in the "concrete" applications:

> Passing now to a second aspect, political economy will naturally be divided according as it is abstract or concrete. The theory of the science consists of those general laws which are so simple in nature, and so deeply grounded in the constitution of man and the outer world, that they remain the same throughout all those ages which are within our consideration. But though the laws are the same they may receive widely different applications in the concrete. The primary laws of motion are the same, whether they be applied to solids, liquids, or gases, though the phenomena obeying those laws are apparently so different. Just as there is a general science of mechanics, so we must have a general science or theory of economy.
> (Jevons [1905] 1965: 198)

But Jevons went farther. He called next for subdivisions of "concrete political economy" along the lines of newly constituted subject matter:

> Concrete political economy, however, can hardly be called one science, but already consists of many extensive branches of inquiry. Currency, banking, the relations of labour and capital, those of landlord and tenant, pauperism, taxation, and finance, are some of the principal portions of applied political economy, all involving the same ultimate laws manifested in most different circumstances. In a subject of such appalling extent and complexity as currency, for instance, we depend upon the laws of supply and demand, of consumption and production of commodities as applied to the precious metals or other materials of money. In the science of banking and the money market we have a very difficult application of the same laws to capital in general. This separation of the concrete branches of the science is, however, sufficiently obvious and recognised, and I need not dwell further on it. The general conclusion, then, to which I come is that political economy must for the future be looked upon as an aggregate of sciences.
> (Jevons [1905] 1965: 200; cf. 206)[20]

In the future, and in contrast with Mill, Jevons envisaged the growth but not the synthesis of such sciences (ibid.: 206). As Steedman has argued in a different context, the theory/practice distinction does not in and of itself imply preeminence of the logical core over application (Steedman 1998: 17). It does seem, however, that in Jevons's mind there was a presumed hierarchy, theory, with its generality and logical consistency, being regarded as superior to "application."

Jevons's *Theory of Political Economy* contained his other major strong plea for subdivision. In this context he alluded to the "remarkable discussion [that] has been lately going on in the reviews and journals concerning the logical method of the science, touching even the question whether there exists any such science at all" (Jevons [1871] 1911: xv). He recognized "a spirit of very active criticism," especially in Leslie's *Hermathena* article, which attempted to "to dissipate altogether the deductive science of Ricardo" (ibid.: xvi).[21] Again he urged that the "present chaotic state of Economics arises from the confusing together of several branches of knowledge" (ibid.: xvi–vii), a problem to be remedied by subdivision:

> Subdivision is the remedy. We must distinguish the empirical element from the abstract theory, from the applied theory, and from the more detailed art of finance and administration. Thus will arise various sciences, such as commercial statistics, the mathematical theory of economics, systematic and descriptive economics, economic sociology, and fiscal science. There may even be a kind of cross subdivision of the sciences; that is to say, there will be division into branches as regards the subject, and division according to the manner of treating the branch of the subject. The manner may be theoretical, empirical, historical, or practical; the subject may be capital and labour, currency, banking, taxation, land tenure, etc. – not to speak of the more fundamental division of the science as it treats of consumption, production, exchange, and distribution of wealth. In fact, the whole subject is so extensive, intricate, and diverse, that it is absurd to suppose it can be treated in any single book or in any single manner. It is no more one science than statistics, dynamics, the theory of heat, optics, magnetoelectricity, telegraphy, navigation, and photographic chemistry are one science.
> (Jevons [1871] 1911: xvii)

Jevons reiterated the case for the universal status of theory:

> But as all the physical sciences have their basis more or less obviously in the general principles of mechanics, so all branches and divisions of economic science must be pervaded by certain general principles. It is to the investigation of such principles – to the tracing out of the mechanics of self-interest and utility – that this essay has been devoted".
> (Jevons [1871] 1911: xvii–xviii)

The theory of political economy, the "logical method" propounded here by Jevons – in opposition to the calls for increased inductive content put forth by Leslie and others – was that advocated by Mill (as well as Cairnes):

> [Mill] considers that we may start from some obvious psychological law, as for instance, that a greater gain is preferred to a smaller one, and we may then reason downwards, and predict the phenomena which will be produced in society by such a law. The causes in action in any community are, indeed, so complicated that we shall seldom be able to discover the undisturbed effects of any one law, but, so far as we can analyse the statistical phenomena observed, we obtain a verification of our reasoning.
> (Jevons [1871] 1911: 16–17)

In contrast with Mill, Jevons called this the "Complete Method," as "implying that it combines observation, deduction, and induction in the most complete and perfect way . . . induction itself in its essential form":

> Possessing certain facts of observation, we frame an hypothesis as to the laws governing those facts; we reason from the hypothesis deductively to the results to be expected; and we then examine these results in connection with the facts in question; coincidence confirms the whole reasoning; conflict obliges us either to seek for disturbing causes, or else to abandon our hypothesis.
>
> (Jevons [1871] 1911: 17–18)

While Jevons concurred with Leslie and Ingram "so far as to allow that historical investigation is of great importance in Social Science," he reiterated his argument that "instead of converting our present science of economics into an historical science, utterly destroying it in the process," he would "perfect and develop" theoretical economics, while "at the same time" erecting "a new branch of social science on an historical foundation" (ibid.: 20).[22]

Jevons's own career very much followed the prescription for subdivision. While he refrained from complementing his theoretical treatment with empirical methods in the *Theory*, he called there for the collection of improved economic data on consumption (Jevons [1871] 1911: 10–11). Further, while alluding to the difficulties involved, he called for complementary statistical endeavors in order to invest theory with the "reality and life of fact" (ibid.: 22; cf. 1905: 195). He was, and remains, well known as an applied, as well as a theoretical, economist.[23]

Most importantly, perhaps, Jevons contributed significant empirical studies throughout his career, contributions that were well known and granted at least qualified approbation by Leslie, Ingram, and other economists of his day. In fact, in correspondence with Jevons, Léon Walras remarked that he knew Jevons's reputation as an applied statistician rather than as a theorist (May 23 1874; Jevons 1972–81, vol. 4: 45). Jevons's work on the value of gold attracted wide attention in the 1860s and well into this century; as a consequence Irving Fisher concluded that Jevons was the "father of index numbers" (Fisher 1922: 459). Keynes praised Jevons's ability in this regard to "survey his material with the prying eyes and fertile, controlled imagination of the natural scientist" (Keynes 1951: 268). Jevons's attempts to decompose time series into secular and cyclical components also earned him high praise (Mitchell 1928: 384) and the title "founder of econometric method" (Robertson 1951: 247).[24]

In Jevons's "reconstruction" of political economy, he made one important additional step, one that Mill would never sanction and which greatly troubled Leslie. In such applications as the gold studies, Jevons argued that causes other than the gold influx "balanced" in the drawing of a mean, and thus could be neglected at least in 'large enough' samples (Peart 1995). Though he was very much in favor of such empirical studies, Leslie – true to his concerns outlined earlier – criticized the method of averages used by Jevons in the gold studies. In a paper that argued strongly in favor of uniting economics and statistics,

Leslie presented a general criticism of the assumption that, in application, one might ignore omitted causes, or presume they "balance":

> And we have in this matter an illustration of the defective character of that kind of statistical inquiry which confines itself to the collection of a multitude of instances of facts, without reference to causes. It must be allowed that the principles laid down by the illustrious Quetelet rather tend to foster the error to which we advert. He assumed that by enlarging the number of instances, we eliminate chance and arrive at general and stable laws of conditions. But a great number of instances does not give us their law, or justify us in any positive conclusion respecting the future. New conditions, for example, have been acting on prices during the last two years, and mere tables of prices for the last twenty or ten years, confound years in which those causes were in operation with years in which they were not.
> (Leslie 1873a: 381)

Thus, Leslie was critical of what he took as Jevons's inadequate attention to the full array of causal factors influencing price data. In opposition to Jevons he stressed that the gold discoveries were not the only cause of the measured price alteration: the method of averages, he contended,

> does not show the real movement of prices or the real depreciation of money; the tables omit some of the chief elements of the cost of living; the prices compared are wholesale prices, while the purchasing power of an income depends on retail prices; and, by ascribing the whole rise of prices to the new gold, this method conceals the material fact that the gold is only one of a plurality of causes lately tending to raise them
> (Leslie 1873b: 349)

Leslie questioned Jevons's assumption that "the new gold [constitutes] the sole cause of the rise in prices arrived at, on the ground that the 'average must, in all reasonable probability, represent some single influence acting on all commodities,'" and argued, in opposition to Jevons, "But why not a plurality of influences?" (ibid.: 353). Leslie's own investigation focused on this very "plurality of causes," and how their influences differed across different prices: "The actual situation of matters in England is, then, that a number of causes, of which the new gold is only one, have raised the cost of living" (ibid.: 355).

Conclusions: implications of the calls for subdivision

These were complex disputes, complicated by Irish policy issues, views on Ricardian distribution theory, and gray areas where the major contributors shared common ground. Neither Mill nor Jevons entirely opposed the historically-based treatment of economic phenomena propounded by Ingram and Leslie. The Historicists' sharpest criticisms were often directed at naïve or narrow economic analysis relied upon by politicians who proclaimed economic theory widely transferable (to Ireland, in particular). Still, the foregoing suggests that economics moved, with Jevons pushing it, a step away from Mill and perhaps two away from the Historicists by the end of the 1870s. Subdivision, with economic theory placed in a position superior to application and few clearly spelled out connections among specialties, reversed the scientific order envisaged by J. K. Ingram and Cliffe Leslie.

It would, of course, be unwise to attribute the development of the economics canon following Jevons's death in 1882, to his contributions to these methodological debates. And it would be simplistic to suggest that Jevons alone is responsible for narrowing the economics canon late in the century, or that the methodology debates occurred without reference to policy issues which were in fact of great significance, especially to Mill, Ingram and Leslie. The Irish question formed a backdrop to these methodological debates throughout the decade, and issues of whether the axioms of political economy were universally relevant or whether economic behavior could be studied in abstraction from the institutional (and, as they often put it) "moral" aspects of the economy, were often framed in terms of the Irish question (Koot 1975).

Certainly also, as outlined earlier, Jevons's own example was by no means narrow.[25] In addition, although there is enough evidence to suggest that Jevons influenced these debates and helped to silence the critics of economics, it would be foolhardy not to recognize two later contributions: by J. M. Keynes, and by Alfred Marshall. But it would be equally foolhardy to neglect, as many have, Jevons's influence on the debate and to conclude that it was Keynes and Marshall alone who caused the demise of Historicism in England.

Whatever the effect of Jevons's methodological recommendations, there is no evidence that he made them strategically, in order to counter the Historicists' influence. Instead, it is much more likely that Jevons called for subdivision because he genuinely believed this was the fruitful methodological approach for the future of his discipline.

It does bear noting, however, that Jevons made something of a virtue of disconnectedness. To some, Jevons's position on the methodology of economics appears rather unfinished. Unlike Mill's *Logic*, there is no section in his 1874 *Principles of Science* on the methodology of social science. Jevons never related the methodological recommendations in the 1876 lecture or the 1879 edition of his *Theory* to his *Principles of Science*. Some have surmised that he might have eventually tried to relate apparently disconnected portions of his work (see the *Guardian*, September 1 1886: 'Review of *Letters and Journal*', p. 1282; Jevons Archive 6/50/20). Others, like Keynes (1951), have concluded that Jevons's best work was finished at the time of his death.

Even beyond the Historicists' concerns, then, there is evidence that Jevons's contemporaries were troubled by his calls for separation of theory and practice, and the resulting disconnected nature of Jevons's work. J. E. Cairnes, for instance, found Jevons's inattention to practice troubling. His distrust of the theory-practice distinction explains, in part, why Cairnes objected to the formalization of economic theory in Jevons:

> When mathematics are carried further than this ["very limited application"] in the moral or social sciences, and used for conducting processes of reasoning, without constant reference to the concrete meaning of the

> terms for which the mathematical symbols are employed, I own I regard the practice with profound distrust.
>
> (Cairnes 1872: 76)

Contemporary summaries of Jevons's achievements also focused on his calls for the separation of theory and practice. Philip Wicksteed's (very favorable) review of the posthumously published *Letters and Journal* suggested that one of Jevons's major achievements lay in his having provided social scientists with the means to separate the historical from the theoretical "with vice-like firmness":

> It would be idle to attempt any exposition here of the precise nature of Jevons's discoveries; but his disciples may claim that he has given them an instrument by which they can hold down any problem of pure economics with vice-like firmness, and submit it to a precise and delicate treatment hitherto undreamed of, that he has provided them with a reagent by which they can *precipitate* the assumptions that pervade, in solution, the works of all the economists, and can separate the theoretical from the historical element in their researches, that he has at last revealed the true nature of "exchange-value" and its relation to "value in use," thereby putting an end to the age-long controversy between England and France and bringing the theory of "supply and demand" out of the clouds, that he has laid the foundations of the true theory of interest, thereby at once confuting the logic and the methods and justifying the aspirations of Mr. Ruskin and the Socialists, and, in a word, that he has made one part of economics actually amenable to the methods of the exact sciences, and has put it beyond the reach of eloquence or ingenuity to make the other parts *appear* to be (as they are not amenable to those methods).
>
> (Wicksteed 1886: 646)

Jevons's calls for subdivision of the discipline provided the means by which the method of Mill could be preserved in the realm of theory, and with the added assertion of universal relevance for the axioms of political economy – extending even to animals! – theory became somewhat more insulated from practice. In contrast with the Historicists, Jevons placed the individual at the heart of economic analysis, and he seems to have elevated universally relevant and logically precise theory to a status above application. Second, Jevons's calls for subdivision allowed for the encouragement of empirical studies as a branch of economic studies, thus garnering at least limited support from the Historicists such as Leslie and Ingram. Within such specialized empirical studies he argued that omitted causes could be presumed to balance, thereby further directing attention away from the process of abstraction underlying the analysis. To this practice, Mill and Leslie both strenuously objected. Finally, as the discipline became more subdivided – and the theory became increasingly regarded as universally applicable – the canon became more narrow, more rigidly defined, and more unassailable.

Notes

A preliminary version of this paper was presented at the Canon Session of the 1999 HES meeting, Greensboro, N.C. I am grateful to David Levy for organizing that session and to Evelyn Forget for encouraging me to write the paper. Jeff Lipkes, Laura Valladādao de Mattos, and Larry Moss provided helpful comments. I am also grateful to Dr Peter McNiven and Dr Peter Noeckles for their assistance and permission to cite material from the Jevons Archives.

1 A leading proponent of the historical school, the Irish political economist Thomas Edward Cliffe Leslie (1825–1882), was Professor of Political Economy and Jurisprudence in Queen's College, Belfast, from 1853 until his death. A second major proponent whose work proved to be of significant popular appeal was John Kells Ingram. Ingram's ([1888] 1967) *History of Political Economy* went through numerous printings and was translated into nine languages.
2 Mill's method has, of course, been widely and carefully studied (see Blaug 1980, DeMarchi 1986, Hausman 1992, Hirsch 1992, Hutchison 1978, Peart 1995). Many investigations have focused on the relative roles of deduction and induction in Mill, with some analysts arguing that his method was "overly" deductive, confident, and irresponsible (Hutchison 1978). It is not my purpose here to repeat this well-known ground. For a recent detailed demonstration of the importance of experience in Mill's method, including several case studies of Mill's practice, see Hollander and Peart 1999.
   On Ireland see "What Is To Be Done With Ireland?" (1848) and "England and Ireland" (1869), (in Mill 1982, vol. 6: 496–503, 505–32). See also Mill's sympathetic review of Leslie's essays, "Leslie on the Land Question" (1870); (Mill 1967, vol. 5: 669–702). In "England and Ireland," Mill advocates wide-ranging land tenure reform transforming tenancy to fixed rents (Mill 1982, vol. 6: 527).
3 On the substantial identity between Mill and Jevons on policy issues, see Peart 1990.
4 Jevons also used the example of the corn laws to make the same argument; cf. *Theory of Political Economy* (Jevons [1871] 1911: 18–19).
5 I agree with Hausman that in some passages Mill writes as though he considers economic reasoning to be an abstraction (and thus hypothetical), while he also on occasion refers to economic laws as qualified by *ceteris paribus* conditions (Hausman 1992: 33–53; see DeMarchi 1986).

6   Not that any political economist was ever so absurd as to suppose that mankind are really thus constituted, but because this is the mode in which science must necessarily proceed. When an effect depends upon a concurrence of causes, those causes must be studied one at a time, and their laws separately investigated, if we wish, through the causes, to obtain the power of either predicting or controlling the effect; since the law of the effect is compounded of the laws of all the causes which determine it.
                                                            (Mill [1836] 1967, vol. 4: 322)

7 A tendency is "a power acting with a certain intensity in that direction" (Mill [1836] 1967, vol. 4: 337).
8 In his *Essay*, Mill seems to imply that the issue is abstraction, instead of *ceteris paribus*:

   The conclusions of Political Economy, consequently, like those of geometry, are only true, as the common phrase is, *in the abstract*; that is, they are only true under certain suppositions, in which none but general causes – causes common to the *whole class* of cases under consideration – are taken into account.
                                                            (Mill [1836] 1967, vol. 4: 326)

9 For additional evidence of Mill's modifications to theory based on experiential evidence, see Hollander and Peart 1999.
10 For an overview of the historical school, see Hutchison 1953. A detailed review of

Leslie's ideas is contained in Koot 1975. The prominent economic historian, J. E. T. Rogers, is also considered an important influence in the historical school. Since his writings are predominantly non-methodological, and since Jevons's responses are directed at the work of Ingram and Leslie, I confine my attention to them. Walter Bagehot (1826–1877), conservative editor of the *Economist* and author of *Lombard Street*, also figured in debates about the generality of the axioms of political economy. He took the Millian position that the conclusions of political economy were of limited relevance, applicable only to countries with institutional structures similar to those of England at the time (Bagehot 1876). He was, however, well disposed towards Jevons, and wrote a March 10 1866 testimonial in favor of Jevons for the Cobden Professorship at Owens College, praising Jevons's "equal knowledge" of "abstract theory" and "statistics" (*Papers and Correspondence of William Stanley Jevons;* Jevons 1972–81, vol. 3: 114).

It would be a mistake not to recognize much admiration for Jevons – and for Mill – among these dissenters, as revealed by their correspondence as well as published remarks. Leslie considered himself a follower of Mill and theirs is a correspondence that reflects much warmth. See Mill's review of Leslie's essays on Ireland, referred to in note 2. See the letter from Ingram to Jevons dated January 21 1881 (Jevons 1972–81, vol. 5: 124–5), in which Ingram acknowledged with great pleasure Jevons's recognition of his BAAS Address in the second edition of the *Theory*. See also Leslie's warm letter to Jevons of 28 August 1878, alluding to the Address by Ingram (Jevons 1972–81, vol. 4: 272–3).

11 Though some common ground is necessary given the intermixture of the issues in the original debates, this investigation confines itself to the theory/practice debates. For a detailed examination of the separation of economics from social phenomena, see Peart 1999.

12 Ingram's Address received wide press. A detailed summary appeared in *The Times* (August 17, p. 10). A leader on the Address appeared in the *Pall Mall Gazette* (August 22 1878). See Leslie's August 28 letter to Jevons, (Jevons 1972–81, vol. 5: 2–3).

13 The significance of such a combination had been revealed in the study of economic fluctuations:

> A theory of decennial recurrence of commercial crises, for example, was based on the occurrence of crises in 1837, 1847, and 1857. Had the causes of commercial crises been examined, it would have been discovered that they are extremely various and uncertain in their occurrence; that a war, a bad harvest, a drain of the precious metals, anything, in short, which produces a panic, may cause a crisis; and as there is no decennial periodicity in the causes, there can be none in the effects.
>
> (Leslie 1873a: 377)

14 Bonamy Price (1807–1888) succeeded Thorold Rogers as Drummand Professor of Political Economy at Oxford in 1868, a position he held until his death. Price acknowledged but downplayed the significance of achievements by J. E. Cairnes as well as Jevons: "they have remoulded, rather than added to, our economical knowledge, and remoulded it in a way rather tentative than final or satisfactory" (Price 1879: 183).

15
> No one, whether agreeing or not, can fail to feel the force, the energy, the extent of knowledge, which distinguish his chapters on peasant proprietors, on co-operation, on the future of the labouring classes. But from these perfectly natural and practical disquisitions he is perpetually being recalled by the artificial sense that he is writing a scientific work. He elaborates the simplest propositions, and puts them in technical form. Sometimes, after a series of complex and cumbrous reasonings, he emerges on a conclusion perfectly naïve in its simplicity.
>
> (Price 1879: 198)

16 Jevons's comment about first principles is, however, a statement about the average: he allowed that individuals make mistakes, but he believed that such mistakes cancel out over time or over a wide group of consumers. See Peart 1996 and, for the similarity with Menger in this respect, Peart 1998.

"M. de Laveleye and Professor Leslie may succeed in constituting a new science, but they will not utterly revolutionise and destroy the old one in the way they seem to suppose" (Jevons [1905] 1965: 197). The Belgian political economist Emile Louis Victor de Laveleye (1822–1892) was a supporter of the historical school and Professor of Political Economy at Liège, from 1864–92.

17 Maas 1998 maintains that Jevons's abacus helped him conceive of economic man as similar to a machine.

18 In support of his calls for subdivision, Jevons invoked the division of labor principle.

19 > [T]he theory of economy . . . will naturally be one science, remaining the same throughout its applications, though it may be broken up into several parts, the theories of utility, of exchange, of labour, of interest, etc. partly corresponding to the old division of the science into the laws of consumption, exchange, distribution, production, and so forth
>
> (Jevons [1905] 1965: 200)

Jevons insisted, of course, that this "general science" or "theory" of economics, was mathematical. See Schabas 1990.

20 "[T]he political economist is expected to teach all parts of his equally extensive and growing science, and is lucky if he escape having to profess also the mental, metaphysical, and moral sciences generally" (Jevons [1905] 1965: 201).

21 He alluded also in this context to Ingram's BAAS Address, as well as – to a "lesser extent" – the work of Thornton. It is important to bear in mind the theoretical debates that occurred throughout this time, and which are linked to the methodological disputes as well: Ricardian wage and distribution theory was being attacked throughout the decade by Historicists (see Leslie 1879b: 160), and, though along other lines, by Jevons as well.

22 Jevons makes a similar argument in the Lecture:

> Now I am far from thinking that the historical treatment of our science is false or useless. On the contrary, I consider it to be indispensable. The present economical state of society cannot possibly be explained by theory alone. We must take into account the long past out of which we are constantly emerging. Whether we call it sociology or not, we must have some scientific treatment of the principles of evolution as manifested in every branch of social existence. . . . every law, custom, or social fact is the product of the past, historical or forgotten.
>
> (Jevons [1905]1965: 195)

23 See the obituary notice in the Royal Society, signed R. H.:

> Problems in applied economics had for Jevons a peculiar attractiveness, because of their bearing on the material welfare of the community. His devotion to abstract studies did not destroy his interest in the progress of society, or in questions touching the practical life of men. While busied with researches on abstract principles, he always kept a window open to the outer world.
>
> (*Proceedings of the Royal Society* 1383: vii–viii)

24 Not surprisingly, Jevons's calls for the use of statistical studies found support in the Manchester Statistical Society, where, in 1871, then President and influential Manchester banker John Mills recognized Jevons's remarkable gold studies, "a beautiful typical illustration of the use of hypothesis in this class of enquiries, [that] may suffice to show the mode in which theoretical Political Economy and Statistics cooperate and render a reciprocal service" (Mills 1871: 8).

25 The obituary in *Nature* points to Jevons's caution in this regard:

> He was too far-seeing and too judicious to overlook the enormous gulf that separates abstract economics from the domain of practice, and he was under no delusion as to the practicability of applying exact methods to phenomena so immensely complex as those of society
>
> (*Nature* 1882: 420).

References

Bagehot, W. (1876) "The Postulates of English Political Economy," *Fortnightly Review* 21 o.s. (15 n.s.)(1): 215–42.

Black, R. D. C. (1972) "W. S. Jevons and the Foundation of Modern Economics," *History of Political Economy* 4(2): 364–78.

Blaug, M. (1980) *The Methodology of Economics or How Economists Explain*, Cambridge: Cambridge University Press.

Cairnes, J. E. (1872) "New Theories of Political Economy," *Fortnightly Review*, 17 o.s. (11 n.s.)(1): 71–6.

DeMarchi, N. (1986) "Mill's Unrevised Philosophy of Economics: A Comment on Hausman," *Philosophy of Science* 53: 89–100.

Economist (1882) "Review of *The State in Relation to Labour*," 40 (July 8): 845.

Fisher, I. (1922) *The Making of Index Numbers*, Boston: Houghton Mifflin.

Guardian (1886) "*Review of Letters and Journal*," (September 1): 1281–2; Jevons Archive 6/50/20.

Hausman, D. (1992) *The Separate and Inexact Science of Economics*, Cambridge: Cambridge University Press.

Hirsch, A. (1992) "John Stuart Mill on Verification and the Business of Science," *History of Political Economy* 24(2): 843–66.

Hollander, S. and Peart, S. (1999) "John Stuart Mill's Method in Principle and in Practice: A Review of the Evidence," *Journal of the History of Economic Thought* 21(4): 369–98.

Hutchison, T. W. (1953) *Review of Economic Doctrines, 1870–1929*, Oxford: Clarendon.

—— (1978) *On Revolutions and Progress in Economic Knowledge*, Cambridge: Cambridge University Press.

Ingram, J. K. (1878) "Address of the President of Section F of the British Association," *Journal of the Royal Statistical Society* 41 (August): 602–29.

—— [1888] (1967) *History of Political Economy*, New York: A. M. Kelley.

Jevons, W. S. [1871] (1911) *Theory of Political Economy*, 4th edn, ed. H. S. Jevons, London: Macmillan.

—— [1882] (1965) *Methods of Social Reform*, London: A. M. Kelley.

—— [1905] (1965) *The Principles of Economics and Other Papers*, ed.H. Higgs, London: Macmillan.

—— (1972–81) *Papers and Correspondence of William Stanley Jevons*, 7 vols, ed. R. D. Collison Black, London: Macmillan.

Keynes, J. M. (1951) *Essays in Biography*, London: Hart-Davis.

Koot, G. M. (1975) "T. E. Cliffe Leslie, Irish Social Reform, and the Origins of the English Historical School of Economics," *History of Political Economy* 7(3): 312–36.

Leslie, T. E. C. (1873a) "Economic Science and Statistics," *Athenaeum* (September 27) (reprinted in *Essays in Political and Moral Philosophy* (1879), Dublin: Hodges, Foster, and Figgis).

—— (1873b) "Prices in England in 1873," *Fortnightly Review* (June) (reprinted in *Essays in Political and Moral Philosophy* (1879), Dublin: Hodges, Foster, and Figgis: 349–55).

—— (1876) "On the Philosophical Method of Political Economy," *Hermathena* iv

(reprinted in *Essays in Political and Moral Philosophy* (1879), Dublin: Hodges, Foster, and Figgis: 216–42).
—— (1879a) "Political Economy and Sociology," *Fortnightly Review* (February 1) (reprinted in *Essays in Political and Moral Philosophy* (1879), Dublin: Hodges, Foster, and Figgis: 383–411).
—— (1879b) "Untitled Review of the Second Edition of *Theory of Political Economy*," *The Academy* 377 n.s. (July 26) (reprinted in *Papers and Correspondence of William Stanley Jevons* ed. R. D. Collison Black, London: Macmillan, vol. 7: 157–62).
Maas, H. (1998) "Mechanical Rationality: Jevons and the Making of Economic Man," *Research Memoranda in History and Methodology of Economics*, Centre for the Philosophy of Natural and Social Science 98(4).
Mill, J. S. [1836] (1967) "On the Definition of Political Economy; and on the Method of Investigation Proper to It," in vol. 4 of *The Collected Works of John Stuart Mill*, ed. J. R. Robson, Toronto: University of Toronto Press.
—— [1843] (1973) *A System of Logic: Ratiocinative and Inductive*, in vols 7–8 of *The Collected Works of John Stuart Mill*, ed. J. R. Robson, Toronto: University of Toronto Press.
—— [1848] (1965(*Principles of Political Economy*, in vols 2–3 of *The Collected Works of John Stuart Mill*, ed. J. R. Robson, Toronto: University of Toronto Press.
—— [1848] (1982) "What is To Be Done With Ireland?,' in vol. 6 of *The Collected Works of John Stuart Mill*, ed. J. R. Robson, Toronto: University of Toronto Press.
—— [1869] (1982) "England and Ireland," in vol. 6 of *The Collected Works of John Stuart Mill*, ed. J. R. Robson, Toronto: University of Toronto Press.
—— [1870] (1967) "Leslie and the Land Question," in vol. 5 of *The Collected Works of John Stuart Mill*, ed. J. R. Robson, Toronto: University of Toronto Press.
Mills, J. (1871) "On the Scope and Method of Statistical Enquiry, and on some Questions of the Day," Manchester Statistical Society Inaugural Address, read Nov. 15, *Transactions of the Society* 1871–2.
Mitchell, W. C. (1928) *Business Cycles: The Problem and Its Setting*, New York: NBER.
Nature (1882) "Obituary," August 31, 420–1.
Peart, S. (1990) "W. S. Jevons's Applications of Utilitarian Theory to Economic Policy," *Utilitas* 2(2): 281–306.
—— (1993) "W. S. Jevons's Methodology of Economics: Some Implications of the Procedures for 'Inductive Quantification'," *History of Political Economy* 25(3): 435–60.
—— (1995) "'Disturbing Causes,' 'Noxious Errors,' and the Theory–Practice Distinction in the Economics of J. S. Mill and W. S. Jevons," *Canadian Journal of Economics* 28(4b):1194–211.
—— (1996) *The Economics of William Stanley Jevons*, London: Routledge.
—— (1998) "Jevons and Menger Re-homogenized: Jaffé After 20 Years," *American Journal of Economics and Sociology* 57(3): 307–26.
—— (1999) "Sociology, Economics and the Demise of the Historicist School in Nineteenth Century England," manuscript.
Price, B. (1879) "Is Political Economy a Science?," *Quarterly Review* 147 (January): 182–202.
Robertson, R. (1951) "Jevons and his Precursors," *Econometrica* 19: 229–49.
Royal Society Proceedings (1883) "Obituary," signed R. H.
Schabas, M. (1990) *A World Ruled by Number: William Stanley Jevons and the Rise of Mathematical Economics*, Princeton: Princeton University Press.
Steedman, I. (1998) "Comments in British HET *Newsletter*," 61 (Winter): 17.
The Times (1878) "The British Association," August 17: 10.
Wicksteed, P. H. (1886) "Review of *Letters and Journal*," in *The Inquirer*, October 2: 645–7; Jevons Archive 6/50/22.
Winch, D. (1972) "Marginalism and the Boundaries of Economic Science," *History of Political Economy* 4(2): 325–43.

20 Canons in the history of economic thought

Alessandro Roncaglia

Introduction

Samuelson's 1978 paper on "The Canonical Classical Model of Political Economy" and the subsequent debate (see in particular Hollander 1980, 1998) raise a number of basic issues for historians of economic thought. First, what sort of tool is the canon for the historian of ideas? Second, is Samuelson's canonical classical model an adequate representation of the views of classical economists? Third, once an adequate canonical classical model has been specified, is it basically similar to an analogous construction for the marginalist approach?

In this chapter, these three issues will be briefly considered (in "What is a canon?" "Is Samuelson's 'the' classical canon?" and "Classical and marginalist canons counterposed"). The chapter suggests: first, that the "canon" is a useful construct, but an ambiguous one, though it is precisely its ambiguity that increases its interest; second, that a classical canon can be constructed in different ways, depending on our basic views of the economy and of economic theory, though a serious rational evaluation of the adequacy of different constructions for the representation of classical political economy is possible; third, that a counterposition between a classical canon and a marginalist one is possible and has some advantages over the construction of a classical canon that flows without loss of continuity into a marginalist canon.

What is a canon?

The term "canon" derives, through Latin, from the ancient Greek κσvvα, the cane used by artisans as measuring tool; but already in Homeric times it had the figurative meaning of rule or norm: for instance, in poetry or in music it indicated a scheme that the composer had to follow. Then in medieval times the term "canon" was used to indicate the juridical norms that the Catholic church imposed on itself, especially those emanated by the synods, in counterposition to the voμοι, the laws emanated by secular authorities; as a transposed meaning, in liturgy it indicates the essential and fixed part in the eucharistic section of the mass.

A number of other usages of the term, also derived from the original

Greek meaning of rule or norm, refer to a set of writings or authors selected as model, to parts of the Bible or to the whole of the holy writings of other religions, to a specific kind of polyphonic music where a theme is imitated at specified intervals of time and tone, and at least in Italian, to the rent on land or to land taxes or to fees to be paid at regular intervals. Only in the adjective form "canonical" is the term used in mathematics to designate any analytic expression when reduced to a simple form, possibly in order to show some intrinsic properties of interest to theoreticians.

We thus have at least four meanings, or groups of meanings: the juridical-ecclesiastical meaning of norm, the derived meaning of reference authority, the musical meaning of a scheme to be filled with one's own composition, and finally the mathematical meaning of a reduced structural form of a model expressing a theory.

Most likely it was the mathematical usage of the term "canonical" that Samuelson had in mind. In fact, his "canonical classical model" is meant to be a simple formulation expressing *in nuce* the main aspects of classical economists' analyses. Moreover, it is a formulation apt to show a most interesting property, namely that the analytic representation of growth in market economies, reduced to its bare bones, must have a substantially unique structure, whether stemming from a classical or a marginalist approach.

The other meanings of the term "canon," however, are also relevant to our discussion.

In order to see why this is so, we must consider the working rules of the historian of economic thought. Historians, exactly like the economists they study, do not replicate in their works the objects of their researches. The world of economic theorizing (interpreted as part of Popper's World Three), is too complex for this, exactly like the real economic world. In order to represent each of these two worlds, a great deal of simplification, abstracting away what we deem important from what we deem irrelevant, is necessary. As we all know, this opens the door to differences in opinion.

Exactly as in economic theorizing, most differences can be solved by reference to the standard rules of the scientific game. In the case of the historian of ideas, this means a rational, open debate based on elements ranging from quotations to the historical context. But there are also what we might call "admissible" differences, where each side in the discussion is personally persuaded of the truth of his/her interpretation (and their respective supporters, when they do exist, are even more certain), but a non-committed observer – perhaps just landed from Mars – finds it difficult to pass a definitive verdict. These admissible differences commonly have something to do with the existence of different "paradigms," as Kuhn (1970) called them: different views of the very nature both of the issue at hand and more generally of the whole course of economic theory and the way of functioning of the economy.

Now, the notion of the canon, as used in the history of economic thought, has precisely to do with this level of the debate. It is a synthesis of our basic vision of the development of economic thought. Thus, admitting that there are different paradigms, the canon is an instrument, indeed the main instrument, for the debate between different paradigms. However, it is precisely because of this that the mathematical notion of the canon is too restrictive for our purposes.

We must recall, here, what Schumpeter stressed at the beginning of his monumental *History of Economic Analysis*: that, after the pre-analytical stage where a vague idea of the problem to be tackled is shaped, we have a most important first stage of theoretical work where we reach for a definition of a set of concepts. Here we define the variables which will then, in a subsequent stage of theorizing, be inserted in formal models.[1]

It is clear, then, that the mathematical notion of the canon is only adequate if economic theorizing is restricted to the activity of model-building. On the contrary, if we take into account the stage of conceptualization, our "canon" cannot be built simply as a set of equations or as a graph. It first and foremost needs a clear indication of the concepts constituting the core of our "vision" of our subject-matter – or, if we prefer to call it so, of our "paradigm." Thus the canon might – possibly, should – take the form of a literary synthesis, rather than, or as a premise to, the set-of-equations form.

The "canon," thus specified, will then first of all constitute a norm, in the sense that it will provide rules for conducting and judging research within the chosen paradigm. Second, it will (after a sufficiently wide and long debate has favored its general acceptance, always within the chosen paradigm) act as an authoritative reference for describing the scenario in which our research takes place. Third, it will provide a musical basic scheme on which to play our variations.[2]

Any canon on which we may choose to research and discuss, including Samuelson's 1978 representation of the classical canon, will have shades of all these different meanings. Our debate will already be a difficult one if we are aware of this; but any debate will be impossible if we try to close our eyes to this multiplicity of meanings and to behave as if only the mathematical meaning were relevant.

Is Samuelson's 'the' classical canon?

Let us now try to evaluate Samuelson's classical canonical model. What is important from our viewpoint is not so much its mathematical formulation, but the conceptual foundation on which it relies.

There is one difficulty in this, that as in any one-commodity model no question of relative price determination arises; hence no theory of value is involved, at least at a first glance. It might seem that there is no scope here for the choice – discussed in the next section – between an "objective" value theory relying on reproducibility conditions and difficulty of production, and a "subjective" value theory relying on preferences and scarcity. Furthermore, Samuelson's canonical classical model really resembles a Clarkian model – as Samuelson himself indicates – based as it is on a well-behaved aggregate production function, with two factors of production, land and capital-cum-labor, and decreasing returns for each factor of production. Thus in equilibrium factor prices are equal to marginal product. It is no surprise, then, that such a model shows no basic contradiction with the marginalist approach: it is, in fact, a marginalist model!

However, since division of labor – both micro, within a given firm, involving increasing returns to scale, and macro, between different sectors of the economy, involving a multi-commodity world – played such a dominant role in the classical economists' representations of economic reality, it is clear that we cannot be content with this simplification. Conceptually, it takes away from the scene what Adam Smith at least considered the main element explaining the wealth of nations.³

Of course, in the writings of classical economists there are a few passages which can be taken at face value as pointing in the direction of Samuelson's interpretation. Also we must recall that analogous interpretations of the classical approach have a long tradition and many supporters, before and after Samuelson's article. Hollander, in a coherent series of writings has developed it most carefully.⁴ With respect to Hollander's interpretation of Ricardo, I have expressed my criticisms elsewhere.⁵ Since each one of us remains unrepentant, this is possibly one of those instances where the opposing interpretations rely on different "paradigms," and a battle of quotations would probably be inconclusive.

Classical and marginalist canons counterposed

The previous two sections thus lead us to two main conclusions. First, the canon can – and probably should – be a "conceptual canon," concentrating attention on the representation of the economy (or of the history of economic thought) as embodied in the set of concepts developed in what Schumpeter stressed to be a necessary stage of theorizing, conceptualization. Second, Samuelson's canonical classical model is the result of a reading of classical economics through marginalist glasses; a widespread reading, one must admit, but certainly not the only possible one, and perhaps not the best.

Leaving aside the issue of choosing between the contending approaches, I will try here only to sketch the differences in the "conceptual vision" of the classical and the marginalist paradigms, and to hint at the different readings of the history of economic thought stemming from them.

Let us begin with the oldest of the two traditions, the subjectivist one. We find hints of it already in Greek and Latin writings, and then in medieval discussions of the "just price." When Galiani proposes a sufficiently clear subjective theory of value based on scarcity and utility, in 1751, he does not present a new way of thinking, but summarizes an already-established traditional vision of economic affairs. What is missing is certainly important. First is the idea of utility as a quantitative magnitude (though the idea that the subjective estimate of a commodity could be indirectly measured by willingness to pay a certain sum for it was already present in various authors).⁶ Second is the idea of interdependence of supply and demand for different commodities (though this too was also occasionally hinted at); third, the mathematical elaboration (though calculus was already half a century old, having been developed independently by Leibnitz and Newton). But the subjective conception of value was clearly there.⁷

According to the subjective "vision," the market is born out of the "double coincidence of wants": economic agents start with different endowments, and soon find that exchanges can improve their position. The mechanism of exchange is modeled on the basis of the experience of the market of the ancient *polis* or of the village fair. It is a physical market where supply and demand meet, in the sense that it is a location in time and space to which both buyers and sellers converge. Thus the idea arises that the price is determined by supply and demand; behind prices, values are explained by the motives inducing economic agents to exchange and by their relative bargaining position: abstracting from not-morally acceptable elements such as physical or military strength, this means relative scarcity of the respective endowments, confronted with needs and desires. This conceptualization of the market is reinforced by the rise of stock exchanges; since Walras, these become the explicit "canon" (in the meaning of term of reference) for the notion of the market.

Slowly, another kind of market economy appeared. While in feudal times only a fraction of the total product passed hands through exchanges, and these mostly concerned luxury goods (see Kula 1970), with the development of the division of labor and the separation of the workers from their traditional means of production, namely common land, exchanges came to involve means of production and subsistence goods. Above all, the relevant reference for the notion of the market was no longer the village fair; slowly the world-wide web of big merchants, and then of industrial firms exchanging their means of production, took a central role in the economy. Thus we have a new notion of the market, no longer as a physical location in time and space, but as a sufficiently stable web of repetitive flows of exchange.[8] Subjective evaluations are rejected, and an "objective" notion of value based on difficulty of production is proposed in its place.[9]

Thus we have a hint about the presence, in the history of economic thought, of different notions of market (village fair or stock exchange versus stable web of commercial flows), of prices (scarcity prices determined by supply and demand versus production prices determined by difficulty of production and conditions of reproduction), of values (subjective versus objective theory of value). And we have, in general, two representations of the working of the economy.

On the one hand we have the classical approach. It starts from the division of labor, seen as the key to the growth of the wealth of nations and in turn explained not by different original endowments but by the social nature of women and men.[10] As a consequence of the division of labor, each subject, be it a firm or an individual, is involved in what Sraffa called a "circular flow of production and consumption"; at the end of the production period, each productive unit has to recover its means of production in the market, by selling in the market (at least part of) its product, and each individual (or family) has to recover in the market its means of subsistence. Thus a repetitive web of exchanges is the necessary counterpart of the division of labor. In a capitalist society, the conditions of reproduction for the economic process involve that each producer is able to reacquire its means of production – that is, to cover its production costs – and to obtain a rate of profit which, under competition (interpreted as the freedom to move capitals from one sector to another, in the search for the highest return), must be analogous to that prevalent in other sectors of the economy. Thus we have the classical notion of natural (or "production") prices, determined on the objective basis of the "difficulty of production," initially expressed as labor contained, then finally as Sraffa's prices.[11]

On the other hand, the subjective theory of value, after the initial steps, found a systematization in a comparison with physics (more precisely, classical mechanics) and the mathematical models developed in that context. The confrontation of endowments and needs in the market (a confrontation possibly mediated by production, but this was only considered a complication to be dealt with in successive approximations) found a theoretical solution in the notion of equilibrium between supply and demand.[12] And this notion, though not a necessary component of the classical notion of natural prices, has so strongly embedded modern economics that we find it very difficult to understand that it has nothing to do with the classical "canon."

Some provisional conclusions

Let me summarize my – admittedly tentative – results. First, the "mathematical" notion of the canon is too restrictive, and attention must also be paid to the "conceptualization" of the different research paradigms. Second, Samuelson's canonical classical model shows no contradiction between the "classical" and the marginalist approach precisely because it is already, in its foundations, a marginalist model. Third, we are confronted with a counterposition between the classical-objective and the marginalist-subjective approaches as different research paradigms.

These two paradigms give rise to two different readings of the history of economic thought. If we adhere to the marginalist-subjective paradigm, the classical approach appears as a rudimentary partial anticipation of modern theory, with no substantial break of continuity in the line of development of economic theory. However, this requires the denial of the different classical conceptualization and theoretical representation of the economic process. If we take this into account, our history loses its simplicity but acquires greater adherence to the flow of the economic debate over the past centuries and greater interest for the contemporary debates on the foundations of economic theory.

Notes

This chapter was written for the Toronto Conference (September 26–28 1998) in honor of Samuel Hollander, a colleague for whom my esteem is as high as our theoretical differences are deep. Thanks, without implication, are due to Nerio Naldi for useful comments on a previous draft. MURST financing (research project on "Teorie dei mercati e processi di sviluppo") is gratefully acknowledged.

1 Cf. Schumpeter 1954: 42, 45.
2 In music, as we know, the true art lies in the way the scheme is filled by the composer, not in the scheme itself.
3 Let us recall here that Ricardo's 1815 corn model is not a one-commodity model: it is a model where only one basic commodity is present, since corn is the only

commodity required for its own production; but other non-basic commodities are explicitly considered. Moreover, the corn model is a very brief interlude in the development of the classical doctrine, no more than three or four years around 1815: Hicks's (1965: 36–8) attempt to attribute such a model to Smith – a rather cautious attempt, one must add – is devoid of any textual foundation.

4 See particularly Hollander 1973 on Smith and 1979 on Ricardo.
5 See Roncaglia 1982.
6 Already in the thirteenth century Albertus Magnus and Thomas Aquinas stressed the role of money for measuring the "common estimate" stemming from the subjective estimates of the protagonists of exchanges.
7 Cf. section II ("*Dell'utilità, e della rarità principi stabili del valore*") of Book I of Galiani (1751). Galiani himself quotes Bernardo Davanzati (1529–1606) as his predecessor as far as the role of scarcity and utility in the determination of value is concerned. Half a century after Galiani, Luigi Molinari Valeriani (1806) counterposes a theory of value based on demand and supply to a theory of value based on cost of production, and sketches a rudimentary mathematical and geometrical analysis for the first kind of theory.
8 A prototype of this notion of the market can be found in William Petty's *Dialogue of Diamonds*. (Cf. Petty [1899] 1963: 624–30 and, for a commentary, Roncaglia 1985: ch. 8.)
9 Cf. again Petty, in the Preface to his *Political Arithmetick*:

> The Method I take . . . is not yet very usual; for . . . I have taken the course . . . to consider only such Causes as have visible Foundations in Nature; leaving those that depend upon the mutable Minds, Opinions, Appetites and Passions of particular Men, to the Consideration of others
> (Petty [1899] 1963: 244)

Petty is here clearly opposing a previous, well-established, subjectivist view of economic matters.

Reference to production costs, especially labor required for production, was already present in the debates on the just price. However, in these debates the "just price" notion was a normative one, not a theoretical variable interpreting the outcome of the main forces in action in a market economy.

10 Smith, who insisted on this point in *The Wealth of Nations* (and it may be stressed that the point has strong connections with the idea that men – and women – are born equal), came in for severe criticism from Pownall 1776: especially 338–9. By contrast, according to the marginalist conception – and Pownall may be considered a precursor of it from this viewpoint – the division of labor arises from differences in the innate abilities and propensities of the various workers.
11 From this perspective, the Smithian distinction between the natural and the market price was a subtle compromise between the old subjective tradition and the then relatively new classical tradition. Let us also recall the insistence of classical economists on treating the natural price as the theoretical variable, and the market price as a sort of empirical notion: most emphatically, not a theoretical variable determined by supply and demand curves. As Ricardo (1951: 382) said, "It is the cost of production which must ultimately regulate the price of commodities, and not, as has been often said, the proportion between the supply and demand." For a discussion of natural and market prices in Smith, see Roncaglia 1990.
12 Wicksteed, "the purist of marginal theory" as Sraffa (1960: v) calls him, by recourse to the opportunity cost notion reached the conclusion that "There is no such thing" as the supply curve (Wicksteed 1935: 785), since the supply price expresses the producers' evaluation for alternative products obtainable if (that quantity of) the commodity under consideration had not been produced. Thus also the supply side is reduced to its subjective foundations.

References

Galiani, F. (1751) *Della Moneta*, Napoli: Giuseppe Raimondi.
Hicks, J. (1965) *Capital and Growth*, Oxford: Clarendon.
Hollander, S. (1973) *The Economics of Adam Smith*, Toronto: University of Toronto Press.
—— (1979) *The Economics of David Ricardo*, Toronto: University of Toronto Press.
—— (1980) "On Professor Samuelson's Canonical Classical Model of Political Economy," *Journal of Economic Literature* 18: 559–74.
—— (1998) "The Canonical Classical Growth Model: Content, Adherence and Priority," *Journal of the History of Economic Thought* 20(3): 253–78.
Kuhn, T. S. (1970) *The Structure of Scientific Revolution*, 2nd edn, Chicago: University of Chicago Press.
Kula, W. [1962] (1970) *Teoria economica del sistema feudale*, Torino: Einaudi. (Original Polish edn, Warsaw 1962.)
Petty, W. [1899] (1963) *Economic Writings*, ed. C. Hull, New York: A. M. Kelley.
Pownall, T. (1776) *A Letter from Governor Pownall to Adam Smith, L.L.D. F.R.S., Being an Examination of Several Points of Doctrine, Laid down in his "Inquiry in to the Nature and Causes of the Wealth of Nations,"* London, repr. in A. Smith (1977) *Correspondence*, ed. E. C. Mossner and I. S. Ross, Oxford: Clarendon: 337–76.
Ricardo, D. [1817] (1951) *On the Principles of Political Economy and Taxation*, vol. 1 of *The Works and Correspondence of David Ricardo*, ed. P. Sraffa, Cambridge: Cambridge University Press.
Roncaglia, A. (1982) "Hollander's Ricardo" and "Rejoinder," *Journal of Post Keynesian Economics* 4(3): 339–59, 373–5.
—— (1985) *Petty: The Origins of Political Economy*, Armonk, N.Y.: Sharpe.
—— (1990) "Is the Notion of Long-Period Positions Compatible with Classical Political Economy?," *Political Economy* 6(1–2): 103–11.
Valeriani, L. M. (1806) *Del Prezzo di cose tutte mercantili*, Bologna: Ulisse Ramponi.
Samuelson, P. A. (1978) "The Canonical Classical Model of Political Economy," *Journal of Economic Literature* 16: 1415–34.
Schumpeter, J. (1954) *History of Economic Analysis*, London: Allen and Unwin (paperback edn 1994, London: Routledge).
Sraffa, P. (1960) *Production of Commodities by Means of Commodities*, Cambridge: Cambridge University Press.
Wicksteed, P. H. (1935) *The Common Sense of Political Economy and Selected Papers and Reviews on Economic Theory*, ed. L. Robbins, London: Routledge.

21 Claiming and reclaiming the past
The legitimizing role of the precursor concept

John K. Whitaker

Historians and methodologists of economics make considerable use of the precursor concept in their attempts to discern meaningful patterns in the economic practices, writings and debates of the past. Ideally they seek to reclaim the past, although their posture of standing dispassionately above the fray may sometimes seem dubious. Other users of the precursor concept seek to claim the past for ulterior purposes. An author seeking acceptance for unorthodox views may attempt to boost their legitimacy and authority by demonstrating their espousal by earlier authors. A "school of thought" in conflict with other schools may seek precursors of its distinctive ideas in order to establish a persuasive intellectual pedigree and capture the hearts and minds of adherents.

These are not the only guises in which the precursor concept may appear. It may be used in a negative way to delegitimize threatening new ideas by claiming that they are not novel.[1] While, at a kind of meta-level, it might feature in analyses of the activities of the historians and methodologists of economics themselves. However, it is the first three contexts for application of the term which will be the focus here. The use of the precursor notion, first by individual authors, second by competing schools of thought, and third by historians and methodologists of economics, will be taken up in turn, the last leading to the vexed question of "the canon." However before going into these matters it is necessary to give consideration to the precursor concept itself and then to its limited scope in a scholarly community practicing the equivalent of "normal science."

The concept of a precursor

The dictionary perhaps offers the best starting point. Of the usages of the word "precursor" listed in the *Oxford English Dictionary* that pertinent to usage in our field is "one who or that which runs before: a forerunner, especially one who precedes or heralds the approach of another, a harbinger." *Merriam Webster's Collegiate Dictionary*, under the definition of "forerunner," gives a sharper delineation between forerunner, precursor and harbinger. Forerunner denotes "anything which serves as a sign or presage," precursor denotes "a person or thing paving the way for the accomplishment of another," while harbinger or herald connote figuratively "one that proclaims or announces the coming or arrival of a notable event."

This definition of a precursor seems to imply that the follower is directly or indirectly influenced by the precursor's "paving the way." My impression though is that usage in our field is more restrictive and that the term precursor is limited to cases where the follower builds independently of the precursor and discovers the pertinence of the latter's work only belatedly, if at all. In other cases a more neutral word such as "predecessor" might be preferred.

Usage in our field seems to imply the following conditions for individual A to be a precursor of later individual B.

1   A must have proceeded to a considerable extent upon the same broad lines as B. Commonality must extend beyond *obiter dicta* by A or agreement on points of detail or modes of expression and must involve central ideas and general principles.
2   B's contributions must have been developed substantially independently of A's rather than as an explicit extension and amplification of them, although B may subsequently discover or recognize the parallels
3   Significant principles common to both A and B must have remained distinctive and not have been substantially adopted by others up to at least the time of B.

A somewhat stricter definition of a precursor is offered by Roy Weintraub, whose discussion of the concept will be considered in the section on "Precursors and the interpretation of past economic thought," later this chapter,

> When we speak of a precursor, we seem to suggest that at time t-2 an individual presented an analysis which can be reconstructed, from a "perspective" placed at time t, as "essentially equivalent" to an analysis "first" done at time t-1.
> (Weintraub 1991: 394: see also 1997: 224–5)

Although a subjective independence of the t-1 contribution from the t-2 contribution is not made explicit here, it does seem to be implied.

It should be observed, however, that the precursor concept is sometimes used to connect not the work of two individuals but the work of an earlier individual or group of individuals to the ideas collectively generated subsequently by an entire group of scholars. Thus, we can speak of Cantillon as a precursor of classical economics or Schumpeter as a precursor of the public choice school, and so on.[2]

The precursor concept in "normal science"

A scholarly community practicing the equivalent of "normal science" has well-established criteria for admission and a shared understanding of the appropriate styles, venues, and organs, for the communication of ideas and new findings. A virtual prerequisite for publication in approved sources is an account of the pertinent prior literature and an indication of how it is proposed to be extended. This requirement is enforced *ex ante* by peer review and *ex post* by peer criticism. To the extent that these procedures are effective, and that they can call upon the collective memory of the community, they restrict the scope for belated discovery of precursors and allow the community to present a public face of the regular and cumulative progression of thought.

The incidence of "unnecessary originality" and duplication of effort is reduced also. The community is aware of its intellectual predecessors, or claims to be so, and is naturally averse to amending its history and public facade to recognize newly-discovered precursors. Of course, if the group pioneers a new area of enquiry it will have to come to terms with the extant literature of the new area, and may discover precursors of its own recent pioneering efforts if it does not dismiss the prior literature imperialistically as irrelevant or misguided. Also, if the community operates in a wider arena, involving conflict with competing schools of thought, then the appropriation of new precursors can help enlarge the community's claim to authority even if the precursorship is doubtful or exiguous (see the section on "Claiming precursors in the 'Conflict of schools'" later in this chapter). However, in general, a community practicing the equivalent of normal science will desire to have an authorized history of its activities already settled upon and will be averse to rewriting it. Precursors will, of course, enter into this authorized history, but the nature of their contributions and their affiliation to later developments will have been long agreed; sometimes in distorted form as with the frequent invocations of Smith's "invisible hand."

An individual member of the community will generally have less knowledge of the past literature than does the community collectively. Despite the incentive to avoid wasted effort by searching early on for pertinent prior work, there must be many cases in which a member develops his or her ideas fully before stumbling upon a precursor who is, however, already known to others in the community. Despite subjective originality any claim to objective originality will be unsustainable in such a case.

If the discovery is made before the member's work is published, this work will probably be represented (falsely) as having been built upon the earlier work. If the discovery is made after publication, an appearance of incompetence may embarrass the member and reduce kudos. However there will sometimes be exceptional cases in which the earlier work was obscure or its full import unrecognized, and then reporting the discovery, even *ex post*, may be regarded as creditable by the community, especially if the precursor was a notable figure.

The emergence of tightly-knit scholarly communities of the kind stereotyped above is a relatively recent phenomenon. In earlier days boundaries were fuzzier and publication practices much less disciplined, while organized access to earlier literature was largely lacking. In such circumstances the scope for the emerging community's discovery of new precursors would be increased considerably.

Invoking precursors to lend authority to new ideas

Discovering and lauding precursors is but one aspect of the more general practice of invoking past literature to strengthen a scholar's claims to respectability and authority. It seems best to lead into the general issues involved by first presenting thumbnail sketches, perhaps caricatures, of the ways in which a few famous economists have drawn upon the past literature in ways going beyond straightforward citation of work drawn upon. The listing is chronological by birth dates.

William Stanley Jevons

Jevons, in his *Theory of Political Economy* (1871) gave considerable, possibly excessive, credit to those foreshadowing his own novel ideas, or ideas he at least believed novel. On utility, besides the obvious case of Bentham, considerable credit was given to Banfield and Jennings (Jevons 1871: 49–51, 65–8, 166–8). On "previous attempts to employ mathematical language in the moral sciences" Hutcheson, Whewell, Tozer, McLeod, Jenkins and Lardner were recognized (ibid.: 14–18). After the work's publication, a vigorous search for prior mathematical work in economics was pursued in alliance with Walras, leading to the extensive list added to the work's second edition (1879). The preface to this edition hailed new precursors, Thünen, Cournot, Dupuit and, above all, Gossen, and recognized handsomely the independent work of Walras. Indeed, Jevons now believed that he had been largely "scooped" by Gossen but found satisfaction in the belief that

> The fact that some four or more independent writers such as Dupuit, Gossen, Walras, and myself, should in such different ways have reached substantially the same views of the fundamental ideas of economic science, cannot but lend great probability, not to say approximate certainty, to those views.
>
> (Jevons 1879: xxxviii–ix)

Henry George

The intellectual roots of George's economics in *Progress and Poverty* (1879) lay very much in the work of the British classical school. Yet he came increasingly to emphasize his affinity to the French physiocrats, stressing the similarity of their "impôt unique" to his own "single tax," although the analytical ideas of the physiocrats seem to have neither influenced him significantly nor appealed to him as relevant. See Baurman (1991).

Alfred Marshall

Marshall vehemently rejected Jevons's claim that Ricardo had "shunted the car of economic science on to a wrong line" so that it was necessary to "pick up the fragments of a shattered science and to start anew" (Jevons 1879: l). Instead Marshall urged recognition of the continuity of development in economic thought. Thus, the work of Ricardo and the classical school, while incomplete and somewhat one-sided, was represented as fully in accord with the new developments, in spirit if not in letter.

Francis Y. Edgeworth

Edgeworth, one of the most original economists, displayed "ostensible reverence for authority and disinclination to say anything definite on his own responsibility" (Keynes [1926] 1972: 265). L. L. Price, a long-time colleague, observed that Edgeworth "was always seeking shelter behind deference to multiple authority" (Price 1926: 371, quoted in Newman 1987: 86). The result was an undue generosity in crediting past writers with ideas they had glimpsed only vaguely, if that, although qualifications sometimes made the implied praise damningly faint.

Eugen von Böhm-Bawerk

Böhm-Bawerk buttressed the validity of his own theory of capital and interest by painstakingly demonstrating to his own satisfaction the errors of all past and current writings on the subject. Erudite and indefatigable, his command of the previous literature was impressive and comprehensive, but the merest hint of confusion or deviation was grounds for excoriation and banishment to the limbo of false ideas.

John Maynard Keynes

In Chapter 23 of his *General Theory* (1936), Keynes assessed the views of various "economic heretics," stressing their resemblance to the revolutionary ideas propounded in his own work.[3] At the same time, he criticized the ideas of Pigou, regarded as an exemplar of the established tradition on monetary and employment theory.

These case studies suggest some obvious general principles:

1 Authors who believe they have revolutionary ideas are likely to search out and laud precursors in order to suggest that the ideas, although apparently novel, have a long but neglected history and are thus more likely to be valid. Such a reaction is more likely the less fully developed is the scholarly community mainly addressed, and the degree to which an additional more general audience is sought. Moreover, the less developed and organized the pertinent scholarly community, the more likely is it that interesting precursors can be found, and the more credible the claims made about them can be. Jevons and George especially, and Keynes to a degree, fit into these patterns. Keynes operating in the milieu of a more professionalized economics, and addressing himself more to this specialized audience, is unable to assemble as compelling a collection of precursors as Jevons's.[4]

2 An alternative strategy for those urging novel ideas is to attempt to discredit by detailed criticism the orthodox position to which they are reacting. Böhm-Bawerk is a prime example of this and Karl Marx might also have been included. George, Jevons and Keynes all adopt such a strategy to some degree. George attacks the classical economists on population and the wage fund, while Jevons attacks their views on value,

but praises them on population and rent. Keynes, as already indicated, uses Pigou as a stalking horse for an attack on received doctrine. George and Marx, seeking to overthrow orthodoxy, could be uninhibited in their criticisms. Keynes and Böhm-Bawerk, seeking rather to reform than to overthrow the well-defined scholarly communities to which they belonged, needed to conform to the accepted canons of scholarly debate, yet nevertheless managed to be exceedingly blunt. Jevons lies somewhere in the middle, seeking to change radically a less organized scholarly community, not yet professionalized.

3   The cases of Marshall and Edgeworth, each of whom introduced significant conceptual innovations, suggest a third strategy for the innovator. This is to present innovations as part and parcel of the normal progression of thinking within the scholarly community and to disguise the extent to which past views are being challenged and modified. In other words, to sneak new ideas in via the back door rather than hammer at the front door, clamoring for admission. Edgeworth's adoption of such a strategy seems almost compulsive, although Stigler (1978: 292–3) has argued that his expository peculiarities served a coherent rhetorical purpose given the subtlety of his thought. Marshall, highly conscious of his leadership role in the rising community of academic economists, might be regarded as attempting by his stress on intellectual continuity to bolster the community's authority and cohesion. Or it could be argued that this stress had a more self-interested basis and was designed to throw doubt upon the claims to originality of some of his contemporaries and strengthen his own claims to authority. Most commentators have regarded his emphasis on the continuity of development from classical to neoclassical economics as overdone: see O'Brien (1990) for a careful adjudication and also Argyrous (1990).

This third broad strategy might be regarded as adherence to the conventions of "normal science" (see "The precursor concept in 'normal science'," earlier). The other two strategies presuppose some degree of revolutionary zeal. The factors leading an intellectual innovator to adopt one or more of the strategies will inevitably be complex and dependent upon the person as well as the situation. Intellectual traits, methodological beliefs, a taste for, or habit of, erudition, a command of foreign language or mathematics, native combativeness, and so on, may all be involved. Jevons was very much a "loner," thinking out problems from scratch and gaining inspiration largely from within. His lack of German cut him off from Thünen's and Gossen's work. Marshall, as Argyrous (1990) has argued, may have been committed to a "growth of knowledge" theory of the continuous accretion of knowledge, whereas Keynes and Jevons might be suspected of tacitly conforming to a more Kuhnian view of revolutionary shifts. Early exposure to the practices of German scholarship may have encouraged Marx or Böhm-Bawerk to place emphasis on commanding and criticizing the extant literature. Böhm-Bawerk's lack of mathematics led him into misunderstanding and pedantic criticism of Marshall's ideas, and so on.

Our sample of innovators is too small in any case for anything but the most tentative of inferences. The same may be true of even the population of successful intellectual innovators in economics. The larger population of unsuccessful would-be innovators might provide interesting insights into the expository strategies aimed at securing recognition, acceptance and authority. Retrospective search for precursors will be one such strategy, but it will only be one of several.[5]

Claiming precursors in the "conflict of schools"

Consider an arena in which differing "schools of thought" compete for recognition and authority.[6] Each school will have claimed its "founding fathers" and "great works." If there is a dominant school it will have established its own view of the genealogy of its current ideas and practices and will be relatively uninterested in revising it. However any less-well-established competitor school will have an incentive to strengthen and extend its pedigree by seeking out precursors of the school's ideas and claiming them as adherents. As a rule, heterodoxy is more interested in exploration of intellectual history than is orthodoxy.

The emerging school of "evolutionary economics" claims Schumpeter, Marshall, Veblen and others as precursors of its views (Hodgson 1994). The "Austrian school" looks to Menger as a founding father but is on the lookout for earlier writers who can be claimed to anticipate the Austrian tradition (Boettke 1994, Rothbard 1995). The claiming of precursors is certainly one aspect of the "conflict of schools" but it should be observed that the same author might validly be claimed as precursor by more than one school, although perhaps with respect to different strands of the author's thought. Marshall, whose thought is complexly stranded, is a good example of this, claimed to some degree by both evolutionists and post-Keynesians as well as by neoclassical orthodoxy.

Precursors and the interpretation of past economic thought

The term "precursor" and its plural are used quite extensively in the literature dealing with the history of economics. A search in the *EconLit* database for the occurrence of both words yields forty-eight pertinent usages, twenty-two of which occur in the titles of the articles listed with bibliographic detail in the appendix.[7] Some of these articles proclaim precursorship, others qualify or deny a prior claim to precursorship. The articles fall into three broad groups.[8]

1   An obscure earlier writer is claimed as precursor of a better known later writer or group of writers (2, 13*, 16, 17, 18, 22*).
2   An obscure earlier writer or group of writers is claimed as precursor of a later phase in economic thought (1, 3*, 4, 5*, 6, 7, 8, 9, 10, 11, 14*, 15, 20*, 21).
3   An unrecognized affinity is claimed between two well known writers, one earlier than the other (12, 19*).

The other twenty-six usages, not occurring in titles but in abstracts, and so on, conform to a similar pattern.[9] There are, of course, many other articles which, while not captured by the above search do in fact focus on precursor issues.[10]

It appears that the dominant usage of the precursor concept in the modern literature on the history of economics is to connect earlier writers to some developed phase of modern economic thought. This dominant usage is reflected in the title of a well-known anthology: *Precursors in Mathematical Economics* (Baumol and Goldfeld 1968). However the more traditional linkage of the non-contemporaneous work of two different authors still retains a place.

Precursorship issues in the literature of the history of economic thought have in the past tended to focus upon three broad areas.

1 Precursors of Adam Smith (see for example Hollander 1987, ch. 2, Meek 1973).
2 Precursors of the marginal revolution (see for example Staley 1989, ch. 12).
3 Classical economics as either precursor or antagonist to neoclassical economics (see for example Hollander 1987, ch. 17).

The last of these topics deals with the question of whether there is a continuous line of analytical development running from Smith to modern mainstream economics, or whether there have been distinctive phases of development involving incompatible conceptual frameworks. Those wedded to a Whiggish view of the development of economic thought as expansive movement along a path preordained by the nature of things will find the concept of a precursor appealingly obvious. Given such a view, foreshadowing involving common travel along the preordained path is naturally to be expected.[11]

Precursorship is then really a special case of unsurprising multiple independent discovery, the discoveries simply being separated in time and the later perhaps more fully developed. Such non-contemporaneous independent discovery is more likely when the later discoverer lacks interest in the history of ideas or suffers intellectual parochialism, due perhaps to a lack of foreign languages or mathematical skills, or when the earlier discoverer has been ignored by contemporaries, perhaps because the time was unripe or communication skills suited to the day lacking. However disinterested historians, as a group at least, can transcend such barriers and limitations and hope to discern *ex post* linkages and parallels remaining obscure to the original authors and perhaps to their contemporaries. In such an event, reconstruction of a detailed genealogy of ideas seems to the Whiggish historian relatively unproblematic and a natural way of making the intellectual past appear comprehensible, rational, and perhaps inevitable.

Even those historians of economics who would view the evolution of economic thought as a conflict of differing paradigms or research programs, reflecting a struggle between competing schools of thought, can expect to attach a significant role to precursors in analyzing the records of the past. Each nascent paradigm can be expected to mature to coherence gradually, and so is likely to have forerunners and precursors who must be identified and integrated into the history to obtain a correct genealogy of ideas. Moreover – as indicated in "Claiming precursors in the 'conflict of schools'," earlier – partisan claims to the ownership of precursors are likely to be made and will need to be assessed in the interests of historical accuracy, but is objectivity possible? This brings us to Weintraub's view (Weintraub 1991: 394–5; 1997: 224–5) that precursorship is largely in the eyes of the beholder and cannot be established objectively.

As was noted earlier, Weintraub defines a precursor as the author of a contribution made at time t-2 and seen from a "perspective" at time t as "essentially equivalent" to an analysis "first" made at time t-1. He sees the terms "first" and "essentially equivalent" as problematic, with meaning entirely dependent on time t's "perspective": "As our perspective changes, as we know different things, what we see as similar and different changes" (Weintraub 1991: 395). Undoubtedly human limitations and intellectual blinkers do constrain and condition all our world views and fundamental methodological presuppositions, creating gaps that cannot always be bridged between one person and another. However this hardly implies that historians of economics or methodologists are necessarily attached to a particular school of economic thought when different schools vie, and so cannot stand disinterestedly above the fray and attempt the adjudication and correction of certain kinds of claims and of the historical record. In other words, it is essential to distinguish the "perspective" brought to bear when the limited subject of the past and present actions of the community of economists is to be judged, from the "perspective," necessarily highly personal, from which each of us judges life and the world. While neither perspective can be claimed as entirely objective it is surely possible to believe, or at least hope, that dispassionate analysis of the past of economics is capable of attaining sufficient objectivity and consensus to allow a common and stable image of it to crystallize and command general assent. In such an image there would surely be a place for precursors.

This is not to deny that the search for precursors by historians of economics may also have self-interested motives. As Weintraub remarks

> Precursor studies seem to function then as legitimizers of a historian's interest in certain past contributors, or possibly marginalized members of a particular scientific community. Rhetorically, calling A "B's precursor," where we can assume a reading community's interest in B, legitimizes an interest in A, if A was not hitherto well noted. In a like manner, if a hitherto unknown current B's contributions can be reconstructed as the fully-articulated version of the past-famous A's almost-analysis, then A's "precursorness" may further enhance a glorious reputation.
>
> (Weintraub 1991: 395)

Or, as I would prefer to put it, professional kudos might be obtainable when studying an obscure economist if that economist can be represented as a precursor of a more famous one or as an anticipator of currently fashionable ideas. While, when studying an already famous economist, credit may be garnered by demonstrating that more of later work was anticipated by that economist than has hitherto been recognized. Conversely:

> A's claim that B is a precursor of A may be an assertion that B has a fame which A can utilize to legitimize A's contribution . . . . the notion that B is my precursor is a rhetorical device which attempts to legitimize certain claims the author otherwise seeks to establish by arguments based on accepted rules of argument within the particular language community.
> (Weintraub 1997: 224)

The argument here differs from that in "Invoking precursors to lend authority to new ideas" earlier, mainly because an author's invocation of precursors is narrowly self-interested rather than driven by intellectual conviction and revolutionary zeal for novel ideas.

A consequence of the kinds of self-interested motivation revealed here may be a tendency to over-representation of precursor claims, but the winds of criticism should winnow out those lacking a kernel of (dare one say it?) truth. The main practical difficulty is that the precursor work typically contains both more and less than the precursee work(s) so that differing views on the extent and centrality of the overlap may be difficult to reconcile.

What of the canon?

How does all this bear on the vexed topic of "the" canon? The controversies associated with the idea of "the canon of great literature" demonstrate the perils and difficulties of the concept, and the term "canon" is itself sufficiently elusive and ambiguous to require elucidation.[12]

Now economics certainly has its roster of "great works," on which there would be considerable although not absolute unanimity. It is arguable though that usage in our field refers to a set of canonical ideas rather than a set of canonical texts. Such a usage of "canon" derives from the mathematical concept of "canonical form" and seems to have been popularized by Samuelson (1978), in his "canonical classical model" for example. The canon then would be a skeletal set of central ideas, more or less a Kuhnian paradigm. On a Whiggish view there will be a unique and gradually crystallizing dominant paradigm expressible in its own canonical form. If a continuing and unresolvable "conflict of schools" is instead taken to be the norm, then each school will develop its own set of canonical ideas. In either case, the search for and appropriation of predecessors and precursors will inevitably be an integral aspect of the construction and defense of a canon, providing supporting texts and additional evidence as to the appeal and inevitability of the canonical ideas. If historians of economics see past economic thought as involving discontinuous shifts between distinct phases, then the canonical ideas of each phase may need to be reconstructed to aid historical understanding.

Appendix: articles from economic literature having the word "precursor(s)" in the title

Boudreaux, D. J. and Selgin, G. A. (1990) "L. Albert Hahn: A Precursor of Keynesianism and the Monetarist Counterrevolution," *History of Political Economy* 22(2) (Summer): 261–79.

Brahmananda, P. R. (1996) "Ganesh Venkatesh Joshi (1851–1911): A Neglected Precursor of Manilesco, Nurkse and Arthur Lewis," *Indian Economic Journal* 43(4) (April–June): 155–69.

Cirillo, R. (1983) "Was Vilfredo Pareto really a 'Precursor' of Fascism?" *American Journal of Economics and Sociology* 42(2) (April): 235–45.

Cowen, T. and Krosener, R. (1992) "German Language Precursors of the New Monetary Economics," *Journal of Institutional and Theoretical Economics* 148(3) (September): 387–410.

Diatkine, S. (1993) "Thomas Attwood: Crude Inflationist or Precursor of Modern Money and Banking Theory?", in R. F. Hébert (ed.), *Perspectives on the History of Economic Thought*, vol. 9, Aldershot: Elgar: 107–18.

Elliott, J. E. and Dowlah, A. F. (1991) "Intellectual Precursors of Perestroika," *International Journal of Social Economics* 18(5–7): 175–206.

Estape, F. (1996) "Ibn Kaldun of Tunis as a Precursor of Economic Science," *Societat Catalana d'Economia Annuari* 13 (Barcelona).

Foss, N. J. (1994) "The Theory of the Firm: The Austrians as Precursors and Critics of Contemporary Theory," *Review of Austrian Economics* 7(1): 31–65.

Hines, L. G. (1973) "Precursors to Benefit Cost Analysis in early US Public Investment Projects," *Land Economics* 49(3) (August): 310–17.

Hodgson, G. M. (1994) "Precursors of Modern Evolutionary Economics: Marx, Marshall, Veblen and Schumpeter" (see listing in *References*).

Humphrey, T. M. (1989) "Precursors of the [FRB] P-star Model," *Federal Reserve Bank of Richmond Economic Review* 75(4) (July–August): 3–9.

Kenzenkamp, H. A. (1991) "A Precursor to Muth: Tinbergen's 1932 Model of Rational Expectations," *Economic Journal* 101(408) (September): 1245–53.

Klotz, G. (1994), "Achylle Nicolas Isnard: Precurseur de Léon Walras?", *Economies et Sociétés* 28(10–11) (October–November): 29–52.

Mitchell, W. C. (1984) "Schumpeter and Public Choice, Part I: Precursor to Public Choice?", *Public Choice* 42(1): 73–88.

Peterson, J. H. (1986) "Three Precursors of Modern Theories of Old Age Pensions," *History of Political Economy* 18(3) (Fall): 405–17.

Robertson, R. M. [1951] (1988) "Jevons and his Precursors," in J. C. Wood (ed), *William Stanley Jevons: Critical Assessments*, vol. 1, London and New York: Routledge: 146–66.

Samuels, W. J. (1969) "The Tableau Economique as a Simple Leontief Model: A Precursor to Phillips," *Indian Economic Journal* 17(1) (July–September): 112–17.

Silagi, M. (1992) "Henry George and Europe: Precursors of Land Reform in Germany; Marx and the Land Question; The Beginnings of the Georgist Movement in the Empire," *American Journal of Economics and Sociology* 51(2) (April): 247–56.

Skinner, A. S. (1994) "National Realities. David Hume: Precursor of Sir James Stewart?", in M. Albertone and A. Masoero (eds), *Political Economy and National Realities*, Luigi Einaudi Foundation, Studi 31, Turin: 31–51.

Streissler, E. and Neudeck, W. (1986), "Are there Intellectual Precursors to the Idea of Second Best Optimization?", *Journal of Economics* (Zeitschrift für Nationalökonomie) Supplementum 5: 227–42.

Waldauer, C. (1996) "Kautilya's Arthashastra: A Neglected Precursor to Classical

Economics," *Indian Economic Review* 31(1) (January–June): 101–8.

Ward, I. D. S. [1959] (1991) "George Berkeley: Precursor of Keynes or Moral Economist on Underdevelopment?", in M. Blaug (ed.), *Pre-Classical Economists*, vol. 2 (Pioneers in Economics Series, vol. 7), Aldershot: Elgar.

Notes

1 I am indebted to Robert Dimand for this point and for other valuable suggestions. He instances reactions to Marx.
2 See the section entitled "Precursors and the interpretation of past economic thought." Weintraub's definition is consistent with such an extension and, of course, equal time intervals from t-2 to t-1 and t-1 to t are not required.
3 The chapter is entitled "Notes on mercantilism, the usury laws, stamped money, and theories of under-consumption." It covers the views of the mercantilists, Smith, Bentham, Gesell, Mandeville, Malthus and Hobson. Interestingly, other and perhaps more significant precursors of the *General Theory*, such as Johannsen 1908 and Walker 1879, on whom see Backhouse 1987, are ignored. Johannsen had even been mentioned in Keynes's *Treatise* (1930).
4 It is perhaps unnecessary to insist in this connection upon a distinction between precursors and predecessors known from the outset to the "revolutionary" author but generally neglected or undervalued.
5 Social interaction provides, of course, another arena for self promotion.
6 This section is obviously perfunctory and included mainly for comprehensiveness. The representation of economic inquiry as the domain of competing "schools of economic thought" – Lakatosian "competing research programs" if you will – seems more plausible to me than an extreme relativism like Weintraub's which makes all flux. This does not exclude evolution within any school.
7 The database covers titles for articles published or republished since 1969 and abstracts, reviews, etc., only from the mid-1980s. The 1990s show considerable usage of the searched-for words, but this perhaps reflects rapid growth in the scale of the pertinent literature rather than increased intensity of usage. Some of the usage might reflect partisan endeavors of the kind indicated in the section "Claiming precursors in the 'conflict of schools'" rather than dispassionate enquiries.
8 The numbers in parentheses indicate the listing numbers of articles in the appendix. An asterisk denotes denial or qualification of a precursorship claim.
9 The distribution among the above categories is as follows: category 1): five cases (one negative); category 2): twenty cases (five negative); category 3): one case.
10 For example Bowley 1972, Brems 1989, Humphrey 1992, Mann [1959] 1991, Samuelson 1993, Syll 1993, Uebe 1992, and so on. I might also mention two of my own articles, Whitaker 1964, 1982.
11 As Weintraub remarks:

> A precursor then is a temporally earlier right idea, where right is equivalent to 'correct from the present viewpoint.' Science as the exemplar of the march of reason . . . leads the Whiggish historian of economics, and the normal economic scientist, to think in terms of successes and failures, precursors and blind alleys, heroes sung and unsung, and all manner of retrospective gold medals and booby prizes.
>
> (Weintraub 1997: 224)

Ingrao, commenting on Weintraub (1997), shares his criticism of "the naive, scientist view that conceives thought as linearly progressing" but warns that extreme relativism can deny a "constructive role for sound interpretation and theoretical appraisal in history writing" (Ingrao 1997: 227).

12 The *Oxford English Dictionary* gives no assistance on modern usage. *Merriam Webster's Collegiate Dictionary* gives two pertinent alternatives: "a sanctioned or accepted group or body of related works" instancing "the canon of great literature" and "a body of principles, rules, standards, or norms." Under "canonical form" it gives "the simplest form of something," with a mathematical example.

References

Argyrous, G. (1990) "The Growth of Knowledge and Economic Science: Marshall's Interpretation of Classical Economics," *History of Political Economy* 22(3) (Fall): 529–37.

Backhouse, R. (1987) "F. A. Walker's Theory of Hard Times," *History of Political Economy* 19(3) (Fall): 435–46.

Baumol, W. J. and Goldfeld, S. M. (1968) *Precursors in Mathematical Economics: An Anthology*, London School of Economics and Political Science, London: Series of Reprints of Scarce Works in Political Economy, 19.

Baurman, G. B. (1991) "A Comparison of the Single Tax Proposals of Henry George and the Physiocrats," *History of Political Economy* 23(3) (Fall): 481–96.

Boettke, P. J. (ed.) (1994) *The Elgar Companion to Austrian Economics*, Aldershot: Elgar.

Bowley, M. (1972) "The Predecessors of Jevons – The Revolution that Wasn't," *Manchester School* 40(1), (March): 9–29.

Brems, H. (1989), "Gustav Cassel Revisited," *History of Political Economy* 21(2), (Summer): 165–78.

George, H. (1879) *Progress and Poverty: An Inquiry into the Cause of Industrial Depressions and of Increase of Want with Increase of Wealth* (privately published, San Francisco: many subsequent editions).

Hodgson, G. M. (1994) "Precursors of Modern Evolutionary Economics: Marx, Marshall, Veblen and Schumpeter," in R. W. England (ed.), *Evolutionary Concepts in Contemporary Economics*, Ann Arbor: University of Michigan Press: 9–35.

Hollander, S. (1987) *Classical Economics*, Oxford and New York: Blackwell.

Humphrey, T. M. (1992) "Marshallian Cross Diagrams and their Uses before Alfred Marshall: The Origins of Supply and Demand Geometry," *Economic Review of the Federal Reserve Bank of Richmond* 78(2), (March–April): 3–23.

Ingrao, B. (1997) comment on Weintraub (1997) in A. Salanti and E. Screpanti (eds), *Pluralism in Economics*, Cheltenham and Brookfield Vt.: Edward Elgar: 227–31.

Jevons, W. S. (1871) *The Theory of Political Economy*, London: Macmillan.

—— (1879) *The Theory of Political Economy*, 2nd edn, London: Macmillan (page references given are to the 3rd edn of 1888).

Johannsen, N. A. L. J. (1908) *A Neglected Point in Connection with Crises*, New York: Bankers' Publishing.

Keynes, J. M. [1926] (1972) "Francis Ysidro Edgeworth," in *Essays in Biography*, London: Macmillan (*Collected Writings* vol. 10): 251–66.

—— (1930) *A Treatise on Money*, London: Macmillan.

—— (1936) *The General Theory of Employment, Interest and Money*, London: Macmillan.

Mann, M. [1959] (1991) "Lord Lauderdale: Underconsumptionist and Keynesian Predecessor," in M. Blaug (ed.), *Pioneers of Economics*, vol. 13, Aldershot: Elgar: 145–54.

Meek, R. L. (ed.) (1973) *Precursors of Adam Smith, 1750-1775*, London: Dent, and Totowa, N.J.: Rowman and Littlefield.

Newman, P. (1987) "Edgeworth, Francis Ysidro (1845-1926)", in J. Eatwell, M. Milgate and P. Newman (eds), *The New Palgrave* 2, London: Macmillan: 84–98.

O'Brien, D. P. (1990) "Marshall's Work in Relation to Classical Economics," in J. K.

Whitaker (ed.), *Centenary Essays on Alfred Marshall*, Cambridge: Cambridge University Press: 127–63.

Price, L. L. F. R. (1926) "Francis Ysidro Edgeworth," *Journal of the Royal Statistical Society* 89 (March): 371–7.

Rothbard, M. N. (1995) *An Austrian Perspective on the History of Economic Thought*, 2 vols, Aldershot: Elgar.

Samuelson, P. A. (1978) "The Canonical Classical Model of Political Economy," *Journal of Economic Literature* 16(4) (December): 1415–34.

—— (1993) "Gustav Cassel's Scientific Innovations: Claims and Realities," *History of Political Economy* 25(3) (Fall): 515–27.

Staley, C. E. (1989) *A History of Economic Thought: From Aristotle to Arrow*, Oxford: Blackwell.

Stigler, S. M. (1978) "Francis Ysidro Edgeworth as Statistician," *Journal of the Royal Statistical Society*, Series A 143: 287–322.

Syll, L. P. (1993) "Cassell and Revealed Preference Theory," *History of Political Economy* 25(3) (Fall): 499–514.

Uebe, G. (1992) "The First Flow of Funds Table: Lang's Tableau of 1815," *History of Political Economy* 24(2) (Summer): 435–53.

Walker, F. A. (1879) *Money in its Relation to Trade and Industry*, New York: Holt.

Weintraub, E. R. (1991) "Allais, Stability, and Liapunov Theory," *History of Political Economy* 23(3) (Fall): 383–96.

—— (1997) "Is 'Is a Precursor of' a Transitive Relation?", in A. Salanti and E. Screpanti (eds), *Pluralism in Economics*, Cheltenham and Brookfield, Vt.: Elgar: 212–6.

Whitaker, J. K. (1964) "A Note on the CES Production Function," *Review of Economic Studies* 31 (April): 166–7.

—— (1982), "A Neglected Classic in the Theory of Distribution," *Journal of Political Economy* 90 (April): 333–55.

22 Economic texts as apocrypha

David M. Levy

Introduction

Samuel Hollander asked me to explain how the classical economists came to be "reactionaries." The otherwise appealing answer "they *were* reactionaries because of Malthusian wage theory" has the difficulty of being demonstrably false. Hollander himself has demolished the lynch-pin of such interpretation "the fixity of the condition of the working class" in his decades in the making *Economics of Thomas Robert Malthus* (Hollander 1997). However if Hollander, and those of us who have come to similar conclusions, are correct then how do we explain the nearly unanimous view to the contrary?[1]

One question can determine who bears the blame for error. In what context did economics become the "dismal science"? The predictable answer "we became the 'dismal science' precisely because of Malthus's theory of the fixed condition of the working class" demonstrates what is so odd about seeing the classics as "reactionary."[2] The correct answer is that we became the "dismal science" as the result of our classical predecessors' role in the abolition of British racial slavery.[3] This claim is not a conjecture; it is a matter of the historical record. Here is the long-forgotten context in which Thomas Carlyle first used the phrase "dismal science" in the December 1849 article in *Fraser's Magazine*, "Occasional Discourse on the Negro Question" (ODNQ) in which he proposed re-enslavement:[4]

> Truly, my philanthropic friends, Exeter Hall Philanthropy is wonderful: and the Social Science – not a "gay science," but a rueful – which finds the secret of this universe in "supply-and-demand," and reduces the duty of human governors to that of letting men alone, is also wonderful. Not a "gay science," I should say, like some we have heard of; no, a dreary, desolate, and indeed quite abject and distressing one; what we might call, by way of eminence, the *dismal science*. These two, Exeter Hall Philanthropy and the Dismal Science, led by any sacred cause of Black Emancipation, or the like, to fall in love and make a wedding of it, will give birth to progenies and prodigies; dark extensive moon-calves, – unnameable abortions, wide-coiled monstrosities, such as the world has not seen hitherto!
>
> (Carlyle 1849: 672–3)

The reader, who cannot imagine to what the unsubtle references to inter-racial sexuality could refer, will learn soon enough.

As Frank Knight has been reported to say on such occasions, it is not ignorance that gets us into so much trouble, but knowing so much which simply isn't true.[5] Widespread error is easy to explain since the truth is very costly.[6] How though is it possible that so many careful scholars make the same error? It would be completely improbable that a large literature would fall into common error if there had been independent research behind the erroneous conclusion.

What might cause a violation of independence of research efforts? I shall argue that there are two violations. First, there is omitted common factor in research, and this will be the topic of the first section of the chapter. What has fallen out of our common knowledge is the fury aimed at economic models of a free society by nineteenth-century defenders of slave society. That Carlyle was the British theorist of an idealized slave system was absolutely clear to those who found themselves in need of a justification for the actually existing slave system in America. Consequently, when George Fitzhugh introduces *Cannibals All!* he defers to the great man across the waters:

> At the very time when we were writing our pamphlet entitled "Slavery Justified," in which we took ground that Free Society had failed, Mr. Carlyle began to write his "*Latter Day Pamphlets*," whose very title is the assertion of the failure of Free Society. The proof derived from this coincidence becomes the stronger, when it is perceived that an ordinary man on this side [of] the Atlantic discovered and was exposing the same social phenomena that an extraordinary one had discovered and *was* exposing on the other. The very titles of our works are synonymous – for the "Latter Day" is the "Failure of Society."
> (Fitzhugh 1857: xx)

How surprising can it be that the American debates in the 1850s, with war impending, provide a vantage from which oblique British defenses of slavery attain transparency?

There is a second violation of research independence. Literary scholars of various persuasions seem enamored of a view of literature, attributed to Carlyle's great disciple, John Ruskin, that literary art moralizes, or as Matthew Arnold put it: "In thus making sweetness and light [S&L] to be characters of perfection, culture is of like spirit with poetry."[7] What does the scholar, for whom this identification of culture and poetry makes sense, do in the presence of great art akin to *Birth of a Nation*? The trick seems to be that S&L does not always come in fixed proportions; one can obtain more S out of the texts by shedding less L in some corners.

The first section of this chapter deals with what seems to be hard to see and the second section deals with that which is easy enough but what all too many scholars seem to prefer not to see.

What has not been seen

We study the past to make sense of the present.[8] Included in the present is some notion of that which distinguishes then from now. This notion, which we call "progress," is not in the past; rather, it is a theoretical claim, with which to organize events imposed upon the past in service to the present. Importantly the notion of progress tells scholars which texts are vital to read and which texts are not.

It is in the context of the independence of research efforts that I propose we think about the canon in economics. Let us call "canonical" the texts one is expected to know to be in the discipline. "Progress" gives reason to consider some texts more important than others. Of course, there is a good economic reason to have a limited canon at some moment in time; the day only has twenty-four hours and one can only read so many words per minute. The debates on the canon have paid insufficient attention to another economic way of making disciplinary demands consistent with one's life. This is to mark off some texts as completely irrelevant, texts that need be read by no one. Just as the deepest economic theory tells us that every market is connected with every other market, the most persuasive philosophy of language tells us that every text is connected to every other text. However these are councils of perfection for a better world.[9]

In our world in which time is scarce, it is helpful, perhaps even necessary, to suppose that there is a boundary across which these connections are remote enough to neglect.[10] Without a convention that there are texts which everyone can ignore (whatever it is they mean, this does not bear upon the important texts) the number of texts can swamp the time available for reading them.

We need a name for books that, as a disciplinary convention, are excluded. Since "canon" is used to name what all need to know, let us use "*apocrypha*" to name what none are expected to know. "*Apocrypha*" is Greek for "hidden"; that seems right.

With such notation in hand let us return to the problem of systematic common error. Suppose that the meaning of a canonical text depends upon a text in the *apocrypha*.[11] Since knowledge of the *apocrypha* is at best second-hand then there is no reason to believe that scholarly conclusions will be independent. Without independence there is no reason to believe that the discipline will correct even gross common errors.

Broad utilitarianism

As an overview to my reading of the larger debate, the missing piece in the equation (the information which neither modern economists nor others have) is the utilitarian basis of the anti-slavery coalition uniting Christian evangelicals and Utilitarian political economists.[12] As there is a mathematical issue involved at the center of the matter, economists ought not expect much guidance from innumerate textual specialists.[13] I propose to distinguish a "narrow" (capitalized) Utilitarianism, as formulated in the position of Jeremy Bentham and associates, and a "broad" utilitarianism which encompasses multiple interpretations of the greatest happiness principle.[14]

Multiple interpretations of the defining slogan of utilitarianism – Francis Hutcheson's "the greatest happiness for the greatest number" – exist. A Platonist knows this as a logical matter. The slogan is mathematically inconsistent: all sentences follow from it.[15] To make coherent policy on the basis of the imperative, one must select one of an infinity of models, of which infinity Bentham's maximizing total happiness approach is just one.[16] As a matter of fact, pre-Benthamite utilitarianism seems to have made judgments on the basis of the happiness of the median individual.[17]

Broad utilitarianism is of necessity a universalist philosophy. One's moral obligations do not stop at an inconsequential border imposed by race, nationality or belief. It is entirely in this spirit that we can find the evangelicals, for whom Adam and Eve were part of the real past, asking on behalf of the slaves: "Am I not a man and a brother?"[18] As any form of utilitarianism must do, it judges overall well-being on the basis of individual well-being. The decisive step to make the evangelical-Utilitarian coalition function is the twofold agreement that first, the well-being of those at the bottom of the distribution of happiness merit our immediate attention and second, the greatest happiness principle of Utilitarianism is formally equivalent to the Golden Rule of Christianity. By focusing exclusively on the condition of slavery, the intra-coalition disagreement as to the nature of happiness was obviated. Utilitarians, then and now, are divided as to whether happiness is anything other than what we, in fact, choose.[19] In the nineteenth century, a heatedly-debated topic concerned the relationship between freely chosen sexuality and happiness.[20] When one focuses on the happiness of slaves – those for whom the range of all choice is radically attenuated – debates over choice vanish and utilitarians unite.[21]

The belief in the formal identity of the Golden Rule of Christianity and the Greatest Happiness Principle of Utilitarianism seems to have passed without notice among twentieth-century commentators.[22] Nonetheless, the texts are exactly where one would expect to find them: in the great debate between T. B. Macaulay and Utilitarians over J. S. Mill's *Government*.[23] Macaulay found nothing to dispute in the Utilitarian formula because it was also a Christian formula:

> The "greatest happiness principle" of Mr Bentham is included in the Christian morality; and, to our thinking, it is there exhibited in an infinitely more sound and philosophical form, than in the Utilitarian speculations. . . . "Do as you would be done by: Love your neighbour as yourself;" these are the precepts of Jesus Christ. Understood in an enlarged sense, these precepts are, in fact, a direction to every man to promote the greatest happiness of the greatest number.[24]
>
> (Lively and Rees 1978: 175)

Macaulay's Utilitarian opponent affected surprise that this needed to be mentioned:

> Nobody ever thought of denying, that the author of Christianity was the first of Utilitarians. . . . Mr. Bentham has demonstrated that for individuals,

societies, nations, to "do as they would be done by," is sound earthly policy. The bigots keep a close lock on their Elysium; but whenever the time comes for the *second* Utilitarian to present himself at the gate, it is presumable the *first* will not wait for their leave, to greet him with "Well done."[25]

(Lively and Rees 1978: 191)

John Stuart Mill, offering his most considered statement of Utilitarianism, found the true spirit of this philosophy in the teachings of Christ.[26] This establishes the coalition agreement on the formal issue.

What evidence is there of agreement that slavery was the worst case? The leader of the "Clapham Sect," William Wilberforce, put forward a series of considerations why we should regard West Indian slavery as the worst state possible for a human. While there may be other reasons he had for thinking this, he gave three strong reasons.[27] The first two considerations appeal to all universalists; the third appeals to all Christians. Here are the claims he put forward. One ought not treat a person as a horse:

> Not being supposed capable of being governed like other human beings, by the hope of reward, or the fear of punishment, they are subjected to the immediate impulse or present terror of the whip, and are driven at their work like brute animals. Lower than this it is scarcely possible for man to be depressed by man.

(Wilberforce 1823: 12)

One ought not to treat a woman as a will-less sexual object:

> No one who reflects on the subject can be at a loss to anticipate one odious use which is too commonly made of this despotism, in extorting, from the fears of the young females who are subject to it, compliances with the licentious desires of the drivers, which they might otherwise have refused from attachment to another, if not from moral feelings and restraints. It is idle and insulting to talk of improving the condition of these poor beings, as rational and moral agents, while they are treated in a manner which precludes self-government, and annihilates all human motives but such as we impose on a maniac, or on a hardened and incorrigible convict.

(Wilberforce 1823: 13)

One ought not to make marriage impossible for men and women:

> I have dwelt the longer, and insisted the more strongly on the universal want of the marriage institution among the slaves, because, among the multiplied abuses of the West Indian system, it appears to me to be one of the most influential in its immoral and degrading effects.... Alas! the injustice with which these poor creatures are treated accompanies them throughout the whole of their progress; and even the cordial drops which

a gracious Providence has elsewhere poured into the cup of poverty and labour, are to them vitiated and embittered.

(Wilberforce 1823: 16)

When challenged with an argument that we shall meet later, Wilberforce selects the sexual slavery argument as the most powerful. Here is the pro-slavery challenge:

> Indeed, the West Indians, in the warmth of argument, have gone still farther, and have even distinctly told us, again and again, – and I am shocked to say that some of their partizans in this country have re-echoed the assertion, – that these poor degraded beings, the Negro slaves, are as well or even better off than our British peasantry.
>
> (Wilberforce 1823: 33–34)

Here is Wilberforce's response:

> Let me therefore ask, is there, in the whole of the three kingdoms, a parent or a husband so sordid and insensible that any sum, which the richest West-Indian proprietor could offer him, would be deemed a compensation for his suffering his wife or his daughter to be subjected to the brutal outrage of the cart-whip – to the savage lust of the driver – to the indecent, and degrading, a merciless punishment of a West-Indian whipping?
>
> (Wilberforce 1823: 35)

The Utilitarians were in agreement that slavery is at the bottom of the distribution of happiness. This too is made abundantly clear in the debate over Mill's *Government*. Mill's worst-case model of government specified it as if it were a slave driver. Mill asked how English gentlemen behave when given slaves in the West Indies:

> The world affords some decisive experiments upon human nature, in exact conformity with these conclusions. An English Gentleman may be taken as a favourable specimen of civilization, of knowledge, of humanity, of all the qualities, in short, that make human nature estimable. . . . In the West Indies, before that vigilant attention of the English nation, which now, for thirty years, has imposed so great a check upon the masters of slaves, there was not a perfect absence of all check upon the dreadful propensities of power. But yet it is true, that these propensities led English Gentlemen, not only to deprive their slaves of property, and to make property of their fellow-creatures, but to treat them with a degree of cruelty, the very description of which froze the blood of those of their countrymen, who were placed in less unfavourable circumstances.
>
> (Lively and Rees 1978: 67)

> if one man has power over others placed in his hands, he will make use of it for an evil purpose; for the purpose of rendering those other men the

abject instruments of his will. If we, then, suppose, that one man has the power of choosing the Representatives of the people, it follows, that he will choose men, who will use their power as Representatives for the promotion of this his sinister interest.

(Lively and Rees 1978: 78)

Macaulay's response takes up several themes, none of which deny slavery its position as the worst case. Rather neatly, he seems to have encountered a paradox of the worse case. If one is thinking of government with the potential to emancipate slaves, what sense does it make to model the government in worst-case slave driving terms?[28] Consequently, Macaulay defends models of government under which the self-interest of the governors needs to be filled in empirically before conclusions can be drawn.[29] Moreover, he asks why Mill's democratic conclusions follow from the axioms of the model.[30] Won't the majority have a sinister interest in exploiting the minority?[31]

It may perhaps be said that, in the long run, it is for the interest of the people that property should be secure, and that therefore they will respect it. We answer thus - It cannot be pretended that it is not for the immediate interest of the people to plunder the rich. Therefore, even if it were quite certain that, in the long run, the people would, as a body, lose by doing so, it would not necessarily follow that the fear of remote ill consequences would overcome the desire of immediate acquisitions. Every individual might flatter himself that the punishment would not fall on him. Mr. Mill himself tells us, in his Essay on Jurisprudence, that no quantity of evil which is remote and uncertain will suffice to prevent crime.

(Lively and Rees 1978: 119)

Surely, Macaulay argues, approbation is desired and this might offset the desire for wealth at what we would say the margin: "the love of approbation, and other kindred feelings, always tend to produce good government" (Lively and Rees 1978: 127).

In response the Utilitarians averted again to racial slavery as a model of despotic government and while conceding the formal "unrealism" of the account defended the value of worst-case models in familiar Humean fashion:

It is true that there are partial exceptions to the rule, that all men use power as badly as they dare. There may have been such things as amiable negro-drivers and sentimental masters of press-gangs . . . But it would be as wise to recommend wolves for nurses at the Foundling, on the credit of Romulus and Remus, as to substitute the exception for the general fact, and advise mankind to take to trusting to arbitrary power on the credit of these specimens.

(Lively and Rees 1978: 135)

On the strength of this debate, Macaulay came to such prominence as to become a member of Parliament where he spoke vigorously for the emancipation of the slaves in the British West Indies. His Parliamentary role in the emancipation of West Indian slaves in 1833 is wonderfully told in Trevelyan's *Life*. The government proposed £20 million to the slave owners and a commitment to a twelve-year transition between slavery and freedom, an "apprenticeship." The money was easy; consenting to even temporary slavery was not.[32] Macaulay found himself, as Trevelyan tells, caught between the hard duty to principles that argued for immediate liberation and the politically possible.[33] He spoke in qualified support for the government after handing in his resignation. First, he argues for the importance of competition:

> In free countries the master has a choice of labourers, and the labourer has a choice of masters; but in slavery it is always necessary to give despotic power to the master. This bill leaves it to the magistrate to keep peace between master and slave. Every time that the slave takes twenty minutes to do that which the master thinks he should do in fifteen, recourse must be had to the magistrate. Society would day and night be in a constant state of litigation, and all differences and difficulties must be solved by judicial interference.
> (Trevelyan 1978, 1: 284–5)

Holding firm to his position in the debate with Mill, Macaulay trusts the government more than he trusts slave owners:

> He did not share in Mr. Buxton's apprehension of gross cruelty as a result of the apprenticeship. "The magistrate would be accountable to the Colonial Office, and the Colonial Office to the House of Commons, in which every lash which was inflicted under magisterial authority would be told and counted. My apprehension is that the result of continuing for twelve years this dead slavery, – this state of society destitute of any vital principle, – will be that the whole negro population will sink into weak and drawling inefficacy, and will be much less fit for liberty at the end of the period than at the commencement. My hope is that the system will die a natural death; that the experience of a few months will so establish its utter inefficiency as to induce the planters to abandon it, and to substitute for it a state of freedom. I have voted," he said, "for the Second Reading, and I shall vote for the Third Reading; but, while the bill is in Committee, I shall join with other honourable gentlemen in doing all that is possible to amend it."
> (Trevelyan 1978, 1: 285)[34]

In a day the Government weakened, proposing a seven-year transition to freedom and the abolitionists, perhaps fearing perfection as the enemy of a great good attainable, accepted.

"Progressive" Fraser's

If economists do not know the racial texts as a matter of disciplinary conventions, what about textual specialists? Physicists report that there is a wraith-like particle, the neutrino, which could pass through a block of lead a light-year thick without collision. Imagine how much more difficult it would be to find a neutrino if the atom which it finally encountered claimed upon inquiry that it was actually visiting the Balkans at the time! The Utilitarian-evangelical agreement of the identity of the Greatest Happiness Principle and the Golden Rule has not only sailed neutrino-like through a century of humanistic texts but one "fact" which everyone knows, Charles Dickens' testimony in the novel *Hard Times* of the opposition of Utilitarian and Christian belief, is a falsification of the historical record.[35] As a consequence, perhaps, the debate over whether policy ought to be focused on black slaves or "white slaves" has not been seen as a debate over just who in fact is at the bottom of the distribution of happiness. Nor has it been appreciated how the issue of slavery obviated debate over choice and happiness.

What is important for humanists is not what is important for economists. "Progress" in the humanistic disciplines involves the triumph of science over traditional Christianity. A defining episode in the warfare of science with theology in Christendom – to recall the title of A. D. White's classic study – is the question of whether Adam and Eve were real people from whom all the human inhabitants of the world descend. In service to this vision of "progress," historians have singled out for special attention a group of Christians who reconciled their beliefs with the emerging scientific consensus that Adam and Eve were not real.[36] In addition to Carlyle himself, these include Samuel Taylor Coleridge, Charles Kingsley and J. Froude.[37]

Emphasis on the universal in evangelical Christianity is replaced by emphasis on the local in progressive Christianity; claims of truth are replaced with claims of belief.[38] In the limit we find progressive religious thinkers asserting that quantum of familiarity being equal, Pan is as good as Christ.[39] The Victorian periodical which perhaps most closely identified itself with such "progressive" Christianity was *Fraser's*. It is worthy of reflection that with the possible exception of Coleridge, this list of religious thinkers is the same list which recent scholars have compiled of Britain's most important "literary" racists.[40] Humanistic scholars have no theoretical explanations for the progressives' racial brutalism.[41] In localized religion, the equivalence of the Greatest Happiness Principle and the Golden Rule breaks down. The only "others" who matter are those near at hand; those who look like us and believe like us.

To see how humanistic scholars have come to grips with the racially-charged texts on this issue, consider the judgment of scholars on the status of *Fraser's Magazine for Town and Country*, the locus for the "dismal science" label. It appears there is one, and only one, book-length scholarly treatment of this magazine in its early days, Miriam Thrall's 1934 "meticulous" *Rebellious Fraser's*.[42] She tells us in great detail (Thrall 1934: 129–145) how, under the leadership of William Maginn, *Fraser's* stood against the economists and for humanity. Here is Thrall's judgment which links Maginn's anti-anti-slavery with Carlyle's attack on economists:[43]

> In condemning the cupidity, heartlessness, and hypocrisy of those political economists who were smirched by the child slavery of the factories, Maginn was as unsparing as Carlyle was later in his Nigger Question. An instance of the kind of slur to which they were subjected . . .

Maginn did not wish it thought that he favored the institution of slavery because he opposed emancipation propaganda. The question in the abstract, he said he was not concerned with. His sole contention was that the economists and their supporters by the policies of free trade and anti-slavery were striking at the prosperity of the colonies, weakening the ties which bound them to England, and in consequence operating to the detriment of the empire.

(Thrall 1934: 145)

Thrall seems to propose that the "child slavery" of the factories is of greater concern than that of real slavery. In the impartial *Wellesley Index*, Houghton (1972: 303), says this about why *Fraser's* became important:

> Whatever else "a magazine" may be, wrote the editor in 1879, "it is primarily an organ of literary expression." That, indeed, was the basic reason for *Fraser's* initial success in the 1830s and its establishment as a major periodical. In the second place, from start to finish, it was an outstanding organ, if not of open revolt, as Thrall would have it (*Rebellious Fraser's*), at least of progressive thought.
>
> (Houghton 1972: 305–8)[44]

In the very first volume of *Fraser's Magazine for Town and Country* in 1830 there is a response by this humane, progressive Maginn to Macaulay, who had written in part as an economic historian in the *Edinburgh Review* challenging the poet laureate Robert Southey's reflections on society. Macaulay was young when he reviewed Southey so Maginn introduced him to *Fraser's* readers as part of the great Christian anti-slavery crusade:

> Our judgment on him for the article which we have just mentioned is not too severe, as the following extract will shew; and, reader, remember, whilst you are enjoying its beauties of diction, and giving the author all credit for the mild spirit of Christianity which it breathes, that that author is the same youth whose existence Mr. William Wilberforce would have involved in the economy of all-gracious Providence, and who is not only the son and heir to the shining virtues of Zachary Macauley [sic], the friend of humanity and of the *nigger* portion of the creation, but has himself spouted at anti-slavery meetings in favour of all black populations, until he received the *accolade paternelle* of the old and enthusiastic Mr. Wilberforce, on account of the fervour and zeal with which he pleaded the cause of universal charity, – and good will and affection towards the *niggers* in particular, not of Sierra Leone, but of our West Indian islands.
>
> ([Maginn] 1830: 584)[45]

The contrast drawn between "humanity and of the *nigger* part of creation," by someone who is paid to use the English language, suggests that, for Maginn "humanity" was exclusively white.[46] The fact that *Fraser's* "from start to finish" is judged "progressive" by the standard reference work in Victorian periodical literature (the very one that I gratefully employ to assign attributions to the *Fraser's* articles) hints, one might say, that there is something very interesting about the authoritative understanding of Victorian literature. However, before we leap to any such substantive conclusions on the basis of one article, actually a few sentences from one article, we should read further.

What seems to be missing in the standard readings of *Fraser's* role in the great debate over emancipation is its persistent denial that slaves occupy the bottom of the distribution of happiness. For example, *Fraser's* February 1831 explained that opposition to slavery was based in an ignorance of the science of philology:

> The West Indians, at the very outset, labour under a serious disadvantage. In no country is liberty so highly extolled, and so little understood, as in Great Britain. And consequently the word *slave*, is associated in the mind of the great mass of the people with every thing that is debasing and cruel. If, however, we examine the origin of the term, much of this cause of offence, this stumbling-block to the uninformed, will vanish. "From the *Sclavi*," observes Sir Walter Raleigh, "came the word, *slave* . . . which is in their language 'glorious;'"
>
> (*Fraser's* February 1831: 114)

After tables comparing the penalties of slaves and of soldiers for various offenses, and concluding that the slaves were punished less harshly, *Fraser's* offers evidence from the slave's cash balances to demonstrate that at least some slaves were richer than some free laborers.

Then, the March 1831 issue, *Fraser's* put forward a real argument that there is reason to believe that slaves will not occupy the bottom of the scale of happiness. Slaves will be well-treated by profit-maximizing masters for the same reasons profit-maximizing farmers treat their horses well:

> It is manifest, by the comparison of their sleekness to that of our English horses, they must be in no bad condition. I have often thought it might occur to anti-slavery writers and speakers, that if there were no higher motive to restrain the planters from whipping their slaves to death, they might be induced to refrain by the consideration that the slaves were their property. What horse-dealer whips his horse to death?
>
> (*Fraser's* March 1831: 205)[47]

Did *Fraser's* really believe this or was this simply a convenient argument? Perhaps, we can see the answer to this question by considering an episode which might serve to illustrate both what was meant by good treatment of slaves and to demonstrate just how *Fraser's* earned its reputation for wit:[48]

> After this he goes on to describe a West Indian execution, as it is set down by Dwarris: –
> "On conviction, sentence of death must be passed without an appeal.

The execution takes place without delay; and, there being no assigned place for the execution, the wretched convict is fastened to the nearest tree, unless, which frequently happens, the owner of the soil is at hand to prevent it. In such cases, the miserable culprit is dragged from tree to tree – from estate to estate; and in one case of then recent occurrence, the constable was at last forced to throw the exhausted sufferer off the town-bridge, securing the rope by a lamp-post."

This speaks the necessity of an established gallows, instead of trusting to the casual hospitality of the planter. A West Indian proprietor may occasionally be a man of such taste, as to object to ornament his plantation with hanging negroes. I submit, that no tree-owners, even in this country, would like to have the culprits of the neighbourhood exhibited as pendants to their estate. George Robins, or one of his tribe, [I fear the story is in Joe Miller,] was so ingenious as to describe, in an advertisement of an estate to be sold, some half dozen gibbets in prospect, as "an agreeable view of hanging woods;" but the story does not say that the purchaser was much delighted with such an ornament to his new estate, when he discovered what it really was.

(*Fraser's* March 1831: 206–7)

The line of argument which Wilberforce encountered, and we read in *Fraser's* in the context of British West Indian slavery, will be recycled for use in an American context.

The sexual use of slaves: arrows "poisoned by truth"

Fraser's appeal to profit-maximizing considerations to argue that slaves will be well-treated might seem an argument to which the stereotypical "free market economist" of the time might assent. This is of course fatuous. Adam Smith thought it obvious that slave owners abuse their slaves precisely because they are not profit maximizing. They get a thrill out of dominating, a thrill for which they are willing to pay:

> The pride of man makes him love to domineer, and nothing mortifies him so much as to be obliged to condescend to persuade his inferiors. Wherever the law allows it, and the nature of the work can afford it, therefore, he will generally prefer the service of slaves to that of freemen.
> (Smith 1976: 388)

Perhaps, the attitude of later economists is best summarized by Richard Whately in a letter to Nassau Senior proposing cannibalism to humanize slavery:

> Only t'other day I heard a man repeat the argument of the "Times" that self-interest is a sufficient security; as in the case of cattle, where, by-the-bye, it is so little a security that we have a law against cruelty to them. But even the most humane master of cattle treats them in a manner which one

could not approve towards men, *e.g.* selling most of the calves that a cow bears; and knocking on the head a horse that is past work. I suggested that it would be an advantage to slaves if the masters could acquire a taste for human flesh. When a negro grows too old to be worth keeping for work, instead of being killed by inches by starvation and over-work, he would be put up to fatten like an ox.

(Whately 1868: 313)

Harriet Martineau in her 1830s visit to America found, as Wilberforce had before, the compelling piece of evidence to distinguish the treatment of slaves and horses.[49] Horse owners do not use them sexually. As a Malthusian, Martineau attends to the trade-off between sex and material income. Unlike Smith and Malthus, who confined themselves to contexts where the Christian convention of one man-one family is generally enforced, she finds in America an instance where a man can have more of both sex and material income by acquiring additional families, only one of which will be white:

Every man who resides on his plantation may have his harem, and has every inducement of custom, and of pecuniary gain,* [*The law declares that the children of slaves are to follow the fortunes of the mother. Hence the practice of planters selling and bequeathing their own children.] to tempt him to the common practice.

(Martineau 1837, vol. 2: 223)

Then she proposes a test for moral motivation: "Those who, notwithstanding, keep their homes undefiled may be considered as of incorruptible purity" (Martineau 1837, vol. 2: 223). Martineau is here responding to the claim that the morality of slavery can be judged by the relative infrequency of prostitution in Southern cities. So, it can, Martineau argues, but not the way the slavery apologists thought. Why, she asked, would a man rent a woman for an hour when he can buy her and keep the children to sell?[50] Thus, the relative infrequency of prostitution in slave cities can provide evidence that slaves were used sexually in sufficient numbers to affect the market demand for irregular sex.[51]

Let me pause to dwell on the simple implication of Martineau's point which differs in subtle ways from Wilberforce's related claim.[52] Martineau's argument that American slavery is a system of sexual exploitation establishes that the relative well-being of free and slave labor will differ between men and women. Thus, when in the great debates over American slavery, the well-being of male "white slaves" and male black slaves is compared, a claim is being made. The reader who knows neither Wilberforce and Martineau may not see the evasion for what it is.

However Carlyle did know Martineau and her works extremely well. Indeed, "ODNQ" gives evidence of close acquaintance with Martineau's *Society in America* in which these arguments are pressed.[53] Thus, we do not have to read at all far to discover what Carlyle means by his linking economics, evangelicals and inter-racial sexuality. The issue is common to Wilberforce and Martineau.

It was another woman who brought new weapons into the war of words over

American slavery. As witness of their novelty, we read from the long version of Senior's *Edinburgh* review of *Uncle Tom's Cabin*:

> Mrs. Stowe came like a heavenly auxiliary, like the divine Twins at the battle of Lake Regillus, or St. Jago in the van of Cortez, using weapons such as they had never thought of, wielded with a skill which they did not possess. She showered on the supporters of the Fugitive Slave Law and the extension of slavery, invective, ridicule, contempt, and defiance, with arrows winged by genius, and barbed and pointed, and poisoned by truth.
> (Senior 1864: 437)[54]

Senior stressed what was uniquely horrible about American slavery:

> the breeding and exporting system, – the system under which the principal use made of men and women is to produce and bring up children, to be torn from them as soon as they attain the age of sale, and never to be seen or heard of again.
> (Senior 1864: 409)[55]

Stowe's attack is on the institution of slavery, regardless of the moral qualities of the slave owners, so she populates her story with slave owners of different moral qualities. This is important for the polemic because in her account, the rational slave will prefer freedom to slavery under even the kindest and most upright master. One never knows what the future will bring: who might next master be?[56] And we the reader are to judge the morality of a slave owner how? Following Martineau the test for moral stature seems to be whether one will use a slave sexually or sell her for such a purpose.[57] Interracial concubinage serves many purposes in the plot. It provides a moment of irony as it explains how it comes to be that an escaping slave darkens himself.[58] More importantly, characters with parents of different races establish on the crudest biological level possible that we are one species.[59]

To appreciate how Stowe uses concubinage as a weapon in the argument against slavery, we ought to compare her discussion with Wilberforce's quoted above, or what the escaped slave and abolitionist William Craft, would write in 1860.[60] When these men write about sexual slavery, they use spectator language to ask how a man would feel about having his wife, sisters or daughters used sexually.[61] They do not pretend to enter into a woman's situation. But Stowe so enters into the heart of this darkness.[62] She has Simon Legree's past and perhaps current concubine, Cassy, talk to her presumptive successor, Emmeline, about how to deaden the inevitable sense of violation:

> "He wanted to make me drink some of his hateful brandy," said Emmeline; "and I hate it so – "
> "You'd better drink," said Cassy. "I hated it, too; and now I can't live without it. One must have something; – things don't look so dreadful, when you take that."
> (Stowe 1982: 438)[63]

As I read the historical record, just as one economist, Smith, provided Macaulay with the analysis of how one adjusts to new possibilities of intoxication for Macaulay's metaphor of intoxication and freedom, it was another who provided Stowe with the poisonous truth.[64] Merely because Martineau's texts are hidden from us, we ought not conclude that Stowe's contemporaries were equally uninformed. It is, I take it, no coincidence that in 1852 and 1853 in the midst of the debate over *Uncle Tom's Cabin*, three massive American attacks on Martineau's claims on slavery and sexual exploitation, published over various times and places, were collected with an unrelated essay into a volume called *The Pro-Slavery Argument*.[65] From the words in these attacks, we can document the origin of this fatal mix of poison and truth.

The first line of argument from William Harper tacitly assumes that the sex is uncoerced. On the basis of this clever postulate, he gives a cogent cost/benefit explanation for why Martineau's account is true:

> In such communities, the unmarried woman who becomes a mother, is an outcast from society – and though sentimentalists lament the hardship of the case, it is justly and necessarily so. She is cut off from the hope of useful and profitable employment, and driven by necessity to further vice. Her misery, and the hopelessness of retrieving, render her desperate, until she sinks into every depth of depravity, and is prepared for every crime that can contaminate and infest society. She has given birth to a human being, who, if it be so unfortunate as to survive its miserable infancy, is commonly educated to a like course of vice, depravity, and crime.
>
> Compare with this the female slave under similar circumstances. She is not a less useful member of society than before. If shame be attached to her conduct, it is such shame as would be elsewhere felt for a venial impropriety. She has not impaired her means of support, nor materially impaired her character, or lowered her station in society; she has done no great injury to herself, or any other human being. Her offspring is not a burden but an acquisition to her owner; his support is provided for, and he is brought up to usefulness; if the fruit of intercourse with a freeman, his condition is, perhaps, raised somewhat above that of his mother. Under these circumstances, with imperfect knowledge, tempted by the strongest of human passions – unrestrained by the motives which operate to restrain, but are so often found insufficient to restrain the conduct of females elsewhere, can it be matter of surprise that she should so often yield to the temptation?
>
> (Harper 1853: 42–3)

Harper attempts to make the case that it is better to have a black concubine than engage a white prostitute (1853: 43–5) which is, of course, Martineau's point although she would say "more profitable" not "better." Harper is not content to respond to – or ratify – Martineau's model. He draws on Coleridge to attack the motives of utilitarians concerned with distant people:

> Are we not justified then in regarding as criminals, the fanatical agitators whose efforts are intended to bring about the evils I have described? It is

sometimes said that their zeal is generous and disinterested, and that their motives may be praised, though their conduct be condemned. But I have little faith in the good motives of those who pursue bad ends. It is not for us to scrutinize the hearts of men, and we can only judge of them by the tendency of their actions. There is much truth in what was said by Coleridge. "I have never known a trader in philanthropy who was not wrong in heart somehow or other. Individuals so distinguished, are usually unhappy in their family relations – men not benevolent or beneficent to individuals, but almost hostile to them, yet lavishing money and labor and time on the race – the abstract notion." The prurient love of notoriety actuates some.

(Harper 1853: 93)[66]

John H. Hammond levels the charge of sexual hysteria against Martineau:

But your grand charge is, that licentiousness in intercourse between the sexes, is a prominent trial of our social system, and that it necessarily arises from Slavery. This is a favorite theme with the abolitionists, male and female. Folios have been written on it. It is a common observation, that there is no subject on which ladies of eminent virtue so much delight to dwell, and on which in especial learned old maids, like Miss Martineau, linger with such an insatiable relish. They expose it in the slave States with the most minute observance and endless iteration. Miss Martineau, with peculiar gusto, relates a series of scandalous stories, which would have made Boccacio jealous of her pen, but which are so ridiculously false as to leave no doubt, that some wicked wag, knowing she would write a book, has furnished her materials – a game too often played on tourists in this country. The constant recurrence of the female abolitionists to this topic, and their bitterness in regard to it, cannot fail to suggest to even the most charitable mind, that "Such rage without betrays the fires within."

(Hammond 1853: 117)

To quiet concerns with the truth of her model, Hammond asks what it is edifying to believe:

But I do not intend to admit that this charge is just or true. Without meaning to profess uncommon modesty, I will say that I wish the topic could be avoided. I am of opinion, and I doubt not every right-minded man will concur, that the public exposure and discussion of this vice, even to rebuke, invariably does more harm than good; and that if it cannot be checked by instilling pure and virtuous sentiments, it is far worse than useless to attempt to do it, by exhibiting its deformities.

(Hammond 1853: 118)

However he does respond to the sharp implication of the model. It is true. As such then, it provides evidence of the love of slave owners for their slaves; hence, slaves really aren't thought of as cattle. Lucky slaves:

> One of your heavy charges against us has been, that we regard and treat these people as brutes; you now charge us with habitually taking them to our bosoms. I will not comment on the inconsistency of these accusations. I will not deny that some intercourse of the sort does take place.
>
> (Hammond 1853: 119)

What is "ridiculous" is *avowedly* buying a slave for sexual use from a woman.

> What Miss Martineau relates of a young man's purchasing a colored concubine from a lady, and avowing his designs, is too absurd even for contradiction. No person would dare to allude to such a subject, in such a manner, to any decent female in this country.
>
> (Hammond 1853: 120)

With arguments like this, one can certainly appreciate why attacking Martineau's motivation was an attractive use of time.

The high point of personal attacks possibly comes from a Dr. W. Gilmore Simms Esq. of South Carolina, who opens his essay by attacking Martineau's motives on the basis that although she is deaf, she makes light of her difficulty, pointing to the beneficial silence in which to think. In this, Simms finds her denial of the providential order.[67] Simms charges her with intellectual dishonesty, forcing the evidence to fit her preconceptions. How so? Carlyle's opinion of slavery is different than hers, and if Carlyle says so who is she to disagree?

> Had it not been for this name of odium, and that Slavery had been assimilated with those features of government policy which it is was her cue to obliterate, we should have seen her, as we have in latter days seen Carlyle, boldly looking through all the mists and mystifications of the subject, and probing it with an independent analysis, with which neither prescription, nor prejudices, nor selfish policy, could be permitted to interfere. Her self-relying nature would have sufficed for this, had she not determined against Slavery, before acquiring any just knowledge of that condition which has received this name.
>
> (Simms 1853: 198)

The example where this dishonesty shows is as follows:

> Alleged rapes, by negroes upon white girls, are frequently stated by Northern journalists. We refer to Mr. Tappan for such particulars as resulted from the examination of the Commissioners of the Magdalen Asylum into the morals of New York; and we regret that Miss Martineau had not looked more closely into the negro quarters, and into the various police trials of negro offenders in the different cities of the free States. Had she done this, she would have spared us the entire chapter on the morals of Slavery.
>
> (Simms 1853: 210–11)

Economic texts as apocrypha 417

The reason it would have been good if Martineau had not included this chapter on the morals of slavery is explained a little while later. Her charges are true:

> There is one painful chapter in these two volumes, under the head of "Morals of Slavery." It is painful, because it is full of truth. It is devoted to the abuses, among slaveholders, of the institution of slavery; and it gives a collection of statements which are, no doubt, in too many cases, founded upon fact, of the illicit and foul conduct of some among us, who make their slaves the victims and instruments, alike, of the most licentious passions. Regarding our slaves as a dependent and inferior people, we are their natural and only guardians; and to treat them brutally, whether by wanton physical injuries, by a neglect, or perversion of their morals, is not more impolitic than it is dishonorable. We do not quarrel with Miss Martineau for this chapter. The truth – though it is not all truth – is quite enough to sustain her and it; and we trust that its utterance may have that beneficial effect upon the relations of master and slave in our country, which the truth is, at all times, most likely to have every where.
> (Simms 1853: 228–9)

So when arguments fail, attack the person:

> Still, we are not satisfied with the spirit with which Miss M. records the grossness which fills this chapter. She has exhibited a zest in searching into the secrets of our prison-house, in the slave States, which she does not seem to have shown in any other quarter.
> (Simms 1853: 229)

Simms's testifies to Martineau's power. The power comes from her command of language and her willingness to apply economics to such matters as sex:

> Miss Martineau is a monstrous proser. She has a terrible power of words, and is tyrannical as she is powerful, in the use of them. We have no doubt she is herself free from stain or reproach; but her tongue is wretchedly incontinent. . . She scruples at no game, fears no opponent, and, whether the meat be washed or unwashed, hawk or heron, it is all the same to her. She discusses the rights of man, and – heaven save the mark! – the rights of women too, with her chambermaid, when she cannot corner a senator. Smart exceedingly, well practised in the minor economies of society, and having at her tongue's end all the standards of value in the grain, cotton, beef and butter markets, she does not scruple to apply them to the mysterious involutions of the mind and society.
> (Simms 1853: 246)[68]

What one prefers not to see

If the "anti-progressive" economists defended competition, what alternative did their opponents point to as superior? The answer is easy: slavery. Of course, it was a slavery supposed without certain "abuses." We now consider a series of three episodes in which the issue of competition or slavery is raised. The criterion by which I selected these episodes is simply that each of them has been extensively discussed by literary scholars. In this way we can see how the judgement of "progressive" is applied. What, I would like to ask, does it take for an opponent of markets to lose his "progressive" credentials?

I have stressed earlier the difficulty which many have had in seeing the coalition of economists and evangelicals in terms of their shared utilitarianism. A coalition which includes J. S. Mill and Biblical literalists is not, as a matter of fact, the easiest group to explain. But there is another aspect of the hidden nature of the debate where the texts are crude and their meaning becomes all to clear. There is a story which literary historians like to tell about how great art moralizes. The consequence which is drawn is that great Victorian literary artists were led to question market relationships. This is doubtless a very comfortable story since, among other things, it suggests that art provides a vantage which is above markets.

Consider the edition of Carlyle's *Past and Present* produced in 1965 by that formidable scholar, Richard Altick. Altick spends his introduction belaboring the horrors of unrestricted markets while noting that Carlyle's own solution looks like "Prussian authoritarianism."[69] In this text Carlyle uses the phrase "Jew Harpies."[70] One presumes that the use of such a term is part and parcel of the historical dehumanization of Jews. Reflect then upon the note which Altick puts after "Jew Harpies" which says this: "Rapacious monsters, half women, half birds." That is all he says.[71] He sees the Harpies but that is all he will see. Turn "Prussian" to "Nazi" and the truth value of "art moralizes" attains transparency.

The first of the three episodes I shall consider is the Poet Laureate Southey's reflections on slavery and competition and Macaulay's attack. (This attack provoked *Fraser's* illuminating outburst which was quoted earlier.) The second is Carlyle's idealization of slavery in *Past and Present* in which the cash nexus is replaced by religious belief carrying moral obligation. The obvious question arises what to do with those who do not share the particulars of the required belief and thus escape moral obligation? Jews are the particular menace. This Carlylean theme continues in Charles Kingsley's novel *Alton Locke* in which the fault of a competitive order is laid on the Jews as outsiders to the religious-moral order. *Alton Locke* is also the focus of the third episode because it contains an enormously influential description of the condition of the "white slaves" of England *vis-à-vis* the black slaves of America. Its influence may have extended to the making of *Uncle Tom's Cabin*.[72]

Southey and Macaulay

Southey's *Sir Thomas More* seems to have been calculated to maximally offend evangelical sensibilities.[73] Defending More against the "libel" of "good old John Fox" (Southey 1829: 88), Southey implicitly sides with More in his persecution and with the judicial murder of William Tyndale, the first translator of the Hebrew scriptures into English.[74] Sir Thomas More describes the benefits of feudalism for the workers secure in their "station." They had attained the state of happy cattle:

Economic texts as apocrypha 419

> The practical difference between the condition of the feudal slave, and of the labouring husbandman, who succeeded to the business of his station, was mainly this, that the former had neither the feeling nor the insecurity of independence. He served one master as long as he lived; and being at all times sure of the same sufficient subsistence, if he belonged to the estate like the cattle, and was accounted with them as part of the live stock, he resembled them also in the exemption which he enjoyed from all cares concerning his own maintenance and that of his family.
> (Southey 1829: 68–9)

After comparing this fixed status with the "vicissitudes" of the modern age, Sir Thomas More points to the virtue of their masters that gives room to hope:

> They had nothing to lose, and they had liberty to hope for; frequently as the reward of their own faithful services, and not seldom from the piety or kindness of their lords. This was a steady hope depending so little upon contingency, that it excited no disquietude or restlessness. They were therefore in general satisfied with the lot to which they were born, as the Greenlander is with his climate, the Bedouin with his deserts, and the Hottentot and the Calmuck with their filthy and odious customs . . .
> (Southey 1829: 69–70)

Southey's spokesman argues with Sir Thomas More: "I am sure it is not your intention to represent slavery otherwise than as an evil, under any modification." Sir Thomas More then responds:

> That which is a great evil in itself, becomes relatively a good, when it prevents or removes a greater evil. . . . But it led immediately to nefarious abuses; and the earliest records which tell us of its existence, show us also that men were kidnapped for sale.
> (Southey 1829: 70–1)

In spite of the stern words about the "abuses" of slavery, as one can easily imagine, the vision of the kindly slave-owner seemed to resonate in certain districts of America.[75]

Before we consider Macaulay's response, let us reflect upon a secondary literature which considers nineteenth-century economics "dismal" because of an alleged "fixed condition" claim. Here we have one of the more energetic critics of nineteenth-century economics, defending a system in which the status of the worker is as fixed as the average weather of his neighborhood.[76]

I have quoted Macaulay's statement of the importance for the worker of a choice of masters, so let us consider how in 1830 Macaulay tackles the question raised by Southey whether the condition of the working class has improved over the last three centuries. For Smith the state of the well-being of the working class, the majority of the population, is critical to his evaluation of the well-being of society (Levy 1995). Macaulay (1961, 2:216) notes that Southey does not "even pretend to maintain that the people in the sixteenth century were better lodged or clothed than at present."[77] Southey claims that the workers were better fed in the sixteenth century so Macaulay (1961, vol. 2: 216) cites evidence from household expenditure records to dispute this. Then he does something quite remarkable; he proposes a novel method of measuring well-being:[78]

> The term of human life is decidedly longer in England than in any former age, respecting which we possess any information on which we can rely. All the rants in the world about picturesque cottages and temples of Mammon will not shake this argument. No test of the physical well-being of society can be named so decisive as that which is furnished by the bills of mortality. That the lives of the people of this country have been gradually lengthening during the course of several generations, is as certain as any fact in statistics; and that the lives of men should become longer and longer, while their bodily condition during life is becoming worse and worse, is utterly incredible.
> (Macaulay 1961, vol.2: 217)

Houghton's judgment is that Macaulay's response to Southey is a "tissue of evasions," Houghton (1957: 415), in particular that "he never comes to grips with the central charge that the poor are being exploited by the rich." K. Curry (1975: 87–8) thinks that the portrayal of More "contributes to the charm of the book" and that Southey is clearly the "progressive" in the debate as he attacks competition. Neither explain what is the matter with using life expectancy as a welfare norm and why the conclusions are not as Macaulay argues. What is remarkable is that neither scholar appears to notice that an inability to switch masters – to regard one's station with the same fatality as one regards the weather – is a more plausible ground for exploitation than a competitive system in which the worker has a choice of masters. Possibly the reading which *Fraser's* offered at the time was more to the point. Macaulay's defense of competition represents a dire threat to the system of slavery in the British West Indies and his attack on Southey's defense of feudal slavery, slavery without "abuses," is just a skirmish in the space of historical memory in the long struggle of a competitive system against a variety of slave systems.

"Just" slavery and the Jewish menace

Carlyle's *Past and Present* has long enjoyed unimpeachable "progressive" credentials because it was so enthusiastically greeted by Frederick Engels.[79] In *Past and Present* Carlyle introduced his notion of "economic chivalry" where the permanence of one's social state is anchored by unquestioned moral imperative. Here he reflects on the need for despotism:

> A question arises here: Whether, in some ulterior, perhaps, some not far-distant stage of this "Chivalry of Labour," your Master-Worker may not find it possible, and needful to grant his Workers permanent *interest* in his enterprise and theirs? So that it become, in practical result, what in

essential fact and justice it ever is, a joint enterprise; all men, from the Chief Master down to the lowest Overseer and Operative, economically as well as loyally concerned for it? – Which question I do not answer. The answer, near or else far, is perhaps, Yes; – and yet one knows the difficulties. Despotism is essential in most enterprises; I am told, they do not tolerate "freedom of debate" on board a Seventy-Four! Republican senate and *plebiscita* would not answer well in Cotton-Mills.

(Carlyle 1965: 278)

To reconcile slavery and freedom? Easy! the voice of the master is the voice of God:[80]

And yet observe there too: Freedom, not nomad's or ape's Freedom, but man's Freedom; this is indispensable. We must have it, and will have it! To reconcile Despotism with Freedom: – well, is that such a mystery? Do you not already know the way? It is to make your Despotism *just*. Rigorous as Destiny; but just too, as Destiny and its Laws. The Laws of God: all men obey these, and have no "Freedom" at all but in obeying them.

(Carlyle 1965: 278)

There was obviously a contemporary demand for the doctrine that "real freedom" is slavery to one's betters as we see from a participant in the debate over *Uncle Tom's Cabin* who found this, and similar doctrines, edifying.[81]

A consequence of the doctrine of "just" slavery is that one's moral obligation is relative to one's status within the hierarchy. One has the obligation of obedience toward those up the hierarchy and the obligation of charity to those down the hierarchy. The slogan of this view of the moral world is that "charity begins at home." It also ends there. Those outside the hierarchy, people in a distant land or with different beliefs, have no claim on us. Here is the passage in *Past and Present*, complete with reference to the ill-spent £20 million, in which the universalism of the anti-slave coalition is contrasted with Carlyle's moral localism:

O Anti-Slavery Convention, loud-sounding long-eared Exeter-Hall – But in thee too is a kind of instinct towards justice, and I will complain of nothing. Only, black Quashee over the seas being once sufficiently attended to, wilt thou not perhaps open thy dull sodden eyes to the "sixty-thousand valets in London itself who are yearly dismissed to the streets, to be what they can, when the season ends"; – or to the hungerstricken, pallid *yellow-*coloured "Free Labourers" in Lancashire, Yorkshire, Buckinghamshire, and all other shires! These Yellow-coloured, for the present, absorb all my sympathies: if I had a Twenty Millions, with Model-Farms and Niger Expeditions, it is to these that I would give it! Quashee has already victuals, clothing; Quashee is not dying of such despair as the yellow-coloured pale man's. Quashee, it must be owned, is hitherto a kind of blockhead. The Haiti Duke of Marmalade, educated now for almost half a century, seems to have next to no sense in him. Why, in one of those Lancashire Weavers, dying of hunger, there is more thought and heart, a greater arithmetical amount of misery and desperation, than in whole gangs of Quashees. It must be owned, thy eyes are of the sodden sort; and with thy emancipations, and thy twenty-millionings and long-eared clamourings, thou, like Robespierre with his pasteboard *Être Suprème*, threatenest to become a bore to us.

(Carlyle 1965: 275)[82]

Carlyle's doctrine of moral localism is represented in Kingsley's novel *Alton Locke*. Here Kingsley has the voice of Carlyle localize moral obligation:

"What do ye ken aboot the Pacific? Which is maist to your business? That bare-backed hizzies that play the harlot o' the other side o' the warld, or these – these thousands o' barebacked hizzies that play the harlot o' your ain side – made out o' your ain flesh and blude? You a poet! True poetry, like true charity, my laddie, begins at hame."

(Kingsley 1850: 85)

"Alton Locke" learns this lesson for his examination:

"I've fearful misgivings about it, just because Irishmen are at the head of it."

"Of course they are – they have the deepest wrongs; and that makes them most earnest in the cause of right. The sympathy of suffering, as they say themselves, has bound them to the English working-man against the same oppressors."

"Then let them fight those oppressors at home, and we'll do the same: that's the true way to show sympathy. Charity begins at home. They are always crying 'Ireland for the Irish;' why can't they leave England for the English?"

(Kingsley 1850: 292)

While the utilitarian coalition supported emancipation regardless of the religion of the slaves, the moral localism of Carlyle and Kingsley, by locating obligation in a hierarchy embodied in religious belief, finds differences in religion to be a threat. Thus, in *Past and Present*'s medieval fantasy, Carlyle's Abbot Samson expels the Jews.[83] As Carlyle says: "Time, Jews, and the task of Governing, will make a man's beard very gray!" [84] If anything the thesis that Jews threaten the moral economic order is pursued more vigorously in *Alton Locke* than it is in *Past and Present*.[85]

In *Alton Locke*, when the old employer dies, the new owner changes policy to emulate that of the Jews who pursue wealth at the expense of all moral obligation in excess of market-based obligation. Jewish economic practice embodies perfectly economic doctrine:[86]

His father had made money very slowly of late; while dozens, who had begun business after him, had now retired to luxurious ease and suburban villas. Why should he remain in the minority? Why should he not get rich as fast as he could? Why should he stick to the old, slow-going, honorable trade? . . . Why should he pay his men two shillings where the government paid them one? Were there not cheap houses even at the West-end, which had saved several thousands a year merely by reducing their workmen's wages? And if the workmen chose to take lower wages, he was not bound actually to make them a present of more than they asked for! They would go to the cheapest market for any thing they wanted, and so must he. . . .

Such, I suppose, were some of the arguments which led to an official announcement, one Saturday night, that our young employer intended to enlarge his establishment, for the purpose of commencing business in the "show trade;" and that, emulous of Messrs. Aaron, Levi, and the rest of that class.

(Kingsley 1850: 96–7)

The chapter "The sweater's den" is Alton's misadventures among the Jewish "sweaters":

As I had expected, a fetid, choking den, with just room enough in it for the seven or eight sallow, starved beings, who, coatless, shoeless, and ragged, sat stitching, each on his truckle-bed. . . .
"Oh! blessed saints, take me out o' this! – take me out, for the love of Jesus! – take me out o' this hell, or I'll go mad intirely! Och! will nobody have pity on poor sowls in purgatory – here in prison like negur slaves?

(Kingsley 1850: 190)

The Jews threatened Christian workers both in this world and the next:

"Och! Mother of Heaven!" he went on, wildly, "when will I get out to the fresh air? For five months I haven't seen the blessed light of sun, nor spoken to the praste, not ate a bit o' mate, barring bread-and-butter. Shure it's all the blessed sabbaths and saints' days I've been a-working like a haythen Jew, and niver seen the insides o' the chapel to confess my sins, and me poor sowl's lost intirely . . ."

(Kingsley 1850: 191)

And in what has to be one of the great surprises in literature, we learn Jews don't fight fairly:

At last, as Downes's life seemed in danger, he wavered; the Jew-boy seized the moment, jumped up, upsetting the constable, dashed like an eel between Crossthwaite and Mackaye, gave me a back-handed blow in passing, which I felt for a week after, and vanished through the street-door, which he locked after him.

(Kingsley 1850: 193)

The role of Jew as menace to the moral economy is worthy of remark if only because a generation of well-informed critics have passed over it in silence.[87] The question naturally should occur: how could *this* be in *Alton Locke* if no one else has read it? Indeed, I would agree that if no one caught the Jewish references they might as well not be there. But then let us reflect upon how a contemporary reader, W. E. Aytoun, reviewing *Alton Locke* for *Blackwood's*, parses the relation of Jews to the competitive order. First, one must make a distinction between "honor" and "competition":

> This is intended, or at all events given, as an accurate picture of a respectable London tailoring establishment, where the men receive decent wages. Such a house is called an "honourable" one, in contradistinction to others, now infinitely the more numerous, which are springing up in every direction under the fostering care of competition.
> (Aytoun 1850: 598)

Second, the competitive establishments employ "sweaters" so they need not deal with workers on a face-to-face basis:

> These sweaters are commonly Jews, to which persuasion also the majority of the dishonourable proprietors belong. Few people who emerge from the Euston Square Station are left in ignorance as to the fact, it being the insolent custom of a gang of hook-nosed and blubber-lipped Israelites to shower their fetid tracts, indicating the localities of the principal dealers of their tribe, into every cab as it issues from the gate. These are, in plain terms, advertisement of a more odious cannibalism than exists in the Sandwich Islands.
> (Aytoun 1850: 598–9)

The moral course of action naturally suggests itself:

> Very often have we wished that the miscreant who so assailed us were within reach of our black-thorn cudgel, that we might have knocked all ideas of fried fish out of his head for at least a fortnight to come! In these days of projected Jewish emancipation, the sentiment may be deemed an atrocious one, but we cannot retract it. Shylock was and is the true type of his class; only that the modern London Jew is six times more personally offensive, mean, sordid, and rapacious than the merchant of the Rialto. And why should we stifle our indignation? Dare any one deny the truth of what we have said? It is notorious to the whole world that these human leeches acquire their wealth, not by honest labour and industry, but by bill-broking, sweating, discounting, and other nefarious arts.
> (Aytoun 1850: 599)

The Jewish link to economics is trivial:

> Talk of Jewish legislation indeed! We have had too much of it already in our time, from the days of Ricardo, the instigator of Sir Robert Peel's

earliest practices upon the currency, down to those of Nathan Rothschild, the first Baron of Jewry, for whose personal character and upright dealings the reader is referred to Mr Francis' Chronicles of the Stock Exchange.
(Aytoun 1850: 599)

Aytoun provides a possible British context for H. S. Chamberlain's pregnant rantings:

> Read the following account by a working tailor of their doings, and then settle the matter with your conscience, whether it is consistent with the character of a Christian gentleman to have dealings with such inhuman vampires.
> (Aytoun 1850: 599)[88]

"White slaves" and black ones

Charles Kingsley's name does not appear on the title page of the first edition of *Alton Locke*. This is how it reads: *Alton Locke, Tailor and Poet. An Autobiography*. Of course, there is an "Ed." who makes various footnote appearances, hardly surprising as the book ends as Alton lies dying, far too weak to bundle the manuscript to the printer. Readers of later editions who know that it is a novel, might know something which the readers in the 1850s might not. "Alton Locke" laments his status as "white slave" (Kingsley 1850: 179). The working men "Alton Locke" encounters view themselves as "nigger slaves" or "negur slaves." What does this mean to the reader?[89] A reader who knows *Alton Locke* to be a novel might conclude the author views the condition of English workers and black slaves as comparable. A reader who does not know *Alton Locke* to be a novel might conclude that the English workers themselves were ready to migrate to America to sell themselves in the New Orleans slave market.

The identification of "white slaves" with black slaves – which we saw earlier in Thrall's commentary on the economists – seems to be a contestation for the role of the minimum of the happiness distribution. This is important to Kingsley, as a Christian, in a way which it is not important to Carlyle. While for Carlyle, blacks and Irish are not morally human so they can be exterminated if they object to their remaking, Kingsley contends with the coalition on their own grounds by putting forward the British working man as contender for the position at the minimum of the distribution of happiness.[90]

The great crisis in slavery, in the form of *Uncle Tom's Cabin*, was published, inviting readers to imagine the fate of mothers seeing their children sold to strangers. In the debate which followed, we find readers who cite *Alton Locke* as offering creditable testimony that the "white slaves" viewed themselves and the black slaves in comparable positions. If modern scholars are correct in thinking that Stowe's view of British laboring conditions comes at least in part from Kingsley, perhaps even from *Alton Locke* itself, then *Uncle Tom's Cabin* authorizes this very response. Here is one attack:

> In bringing forward the condition of the English labouring class, then, I do it from no vile motive of recrimination. I do it, because the subject is

introduced into the work I am commenting on, and because my *argument* requires it.

(Stearns 1853: 81)

Stearns takes note of Helps' *Letter*. He brings up the question of women working in gangs:

> "White slaves," in the words of the London Times, . . . "of a sex and age least qualified to struggle with the hardships of their lot – young women, for the most part, between sixteen and thirty years of age, *worked in gangs* in ill-ventilated rooms . . ." sewing "from morning till night, *and night till morning . . .*"
>
> (Stearns 1853: 87)

Then *Alton Locke* is offered as testimony:

> And these things are done in "*merry* England!" Ay, and not these alone. The milliners and dressmakers are not the only ones who thrive on the miseries of their fellows; the keepers of "furnishing" shops are in the same category, – witness the "song of the shirt;" and so are the "fashionable tailors," as many an Alton Locke could testify.
>
> (Stearns 1853: 89)

A second attack occurs in a pamphlet reprinted in *Fraser's* which mixes statistics and fiction promiscuously:[91]

> This power that slavery gives to one man over another is met with everywhere in society. Caleb Williams! Alton Locke! Mary Barton! Parliamentary Blue Books! Mining Districts! Manufacturing Districts! Combinations of Workers! Combinations of Masters! – to which shall we point especially? In all is the lesson of one man's power over another.
>
> (Pringle 1852a: 20; Pringle 1852b: 481)

If all work is slavery and we are interested in those who are the worst off then what difference is there between "white slavery" and black slavery?[92] Moral localism would not in fact contradict universalism since the "white slaves" of Britain would merit our concern as much as do the black slaves of America. But there is a trap in this line of argument: all those who lament their status as "white slaves" in *Alton Locke* are male.

And we see the trap sprung in the response to the critics of *Uncle Tom's Cabin* taking withering variations on the sexual slavery theme of Wilberforce and Martineau. Writing with an ink capable of etching steel, "Nicholas Brimblecomb" retold the story from a "pro-slavery" point of view:[93]

> He sought to secure Harry's young and beautiful mother, as judging her suitable to accommodate and please one of those numerous

southern gentlemen who not only have field and house servants, but also certain house servants of a peculiar character.

(Brimblecomb 1853: 13–14)

Slavery gave him power to compel such slaves to be his concubines as he saw fit; he acted accordingly, and when he was weary of one, he would buy another for his particular purpose.
. . . Whosoever would see slavery – see it in its genuine nature, operations, and character – must not look at such an awkward case as that of St. Clare; but he must look at Legree.

(Brimblecomb 1853: 115)

F. C. Adams explicitly challenges P[ringle]'s doctrine that slavery moralizes:

In all our intercourse with Southerners, we never heard one claim moral caste for the institution of slavery; but not unfrequently have we heard them denounce instances of outrage upon chastity, sustained in the rights of the master, and beyond the remedy of laws made to govern the outraged. With our knowledge of social life in Charleston, we feel no hesitation in saying, that Mr. P – 's erudition in behalf of the divine precepts of slavery will prove as novel to Southern readers, as it will be forcible to those of more Northern sensibility.

(Adams 1853: 15–16)

The conflict of universality and "progressive," localizing moralizing is clearly explained:

But the reader must remember that the quality, depth, and attributes of Christianity, according to the rule of progress, are at the present day measured by a scale of locality. That which is made the medium of an accommodating morality in Charleston, would be rejected as unwholesome by the sterner judgment of the New Englander.

(Adams 1853: 16)

Literary scholars who restrict their attention to British publications, and who take seriously neither economists like Martineau nor evangelicals like Wilberforce, evidently do not see what is so odd about comparing "white slaves" to black slaves on the basis of male well-being.[94] Slavery was not the same burden for men and women.[95] This was the contention of the broad utilitarian coalition and to silently suppress this issue is to take a position in the debate.

Conclusion

The real past is complicated. British economists not only studied the world but they helped to change it. Indeed, they helped change it so radically that without considerable effort we cannot see what is so radical about their views. The "reactionary" status of the classical economists, it seems to me, comes from the lazy habit of making a judgment from the comfortable vantage of the status quo.

The mathematician-philosopher A. N. Whitehead said that a science which hesitates to forget its past is lost. I think this is precisely wrong, it is by remembering our past that we shall deserve to be saved. The past has always been contested ground. "Who controls the past controls the future." Orwell told us that.

> The mutability of the past is the central tenet of Ingsoc. Past events, it is argued, have no objective existence, but survive only in written records and in human memories. The past is whatever the records and the memories agree upon.
> (Orwell 1961: 176)

If we do not remember our past, others with no love for the sort of market or political organizations which economists study, will be all-too-willing to provide a "past" for us. It ill becomes economists, of all people, to have our understanding of our place in the world depend on the kindness of strangers.

Appendix: some dismal results

Thanks to the generosity of the Mellon family, economists and others have the capability to do on-line searches of the content by character strings of major journals for the entire period of their run in the database JSTOR.[96] The ten economics journals so accessible at the time of the study were as follows: *American Economic Review, Econometrica, the Journal of Economic History, the Journal of Industrial Economics, Journal of Money, Credit and Banking, the Journal of Political Economy, the Quarterly Journal of Economics, the Review of Economics and Statistics, Journal of Applied Econometrics, and the Journal of Economic Perspectives.*

Searching the articles in these journals found sixty nine uses of the "dismal science." Searching for "dismal science" and ("Malthus" or "Malthusian" or "wage") found forty-seven. Searching for "dismal science" and ("nigger" or "negro") found exactly two germane articles.[97] These are E. Hamilton (1952) and J. Persky (1990).

Notes

Thanks are due to comments on earlier drafts from James Buchanan and Larry Moss, and thanks too to Wendy Motooka and Gordon Wood for clarifying conversations. Most of my reading was done at the Library of Congress. I am in the particular debt of Cynthia Earman of the Rare Book Room who initiated me into the mysteries of the collection-specific shelf list. Andrew Farrant, Maria Pia Paganelli and Nicola Tynan saved me many errors when they helped me check the quotations. I would also like to express my gratitude to the organizers of the Hollander Conference, Evelyn Forget and Sandra Peart, for arranging such a wonderful party for Sam. I also thank the Center for Study of Public Choice for a research grant. All the errors are my responsibility.

1 George Stigler asked precisely this question when I proposed my version of the "new" view of Malthus and Ricardo. It has taken me close to thirty years to find an

answer worth even taking seriously. My stubbornness on this issue was largely influenced by a lesson which I learned from Earl Hamilton.
2   For some dismal results of an electronic survey of the economics literature see the Appendix. The reader will then appreciate why Earl Hamilton mattered to my education.
3   The details of the Carlyle–Mill controversy and the background are studied by Persky 1990 and Levy 2001.
4   Some reference works give the first of Carlyle's *Latter-Day Pamphlets*, the February 1850 "The Present Time," as the source for the "dismal science." In this piece, enlarging on "ODNQ" and responding to John Stuart Mill (1850), Carlyle asserts that if slavery does not humanize blacks, they ought to be exterminated (Carlyle 1850: 40). "ODNQ" was itself expanded and published as *Occasional Discourse on the Nigger Question* (*ODNQ*) in 1853. Because the pamphlet was reprinted in Carlyle's works with the assertion that *it* had appeared in the 1849 *Fraser's*, there has been endless confusion about the name. This confusion matters only because it demonstrates scholars' reluctance to work with original periodicals. The fact that the error appears in the *Oxford English Dictionary* is a consequence of its general reliance upon collected works.

The importance of this sequence of articles is explained by Froude (1897, vol. 2: 25): "A paper on the Negro or Nigger question, properly the first of the 'Latter-day Pamphlets,' was Carlyle's declaration of war against modern Radicalism." Wilson (1927: 217) is in rare agreement with Froude, "But what most of all astonished the pundits of the Dismal Science was his insistence on a right principle which took the ugliness out of slavery." "ODNQ" broke Mill's friendship with Carlyle (Froude 1897: 2, 28). Carlyle's awful candor is hard to emulate. For example, in an edition of Carlyle for students, when G. B. Tennyson lists the Carlyle chronology (Tennyson 1984: xliv–xlv), there is no mention of any version of the "ODNQ" or *ODNQ* even though there is a now standard edition as Morgan (1985: 162) points out. Carlyle's most recent biographer offers an intriguing defense of *ODNQ* that economists (and liberals more generally) were actually the real target but its readers have not been bright enough to figure this out:

> Carlyle did not feel he was attacking the blacks; his targets were the liberals who were destroying them. This was not, though, how his audience saw it. He was so open to interpretation because of the callous, heartless and brutally sarcastic language he used.
>
> (Heffer 1995: 276)

Recent interest in the Governor Eyre controversy, (Semmel 1962) has rekindled interest in the Carlyle–Mill exchange, e.g., Hall 1992, Young 1995, and raised questions whether aspects of Carlyle's thought are really such paradigms of authentic progressive thought, as some might suggest, e.g., Willey 1949: 126–31, Williams 1958: 71–86.
5   J. M. Buchanan in Knight (1982: xi–xii): "I have personally heard Knight repeat many times the Josh Billings aphorism: 'It ain't what we don't know that hurts us. It's knowing so darned much that ain't so.'"
6   This is so if for no other reason that we must combat our inclination to believe that which is most pleasing to us, Feigenbaum and Levy 1996.
7   On Ruskin, see Belsey (1980: 8), Arnold (1993: 67). Arnold criticizes Carlyle's "aristocracy" for insufficient L (Arnold 1993: 90). Denise Albanese gave me these references.
8   Levine (1993: 5) writes that historical research "involves not changing interpretations of well-agreed-upon standard events but changing notions of which events – and which people – should constitute the focus of the historian's study." Levine 1996: 96–7 continues the argument.
9   Hill (1993: 436): " we impoverish our understanding of the past if we chop it up into

little bits labelled 'constitutional history', 'economic history', 'literary history', 'political history' and so on."
10 The philosophical correlative to an economic general equilibrium point of view is W. V. Quine's (1961) doctrine that "The meaning of words is defined in the whole of the language." The correlative to a partial equilibrium point of view is found in Putnam's "linguistic division of labor." Not everyone in a language community is knowledgeable about what the various words we all use actually mean.

> in giving up my right to be the authority on the denotation of my own words, I give up, often, the ability to give any satisfactory description of my own denotations. I can refer to elms as well as the next man; but I probably couldn't tell an elm from a beech if my life depended upon it.
> (Putnam 1975, vol. 2: 274–5)

11 This problem occurs even in a Biblical context in which canonical books contain citations to the non-canonical, Charlesworth 1983.
12 When John Stuart Mill responded to Carlyle's "ODNQ" he began by making clear who was the majority partner in the coalition:

> I must first set my anti-philanthropic opponent right on a matter of fact. He entirely misunderstands the great national revolt of the conscience of this country against slavery and the slave-trade, if he supposes it to have been an affair of sentiments. It depended no more on humane feelings than any cause which so irresistibly appealed to them must necessarily do. Its first victories were gained while the lash yet ruled uncontested in the barrack-yard and the rod in schools, and while men were still hanged by dozens for stealing to the value of forty shillings. It triumphed because it was the cause of justice; and, in the estimation of the great majority of its supporters, of religion. Its originators and leaders were persons of a stern sense of moral obligation, who, in the spirit of the religion of their time, seldom spoke much of benevolence and philanthropy, but often of duty, crime, and sin.
> (Mill 1850: 26)

His tribute is all the more striking coming from perhaps the greatest opponent Christianity faced in the nineteenth century. J. Hunt (1866) – the driving force behind mid-century British racial anthropology – testifies to this coalition. Hunt's importance is now widely discussed, for example, Young 1995 and Levy 2001.

13 Indeed, even the modern student of the evangelicals and economists does not see the coalition in utilitarian terms. "They supported slave emancipation because slavery was obviously incompatible with free will individualism, but were notoriously much less concerned about wage [sic] slavery, and the other social evils of their own land." (Hilton 1988: 98). Some classics are hopeless, for example, L. Stephen finds it incomprehensible that slavery could be defended: "The conflict with morality, again, was so plain as to need no demonstration. It seems to be a questionable logic which assumes the merit of a reformer to be proportional to the flagrancy of the evil assailed" (Stephen 1900, vol.1: 113). Questionable it is, but one might have thought that an authority on the history of Utilitarianism would recognize the principle of attacking the worse evils first.

14 The adjective "broad" I hope resonates with the celebrated description of the Church of England as "not High, or Low, but Broad." Credit is claimed for this coinage by A. Stanley (1870: 8) in his 1850 *Edinburgh Review* article on the "Gorham Controversy." This controversy generated – by *DNB* count – over fifty pamphlets, all forgotten even before the *DNB* was printed. Forgotten or not, Gorham shows the hand of the broad utilitarian coalition playing real power politics. The flavor of the coalition caught in the *Christian Remembrancer* which noted:

> and we see hoary liberals, who have all their life been sneering at kings, and

scoffing at Churches, gravely rise up in their place in Parliament, to interrogate the Prime Minister, whether he has done his duty in upholding the endangered prerogative of her gracious Majesty, as the 'Supreme Head of the Church.'

(*Christian Remembrancer* 1850: 13–14)

At issue was whether an Anglo-Catholic Bishop (H. Phillpotts) could deny an office to an otherwise qualified candidate (George Gorham) because of Gorham's evangelical views on the sacraments. Phillpotts blamed the Privy Council's decision – evangelical views must be tolerated – on J. B. Sumner who held office as Archbishop of Canterbury (Phillpotts 1850). Another Christian Malthusian, Whately (1850), weighed in as Archbishop of Dublin with a subtle explanation of why one would expect variation in interpretation of hard texts. Sumner and Whately are studied in Hilton (1988), Waterman (1991) and Winch (1996). Only Hilton's research extends through the 1850s, but he does not study the Gorham decision.

The rowdy world of seventeenth-century evangelicalism (Hill 1993), was alive and well in the Gorham controversy, as we learn from William Bennett:

> I wish to inform you, my Lord, that on Sunday 10th November, while I was performing the duties of Divine service in the church of S. Barnabas, a tumultuous crowd assembled in the streets round about the church, and that a band of persons who had congregated together no doubt for this purpose within the very church walls, was guilty of violent outrage against all decency, in uttering hisses, and exclaiming, 'No mummery! No popery!' and other similar cries, alarming the decent worshippers.
>
> (Bennett 1850: 1–2)

William Tyndale, whose views on sacraments were cited in the controversy (Maskell 1850), dramatically characterizes evangelical views and suggests why Anglo-Catholics would find them unhappy:

> Testament here, is an appointment made between God and man, and God's promises. And a sacrament is a sign representing such an appointment and promises: as the rainbow representeth the promise made to Noe, that God will no more drown the world. And circumcision representeth the promises of God to Abraham ... as baptism which is come in the room thereof, now signifieth.
>
> (Tyndale 1992: 82–3)

Tyndale's view of sacraments – Judaism is in Tyndale's representation a sacramental religion – helps predict on which side of the debate anti-Semitism will be found.

15 "The principle of greatest happiness may have gained its popularity, but it lost its meaning, by the addition '*of the greatest number*.'" (Edgeworth 1881: 118) Here is a way to see the technical issue without appeal to the calculus of variations. Utilitarianism proposes to move from facts of individual happiness to claims about social happiness. Consider the same three individuals in two possible states of the world. Each state of the world is described in terms of the ordered triple of the individuals' happiness. Consider the case of A = {1,2,9} and B = {2,3,4}. Which has the "greater happiness of the greater number"? A has the higher mean happiness [4>3] – and since the population is fixed, the higher total happiness – but B has the higher median happiness [3>2]. Hutcheson's slogan encourages one to believe, wrongly, that a utilitarian will never have to choose between a higher mean and median of happiness.

16 Francis Hutcheson emphasizes the *number* of those benefitting:

> In comparing the *moral Qualities* of Actions, in order to regulate our *Election* among various Actions propos'd, or to find which of them has the greatest

> *moral Excellency*, we are led by *our moral Sense* of *Virtue* to judge thus; that in *equal Degrees* of Happiness, expected to proceed from the Action, the *Virtue* is in proportion to the *Number* of Persons to whom the Happiness shall extend; (and here the *Dignity*, or *moral Importance* of Person, may compensate Numbers) and in equal *Numbers*, the *Virtue* is as the *Quantity* of the Happiness, or natural Good; or that the *Virtue* is in a *compound Ratio* of the *Quantity* of Good, and *Number* of Enjoyers. In the same manner, the *moral Evil*, or *Vice*, is as the *Degree* of Misery, and *Number* of Sufferers; so that, *that Action is best* which procures the *greatest Happiness* for the *greatest Number*, . . .
>
> (Hutcheson 1726: 177)

Darwall (1995) is in my opinion the single most important work treating utilitarianism in broad terms. The accounts of Stephen 1900 and Halévy 1955, for all their erudition and sympathy, take utilitarianism in a narrow sense of Bentham and his school, relegating Francis Hutcheson, Adam Smith *qua* moral philosopher and William Paley to the role as predecessors *avant la lettre*. The decisive test for analytical seriousness of a study of utilitarianism is whether it recognizes the incoherence of the "greatest happiness of the greatest number." The fact that neither Stephen nor Halévy seems even to know of Edgeworth's work hints at a failure to understand why there must be more than one way of utilitarianism.

17 I read Smith as supposing a utilitarianism based on medians (Levy 1995). Paley's utilitarian calculus is based on a count of those who benefit and those who lose from policy, for example:

> It may be useful to rob a miser, and give the money to the poor; as the money no doubt would produce more happiness, by being laid out in food and cloathing for half a dozen distressed families, than by continuing locked up in the miser's chest.
>
> (Paley 1785: 62)

However, as Paley adds in his defense of general rules: "a disposition of affairs which would presently fill the world with misery and confusion; and ere long put an end to human society, if not to the human species." (Paley 1785: 64). Hollander (1997: 830–1) points out how Malthus's welfare arguments depend upon the well-being of the *majority* of society.

18   Wedgwood, the celebrated potter, had made another effective contribution to the cause. He designed a cameo showing, on a white background, a Negro kneeling in supplication, while he utters the plea to become so famous, "Am I not a man and a brother?"

> (Howse 1952: 40–1)

The debate between the economists, who affirmed, and the racists, who denied, fully human status to distant people is studied in Levy 2001.

19 Here is where the doctrine of "revealed preference" – happiness is what we have freely chosen – makes modern economists followers of Bernard Mandeville (Levy 1992).

20 Levy 1999 identifies four major positions taken by Christians and Utilitarians in the Malthusian controversy, three of which were publicly defended in the nineteenth century. Only in the twentieth century would we see publication of the fourth position, sexually-liberated Utilitarianism. Stephen (1900, vol. 1: 326) knows that the mss. of *Not Paul but Jesus* has Bentham's defense of the decriminalization of homosexuality but he is not going to tell the reader anything about that. I conjecture the vote reconciling Anglican Christianity to neo-Malthusianism at the 1930 Lambeth Conference was a consequence of the utilitarian coalition. I have two independent reasons to think so. First, there is a simple public choice calculation: Anglo-Catholics separated themselves from the Church of England after Gorham and so

Economic texts as apocrypha   433

changed the distribution of votes on the issue. Second, no one of any evangelical sympathies could doubt J. S. Mill's moral seriousness; hence, his neo-Malthusian views earned reflection and consideration.

21 Thus I disagree with Cunliffe who reads the larger debate as one in which the participants viewed chattel slavery and "white slavery" as composed of the same fundamentals:

> Moreover, if slavery in general were evil, and if chattel slavery were arguably the most ominous form, then the abolitionists had a good case for attacking the problem on this particular front.... Reform must begin *somewhere* .... their crusade would have been altered out of all recognition if they had endeavored to direct a dual assault, on both chattel slavery and wage [sic] slavery.
>
> (Cunliffe 1979: 26–7)

Working for money wages instead of approbation is a choice in both Adam Smith's and Mill's models of utilitarianism.

22 The accounts in Halévy 1955 and Stephen 1900 would not suggest such exists. Indeed, although Stephen (1900, vol. 3: 300) notes Mill's identification of the Golden Rule with the Greatest Happiness Principle, he completely ignores this agreement in the Macaulay-Mill exchange, Stephen (1900, vol. 2: 85–98). Moreover, he neglects Bentham's own Utilitarianization of Christ when he dismisses *Not Paul but Jesus* as irrelevant to his concerns, Stephen (1900, vol. 1: 323–4).

23 The papers in the debate are most conveniently available in Lively and Rees 1978, from which source I cite. The debate is rather more central to various open public choice problems than standard accounts suggest, for example, Schumpeter 1954: 432. Scholars have long speculated about the reasons Macaulay declined to republish his attack on Mill, for example, Stephen (1900, vol. 2: 85) suggests "gratitude for Mill's generosity in regard to the Indian appointment." Perhaps the importance of the solidarity of the anti-slavery coalition dominated the importance of old intra-coalition debates? In any event Macaulay's arguments are not forgotten in Mill 1861.

24 Macaulay in Lively and Rees (1978: 175). Paley 1785 gave definite form to the Christian version of utilitarianism. Wilberforce (1823: 18) refers to Paley as a "most sagacious observer of human nature."

25 The critical Bentham text is *Not Paul, but Jesus* in which the non-Utilitarian aspects of Christianity are blamed on St. Paul's teaching: "Not so Jesus: no harm did he see in eating and drinking, unless with the pleasure it produced greater pain. With this reserve, no harm ... did he see in any thing that gives pleasure" (Bentham 1823: 394). The role of this text in the intra-coalition debate is discussed in Levy 1999.

26
> I must again repeat, what the assailants of utilitarianism seldom have the justice to acknowledge, that the happiness which forms the utilitarian standard of what is right in conduct, is not the agent's own happiness, but that of all concerned. As between his own happiness and that of others, utilitarianism requires him to be as strictly impartial as a disinterested and benevolent spectator. In the golden rule of Jesus of Nazareth, we read the complete spirit of the ethics of utility. To do as you would be done by, and to love your neighbour as yourself, constitute the ideal perfection of utilitarian morality.
>
> (Mill 1861: 401)

27 Evangelicals such as Wilberforce are under obligation to oppose any system restricting access to the Word of God. The pro-slavery writers were sensitive to the charges that the slaves were kept from the Bible and thus their salvation itself jeopardized. Fletcher (1852: 23) confronts an argument from F. Wayland that slavery "renders the eternal happiness of the one party subservient to the temporal

happiness of the other." Pringle (1852a: 20) cites "the taunt that we should not boast of the education of the slave as long as the reading of the Bible is shut out from him by our laws." He responds:

> The slave's inability to read has given rise to a more kindly feeling, and to a closer connection between the races, than if each slave could read his own Bible. It has induced oral teaching; and the effect of this upon both races no man at the North can conceive.
>
> (Pringle 1852b: 482)

The always illuminating "Nicholas Brimblecomb" (1853: 80) emphasizes how orality restricts the slave's ability to select which of the Biblical texts on slavery to read, as well as to learn other lessons.

Evangelicals, for whom the Bible was the Word of God, would be vastly unhappy with a second-hand encounter with the Word. If orality suffices then what exactly is wrong with having a priest explain the Latin Bible? Wilberforce (1982: 3) compares two systems of belief: real Christianity versus one in which "The Bible lies on a shelf unopened." W. Tyndale, in his *Letter to Fryth*, explains translation as an act for which *his* salvation was at risk: "I call God to record against the day we shall appear before our Lord Jesus, to give a reckoning of our doings, that I never altered one syllable of God's Word against my conscience." I modernized the spelling and quote the epigram of Tyndale's nineteenth-century biographer, Demaus (1871). Tyndale's moral seriousness was of great consequence. Hammond (1983: 44ff) establishes just how Tyndale's translation attains the stupendous feat of preserving both semantics and syntax of the Hebrew original by bending English itself as when he introduced the syntactical form "X-of-X" as an English superlative, for example, "the Song of Songs."

The anti-slavery movement's link to Reformation controversy is suggested by Senior (1864: 434) when he poses the puzzle: "If we did not know that 'Uncle Tom' has been prohibited by the Pope, we should have supposed that there was no form of Christian faith in which it would not find grateful admirers." He suggests an answer:

> It is possible, too, that the Papal authorities were alarmed by hearing of one of the effects produced by the work in Paris – a general demand, among the ouvriers, for bibles. . . . All the stalls were full of them; and the purchasers, to most of whom the book was unknown, asked anxiously whether what they were buying was the 'real bible,' – 'Uncle Tom's bible?'
>
> (Senior 1864: 435)

28 Worst-case theorizing has a long and distinguished history:

> Political writers have established it as a maxim, that, in contriving any system of government, and fixing the several checks and controuls of the constitution, every man ought to be supposed a knave, and to have no other end, in all his actions, than private interest.
>
> (Hume 1987: 42)

The modern revival of this Humean point of view comes in Buchanan and Brennan 1980. The analogue in mathematical statistics is that developed in the various robust schools of thought, for example, Mosteller and Tukey (1977) and Huber 1981. The worst-case paradox seems to be avoided when one describes the decision abstractly, for example, minimizing the maximum loss, and not concretely, for example, supposing the government "is" a slave driver. One must be cautious here because I am not aware of any attention paid the possibility of this paradox in the theoretical literatures.

29   When we see the actions of a man, we know with certainty what he thinks his

interest to be. But it is impossible to reason with certainty from what we take to be his interest to his actions. One man goes without a dinner, that he may add a shilling to a hundred thousand pounds: another runs in debt to give balls and masquerades. One man cuts his father's throat to get possession of his old clothes: another hazards his life to save that of an enemy. One man volunteers on a forlorn hope: another is drummed out of a regiment for cowardice. Each of these men has, no doubt, acted from self-interest. But we gain nothing by knowing this, except the pleasure, if it be one, of multiplying useless words. In fact, this principle is just as recondite, and just as important, as the great truth, that whatever is, is.

(Lively and Rees 1978: 125)

30 And why Mill excludes women since the same reasoning which argues for universal manhood suffrage argues for universal suffrage, (Lively and Rees 1978: 116).
31 This exchange might be central to Jeremy Bentham's attack on what seems to be utilitarianism based on medians (Levy 1995). Macaulay's demonstration of the importance of time preference to Utilitarian claims – a point which one can find in Mill (Lively and Rees 1978: 75) – may have had something to do with Bentham's *Auto-Icon* (Levy 1992). Andrew Farrant found the point in Mill for me.
32 A useful test for any edition of a Carlyle text designed for students is whether the editor glosses Carlyle's customary grumping at the "wasted" £20 million. If not, one ought to ask why.
33 His principles were announced in the great essay on Milton:

There is only one cure for the evils that newly acquired freedom produces; and that cure is freedom. When a prisoner first leaves his cell he cannot bear the light of day; he is unable to discriminate colours, or recognize faces. But the remedy is, not to remand him into his dungeon, but to accustom him to the rays of the sun. The blaze of truth and liberty may at first dazzle and bewilder nations which have become half blind in the house of bondage. But let them gaze on, and they will soon be able to bear it.

(Macaulay 1961, vol. 1: 179–80)

Many politicians of our time are in the habit of laying it down as a self-evident proposition, that no people ought to be free until they are fit to use their freedom. The maxim is worthy of the fool in the old story, who resolved not to go into the water till he had learnt to swim. If men are to wait for liberty till they become wise and good in slavery, they may indeed wait for ever.

(Macaulay 1961, vol. 1: 178–9)

Maucalay uses the analogy of people adjusting to inexpensive alcohol to make the case The reader who does not know the tacit reference to the *Wealth of Nations* (Smith 1976: 492) will not catch the division of labor within the coalition.
34 Trevelyan (1978, vol. 1: 285). A view of Buxton from *Fraser's* is found in May 1831.
35 after eight weeks of induction into the elements of Political Economy, she had only yesterday been set right by a prattler three feet high, for returning to the question 'What is the first principle of this science?' the absurd answer, 'To do unto others as I would that they should do unto me.

(Dickens 1972: 95)

Hard Times requires a detailed examination as a key text in the anti-anti-slavery movement.
36 Thus, Willey (1956: 144–7) defines "liberal" Christians in terms of their denial of "uncritical bibliolatry" and their acceptance of Darwin's theory.
37 A liberal effort to free the mind from these 'Hebrew old clothes' seemed to many thinkers the major need of the age. Only then could religious truth be

> reembodied in a believable form. 'It was clearly the part of every noble heart,' said Carlyle, thinking of himself and his work, 'to expend all its lightnings and energies burning-up without delay, and sweeping into their native Chaos' these 'incredible uncredited traditions...'
>
> (Houghton 1957: 49)

38 Carlyle is remembered, and his influence was felt, as an upholder of the spiritual view of the world in an age of increasing materialism and unbelief. Yet he is the most remarkable example of a phenomenon which I take to be typical of the nineteenth century, that of the religious temperament severed from 'religion.'

(Willey 1949: 105)

"The strength of Carlyle lay in the passionate sincerity with which he believed in his own 'God'." (Willey 1949: 117)

39 Here is an extract from Froude's *Nemesis of Faith*:

> Whatever after evidence we may find, if we are so happy as to find any, to strengthen our religious convictions, it is down in childhood their roots are struck, and it is on old association that they feed. Evidence can be nothing but a stay to prevent the grown tree from falling; it can never make it grow or assist its powers of life. The old family prayers, which taught us to reverence prayer, however little we understood its meaning; the far dearer private prayers at our own bedside; the dear friends for whom we prayed; the still calm Sunday, with its best clothes and tiresome services, which we little thought were going so deep into our heart, when we thought them so long and tedious.
>
> (Froude 1849: 28)

> Pan, almighty Pan! Had the water-nymphs forsaken their grottoes where the fountains were flowing as of old? Were the shadows of the deep woods less holy? Did the enchanted nightingale speak less surely the tale of her sorrow? As it was in the days of their fathers so it was in theirs – their fathers had gone down to the dust in the old ways, and so would they go down and join them. ... Who shall say that those poor peasants were not acting in the spirit we most venerate, most adore.
>
> (Froude 1849: 32)

40 The texts are discussed in Levy 2001 where I propose "quackery" as the unifying principle of "literary" and "scientific" racists. Thomas caught the spirit of quackery:

> Here we are reminded of the dogma laid down by a certain class of ethnologists, to the effect that intellectuality, when displayed by a person of mixed European and African blood, must always be assigned to the European side of the parentage.
>
> (Thomas 1889: 134–5)

"Racism" is not simply a retrospective judgment from the comfortable vantage of the passing of our ghastly twentieth century.

Nineteenth-century attacks on racial aspects of Carlyle, Froude and Kingsley respectively are found in Mill 1850, Thomas 1889 and Robertson 1897. Cunliffe (1979: 13) describes Carlyle's *Latter-Day Pamphlets* as "radically conservative" and as far as I can see never mentions his opinions on race. This is odd because he sees J. Campbell's *Negro-Mania* for exactly what it is, "a vehemently anti-black compendium" (Cunliffe 1979: 22). Carlyle's "ODNQ" is reprinted in *Negro-Mania*. Kingsley's *Alton Locke* – which Cunliffe (1979: 14) describes as one of a list of novels with "socially conscious titles" – will be considered later in detail.

41 Willey's analysis of Carlyle does not comment on the racism (Willey 1949: 128–9).

> Sadistic brutality of this kind is pathological, and no doubt the desire to 'smash 'em good' in Carlyle and Froude as well as Kingsley had personal origins. But nationalism and racism, sanctioned by Old Testament Puritanism and social Darwinism, created an atmosphere in which the normal control of the beast in man could be seriously weakened.
>
> (Houghton 1957: 213)

One stares at such claims. Does Houghton mean to blame the anti-slavery evangelicals for Carlyle's racist brutality? Even that makes more sense than blaming post-1859 texts (didn't social Darwinism have to wait for Darwin?) for arguments in the late 1840s–early 1850s. Williams 1958 mentions neither racial issues nor slavery. Hall 1992 thinks different conceptions of masculinity motivate the debate between Carlyle and Mill. Stephen has a characteristically dense version of this argument:

> His feelings, however, were I take it, as tender as a woman's. They were wanting, not in keenness, but in the massiveness which implies more masculine fibre. And this, indeed, is what seems to indicate the truth. Mill could never admit any fundamental difference between the sexes. That is, I believe, a great but natural misconception for one who was in character as much feminine as masculine. He had some of the amiable weaknesses which we at present – perhaps on account of the debased state of society – regard as especially feminine. The most eminent women, hitherto at least, are remarkable rather for docility than originality.
>
> (Stephen 1900, vol. 3: 72–3)

The parallel "masculinization" of Harriet Martineau is documented later.

42   Sixty years after it was written, Thrall's book remains the only full-length study of the magazine. Her scholarship was so meticulous, and many of her sources now so irrecoverable, that anyone who writes anything at all about *Fraser's* must be deeply indebted to her work.

> (Leary 1994: 123)

43 Thrall's study does not extend through the later role of *Fraser's* as an organ of racist thought during the Governor Eyre controversy, Greg 1866 and *Fraser's* February 1866. Semmel 1962 remains the definitive study of the British debates over Eyre. Mill and the last of the utilitarian coalition wish to have Eyre tried for murdering blacks. Carlyle and associates triumphed with the argument that non-people cannot be murdered. All the "progressives" – Dickens, Kingsley, Ruskin – sided with Carlyle.

44 Houghton considers in detail Maginn's wickedly unkind attack on the economist F. Place, then the founder of neo-Malthusianism and later the author of the People's Charter. Maginn's untrue attack on Harriet Martineau for neo-Malthusianism is considered in Levy 2001. Marks (1986: 29) is puzzled that the attack is in personal not intellectual terms. Rather, systematic personal attacks on Martineau will be documented later in a context which is easy to explain. When facts or law could be quoted against her, the argument was completely polite by the standards of the time. Austin (1839: 45) calls her "this intrusive stranger," gives his evidence and then proceeds to his next point.

45 Please note that these are not my italics; they are there in the original. Macaulay's speech is quoted in Trevelyan (1978:, vol. 1: 103–5); *Fraser's* attack is not discussed at all. Contemporary judgments of the anti-slave movement often characterize it as Wilberforce and Co. Here is testimony from the industrious pro-slavery American publisher responsible for considerable reproduction of British racial anthropology, J. H. van Evrie:

> And if the Father of Lies, Lucifer himself, had plotted a plan or scheme for concealing a great truth, and embarrassing a great cause, he could have

> accomplished nothing more effective than the movement that Wilberforce inaugurated for the professed benefit of the negro and other subordinate races of mankind, which, masked under the form of religious duty, and appealing to the conscience, the love of proselytism, the enthusiasm, and even the bigotries of the religious world, has, for more than half a century, held in thrall the conscience as well as the reason of Christendom.
>
> (van Evrie 1868: 27)

46 It also suggests that Carlyle's contribution to the language is rather less original than recently urged. Hall thinks Carlyle's use of the emphasized word in 1853 to be worthy of note: "It was the Mutiny which brought the term 'niggers' into common parlance. This was the term that Carlyle had seen fit to use publically in 1853" (Hall 1992: 275). In *Alton Locke*, the word is used only by characters without pretensions to education, for example, Kingsley 1850: 190, 246. The "author" speaking on his own behalf does not descend to this vulgarity; for example, he uses "negro" or "black man" at Kingsley 1850: 343 and elsewhere.

47 One can find this argument in Stearns 1853: 46. Lockhart, in the *Quarterly Review* made the perfectly correct observation that this sort of argument assumes that the *owner* of the slaves is directly responsible for punishment:

> Absenteeism all the world over is the greatest of evils that can befall a labouring population; and it is impossible not to admit that if the West India proprietors had generally visited their estates in person, and endeared themselves, as Lewis did, to their dependents, it would have been a hard matter indeed for all the fanatics, backed by all the liberals, and all the East India sugar-dealers, to consummate their ruin.
>
> (Lockhart 1833: 397)

48 Testimony to *Fraser's* wit is well-nigh universal, for example, Houghton 1972: 304.

> At Maginn's death *Punch* claimed him as its own by donning for the first time in its as yet brief course the black border, which has ever since been famous as its symbol of mourning for the passing of those who have had the wit to make the world laugh at folly.
>
> (Thrall 1934: 10)

49 If modern economists have heard of Harriet Martineau, it is as the pre-eminent popularizer of classical economics (Blaug 1958: 129–38). Blaug suggests she should be judged as a journalist not as an economist because she bears some responsibility for our discipline becoming the "dismal science" (ibid.: 138–9). By this Blaug does not mean the possibility that her willingness to discuss interracial sex in public made economics "dismal." If there is a Malthusian link, the references to interracial sexuality in Carlyle's "ODNQ" suggest this would be it. There is a recent account of Martineau which takes the charming line that since she is too radical to be a real economist, she must be something else, the first woman sociologist! (Hoecker-Drysdale 1992).

50 The lease-purchase analysis is easy to find. Here it is expounded by someone writing as Amor Patriæ: "A highly civilized, intelligent and refined society, cannot exist without servants of some kind – and the difference between purchase and hiring, is just about the difference between buying and hiring a horse; the former is generally the best used." (Amor Patriæ 1858: 14–5) Karl Marx attacked Carlyle for just such an argument:

> Finally, spake the oracle, Thomas Carlyle . . . In a short parable, he reduces the one great event of contemporary history, the American Civil War, to this level, that the Peter of the North wants to break the head of the Paul of the South with all his might, because the Peter of the North hires his labour by the day,

and the Paul of the South hires his by the life.... The bubble of Tory sympathy for the urban workers – but no means for the rural – has burst at last. The sum of all is – slavery!

(Marx 1887: 255–6)

Is Mill (1850: 27) – "the oracle of which your contributor is the prophet" – the source of Marx's "oracle"? If so there is a tighter relationship between these authorities than their ideological heirs would suggest.

51 "It is a common boast in the south that there is less vice in their cities than in those of the north." (Martineau 1837, vol. 2: 325) She then goes on to develop the argument that owning a sexual object as slave is a good substitute for renting one in a brothel. The argument to which Martineau refers can be found in the anonymous 1844 *Slavery* together with an added homosexual twist (anon. 1844: 27):

> who, on entering any large Northern city, is not made painfully aware of the low state of moral feelings, in noting the innumerable evidences of prostitution that meet his eye on every side? What visitor of New York city, has failed to notice with what unblushing effrontery prostitutes of both sexes make Broadway their place of assignation?
>
> (Martineau 1837, vol. 2: 325)

Motooka asks whether the Martineau procedure for estimating the hidden economy of inter-racial sex might not be applicable here too? Responding to *Uncle Tom's Cabin*, Stearns (1853: 82–3) discusses prostitution and concubinage as substitutes.

52 As a Christian Wilberforce is bound by the Book of Common Prayer's injunction to marry early to avoid fornication, as a Malthusian Martineau will allow people to choose when to marry to find happiness as they perceive it. Christian Malthusians had a very narrow line to walk between competing conceptions of happiness.

53 Levy 2001 gives the Martineau reference missing in E. August (Carlyle 1971: 8).

54 Senior 1864: 437. The long version of the review is available as the very rare *American Slavery* (Senior 1862), which is in turn reprinted in Senior 1864. Gosset (1985: 240–3) emphasizes the importance of this review. Fiedler (1979: 37) cannot see why all the fuss about *Uncle Tom*, but then he shows no interest in the actual debates over slavery and sexuality.

55 Senior 1864: 409. Senior's demographic analysis argues that child-selling is important. Senior's role in this debate is unremarked in economic scholarship even by Bowley 1937.

56 Stowe 1982: 30, and then in case the reader missed it the first time, Stowe 1982: 512.

57 Stowe begins *Uncle Tom's Cabin* with a respectable owner, reflecting upon his wife's reaction, refusing to a sell a woman for sexual usage even though it is clear she "might make your future on that ar gal in Orleans, any day. I've seen over a thousand, in my day, paid down for gals not a bit handsomer" (Stowe 1982: 14–15). Simon Legree, the embodiment of all evil, has an old concubine, Cassy, and has recently acquired the fifteen-year-old Emmeline as her replacement. Obviously, I disagree with J. Donovan: "Most wrongdoing and evil behavior in the novel are shown to have monetary motives. In this, Stowe links slavery with capitalism, and her critique of the profit motive therefore remains relevant today" (Donovan 1991: 40). But surely it is Mrs Shelby who puts the iron in Mr. Shelby's spine about selling Eliza for sexual use, and she is certainly the more competent capitalist. Donovan testifies how sturdy the faith that any progressive opposes markets. Emancipation would put the former slaves in what institution?

58 "[George's] mother was one of those unfortunates of her race, marked out by personal beauty to be the slave of the passions of her possessor, and the mother of children who may never know a father" (Stowe 1982: 133). "It may be remembered that slavery in America is not at all confined to persons of any particular

complexion; there are a very large number of slaves as white as any one" (Craft 1860: 2). It is possibly relevant that in *Hard Times*, Tom Gradgrind darkens himself to escape (Dickens 1972: 298–9).

59 Gossett emphasizes Senior's claim that many Britons had actually never seen a black person (Gossett 1985: 242). Carlyle detested that part of *Uncle Tom's Cabin* he would read (ibid.: 247). Carlyle's argument that blacks and whites are a species apart is considered in Levy 2001.

60
> For instance, it is a common practice in the slave States for ladies, when angry with their maids, to send them to the calybuce sugar-house, or to some other place established for the purpose of punishing slaves, and have them severely flogged; and I am sorry it is a fact, that the villains to whom those defenceless creatures are sent, not only flog them as they are ordered, but frequently compel them to submit to the greatest indignity. Oh! If there is any one thing under the wide canopy of heaven, horrible enough to stir a man's soul, and to make his very blood boil, it is the thought of his dear wife, his unprotected sister, or his young and virtuous daughters, struggling to save themselves from falling a prey to such demons!
>
> (Craft 1860: 8)

Craft's mixed-race status which kept him from falsifying the racists' claim "all blacks were stupid" – he was too smart to be "black" – did not exempt him from "black" slavery (Young 1995, Levy 2001). The spectator move is found in *Suppressed Book* (1864: 128).

61 Motooka (1998: 213) argues from Adam Smith's texts that spectating is gendered. I only saw the connection here as a result of a conversation with Gordon Wood. The general principle in Smith's account is that we imagine new situations in which our current consciousness is placed (Levy 1995). Thus, without reflection we get many things wrong in our judgments as Smith explains, for example, we think that the problem with being dead is the cold and the gnawing vermin.

62 Senior explained the importance of *Uncle Tom's Cabin* as partly resulting from the fact that there are no unmarried lovers with whom the reader is invited to sympathize (Senior 1864: 441–2). He notes that it was a novel that the evangelicals were permitted to read: "Even in this country in some classes, particularly among the Dissenters, novel reading is forbidden, and here, as in America, 'Uncle Tom' is excepted from the general prohibition" (ibid.: 436). Most of the unmarried sexuality, lacking consent, is deeply sinful on broad utilitarian grounds.

63 Stowe 1982: 438. Tom's murder at Legree's hands results from his assistance in Cassy's and Emmeline's escape (Stowe 1982: 479). In a famous essay, Fiedler (1979: 35–6) reads unproblematical rape into the story. However Stowe insists that bought concubinage as a long-term relationship can have strange effects on the owner-rapist:

> The influence of Cassy over [Legree] was of a strange and singular kind. He was her owner, her tyrant and tormentor. . . . the most brutal man cannot live in constant association with a strong female influence, and not be greatly controlled by it. When he first bought her, she was, as she had said, a woman delicately bred; and then he crushed her, without scruple, beneath the foot of his brutality. But, as time, and debasing influences and despair, hardened womanhood within her, and waked the fires of fiercer passions, she had become in a measure his mistress, and he alternately tyrannized over and dreaded her.
>
> (Stowe 1982: 466–7)

64 Hedrick (1994: 264) documents that the teenage Harriet Beecher had been compared to Harriet Martineau even when the latter was on her famous American tour.

65 Two of the three authors are mentioned in the *Suppressed Book*, Hammond (1864: 26) and Harper (1864: 34). The 1852 collection claims to be published in Charleston, the 1853 in Philadelphia. Spot comparison of the two suggests that the

same type was used for both editions. Indeed, the page number 132 is transposed in both editions to 231 and page number 120 is set in broken type in both editions, although that of the 1853 version seems less damaged. The margins of the Philadelphia edition are more generous, which suggests it was a more expensive edition. It seems odd that a more expensive edition would be printed with the same type after a less expensive edition.

Uncle Tom's Cabin had the property of reviving classics. Ker (1840, 1842) attained a decade-delayed third edition with addition of a discussion of *Uncle Tom* (Ker 1853). Ker provides a treasure chest of the commonplace defense of slavery which might be useful to read in conjunction with Carlyle, for example, on the £20 million needed to ransom the West Indian slaves: "from her oppressed, starving and over-wrought population at home, to emancipate her slaves in the West Indies, which slaves labored less, and were better fed, clothed and lodged, than half the operatives of England" (Ker 1853: 34–5). We find Carlylean moral localism in the new material: "There *was* a time, when philanthropy, like charity, began at home" (ibid.: vi). And on why despots so like *Uncle Tom*: "they can get a club by which they will be able to dash out the brains of the young Western Lion of Liberty ... [they] prefer *white* slaves to black" (ibid.: iv). On Ker, the *Suppressed Book* (1864: 75–6).

66 The reference in *Table Talk* is Coleridge (1990, vol. 14: 416). Perhaps it is not a surprise that Harper (1853: 92) cites Coleridge's racist reading of *Othello*: "as Coleridge has said, we are to conceive of him not as a negro, but as a high bred Moorish chief." *Fraser's* in September 1849 proposed to amend the established text of *Anthony and Cleopatra* to rid it of the blackness of Cleopatra.

67   What person beside herself would undertake to argue for the advantages of being deaf? To prove that the ears are but surplusage, is certainly to suggest to the deity a process of improvement, by which the curtailment of a sense will help the endowments of a philosopher.

(Simms 1853: 188–9)

68 Simms' masculinization of Martineau is rather more interesting than the later Stephen-Hall feminization of Mill, if only because it helps Simms see the robust utilitarianism which underlies the economics Martineau wields as a weapon of terror.

> With her, as with most European philosophers of her order, they are assumptions only – specious or imposing – which have been taken on trust; according, perhaps, with the particular temperament of the individual. To a woman of the bold, free, masculine nature of Miss Martineau, impatient of the restraints of her sex, and compelled to seek her distinction in fields which women are rarely permitted to penetrate, democracy is one of the most attractive of social philosophies, as conservatism must be necessarily the most offensive. With her, the doctrine of the majorities is the voice of God.

(Simms 1853: 247)

F. C. Adams (1853: 38–141) responds to Simm's attack on *Uncle Tom's Cabin*.

69 "these made the lot of the industrialized masses brutal beyond anything ever before experienced in England, and unmatched anywhere in the western world" (Altick in Carlyle 1965: x). "The intellectual rationalization of the get-rich-quick, dog-eat-dog, and devil-take-the-hindmost spirit that dominated British economic life in the age of *Past and Present* was supplied by Benthamite utilitarianism"(ibid.).

> the cure, for its part, strikes one as being a substitution, for the justly maligned Morison's pill, of something uncomfortably like Prussian authoritarianism. But if Carlyle's remedy fails to satisfy, the acuteness with which he recognized the symptoms of a diseased society compels our imagination.

(Altick in Carlyle 1965: xvii)

70 Carlyle (1965: 91): "Jew Harpies"; (ibid.: 96): "harpy Jews"; (ibid.: 95) is ecumenical: "ravening flights of Jew and Christian creditors, pouncing on him like obscene harpies."
71 Altick in Carlyle 1965: 91. Altick's gloss on page 95 gives a reference to the *Aeneid*. One might have expected Apollonius but then he misses the £20 million.
72 In *Uncle Tom's Cabin*, Stowe's character St Clare, who sometimes sounds a great deal like Carlyle in *ODNQ*, Stowe (1982: 261), makes the following assertion:

> Well, I've travelled in England some, and I've looked over a good many documents as to the state of their lower classes; and I really think there is no denying Alfred, when he says that his slaves are better off than a large class of the population of England.
>
> (Stowe 1982: 270)

Dickens's review singled out St Clare for special praise (Dickens and Morley 1852). Needless to say, the comparison drew comment. A. Helps (1852a: 6, 1852b: 238): "there is, I am sorry to say, an exaggeration in the statements which are made in the course of the volume, and are not contradicted, respecting the condition of the English laborer" (Gossett 1985: 243–5). Stowe's response to Helps was twofold: first, this is how the slave-owners in fact defended themselves, and second, this is what she learned from "the works of Charles Dickens and Charles Kingsley" and others (Hedrick 1994: 243). Stowe talked to an economist about this "evidence":

> When Stowe broached the subject with Richard Whately, the English Archbishop of Dublin, he assured her that her literary evidence was suspect, especially her use of Charles Kingsley: "He, & a Profr Maurice, & some others, are what are called Christian Socialists; giving such a representation of Christianity as would have justified the Roman Emperors in putting it down by force, as leading straight to anarchy."
>
> (Hedrick 1994: 243)

73 Macaulay did not take the bait, treating More as saint and statesman.
74 Explicitly, Southey claims such things as persecution are morally random:

> Had it been my fortune to have associated with Bilney, or Tindal and Frith, I might have partaken their zeal and their fate. On the other hand, had I been acquainted with you and Cuthbert Tonstal, it is not less likely that I should have received the stamp of your opinions.
>
> (Southey 1829: 245–6)

On More, Bilney and Tyndale (Foxe 1829: 117–19):

> William Tyndale gave us our English Bible. The sages assembled by King James to prepare the Authorised Version of 1611, so often praised for unlikely corporate inspiration, took over Tyndale's work. Nine-tenths of the Authorized Version's New Testament is Tyndale's. The same is true of the first half of the Old Testament, which is as far as he was able to get before he was executed outside Brussels in 1536.
>
> (Daniell 1994: 1)

Daniell (1994: 262ff) demonstrates that the dispute between Tyndale and More is alive and well.

Kingsley testifies the importance of the Hebrew scriptures for nineteenth-century evangelicals: "As for the Bible, I knew nothing of it really, beyond the Old Testament" (Kingsley 1850: 12). Hill expresses his surprise that his study of the Biblical basis of seventeenth-century radicalism ended up almost exclusively focusing on the Hebrew Bible (Hill 1993: 440). On Foxe's importance: "All East

India vessels carried the Bible as reading matter, together with Foxe's *Book of Martyrs* and Hakluty's *Voyages*" (ibid.: 18).

75 Thus, one of the responses to *Uncle Tom's Cabin* passed along the following intelligence:

> What says Southy [sic], the English poet, of the great mass of the English poor? He says that "they are deprived, in childhood, of all instruction, and enjoyment. They grow up without decency; without comfort; without hope; without morals, and without shame."
>
> (Woodward 1853: 25)

76 Winch 1996: 290–1 has a discussion of Southey's *More* without mentioning the idealization of slavery.

77 "It is but equity, besides, that they who feed, clothe, and lodge the whole body of the people, should have such a share of the produce of their own labour as to be themselves tolerably well fed, clothed, and lodged" (Smith 1976: 96).

78 The Smithian roots of the idea of using life expectancy as a measure of well-being is discussed in Levy 1995. It has been revived by Sen 1993.

79 When one views the world through traditional Marxist preconceptions, one tends not to see much racial conflict. Engel's opinion signifies one thing for a world split on class among white people; perhaps, it implies something else when we introduce racial considerations Poliakov (1974: 244–6) discusses Engels and Marx's racism. Engels claimed that "Blacks were congenitally incapable of understanding mathematics." The problem for friends of Carlyle is explained this way: "Yet the Carlyle who kindled the enthusiasm of Emerson and Engels and Whitman . . . is not another creature from the Carlyle who brought tears of hope to the eyes of Hitler" (Rosenberg 1985: 117).

80 Carlyle lives as a "progressive" in textbook accounts because of his impact on religious thinking. It is remarkable, though, how many "Hebrew old clothes" Carlyle presupposes. God in Carlyle's account does not want to use His slaves sexually, or any other way for that matter. This presupposes the God of Abraham and not Pan and the old Homeric crew of raping optimizers. C. Gore made the point with perfect clarity:

> There was an old dilemma invented I think at the time of the Reformation: 'either Jesus was God or He was not a good man'; and the modern critic often laughs at it as ridiculous. I do not think I can laugh at it as ridiculous. What is, after all, the worst kind of spiritual crime? Is it not spiritual arrogance? What makes men hate with a profound hatred the wrong sort of sacerdotalism? It is that it exercises tyranny over human souls. Every man has the right to be himself; he ought not to be dominated or mastered by any other except God.
>
> (Gore 1922: 18–19)

For an account of the Homeric divinity as optimizers who differ from mortals only by their constraints, see Levy 1992: 108–34.

81   if there is any inalienable right of another class, it is that so ably set forth by Carlyle, – the right of every man to be compelled to do what he is fit for, if he won't do it voluntarily; and this brings us back to Quashy.

    (Stearns 1853: 21)

82 Cunliffe 1979: 108 gives references to Carlyle's influence.

83   In less than four years, says Jocelin, the Convent Debts were all liquidated: the harpy Jews not only settled with, but banished, bag and baggage, out of the *Bannaleuca* (Liberties, *Banlieue*) of St. Edmundsbury, – so has the King's Majesty been persuaded to permit. Farewell to you, at any rate: let us, in no extremity, apply again to you! Armed men march them over the borders,

dismiss them under stern penalties, – sentence of excommunication on all that shall again harbour them here: there were many dry eyes at their departure.

(Carlyle 1965: 96)

84 Carlyle 1965: 104.
85 S. Harris 1981: 16 describes two letters to *The Times* in 1862 protesting Kingsley's views on Jews.
86 "his wages, thanks to your competitive system, were beaten down deliberately and conscientiously (for was it not according to political economy, and the laws thereof?) to the minimum on which he could or would work" (Kingsley 1850: 245).

87   In part, *Alton Locke* is in the orthodox sense an 'exposure': an informed, angry and sustained account of sweated labour in the 'Cheap and Nasty' clothing trade. Much of it can still be read in these terms, with attention and sympathy. It is fair to note, however, that in respect of this theme the Preface is more effective than the novel.

(Williams 1958: 100)

There is no preface in the first edition. Houghton 1957 has an extensive discussion of *Alton Locke* without mentioning the role of Jews as "sweaters." Lodge continues in the tradition even as he emphasizes that Kingsley late in life took a "right-wing line" on the American Civil War and Gov. Eyre (Lodge 1967: xviii). Cripps' notes in her edition of *Alton Locke* (1983: 409) helpfully explain that "guanaco" is a "reddish-brown wool from the South American llama," but doesn't explain why Jews might be "sweaters." This is obvious to the reader? Hawley 1986 also reads the Jews out of the story.

88 Aytoun 1850: 599. The reader ought not think "vampire" refers to the suave, elegant, highly erotic creatures of late Victorian fiction or modern movies with whom one might well spend an enchanting evening. Barber 1988 describes the loathsome folkloric monster as a belief evolved to rationalize the nasty facts of bodily decomposition.
89 This problem, an example of reader-response criticism, (Fish 1967) seems not to be noted by literary commentators. Both the reviews in *Fraser's* (November 1850) and in *Blackwood's* (Aytoun 1850), warn their readers that it isn't really what it purports to be. The extract reprinted in *Harper's* has this preface:

It was an error to call this work the autobiography of an individual. It is a picturing – faithful, minute, and eloquent – of the hardships, the suffering, and the miseries endured by a large mass of our fellow men. It is an earnest and honest exposure of the hollowness that infests English society.

(*Harpers* 1850: 803)

The reviewer in the American *Southern Quarterly* considers it an "auto-biography" which testifies truthfully:

There is a vivid reality about his descriptions which too well vouches for their truth, and touches us home – we of these Southern United States – by the great contrast which such a state of society presents, with the far happier, and every way more elevated, position of *our* labouring classes. Aye – negro and slave though these be – the white slave of England – great, proud, glorious England – has sunk far lower than they, in the weltering abyss of misery and hopeless wretchedness.

(*Southern Quarterly* 1851: 120–1)

Westward the course of rationalization? However, the extensive reprinting of *Alton Locke* in Cobden contains this information: "In Charles Kingsley's popular novel, 'Alton Locke,' we find a vivid and truthful picture of the London tailor's workshop, and the slavery of the workmen" (Cobden 1859: 193ff). Cunliffe (1979: 43) cites a 1853 edition which I have not seen.

90 Even though Kingsley asserts in *Alton Locke*, and everywhere else the question comes up, the doctrine of racial hierarchy, his social theorizing is constrained by Christian doctrine:

> Abstract rights? They are sure to end, in practice, only in the tyranny of their father's opinion. In favored England here, the notion of abstract right among the many are not so incorrect, thanks to three centuries of Protestant civilization; but only because the right notions suit the many at this moment. But in America, even now, the same ideas of abstract right do not interfere with the tyranny of the white man over the black. Why should they? The white man is handsomer, stronger, cunninger, worthier than the black. The black is more like an ape than the white man; he is; the fact is there; and no notions of an abstract right will put that down: nothing but another fact; a mightier, more universal fact; Jesus of Nazareth died for the negro as well as for the white.
>
> (Kingsley 1850: 343–4)

Kingsley wrote to Stowe agreeing with her doctrine of racial differences (Gossett 1985: 246). Levy 2001 describes Kingsley's racial quackery.

91 The attack was bracketed by an earlier most favorable review (Helps August 1852) and a favorable discussion of the Beecher family (November 1852). Pringle's attack was prefaced by the editor's (J. Parker) announced policy of publishing both sides. Parker calls attention to the exchange over the "Negro question." Modern authorities on *Fraser's Magazine* pass Parker's policy over in silence. Both the Helps and Pringle articles are reprinted from pamphlets. Ashton (1977) only catches the Helps reprint.

92 Economists ought to have learned from the Soviet era to be cautious of claims that the standard of living in an area people flee *from* is higher than the standard of living in an area people flee *to*. Some particularly embarrassing "data" are considered in Levy 1993.

93 Ashton (1977: 10) regards this as "possibly satire." It is possible that I am an economist.

94 As far as I can see this is even the case in Cunliffe 1979, who carefully attends to the interrelations between the American and British discussions. His references to Martineau are decorative and to Wilberforce nonexistent.

95 This issue has not vanished, as the debate over the Thomas Jefferson-Sally Hemings affair testifies (E. Foster *et al.* 1998).

96 The URL is www.jstor.org. The search was conducted in September 1998.

97 A third "article" was actually a series of independently authored comments. One author used "dismal science" and another used "Negro." JSTOR can search the whole of journals, for example, the table of contents and lists of publications received and the like. Needless to say, searches in such heterogeneous material turn up many such illusory hits.

References

Known or attributed authors

Adams, F. C. (1853) *Uncle Tom at Home*, Philadelphia.
Arnold, M. (1993) *Culture and Anarchy and other Writings*, ed. S. Collini, Cambridge: Cambridge University Press.
Ashton, J. W. (1977) *Harriet Beecher Stowe: A Reference Guide*, Boston: G. K. Hall.

[Austin, J. T.] (1839) *Review of the Rev. Dr. Channing's Letter to Jonathan Phillips, Esq. On the Slavery Question*, Boston.
[Aytoun, W. E.] (1850) "Alton Locke, Tailor and Poet: An Autobiography," *Blackwood's Edinburgh Magazine* 68: 592–610.
Barber, P. (1988) *Vampires, Burial and Death: Folklore and Reality*, New Haven: Yale University Press.
Belsey, C. (1980) *Critical Practice*, London: Routledge.
Bennett, W. J. E. (1850) *A First Letter to the Right Honourable Lord John Russell, M.P. on the Present Persecution of A Certain Portion of the English Church*, 6th edn, London.
[(Bentham, J. ed.) F. Place and G. Smith] (1823) *Not Paul, But Jesus*, London.
Blaug, M. (1958) *Ricardian Economics*, New Haven: Yale University Press.
Bowley, M. (1937) *Nassau Senior and Classical Economics*, London.
Brimblecomb, N. (1853) *Uncle Tom's Cabin in Ruins! Triumphant Defence of Slavery!* Boston.
Buchanan, J. M. and Brennan, G. (1980) *The Power to Tax: Analytical Foundations of a Fiscal Constitution*, Cambridge: Cambridge University Press.
[Carlyle, T.] (December 1849) "Occasional Discourse on the Negro Question," *Fraser's Magazine for Town and Country* 40: 670–9.
—— (1850) *Latter-Day Pamphlets*, London.
—— (1965) *Past and Present*, ed. R. D. Altick, Boston: Houghton Mifflin.
—— (1971) *The Nigger Question*, J. S. Mill, *The Negro Question*, ed. E. R. August, New York: Appleton Century Crofts.
Charlesworth, J. H. (ed) (1983) *The Old Testament Pseudepigrapha*, Garden City, N.Y.: Doubleday.
Coleridge, S. T. (1990) *Table Talk I.*, ed. C. Woodring, vol. 14 of *The Collected Works of Samuel Taylor Coleridge*, Princeton, N.J.: Princeton University Press.
Cobden, J. C. (1859) *The White Slaves of England*, New York.
Craft, W. (1860) *Running a Thousand Miles for Freedom; or, The Escape of William and Ellen Craft from Slavery*, London.
Cunliffe, M. (1979) *Chattel Slavery and Wage Slavery: The Anglo-American Context, 1830–1860*, Athens: University of Georgia Press.
Curry, K. (1975) *Southey*, London: Routledge and Kegan Paul.
Daniell, D. (1994) *William Tyndale*, New Haven: Yale University Press..
Darwall, S. L. (1995) *The British Moralists and the Internal "Ought," 1640–1740*, Cambridge: Cambridge University Press.
Demaus, R. (1871) *William Tyndale: A Biography*, London.
[Dickens, C. and Henry Morley] (September 18, 1852) "North American Slavery," *Household Words. A Weekly Journal Conducted by Charles Dickens* 6(130): 1–6.
Dickens, C. (1972) *Hard Times*, ed. D. Craig, Harmondsworth: Penguin.
Donovan, J. (1991) *Uncle Tom's Cabin: Evil, Affliction and Redemptive Love*, Boston: Twayne.
Edgeworth, F. Y. (1881) *Mathematical Psychics*, London.
Feigenbaum, S. and Levy, D. M. (1996) "The Technological Obsolescence of Scientific Fraud," *Rationality and Society* 8: 261–76.
Fletcher, J. (1852) *Studies in Slavery, in Easy Lessons*, Natchez.
Fielder, L. (1979) *The Inadvertent Epic: From Uncle Tom's Cabin to Roots*, New York: Simon and Schuster.
Fish, S. (1967) *Surprised by Sin: The Reader in Paradise Lost*, Berkeley: University of California Press.
Fitzhugh, G. (1857) *Cannibals All! or, Slaves without Masters*, Richmond.
Foster, E. A., et al. (5 November 1998) "Jefferson Fathered Slave's Last Child," *Nature* 396: 27–8.

[Foxe, J.] (1829) *Fox's Book of Martyrs; or, The Acts and Monuments of the Christian Church*, rev. J. Malham, New York.
Froude, J. A. (1849) *The Nemesis of Faith*, London.
—— (1897) *Thomas Carlyle. A History of His Life in London*, new edn, London.
Gore, C. (1922) *The Deity of Christ*, London.
Gossett, T. F. (1985) *Uncle Tom's Cabin and American Culture*, Dallas: Southern Methodist University Press.
[Greg, W. R.] (March 1866) "The Jamaica Problem," *Fraser's* 73: 277–305.
Halévy, E. (1955) *The Growth of Philosophic Radicalism*, trans. Mary Morris, Boston: Beacon Press.
Hall, C. (1992) *White, Male and Middle-Class: Explorations in Feminism and History*, New York: Routledge.
Hamilton, E. J. (1952) "Prices as a Factor in Business Growth: Prices and Progress," *Journal of Economic History* 12: 325–349.
Hammond, G. (1983) *The Making of the English Bible*, New York: Philosophical Library.
Hammond, J. H. (1853) "Hammond's Letters on Slavery," *The Pro-Slavery Argument*, Philadelphia.
Harris. S. (1981) *Charles Kingsley: A Reference Guide*, Boston: G. K. Hall.
Harper, W. (1853) "Harper on Slavery," *The Pro-Slavery Argument*, Philadelphia.
Hawley, J. C. (Winter 1986) "Responses to Charles Kingsley's Attack on Political Economy," *Victorian Periodical Review* 19: 131–7.
Hedrick, J. D. (1994) *Harriet Beecher Stowe: A Life*, New York: Oxford University Press.
Heffer, S. (1995) *Moral Desperado*, London: Weidenfeld and Nicolson.
[Helps, A.] (1852a) *A Letter on "Uncle Tom's Cabin,"* Cambridge, Mass.
—— (August 1852b) "Uncle Tom's Cabin," *Fraser's* 46: 237–44.
Hill, C. (1993) *The English Bible and the Seventeenth-Century Revolution*, London: Penguin.
Hilton, B. (1988) *The Age of Atonement: The Influence of Evangelicalism on Social and Economic Thought, 1795–1865*, Oxford: Clarendon.
Hoecker-Drysdale, S. (1992) *Harriet Martineau: First Woman Sociologist*, Oxford: Berg.
Hollander, S. (1997) *The Economics of Thomas Robert Malthus*, Toronto: University of Toronto Press.
Houghton, W. E. (1957) *The Victorian Frame of Mind*, New Haven: Yale University Press.
—— (1972) "Fraser's Magazine for Town and Country, 1830-1882," *Wellesley Index to Victorian Periodicals* , ed. W. E. Houghon, Toronto.
Howse, E. M. (1952) *Saints in Politics: The "Clapham Sect" and the Growth of Freedom*, London: Allen and Unwin.
Huber, P. J. (1981) *Robust Statistics*, New York: Wiley.
Hume, D. (1987) *Essays Moral Political, and Literary*, ed. E. F. Miller, rev. edn, Indianapolis: Liberty Classics.
[Hunt, J.] (1866) "Race in Legislation and Political Economy," *Anthropological Review* 4: 113–35.
[Hutcheson, F.] (1726) *An Inquiry into the Original of Our Ideas of Beauty and Virtue; Concerning Moral Good and Evil*, 2nd edn, London.
Ker, L. (1840) *Slavery Consistent with Christianity*, Baltimore.
—— (1842) *Slavery Consistent with Christianity*, 2nd edn, Jefferson City.
—— (1853) *Slavery Consistent with Christianity, with an Introduction, Embracing a Notice of the "Uncle Tom's Cabin" Movement in England*, 3rd edn, Weston, Mo.
[Kingsley, C.] (1850) *Alton Locke, Tailor and Poet. An Autobiography*, New York.
—— (June–November 1850) "Sketches of a Life. By a Radical," *Harper's* 1: 803–7.
—— (1983) *Alton Locke. Tailor and Poet. An Autobiography*, ed. E. A. Cripps, Oxford: Oxford University Press.
Knight, F. H. (1982) *Freedom and Reform*, intro. J. M. Buchanan, Indianapolis: Liberty Classics.

Leary, P. (1994) "*Fraser's Magazine* and the Literary Life," *Victorian Periodicals Review* 27: 105–26.
Levine, L. W. (1993) *The Unpredictable Past*, New York: Oxford University Press.
—— (1996) *The Opening of the American Mind*, Boston: Beacon.
Levy, D. M. (1992) *The Economic Ideas of Ordinary People: From Preferences to Trade*, London: Routledge.
—— (1993) "The Public Choice of Data Provision," *Accountability in Research* 3: 157–63.
—— (1995) "The Partial Spectator in the Wealth of Nations: A Robust Utilitarianism," *European Journal of the History of Economic Thought* 2: 299–326.
—— (1997) "Adam Smith's Rational Choice Linguistics," *Economic Inquiry* 35: 672–8.
—— (1999) "Malthusianism or Christianity: The Invisibility of a Successful Radical," *Historical Reflections/Réflexions Historiques* 25: 61–93.
—— (2001) "Debating Racial Quacks: How the Dismal Science Got Its Name," *Journal of the History of Economic Thought*.
Lively, J. and Rees, J. (1978) *Utilitarian Logic and Politics*, Oxford: Clarendon.
[Lockhart, J. G.] (1833) "M. G. Lewis' West India Journals," *Quarterly Review* 50: 374–99.
Lodge, D. (1967) "Introduction," Charles Kingsley, *Alton Locke: Tailor and Poet*, London: Cassell.
Macaulay, T. B. (1961) *Critical and Historical Essays*, London: Everyman.
[Maginn, W.] (June 1830) "*The Edinburgh Review.* No. C Art. XI, Southey's Colloquies on Society," *Fraser's* 1: 584–600.
Martineau, H. (1837) *Society in America*, London.
Marks, P. (1986) "Harriet Martineau: Fraser's 'Maid of Dishonour,'" *Victorian Periodicals Review* 19: 28–33.
Marx, K. [1887] *Capital*, ed. F. Engels, trans. S. Moore and E. Aveling, Moscow.
Maskell, W. (1850) *A Second Letter on the Present Position of the High Church Party in the Church of England*, London.
[Mill, J. S.] (January 1850) "The Negro Question," *Fraser's* 41: 25–31.
—— (1861) "Utilitarianism," *Fraser's* 64: 391–406.
Morgan, P. (1985) "Review of G. B. Tennyson's Carlyle Reader," *Victorian Periodicals Review* 18: 162.
Mosteller, F. and J. W. Tukey (1977) *Data Analysis and Regression: A Second Course in Statistics*, Reading, Mass.: Addison-Welsey.
Motooka, W. (1998) *The Age of Reasons: Quixotism, Sentimentalism and political economy in Eighteenth-Century Britain*, London: Routledge.
Orwell, G. (1961) *1984*, New York: New American Library.
Paley, W. (1785) *The Principles of Moral and Political Philosophy*, London.
Poliakov, L. (1974) *The Aryan Myth*, trans. E. Howard, New York: Basic Books.
Persky, J. (Autumn 1990) "Retrospectives: A Dismal Romantic," *Journal of Economic Perspectives* 4: 165–72.
[Phillpotts, H. 'Bishop of Exeter'] (1850) *A Letter to the Archbishop of Canterbury*, London.
[Pringle, E. J.] (1852) *Slavery in the Southern States*, 2nd edn, Cambridge.
[Pringle, E. J.] (October 1852b) "Slavery in the Southern States," *Fraser's* 46:476–90.
Putnam, H. (1975) *Mind, Language and Reality*, Cambridge, Cambridge University Press.
Quine, W. V. O. (1961) "Two Dogmas of Empiricism," *From a Logical Point of View: Logico-Philosophical Essays*, 2nd edn, Cambridge, Mass.: Harvard University Press.
Robertson, J. M. (1897) *The Saxon and the Celt*, London.
Rosenberg, J. D. (1985) *Carlyle and the Burden of History*, Cambridge, Mass.: Harvard University Press.
Schumpeter, J. A. (1954) *A History of Economic Analysis*, New York: Oxford University Press.
Semmel, B. (1962) *The Governor Eyre Controversy*, London.

Sen, A. (May 1993) "The Economics of Life and Death," *Scientific American* 268: 40–47.
Senior, N. W. (1862) *American Slavery*, London.
—— (1864) *Essays in Fiction*, London.
Simms, W. G. (1853) "The Morals of Slavery," *The Pro-Slavery Argument*, Philadelphia.
Smith, A. (1976) *An Inquiry into the Nature and Causes of the Wealth of Nations*, ed. W. B. Todd, Oxford: Clarendon Press.
Southey, R. (1829) *Sir Thomas More: or, Colloquies on the Progress and Prospects of Society*, London.
Stanley, A. P. (1870) *Essays Chiefly on Questions of Church and State from 1850 to 1870*, London.
Stearns, E. J. (1853) *Notes on Uncle Tom's Cabin: Being a Logical Answer to its Allegations and Inferences against Slavery as an Institution*, Philadelphia.
Stephen, L. (1900) *The English Utilitarians*, London.
Stowe, H. B. (1982) *Three Novels*, New York: Library of America.
Tennyson, G. B., ed. (1984) *A Carlyle Reader*. Cambridge: Cambridge University Press.
Thomas, J. J. (1889) *Froudacity*, London.
Thrall, M. (1934) *Rebellious Fraser's: Nol Yorke's Magazine in the Days of Maginn, Thackeray, and Carlyle*, New York: Columbia University Press.
Trevelyan, G. O. (1978) *The Life and Letters of Lord Macaulay*, Oxford: Oxford University Press.
Tyndale, W. (1992) *Tyndale's Old Testament*, ed. D. Daniell, New Haven: Yale University Press.
Van Evrie, J. H. (1868) *White Supremacy and Negro Subordination; or, Negroes a Subordinate Race, and (so-called) Slavery Its Normal Condition*, New York.
Waterman, A. M. C. (1991) *Revolution, Economics and Religion*, Cambridge: Cambridge University Press.
Whately, R. (1850) *Infant-Baptism Considered, in a Charge*, 2nd edn, London.
Whately, E. J. (1868) *Life and Correspondence of Richard Whately, D.D*, new edn, London.
White, A. D. (1993) *A History of the Warfare of Science with Theology in Christendom*, New York: Prometheus.
Wilberforce, W. (1823) *An Appeal to the Religion, Justice, and Humanity of the Inhabitants of the British Empire, in Behalf of the Negro Slaves in the West Indies*, new edn, London.
—— (1982) *Real Christianity: Contrasted with the Prevailing Religious System*, ed. J. M. Houston, Portland, Ore.: Multnomah Press.
Williams, R. (1958) *Culture and Society: 1780–1950*, New York: Columbia University Press.
Willey, B. (1949) *Nineteenth Century Studies*, New York: Columbia University Press.
—— (1956) *More Nineteenth Century Studies*, New York: Columbia University Press.
Wilson, D. A. (1927) *Carlyle at his Zenith*, London.
Winch, D. (1996) *Riches and Poverty: An Intellectual History of Political Economy in Britain, 1750–1834*, Cambridge: Cambridge University Press.
Woodward, A. (1853) *Review of Uncle Tom's Cabin; or, An Essay on Slavery*, Cincinnati.
Young, R. J. C. (1995) *Colonial Desire*, London: Routledge.

Unattributed articles and books

(February 1831) "The Colonists versus the Anti-Slave Society," *Fraser's* 3: 114–25.
(March 1831) "Stray Notes on the Anti-Slavery Monthly Reporter," *Fraser's* 3: 205–8.
(May 1831) "Mr. Buxton and West Indians," *Fraser's* 3: 509–11.
(1844) *Slavery: A Treatise, Showing that Slavery neither a Moral, Political, nor Social Evil*, Penfield, Ga.
(September 1849) "Shakespeare's Character of Cleopatra," *Fraser's* 40: 277–291.
(September 1849) "Babel," *Fraser's* 40: 318–27.

(November 1850) "A Triad of Novels. Alton Locke, Tailor and Poet," *Fraser's* 42: 576–85.
(April 1850) *Church and State.* Reprinted from the Last Number of *The Christian Remembrancer*, London.
(July 1851) "Negro and White Slavery; Wherein do they Differ? *Alton Locke, Tailor and Poet*, an auto-biography," *Southern Quarterly Review* 4 (n.s.): 118–32.
Amor Patriæ (1858) *Slavery, Con. And Pro. Or, A Sermon and its Answer*, Washington.
(1864) *The Suppressed Book about Slavery*, New York.
(February 1866) "Jamaica, and the Recent Insurrection There," *Fraser's* 73: 161–79.

23 Women in the canon of economics

Robert W. Dimand

When the gamblers at the Casino du Hull interrupt their efforts to accumulate capital despite the odds at the gaming tables and go to grab a quick snack, they do so by a forty-metre-wide mural, *L'Hommage à Rosa Luxemburg*, by Jean-Paul Riopelle, which looks out over the slot machines (Guly 1997). Lest their snack-time be unremunerative, they can "Count the number of snow geese in *L'Hommage à Rosa Luxemburg* located on the third level of the Casino de Hull to earn a chance to win $15,000 in prizes, including a stay at Île-aux-Grues, where this masterpiece was created" (advertisement in *Ottawa Citizen*, August 10 1997). Perhaps a few of them may be moved to reflect on comparisons of capitalism to a casino. The mural may serve to remind us that, if one looks for them, women economists turn up in all sorts of contexts where the generally accepted canon of economics would not lead one to expect them.

At least until very recently, the textbook presentation of the history of economics has suggested that it was (with the exception of Joan Robinson on imperfect competition and of Anna J. Schwartz's work with Milton Friedman on monetary history) what J. H. Hexter notoriously claimed history was more generally: a stag affair (Zinsser 1993: 34). The participation of women in the economics profession, exemplified by the election of Alice Rivlin as president of the American Economic Association and of Alice Orcutt Nakamura as president of the Canadian Economic Association (and of Tansu Ciller, a University of Connecticut economics Ph.D., as prime minister of Turkey), is regarded as comparatively recent, a tribute to how progressive we moderns are: the past is a foreign country, they do things differently there. Women are still a minority in the discipline, especially in tenured ranks and at the most prestigious institutions, but they are represented, providing for instance just under 5 percent of the contributors to *The New Palgrave: A Dictionary of Economics*. A clear example of the belief that almost no women contributed to economics until very recently is provided by William J. Baumol in his "Digression: On Earlier Writings by Women," in an article on the centenary of the American Economic Association. Baumol reported the "observation . . . that before the first World War, as today, a (distressingly) few women *were* contributing to the literature" (Baumol 1985: 11), as his research assistant Nicola Pearson had found seven articles (one in two parts) by four women, not all before the First World War – although missing even the article by Katharine Coman that fills the first nineteen pages of Volume 1, Number 1, of the *American Economic Review*.

In this chapter, I argue to the contrary that, although their level of participation has fluctuated and despite barriers to academic employment, women participated in and made significant contributions to the discipline of economics in the nineteenth and early twentieth centuries. I also argue that forgetfulness of their contributions has hampered understanding of the economic experience of half of humanity, as female political economists paid particular attention to the economic role of women, and brought to its analysis points of view and concerns absent from what Michèle Pujol termed the "malestream" of the discipline (with the important exception of John Stuart Mill). This greater concern by women economists with "women's issues" contributed in turn to the neglect of their contributions, as did an emphasis in the history of economic thought on advances in theory rather than in empirical economics, and a myopia that simplifies the past by envisioning it as the achievements of a handful of outstanding individuals (history as the names of kings).

Women took the lead in popularizing English classical political economy, and were active in the turn of the century monetary controversy and in the Stockholm School in the 1920s and 1930s, in *The Australian Economist* in the 1890s (Butlin *et al.* 1986) and the *Journal des Économistes* in the 1860s, in Marxian political economy and in Chicago monetarism, in the massive statistical studies leading to the creation of national accounts and in the early stages of "the new home economics." Niels Kaergaard (in Dimand, Dimand and Forget, 2000) writes about a Danish family with four generations of women economists. They were always outnumbered by male economists, but the proportion of women among contributors to the "Old Palgrave," R. H. Inglis Palgrave's *Dictionary of Political Economy*, was slightly higher than that of *The New Palgrave* nine decades later (see Dimand 1999a).

In surveying the contributions to economics made by women in the nineteenth and early twentieth centuries, I make use of research carried out for *A Biographical Dictionary of Women Economics*, which I am editing with Mary Ann Dimand and Evelyn L. Forget for publication by Edward Elgar, and for an earlier volume of essays (Dimand, Dimand, and Forget 1995). An important University of Sydney working paper by Peter Groenewegen and Susan King (1994) lists 112 women (6.78 percent of contributors) who published 222 articles (5.3 percent of the total) in five core British and US economics journals from 1900–39 (a preliminary list that will be longer in final form): a list rather different from Baumol's. For three of these journals, the *Quarterly Journal of Economics* (founded 1886), the *Economic Journal* (founded 1891), and the *Journal of Political Economy* (founded 1892), I have counted forty-four articles by thirty women in the 1890s (for a list, see the bibiliography to Dimand 1999a). (The other two journals used by Groenewegen and King, *Economica* and the *American Economic Review*, did not yet exist in the 1890s). Of those forty-four articles, the only ones coauthored by a man were two that Beatrice Webb wrote with Sidney Webb. Other important "reviews of the troops" (to use Schumpeter's term) were presented to History of Economics Society conferences in Vancouver in1996 by the late Michèle Pujol (based on preparatory work for her multivolume Routledge anthology of pre-1900 economics by women, now being completed by Janet Seiz) and in Montreal by Kirsten Madden (1998).

In a series of papers to the Economic and Business Historical Society, Barbara Libby (1984, 1987, 1990, 1996) has conducted a quantitative study of the participation of women in the USA economics profession 1900–40 (cf. Forget 1995), while Judith Alexander (1995) surveys their participation in Canada, which began with Irene Biss (later Spry) and the economic historian Mary Quayle Innis between the wars (cf. Wargon 1992 on Canadian women in the neighboring field of demography). With these studies, historians of economics are well on the way to achieving the awareness of past contributions by women to the discipline of economics that has provided for neighboring disciplines by such works as Mary Jo Deegan's *Women in Sociology* (1991) (cf. Gregson and Rose 1997 on feminist history of geography).

It should be kept in mind that women could be very productive economists, without publishing in the five core journals used by Groenewegen and King (1994), given the greater importance of books relative to journals in the economic profession in the late nineteenth and early twentieth centuries. For instance, Margaret Good Myers taught economics for many years at Vassar, and published books on *The New York Money Market* (2 vols, 1931, her Columbia Ph.D. dissertation), *Paris as a Financial Centre* (1936), *Monetary Proposals for Social Reform* (1940), and *A Financial History of the United States* (1970), while her journal contributions include "Monthly Production of Pig Iron, 1884 to 1903" in the *Journal of the American Statistical Association* (June 1922) and "The Attempted Nationalization of Banks in Australia, 1947" in the *Economic Record* (August 1959), but nothing in her long career in those five selected economics journals. Faith Moors Williams published articles in three consecutive issues of the *Journal of the American Statistical Association* in 1921, on French war finance, the origin and development of modern trade statistics, and the business indices of the *Frankfurter Zeitung*, and other articles in the same journal in 1929 (on measuring demand for food), 1930, 1934, 1937, 1940, 1942, and 1943, and with Dorothy S. Brady in the *Journal of Farm Economics* in 1945 (on estimating consumption expenditure), but her first appearance in one of those five core economics journals was in the *American Economic Review* in 1959, long after the 1940 cut-off date for the Groenewegen and King sample.

In the classical era

The earliest appearance known to me of a woman in the history of classical political economy is Priscilla Wakefield's criticism of *The Wealth of Nations* for insufficient attention to the economic activity of women, not only in the sphere of household production (which Smith excluded from the rational self-interest that guided behavior in the market sphere) but also outside the home in wage work and market activity (Wakefield [1798] 1817, discussed by Kathryn Sutherland 1995). Sophie Grouchy, Marquise de Condorcet, had known Adam Smith and translated Smith's *Theory of Moral Sentiments* into French in 1798 with a lengthy commentary in the form of eight letters on sympathy (disapproving of inequality of wealth more sharply than Smith had), but not *The Wealth of Nations* (McDonald 1994: 131–2; 1998b: 125–7). Wakefield's *critique* of classical political economy for neglecting women had little effect on her son Edward Wakefield, writer on Ireland and friend of James Mill, or her grandson Edward Gibbon Wakefield, who, apart from his colonizing activities, edited *The Wealth of Nations* with extensive commentary.

Michèle Pujol (1992: 17) noted that "except for all of one page in the two-volume *Wealth of Nations*, and in spite of Smith's own acknowledgement of the common and necessary nature of their employment, women are conspicuously absent from his seminal discussion of the nature, organization and operations of capitalist production" (cf. Rendall 1987), while "Women, the domestic sphere and reproductive activities are nowhere mentioned in Ricardo's *Principles of Political Economy and Taxation* and in Malthus's *Principles of Political Economy*" (Pujol 1992: 23). In contrast, Jean-Baptiste Say explicitly presented a patriarchal analysis of the household sphere alongside his discussion of the market economy (Forget 1997).

Pujol raised the

> pertinent question ... whether the doctrine of the "invisible hand" developed in *The Wealth of Nations* can be reconciled with the candid, patriarchal beliefs informing Smith's discourse in *The Theory of Moral Sentiments* and, to some extent, in *The Wealth of Nations*. Does it matter to the relevance of his doctrine that at least half of the human race is not allowed to be freely guided by self-interest?
>
> (Pujol 1992: 22)

Priscilla Wakefield protested against such neglect and raised such questions at the time. In his unpublished Glasgow lectures, however, Adam Smith had followed Montesquieu in discussing the social status of women in different historical stages of economic development (Nyland 1993, cf. Bowles 1984, Clark 1993, Nyland 1997).

Women's work was not restricted to the household in Smith's time. The workers in the pin factory described by Adam Smith (based on an article in Diderot's *Encyclopédie* and on the example of nailers near Kirkcaldy) were male, but this was not the case in such trades as nailmaking in England:

> In the Black Country [of the West Midlands] trades there was no lighter alternative work open to women, and they worked beside the men in heavy industry – on the pitbank, in the nail manufacture, and in the manufacture of chains, saddlery, harness and hollow ware. But in many of these trades, and in particular in nailmaking, they had long been degraded workers.
>
> (Berg 1985: 312)

A survey of *Aris's Gazette* [in Birmingham] from 1752–90 indicates that women were taking over husbands' businesses or dealing with various problems which arose in the trades over a wide range of processes. Notices appeared from nine female ironmongers, eight plumbers and glaziers, seven buttonmakers and seven bucklemakers, six watchmakers, five brass manufacturers and braziers, five toolmakers, and five chain- and toymakers. There were notices from three women running ironworks, three women plateworkers, two nailworkers, two women running coalworks, as well as individual locksmiths, japanners, wireworkers, and file cutters.

(Berg 1985: 313)

Such diverse economic activity by women (particularly by widows) was not a new phenomenon in Smith's time: David Herlihy (1990, 142–50) reports that Paris tax records listed 172 occupations of female heads of households in 1292 (compared to 325 for male heads of households) and 130 in 1313 (compared to 276 for men). Not only did women undertake the bulk of the household production necessary for the reproduction of the work force, but a significant number of them engaged in a great variety of productive activities outside the household.

In addition to Priscilla Wakefield, another outspoken feminist with personal ties to circles close to leading classical economists was Frances "Fanny" Wright, who, as Joseph Dorfman wrote,

was one of the most remarkable characters of the period. Her father had been an intimate of Adam Smith, and she had sat at the feet of Bentham. She interested herself in all sorts of reforms, from the ending of slavery to equal rights for women

(Dorfman 1946: 642)

as a popular lecturer and as a leading figure in utopian communities at Nashoba, Tennessee (providing land and training to blacks she had bought to free from slavery, and whom she later helped to settle in Haiti), and, with Robert Dale Owen, at New Harmony, Indiana. Although one of the few women mentioned in Dorfman's monumental *The Economic Mind in American Civilization*, Wright was a social reformer with outspoken views on religion, marriage, and education rather than a political economist applying formal economic reasoning or, as Priscilla Wakefield had done, critiquing the writings of economists. (In my comments on Dorfman's book in my 1995 paper, I overlooked his remarks on Wright, which were indexed under the male name Francis Wright.)

Priscilla Wakefield, a pioneer in founding savings banks, was a popularizer and educator, writing extensively on botany. Like Wakefield, Jane Marcet was a popularizer of science, writing nearly thirty books, and she popularized classical political economy in three books from 1816 to 1851. Marcet (1816) and Harriet Martineau (1832–4) sold more copies, by an order of magnitude, than did such eminent classical economic theorists as Ricardo (see Polkinghorn 1993, 1995, Polkinghorn on Marcet and Forget on Martineau in *Biographical Dictionary*, and Shackleton 1990, Henderson 1992, 1994). Martineau's monthly *Illustrations of Political Economy* even sold better than the monthly installments of Dickens's novels! More readers would have seen Marcet's simplified and dogmatic exposition of wage-fund theory than would have read, say, John Stuart Mill on the subject. Mrs Marcet's *Conversations on Political Economy* sometimes receives passing mention in textbooks on the history of economics for presenting Ricardo's political economy in more accessible form, which would be remarkable since her book appeared the year before Ricardo's *Principles* (see Dimand 1995: 12–13). While she knew Ricardo (who recommended her 1816 book to his daughter) and Malthus, her account of value theory was in fact closer to Say's emphasis on utility (an emphasis with which Malthus disagreed in a letter to Marcet), and she was less concerned than Ricardo or Malthus about population growth and natural resource scarcity as threats to a rising standard of living (Polkinghorn 1993: 52–5).

Harriet Martineau's twenty-five best-selling *Illustrations of Political Economy* (1832–4), a total of some 3,000 pages, also served to make the accepted ideas of classical political economy generally accessible, although in her autobiography she distanced herself from these expositions of

> what I then took to be a science ... After an interval of above twenty years, I have not courage to look at a single number – convinced that I should be disgusted by bad taste and metaphysics in almost every page.
> (Martineau 1877, vol. 1: 194–5)

Martineau (1855) rejected some, but not all, factory legislation as discriminating against women's opportunities for employment: some of the public may taken note of a political economist opposing the Factory Acts (and of the National Association of Factory Operators publishing her work) without appreciating why she was opposed. She was an innovator in social science or political economy more generally, rather than in economic theory.

Martineau's *Society in America* ([1837] 1962) was a pioneering work of comparative sociology which she had wished to entitle *The Theory and Practice of Society* (a title the publisher did not think would enhance sales). Unlike Tocqueville, Martineau included a chapter on the status of women in America, contrasting their low wages and restricted property rights with the American ideology of equality (Frawley 1992). Martineau's *How to Observe Morals and Manners* ([1838] 1989) was a companion piece, an innovative methodological essay on comparative social science. Her contributions to social science (including, I hope, her writings on economics) will receive increasing attention because of the Harriet Martineau Sociological Association, founded at the Amsterdam meeting of the International Sociological Association's History of Sociology Section in 1996, with its first working meeting at Mackinac Island in 1997 (McDonald 1998b: vii).

Joseph Dorfman (1946: 848) identified Louisa Cheves McCord, who in 1848 translated Bastiat's satire against protective tariffs into English at her husband's request, as "The Harriet Martineau of the South." Given Martineau's views on women's rights, slavery, and Jefferson's ideal of equality, she might have dissented from this identification, since McCord, daughter of the second president of the second Bank of the United States, "traced abolitionism, socialism, and women's rights to Jefferson's error in holding that all men are created equal.... She devoted most of her literary talents to the defense of slavery as an absolute blessing" (Dorfman 1946: 848). After the American Civil War, McCord moved from South Carolina to Cobourg, Ontario, for two years, rather than take the oath of allegiance to the Union.

Mme Mary Meynieu (died 1877), born in England, wrote successful books on *Elements d'économie politique* (1839, presented as conversations as Marcet had done) and *Paupérisme anglais* (1841). She published in the *Journal des Économistes* in 1859, and the following year published a pamphlet on women's work, responding to an article by Jules Simon (Meynieu 1860).

Mlle Clémence-Auguste Royer (1830–1902) published a two-volume *Théorie de l'impôt, ou la dîme sociale* (Royer 1862), "*Ouvrage couronné par le Conseil d'état du canton de Vaud*," in the same year as her translation of Darwin's *Origins of Species*. In 1868, some chapters of this work on taxation (*Capitoli estratti dalla Teoria dell'imposta*) appeared in Italian in Turin as part of the prestigious *Bibliotheca dell'economista* (2e serie, Tratti speciali, vol. 10). Primarily an anthropologist in the 1870s and a writer on scientific topics ranging from optics (Royer 1892) to physics (Royer 1900, her 800-page *magnum opus*), Royer published in the *Journal des Économistes* in 1875, 1876, 1877, and 1878. These articles were on broad social or anthropological topics (such as "*Les phases sociales des nations*" in 1876), apart from one on the proposed Panama canal (Royer 1875).

Julie-Victoire Daubié was "a young governess and virtually unknown" (Scott 1987: 132) until she won the Academy of Lyon's competition in 1859 with an essay, "*La Femme pauvre au XIXe siècle*" which she published in part as a series of articles in the *Journal des Économistes* in 1862 and 1863 and then, enlarged, as a book in 1866.

> She was a self-defined feminist, who would earn the first baccalaureat awarded to a woman (in 1862) and who would lead campaigns against government regulation of prostitution and for women's suffrage in the early years of the Third Republic.
>
> (Scott 1987: 134)

Denying any inherent difference in productivity between men and women, Daubié called for equal hourly wages, equal access to training, apprenticeship and jobs (ending, for instance, the male monopoly of such trades as printing), equal participation in law-making, and legal enforcement of men's obligation to acknowledge paternity and provide financial support for their children. This last demand called for restoration of a legal right held by French women until 1793 (Folbre 1994: 145). Daubié attributed women's low wages and poverty to the monopoly by men of trades suited to women or formerly all-female, crowding wage-earning women in a restricted range of trades and thus depressing wages in those trades, and to the failure of some men to contribute to the support of their children.

Joan Wallach Scott asserts that Daubié's support for the legal power of women to enforce paternal responsibility "cancelled the radical import" of her call for equality in the job market

> for it suggested that equality was a compensatory measure for women who had not yet married, or who could not marry, or whose husbands were delinquent providers ... endorsing political economy's view of men as the major source of subsistence ... though gender power relationships were

the cornerstone of her analysis, Daubié remained within the conceptual boundaries earlier set by political economy, accepting the notion that work and family (economics and morality) were separate spheres.

(Scott 1987: 141)

I do not see that insisting on legal responsibility of both parents to provide for the support of children detracts from the radicalism of Daubié's analysis (radical in the sense of going to the root of the matter), which is well brought out in Scott's valuable essay on how French political economy viewed women workers in the mid-nineteenth century. However radical its analysis, Daubié's prize-winning work, published in the *Journal des Économistes*, was accepted as part of the discourse of political economy in France, while Flora Tristan's criticisms of classical political economy in her *London Journal* in 1840 had been received as the criticisms of an outsider (see Christine Ivory on Daubie and Jean Shackelford on Tristan in the *Biographical Dictionary*).

Ekelund and Hébert (1999: 427) quote a letter from Walras to Mlle Guillaumin "who took over her father's publishing business on his death [in 1864] and acted as de facto editor of the *Journal des Économistes*." Palgrave's *Dictionary* recorded, in its article on Urbain Gilbert Guillaumin, that "Guillaumin's two daughters, of whom the eldest, Félicité, died in 1885 at the age of fifty six, inherited both his administrative ability and his devotion to economic science."

Caroline Healey Dall acted as the Toronto agent for a society helping fugitive slaves flee to Canada, reported to a women's rights convention in Boston in 1855 on the legal status of Massachusetts women, and organized the New England Woman's Rights Convention, also in Boston, in 1859. A precursor of Charlotte Perkins Gilman among American feminists, Dall went beyond the suffrage question and unequal laws on property rights to a critique of the economic role of women in series of public lectures in Boston, published as *"Women's Right to Labor"; or Low Wages and Hard Work* (1860) and *The College, the Market, and the Courts; or Women's Relation to Education, Labor and the Law* ([1867] 1914). Beyond calling for educational and legal equality, Dall ([1867] 1914: 179) attributed women's discontent to restricted opportunities for paid employment, for it was no longer the case that "every woman found, in spinning, weaving, and sewing, in the active labor of a ... household, full employment for time and thought."

Dall served on the executive committee of the American Social Science Association (ASSA) from its foundation in 1865 until 1905 (seven years before her death at the age of ninety, and four years before the dissolution of the ASSA), initially as a director and from 1880 as a vice-president. Indeed, Bernard and Bernard (1943: 539–40) suggest that Dall instigated the circular convening the founding meeting of the ASSA, as she had been in communication with the secretary and assistant secretary (Isa Craig, of the Langham Place group) of the National Association for the Promotion of Social Science. The American Social Science Association was the professional association for economists until the American Economic Association (AEA) was founded at the 1885 ASSA annual meeting as a breakaway specialist group, with the support of the secretaries of the ASSA's Finance and Social Economy sections, and remained the professional association for the rest of the social sciences until separate societies were organized by the sociologists in 1905 and political scientists in 1909 (Furner 1975, Haskell 1977). There were six women among the 185 founding members of the AEA. Women were also active in the ASSA's British counterpart, the National Association for the Promotion of Social Science, from its founding meeting in 1857 to its demise in 1886 (Cobbe 1861, Rogers 1952, Martel 1986). The Massachusetts feminists kept in touch with developments in England, with Sarah Grimké, at the age of seventy-nine, trudging door to door in 1871 to sell 150 copies of John Stuart Mill's 1869 essay *On the Subjection of Women* (Rossi 1973: 296; Mill's essay is reprinted in Robson and Robson 1994).

Margaret McFadden, in her article "Boston Teenagers Debate the Woman Question, 1837–1838" (1990), gives a fascinating account of the origins of Dall's feminism in a correspondence between Caroline Wells Healey (later Dall), aged fifteen, and her friend Ednah Dow Littledale (later Cheney), aged thirteen, in which Healey was the one opposing women's rights. This correspondence was significantly influenced by Martineau's chapter on "The Political Non-Existence of Women" (Martineau [1837] 1962) and by what Cheney termed "a brave address on Woman's Rights at the Lyceum" by Amasa Walker, "underground railway" activist, soon to be professor of political economy at Oberlin and later lecturer at Amherst, and from 1853 to 1860 an examiner in political economy at Harvard. McFadden notes that

> The Boston Lyceum sponsored a debate on the equality of the sexes in January 1838. Amasa Walker (1799–1875), one of the founders of the Lyceum, spoke in favor of the proposition, but the Lyceum voted against it (see the *Liberator* [January 12, 1838]: 7).
>
> (McFadden 1990: 836n)

The *Liberator* was the abolitionist journal, edited by William Lloyd Garrison, that published Angelina and Sarah Grimke's letters on equality of the sexes from 1836 to 1838, and in which Dall in 1849 first published in support of women's rights. The role of Walker's talk in converting Dall to women's rights is interesting both as a link between her work and that of an academic economist, and because Walker's position on women's wages has been misunderstood in the literature. In an otherwise exemplary article in the volume of *Signs* following McFadden's article, Nancy Folbre (1991: 474) refers to "the well-known political economist Amasa Walker's insistence that women's wages should be low because 'the prevailing ideas of the community restrict them to easily dispensable occupations'", where the passage she quotes is from Joseph Dorfman (1946: 750). Unfortunately, Dorfman, and following him Folbre, mistook Walker's account of what had occurred for his belief about what should occur.

In *The Science of Wealth* (1872: 286), Walker reported that "Women receive less wages than men . . . not only where the services of the two sexes differ, but where they are identical, as in school-teaching, type-setting, etc." He reported that in the public schools of Massachusetts in 1857–8, the average monthly wage of male teachers was $49.87, that of female teachers $19.63. "Political economists, so far as we know, have not troubled themselves much about" such disparities, but Walker offered an explanation in terms of supply and demand. Numbers of men and women were roughly the same, but "while almost all occupations and employments are open to the male sex, but comparatively few are, by the opinions and customs of society, regarded as proper for women" so that the supply of women, crowded into a few occupations, forced their wages down (1872: 266–7). Far from approving of this state of affairs, Walker held that

> An increase of her wages can result only from an increase of her employments, – of employments, too, of an equally indispensable character as those of the other sex. That a change of this sort is fortunately in progress in most civilized countries, and especially in the United States, is apparent.
> (Walker 1872: 268)

Folbre (1991: 475) also remarks that "Like his father," Amasa Walker's better-known son General Francis Amasa Walker (Superintendent of the Censuses of 1870 and 1880, President of MIT 1881–97, of the American Economic Association 1885–92, and of the American Statistical Association 1882–97) "had a low opinion of women's productive capacities." However, the elder Walker argued that with the introduction of machinery,

> Water and steam are now made to accomplish that which could once be done only by human strength, leaving the residue of labor, which is, to a great extent, the exercise of intelligence and attention, to be performed by persons of either sex. . . . There is less demand for muscle, and more for mind: this brings woman nearer an equality with man.
> (Walker 1872: 268)

Bernard and Bernard (1943: 541) mention Dall and Walker as working together at the organizing meeting of the ASSA in 1865 to oppose creating a special department to study crime prevention and reformation of criminals, so they clearly remained in contact.

After a publisher refused financial support, Virginia Penny used her inheritance to produce her book *The Employments of Women: A Cyclopaedia of Woman's Work* (1863), whose second printing was entitled *Five Hundred Occupations Adapted to Women; with the Average Rate of Pay in Each* and third printing *How Women Can Make Money, Married or Single*. A German translation appeared in 1867. Issued through the same Boston publisher as Dall (1860), Penny (1863) was favorably reviewed by the *English Woman's Journal* (of the Langham Place group around Barbara Bodichon) and, with reservations about Penny's mixing of advocacy with information, the *New York Times*. The book reported on wages, gender pay differentials (with reasons, both as stated by employers and as seen by the author), necessary skills and education, time needed to learn the job, seasonality of employment, paid or unpaid apprenticeship, and availability of jobs to women for 500 occupations, from medicine to beekeeping to artificial eye making. Her second book, *Think and Act: A Series Articles Pertaining to Men and Women, Work and Wages* (1869), analyzed such economic topics as married women's property rights and desired changes, use value of women in the domestic sphere, the undesirability of women's lack of non-marriage market opportunities, importance of even a married woman possessing human capital given the possibility of her husband's death, poverty rate of women relative to men, and economic changes, especially for women, wrought by the Civil War.

(Susan H. Gensemer on Penny in Dimand, Dimand, and Forget 2000)

In later years, she returned to school teaching and worked for the US Census Bureau, and in 1892 the *New York Times* reported her lecture at Cooper Union on "How Women Can Earn Money." In 1901, the *New York Times* reported that Penny, "who has spent almost a lifetime in seeking occupations for women in the United States," was living destitute in a tenement in New York City at the age of seventy-six.

Barbara Leigh Smith Bodichon drafted the petition to Parliament that led to the Married Women's Property Act of 1857 and the petition for women's suffrage that John Stuart Mill presented to Parliament in 1866 (Robson and Robson 1994: xxv–xxviii), founded the Society for Promoting the Employment of Women and the *Englishwoman's Journal*, and wrote on *Women and Work* (1857) and on laws affecting women. Reading the first edition of John Stuart Mill's *Principles of Political Economy* in 1849 when she was twenty-two, Bodichon regretted that "one who carries so much weight" failed to mention "the injustice of their [men's] laws to women and the absurdity of the present Laws of Marriage and Divorce" since "philosophers and reformers have generally been afraid to say anything about the unjust laws both of society and country which crush women" (quoted by Pujol 1992: 37, Sockwell 1995: 107). In the 1860s, Bodichon and her Langham Place associates were brought into contact with Mill by his stepdaughter, Helen Taylor, and were active in the National Association for the Promotion of Social Science. In *Women and Work*, Bodichon analysed the causes of women's low wages as lack of training and the crowding of women in a few occupations such as governesses or, later, school teachers, exacerbated by undervaluation of non-market household production by women (see Sockwell 1995 and in *Biographical Dictionary*).

John Stuart Mill also held a crowding theory of women's low wages, as did the suffragist leader Millicent Garrett Fawcett (1892, 1918), a visitor to Langham Place and (by the time of her *Economic Journal* articles) widow of Henry Fawcett, MP and professor of political economy at Cambridge. Mill's views on the economic and social position of women, and on liberty, were influenced by his future wife Harriet Taylor (see Robson and Robson 1994 and Hayek 1951 for primary sources, and Pujol 1992, 1995, for an argument that Harriet Taylor Mill's feminist economics was more radical and far-reaching than that of John Stuart Mill). Priscilla Wakefield, Frances Wright, Anna Wheeler, Harriet Martineau, Harriet Taylor Mill, Julie-Victoire Daubié, Caroline Dall, Virginia Penny, Barbara Bodichon, and Millicent Garrett Fawcett provided feminist *critiques* and analyses of the economic role of women (as did a few male economists, notably John Stuart Mill, Amasa Walker, and, outside the mainstream, the socialist William Thompson), while Jane Marcet,

Harriet Martineau, and Millicent Garrett Fawcett wrote best-selling popular accounts of classical political economy. Mention ought also be made of Florence Nightingale, who, after meeting Adolphe Quetelet at the London congress of the International Statistical Association in 1860, made extensive notes on the application of probability theory to social science, and thirty years later attempted to endow a professorship at Oxford to teach Quetelet's probability theory and statistical approach, "social physics and its practical applications" (McDonald 1994: 183–206, 1998b: 175–80; Diamond and Stone 1981).

Economics of consumption and the household

The "new home economics" of Nobel laureate Gary Becker of the University of Chicago, concerned with rational allocation of time and other resources within the household and family, represents a break with the idea shared by writers as diverse as Adam Smith and Catherine Beecher that the household is outside the sphere of rational calculation and self-interest, enlightened or otherwise. It also represents the fruition of a line of research initiated, at Iowa State College and the University of Chicago, by Elizabeth Ellis Hoyt (*The Consumption of Wealth* 1928, *Consumption in Our Society* 1938), Hazel Kyrk (*Theory of Consumption*, 1923, *Economic Problems of the Family*, 1933), and Margaret Gilpin Reid (*Economics of Household Production*, 1934), a body of work belatedly honored by the selection of Margaret Reid in 1980 as the first female Distinguished Fellow of the American Economic Association at the age of eighty-three (see Thorne 1995, Forget 1996, Yi 1996; cf. Thorne 1936, Zuckerman and Carsky 1990). In addition, Dorothy Stahl Brady and Rose Director Friedman (1946) anticipated the relative income hypothesis of consumption, for which the slightly later publications of James Duesenberry are almost always cited (see R. Dimand 1995: 13–14). The other two postwar theories of consumption (of greater lasting influence than the relative income hypothesis), the permanent income hypothesis of Milton Friedman (1957) and the lifecycle theory of Franco Modigliani and his associates, built upon empirical studies by Dorothy Brady, Rose Friedman, and Margaret Reid. Despite full and proper acknowledgement by Nobel Prize winners M. Friedman and Modigliani of these valuable earlier contributions by women, textbook accounts of consumption economics ignore these contributions.

Hazel Kyrk, who won the Hart, Schaffner and Marx Prize for the 1920 Chicago dissertation that became her 1923 book, worked briefly at the Food Research Institute at Stanford and at Iowa State College before returning in 1925 to the University of Chicago (with Hoyt hired to replace her), where she became a full professor (in 1941) appointed jointly to the Department of Economics and to that of Home Economics. At Iowa State, Hoyt and Reid were also full professors (Hoyt from 1931, Reid from 1940) in both economics and home economics (with their offices with other home economists, not economists), and Hoyt was also a pioneering economic anthropologist (*Primitive Trade*, 1926).

In 1952, a year before Kyrk's retirement, her former doctoral student Reid came to Chicago as a full professor of both economics and home economics (an appointment influenced by the fact that the chair of Chicago's Economics

Department, the future Nobel laureate Theodore Schultz, had previously headed the department at Iowa State, and so was familiar with Reid's ability and work). Along with women's colleges and the position of dean of women at coeducational institutions, home economics provided an opportunity for American women economists to enter the academic world: "An economist, Sarah Gibson Blanding, moved from dean of women and associate professor of political science at the University of Kentucky (1928) to dean of home economics at Cornell University (1941), to president of Vassar College (1946)" (Clifford 1989: 17). These consumption economists brought an interdisciplinary social science perspective to their work: from 1951 to 1960, Hoyt published in the *Journal of Political Economy*, the *British Journal of Sociology*, and *Current Anthropology*.

Milton Friedman stated that

> Miss Reid, with characteristic enthusiasm, persistence, and ingenuity, proceeded to put to a critical test the hypothesis that had been evolving out of the conversations. When it seemed to be passing the test with flying colors, she pressed me to write up the underlying theory so that she could refer to it in a paper presenting her conclusions. This book is the result, and though my hand held the pen, and though I am fully responsible for all its defects, it is in essential respects a joint product of the group, each member of which not only participated in its development, but read and criticized the manuscript in its various stages.
>
> (Friedman 1957: ix)

The group to which Friedman refers was himself, Dorothy Brady, Rose Friedman, and Margaret Reid.

In his 1985 Nobel lecture, Franco Modigliani (quoted by Yun-Ae Yi) acknowledged that

> The third fundamental contribution was the highly imaginative analysis of Margaret Reid ('The relation of the within-group permanent component of income to the income elasticity of expenditure,' unpublished paper) which pointed to a totally different explanation for the association between the saving ratio and relative income, namely that consumption was controlled by normal or 'permanent, rather than current,' income. This contribution was an important source of inspiration, both for the Life Cycle and for the roughly contemporaneous Permanent Income Hypothesis (PIH) of Milton Friedman (1957).
>
> (Yi 1996: 20–1)

(See also Reid 1952, Friedman and Friedman 1998, and *New Palgrave* articles by Reid on Brady and by Mary Jean Bowman on Reid.) Despite these clear statements by Milton Friedman and Franco Modigliani, the tendency of the economics profession is to associate each theory with a single economist (as though each theory results when a light bulb appears over the head of a Great Man or, less often in the consciousness of economists, a Great Woman). Thus, economists think only of Milton Friedman when they think of the permanent income hypothesis, only of Franco Modigliani when they think of the lifecycle theory, and only of James Duesenberry when they think of the relative income hypothesis. This narrowing of the canon to a single person per theory distorts historical perspective and, in the case of consumption economics, turns the spotlight from several women who made important, but not quite Nobel prize-winning, contributions.

Yun-Ae Yi notes that

> The core of Becker's "theory of the allocation of time" corresponds with Reid's ideas of time-good substitutability in housework – the very definition of Reid's household production and monetary valuation of an individual's housework with the value of what women give up (Reid 1934: 160).
>
> (Yi 1996: 31)

and that another of Kyrk's Chicago students, Maud Wilson, provided Reid with a large amount of useful time-study data. As in the case of theories of consumption, the collective memory of the economics profession has shrunk the story of the "new home economics" to the work of a single outstanding individual, Gary Becker, even a full, balanced account involves several significant contributors (Ferber and Birnbaum 1977, Reid 1977).

Some continental European women economists after Luxemburg

In this section, I am greatly indebted to Harald Hagemann for research he undertook on German-speaking economists who emigrated after 1933 (Hagemann and Krohn 1992, Hagemann 1997), which he has generously shared with the *Biographical Dictionary of Women Economists*.

Rosa Luxemburg's 1897 University of Zurich doctoral dissertation in political science (i.e. political economy) was published the next year as *The Industrial Development of Poland* ([1898] 1977; the publishers, Duncker und Humblot of Leipzig, cavilled at the phrase *Capitalist Development*). This empirically-based and theoretically-informed work of historical analysis compares favorably with Lenin's *Development of Capitalism in Russia* (1899), published the next year. Her major work, *The Accumulation of Capital* ([1913] 1951), stands as a landmark in the development of growth theory and Marxian macroeconomics, as Joan Robinson emphasized in her introduction to the English translation. In tandem with her political activity, Luxemburg taught political economy at the Social Democratic Party's academy in Berlin, giving lectures that were published posthumously in German in 1925 and translated into French in 1971. She was murdered in 1919, after the failure of the Spartacist uprising. Like Rosa Luxemburg, the life stories of later Continental European women economists were profoundly affected by the upheavals that convulsed Europe from 1914–45. The following examples are illustrative of the participation of women in Continental European economics.

Naum Jasny reported that

Russia was ahead of other countries as regards studies of peasant economy and peasant life by the survey method. This type of research dates back to the early 1890s, F. A. Scherbina having been the greatest name in this field. See her *Krest'yanskie byudzhety* (Peasant Budgets), Voronezh, 1900.

(Jasny 1972: 200–1)

and mentioned S. Platova as one of the authors of *Methods of Quantitative Calculation of the Effectiveness of Land*, a 1925 study edited by A. V. Chayanov as director of the Scientific Research Institute for Agricultural Economics (the so-called Chayanov Institute, destroyed along with N. D. Kondratiev's Business Cycle Institute after the arrest and disappearance of Chayanov and Kondrat'ev). Solzhenitsyn (1974: 100, 627) reports of the economist Revekka Saulovna Levina (1899–1964) that "After the war, they tortured Corresponding Member of the Academy of Sciences Levina because she and the Alliluyevs had acquaintances in common," the Alliluyevs being the family of Stalin's wife, who had committed suicide. Much later, when serious scholarly activity resumed in the Soviet Union after the catastrophe of Stalinism, Olga Bondareva was an outstanding game theorist of international stature, author of seventy papers and a book, and member of the editorial board of *Games and Economic Behavior* (see, for example, Bondareva 1963). Two of her students and colleagues, Tatiana Kulakovskaja and Natalja Naumova, report that

> Beginning in 1968 she was invited to almost all international conferences on Game Theory but only in 1988 did she obtain a permission to participate – thus she went to conferences in Columbus, Brussels, Oberwolfach, Ulm, Bielefeld, New Delhi, and Stony Brook.
>
> (Kulakovskaja and Naumova 1992: 310)

She was a senior research fellow of the economics faculty at Leningrad State University from 1972–84 (and at the Institute of Physics 1984–9), after her expulsion from the mathematics faculty in 1972 for refusing to go along with what Kulakovskaja and Naumova term "a political 'hate lesson'" aimed at one of Bondareva's students who had applied for permission to emigrate to Israel. With the coming of perestroika, Bondareva was permitted to travel abroad and then to rejoin the mathematics faculty in 1989, two years before her death in a traffic accident in what was once again Saint Petersburg. Her path-breaking 1963 Ph.D. dissertation in mathematics was on "Theory of the Core in an n-Person Game," while her 1984 Dr. Sci. thesis in mathematics was on "Methods of solving cooperative games and their applications."

Natalie Moszkowska, the outstanding woman Marxist economist after Rosa Luxemburg, took her doctorate at the University of Zurich in 1917, with a dissertation on workers' savings banks in the Polish coal and steel industries, published by Dietz in Stuttgart the same year. Originally from Warsaw, she lived in or near Zurich from 1923, working as a private tutor and writing for the trade union and socialist press. She provided a critique of Marx's theory of the tendency of the profit rate to fall in her books *Das Marxsche System* (1929) and *Zur Dynamik des Spätkapitalismus* (1943), and advanced an underconsumptionist theory of crises in *Zur Kritik Moderner Krisentheorien* (1935). She published three articles in a leading mainstream economics journal, *Schmollers Jahrbuch*, in 1959, 1963, and 1965. The first of these, (Moszkowska 1959) compared Marx and Keynes on crisis theory to the disadvantage of Keynes, and was published when she was seventy-three years old (Howard and King 1989–92, and their *Biographical Dictionary* entry on Moszkowska).

Another Polish scholar with a connection with Switzerland, the historian of economic thought Sophie Daszynska-Golinska, published a thirty-page pamphlet on China and French Physiocracy, in French in Warsaw in 1923. As Zofia Daszynska (1889), she had previously published in German in Berne a book on the historical population statistics of Zurich.

Else von Richthofen

> earned a doctorate in economics at the University of Heidelberg in 1901; she had taught school since she was seventeen in order to pay for her university studies. She was Max Weber's "first woman student," and he helped her get an appointment in 1900 as the first woman factory inspector, responsible for the protection of women workers in the state of Badenia.
>
> (Kandal 1988: 114, cf. Green 1974).

Frieda Wunderlich received her doctorate at the University of Freiburg in 1919, and rose to a professorship at the University of Berlin, before emigrating to be a professor of economics at the New School for Social Research in New York from 1933 to her retirement in 1954 (the New School's Graduate Faculty originated in 1933 as the "University in Exile"). Before emigrating, she had published in the *Quarterly Journal of Economics* in 1928 on German unemployment insurance. Afterwards she published fourteen articles from 1934 to 1953 in the New School's journal *Social Research* (founded 1934) on women's work in Germany, unemployment insurance, health insurance, and the Beveridge plan, and another in *QJE* in 1938 on "Germany's defense economy and the decay of capitalism," as well as books on *German Labor Courts* (1946) and *Farm Labor in Germany 1810-1945* (1961).

Steffy Browne (born Martha Stephanie Hermann) was, in 1921, the first woman to take a doctorate in economics at the University of Vienna (with a thesis in monetary theory supervised by Wieser). She served in the US Office of Strategic Services in the Second World War (as did Wunderlich), and was professor of economics at Brooklyn College from 1947 to 1969 and a lecturer at New York University from 1970 to 1981.

Charlotte A. P. Leubuscher received her doctorate at the University of Berlin in 1913 and her habilitation as a lecturer (docent) there in 1921, with promotion to associate professor (extraordinary professor) in 1929, publishing a book on *Liberalismus und Protektionismus unter englischen Wirtschaftspolitik seit dem Kriege* in 1927. She was a research fellow at Lady Margaret Hall, Oxford (1936–42), LSE (1942–4), and the University of Manchester (1952–5), and worked for the Colonial Office in London (1945–51). The Free University of Berlin made her a professor emerita in 1956.

Marie Dessauer, who took her doctorate at the University of Frankfurt in 1933 with a thesis on the "Big Five" English deposit banks (published in Stuttgart), had studied at LSE in 1928–9. She returned to LSE as a student in 1934–6 and as a research assistant to T. E. Gregory and Friedrich Hayek 1937–41. She contributed an article on the German Bank Act of 1934 to the second volume of the *Review of Economic Studies* in 1935, and published on "Unemployment Records, 1848–59" in the *Economic History Review* (February 1940) and "Monthly Unemployment Records 1854–1892" in *Economica* (August 1940).

In August 1940 she married and took the name Meinhardt. Her activity at the LSE ended when the School was exiled to Cambridge in 1941, due to German bomb raids on London. In the 1960s Marie Meinhardt, now living in Bournemouth, published a long and a short article for a German readership in which she described the legal status and accounting practices of British joint-stock companies for a German readership.

(Hans-Michael Trautwein in Dimand, Dimand, and Forget 2000)

Clare Tisch, whose 1931 Bonn doctoral dissertation on economic calculation and distribution in a socialist society (published as a book in 1932) was supervised by Schumpeter, did not emigrate. In two years as a research assistant to Arthur Spiethoff at the University of Bonn (until she was dismissed by the Nazis in 1933), she wrote two more books (both published in 1934), one on the German Cartel Court and the other on small and medium-sized firms in German industry.

She earned her living as a shorthand typist in Cologne and a girl clerk in a shoeshop in Solingen before she became head of the central office for orphans of the Jewish Women League in Wuppertal in 1936. She let skip several possibilities to emigrate and sacrificed herself to take care of the Jewish orphans. She probably was killed immediately after arrival in the Jewish ghetto in Minsk at the end of 1941.

(Harald Hagemann in Dimand, Dimand, and Forget 2000)

Kaethe Leichter took her doctorate at Heidelberg in 1918 with a thesis on Austro-Hungarian trade policy towards Italy. She was arrested by the Gestapo in Vienna in 1938 and murdered in 1942.

Ilse Schueller Mintz, who received a doctorate at the University of Vienna in 1927 (supervised by Ludwig von Mises) and worked at the Austrian Institute for Business Cycle Research, earned a second doctorate at Columbia University in 1951 (supervised by Arthur Burns), taught at Columbia from 1948–69, and from 1951–73 was a Senior Research Associate at the National Bureau of Economic Research (which published her dissertation, four books by her on business cycles, and a book by her on import quotas). Hanna Stern, who took her doctorate at the University of Frankfurt with a thesis in public finance in 1928, worked at that university until 1933 and then emigrated, initially to Paris, but from 1942 she also was at the National Bureau of Economic Research. While Ilse Mintz was able to resume a highly productive academic career at the cost of doing another doctorate (as happened to John Harsanyi), Elisabeth Maresch, who took a doctorate at the University of Vienna in 1938 and then emigrated to the USA, became a housewife.

Fanny Ginor (born Dulberg), born in Galicia and raised in Stuttgart, was a student at the universities of Frankfurt, Heidelberg, and Munich, but took her PhD at the University of Basle in 1934 (at the age of twenty-three). She was economic advisor to the Israeli Finance Ministry from 1949–1953 and to the Governor of the Bank of Israel from 1953–71, and taught at Tel Aviv University until 1978 (Ginor 1997).

Lola (Helene) Zahn studied at the Universities of Hamburg, Freiburg, and Heidelberg, before emigrating in 1933 to France, where she took her doctorate at the University of Paris in 1937. She moved to the United States in 1941, and returned to the German Democratic Republic in 1947, first as professor of economic planning at the University of Rostock and then as professor of political economy at Humboldt University in East Berlin.

Elisabeth Caroline van Dorp published in the *Economic Journal* on "The deviation of exchanges" in 1919 and on "Abnormal Deviations in International Exchanges" in 1920, but most of her work on economic theory was published in Dutch. She served as a Dutch member of Parliament, and died in a Japanese internment camp in the Netherlands East Indies during the Second World War.

Costanza Costantino earned her doctorate in economic and commercial sciences at the University of Torino (Turin) with a thesis on long-term economic fluctuations. Although excluded from the university in 1938 by newly enacted anti-Semitic laws, she published an article based on her dissertation (Costantino 1939) and continued her studies independently, publishing on women's right to work (Costantino 1941). After the war, she taught finance and financial law in the Department of Jurisprudence of the University of Torino, becoming professor of finance and financial law in 1967, and of the economics of transportation in 1970, retiring at the age of seventy-seven in 1990, the year of her last book (Graziella Fornengo in Dimand, Dimand, and Forget 2000).

Huguette Biaujeaud received a doctorate from the University of Paris in 1933 with a thesis entitled *Essai sur la théorie ricardienne de la valeur* ([1934] 1988), which attracted notice and eventual republication because Piero Sraffa quoted it in the introduction to his edition of Ricardo's *Principles* for her statement of the determining role of agricultural profits in Ricardo's early writings and for her argument that Ricardo strengthened his claim that embodied labor is the regulator of value in later editions of his *Principles*. De Vivo (1991: 85) reports that "Biaujeaud apparently did not pursue her career as an economist any further." This may well have been due to limited opportunities for academic employment: the only woman to hold a professorship in any discipline in interwar France was Marie Curie (after her first Nobel prize), and French women did not win the right to vote until the establishment of the Fourth Republic at the end of the Second World War. A check of fourteen volumes of the *Revue d'Économie Politique* from 1921 to 1934 reveals only two articles by women: a contribution by the Swedish economist Karin Kock to a 1932 symposium on monetary issues, and Fernande Dauriac (1933) on "*Le travail des femmes en France devant la statistique* (1906–26)."

Karin Kock's Stockholm doctoral dissertation translated into English as *A Study of Interest Rates* (1929). Although she published primarily in Swedish (e.g. Kock 1961–2), she also published internationally on monetary economics and trade policy (e.g. Kock 1927, 1933, 1943, 1969) and collaborated on the construction of retrospective national income accounts for Sweden (Lindahl, Dahlgren and Kock 1937). After teaching at the University of Stockholm, she became, in the 1940s, Sweden's first female cabinet minister (1947–50), and was head of Sweden's Central Bureau of Statistics from 1950–58 and of the Swedish delegation to the United Nations Economic Commission for Europe from 1947 to 1960, chairing the Commission from 1950–2 (see Rolf Henriksson in Dimand, Dimand, and Forget 2000). She was elected a Fellow of the American Statistical Association in 1956.

Politics and world events also impinged on the careers of some North American economists. Agatha Chapman of Canada's Dominion Bureau of Statistics was tried for espionage as a supposed Soviet agent. After her acquittal, she moved in 1947 to the Department of Applied Economics at the University of Cambridge, and published *Wages and Salaries in the United Kingdom, 1920–1938* (1952). She returned to Montreal in the mid-1950s, married a refugee from the McCarthy investigations in the US, and with him established a consulting firm specializing in labor economics, but fell from her apartment window, an apparent suicide, in 1963 (see Judith A. Alexander on Chapman in Dimand, Dimand, and Forget 2000). Vera Shlakman published her dissertation, *Economic History of a Factory Town* (concering Chicopee, Massachusetts), as Volume 20 of the *Smith College Studies in History* in 1935, and in 1950–1 published four articles about white-collar unionism in the Marxist quarterly *Science and Society*, about the time that, for political reasons, she lost her job in the Economics Department at the City College of New York. Mark Blaug was among the faculty who supported students objecting to this infringement of academic freedom.

A more inclusive canon

Few women have received a secure place in the accepted canon of economics, as measured by coverage in textbooks of the history of economic thought. Two have generally received mention in such textbooks, when what they might very plausibly have received is the Nobel Memorial Award in Economic Science. For Joan Robinson to have shared a Nobel prize with Robert Solow for capital and growth theory would have represented no greater a range of political opinion and economic theory than the prize shared by Friedrich Hayek and Gunnar Myrdal, or that shared by Theodore Schultz and W. Arthur Lewis, recognitions of scholarly achievement that honored the Swedish Academy of Sciences as well as the recipients. Milton Friedman's Nobel prize was awarded for *A Theory of the Consumption Function* (1957) but, granted that the permanent-income hypothesis was a distinguished contribution, is it as obvious a candidate for a Nobel prize as the monumental joint work of Friedman and Anna Jacobson

Schwartz, *A Monetary History of the United States, 1867–1960* (1963)? The impact of Friedman and Schwartz's *Monetary History* (supplemented with subsequent Friedman and Schwartz volumes on *Monetary Statistics* and *Monetary Trends*) is surveyed in the special issue of the *Journal of Monetary Economics* on the thirtieth anniversary of the book's publication.

The situation is reversed in the case of Emily Greene Balch, a colleague of Katharine Coman as an economics professor at Wellesley College from 1894 to 1918, who is neglected by textbooks of the history of economic thought but did share a Nobel prize (for Peace, in 1947), awarded for the same pacifist and social reform activism which had led Wellesley College to refuse to renew her full professorship in 1918 for her "outspoken pacifist position and her radical economic views" (Randall, introduction to Balch 1972: xxvi; see Randall 1964).

At a time when economists as eminent and varied as Thomas Nixon Carver, John R. Commons, Frank A. Fetter, Irving Fisher, and Francis Amasa Walker advocated immigration restriction on the grounds of the supposed racial inferiority of immigrants from southern and eastern Europe, Balch argued in the *American Economic Review* Supplement (March 1912) and in books that intelligence tests given to immigrants were culturally biased, testing primarily whether people had grown up speaking English, and that immigration brought economic and cultural benefits, a point stressed in the title of her 1939 pamphlet *Refugees as Assets* (Balch 1972: 60–2; McDonald 1998b: 289–90, but contrast Folbre (1994: 185–6), on a eugenic argument against free school lunches by Balch in the *American Journal of Sociology* in 1907). Her proposal for a United Nations Maritime Authority (Balch 1972: 169–73; McDonald 1998b: 292–3) included a concern that the oceans would be over-fished if left as a global commons, an early environmental economic concern. Balch has been rediscovered as a precursor of ecological and pacifist feminism (Pois 1995), but the role of economic reasoning in her thought has not received as much attention as it would if economists had made the rediscovery.

Research for this paper has identified several specific areas in which I feel that the generally accepted canon of economics, as taught in the literature of the history of economics, needs to be broadened, if economics is not to ignore the economic experience of half of humanity. I offer the following, undoubtedly idiosyncratic, suggestions for reloading the canon of economics.

1   Teaching of institutionalist economics needs to include analysis of the economic institutions affecting gender relations, with Charlotte Perkins Gilman being considered along with such established institutionalist giants as Veblen, John R. Commons, and, in Canada, Harold Innis. (See Gilman 1898, [1903] 1970, Hill 1904, M. A. Dimand 1995, 1996, O'Donnell 1985, 1996, Sheth and Prasch 1996.)
2   From Priscilla Wakefield ([1798] 1817) and Julie-Victoire Daubié (1862, 1863) to Michèle Pujol (1992) and Heidi Hartmann (1981), feminist critics have questioned the extent to which economic theories, whether classical, neoclassical, or Marxist, inconsistently exclude household production and reproductive work from their analysis: such critics and their questions should be considered when evaluating such bodies of

theory (cf. J. Madden 1972). At the same time, contemporary feminist economics can benefit from knowing past feminist analyses.
3   The rich heritage of pre-1940 work by women on the economic history of women (e.g. Edith Abbott 1910, Alice Clark 1919, Elizabeth Dexter 1931, 1950, Bessie Leigh Hutchins 1915, Annie Meyer 1891, Ivy Pinchbeck 1930, Helen Sumner 1910, Caroline Ware 1931) and occasionally by men (Frederick W. Tickner 1923) offers much information and insight directly about the past work experience of half the population, both in the household and in the marketplace, and indirectly about the experience of the other half. (See R. Dimand 1995: 14–16, on the paucity of references to this literature in recent textbooks in economic history.)
4   The widely-held impression that female participation in the discipline of economics is a very recent phenomenon is mistaken. Participation by women in economics, as in other disciplines, has recovered in recent decades from the squeeze on academic jobs for women during the Depression and the absorption of women academics into public service during the Second World War: in 1962 "women as a percentage of all [US] academics reached their lowest point in over seventy years", 22 percent, about double the proportion for Canada (Clifford 1989: 37). Women were 8 percent of the University of Chicago faculty in 1892, 2 percent in 1970; three of fifteen members of the Berkeley mathematics department in 1928, none of eighty-one in 1968 (Clifford 1989: 32, 36).

Women economists now have much better academic job prospects that they did in the past, yet, despite obstacles to employment, a significant number of women made contributions to economics in the nineteenth and early twentieth centuries. The quantity of their contributions can be seen by examining what they published in journals, in books, and in collective reference works such as *Palgrave's Dictionary*: as that underrated methodologist Yogi Berra said, you can observe a lot just by looking. They paid far more attention, proportionately, than men did to "women's issues" of social policy and gender pay differentials, but also wrote on topics from Marxian macroeconomics (Rosa Luxemburg, Natalie Moszkowska) to exchange rates (Elisabeth Caroline Van Dorp, Joan Robinson), international trade theory (Marion Crawford Samuelson on the Australian case for protection), monetary economics (Eleanor Lansing Dulles, Sara McLean Hardy), the theory of the firm (Joan Robinson on imperfect competition, Edith Penrose), public finance, and economic development.

Their political range has also been vast, from the revolutionary Marxism of Rosa Luxemburg and Raya Dunayevskaya to Vera Smith Lutz's case for the free banking alternative to a central bank, put forward in an LSE doctoral dissertation supervised by Hayek (Smith 1936), and the anti-statist views of Suzanne LaFollette (1926; Rossi 1973: 537-565), which have been taken up by the Association of Libertarian Feminists (McElroy 1988).

Most especially, the whole area of the "new home economics" and theories of consumption and time-allocation should be recognized as indebted to the high-quality achievements of Dorothy S. Brady, Rose Director Friedman, Elizabeth Ellis Hoyt, Hazel Kyrk, Ruby Turner Morris (1941), and Margaret G. Reid. Economic history was another area of top-quality, innovative work by women, including Mabel Ping-Hua Lee's *Economic History of China* (1921), Margaret Stephenson Miller's *Economic Development of Russia* (1925, cf. Miller 1921, Miller and T'ang 1925), Vera Anstey's *Economic Development of India* (1929), Mabel Buer (1926) on health, wealth, and population in the Industrial Revolution (see Buer 1921 for self-identification as an economist rather than a historian), Ivy Pinchbeck (1930) on women's work in the Industrial Revolution, Elizabeth Gilboy (1932, 1934) on demand as a factor in the Industrial Revolution and on wage history, Miriam Beard's *History of Business* (1938), Alice Hanson Jones's massive study of wealth distribution in colonial America (culminating in Jones 1978, 1980), and Anne Bezanson's work in price history (Bezanson *et al.* 1935, 1936–7, Bezanson 1948, Bezanson *et al.* 1951, a publishing career that began with three *QJE* articles in 1921–2). In addition to her own books, Lillian Knowles merits notice as the teacher of Clark, Buer, Anstey, and Pinchbeck (and perhaps of Miller) at LSE. Maxine Berg (1992: 320–1) notes that one-fifth of the Economic History Society's 500 members were women in 1927, while in 1989 women were only a tenth of the society's 1,800 members.

5 Would it be too much to hope for that more textbooks on the history of economic thought might mention Joan Robinson not only for imperfect competition, but also include her criticism in the chapter presenting the capital theory of Böhm-Bawerk and Irving Fisher?

6 I hope that the information in this paper will serve as a stimulus and change to historians of economic thought, suggesting to them past issues, controversies, theories, and economists with interesting stories still to be told. Having attempted to draw attention to the significant contributions to macroeconomics made from 1906 to 1915 by Minnie Throop England of the University of Nebraska (R. Dimand 1995: 4, and 1999b, a paper presented to the York-Toronto workshop on the history of economic thought founded by Sam Hollander), I am pleased to note that Part 6 of Dennis O'Brien's Elgar Reference Collection, *The Foundations of Business Cycle Theory* (1997), reprints Irving Fisher on booms and depressions together with Minnie Throop England's criticism of Fisher.

Not only is the substance of women's contributions worthy of study, but their career paths were diverse and interesting. Helen Sumner (later Woodbury), a labor historian trained by Ely and Commons, went into government service after being told that she could not be offered a permanent faculty position (Zinsser 1993: 64). Mabel Frances Timlin was a secretary at the University of Saskatchewan for twenty years, becoming an assistant professor there at forty-nine after finishing the University of Washington Ph.D. dissertation published, when she was fifty, as *Keynesian Economics* (Timlin 1942), and went on to become a full professor, Fellow of the Royal Society of Canada, first female President of the Canadian Political Science Association (then including economics), a member of the executive committee of the American Economic Association, a participant in International Economic Association roundtables, and a frequent contributor to the *Canadian Journal of Economics and Political Science*. Perhaps most startling,

> In 1926, when Theresa McMahon was promoted to associate professor, Shirley Jay Coon, a new PhD that very year from the University of Chicago was brought in as full professor. . . . Coon was brought in, apparently, to teach theoretical courses; in "My Story," McMahon says she was never interested in being a theorist.
>
> (Howe 1989: 237)

Coon's 1929 *AER* article on "Collective bargaining and productivity" appears appropriate for a theorist; her only other paper listed in the *AEA Index of Economic Journals*, a 1930 *JPE* paper on "Influence of the Gold Camps on the Economic Development of Western Montana," is more surprising.

This survey of women's past contributions to economics has of course been woefully incomplete: no discussion has been given of Helen Campbell's work in the 1880s and 1890s on women's wages, poverty, and home economics (John Davis in Dimand, Dimand, and Forget, in preparation), Edith Penrose's theory of the growth of the firm, Elizabeth Boody Schumpeter's books on Japanese economic development and on seventeenth and eighteenth-century English overseas commercial statistics, Elizabeth Reade Brown's Georgist work on site value taxation (nineteen articles in the *American Journal of Economics and Sociology* in the 1950s and 1960s), Eleanor Lansing Dulles as monetary economist and diplomat, Barbara Wootton's *Lament for Economics*, Irma Adelman, Ester Boserup, Polly Hill, Cynthia Taft Morris, and Barbara Ward on economic development, Ursula Hicks, Mabel Newcomer, and Selma Mushkin in public finance, Marian Bowley, Marjorie Grice-Hutchinson, and Jacqueline Hecht as historians of economics (and Bowley on the housing market and construction industry), Mary Jean Bowman on income distribution (in a career that led to ten books, over a hundred articles, and editorship of *JPE*), Bowman (and also Sophie Willock Bryant 1894) on the economics of education, Helen Makower on activity analysis and on asset prices in monetary theory, Ruth Cohen on the hog cycle and on the "Ruth Cohen curiosum" (reswitching of techniques), Krishna Bharadwaj's contributions to Cambridge capital theory, Selma Goldsmith on income distribution, Vera Smith Lutz's work on the economic development of southern Italy, Julia Bowman Robinson on "fictitious play" in game theory. Let me close with reference to a distant cousin of Sam Hollander, and draw attention to an insight into economic base and social superstructure by a woman who was not a professional economist, "a letter by Henrietta Marx to her son in the first year as a student at the University of Bonn urging him to look after himself, since "economic needs come first'" (Marcuzzo 1998: 375).

Note

I am grateful to all the contributors to the *Biographical Dictionary of Women Economists* for all that I have learned from their research.

References

Abbott, E. (1910) *Women in Industry: A Study in American Economic History*, New York: D. Appleton (reprinted New York: Arno Press, 1969).

Alexander, J. A. (1995) "Our Ancestors in Their Successive Generations," *Canadian Journal of Economics* 28(1): 205–24.
Anstey, V. (1929) *The Economic Development of India*, London: Longmans, Green (4th edn 1952).
Balch, E. G. (1972) *Beyond Nationalism: The Social Thought of Emily Greene Balch*, ed. M. M. Randall, New York: Twayne.
Baumol, W. J. (1985) "On Method in U. S. Economics a Century Earlier," *American Economic Review* 75(6): 1–12.
Beard, M. (1938) *A History of Business*, 2 vols (reprinted Ann Arbor: University of Michigan Press, 1962).
Berg, M. (1985) *The Age of Manufactures: Industry, Innovation and Work in Britain 1700–1820*, London: Fontana.
—— (1992) "The First Women Economic Historians," *Economic History Review* 45(2): 308–29.
Bernard, L. L. and Bernard, J. (1943) *Origins of American Sociology*, New York: Thomas Y. Crowell (reprinted New York: Russell and Russell, 1965).
Bezanson, A. (1948) "Inflation and Controls, Pennsylvania, 1774–1779," *Journal of Economic History* 8, Supplement: 1–20.
Bezanson, A., Daley, B., Denison, M. and Hussey, M. (1951) *Prices and Inflation during the American Revolution, Pennsylvania 1770–1790*. Philadelphia: University of Pennsylvania Press.
Bezanson, A., Gray, R. D. and Hussey, M. (1935) *Prices in Colonial Pennsylvania 1770–1790*, Philadelphia: University of Pennsylvania Press.
—— (1936–7) *Wholesale Prices in Philadelphia 1784–1861*, 2 vols, Philadelphia: University of Pennsylvania Press.
Biaujeaud, H. ([1934] 1988) *Essai sur la théorie ricardienne de la valeur*, with 1934 preface by Gaetan Pirou and 1988 foreword by C. Abraham-Frois, Paris: Economica.
Bodichon, B. L. S. [1857] (1987) *Women and Work*, London, as reprinted in C. A. Lacey (ed.), *Barbara Leigh Smith Bodichon and the Langham Place Group*, London and New York: Routledge: 36–73.
Bondareva, O. N. [1963] (1968) "Some Applications of Linear Programming to the Theory of Cooperative Games," trans. in *Selected Russian Papers in Game Theory 1959–1965*, Princeton, N.J.: Princeton University Press.
Bowles, P. (1984) "John Millar, the Four-Stages Theory, and Women's Position in Society," *History of Political Economy* 16(4): 619–37.
Brady, D. S. and Friedman, R. D. (1947) "Savings and the Income Distribution," *Studies in Income and Wealth* vol. 10: 247–65, New York: National Bureau of Economic Research.
Buer, M. C. (1921) *Economics for Beginners*, London: Routledge (3rd edn 1935).
—— (1926) *Health, Wealth, and Population in the Early Days of the Industrial Revolution*, London: Routledge.
Butlin, N. G., Fitzgerald, V. W., and Scott, R. H. (eds) (1986) *The Australian Economist 1888–98*, 2 vols, facsimile edn, Sydney: Australian National University Press.
Chapman, A. L. (1952) *Wages and Salaries in the United Kingdom, 1920–1938*, assisted by Rose Knight, Cambridge: Cambridge University Press, Studies in National Income and Expenditure of the United Kingdom, no. 5.
Clark, A. (1919) *The Working Life of Women in the Seventeenth Century*, London: Routledge.
Clark, H. C. (1993) "Women and Humanity in Scottish Enlightenment Social Thought: The Case of Adam Smith," *Historical Reflections* 19: 335–61.
Clifford, G. J. (1989) "Introduction" to G. C. Clifford (ed.), *Lone Voyagers: Academic Women in Coeducational Institutions, 1870–1937*. New York: Feminist Press at City University of New York.
Cobbe, F. P. (1861) "Social Science Congresses and Women's Part in Them," *Macmillan's*

Magazine (December).
Coman, K. (1911) "Some Problems of Irrigation," *American Economic Review* 1(1): 1–19.
Coon, Shirley Jay (1929) "Collective Bargaining and Productivity," *American Economic Review* 19 (September): 419–27.
—— (1930) "Influence of the Gold Camps on the Economic Development of Western Montana," *Journal of Political Economy* 38 (October): 580–99.
Copley, S. and Sutherland, K. (eds) (1995) *Adam Smith's Wealth of Nations: New Interdisciplinary Essays*, Manchester: Manchester University Press.
Costantino, C. (1939) "Sulle fluttuazioni economiche di lunga durata," *Rivista Internazionale di Scienze Sociali* 794–809.
—— (1941) "Di alcuni aspetti del problema del lavoro femminile nel quadro della ricostruzione europea," *Rivista di Politica Economica* 677–84.
Dall, C. (1860) *"Woman's Right to Labor"; or Low Wages and Hard Work: In Three Lectures Delivered in Boston, November, 1859*, Boston: Walker, Wise.
—— [1867] (1914) *The College, the Market, and the Court, or Woman's Relation to Education, Labor, and Law*, Concord, N.H.: Rumford Press.
Daszynska, Z. (1889) *Zurichs Bevolkerung im XVII. Jahrhundert. Ein Beitrag zur historischen Stadtestatistik*, Berne.
Daszynska-Golinska, S. (1923) *La Chine et le système physiocratique en France*, Varsovie (Warsaw): Bibliotheca Universitatis Liberae Polonae.
Daubié, J-V. (1862) "Quels moyens de subsistance ont les femmes?" *Journal des Économistes*, 2e serie, no. 34.
—— (1863) "Travail manuel des femmes," *Journal des Économistes*, 2e serie, nos. 38 et 39.
Dauriac, F. (1933) "Le travail des femmes en France devant la statistique (1906–1926)," *Revue d'Économie Politique* 47: 91–109.
Deegan, M. J. (ed.) (1991) *Women in Sociology: A Bio-Bibliographical Sourcebook*, New York: Greenwood.
Dexter, E. A. (1931) *Colonial Women of Affairs: Women in Business and Affairs in America before 1776*, 2nd ed. Boston, Mass.: Houghton Mifflin.
—— (1950) *Career Women in America: 1776–1840*. Francestown, N.H.: M. Jones.
Diamond, M. and Stone, M. (1981) "Nightingale on Quetelet," *Journal of the Royal Statistical Society*, Series A, vol. 144: 66–79, 176–213, 332–51.
Dimand, M. A. (1995) "The Economics of Charlotte Perkins Gilman," in M. A. Dimand, R. W. Dimand and E. Forget (eds), *Women of Value: Feminist Essays on the History of Women in Economics*, Aldershot, UK, and Brookfield, Vt.: Elgar: 124–49.
—— (1996) "Review of 1994 reprint of Gilman (1898)," *Feminist Economics* 2(3): 167–75.
Dimand, M. A., Dimand, R. W. and Forget, E. L. (eds) (1995) *Women of Value: Feminist Essays on the History of Women in Economics*, Aldershot, UK, and Brookfield, Vt.: Elgar.
Dimand, R. W. (1995) "The Neglect of Women's Contributions to Economics," in M. A. Dimand, R. W. Dimand and E. Forget (eds), *Women of Value: Feminist Essays on the History of Women in Economics*, Aldershot, UK, and Brookfield, Vt.: Elgar: 1–24.
—— (1999a) "Women Economists in the 1890s: Journals, Books and the Old Palgrave," *Journal of the History of Economic Thought* 21(3): 269–88.
—— (1999b) "Minnie Throop England on Crises and Cycles: A Neglected Early Macroeconomist," *Feminist Economics* 5(3): 107–26.
Dimand, R. W., Dimand, M. A. and Forget, E. L. (eds) (2000) *A Biographical Dictionary of Women Economists*, Cheltenham, UK, and Lyme, N.H.: Elgar.
Dorfman, J. (1946) *The Economic Mind in American Civilization 1606–1865*, 2 vols, New York: Viking.
—— (1959) *The Economic Mind in American Civilization*, vols 4 and 5: 1918–33, New York: Viking.
Eatwell, J., Milgate, M. and Newman, P. (eds) (1987) *The New Palgrave: A Dictionary of Economics*, 4 vols, London: Stockton.

Ekelund Jr, R. B. and Hébert, R. F. (1999) *Secret Origins of Modern Microeconomics: Dupuit and the Engineers*, Chicago: University of Chicago Press.

Fawcett, M. G. [1918] (1995) "Equal Pay for Equal Work," *Economic Journal* 28(1): 1–6 (as reprinted in W. A. Darity, Jr. (ed.), *Economics and Discrimination*, vol. 1, Aldershot, UK, and Brookfield, Vt.: Elgar.)

Ferber, M. A. and Birnbaum, B. G. (1977) "The 'New Home Economics': Retrospects and Prospects," *Journal of Consumer Research* 4(1): 19–28.

Folbre, N. (1991) "The Unproductive Housewife: Her Evolution in Nineteenth-Century Economic Thought," *Signs* 16(3): 463–84.

—— (1994) *Who Pays for the Kids? Gender and the Structures of Constraint*, New York and London: Routledge.

Forget, E. L. (1995) "American Women Economists, 1900–1940: Doctoral Dissertations and Research Specialization," in M. A. Dimand, R. W. Dimand and E. Forget (eds), *Women of Value: Feminist Essays on the History of Women in Economics*, Aldershot, UK, and Brookfield, Vt.: Elgar: 25–38.

—— (1996) "Margaret Gilpin Reid: A Manitoba Home Economist Goes to Chicago," *Feminist Economics* 2(3): 1–16.

—— (1997) "The Market for Virtue: Jean-Baptiste Say on Women in the Economy and Society," *Feminist Economics* 3(1): 95–111.

Frawley, M. H. (1992) "Harriet Martineau in America: Gender and the Discourse of Sociology," *Victorian Newsletter* 81: 13–20.

Friedman, M. (1957) *A Theory of the Consumption Function*, Princeton, N.J.: Princeton University Press.

Friedman, M. and Friedman, R. D. (1998) *Two Lucky People*, Chicago: University of Chicago Press.

Friedman, M. and Schwartz, A. J. (1963) *A Monetary History of the United States, 1867–1960*. Princeton, N.J.: Princeton University Press for National Bureau of Economic Research.

Furner, M. O. (1975) *Advocacy and Objectivity: A Crisis in the Professionalization of American Social Science, 1865–1905*, Lexington, Ky.: University Press of Kentucky.

Gilboy, E. W. (1932) "Demand as a Factor in the Industrial Revolution," in A. H. Cole (ed.), *Facts and Factors in Economic History*, Cambridge, Mass.: Harvard University Press. (Reprinted in R. M. Hartwell (ed.), *The Causes of the Industrial Revolution*, London: Methuen, 1967.)

—— (1934) *Wages in Eighteenth Century England*, Cambridge, Mass.: Harvard University Press, Harvard Economic Studies.

Gilman, C. P. (1898) *Women and Economics: The Economic Factor Between Men and Women as a Factor in Social Evolution*, Boston: Small, Maynard (reprinted (with intro.by C. Degler) New York: Harper Torchbooks, 1966; reprinted Amherst, N.Y.: Prometheus, 1994).

—— [1903](1970) *The Home: Its Work and Influence*, New York: Source Book Press.

Ginor, F. (1997) "Krise des Uebergangs in einen anderen Kulturkreis," in H. Hagemann (ed.) *Zur deutschsprachigen wirtschaftslichen Emigration nach 1933*, Marburg: Metropolis Verlag.

Gregson, N. and Rose, G. (1997) "Contested and Negotiated Histories of Feminist Geography," in Women and Geography Study Group of the Royal Geographical Society with the Institute of British Geographers, *Feminist Geographies: Explorations in Diversity and Difference*, London: Longman: 13–48.

Green, M. (1974) *The Von Richthofen Sisters: The Triumphant and the Tragic Modes of Love: Else and Frieda von Richthofen, Otto Gross, Max Weber, and D. H. Lawrence, in the Years 1870–1970*, New York: Basic Books.

Groenewegen, P. D. (ed.) (1994) *Feminism and Political Economy in Victorian England*, Aldershot, UK, and Brookfield, Vt.: Elgar.

Groenewegen, P. D. and King, S. (1994) "Women as Producers of Economic Articles: A Statistical Assessment of the Nature and Extent of Female Participation in Five British and North American Journals 1900-1939," *University of Sydney Working Papers in Economics* no. 201.
Guly, C. (1997) "Casino's Mural a Safe Bet for Museum," *Globe and Mail* (May 31).
Hagemann, H. (ed.) (1997) *Zur deutschsprachigen wirtschaftslichen Emigration nach 1933*, Marburg: Metropolis Verlag.
Hagemann, H. and Krohn, C-D. (1992) *Die Emigration Deutschsprachiger Wirtschaftswissenschaftler Nach 1933: Biographische Gesamtuebericht unter Mitarbeit von Hans Ulrich Esslinger*, Diskussionbeitraege nr. 72 aus dem Institut für Volkswirtschaftslehre, Universitaet Hohenheim, Stuttgart.
Hartmann, H. (1981) "The Unhappy Marriage of Marxism and Feminism: Towards a More Progressive Union," in L. Sargent (ed.), *Women and Revolution*, Boston: South End: 1–41.
Haskell, T. L. (1977) *The Emergence of Professional Social Science: The American Social Science Association and the Nineteenth Century Crisis of Authority*, Urbana: University of Illinois Press.
Hayek, F. A. (1951) *John Stuart Mill and Harriet Taylor: Their Friendship and Subsequent Marriage*, Chicago: University of Chicago Press.
Henderson, W. (1992) "Harriet Martineau or 'When Political Economy Was Popular'," *History of Education* 21: 383–403.
—— (1994) "Jane Marcet's Conversations on Political Economy," *History of Education* 23: 423–37.
Herlihy, D. (1990) *Opera Muliebra: Women and Work in Medieval Europe*, New York: McGraw-Hill.
Hill, C. (1904) "The Economic Value of the Home," *Journal of Political Economy* 12(3): 408–19.
Howard, M. C. and King, J. E. (1989–92) *A History of Marxian Economics*, 2 vols, Princeton, N.J.: Princeton University Press.
Howe, F. (1989) "Practical in Her Theories: Theresa McMahon, 1878–1961," in G. J. Clifford (ed.), *Lone Voyagers: Academic Women in Coeducational Institutions, 1870–1937*, New York: Feminist Press at City University of New York: 223–80.
Hoyt, E. E. (1926) *Primitive Trade: Its Psychology and Economics*. London: Kegan Paul (reprinted New York: Augustus M. Kelley, Reprints of Economic Classics, 1968).
—— (1928) *Consumption of Wealth*, New York: Macmillan.
—— (1938) *Consumption in Our Society*, New York: McGraw-Hill.
Hutchins, B. L. (1915) *Women in Modern Industry*, London: G. Bell (reprinted West Yorkshire: E. P. Publishing).
Jasny, N. (1972) *Soviet Economists of the Twenties: Names to be Remembered*, Cambridge: Cambridge University Press.
Jones, A. H. (1978) *American Colonial Wealth: Documents and Methods*, 2nd edn, 3 vols, New York: Arno Press.
—— (1980) *Wealth of a Nation to Be: The American Colonies on the Eve of the Revolution*. New York: Columbia University Press.
Kandal, T. R. (1988) *The Woman Question in Classical Sociological Theory*, Miami: Florida International University Press.
Kock, K. (1927) "The Organisation of the Swedish Money Market," *Economica* 7 (March): 63–73.
—— (1929) *A Study of Interest Rates, Stockholm Economic Studies* no. 1, London: P. S. King.
—— (1933) "Paper Currency and Monetary Policy in Sweden," in *Economic Essays in Honour of Gustav Cassel*, London: Allen and Unwin: 343–56.
—— (1943) "Swedish Economic Policy During the War," *Review of Economic Studies* 10(2): 75–80.

—— (1961–2) *Kreditmarknad och rantepolitik 1924–1958*, 2 vols, Uppsala.

—— (1969) *International Trade Policy and the GATT, 1947–1967*, Stockholm Economic Studies, New Series. Stockholm: Almqvist and Wiksell.

Kulakovskaja, T. E. and Naumova, N. I., assisted by Ramovsky, J. V. (1992) "Obituary: Olga Nikolajevna Bondareva 1937–1991," *International Journal of Game Theory* 20: 309–12.

Kyrk, H. (1923) *A Theory of Consumption*, Cambridge, Mass.: Houghton Mifflin, Riverside Press.

—— (1933) *Economic Problems of the Family*, New York: Harper and Brothers.

LaFollette, S. (1926) *Concerning Women*, New York: Albert and Charles Boni.

Lee, M. P-H. (1921) *The Economic History of China, with Special Reference to Agriculture*, New York: Columbia University Press.

Lenin, V. I. [1899] (1956) *The Development of Capitalism in Russia*, Moscow: Foreign Languages Publishing House.

Leubuscher, C. (1927) *Liberalismus und Protektionismus unter englischen Wirtschaftspolitik seit dem Kriege*, Iena: Verlag von Gustav Fischer.

Libby, B. (1984) "Women in Economics before 1940," *Essays in Economic and Business History* 3: 273–90.

—— (1987) "Statistical Analysis of Women in the Economics Profession," *Essays in Economic and Business History* 5: 179–89.

—— (1990) "Women in the Economics Profession 1900–1940: Factors in Declining Visibility," *Essays in Economic and Business History* 8: 121–30.

—— (1996) "As Time Goes By: A Chronological Study of Women in the Economics Profession 1900–1940," Niagara University, forthcoming in *Essays in Economic and Business History*.

Lindahl, E., Dahlgren, E. and Kock, K. (1937) *National Income of Sweden, 1861–1930*, 2 vols, London: P. S. King, Stockholm Economic Studies nos. 5A and 5B.

Luxemburg, R. [1898] (1977) *The Industrial Development of Poland*, trans. Tessa DeCarlo, with an introduction by L. H. LaRouche, Jr., New York: Campaigner.

—— [1913] (1951) *The Accumulation of Capital*, trans. Agnes Schwarzchild, with an introduction by Joan Robinson, London: Routledge and Kegan Paul, and New Haven: Yale University Press.

Madden, J. F. (1972) "The Development of Economic Thought on the 'Women Problem'," *Review of Radical Political Economics* 4(3): 21–39.

Madden, K. (1998) "Female Economists in the History of Economic Thought: Methodological Issues and a Case Study in Consumption Theory," Millersville University, presented to History of Economics Society, Montreal, June.

Malveaux, J. (1991) "Missed Opportunity: Sadie Tanner Mossell Alexander and the Economics Profession," *American Economic Review* 81(2): 307–10 (reprinted in T. D. Boston (ed.), *A Different Vision*, vol. 1: *African American Economic Thought*, London and New York: Routledge, 1997).

Marcet, J. (1816) *Conversations on Political Economy*, London: Longman. (Extracts from 6th edn of 1827 in University of Sydney, Reprints of Economic Classics, Series 1, no. 6, c. 1954.)

Marcuzzo, M. C. (1998) "Review of B. Ingrao and F. Ranchetti, *Il mercato nel pensiero economico*," *European Journal of the History of Economic Thought* 5(2): 374–7.

Marshall, A. and Marshall, M. P. (1879) *The Economics of Industry*, London: Macmillan (reprinted with a new intro. by D. P. O'Brien, Bristol: Thoemmes Press, 1994).

Martel, C. F. (1986) "British Women in the National Association for the Promotion of Social Science, 1857–1886," Ph.D. dissertation, Arizona State University (Dissertation Abstracts International 47, 4169A, 1987).

Martineau, H. (1832–4) *Illustrations of Political Economy*, 9 vols, London: Charles Fox.

—— [1837] (1962) *Society in America*, abridged and ed. S. M. Lipset, Garden City, N.Y.:

Doubleday Anchor (reprinted New Brunswick, N.J.: Transaction, 1981).
—— [1838] (1989) *How to Observe Morals and Manners*, ed. Michael R. Hill. New Brunswick, N.J.: Transaction.
—— (1855) *The Factory Controversy: A Warning Against "Meddling Legislation"*, Manchester: Ireland and National Association of Factory Operators.
—— (1877) *Autobiography*, ed. M. W. Chapman, 2 vols, Boston.
McDonald, L. (1994) *The Women Founders of the Social Sciences*, Ottawa: Carleton University Press.
—— (1998a) "Classical Social Theory with the Women Founders Included," in C.Camic (ed.), *Reclaiming the Sociological Classics*, Oxford: Blackwell.
—— (ed.) (1998b) *Women Theorists on Society and Politics*, Waterloo, On.: Wilfrid Laurier University Press.
McElroy, W. (ed.) (1988) *Freedom, Feminism and the State*, Boulder, Co.: Westview Press for Independent Institute, Independent Studies in Political Economy.
McFadden, M. (1990) "Boston Teenagers Debate the Woman Question, 1837–1838," *Signs* 15(4): 832–47.
McMahon, T. (1912) *Women and Economic Evolution*, Madison, Wis.: University of Wisconsin Bulletin, no. 496.
Meade, E. F. (1901) "The Place of Advertising in Modern Business," *Journal of Political Economy* 9 (March): 218–42.
Meyer, A. (ed.) (1891) *Women's Work in America*, New York: Holt.
Meynieu, M. (1839) *Elements d'économie politique, exposés dans une suite de dialogues entre un instituteur et son élève, a l'usage des écoles normales primaires*, Paris: A. Cherbuliez.
—— (1841) *Du Paupérisme anglais*, Paris: A. Cherbuliez.
—— (1859) "Observations sur l'économie politique, a propos du Manuel de M. Baudrillart," *Journal des Économistes* 65 (May).
—— (1860) *Quelques mots sur le travail des femmes, a l'occasion d'un article de M. Jules Simon*, Paris: Imprimerie du Corps legislatif, A. H. Noblet.
Miller, M. S. (1921) "Co-operation in Russia," *Economica* 1 (October): 291–301.
—— (1925) *Economic Development of Russia*, London: P. S. King.
Miller, M. S. and Tang, L. -L. (1925) "The Political Aspect of International Finance in Russia and China," *Economica* 5 (March): 69–88.
Morris, R. T. (1941) *The Theory of Consumer's Demand*, New Haven: Yale University Press (rev. edn 1952).
Moszkowska, N. (1929) *Das Marxsche System*, Berlin: Verlag Hans Robert Engelmann.
—— (1935) *Zur Kritik Moderner Krisentheorien*, Prague: Michael Kacha Verlag.
—— (1943) *Zur Dynamik des Spätkapitalismus*, Zurich and New York: Verlag "Der Aufbruch."
—— (1959) "Das Krisenproblem bei Marx und Keynes," *Schmollers Jahrbuch* 79, 6: 665–701.
Myers, M. G. (1931) *The New York Money Market*, 2 vols, New York: Columbia University Press.
—— (1936) *Paris as a Financial Centre*, London: P. S. King.
—— (1940) *Monetary Proposals for Social Reform*, New York: Columbia University Press.
Nyland, C. (1993) "Adam Smith, Stage Theory, and the Status of Women," *History of Political Economy* 25(4): 617–40.
—— (1997) "Biology and Environment: Montesquieu's Relativist Analysis of Gender Behavior," *History of Political Economy* 29(3): 391–412.
O'Brien, D. P. (ed.) (1997) *The Foundations of Business Cycle Theory*, 3 vols, Cheltenham, UK, and Lyme, N.H.: Edward Elgar.
O'Donnell, M. (1985) "Charlotte Perkins Gilman's Economic Interpretation of the Role of Women at the Turn of the Century," *Social Science Quarterly* 69(1): 177–92.
—— (1996) "A Reply to 'Charlotte Perkins Gilman: Reassessing Her Significance for

Feminism and Social Economics'," *Review of Social Economy* 54(3): 337–40.

Palgrave, R. H. I. (ed.) [1894–9] (1910) *Dictionary of Political Economy*, 3 vols, London: Macmillan.

Penny, V. (1863) *The Employments of Women: A Cyclopaedia of Woman's Work*. Boston: Walker, Wise and Company. Reprinted as *How Women Can Make Money, Married or Single* (title of 3rd printing), with intro. by L. Stein and P. Taft, New York: Arno Press and *New York Times*, 1971. (Second printing entitled *Five Hundred Occupations Adapted to Women; with the Average Rate of Pay in Each*.)

—— (1869) *Think and Act: A Series of Articles Pertaining to Men and Women, Work and Wages*, Philadelphia: Claxton, Remsen, and Haffelfinger (reprinted New York: Arno Press and *New York Times*, 1971).

Pinchbeck, I. (1930) *Women Workers and the Industrial Revolution, 1750–1850*. London: Routledge (reprinted London: Virago, 1969).

Pois, A. M. (1995) "Foreshadowings: Ecofeminist/Pacifist Feminism of the 1980s," *Peace and Change* 20(4): 439–65.

Polkinghorn, B. (1993) *Jane Marcet: An Uncommon Woman*, Aldermaston, Berkshire: Forestwood.

—— (1995) "Jane Marcet and Harriet Martineau: Motive, Market Experience and Reception of their Works Popularizing Classical Political Economy," in M. A. Dimand, R. W. Dimand and E. Forget (eds), *Women of Value: Feminist Essays on the History of Women in Economics*, Aldershot, UK, and Brookfield, Vt.: Elgar: 71–82.

Pujol, M. (1992) *Feminism and Anti-Feminism in Early Economic Thought*, Aldershot, UK, and Brookfield, Vt.: Elgar.

—— (1995) "The Feminist Economic Thought of Harriet Taylor (1807–58)," in M. A. Dimand, R. W. Dimand and E. Forget (eds), *Women of Value: Feminist Essays on the History of Women in Economics*, Aldershot, UK, and Brookfield, Vt.: Elgar: 82–102.

Randall, M. M. (1964) *Improper Bostonian: Emily Greene Balch*, New York: Twayne.

Reid, Margaret G. (1934) *Economics of Household Production*, New York: Wiley.

—— (1952) "Effect of Income Concept upon Expenditure Curves of Farm Families," *Studies in Income and Wealth* 15, New York: National Bureau of Economic Research.

—— (1977) "How New is the 'New Home Economics'?" *Journal of Consumer Research* 4(3): 181–3.

—— (no date) "The Relation of the Within-Group Permanent Component of Income to the Income Elasticity of Expenditur," unpublished paper.

Rendall, J. (1987) "Virtue and Commerce: Women in the Making of Adam Smith's Political Economy," in E. Kennedy and S. Mendus (eds), *Women in Western Political Philosophy, Kant to Nietzsche*, Brighton: Wheatsheaf.

Roberts, H. V. D. (1935) *Boisguilbert, Economist of the Reign of Louis XIV*, New York: Columbia University Press.

Robson, A. P. and Robson, J. M. (eds) (1994) *Sexual Equality: Writings by John Stuart Mill, Harriet Taylor Mill, and Helen Taylor*, Toronto: University of Toronto Press.

Rogers, B. (1952) "The Social Science Association, 1857–1886," *Manchester School* 20(3).

Rossi, A. S. (1973) *The Feminist Papers: From Adams to de Beauvoir*, New York: Bantam.

Royer, C. -A. (1862) *Théorie de l'impôt, ou la dîme sociale*, 2 vols, Paris: Guillaumin.

—— (1875) *Du Percement de l'isthme américain*, Paris: Guillaumin (reprint from *Journal des Économistes*).

—— (1892) *Recherches d'optique physiologique et physique*, Bruxelles: Imp.Veuve Monnom.

—— (1900) *Natura Rerum. La Constitution du monde. Dynamique des atomes. Nouveaux principes de philosophie naturelle*. Paris: Schleicher Frères.

Scott, J. W. (1987) "'L'ouvrière! Mot impie, sordide ...': Women Workers in the Discourse of French Political Economy, 1840–1860," in P. Joyce (ed.), *The Historical Meanings of Work*, Cambridge: Cambridge University Press: 119–142.

Sockwell, W. D. (1995) "Barbara Bodichon and the Women of Langham Place," in M.

A. Dimand, R. W. Dimand and E. Forget (eds), *Women of Value: Feminist Essays on the History of Women in Economics*, Aldershot, UK, and Brookfield, Vt.: Elgar: 103–23.

Shackleton, J. R. (1990) "Jane Marcet and Harriet Martineau: Pioneers of Economics Education," *History of Education* 19: 283–97.

Sheth, F. A. and Prasch, R. E. (1996) "Charlotte Perkins Gilman: Reassessing Her Significance for Feminism and Social Economics," *Review of Social Economy* 54(3): 323–35.

Sinclair, A. (1965) *The Emancipation of the American Woman*, New York: Harper and Row.

Smith, V. (1936) *The Rationale of Central Banking: And the Free Banking Alternative*, London: P. S. King (reprinted with intro. by L. Yeager, Indianapolis: Liberty Fund, 1990. (Later V. Smith Lutz.)

Solzhenitsyn, A. (1974) *The Gulag Archipelago 1918–1956*, Parts I–II, trans. T. P. Whitney. New York: Harper and Row.

Sumner, H. L. (1910) *History of Women in Industry in the United States*. Washington, D.C.: Senate Report on Condition of Women and Child Wage-Earners in the United States, vol. 9 (Doc. no. 645, 61st Congress, 2nd session). (Later H. Sumner Woodbury.)

Sutherland, K. (1995) "Adam Smith's Master Narrative: Women and the Wealth of Nations," in S. Copley and K. Sutherland (eds), *Adam Smith's Wealth of Nations: New Interdisciplinary Essays*, Manchester: Manchester University Press: 97–121.

Thorne, A. C. (1936) "Capacity to Consume," *American Economic Review* 26 (June): 292–5.

—— (1995) "Women Mentoring Women in Economics in the 1930s," in M. A. Dimand, R. W. Dimand and E. Forget (eds), *Women of Value: Feminist Essays on the History of Women in Economics*, Aldershot, UK, and Brookfield, Vt.: Elgar: 60–70.

Tickner, F. W. (1923) *Women in English Economic History*, London and Toronto: Dent.

Timlin, M. F. (1942) *Keynesian Economics*, Toronto: University of Toronto Press (reprinted, with biographical note by A. E. Safarian and foreword by L. Tarshis, Toronto: McClelland and Stewart, Carleton Library no. 107, 1977).

Veblen, T. [1899] (1979) *The Theory of the Leisure Class*, New York: Penguin.

Vivo, G. de (1991) Review of Biaujeaud, *Essai sur la théorie ricardienne de la valeur*, *Contributions to Political Economy* 10: 85–7.

Wakefield, P. [1798] (1817) *Reflections on the Present Condition of the Female Sex, with Suggestions for its Improvement*, 2nd edn, London: Darton, Harvey, and Darton.

Walker, A. (1872) *The Science of Wealth*, student's edn (condensed from 6th edn of 1871), Philadelphia: Lippincott.

Ware, C. F. (1931) *The Early New England Cotton Manufacture*, Boston: Houghton Mifflin (Repr. New York: Russell and Russell, 1966).

Wargon, S. T. (1992) "Women in Demography in Canada: The 1940s to the Late 1960s," *Canadian Studies in Population* 19(2): 181–215.

Wunderlich, F. (1946) *German Labor Courts*, Chapel Hill: University of North Carolina Press.

—— (1961) *Farm Labor in Germany 1810–1945*, Princeton, N.J.: Princeton University Press.

Yi, Yun-Ae (1996) "Margaret G. Reid: Life and Achievements," *Feminist Economics* 2(3): 17–36.

Zinsser, J. P. (1993) *History and Feminism: A Glass Half Full*, New York: Twayne.

Zuckerman, M. E. and Carsky, M. L. (1990) "Contributions of Women to U.S. Marketing Thought: The Consumers' Perspective, 1900–1940," *Journal of the Academy of Marketing Science* 18(4): 313–8.

24 The canon in economics

Warren J. Samuels

In this chapter I want to explore, as objectively and analytically as possible, the problem of the canon in economics. The first part of the chapter treats canonical literature and canonical interpretation in economics. The second part treats the economics canon in a manner parallel to the general cultural, or literary, canon.

The nature and structure of the canon

The meaning and existence of an economics canon

The canon in economics is whatever literature – readings – scholars in economics revere, recommend and assign. The canon has no independent existence. It is socially constructed, on the basis of, first, what individual scholars see fit so to treat as relevant to their own interests, including their research and the training of their students, and, second, what scholars perceive as having professional status.

A strong argument can be made that the books most historians of economic thought, and perhaps most older economists, would include in the economics canon are not widely read by most (younger) economists, certainly not as part of their graduate training. To the extent that this is true, the canon in the traditional sense, of venerated "ancient" literature, may not apply to economics. I have in mind at least Adam Smith's *The Wealth of Nations*, David Ricardo's *Principles of Political Economy and Taxation*, Karl Marx's *Capital*, Alfred Marshall's *Principles of Economics*, John Maynard Keynes's *General Theory of Employment, Interest and Money*, and Paul Samuelson's *Foundations of Economic Analysis*. These books may be consulted like other references but consultation *per se* is not enough to constitute canonical status. Nor is it enough to say that in any case, no matter what is and what is not read, these (and perhaps other works) necessarily and inexorably constitute the canon of economics. Reading, however, may not be the only basis of canonical status: authors and works important when they were published but now largely unread may have become absorbed in the corpus of knowledge and belief in the discipline, though such a consideration would make the canon even more amorphous than it is already.

One could speak of a canonical literature in economics in other ways. First, there may be canonical reading lists in specialized fields. For example, Abram

Bergson's article on the reformulation of welfare economics, Paul Samuelson's article on the pure theory of public expenditure, Ronald Coase's articles on the theory of the firm and the problem of social cost, and Milton Friedman's on methodology surely are read as canonical in their respective fields, at least in the sense of venerated seminal or decisive statements, if only from a particular point of view. Second, if one consults graduate reading lists in most fields, the canon in economics may largely, if not entirely, consist of recent leading articles, with the emphasis on recent. Lately, economists seem to have increased their reliance on – and prestige assigned to – more or less contemporary journal articles compared with books.

However in neither of the two latter cases – specialized fields and recent leading articles – does this literature have a perennial and transcendent canonical status for economics; neither accurately defines economics as a whole. In the second case, because the canon thus understood is a shifting phenomenon, reflecting the current interests of graduate instructors, this literature arguably does not constitute a canon at all. To some persons, this would be disgraceful; for others, healthy.

An enormous percentage of all economics literature has been published in the last thirty or so years (a statement which must remain ambiguous as to both what constitutes "economics literature" and the nonquantifiability of the percentage itself). Two implications follow: first, attention to relatively recent publications should be great (due also to other causes, such as membership in the mutually citing invisible college and the commonality of contemporary interests); and, second, canonical status accruing to much earlier writings is likely to be more honorific and less substantive.

Further *apropos* of citations, referencing canonical literature may principally serve as a mode of legitimation, the clothing of one's ideas, as it were, in the wraps of prestigious authors and works. Conversely, the invocation of certain sources for the purpose of legitimation may serve to create and/or reenforce canonical status. (I return to the canon as independent versus dependent variable and cumulative causation later.)

Canonical status in economics may arise and accrue in a yet quite different manner. A serious case can be made that in economics neither authors nor particular works acquire canonical status, or do not do so alone. Canonical status can, and perhaps widely does accrue to particular models, more or less independent of the principal figure(s) who developed them: the multiplier, Harrod-Domar growth models, the quantity theory, the overlapping generations model, opportunity cost, transaction cost, Post Keynesian and New Keynesian macroeconomic models, and so on. Canonical models, along with their canonical interpretations, may well constitute the economics canon, at least a significant part thereof.

In general, canonical status accrues to literature which has had a major impact on subsequent thought, action and events, and which continues to instruct and inspire. However, the meaning of "major," the time frame pertaining to "subsequent" and the domain of potential impact can vary.

Notwithstanding the foregoing ambiguities, in what follows I nonetheless assume that an economics canon exists.[1] It will be seen that the same problems of ontology, epistemology and political sociology that pertain to the study of the economy also apply to the study of the economics canon.

However the assumption that an economics canon exists can be incomplete and misleading in a number of ways. First, canonical texts can be used in noncanonical ways, for example, the texts can be raw material for rational reconstruction and for structuralist interpretation in the manner of Michel Foucault. Second, canonical texts and/or authors can be used selectively, that is, one part of a text or an author's total system can be taken, perhaps out of context, and the remainder ignored. And third, taking one of an author's texts as canonical may obfuscate the evolutionary or transformative nature of the author's work, so that even the author's last publication or writing can represent a stage in a work in progress. Canonical status, in other words, involves considerable abstraction and potential over-generalization.

Both specification of the canon and the canon itself serve a number of functions. The canon helps define the discipline, even though our definition of the discipline helps identify the canon, in a process of cumulative causation. The canon is a means of establishing historical credentials and legitimacy; for some, almost a mode of confirmation. The canon is an intellectual battleground for contests between continuity and change, as well as for the continued redefinition and/or recasting of each; alternatively, or simultaneously, the canon is a set of weapons in such contests, always a set of intellectual tools in the quest for definition and meaning. The canon contributes to the myths by which some know the discipline, if not also the economy; and *vice versa*. The canon constitutes a mode of discourse, of thinking and of rethinking. The canon is a mode of working out relevance: on the one hand, if may be difficult for something to be given canonical status if it is not presently relevant; on the other hand, what is of present relevance may influence what is given canonical status.

Two further introductory considerations: initially, this chapter deals with neither epistemology nor philosophy of science, but, especially in light of the fact that discussions of canonical status have generally dealt with fictional literature, it is not inapposite to point out that in at least three interrelated respects the literature of economics is fictional, literally economic science fiction. First, contrary to the laudable goal of science being "truth," well-known contemporary work on the rhetoric or discourse of economics leads to the widely accepted conclusion that economics consists of a group of stories (for example, "In a neoclassical world, . . ."). I consider this point further later. Second, because both economic theories and models abstract by assumption from certain variables and relationships recognized to be operative in actual economies, economic theories and models are necessarily unrealistic and, as the products of acts of imagination, literally fiction. Third, economic paradigms, models and theories represent idealizations of aspects of actual economies, not actual economies themselves. The combination of limiting assumptions and ideal types serves several functions – psychic balm, social control, and knowledge production – and jointly and severally are tools to be utilized in the construction of stories which only then become instruments in the construction of putative economic knowledge.

Further, nothing in this chapter should be taken to mean that the economics canon is empty, sterile, irrelevant, or exploitative – claims sometimes made about the literary canon. While the economics canon has no independent ontological existence and its content and meaning must be worked out as a function of selective perception in a process of social construction, judgements such as these are part of the process through which the economics canon is continually reconstructed.

The domain and structure of the canon

The canon in economics consists of first, a body of canonical authors and literature and second, a body of canonical interpretations. As for the body of canonical authors and literature, disagreement concerns who is an "authentic," that is, canonical, author (who is a "true" as opposed to a "false" member or practitioner) and therefore qualifies to have his or her work be candidates for canonical status – as well as membership in the relevant in-group. The canonical interpretations are of, first, the canonical and other literature, piece by piece and/or author by author; and second, the history of economic thought writ large. Also relevant is the history of economics as a sociological enterprise. The further distinction should be made between who and what is canonical for economics as a whole and who and what is canonical for, or within, a school or field within economics.

Formation of individual visions of the past

Each economist has a vision of the discipline's past, probably largely inchoate and a mixture of sophisticated and naive understandings. The visions that most if not all economists have of the discipline's past have been subjectively and selectively formed. Economists have learned their visions, in part, from similarly more or less informed/ignorant teachers, whose visions were formed in the same way and whose views they to some extent perpetuate and may even narrow. Or they have formed their visions more or less subconsciously in the light and on the basis of their own individual interests, work, expectations and projections.

Heterogeneity and multiple interpretation

Economics has had a heterogeneous existence.[2] Throughout its history, at every point in time, economics has been comprised of multiple schools of economic thought. Moreover, each school of economic thought (and its theories and doctrines) has been given multiple interpretations. If several schools of economic thought exist, A, B, C, . . . N, and if each of them has several different interpretations, A1, A2 . . ., B1, B2 . . ., N1, N2 . . ., then one can, first, define economics in terms of any one interpretation of any one school, say D4, and, second, identify the history of economic thought and the corpus of canonical literature in the light, and in the image, of D4. Or one can define economics and understand its literature (canonical and otherwise) in terms of the matrix formed by all schools of thought and all interpretations of each school (Samuels 1974). The history of economic thought and the content of the canon depend on which interpretive route is taken. No one route is necessarily canonical, though a hegemonic school's view of itself and of its past (neoclassicism in the West and Marxism in the former USSR), in a hagiographic, Whiggish and presentist sort of way, is common.

Canonical interpretations

In economics, the case can be made that at least as, if not more important than a defining set of canonical literature is a defining set of canonical interpretations. Adam Smith's *The Wealth of Nations* enjoys discipline-wide canonical status (though not by every economist). However it is given very different interpretations by different writers, readings which arguably are typically, if not inevitably, incomplete and myopic. None of Carl Menger's and Vilfredo Pareto's work seems to be canonical for economics as a whole (though canonical for certain schools of thought); what is important is the canonical reading given them, which defines their meaning for later economists – readings which arguably are typically incomplete and myopic.

The canonical interpretation of *The Wealth of Nations* is in the image of modern individualism, noninterventionism and pure-market theory. *The Wealth of Nations* though has also been interpreted in conjunction with his other work and lectures, yielding a much broader and more complex view of economy, polity, society and social science, more room for legal and nonlegal social control and less for sacralization of the market. One will "know" Adam Smith on such topics as rationality and *laissez-faire* quite differently because one knows one reading of Smith and not another. One will "know" David Ricardo's theory of value depending on which one of over half a dozen interpretations of it one has been taught or come to adopt as one's own. One will "know" Karl Marx differently depending on whether one interprets him through Eduard Bernstein, Karl Kautsky, V. I. Lenin, or Josef Stalin, or for that matter Paul Samuelson, John Romer, Howard Sherman, Samuel Bowles, Herbert Gintis, or Stephen Resnick and Richard Wolff. One may interpret Alfred Marshall as a proto-neoclassical, as neoclassical, or as something more than neoclassical. One will "know" John Maynard Keynes depending on which interpretation of his *Treatise on Money* and *General Theory* one has been taught or come to adopt as one's own. Neoclassical economics will look different if it is defined by Armen Alchian's or by Tibor Scitovsky's understanding of it, just as institutional economics will look different if defined by those writing in the tradition of John R. Commons rather than those writing in the tradition of Clarence Ayres.

Perhaps no example is more telling of both heterogeneity of interpretation and its associated interpretive conflicts than Samuel Hollander's work on the classical economists and the relation of their ideas to neoclassical theory, and the criticism and attacks which his reinterpretation has engendered, and so on. Which of these or still other examples one centers on, and how they are interpreted, will determine one's understanding of the history of the discipline. The history of economic thought and, to no small degree, the content and meaning of the canon depend on which interpretive route is taken. Or one can take the aforementioned matrix approach to meaning.

The social construction of the canon

The politics of construction

What becomes canonical for economics as a whole depends on, first, the results of the process by which the canonical literature of the school which becomes dominant thereby becomes canonical for economics as a whole, and, second, the canonical interpretation given that literature.

Both doing economics and constructing an economics canon are political acts. By "political" I mean (as in my work in law and economics) having to do with the exercise of power and choice. The political nature of both economics and the economics canon resides in the resultant construction of a definition of economic reality as both putative knowledge and basis for policy. Part of the meaning and significance of economic theories – not least those given further sanction through canonization of text and/or author and/or interpretation – resides in their political attractiveness to certain interests and/or points of view.

One problem with having a canonical literature is the correlative obfuscation and neglect of literature not given canonical status. Concentration of attention on the canonical literature by specialists and nonspecialists, including specialists in other disciplines and the lay public, misrepresents the literature of the totality of the discipline. It does so in much the same way that concentration of attention on heads of schools and other luminaries obfuscates and neglects the vast array of practitioners and thereby misrepresents the work of the discipline or a school, including understating the diversity of formulation of doctrines within the school.[3] The same is true of canonical interpretations.

The discipline as a whole and each school within it are comprised of both the work of innovators and system-builders and the work of conventional and non-conventional practitioners. Just as different pictures of a distribution are formed by focusing on its mean or average, or by focusing on, say, the top decile, or the ratio of top to bottom decile, focusing on the most sophisticated authors and/or on the innovators and system-builders gives a different picture than that provided by focusing on the range of average or typical practitioners. Both the self-identity and social promotion of a discipline or a school inevitably tend to focus on what is considered "the best" or the most sophisticated rather than on the average, most common, most representative, or most naive. However this is an insufficient basis for understanding all of what goes on in or characterizes the discipline or school. It does say something about both the state of selectively and subjectively recognized "achievement" and the roles of status emulation and promotion. The same is true of canonical interpretations.

The significance of the canon for the historian of economic thought depends on context or purpose. For those interested in the history of the discipline, the canon has an indicative role, but much more is, or should be, involved in the history than the canon. For those interested in how the past led to the present and/or how the past can inform the present, the canon also has an indicative role, though presumably more can be involved than the canon. For those interested in the establishment of the current hegemonic school, the canon may be of particular, perhaps more or less exclusive, importance (but see below, regarding the canon as independent versus dependent variable). For those interested in the entire history of ideas and/or the history of economics (the former is an intellectual and the latter a sociological study), the canon is not only not enough but may itself be an object of inquiry.

Until relatively recently – the last two decades or so – much history of economic thought was Whiggish (viewing the past from the standpoint of the perspective of the currently hegemonic school or in terms of certain canonical interpretations largely driven by the perspective of that school) and presentist (viewing the past as prelude to the present and either ignoring or denigrating what was not prelude). Recently, many historians of economic thought have criticized and largely cast aside these approaches, except to consider them as part of the sociology of the discipline. They have examined the past on its own terms (or what is thought to be its own terms) and independent of whether or not it conflicted with the canon and/or the perspective of the currently hegemonic school, and so on.

Somewhat more pointedly, the history of thought is oriented less toward the record of progress from error to truth (with truth more or less the doctrines of the currently hegemonic school) and more toward a more complete account of the discipline's past; that is, from a seeming interment of past writers and ideas not consistent with the current mainstream, to a program recovering, understanding them and their place, and storing them, ready for future use as so much intellectual capital. In the former approach, ostensibly marginal figures are further marginalized. From the latter approach they are given serious recognition. In the sociology of economics approach, the processes and results of marginalization and recovery are treated as so many sociological phenomena. In neither of the latter approaches is the Whig/presentist definition of status taken at face value; in the sociological approach, the definitions are taken as objects of study.

Both self-fulfilling and instrumental

A self-fulfilling force is operative. If, say, D4 is the interpretation given, this will govern not only perceived identity but the training of future economists – their work, and thus what economics becomes, and their perception of what constitutes economics and the canon – in each respect giving effect to, reenforcing, and seemingly (further) warranting D4. If the potential domain and the potential evolutionary route is defined in terms of A, B, . . . N, then the adoption of D4 means that the development of economics is governed by the content of D4 and how D4 differs from other D than D4 and from all A, B, C, E, . . . N. This is accomplished in part through the hiring solely or largely of like-minded and/or like-trained colleagues and only them, and publishing only their work.

The self-fulfilling force is functional and sometimes intentional. Hagiography and Whig history are the product of selectively true belief, and they function to generate its perpetuation. Hagiography and Whig history are tools of social construction.

The question of truth

Literature which is given or somehow achieves canonical status often, perhaps generally, has the aura of possessing "truth." That such is both problematic and a conceit is apparent from the foregoing: which literature and which interpretation of a particular work becomes canonical depends upon the entire set of sociological forces which generates results. There is no necessary reason to believe, within either a dominant school or a nondominant, heterodox school, that a particular canon and its particular interpretation represent either accurate description or correct explanation, whatever the agreed-upon domain of social space to which the canonical literature is believed to apply, and how it applies (which are themselves products of social forces). Every hegemonic school and every hegemonic interpretation, along with their respective canonical literature and reading, is hubristically self-assigned the status of truth.

Still, one does not want to overdo the emphasis on truth status. Given the contradictions among canonical writings and among canonical authors, perhaps even among canonical interpretations, the notion of truth status may make little or no sense, unless one assumes considerable ignorance of the content of canonical works and the positions of canonical authors. Perhaps more important than truth status (though see later) is simple status in a world, and discipline, driven by status emulation. When one considers the diverse and conflicting theories and positions held by the Nobel Laureates in economics, status seems to be the more relevant context than putative truth.

Evolution of the canon

The canon in economics, like the canon in general literature, evolves (the argument of this section is an application and extension of Samuels 1991b). It is not written in stone. Its content is also, and most especially, an object of control, as different schools of economic thought and different interpretations of particular schools contest in order to influence, if not control, the future evolution of economics. An overt war over "the canon" has raged for some time in the field of general literature, as critics and defenders of the putatively great books of Western civilization have fought over the relevance of other literature. A much more subtle tension, if not war, has taken place both between and within the several schools comprising economics. Some figures in the general cultural war over the canon would exclude certain literature from the canon. In economics the same, or at least a similar, process has taken place through omission versus inclusion on reading lists of work representing schools and interpretations not favored by the instructor and through the hiring of likeminded and/or like-trained colleagues and only them. Instead of exposing students to the entire menu of the discipline, they are given only one diet. Most if not all combatants argue as if their canon, and their conceptions of the economy and of economics, are the canon and the conception, as if having unequivocal ontological status. Yet willy nilly each behaves thereby in a manner instrumental to the social construction of the canon and the discipline. All the recent controversy over, and the petitions and reports on, the training of graduate students in economics is, by almost any reckoning, controversy over the future social construction of economics and thereby of its canon. If canonical status within the discipline or a school connotes perennial importance, it is a function of the interests of practitioners and of how practitioners become practitioners.

The literature acquiring canonical status within a school and/or within economics as a whole is a function of the history and sociology of each school and of economics as a whole. This means that the same forces at work in both literature and culture as a whole, forces which include uncertain blends of deliberative and nondeliberative decision making, also operate within both each school of economics and economics as a whole. These forces include ideology and power, as well as status emulation.

Controversy over the canon is an ineluctable facet of the dynamics of cultural and intellectual change, in a world in which culture and the works of the intellect are admittedly artifacts and therefore the products of the social reconstruction of extant reality.

The western canon

What is commonly debated as the canon in literature is substantially European (inclusive of the ancient Near East and modern North America as well as, selectively, a few other areas). Modern western civilization is essentially European, and its notions of what civilization is all about are European and, increasingly, North American, especially US. Similarly the canon in economics is European and US and, within that category, neoclassical.

At the foundation of most if not all of relevant literary thought is the fundamental ethnocentric tautology of civilization and European. The hegemonic definitions of social reality and values are those of European/North American civilization. The fundamental conceptions of the humanities and social sciences in the west are largely western. They give effect to western modes of observation and interpretation. Similarly with economics: for many economists, to speak of economics is to speak of neoclassical economics and to speak of neoclassical economics is for them to exhaust economics; a fundamental tautology of economics and neoclassicism pervades. (Within some dissident schools the identification of their school, or a particular interpretation thereof, with economics is latent. In the former USSR, the identification and tautology was with some version of Marxian economics.)

The hegemonic definitions of economic reality and values are those of neoclassical economics, from both European and especially North American civilization. Neoclassical economics is an emanation from and self-definition of western civilization (no more and no less than Marxian economics); its hegemony in economics is hardly a surprise. Neoclassical economics is also a continuing reinforcer and shaper of western civilization. The fundamental conceptions constituting the discipline are largely neoclassical. They give effect to neoclassical modes of observation and interpretation. All this helps explain the content of the economics canon, though, with Marx and Keynes included therein, the canon is more catholic than neoclassical hegemony might lead one to expect.

The foregoing argument has been expressed in statements which are intentionally severely constrained; I have used "substantially," "essentially," and "largely." In matters of culture, this is in part because throughout its history what we have come to call western civilization – which has from time to time been associated with different areas within what we now call the west – has been both an exporter and an importer of cultural features to and from other parts of the planet. What we now call western civilization, and what western civilization has been at any point in time, is the changing amalgam of elements, some home-grown, some derived from elsewhere. The result has been an interpretive vision about man and society, a vision which has been both consequence and, as regulatory or socialization mechanism, cause.

Much the same is true of economics. Until relatively recently, economics has been pervasively if not "officially" recognized to be comprised of many schools of thought; it had been thus since at least the early nineteenth century. Neoclassical economics is often, and not entirely incorrectly, understood to have effectuated both a narrowing of "economic" categories and a model of a pure abstract economy. Neoclassical economics has evolved largely endogenously (on the basis of the interests of its members). Yet neoclassical economics has imported (often unconsciously) problems and theories from other schools. Furthermore, neoclassical economics has always been heterogeneous in character, the differences among some nominally neoclassical economists being almost as serious as the differences between neoclassical and other economists.

Both economics and neoclassical economics are heterogeneous, no less than western culture is heterogeneous. What appears homogeneous is so because we tend to identify the elements as parts of a cultural whole, or to identify the whole in terms of one of its parts. I shall return to the matter of heterogeneity later.

It also means that economics, not unlike western culture, has exhibited the problem of continuity versus change. At all times there have been forces operating to selectively change economics along with forces operating to selectively continue economics as practiced. The conflict of continuity and change is an inescapable facet of social, cultural and intellectual life. Some changes derive from pressures internal to the discipline and others from without. Continuity may signify only the continuation of the old modes of change, not fixity of social arrangements or of theory within the discipline (perceptions of "revolution" notwithstanding). The balancing, as it were, of continuity with change is very complex but it is an ongoing facet of individual, collective and intellectual life.

One facet of the conflict between continuity and change is the contest over particular elements of economics (general culture). Another is the contest over the structure of power, over the balancing of hierarchical and egalitarian tendencies within the discipline (culture). Still another is over operative values (pretensions to the status of a value-free science notwithstanding). One facet, therefore, of the multifaceted struggle for power in the discipline (culture) is participation in the contest over continuity versus change of all sorts of details, large and small, of the work and organizations of the discipline (culture).

There is therefore a struggle between interested groups within economics (general culture), each group being a culture carrier, over the continuity versus change of both economics and culture. Intermixed with that struggle is another, the contest between European and North American economics and economics as intellectualized in other cultures. Although this contest is in some respects nugatory, inasmuch as proximity and interaction necessarily engender import and export of cultural features, western economics has been highly resistant to influences from other areas of the world; indeed, the export of neoclassical economics to other parts of the world has been infinitely stronger. Correlative to the struggles over continuity versus change within western economics (general culture) and between western and other economics (cultures) is the comparable struggle within those other bodies of economic thought and cultures, in part over the impact of "modernization," which is often a euphemism for the spread of western economic culture and western economics.

I have witnessed Maoris of various ages in New Zealand and youths in Russia wearing sweat shirts with the logos of teams from the US National Football League. American culture, both general culture and entertainment culture in particular, constitute the US's major, not so invisible, export. Much the same is true of its neoclassical economics, indeed of Western economics more or less as a whole. Maoris in New Zealand colleges and universities are more than likely to read Western economics textbooks, to be more or less conversant with the western economics canon. It is telling that anticolonial and other so-called liberation movements around the world have taken at least part of their lead from Marx; his work ironically represents the canonical western export to the dispossessed and disaffected. For the most part, as they see it, it seems, they have no one else to whom to turn; mainstream western economics seems to them to offer subtle rationalizations and legitimations for the socioeconomic orders and elitist structures they find so repugnant.

The humanities and the social sciences, for us notably economics, are artifacts; they do not exist independent of mankind. They are both the product and the progenitor of culture. They are instruments in the social reconstruction of social reality. They are therefore the battleground for contests over the continuity versus change of social arrangements, over particular elements of culture, over power structure, over values. They are, not surprisingly, the battleground over "the canon."

Should a transcultural world civilization or society develop, there will still be conflicts over continuity versus change of particular features. The same is true of a transcultural economics and its canon.

Whether a transcultural economics will emerge is an interesting question. Some of the social sciences may presently be more advanced in this direction than economics, but the very meaning of "advanced" is itself a matter of debate. But should a transcultural economics develop, there will still be conflicts over continuity versus change of particular features.

Heterogeneity, conflict and evolution

Both economics and culture are, as a matter of putative fact, evolutionary in nature. Two features of western civilization, especially and increasingly so within the last millennium, have been both the recognition and the lauding of social and cultural evolution. There has therefore developed the curious and tendentious situation or dilemma that on the one hand cultural evolution is recognized and lauded, while on the other hand individuals and subgroups affirm particular values and arrangements to the point of absolutist legitimation and reification of those values and arrangements. These affirmations are due to diverse causes: ideological congruence, socialization, institutional identification, and, *inter alia*, personal identity formation. The dilemma is exacerbated by the situation that some people manifest a psychological propensity or need for determinacy and closure, and others a tolerance for ambiguity and openness. Whereas the former in general loathe any semblance of relativism, nihilism, heterodoxy, and diversity, the latter in general cannot fathom the opposite.[4]

All this certainly characterizes the discipline of economics, as well as general culture. Neoclassical economists have largely both avoided considerations of structural and systemic evolution and resisted challenges to their disciplinary hegemony. None of this is surprising, since, for example, neoclassical tools and research protocol focus on static problems, the neoclassical world view is congruent with the dominant cultural world view, and no one expects a hegemonic school to unilaterally abdicate its position.

Yet the received discipline (culture) and its canon are heterogeneous. They have heterogeneity which may be perceived and assessed from different perspectives or standpoints. And they have heterogeneity in part because certain literature which might seen suspect by some criteria is deemed to qualify by other criteria. That is why, for example, Marx and Keynes are included in the pantheon of canonical economists in an otherwise largely mainstream if not neoclassical population; not for their putative radicalism but because, first, they did have manifest impact, and, second, their mode of procedure – models more or less neatly stated in mathematical terms – was congruent with the familiar practices of neoclassical economists. However, while they are included today, they may not be given membership a century from now.

To speak, therefore, of "the canon" is to selectively specify what received economics (culture) is all about, to selectively reify an aspect of what is heterogeneous and in a transient stage of a process of evolution, to take a position on something which by its very nature is problematic. Above all it is to participate in the process of cultural change. To even identify "the canon" with certain works is to selectively identify and define received economics (culture) and thereby to contribute to its selective evolution along one channel or another.

The important matters are, first, that received economics (culture) and its canon is heterogeneous; second, that it is subject to change and third, that participation in the process of selective change is what affirmation and critique of "the canon" is all about.[5] Affirmation of certain adduced substantive content to "the canon" is affirmation of some elements of received economics (culture) and not others; it is affirmation of one interpretation of received economics (culture) and not others. Affirmation of "the canon" is always selective and contributes, intentionally or otherwise, to the reformation of economics (culture).

Consider that in every field of economics there have been diverse and often mutually exclusive schools of thought and lines of reasoning; that on every issue there are two, often more, quite different perspectives; – each distinctly, albeit differently, congruous with western economic culture. Consider that every element adduced to constitute "the canon" was often from the start a controversial contribution to economics (culture). Each was novel and incongruous with something; each represented change was in conflict with some facet of continuity. Each present element of "the canon" represents the accumulation of past innovations, somehow socially chosen to be innovations. At every point in time, certain advocates of the past, selectively perceived and propagated, desired to privilege certain preferred elements of the past so as to reinforce them against the new; and when the new became part of the past, for later generations, it too was selectively given privileged status by some.

Economics (culture) changes, and it changes in part through the continuous contest over continuity versus change of economics (culture), with each position (continuity and change) being selectively advanced, itself a mode of change. Reification and dereification of what is taken to be "the canon" are facets of this process. Economics (culture) is an artifact subject to continuing social reconstruction, a process in which reification of elements into putative absolutes is part of the contest over continuity and change of the discipline (culture) and is therefore part and parcel of the reconstruction process.

The fact is that even if we all affirmed our allegiance to "the economics canon," we would disagree in many ways as to what constituted economics or the canon. It may be that professional socialization or acculturation is so complete that we do not have to rely on overt affirmation of allegiance; surely such would be difficult in our society (though hegemony is enforced through examinations and hiring and publication policy). Even though economists are largely products of western economics and economic culture, we nonetheless disagree as to what constitutes economics (culture) or in the assemblage of agreed-upon details. Some disagreement will disappear and the rest may narrow through social control exercised by hegemonic interests. (Lest one think I am picking on neoclassicism, my argument must be understood to apply to any hegemonic school. Where applicable, one could use the example of Marxism in the former USSR) For a long time, some economists, motivated by a belief in Truth and "sound" policy and a desire for scientific and cultural status, have wished that economists would speak with one voice. This has been impossible to achieve.[6]

It may be noted that conflicts over economics, as in general culture, are often, at least some times, conflicts between intra-elite rivals (Vilfredo Pareto's circulation of the elite). In such a situation it is difficult if not impossible unequivocally to declare which conflict is preeminent, that over economics *per se* or that over power (or status). Different social science models (for example, idealist versus materialist models) define the situation quite differently.

Conclusion

The existence of a canon in economics (to the extent there is one, and abstracting from its heterogeneity) enables recognition of social control within the discipline and therefore of two rival formulations. One formulation affirms the organic integrity of received social arrangements, customs, and institutions in the discipline. It affirms certain doctrines to be truth. It also affirms the established disciplinary hierarchical elite as duly constituted authority. The other affirms the exercise of individual freedom of choice, subject to the presumably most minimal possible constraints. It also affirms governance as negative, as an evil even when necessary, as the source rather than the solution of problems, as something to be denigrated, debased, and avoided. Quite aside from the opportunistic use of these aprioristic doctrines as arguments by interested parties, these dichotomies represent combinations of conflicts between continuity and change and between freedom and control within the discipline. The approbation and disapprobation of continuity, change, freedom, and control in an institutionally and culturally heterogeneous discipline (society) are always a matter of selective perception.

Given the existence of a body of canonical literature – literature which (as earlier) is canonical because it has had a major impact on subsequent thought, action and events – that literature has further impact because it is taught as canon. Construction, or reconstruction, of the canon thereby becomes an object of influence as scholars interested in controlling the future development of the discipline (culture) endeavor to establish their preferred literature in place of others. On the one hand, canons are put together to help us make sense of how we got to where we are in the present, which is to say, they evolve. On the other hand, not all the evolution is nondeliberative; some is deliberative, as to inclusion and exclusion. Canons help set the agenda for current work. Those who want to influence or control that agenda – and therefore the future of the discipline – will both deliberatively and nondeliberatively work to reconstitute the canon.

Canons, therefore, obviously arise and evolve in a process of cumulative causation. Among the operative variables are the further impacts of canonical literature which is canonical in part because of their past impacts and in part because of the exercise of disciplinary power, both deliberative and nondeliberative, in elevating certain literature and not others to canonical status, which is one set of facets in comprehending their initial impact. For canons to exist is probably inevitable. The questions remaining concern the determination of their content and the mode of such determination.

Enlightenment values are an important part of the heritage of western culture in general and economics in particular: a zone of individual autonomy relative to state and society; institutional pluralism; empiricism; free expression; secularism, that is, antagonism to ideological and other pretense and superstition; skepticism; rule of law; liberal democracy; preoccupation with material living conditions; and so on. Yet none of these values is uniquely and unequivocally conclusively dispositive of particular issues in either general society or in organized economics, and these are not the only values constituting the cultural heritage of western society. Their opposites ("some considerations ought not to be discussed in public"; maintenance of established authoritative if not authoritarian institutions; etc.) often enter discussion and policy. (One irony resides in the simultaneous affirmation of freedom of choice and practice of elitism in mainstream economics, the latter rationalized by identifying hegemonic doctrines as "truth.")

Both Enlightenment and anti-Enlightenment values participate in the grand social valuational process of the discipline (culture) in which values are defined, juxtaposed to each other, explored, and reevaluated – a process in which the conflict between continuity and change is addressed both directly and obliquely through a process which itself manifests the conflict. Beliefs in pluralism, candor, tolerance, and constructive critique from within neither unequivocally resolve the conflicts between continuity and change and between hierarchy and equality nor are they unequivocally held.

Concern over maintenance of "the canon" in the university classroom, as well as in the larger society, can properly take the form of affirmations of particular specifications of "the canon." However it can also take the form of promoting the marketplace of ideas coupled with deep-level understanding of the fundamental issues with respect to which different formulations of "the canon" take positions, teaching a broad or full menu and not a slim diet. One can emphasize substance or process. It is the case, of course, that certain attitudes toward "the canon" are more prescriptive, and their advocates see in such a perspective a relativism and nihilism that must be countered and overcome, lest the integrity of western culture be compromised.

One source of these attitudes resides in the almost ubiquitous tendency to use the canon to render absolute that which is relative. Another is the tendency to employ words designating categories as if they were self-subsistent and uniquely dispositive of the issues involved. (Other sources abound, including the functionality of myths for ruling elites.) The former, and perhaps also the latter, is itself due in part to the desire for an apolitical world and reflects the mind set which requires determinacy and closure and is unable to tolerate open-endedness, ambiguity and recognition of both selective perception, social constructivism, and the need to work things out – all given effect and channeled by the socially constructed canon. Among the words I have in mind are justice, good, bad, rationality, morality, property (and other) rights, efficiency and so on. Our interpretations of these terms both help determine their substantive content and conflate "is" and "ought" (Samuels 1992) with regard to what we seemingly purport only to describe, in both respects the selective perception which both forms and is formed by our larger cognitive frameworks.[7]

This brings me to the penultimate matter. Canons both can and cannot be legislated by academic high priests. Canons evolve largely nondeliberatively, in the manner of organic development underscored by Adam Smith, Adam Ferguson, Carl Menger and Friedrich von Hayek, and in that respect are not legislated. However canons are also profoundly influenced by power structure and decisions made on the basis of power and with future power in mind. Decisions as to the content of reading lists, journal acceptances, and faculty hiring help govern both who and what writings will count in the future. Indeed, while most discussion of "the canon" is either backward-looking or presentist, the critical matter is decisions made today which, in the aggregate, determine the structure of the discipline and the content of the canon in the future. The resolution of conflicts between continuity and change and between hierarchy and equality in economics will determine the structure and content of economics in the future and thereby of the economics canon. That is, in addition to status emulation and career advancement in the present, what the conflicts are all about. Such conflicts are fundamental to the human predicament and constitute some of the facts of social life which most arguments over "the canon" fail to recognize and articulate, all the while participating in and contributing to the fundamental social and disciplinary processes involved.

For "the canon" is arguably much more a matter of the sociology of economics than of economic Truth. It is the working out of the sociology of economics which governs the economics canon. What is worked out is whose economics the discipline of economics is to represent and teach. The answer to this question cannot be set down once and for all time; it must be worked out – and positions as to what constitutes the canon are contributions to the process of working this out.

Because the subject is so important, in concluding this essay I turn normative. First, notwithstanding the rather cold-blooded way in which the subject of the canon is approached earlier, canons perform functions and, given that performance, are, at a certain level of abstraction, "good." Canons serve the function of helping to crystallize the doctrinal and valuational content of a discipline (culture), thereby serving a pedagogical role. Canons in some sense are perhaps inevitable.

Second, the question must arise as to the exclusivity or nonexclusivity with which a particular canon is held. Given that the very role of a canon is to elevate certain literature, and therefore certain practices and conceptions of the discipline (culture) over others, the existence of a canon can have a putatively negative influence if used to rule non-canonical thinking out of disciplinary bounds.

Third, one function of having a canon is particularly laudatory and to be especially noticed. Although having a canon can unduly narrow perspective, perception and understanding, having a canon of old, established works serves as a reminder that economics encompasses more than is presently pursued and unduly narrowly studied. Such a canon can inform and enrich present studies, but it can especially remind us that there both has been and is more to economics than is presently hegemonically recognized.

What is at stake, in my opinion, is not the integrity of some presumptive content of the canon of either economics or western culture but the nature of economics and by extension the larger society itself. Is a pluralist and open economics possible and desirable? If we proceed on the basis of a negative answer to that question, we may be undermining the vitality of economics, the Enlightenment values which economics has absorbed, and the larger society. There is a considerable difference between the university classroom and discipline in which the high priest preaches absolute truth and reifies certain economic and social arrangements, and the university classroom and discipline in which the student is taught the fundamental problems with respect to which the theories of all schools, the preachings of all economic ideologies, and all policy programs take positions, as well as the contents of the theories, ideologies and policies themselves. If there is to be a canon, therefore, let it be a diverse and open one.[8] If there is to be a canonical interpretation, too, let those who honor and use it appreciate that they are thereby taking a position as to which interpretation is to count.

Notes

I am considerably indebted to Jeff Biddle, Steven Medema and Paul Strassmann for comments on an early draft of this essay.

1 Questions about the existence and specific content of the canon are similar to those about the existence and specific content of a (hegemonic or nonhegemonic) school. In this essay I assume the existence of both an economics canon and a hegemonic school, but also consider questions of heterogeneity.
2 The sources and significance of heterogeneity are discussed in Samuels 1991a, 1995a, 1995c, 1997a and 1997b. In general, the economy is sufficiently multifaceted that it can be given different interpretations, and people do in fact examine it from different perspectives and do interpret it differently.
3 The situation in general is aptly summarized by Ylikoski:

> there are non-cognitive factors working in science. Sociological studies on both contemporary science and the history of science show that scientists do not live up to their idealized public image. Scientists are certainly interested in other things than the truth. They have all kinds of non-cognitive commitments and interests. The interests vary from different kinds of purely extra-scientific interests to professional interests that are internal to science. Even if, as one might hopefully suggest, all scientists had a common interest in finding the truth, they have very different conceptions of how to get there. And of course truth is not the only interest. There is of course much controversy about interests and their consequences in science, but their existence is not in question. One can say that scientists are interested, which contradicts the usual picture of disinterested scientists.
>
> (Ylikoski 1995: 35)

4 Interestingly, one reaction to this essay has been discomfort with the picture of fluidity and problematicity it draws of the economics canon and thereby of economics. One person found it difficult to accept the enormous variability of specification of economic concepts; another wished to establish mathematics (if not also physics), at least, as a harder discipline not manifesting the conflicts and ambiguities of a heterogeneous economics – a determination which is simply not warranted.
5 Some sources of change in economics are internal to the discipline and others are external. The forces determining when a problem becomes a problem for study, and when something does or does not "work," are vast.
6 Writing in his Diary for April 14 1891 about the prospects for a syllabus in political economy for candidates for the open competition for Indian Civil Service positions, John Neville Keynes noted that "We are so little agreed among ourselves that I do not think much will come of it." Whitaker (1996, vol. 2: 32). The "we" also included Alfred Marshall, James Bonar, H. S. Foxwell and J. S. Nicholson.
7 The inability of many people to accept the idea of social constructivism is particularly ironic. If social constructivism were false, and if government were not to be used to socially construct along desired lines, why bother, not only with electing representatives sharing our desired values but with arguing about government at all?
8 The case for various modes of disciplinary pluralism *per se* is made in Samuels 1991a, 1992, 1993, 1993–4, 1995a, 1995b, 1996, 1997a, 1997b.

References

Samuels, W. J. (1974) "The History of Economic Thought as Intellectual History," *History of Political Economy* 6 (Fall): 305–23.

—— (1990) "On Causation, the Principle of Unforeseen Consequences, and the Matrix of Human Action: The Case of the Iraqi Conquest of Kuwait," *Methodus* 2 (December): 9–15.

—— (1991a) "'Truth' and 'Discourse' in the Social Construction of Economic Reality: An Essay on the Relation of Knowledge to Socioeconomic Policy," *Journal of Post Keynesian Economics* 13 (Summer): 511–24.

—— (1991b) "Dynamics of Cultural Change," *Society* 29 (November/December): 23–6.

—— (1992) "The Pervasive Proposition, 'What Is, Is and Ought to Be': A Critique," in W. S. Millberg (ed.), *The Megacorp and Macrodynamics: Essays in Memory of Alfred Eichner*, Armonk, N.Y.: M. E. Sharpe: 273–85.

—— (1993) "In (Limited but Affirmative) Defence of Nihilism," *Review of Political Economy* 5 (April): 236–44.

—— (1993–4) "On the Conclusivity of Certain Lines of Reasoning in Economic Policy Analysis," *Journal of Post Keynesian Economics* 16 (Winter): 241–9.

—— (1995a) "Richard Reeve's Study of the Kennedy Presidency: Implications for Studying Economics and the History of Economic Thought," *History of Economics Review* 23 (Winter): 108–16.

—— (1995b) "The Making of a Relativist and Social Constructivist: Remarks upon Receiving the Veblen-Commons Award," *Journal of Economic Issues*, 29 (June): 343–58.

—— (1995c) "Some Thoughts on Multiplicity," *Journal Of Economic Methodology* 2 (December): 287–91.

—— (1996) "Postmodernism and Knowledge: A Middlebrow View," *Journal of Economic Methodology* 3 (June): 113–20

—— (1997a) "The Case for Methodological Pluralism," in A. Salanti and E. Screpanti (eds), *Pluralism in Economics*, Brookfield, Vt.: Edward Elgar: 67–79.

—— (1997b) "Methodological Pluralism: The Discussion in Retrospect," in A. Salanti and E. Screpanti (eds), *Pluralism in Economics*, Brookfield, Vt.: Edward Elgar: 308–9.

Whitaker, J. K. (ed.) (1996) *The Correspondence of Alfred Marshall, Economist*, vol. 2, New York: Cambridge University Press.

Ylikoski, P. (1995) "The Invisible Hand in Science," *Science Studies* 8: 32–43.

Appendix

The chapters in this book were among papers presented at a conference held to honor Samuel Hollander, as he retired from the Department of Economics at the University of Toronto. Among the tributes Samuel Hollander received was that of Paul Samuelson:

Samuel Hollander, our master and co-worker

Paul A. Samuelson

Of Works and the Man I sing. But for a scholar like Samuel Hollander, to sing of his work is to praise *him* as a scholar. The immortality a thinker can have – and the only immortality worth having – lives on in the value-added that we each contribute to the accumulating body of knowledge.

I have known most of the great economists since 1930. They have taught me. I have taught some of them. I could contrive to rank them in a strong transitive ordering. My motto has been . . . nay, my experience has been: "Chocolate is good. Good too is herring. How good then must be chocolate and herring." The only thing better than a Hollander article is a Hollander book. Or do I have it vice versa?

When John Stuart Mill wished to analyze bilateral monopoly, he sought for the wildest spot in the Victorian world in order to discuss how much an explorer going into the bush would give for a musical snuff box to a veteran returning toward London civilization. The woods north of Minneapolis and south of Winnipeg, Mill thought to be the wildest place imaginable. (I may digress to add that those International Falls still are untamed wilderness.) But Toronto, our Toronto, is not that far away. Reading Sam Hollander's 1995 autobiography, I was struck again by the remarkable Canadian tradition of importing English scientists and giving them their first chance to develop individual genius. Sir William Osler in medicine at McGill; Ernest Rutherford in physics, from New Zealand on to the home counties before moving to Montreal is another example. And scientist Samuel Hollander, from LSE to Princeton to Toronto, is just one more instance of what I hope will be a continuing tradition.

Did you notice that I applied the noun "scientist" to this World Master of the History of Thought? That was no slip of my pen. To analyze cogently, fairly and correctly the structure of classical economic studies accords completely with my understanding of what constitutes science and scientific method.

Jacob Viner was my teacher. Viner was a great theorist; Viner was a great expert on international economics; Viner was a great historian of economic thought. Frank Knight was Chicago's other great master when I was an undergraduate there in the early 1930s. Knight was a great theorist; Knight was a subtle philosopher of the social sciences; Knight also wrote sparingly on the history of economics. As a juvenile admirer, I scored Knight on Ricardo much the way I scored Viner on Ricardo. Now I note the difference between the learned sage and the hit-and-run amateur. Samuel Hollander is not your run of the mill *dilettante*. In his field he is a Viner not a Knight.

Because I am an absent-minded professor, I want right now to accomplish the task I am setting out for myself in today's lecture. I am here to make a nomination for a new member to the venerable Hall of Fame for Doctrinal History. Along with Edwin Cannan, Frank Taussig, Edwin R. A. Seligman, Jacob Viner, Piero Sraffa, Lionel Robbins, and Joseph Schumpeter, and with another (secondary), Jacob Hollander, I want to nominate our Samuel for this immortal Hall of Fame. Since it is *my* Hall of Fame, nomination by me is equivalent to *election*. So consider it done.

The quadriad of masterpieces – books by Professor Hollander on Smith, Ricardo, the young Mill and Malthus – makes this choice a lay-down hand. If Dr Hollander later gilds the lily with a masterpiece on Karl Marx, well that will only gild the lily.

My praise is perforce fulsome praise. All of you here in this audience realize that, for once, a commemorative speaker is spouting the unvarnished truth. Our Master has earned from us our just appreciation.

In concluding I want to strike a different note. The discipline of doctrinal analytic history lives on in a lean season. We are gathered as a band of beleaguered martyrs. Topological dynamics and stochastic matrices vie for research grants and these days elbow out the humanist scholars.

When I think of Sam Hollander, I am reminded of Frank Sinatra. The audience goes wild when they hear Sinatra sing about doing things His Way. At the end of the day, Samuel Hollander can say to himself and say to the world

> I kept the faith
> I passed on the torch of learning and truth to a devoted band of student scholars.
> We advanced the corpus of knowledge together and enriched the canon.

Therefore, I propose on behalf of all of us the toast.

> Hail Apollo!
> Hail Solon!
> Hail Hollander!

Samuel Hollander responds

Dear Paul; if only 10 percent of what you said was accurate I would be a happy man. But I am not going to argue with you.

Imagine, if you will, a life tree – a life tree such as I have, in fact, in my possession. On the top line there is a reference to Hillel the Elder, circa 30 BC to AD 10. We are not absolutely sure of the ten generations going back from 1000, but tradition has it that he is an ancestor and it is quite a firmly established tradition. Now given this history, it is difficult for me to take the new millennium very seriously. There is a reference here that he had eighty students. Thirty of them were so splendid that they had the great merit that the sun should stay and move in the sky because of their greatness, and thirty of them had the great merit that the spirit of God would pass over them, and then there were twenty that were just average. The least of them was an expert in numerology, and could also understand angels and ghosts and speak to trees and understand what they said. That was the least of the students. The rest of them could do all this, plus some. Now I have only 10 percent of the students. Only 10 percent unless I include my undergraduate students. However there are a number of differences where I think I outshine him.

First of all, well over 50 percent of my students are female, versus zero. This is enormous progress in 2,000 years. Second, my students can also do weird and wonderful things. One of them is an expert in the history of science, and I mean an expert. Several of them are experts in philosophy. All are expert in mathematics and economics. Every one of them! The modern day numerologist. Or as my teacher Lionel Robbins would say, "Acrobats, acrobats in the upper stratosphere!" One has read all the papers collected in the handout today. Above all there is no record in the Talmud or the glossaries or commentaries that Hillel's students arranged a grander kind of conference.

All of this takes me to the gist of my remarks, the focus of this lengthy introduction which is a serious one. To express my appreciation, and I use the loose word for I cannot find the right one, to Evelyn Forget and Sandy Peart for all that they have done from afar and, of course, for all the initiative taken in the first place. I am quite overwhelmed by this. I believe it is fair to say that this is a unique manifestation of affection and, if you will permit me to say so, of loyalty. I don't think it is possible for most professors, for many professors, to say at the end of a long – excuse me, I take that back – to say after thirty-five years, that they have received such an affectionate treatment from their students. Also my gratitude to Karolina Sygula, for the local arrangements undertaken with exquisite sensitivity. These friends have turned a winter of discontent into glorious summer.

The presence of our guest speaker, our master of ceremonies, so many friends and family from near and far, the enormous honor that I should say I do not deserve. (My late mother would expect me to.) Now my nearest guests are my literal next door neighbors to the south. I hear they have not brought their dog Chips with them. He must have had another engagement. Pity. I might have use for him. The furthest of my friends are from Japan and New Zealand. The largest single contingent is from France. *Et vous êtes bienvenu.* The next largest contingent is from Italy. I'll just say, "You're welcome."

I recall that I was in Italy and Alessandro Roncaglia was organizing interviews on the Italian television. It was quite a long time and it was quite difficult. When I came back I told people I had been on Italian television. They said, "How was your Italian?" I replied, "It was in English. Had it been in Italian, they would have had to have dubbed it." So I won't try to translate. I am particularly delighted with our Italian Sraffian whom I just mentioned. As he put it, I am his best enemy. Because there is something serious in that. It is perfectly possible to take sharply divergent positions on technical matters and yet remain excellent friends. This is the spirit of the relationship between Malthus and Ricardo. Everyone – well, not everyone – most people will recognize Malthus's letter from Ricardo penned only a few days, literally a few days, before he died: "And now my dear Malthus, I have done. We each retain our own opinions. These discussions, however, never influence our friendship. I should not like you more than I do if you agreed in your opinion with me." Fewer are familiar with Malthus's own comments about Ricardo after he had died.

> I never loved anybody out of my own family so much. Our interchange of opinions was so unreserved and the object after which we were both inquiring was so entirely the truth and nothing else, that I cannot but think that sooner or later we must have agreed.

I have my doubts about that, however. I trust that someday we will continue this?

When I look back over some three and a half decades, I am amazed not only by some of the harsh criticisms of my work, and I do not mean Alessandro Roncaglia's here. His were criticisms, but never harsh. Of the harsh criticisms, they do not unfortunately have the qualities of the Ricardo-Malthus relationship. I am amazed by that, but also by the extraordinary disparity of opinion. The disparity of opinion really surprises me. For example, one referee of a project for which I requested research funds tried to convince the prospective grantors not to make the modest award on the grounds of the total rejection of my earlier book on Ricardo. Yet we have the late Lord Robbins' opinion, expressed to his students twenty years ago but only recently published by Princeton. My Ricardo, he wrote, "is a book to put an end to prayer about Ricardo." So I have to live with these diverse opinions.

I mention Lionel Robbins because he has provided moral support for me since 1958 in my final undergraduate year, and he continues to do so. When I read what he had written in these lectures as soon as they were published, two or three weeks ago, the emotion that I felt is not to be described.

Now, because this is a happy occasion, I want to concentrate on the truly hostile reviews, but before I do that, I might mention that my graduate students have themselves suffered a little. Here are two comments by a referee of an ex-student's article for a journal. He or she knows who it is. "I do grow weary of these Hollander students who have imbibed from their master the principle that their ignorance of the history of science is actually a warrant to assert that the history of science is unimportant to economics." Here is another one: "This author demonstrated elsewhere that if the quote offends they merely pluck it from conscience." Now all this is very strange. I always thought that I practiced the rule: "Be one's own worst enemy." In any event, as Antonia Fraser wrote in her book on Cromwell, "No man is a stranger to self doubt," and what's with this "master" business? Still, I am gratified that my students did not hold it against me that I am responsible for their occasional rejection.

I focus on hostile reactions for a more specific reason. It may turn out to be a source of financial gain. A retiree cannot afford to sneeze at these matters. Thus one reviewer wrote that, "reading Hollander is always irritating and sometimes dangerous to one's mental health." Now, I have in hand a journal, *US Cavalry, The World's Finest Military Equipment.* I don't subscribe, of course, but my wife does. What she would want with commando training weapons, or a Tiger Tank model, I have not dared ask. The point, though, is this: when I read in this journal of the Intimidator Stun Gun that it can cause a dazed mental state, loss of muscle control and disorientation and that the ultrasonic deterrent may cause aggressive dogs to become dazed, confused and retreat to a safe distance, I thought for a moment I was reading a review. Then it came to me: if I could miniaturize these books, I might make a fortune!

And now a perfect reason to focus on the confused state of mind my work allegedly engenders, takes us back to the imaginary life chart. In the middle there, you would find in the fifteenth and sixteenth centuries are two individuals; a certain Rabbi Jehiel Luria the second and a Rabbi Israel Isserlein of Krakow and his wife Dinah. We share common ancestry, Marx and I. Reading Marx has the same effect for many as reading my work. So I am well placed to complete my fifth volume in the series *Classical Political Economy.* I say complete, not start, because I am on my way. The point is that it takes one to know one, and that is what I, in fact, propose to do in the immediate future.

Sir John Hicks wrote to me back in 1972 the following, "I hope I shall live long enough to read your Marx volume." I regret, Sir John, the delay. Ricardo, Mill and Malthus got in the way, but I do have the dedicatee. My late friend Martin Bronfenbrenner also gives me courage. He wrote the following two years ago: "After twelve years as Professor Demeritus at Duke and five in similar incapacity elsewhere, I sometimes ask prospective fellow retirees what they propose to do with their lives after catching all those fish, playing all that golf and/or chess, and visiting all the tourist traps of all six continents. But with you," he wrote to me, "there will be no problem. You will just go on indefinitely, between visits to doctors and the hospital, on what some call scholarship sublime, and others call idle curiosity, to the last syllable of recorded time. Congratulations."

Thank you Martin. I had a wonderful correspondence with him over years and years, and would like to reiterate the tribute to him that I prepared last summer.

There is a problem that I am facing: I am not retiring. I feel that I have enjoyed dinner under false pretences. Like John Mortimer's Horace Rumpole that some might recognize, when his law firm made a great dinner for him on the assumption that he was going to retire and gave him wonderful presents. So he pocketed the presents, drank the excellent wine, and it wasn't Thames Embankment Wine, it was good wine. And then he announced that since his colleagues in chambers showed such affection for him, he wouldn't retire. I am not retiring in the sense that whatever happens – about which I shall say a few words in a moment – I pray that I will continue my work as if nothing has changed at all.

Can a historian of economics who questions the Marx-Sraffa reading of the history of economics do a fair job on Marx? I think so. Years ago I had a pleasing review in an East German journal, probably no longer extant. The author attacks distortions which are standard in the *bourgeois* literature on Adam Smith, and he adds, "They do not entirely govern the history of classical economic theory. There can be found serious analysis. In the first rank of these exceptions, belongs Samuel Hollander's *Economics of Adam Smith* which must be included amongst the best *bourgeois* studies." Exactly what it was that appealed to the reviewer I do not now recall, but this expression of confidence from the past and another world that no longer exists, means a great deal to me as I approach my long delayed task to deal with my distant cousin.

However do not the current or recent Chinese and Russian attempts to transfer from central control to market capitalism constitute such a massive and empirical refutation of Marx's prediction as to undermine all interest in the model? Not at all. The predictive power of Marx's model was, so to speak, undermined by the very establishment of the Soviet command system some three-quarters of a century ago. Marx never expected what happened in 1917. He would have expected the collapse of the USSR for that very reason. That is the other side of the coin. For, of course, the story is not over yet. The point is that the absence of Marx's picture from Red Square is no reason for historians of Marxist thought to alter their research programs. And, refuted or not, logically or empirically, Marx is in an old Scottish tradition that merits continued investigation. And there are fascinating comparisons and contrasts that can be made. Malthus, after all, predicted in a purely mental exercise that the adoption of communism would occur first in economies under pressure of scarcity. By the way, Marx himself believed one would only get true, permanent communism after the collapse of capitalism. All this remains as important as ever and I feel excited by the prospect of continuing my work.

Why have I chosen to retire from the University of Toronto when there is so much to be done and when I still have the enthusiasm to carry on? Maybe it is time for you all to doze off while I come to sensitive matters. Not for an extended time, perhaps just forty winks. I say these things because I feel them strongly and because this is a group of historian economists. Largely this is why this conference exists.

I discuss the matter of the departmental policy regarding the abandonment of the requirement for Ph.D. students to take a history course. In line with elsewhere, this rather arcane condition was to be abandoned. It wasn't a requirement to take a course in the history of economic thought only. It was either history of economic thought or economic history. Back in the past the department heard the word "history" and thought, "oh well, one or the other." Of course they ought both have been required. Although I was the professor most affected by the change, no opportunity was provided for debate, and this, despite a 1982 commitment when economics split from political science. It was, and it is, my belief that the decision was an error. I don't mean an error for me. I mean an intellectual error. The largest of Canada's economics departments should build on its strengths and follow a distinct line. And this without diluting the essential technical training required of an economist in this day and age.

Actually Martin Bronfenbrenner tried to convince me that I was wrong. Excuse Martin's strong language, I'm quoting:

> I think we disagree on the advisability of subjecting the desiccated robots and computer jockeys who are the graduate student body to the horrors of doctrinal history and textual exegesis. If their little worlds are to be bounded by a few computer programs to do their thinking for them, all the rest is pure sadistic torture, like the famous language requirement, only more so.

Strong language, indeed. I agree, up to a point only.

Certainly a *pro forma* course by a disinterested professor corralled from important tasks and using some imported textbook is of no use whatsoever. Certainly better get rid of such a course, but students at the University of Toronto were getting a very different sort of course. My students will assure you of that. Here I am compelled to say, so there should be no misunderstanding, that my personal relations with my department, faculty and I might add the staff, are warm and friendly. I sense a degree of sympathy and affection on the part of many, and I fully reciprocate.

Now, notwithstanding all this, I might have stayed on, but I found myself caught up in a single issue that a voluntary early retirement package could be picked up by midnight on a certain date or forever surrendered. There was no opportunity whatsoever to discuss the intellectual or scholarly costs either to me or to the university, and notwithstanding my university professorship. Now I am fully aware that this is pretty common worldwide. I do wish the University of Toronto well, for it has given me the opportunity to flourish for three and a half decades, and for that I am and always will be grateful. It is only that it might have been nice for me, as the university marches into the long run under a frayed banner declaring "Great Minds for a Great Future" – you will see them flying down St George Street all the way – to have contributed towards that future. Some input from the old guard might have helped the institution, especially since university professors were always led to believe that their judgement was valued.

For example, I might have recommended a little theoretical activity on the basis of some clear principle in any housecleaning, in any great budget cuts. Malthus touched on this matter. As the best means of proceeding to a reformed system, he wrote as follows:

The question between the theorist who calls himself practical and a genuine theorist is whether he should prompt us to look in all the holes and corners of workhouses, and content ourselves with mounting [mounting means whining or punishing] the parish officers for their waste of cheese parings and candle ends. Or whether to recur to general principles.

(Malthus [1798] 1986: 558–9)

In fact, in the recent episode, the order came down from on high, from our political masters, to cut down on the cheese and candles. This was done by a process of slashing and burning. I suspect at an unnecessarily high cost, but only the future will tell. I would press the University, indeed any university, to try and decide what sort of institution it is. And what it is it thinks it is trying to produce. In this regard I find a paradoxical situation exists, and it needs looking into. I refer to the merit award process and all of that.

Most of you will know that the administration requires professors to go through an annual review of their output in excruciating detail, specifying books, chapters in books, articles (those that are refereed, those that are not refereed). I have serious doubts about the meaningfulness of the system, especially in light of the fact that the administration pays such serious consideration to outside offices, suggesting a preoccupation with a sniffing out of economic relics. Now the model for sniffing out relics is the economist's bread and butter – opportunity costs, all of that – it is the market model, but the model for recognizing merit is something else. It shows the concern for morale, for fairness, for the relations between individuals, and for the relation between an individual and the institution. I am concerned, and I am talking quite generally here, that the annual exercise is a facade, counting for little except under threat of departure to major centers. It reflects something of an inferiority complex, if one believes that the only people worthwhile are those who are sought after by the Harvards. Adam Smith has much to say on this. I forgot why I brought John Stuart Mill with me, but I see I have a note here. I'd like to read a poem by John Stuart Mill. He wrote this in the late-1860s:

> The founders of political economy have left two sorts of disciples – those who have inherited their methods and those who have stopped short at their phrases. Those who have carried on the work of the masters and those who think their masters had left them no work to do. The former follow the example of their teachers in endeavouring to discern what principles are applicable to a particular case by analyzing circumstances. The latter believe themselves to be provided with a set of catchwords which they mistake for principles. "Free Trade", "Freedom of Contract", "Competition", "Demand and Supply", etc., etc.
>
> (Mill 1967: 671)

The art of being an economist is to know when to apply economic reasoning. I don't think that there are many departments that teach the art of economics. Now for me these issues are purely academic, and I've had to come to earth after all this musing. Please wake up. Forget you were dozing.

I shall, in fact, miss the University. One of its agencies, in particular, deserves mention. It is the University's "Tenure Appeals Committee." I congratulate the University for having years ago set up and supported the structure whereby to correct potential injustices related to the denial of tenure. During my fifteen-year involvement with the Tenure Appeals Committee, I have been amazed by the dedication and utter honesty of its members, some of whom are here tonight, and by their concern to do justice to both individual and institution, for the two objectives are compatible. I pray that the committee will continue in its independent role long into the future.

There is another agency or institution – I don't know the legal relationship – but I want to say a word on it. It is the University of Toronto Press. To my mind the Press stands among the very best in their beautiful production, and more importantly perhaps, they stand also at the very top in their old-fashioned concern for accuracy in proofreading their work and the like. You would be surprised at some of the great names in publishing who do not pay adequate attention to those things. Above all though, I appreciate the University Press because they have allowed me (and no other press would do so), thousand-page books. Now perhaps they are less liberal than it appears. I have the following anecdote to tell you, which is true.

I went away for two weeks on a vacation and when I came back – I had finished the bulk of my Malthus, but I had left certain materials that were going to be two additional chapters on the window ledge – when I came back, I was shocked to see that they had been nibbled away and eaten up, it turns out, by squirrels that had entered through my Italian-made air conditioner. Now it is possible that the Press is less liberal than it appears. Could it be that they have a Squirrel Department to deal with authors like me? But at least I felt that someone liked my research. Now these stray documents and also the letters and much else are all to be found in the National Archives in Ottawa.

And that reminds me that it will be Yom Kippur in two days. At the evening service we read in the confessional that God tests us, and tests and examines archives. I'm not sure He will be too impressed by my collection. He may be amused. And we also read the following: "What can we say before You, our God and God of our forefathers? Are not all the heroes like nothing before You? The famous as if they have never existed? The wise as if devoid of wisdom and the perceptive as if devoid of intelligence?" Wait a minute, there's a footnote: "This passage does not apply to out-of-town guests."

I would not like the Creator to get the wrong idea from my remarks tonight. Let me assure Him that I do not take myself too seriously. It is only that if we decide to play the game, we must do it properly or not at all.

Now I come back to my imaginary Life Chart. There is a great empty space down here. I've said nothing about the most important part of my chart. Whatever it is that I plan to accomplish would have been – I am absolutely convinced – aborted years ago, or not been commenced, without the support of my wife, my companion and my help-mate, Arlette.

I admire (I have to come back to myself) the perspicuity and far-sightedness of that twenty year-old in Paris, forty-one years ago, when he decided to propose. Economists sometimes get their own house right. Now I will ask you to be upstanding for Arlette.

I have one question my dear: What do you do with those Commando-in-training weapons?

Among the honored guests at the dinner, were Samuel Hollander's two children, Isaac and Frances.

Isaac Hollander

There is a saying that goes some distance in explaining the quality of my father's scholarship: "If you have nothing to say, don't say it." This dictum was voiced at home quite often. I'm not about to abuse its wisdom on this particular occasion. So to be on the safe side, I have taken the liberty of drawing freely on my father's own biographical background. My concerns are with the intimate rather than the academic. Given, I will tell the truth but not the whole truth, certainly not in five minutes.

I've chosen to start with the beginning and with my first conscious religious experience. That experience did not occur in a milk delivery van. It took place outside a mosque somewhere in downtown Toronto with my mother explaining to me that I may have prayed myself like the other congregants if necessary. This was because both Jerusalem and Mecca were somewhere behind the same wall. Not much later I found myself at the school of my father's childhood teacher in London translating some analytical texts from Aramaic into Yiddish, but not before I was given a good idea of what Florence had to offer a nine year-old boy. Now here is a pattern I cannot quite appreciate, but I am trying to. So much so that my own search occurs around meeting places of some of these cultures.

My parents' home was never very competitive in the area of creature comforts. Their 1964 Valiant held up til 1973; their 1974 Beetle til 1983; the 1983 Tercel only this week faces the speedways of southeast Michigan. Their vintage black and white TV set lasted up until the early 1990s when it succumbed with the original channel dial. It finally submitted to the pair of pliers used to turn it. So did the fridge, which for about nineteen years, would close only if kicked in the right place. That, and the stove, were the only electrical appliances to be found in the kitchen. A stereo was first purchased in the mid-1980s. It sat in the living room. As to the living room. . . .

Rather it is the exceptional blend of culture and morality, and of intellect and honesty, to be found at my parents' home which attracted the people who chose to drop by on Saturdays or on other days for a drink or a meal. It is not to suggest, of course, that the meals themselves were not attractive, or the drink. Such was the case wherever they set up house. In Downsview or the Annex, in Florence or London, or in Jerusalem. Growing up in this home was a rare privilege.

Dad, of course we are not celebrating your retirement. Allow me to claim at least partial credit for this state of affairs. If not for my beleaguering, you would probably have handled Marx long ago and been ready to retire. Or would you?

Speaking of relations, I think it was my Uncle Harry who soundproofed the office or tried to. Now is the time to thank him for overlooking the heating ducts. It made my life as a kid so much easier.

Dad, the time also has come to admit that as a kid I was aware of every book you published and every translation that appeared. I was always proud. You would have found that out, had you asked my classmates. I also know that your father was immensely proud of you and of your accomplishments. You would have found that out had you asked me. I remember, too, every award you received. I'll never forget that sunny day in spring back in 1973 when you were notified of having landed the Killam Award, but I'll spare the audience the details. I will, however, say to the sponsors of this event, to the precious individuals who for the past year have applied themselves so sensitively to piecing this conference together, to the participating scholars and to the friends and family who have come to be here with us, that by doing so you have presented my father and my mother with a gift rivaling any award. On behalf of my sister Frances and myself, I thank each of you for marking so splendidly this evening. Thanks.

Frances Bogot

A few weeks ago I came across a yellowed clipping from a student newspaper dated 1984. Sam had just become a university professor and the title read, "Scholar in History of Economic Thought Enjoys Proving Accepted Opinions Wrong." It went on to quote a student as saying, "even a dead man would find Professor Hollander interesting."

I grew up with Adam Smith and David Ricardo. They lived in the Holy of Holies that was my father's office. It was a soundproofed room as my brother described, accessed by two heavy doors and jealously guarded by my mother. Looking back, I'm surprised there wasn't a drawbridge.

We tend to romanticize our childhood and I may be guilty of doing so, but I can safely say it was both weird and wonderful. We spent a year in Florence when I was thirteen. Because of the oil crisis, cars were not allowed to drive on Sunday and every Sunday we would emerge into a truly Renaissance street or avenue and visit some museum or art gallery or piazza. There was a year in London, too. I remember visiting Walter Eltis in Oxford. It was a cold autumn day and his home was warm and comfortable and we were treated to freshly baked bread. Back in Toronto there were always interesting visitors around my mother's dinner table. Larry Moss was a particular favorite guest as he was also a skilled magician, and of course there was always the specter of Mark Blaug. Even as a grownup, he enchanted me, but more importantly it is my children who benefit now. Although we live far apart, there is a wonderful closeness to their grandparents. They always return from visits to Sammy and Arlette happier, wiser and visibly more secure.

This is a difficult transition period. You are being forced to look back without knowing where forward is. My husband, by the way, and my eldest son are very much in favor of Nice for their own reasons.

What I want to say is that, however frightening the unknown may be, the world *is* your oyster and you already have your pearl beside you. Wherever you go, you will certainly attract the weird and the wonderful. And what more can one ask of heaven?

References

Malthus, T. R. [1798] (1986) "An Essay on the Principle of Population", in *The Works of Thomas Robert Malthus*, ed. E. A. Wrigley and D. Souden vol. 3, London: Pickering

Mill, J. S. (1967) "Leslie on the Land Question", in *Collected Works of John Stuart Mill*, vol. 5: 669–85, Toronto: University of Toronto Press.

Index

Abbot, E. 471
Abraham-Frois, G. 287n12
Académie des Sciences Morales et Politiques 216
Accumulation of Capital, The 464
Adams, F. C. 427
Adelman, I. 473
agents: economic 4, 47, 51, 55n8, 58, 107, 129, 158, 173, 341, 350, 381, 382, 433n26 (statesmen as 151–2); individual 211–12, 214, 342; moral 129, 181n 404; of state 189
agriculture 9, 13–15, 19, 44–8, 50, 51, 62–4, 77–8, 92, 94, 96, 156–7, 160, 165n5, 189–93, 196–7, 199, 201n3, 249, 260, 267n22, 270–87, 295–7 *passim*, 301, 305, 314n13, 319, 321–3 *passim*; and demand 44, 57, 81, 82, 86, 87, 92, 94, 189, 191, 279, 296, 327n6, 328n20, 352; depression 18, 20–22, 324–5, 326; investment 62–3, 64, 157, 190, 192; profit/productivity 270–87, 314n10; *see also* land
Alchian, A. A. 312n2, 312n5, 486
Alexander, J. 453
Allais, M. 97
allocation: theory 11, 462, 464; misallocated capital 318, 322, 323, 326
allocative structure (capital formation) 67–8
Alton Locke 422–6
American Economic Association 458–9, 460, 462, 472
American Economic Review 201n1, 246, 451, 452, 470
American Social Science Association 458–9, 460
American Statistical Association 460
ami des hommes, L' 143, 190, 192
analytics of classicism, pure 8–9, 16
Annual Register 326
Anti Duhring 239n8
Arena, A. 4, 209, 210, 217

Arestis, P. 312n3
Argenson, Marquis de 188, 189
Argyrous, G. 391
Aristotle 125, 137
Arkwright, R. 96
Arnold, M. 401
Arrow, K. J. 17, 243
Ashley, Sir W. 243, 259
Athénée 217
Aytoun, W. E. 424–5

Babbage, C. 76–7, 89, 98–103, 112–13, 114n4, 117n32, 118n33–4, 118n36, 118n39–40, 119n43; Babbage Principle 98–9, 102
Bailey, S. 17, 312n4
Balch, E. G. 470
Banfield 389
Bank of England 72n9, 327n4, 334–42 *passim*
banking: Central Banks 350, 351; lending 62; notes 162, 163–4, 327n4, 331–43 *passim*, 349; Parisian 217; private 61, 162 (failure 131, 163); reserves 338, 350; Scottish 145; security of Banks of Amsterdam and Hamburg 335, 337, 338
bankruptcy 59, 72n9, 215
Bastiat, F. 215, 218
Baudrillart, H. 209, 217
Baumol, W. 4, 119n42, 327n1, 393, 451, 452
Beard, M. 472
Becker, G. 462
Beecher, C. 462
Bentham, J. 3, 43–56, 77, 114n7, 335, 337, 389, 397n3, 402, 403–4, 432n16, 432n20, 433n22, 433n25, 435n31, 441n69; pre-Benthamite utilitarianism 403; and usury 49
Berg, M. 75, 76, 77, 79, 113, 114n1, 114n7, 117n29, 118n40, 454, 472
Bernard, J. 458

Bernard, L. L. 458
Berrebi, E. 287n12
Bezanson, A. 472
Bharadwaj, K. 251, 473
Biaujeaud, H. 286n2, 468–9
Bidard, C. 287n12
Biographical Dictionary of Women Economics 452, 455, 464, 466
Biss, I. 453
Bitterman, H. J. 174, 181n5
Black, R. D. C. 356
Blanding, S. G. 463
Blanqui, J. A. 209, 215, 216, 217
Blaug, M. 154, 166n6, 244, 296, 313n1, 331
Bodichon, B. L. S. 460–1
Boettke, P. J. 392
Böhm-Bawerk, E. von 390, 391, 472
Bonar, J. 43
Bondareva, O. N. 465
Boserup, E. 473
Boulding, K. E. 140, 148–9
Bourricaud, F. 212
Bowley, M. 58, 72n16, 95, 177, 473
Bowman, M. J. 473
Brady, D. S. 453, 462, 463, 471
Brennan, G. 17
Brewer, A. 75, 76, 83, 84, 87, 102, 106, 113, 114n5, 119n47
Brimblecomb, N. 426–7
British Association for the Advancement of Science 362
Brown, E. R. 473
Brown, V. 57, 85, 125, 128–9, 130, 140, 145, 148, 154–5, 156, 164, 172, 176, 177–8, 181n4–5
Browne, S. 466
Bryant, S. W. 473
Buckle, H. T. 169–70, 171, 176, 181n2
Buer, M. 472
bullion 331–43, 344n3–4; premium on 339–43; *see also* specie
Burke, E. 131, 134, 139, 141

Cairnes, J. E. 17, 75, 255, 256, 257, 290, 292, 314n14, 363, 368, 371–2
Campbell, H. 472
Campbell, W. F. 181n5–6
Canadian Political Science Association 472
Cannan, E. 75–7, 83, 97, 112, 113, 114n3–4, 117n23, 119n47, 168, 170, 176, 243, 248–9, 254, 256
Cannibals All! 401
canon: ambiguity of 5, 391, 485–6; and Bentham 43–55; definition of 1–2, 353n3, 378–80, 402; differing 242, 243, 485–6; diffusion of 309–11; evolution of 1–2, 24n2, 142, 176–9, 219, 241, 371, 381–3; first 347–9, 489–90, 492–4, 495; French 4, 185–202, 205–22; in history of economic thought 378–84; independent 169–76; interpretations of Malthus 346–53; narrowing in late nineteenth century 356–7, 371, 372; nature/structure of 482–5; nineteenth and twentieth centuries 195–201; orthodox 331; Quesnay's contribution 188–95; Ricardian 270–88; Samuelson's 378, 380–1, 383; Schumpeter's 241; second 349–50, 353; selection and omission 2, 6, 381–3, 402, 496–7, 498n1; Smith in 148–9, 165n1, 165n3, 168–82, 185, 195–199; social construction 487–8; theory and application 356–76; Western 490–2; women 451–81 (dearth of 6, 451, 469–73)
canonical model 13, 16, 17, 27, 28, 40–1, 43, 44, 57–74, 75, 77, 80, 81, 89, 91, 92, 95, 97, 102, 103, 113, 114, 114n1, 125, 225, 346–7, 378, 381–3; contemporary 139–42; historiography 57–8; in Smith's analysis of profit; in Smith on security of capital 58–65; 58–60; in Smith on security and investment 60–70; uncanonical/pre-classical 27–42 (characteristics 28–31)
Cantillon, R. 21, 28, 71n5, 187, 189, 193, 194, 387
capital: accumulation 2, 9, 11, 13, 22, 23, 25n11, 41, 44, 53n1, 58, 64, 65, 66, 69, 71, 75, 80, 85–6, 88, 96, 104–8 *passim*, 110, 114n1, 114n5, 130, 135, 157, 177, 197–201, 202n8, 272, 304, 346, 347–8, 350, 352, 354n8–9, 352, 354n9 (unsustainable 16) (upon the land 81, 82, 94); and agriculture 44, 57, 86, 87, 92, 94, 189, 191, 287n6, 296, 323, 324; allocation 10, 11, 12, 14, 15, 19, 23, 58, 59–64 *passim*, 66, 69–71, 157, 186, 296–7, 299, 300, 328 (misallocated 322, 323, 326); competition of 13, 15, 38–9, 92; formation 58, 65, 66–8, 69, 70, 210; and growth 28, 87–8; capital-intensive processes 11; and labour 9, 11, 13, 25n11, 27, 44, 229, 258, 314n18; and manufacturing 85, 297, 323; markets 3, 57–72; Marx 231, 232, 233–6, 238, 260; movement 10, 19, 53n1, 66, 138, 296, 297, 321, 321–2; need for 215; return on 9, 11, 14, 15, 22–3, 60, 70, 75, 83, 100, 102, 105, 106, 113, 163, 226, 227, 235–6, 272–3, 297–9, 346, 348, 350; Ricardo 225, 227, 229–30, 261, 274, 276, 279, 287n6; security 60–5, 66, 70; supply 23, 59–60, 70, 75, 80, 328n7

Index

Capital 196, 225, 231, 232, 233, 234, 235, 236, 237, 239n9, 253, 482
capital-intensive: processes 11; farming 189
Carbon, B. de 214, 217
Carlyle, T. 5–6, 400, 401, 408, 412, 416, 418, 420–2, 425
Carsky, M. L. 462
Cassell, G. 257
Castlereagh, Viscount 326
Catéchisme d'Economie Politique 206
Cauwès, P. 216
Censeur Européen, Le 215, 218
Chalmers, T. 17, 96, 117n26
Chamberlain, H. S. 425
Chapman, A. 469
Chardin, D. 264
Charles, L. 192, 201, 202n6
Charlier, C. 176
Chayanov, A. V. 465
Chayanov, S. 465
Chevalier, M. 217, 218
Choi, Y. B. 180
Church: income 189, 191; *see also* religion
Cicero 129
Ciller, T. 451
Clark, A. 471
Clark, J. B. 254
classical economics: definition 3, 7; development 3, 185; key elements 4; and Marx 262; neoclassical 141; nineteenth-century 75, 76, 77, 91–2, 113; reappraisal 241; schism 3, 27
Classical Economics 2, 7, 9
Cliffe Leslie, T. E. 356, 362, 363, 364, 365, 366, 368, 369, 370, 371, 372, 373n1
Clinton, W. 292
Coase, R. 65, 483; theorem 162
Cobbe, F. P. 459
Cobbett, W. 116n16
Cobden, R. 309
Cohen, R. 473
Colbert, J. B. 152, 186
Coleridge, S. T. 408
Collège de France 217
colonies 13, 138, 191; American 131, 193–4
Colson, C. 217
Coman, K. 451
commerce et le gouvernement considérés relativement l'un à l'autre, Le 197, 207–8
comparative advantage, theory of 11, 299
competition 4, 15, 18, 24n1, 39, 99–100, 109, 112, 118n34, 134, 138, 144, 154, 155, 163, 175, 185–7, 189, 194–5, 198, 201, 271, 279 *see also* capital
Comte, C. 216, 362, 363
Condillac, abbé de 186, 188, 197, 207
Condorcet, Marquise de 134, 187, 453

Confessions 143
Conservatoire des Arts et Métiers 217
Constantino, C. 468
Consumption of Wealth, The 462
Conversations on Political Economy 455
Coon, S. J. 473
Corn Law 19, 21, 95, 165n5, 200, 225, 226, 239n1 308–9; *Report of the Commons Committee on the Corn Law* 325
corn profit model 246–7, 276–8, 280, 314n13, 383n3
corn wage 8, 9, 116n22, 193, 197, 257, 260, 279
Corsi, M. 117n30
cost price 14, 233; and demand and supply 10–12
costs of production 10, 14, 16, 96, 131, 185, 225–6, 227, 233, 239n5, 247, 248, 259, 260, 267n21, 272, 274–5, 276, 278, 280, 304, 347, 382, 384n7, 384n9, 384n11, 347, 382; agricultural 325
Courcelle-Seneuil, J. C. 210, 216, 218
Cournot, A. 389
Craft, W. 413
Craig, I. 458
crisis theory 466
Critique of the Gotha Programme 231, 234, 238
Cromwell, O. 186
Cropsey, J. 127, 137, 138
Curry, K. 420

d'Épinay, L. 197
Dall, C. H. 458, 460, 461
Dangeul, P. de 187, 188
Das Marxsche System 465
Daszynska-Golinska, S. 466
Daubié, J-V. 457–8, 461, 470
Davenport, C. 257
Davis, J. B. 226, 227, 239n4, 473
Davis, T. 5, 21, 343
Décade Philosophique, Politique et Littéraire 207
Deegan, M. J. 453
Defence of a Maximum 54n3
Deleplace, G. 5, 53
demand and supply 3, 10–11, 12, 14, 28, 29–33, 38, 40, 45–7, 83, 84, 100, 132, 142, 171–2, 190, 214, 259, 294, 301, 320, 349, 352, 367, 372, 381–2, 384n7, 384n11, 472n4; in depression 320; Say's law 198, 210
Demier, F. 215
depression, post-Napoleonic 318–28
Derrida, J. 128
Dessauer, M. 466–7
Development of Capitalism in Russia 464
Dexter, E. 471
Dialogues Concerning Natural Religion 143

Index   515

Diamond, M. 462
Dickey, L. 178, 179
Dictionary of Political Economy 452
Dictionnaire de l'Economie Politique 218
Dictionnaire du Commerce 218
Diderot, D. 189, 454
Dimand, M. A. 452, 470
Dimand, R. 6, 119n45, 396, 452, 456, 462, 471, 472
Discours Préliminaire 206–7, 208
Discourse on Inequality 134, 136
"dismal science" 400
Disraeli, B. 308–9
Dobb, M. 21–2, 257
Dorfman, J. 455, 456, 459
Dorp, E. C. van 468, 471
Duesenberry, J. 464
Dulles, E. L. 471, 473
Dunayevskaya, R. 471
Dunoyer, C. 209, 215, 216, 218
Dupuit, A. 389
Dutot, C. 141

Eatwell, J. 251, 271–2, 280, 281–3, 284
Ecole: Commerciale 217; Libre des Sciences Politiques 217–18; des Ponts et Chaussées 217; Spéciale de Commerce 215, 217
EconLit database 392–3, 395–6
economic agents *see* agents, economic
Economic Development of India 472
Economic Development of Russia 472
Economic History of China 472
Economic History of a Factory Town 469
Economic History Society 472
Economic Problems of the Family 462
economic publication, growth in 1750s 187
Economical and Philosophical Manuscripts 237
Economics of Adam Smith, The 2
Economics of David Ricardo, The 2, 339
Economics of Household Production 462
Economics of John Stuart Mill, The 2, 7
Economics of Thomas Robert Malthus, The 2, 5, 347, 400
Economie Politique Chrétienne 215
economy, closed/open 28ff, 210, 292, 314n17
Edgeworth, F. Y. 350, 390, 391
Einaudi, L. 243
Ekelund, Jr, R. B. 458
Elements d'economie politique 457
Elements d'Economie Pure 211
Elements of Political Economy 89, 90
Ellis, W. 76
Elmslie, B. 114n1
Eltis, W. 4, 24n2, 25n10, 72n7, 78, 113, 114n1, 189, 201n2, 201n5, 347, 353, 354n6

Emmett, R. 264
Employments of Women, The 460
Encyclopaedia Britannica 90, 117n25
Encyclopaedia Metropolitana 117n28, 117n31
Encyclopédie 189, 192, 454
Engels, F. 231, 234, 235, 237, 239n7–9, 420
England, M. T. 472
English tradition 4, 254
Enlightenment 126, 145; Scottish 141, 133
entrepreneurs 4, 24n1, 49, 72n10, 107, 108–11 *passim*, 129, 152, 185, 186, 207, 214–15, 216, 217, 231
Epicureanism 169
Essai sur l'amélioration des terres 192, 194
Essai sur la nature du commerce 187
Essai sur la police générale des grains 186
Essai sur la théorie Ricardienne de la valeur 468
Essay on Population 7, 15, 28, 82, 93, 115n11–12
Essay on Profit 79, 115n9, 226, 245, 270–88 *passim*
Essay on the Application of Capital to Land 270
Essay on the External Corn Trade 87
Essay on the Principles of Population 27–8
Essay on the Production of Wealth 84
Essays in Biography 318
Essays on Philosophical Subjects (EPS) 133
Essays on the Active Powers of Man 177
Essays on the Principles of Morality and Natural Religion 180
ethical theory 168–73, 178, 179, 180, 182n8
Evensky, J. 182n10
Everett, A. H. 113, 119n46

Fable of the Bees 37, 134, 141
Factory Acts 456
Farm Labor in Germany 466
Faucher, L. 217
Fawcett, M. G. 461, 462
Ferguson, A. 142, 496
Ferrara, F.: *Lectures* 243
Fetter, F. W. 116n20, 259, 470
Financial History of the United States, A 453
Fisher, I. 369, 472
Fitzgibbons, A. 66, 71n3, 125, 130, 140, 182n8
Fitzhugh, G. 401
Fitzpatrick, M. 144
Five Hundred Occupations Adapted to Women 460
Fletcher, A. 141
Folbre, N. 459, 460
Fontaine, P. 181n4

516 *Index*

Forbes, D. 137
Forbonnais 187
Forget, E. 181, 219, 452, 455, 458, 462
Foucault, M. 128, 484
Foxwell, H. 286n1
France 131, 144, 152, 185–202, 322; Adam Smith in 169, 194, 202n8; famines 188; foundations of classical canon 185–202; interest on government debt 188; July Monarchy 215–6; liberal tradition 4, 12, 14, 24n2, 149, 186, 187–95, 197, 199, 201, 205–22 (family ties in 216–17); Smith in 169–71, 176, 181n1, 185, 186, 194, 202n8
Franklin, R. S. 175
Frasers Magazine for Town and Country 407–11, 420
Frawley, M. H. 456
free markets *see* markets, free
free trade/competition 24n2, 116n22, 138, 152, 154, 157, 165n5, 185, 189, 191, 199, 200, 215, 225; *see also* markets, trade
French Revolution 78, 131
Friedman, M. 451, 462, 463, 469, 483
Friedman, R. 462, 463, 471
Froude, J. 408
Furner, M. O. 459

Galiani, abbé 197, 381
Galton, Sir F. 362
Garegnani, G. 251, 264, 274, 287n8
Garnier, J. 210, 213–14, 215, 216, 217, 218, 219
Garrison, W. L. 459
Gee, J. M. A. 181n5
General Theory of Employment, Interest and Money 198, 318, 348, 351, 354n7, 390, 486
General View of a Complete Code of Laws, A 54n3
Gensemer, S. H. 461
George, H. 389, 390, 391
German Ideology, The 239n8
German Labor Courts 466
Gide, C. 216, 217
Gilboy, E. 472
Gilman, C. P. 458–9, 470
Ginor, F. 468
Giornale degli economisti 243
Globe 218
Godwin, W. 134
Goldsmith, O. 134
Goldsmith, S. 473
Gordon, B. 160, 174–5, 239n3
Gossen, H. 389
Gournay, J. V. de 187, 191
government 18, 20, 24n2, 61–70 *passim*, 112, 119n42, 126–7, 133, 134, 136, 137, 139, 141, 143, 145, 148–65 *passim*, 174, 188, 197
Grampp, W. D. 173, 174, 181n5, 309, 315n21
Graziani, A. 264
Grice-Hutchinson, M. 473
Grimke, A. 459
Grimke, S. 459
Groenewegen, P. D. 452, 453
Grotius 130, 136, 142
growth: economic 4, 24, 28, 38, 39–41, 48, 51, 58, 60–5, 69, 71, 77, 78, 86, 96, 98, 102, 115n13, 130, 136, 137, 178, 182n8, 185, 191, 193–5, 201, 202n8, 215, 225, 226; and development 39; threat to 87
growth and knowledge 75, 77, 80, 87, 89, 90, 91–4, 98, 102, 112, 113–4, 114n6, 118n39 (John Rae 105–11)
growth model 2, 3, 13, 27, 43, 75, 77, 80, 81, 89, 91, 92, 95, 97, 102, 112–14 *passim*, 114n1, 331, 346, 347
growth: population 13, 14, 35, 44–5, 46, 47, 48, 75, 88, 90, 92–5, 116n22, 117n27, 194, 199, 200, 202n6: control 20, 47–8; equilibrium 31–3, 36, 37, 40, 41, 51, 193, 294; mechanism 2, 4, 30; land output 29–31; sustainable/non-sustainable 15–16, 21
growth theory 8–9, 10, 15, 17, 19, 43–5, 77, 80, 102, 103–11, 112–14 *passim*, 114n1, 114n5, 115n8, 118n39, 175
Grundrisse 213, 237
Guillamin, F. 458
Guillamin, U. G. 458
Guillaumin Publishing House 218
Guizot, F. 218
Guly, C. 451
Guyot, Y. 209, 218

Haakonssen, K. 68, 137, 146n1, 155, 158, 164
Hagemann, H. 463
Hamilton, A. 140
Hamilton, E. 428
Hammond, J. H. 415–16
Hamouda, O. 219
Hardy, S. M. 471
Harper, W. 414–15
Harriet Martineau Sociological Association 456
Harrington, J. 141
Hartmann, H. 470
Harvard Business Review 310
Haskell, T. L. 459
Hausman, D. 359
Healey, C. W. 459
Hébert, R. F. 458

Hecht, J. 188, 473
Hegel, G. W. F. 254
Henderson, J. P. 225, 239n4, 257
Henderson, W. 455
Herbert, C-J. 186, 187
Herlihy, D. 455
Hexter, J. H. 451
Hicks, Sir J. 17, 188, 205, 210, 301, 327n3
Hicks, U. 473
High Price of Bullion 334, 335, 341
Hill, P. 473
Histoire de l'économie politique en Europe 209
historical school 5, 210
"History of Astronomy" 159–60
History of Business 472
History of Civilization in England 169
History of Doctrines 253
History of Political Economy 362–3
Hobbes, T. 128, 130, 131, 254
Hodgskin, T. 252, 254
Hollander, S. 2, 4, 5, 12, 14, 21, 24n4, 24n5, 24n9, 27, 41, 57, 59, 63, 65, 72n14, 72n16, 75, 79, 82, 93, 111, 114n1, 114n6, 115n8–12, 116n20, 116n22, 117n45, 152, 165n5, 181, 199, 200, 201, 224, 225, 241, 244, 246, 257, 262–3, 264, 265n3, 265n8, 266n9, 266n13–14, 268n24, 270–2; challenge 278–84, 285, 287n6, 287n18, 288n19, 288n22, 291–3 *passim*, 296, 297, 301, 304, 307, 309, 312n1, 312n4, 313n10, 314n13–15, 315n18, 315n20, 323, 328n7–8, 328n10, 331, 339, 340, 341, 346–9 *passim*, 351, 353, 381, 383, 400, 486; works of 2
home economics 462, 473
Hommage à Rosa Luxemburg, L' 451
homme aux quarante écus, L' 196
Hont, I. 136
How to Observe Morals and Manners 456
How Women Can Make Money 460
Hoyt, E. E. 462
Hume, D. 8. 28, 34, 71n5, 72n9, 90–1, 126, 131, 132, 133, 134, 142, 143, 165n4, 166n7–8, 169, 170, 185, 186, 187, 254, 291–2, 299, 300, 304
Hutcheson, F. 71n5, 129, 132, 142, 166n9, 169, 254, 389, 403
Hutchins, B. L. 471
Hutchison, T. W.. 7, 187, 327n2

Ignatieff, M. 136
llustrations of Political Economy 455–6
Industrial Development of Poland, The 464
Inequality, Discourse on 134, 136
Inglis Palgrave, R. H. 452
ingot plan 331, 334–9, 344n9
Ingram, J. K. 356, 362–3, 364, 369, 370, 371, 372, 373n1

Innes, M. Q. 453
innovation 13, 48, 49, 80, 81, 98; microeconomic analysis of 98–103, 106–8 *passim*, 114n1–2, 239n3
Inquiry into the Nature and Progress of Rent 270
Inquiry into the Principles of Political Economy (Steuart, Sir J.) 146, 151
insurance 59–60
interest/financial return 8, 12, 14, 17, 19, 23, 58, 59, 61, 62, 70, 78, 82, 132, 136, 162–4, 188, 233, 236, 239n2, 261, 273, 298–9, 323, 347, 351, 352, 353; on French government loans 188; regulation 62; *see also* capital
investment 4, 23, 24n1, 24n3, 39, 57–73, 100, 103, 185, 186, 201, 229, 235, 236, 239n10; agricultural 62–3, 64, 157, 190, 192; educational 111; security/risk 59–61, 63–4, 65–70; state 20, 198

Jasny, N. 464–5
Jealousy of Trade, The 143
Jenkins, F. 389
Jennings, R. 389
Jessua, C. 201
Jevons, W. S. 5, 8, 16, 17–18, 118n39, 244, 251, 252, 253, 255, 256, 259, 262, 267n19, 356–7, 358, 364, 365–70, 371, 372, 389, 390, 391
Jewish "menace" 418, 420–5
John Stuart Mill on Economic Theory and Method 2
Johnson 134
Jones, A. H. 472
Jonsson, P. 322
journals, economic 187, 201n1, 218, 243, 245, 270, 284, 452, 458, 466
JSTOR 428
Jurisprudence, Lectures on 65, 127, 129, 134, 136, 150, 157, 161, 165, 165n1, 168, 170, 173, 176–80
justice 66, 69, 71, 71n5, 72n10, 126, 129–38 *passim*, 149, 150, 155–65 *passim*, 169, 174, 175, 178, 181n5–7, 195

Kaldor, N. 274
Kames, Lord 132, 180
Kandal, T. R. 466
Kant, I. 254
Kaplan, S. 202n7
Keynes, J. M. 5, 8, 21, 198, 243, 254, 286n1, 318, 327n3, 331, 338, 344n6–7, 348–9, 350–3, 354n8, 369, 371, 390–2, 482, 486, 490
King, S. 452, 453
Kingsley, C. 408, 418, 422–4, 425, 426

518 *Index*

Kleer, R. A. 3, 53, 54n4, 146n2
Knight, C. 76
Knight, F. 401
knowledge 3, 75–119: collective 186; creation/growth of 77, 82, 89, 90, 91, 96, 98, 102, 111–12, 114n6, 117n28; definition 114n2; economic 218; of entrepreneur 214; fixed 5; gap in 75; and growth 75, 77, 80, 87, 89, 90, 91–4, 98, 102, 112, 113–4, 114n6, 118n39 (John Rae 105–11); increase of 76, 251; as public good 76, 112, 113; Ricardian (first generation 78–91, 113) (second generation 98, 113); of wage rate 21
Knowles, L. 472
Kock, K. 469
Kondratiev, N. D. 465
Koot, G. M. 371
Krugman, P. 290, 292–3, 310–11, 312, 313n7
Kuhn, T. 17, 379
Kula, W. 382
Kulakovskaja, T. 465
Kurdas, C. 57, 114
Kurz, H. D. 24n8, 260, 263, 266n14, 287n12
Kyrk, H. 462–3

labor 13, 44, 57, 83, 85, 131, 153, 196, 236, 256–61, 274, 314n18, 322; agricultural/rural 29, 46, 92, 117n28, 196, 294–5; demand for 9, 11, 24n2, 39, 46, 54n1, 58, 82, 88, 185, 274, 320; distribution 18–19, 90; division of 37, 44, 76, 77, 82, 83, 84, 85, 87, 89, 90, 91, 98–100, 101, 102, 112, 114n1, 118n32–33, 126, 127, 130, 132, 135, 136, 152, 198, 210, 235, 237, 239n8, 381 (Mill's case for specializaton 357–62); inputs 10; market 22, 132, 134, 294; and natural rights 133; and profit 9, 15, 20, 64, 111 (*see also* wage–profit relationship); and price/value 225–226, 226–31, 232–3, 239, 247, 248, 254, 275; productivity 9, 10, 76, 89, 91, 92, 134, 135, 196, 201, 304; labor-saving 80–1, 89, 96, 115n11; subsistence 64, 294; supply 20, 80, 85, 86, 88, 274, 294; surplus time 23; surplus value 231–2, 238, 249, 252; unions 20, 307–8, 315n20; unproductive 29–32 *passim*, 37, 38, 177, 196; *see also* corn wages, value theory, wages
laboring classes, condition of 87–8, 94–5, 111, 115n12, 116n22, 136, 193, 225, 237–8, 294, 313n9, 327n7
labor-intensive processes 11, 64

labor theory of price/value 224, 225, 226–7, 233, 260, 261, 308; *see also* value theory
LaFollette, S. 471
Laidler, D. 21
Lamb, R. B. 178
Lament for Economics 473
land 5, 14, 17, 28, 44, 54, 62, 69, 83, 92, 115n11, 117n28, 225, 276, 282, 286, 295, 347; scarcity 3, 9, 12–18 *passim*, 27, 28, 38, 44, 47, 53, 77, 81, 82, 298, 351–3; *see also* agriculture
Langham Place group 458, 461
Lapidus, A. 4–5, 53, 219, 287n13
Lardner, D. 389
Lassalle, F. 232
Lauderdale, Earl of 77, 114n7, 313n10
law 48–9, 54n5, 65–6, 69, 70, 88, 95, 116n22, 126, 130–2, 134, 141, 150–1, 155–6, 157–64 *passim*, 165n1, 165n5, 176, 178, 182n10, 195, 198; canon 270; French 191; of usury 24n6, 163, 352; of war 161; *see also* Corn Laws, Navigation Act
Law, J. 152
Laws and Policy of England Relating to Trade 146
Lectures on Jurisprudence, The 65, 127, 129, 134, 136, 150, 157, 161, 165, 165n1, 168, 170, 173, 176–80
Lectures on Justice, Police, Revenue and Arms 178
Leichter, K. 457
Lenin, V. I. 464
Lerner, A. P. 352, 353
Leroy-Beaulieu family 216–7
Leroy-Beaulieu, A. 217
Leroy-Beaulieu, P. 209, 215, 217, 218
Letter to Lord Horwick 116n21
Leubuscher, C. A. 466
Levan-Lesmesle, L. 216, 218
Levasseur, E. 218
Levina, R. S. 465
Levy, D. 2, 5, 114n3, 181, 182n10, 301, 419
Libby, B. 453
Liberalismus und Protektionismus 466
Liberator 459
liberty 61, 66, 68–9, 72n10, 73n21, 126, 129, 130, 132, 137, 138, 143, 144, 152, 155–9 *passim*, 156–165 *passim*, 177, 195
Libre-Echange, Le 218
Link, R. 327n5
Literature of Political Economy, The 2
Littledale, E. D. 459
Lively, J 403, 404, 405, 406
Liverpool, Lord 325
Locke, J. 137, 142; scholarship 144, 254
Longfield, M. 290, 292, 301, 303, 314n14

Louis XV 187–8, 195
Lutfalla, M. 216
Lutz, V. S. 471, 473
Luxemburg, R. 464, 471
luxuries 29, 34, 36, 38, 49–50, 53, 119n45, 274, 277, 291, 348; Hume on 143; prodigality debate 134–5, 136

Macaulay, T. B. 403, 406, 407, 409, 418–20
McCord, L. C. 456
McCulloch, J. R. 12, 17, 63, 76, 77, 91, 96–8, 102–4 *passim*, 112, 113, 117n26–9, 119n47, 257–9 *passim*, 261, 292, 314n14
McDonald, L. 462
McElroy, W. 471
McFadden, M. 459
McFie, A. L. 170, 171–2, 176, 178, 179, 181n1–2, 181n5
Machiavelli, N. 130, 141, 142
McLeod, H. 389
McMahon, T. 473
Madden, K. 453
Maginn, W. 408, 409
Makower, H. 473
Malthus, T. R. 2, 3, 12, 13, 14–16, 17, 19, 24n4, 27, 75, 80–2, 111, 115n11, 115n13, 118n38, 118n40, 141, 200, 206–8 *passim*, 210, 253, 270, 287n7, 290, 292, 313n10, 326, 327, 327n5–7, 328n17, 347–9 *passim*, 351, 353, 400, 412, 456; and Babbage 102, 118n33; influence on Bentham 45, 54n3; and Corn Laws 21, 165n5, 200; and McCulloch 96–8 *passim*; on population 20, 113, 233, 239n10; on postwar depression 319–20; pre-Malthusian thought 28, 194; and Ricardo 78, 227, 228, 239n5, 247, 248, 249, 258, 259, 265n8, 273, 278–9, 283, 299, 318, 321–2, 322–3, 327n2, 328n9, 350; and Nassau Senior 87, 92–5, 116n22
Malthus, Economics of 5, 7
Manchester School 309
Mandeville, J. 28, 34, 37, 131, 134, 135, 141, 142, 143, 169
Manifesto of the Communist Party 235
Manual of Political Economy 47
Marabeau, Marquis de 141, 143, 187, 190, 191, 192, 195, 200
Marcet, J. 455–6, 461
Marco, L. 210
Marginal Notes on Adolph Wagner 231
market 13, 16, 22, 23, 24n1, 35, 58, 61, 64, 65, 69–71, 72n13, 84, 103, 106, 109, 126, 129–31 *passim*, 141, 142, 144, 145, 153, 162–3, 171–2, 175, 181n4–5, 185, 186, 189, 194, 198, 201n3, 202n7, 218, 228, 229, 232, 236; adjustments 3;

different notions of 382; free 4, 139, 153, 171, 194, 195, 202n7 (*see also* free trade); imperfect capital 3; labor 15, 22, 134, 136, 139, 294; law of 12, 15, 18, 198, 321, 323, 326, 328n17; mechanism 4, 294; non-market motives 107; market-society 28, 34
Marmontel, J-F. 190
Married Women's Property Act 461
Marshall, A. 252, 253, 254, 255, 259, 260, 261, 346, 349, 352, 371, 389–90, 391, 392, 482, 486
Martel, C. F. 459
Martineau, H. 6, 76, 412, 413, 414, 415, 416, 417, 426, 455, 456, 459, 461, 462
Marx, K. 2, 3, 4, 8, 21, 22, 23, 24n1, 27, 28, 77, 113, 119n40, 190, 196, 225, 226, 227, 238n8–10, 241, 250–64 *passim*, 390, 391, 482, 486, 490; alienation and production 237–8; and morality of distribution 231–2; productivity 235–6; values and price 232–5;
masters 28–30, 34, 39, 196, 295, 304; agriculturalist as master 64; inn keeper not 71
Mechanics Institute 76
Meek, R. L. 149, 152–3, 166n9, 177, 191, 201n2, 201n5
Meinhardt, M. *see* Dessauer, M.
Melon, J. F. 141
mercantilism 18, 130, 132, 133, 138, 151, 152, 154, 155, 165 n4, 177–8, 185
Methods of Quantitative Calculation of the Effectiveness of Land 465
Meyer, A. 471
Meynieu, M. 457
Mildmay, W. 146
Mill, H. T. 461
Mill, J. S. 2–6 *passim*, 7, 12, 16–20 *passim*, 23, 27, 76, 77, 78, 118n33, 118n40, 119n47, 207, 291, 292, 296, 300, 307–11 *passim*, 314n14, 356, 362–72 *passim*, 403–7 *passim*, 418, 451, 452, 461; law of distribution/wage–profit theorem 302–6, 315n20; and Ricardo 16, 20, 226, 252, 255, 256; and Smith 303; case for specialization 357–62; *see also* works by name
Mill, James 76, 87, 89–91, 98, 116n19, 249–50, 291, 292, 314n14, 314n16, 454
Miller, M. S. 126, 472
Minowitz, P. 125, 127–8, 140, 176, 181n5
Mintz, I. S. 467
Mirabeau, Marquis de 187, 191, 195
Mitchell, W. C. 43, 286n2, 369
Modigliani, F. 463, 464
Molinari, G. de 218
Monetary History of the United States, A 470

520 Index

Monetary Proposals for Social Reform 453
money: notes and bullion (ingot plan) 331, 334–43 (*see also* banking); relation between quantity and value 332–4; stocks of metallic 346; theory of 331–43
Mongiovi, G. 264
Montesquieu 142, 143
Moral Sentiments, Theory of 62, 65, 70, 72n11, 72n13, 127–8, 129, 131, 133, 134, 135, 137, 149, 150, 158, 159, 160, 161, 454; and *The Wealth of Nations* 4, 148–64, 162–82
More, Sir T. 418–9
Morris, C. T. 473
Morris, R. T. 471
Morrow, G. R. 171, 172, 174, 175, 181n3, 181n5
Moss, L. 5, 291, 314n13
Moszkowska, N. 465–6, 471
Muller, G. Z. 125–6, 128, 130, 140
Mushkin, S. 473
Myers, M. G. 453

Nakamura, A. O. 451
Napoleon I 198
Napoleoni, C. 277n13
National Association of Factory Operators 456
National Association for the Promotion of Social Science 458–9, 461
National Debt 145, 199; Sully's view 193
Natural Religion, Dialogues Concerning 143
Naumova, N. 465
Navigation Acts 138
Negishi, T. 20, 63, 201n3
Newcomer, M. 473
New England Women's Rights Convention 458
"new home economics" 462
New Palgrave: A Dictionary of Economics 451, 463, 471
New Principles (Rae) 106, 119n46
New York Money Market, The 453
Newman, P. 287n9
Nightingale, F. 462
North America 81, 88, 92–4, 111, 193–4, 199, 312, 323; Revolution 131
North, D. C. 65, 66, 70
Nouvelles Éphémérides 187

O'Brien, D. P. 96, 117n24, 117n28–9, 118n37, 119n47, 391, 472
Of the Balance of Trade 187
Of the Tendency of Profits to a Minimum 199
Olbie ou Essai sur les Moyens de Réformer les Moeurs d'une Nation 211
On the Canonical Classical Model of Political Economy 2

On the Definition of Political Economy 356
On the Economy of Machinery and Manufactures 76, 98, 118n33
On the Subjection of Women 459
On Wages and Combination 87
Oncken, A. 176
Orwell, G. 428
output and population 29–31
Owen, R. 252, 455

Pack, S. J. 181n6
Paglin, M. 327n2
Paine, T. 134, 143
Paley, W. 28, 34, 35
Pannomial Fragments 54n5
Paretian ophelimity 213
Paris as a Financial Centre 453
Pasinetti, L. 264, 266n13, 274, 287n12
Passy, L. 217
Past and Present 418, 420–1
patents 49, 101, 112
Patullo, H. 192, 193–4, 210n6
Pauperisme anglais 457
Peach, T. 288n22, 323
Pearson, N. 451
Peart, S. 5, 118n39, 181, 356, 358, 369, 370
Peel, Sir R. 326
Pénin, M. 215
Penny, V. 460–1
Penrose, E. 471, 473
Persky, J. 428
Pesciarelli, E. 72n8, 72n10–11, 114n7
Peters-Fransen, I. 4, 71
Petty, Sir W. 21, 24n1, 189, 252, 254, 256, 257, 259–60, 269n19
Philosophie rurale 191, 192
Physiocratie 194–5
physiocrats 4, 14, 15, 21, 62, 116n16, 152, 130, 156, 157, 165n4–5, 169, 176, 177, 179, 185, 187, 191, 194, 196, 197, 207, 209, 253, 257, 259, 260, 261, 267n22, 389
Pinchbeck, I. 471, 472
Plato 125, 127, 137
Platova, S. 465
Political Economy Club 200, 309, 362
Political Economy, Dictionary of 452
Political Economy, Principles of see Principles
Polkinghorn, B. 455
Pompadour, Marquise de 192, 194
population growth *see* growth
Population, Two Lectures on 87, 92
Porta, P. L. 263
Porter, P. L. 4
Poynter, J. R. 44, 54n3
Precursors in Mathematical Economics 393
Pribram, K. 43
price 24n3; 28, 29, 37, 80, 84, 87, 136,

142, 157, 191–3 *passim*, 197, 198, 213, 224–30 *passim*, 258, 260, 303–5, 321, 352, 370, 382–3; and demand and supply 10–12, 17; determination 3, 4, 132, 232–5; inflation 17, 45, 46, 195, 304, 308; just 136; market 4; mechanism 132, 292, 299, 301, 304; natural 174, 276–7 (*see also* costs of production); of production *see* costs of production; system 65; *see also* value theory, wage–price relationship
price theory *see* value theory
Price, B. 134, 365
Primitive Trade 462
Principles of Political Economy (Malthus) 7, 15, 20, 28, 80, 82, 320, 323, 353n5, 454
Principles of Political Economy (McCulloch) 97, 113
Principles of Political Economy (Mill) 7, 77, 302, 303–9 *passim*
Principles of Political Economy (Ricardo) 7, 12, 14, 22, 76, 96, 206, 225, 226, 227, 242, 244, 245, 246, 247, 248, 250, 262, 271, 273–4, 276, 277–84 *passim*, 286n2, 287n8, 293, 296, 297, 301, 314n16, 326, 327n2, 331, 332, 454, 482
Principles of Population and Production (Weyland) 115n11
Production of Commodities by Means of Commodities 244, 245–6, 274–6, 271, 274–5, 276, 277, 286n1
profit 10, 13, 16, 18, 21, 22, 23, 24n4, 25n11, 29, 38–9, 41, 43, 49, 61–6 *passim*, 70, 71, 71n4, 71n6, 77, 78, 81–4 *passim*, 90, 99–101 *passim*, 108–11 *passim*, 115n11, 117n28, 132, 157, 196, 199–201 *passim*, 226–33 *passim*, 235, 236–8 *passim*, 239n2, 239n5–6, 247–9 *passim*, 261, 265n8, 266n11, 270–86 *passim*, 287n6, 287n16, 288n19–22: decline 9, 11, 12–13, 15, 16, 19–20, 27, 44, 75, 82, 200, 227, 229, 231, 238, 240n10, 297, 299; Smith's analysis of 59–60, 145; *see also* interest, wage–profit relation
Profit, Essay on 79, 115n9, 226, 245, 270–88 *passim*
Progress and Poverty 389
property 18, 24n2, 53, 66, 136, 166n9; justice 139, 141, 185; rights 4, 24n2, 48, 50, 69, 185, 195; *see also* patents
Proposals for an Economical and Secure Currency 334, 335
Pro-Slavery Argument, The 414
Proudhon, P. J. 254, 256
prudence 126, 128, 129, 130, 151, 173–6 *passim*, 178, 181n5–6, 182n9
Pufendorf, S. 130, 136, 142
Pujol, M. 452, 454, 461, 470

Pulteney, W. 151

Quesnay, F. 17, 21, 28, 149, 152–3, 154, 156, 187–8, 196, 206, 210; contribution to French canon 188–95; Mirabeau-Quesnay Tuesdays 200; 187, 189–90, 191, 193, 194
queuing phenomenon 45–6

Rae, J. 106, 119n46, 347, 348
Raphael, B. B. 161, 165n1, 166n7–8, 170, 172–3, 176–7, 178, 179, 181n1–2
Rationale of Reward, The 55n7
Read, S. 77, 114n7
Rebellious Fraser's 408–9
Recktenwald, H. C. 175, 177–8
Rees, J. 403, 404, 405, 406
Reid, M. 462, 463, 471
Reid, T. 177, 179, 180, 464
Remarques sur les avantages et les desavantages de la France et de la Grande-Bretagne 188
Renaissance 126, 130
rent 9, 14, 27, 82, 116n20, 136, 145, 157, 165n5, 189, 191, 196–7, 200–1, 226, 233, 236, 239n2, 248–9, 266n11, 272, 274, 276, 295, 298, 305, 348, 390
Report of the Commons Committee on the Corn Law 325
Republic 127
republicans 126–7
resources 17, 64, 65, 87, 105, 118n39, 157; allocation 10, 11, 14, 19, 157; natural 3, 27, 107; state stewardship of 149, 153, 154, 157, 186; *see also* land
returns, diminishing 9, 13, 15, 19, 27–8, 40, 44, 57, 75, 77–84 *passim*, 86,92, 102, 105, 106, 114n1, 115n11, 117n28, 199, 249, 272, 301, 313n8
Revue d'Economie Politique 216, 219
Reybaud, L. 209, 214
Ricardo, D. 2, 3, 4, 7, 12, 16–23, 27, 57, 63, 75, 78–80, 81, 112, 115n9–10, 115n13, 116n20, 117n28, 118n40, 199, 200, 206, 207, 208, 210, 224–32, 236, 238, 239n3, 239n5–6, 241–68, 270–88, 290–315, 328n12, 328n17, 351, 365, 368, 454, 456, 482; analytics 226–32; and corn laws 19; corn-profit model 276–8; and growth model 13; and Malthus 15, 17, 21, 299, 318, 321–2, 322–3, 328n9, 350; and Mill 16, 20; *Production of Commodities* 274–6; and Say's law 318–28; and Smith 14, 15, 17, 296–8, 299, 303, 328n14; theory of money 331–43; value theory 227–32, 249–50, 486; wage–profit mechanism 293–301; *see also* works by name

Ricardo, Works and Correspondence of 4, 43, 244, 245, 270
Ricardo – The New View 2, 7
Richter, R. 72n18
Richthofen, E. von 466
Riopelle, J-P. 451
Rivlin, A. 451
Robbins, Lord L. 15, 20, 75, 76, 77, 102, 112, 113, 114n3, 116n17–19, 119n47, 309
Robertson, R. 369
Robinson, Sir A. 244
Robinson, J. 287n13, 352, 353, 354n8, 451, 469, 471, 472, 473
Robson, A. P. 459, 461
Robson, J. M. 459, 461
Rogers, B. 459
Rogers, C. 351
Romano, R. M. 117n30, 118n34, 118n38, 119n43
Roncaglia, A. 5, 251
Rorty, R. 125, 128, 141–3 *passim*
Rosenberg, N. 65, 71n3, 99, 114n6, 117n30, 118n32, 118n39
Ross, I. S. 125, 131–2, 141, 144, 145
Rossi, A. S. 459, 471
Rossi, P. 209, 215, 217, 220n10
Rothbart, M. 314n16, 392
Rothschild, E. 144, 159, 165n3
Rousseau, J. J. 130, 132, 134, 136, 141, 142, 143
Royal Economic Society 201n1, 286n1
Royal Society 118n38, 189
Royer, C-A. 457
Ruskin, J. 401
Russia 111, 194, 465, 492; Alexandre I 198
Rutherford, R. P. 350
Rymes, T. K. 5, 350

Salleron, L. 191
Salvadori, N. 24n7, 263, 287n12
Samuels, W. 6, 485, 489
Samuelson, P. 2, 3, 5, 8, 13, 17, 27, 33, 41, 57–8, 59, 71, 71n1, 114n1, 199, 200, 225, 245, 264, 265n5, 301, 331, 352, 378, 379, 380–1, 383, 482, 483, 486
Sawyer, M. 312n3
Say family 216
Say, J.-B. 4, 5, 16, 77, 114n7, 205–22, 323; extension to canon 198–9; Say's law 198, 318–27, 327n1–2, 454
Say's equality and identity 12, 318, 327n1
scarcity 3, 27, 28, 207, 214, 382; land 8, 11–14 *passim*, 16, 17, 20, 21, 38, 44, 47, 53, 105, 107, 346
Schefold, B. 242, 245, 265, 265n8
Schumpeter, J. A. 16, 78, 205, 322, 331, 380, 392, 452
Schumpeter, E. B. 473

Schwartz, A. J. 291, 451, 469–70
Science of Wealth, The 459
Scott, J. W. 457–8
Scrope, G. P. 77, 114n7, 119n40
security 43, 48–9, 50, 51, 53, 58, 71, 72n7, 72n9, 72n11, 72n13, 72n19, 72n21, 92, 127, 162–3; in a growing economy 60–5; as institutional constraint 65–70
Seiz, J. 453
self-interest 4, 61, 65, 128, 130, 133, 135, 140, 159, 168–77 *passim*, 180, 181n5, 182n9, 211
Senior, N. 76, 77, 87–8, 91–5, 113, 114n3, 116n17, 116n20–23, 117n27–8, 121n47, 255, 256–7, 292, 411, 413
Shackleford, J. 458
Shackleton, J. R. 455
Shaftesbury, Earl of 142
Shinohara, H. 176–7
Sigot, N. 3, 4–5, 44, 54n5, 55n7
Simms, Dr W. G. 416–7
Simon, J. 457
Singer, K. 43
Skarżyński, W. von 169, 170, 173–4, 177, 181n1
Skinner, A. S. 151, 165n1, 165n4, 202n8
slavery 5–6, 400, 401, 403–28, 458; child 409; sexual 411–18
Smith, A. 2, 3, 4, 7, 12, 18, 21, 22, 27, 28, 34, 43, 57–73, 76, 77, 85, 89–93 *passim*, 97, 111–4 *passim*, 117n32, 118n33, 118n40, 125–146, 185, 186–7, 188, 195, 199, 201, 205–8 *passim*, 210, 221n12, 225, 227, 233, 243, 252, 253, 254, 260, 261, 290, 291, 307, 313n8, 313n10–12, 341, 347, 388, 411, 412, 414, 453, 454, 482, 486, 496; and agriculture 15; and Bentham 49; competition of capital 92; *Correspondence* 151; cost-push doctrine 313n10; division of labor 76, 85, 89, 91, 98, 102, 112, 114n1, 381; in France 169, 194, 202n8; and growth 13, 40, 114n5, 130, 137; and justice/ expediency 126, 129–31 *passim*, 133, 135, 136, 138, 139, 141, 145, 148–66, 169; and Malthus 15, 17; and Mill 303; and price/cost 14, 136, 247–9, 255–7, 266n9–11; and profit 58–60; relationship between books 4, 148–64, 168–82; and Ricardo 14, 15, 17, 296–8, 299–301, 303, 328n14; in Scotland 169; and security 60–70; transformation of canon 195–8; and usury 24n6, 49; *see also* works by name
Smith, J. 251, 264
Société d'Economie Politique 217, 218

Society in America 456
Society for the Diffusion of Useful Knowledge 76
Society for Promoting the Employment of Women 461
Sockwell, W. D. 461
Solzhenitsyn, A. 465
Southey, R. 409, 418–20
Sowell, T. 322
specie flow 294, 299, 300; adjustments 132; mechanism 8, 291–2, 299, 301, 304, 305, 311; *see also* bullion, ingot plan
Spengler, J. J. 177, 201n3
Sraffa, P. 4, 8, 21–3, 43, 241–68, 270–82, 284, 286n1–2, , 287n3–4, 287n6–7–8, 287n10–15, 382; lectures on value 257–64
Stark, W. 43, 54
state of nature 3, 58, 211, 232
Stearns, E. J. 426
Steedman, I. 367
Steiner, P. 201n4, 216, 217
Stern, H. 467–8
Steuart, Sir J. 146, 151, 344n5
Stewart, D. 169, 170
Stigler, G. J. 115n13, 117n30, 118n32, 118n38, 239n6, 246, 312n1, 391
Stiglitz, J. E 75
Stoicism 128–31 *passim*, 173
Stone, M. 462
Stowe, H. B. 413, 425
Study of Interest Rates, A 469
subsistence 48, 49, 55n7, 58, 64, 87, 88–97 *passim*, 135, 152, 193, 227, 260, 279; and abundance 48; economy 37, 189; goods 46, 278; and population 44–5, 53, 53n1, 54n2–3, 92, 97, 116n23, 117n27, 198, 232; rate 31; wage 9, 17, 28, 31, 32, 35, 226, 232
Sully, Duc de 193
Sumner, H. 471, 472
Sur les prix 44, 54n3
surplus 4, 15, 21, 23, 28, 31, 36, 37, 45, 46, 50, 58, 59, 64, 87, 135, 189, 191, 194–7 *passim*, 201, 245, 252, 260, 262, 267n21, 270, 274, 285; value 225, 232, 233, 235–8 *passim*, 239n2, 240n10, 252, 267n22
Sutherland, K. 453

tableau économique see Quesnay
Taylor, H. 461
tax 11, 19, 23, 24n2, 96 131, 185, 189, 190, 191, 193, 196, 197, 294–300 *passim*, 302, 304, 306, 313n10, 321; import duties 19
Teichgraeber III, R. F. 178
Théorie de l'impôt, ou la dime sociale 457

theory: of distribution 258, 281; of general economic equilibrium 214; of marginal utility 259; of prices of production 276, 278, 280; of production and distribution 249; and text 241; *see also* allocation theory, comparative advantage, ethical theory, growth theory, labour theory of pricing, theory of profit, price theory, the theory of general economic equilibrium, value theory
theory of profit 250; corn-ratio 247, 250, 263n8, 278, 280, 281, 314n13
Theory of Consumption 462
Theory of the Consumption Function 469
Theory of Moral Sentiments 62, 65, 70, 72n11, 72n13, 127–8, 129, 131, 133, 134, 135, 137, 149, 150, 158, 159, 160, 161, 454; and *The Wealth of Nations* 4, 148–64, 162–82
Theory of Political Economy (Mill) 357
Théré, C. 187
Think and Act 460
Thompson, W. 461
Thomson, H. F. 173
Thorne, A. C. 462
Thrall, M. 408–9, 425
Three Lectures on the Rate of Wages 116n17
Thünen, J. von 389
Tickner, F. W. 471
Timlin, M. F. 472
Tiran, A. 212
Tisch, C. 467
Tocqueville, A. de 456
Tooke, T. 116n23, 118n33, 327n5
Torrens, R. 13, 17, 75, 77, 78, 84–9, 115n15, 116n16–18, 259
Tozer, J. 389
Tracy, D. de 207
trade, colonial 69, 138; cycle 16; free 116n22, 138, 152, 154, 157, 165n5, 195, 199, 200, 309 (*see also* Corn Law); foreign/international 11, 16, 18, 23, 29, 62–4, 112, 118n40, 119n45, 131, 154, 191, 201n3, 291, 294–5, 299–301, 310, 324
Traité d'Économie Politique 198, 205, 207, 216
Traités de législation civile et pénale 45, 48
Tristan, F. 458
Tucker, G. 34, 141
Turgot, A. 141, 187, 190, 195, 202n8, 207
Two Lectures on Population 87, 92

Uncle Tom's Cabin 413–14, 418, 421, 425, 426
Ure, A. 117n29
USA *see* North America
usury 24n6, 49, 163, 352

utilitarianism 133, 149, 158, 160, 164, 166n7, 171–4 *passim*, 403, 405, 406, 408
utility 4, 54n4, 127, 142, 159, 160, 162, 169, 172–4, 179, 207, 211, 251, 252, 256, 259; and justice 149, 158–63, 166n7–8; money 12; social 212–14

Vaggi, G. 201n2
value theory 4, 8, 10, 14–17 *passim*, 29, 115n8, 214, 216, 224, 225, 227–32, 233, 234, 236, 237, 238, 239, 239n6, 245, 255, 256, 258, 259, 260, 261, 263, 263n8, 272–5, 281, 286n2, 383; adding-up theory 247–9, 266n9; classical 5; labour theory of 9–10, 37, 20; standard of value 249–51
Villeneuve-Bargemont, A. de 215
Viner, J. 171, 172, 174, 224
virtue 174, 176, 178
Vivo, G. de 242
Voltaire, F-M. 126, 188, 196

wage–profit/price relationship 5, 10, 11, 12, 13, 15, 17, 20, 21, 23, 38, 44, 75, 108, 226, 227, 229, 248, 285–6, 290–1, 293–301, 302–12, 313n5, 315n20
wages 4, 10–17, 19–21, 23, 24n2, 25n11, 28–32 *passim*, 35, 38, 40, 44, 54n7, 75, 80, 82, 89, 99, 109–11, 130, 133, 134, 136, 144, 145, 193, 194, 197–8, 199, 201, 248, 291, 299, 305, 308; competitive 29, 40, 134; fixed 5; minimum 13; real 2, 8–9, 19, 21, 31, 32, 79, 116n22, 185, 200, 201, 271–88 *passim*, 294–6, 298, 302, 347; *see also* corn wage
Wages and Salaries in the United Kingdom 469
Wakatabe, M. 3, 114, 114n5
Wakefield, E. 454
Wakefield, P. 453–4, 455, 461, 470
Walker, A. 459–60, 461
Walker, F. A. 460
Walpole, R. 152
Walras, L. 17, 211–14, 216, 251, 255, 265n3, 382, 389, 458; Walrasian economics 58, 205
war 44, 98, 126, 131, 139, 193, 328n13; laws of 161; Napoleonic 53n1, 78, 81, 96, 199, 318, 320; rehabilitation of soldiers after 139, 328n8
Ward, B. 473
Ware, C. 471
Waterman, A. 3, 27, 35, 37
Watt, J. 96, 107
Wealth of Nations, The 7, 13, 14, 24n2, 27, 57–72, 125–46, 150, 165n2, 168–82, 188, 194, 195–6, 201, 202n8, 205, 206, 248, 292, 293, 295, 308, 313n10, 454, 482, 486; anti-political economy 154–50; in contemprary canon 139–42; purpose of 4; studies of 125–39; and *The Theory of Moral Sentiment* 4, 148–64, 168–82
Webb, B. 452
Webb, S. 452
Wedgwood, J. 96
Weintraub, E. R. 387, 394
Werhane, P. 66, 72n10
West, Sir Edward 13, 17, 75, 77, 78, 82–4, 91, 92, 112, 115n13–14, 270
West, Edwin 17, 61, 69, 114n1
Weyland, J. 115
Whateley, R. 411
Wheeler, A. 461
Whewell, W. 389
Whig: party 145; view of history 393, 486, 488
Whitaker, J. 5
Wicksell, K. 17, 350
Wicksteed, P. 372
Wilberforce, W. 404–5, 411, 412, 413, 426
Williams, F. M. 453
Williamson, O. E. 70
Winch, D. 27, 66, 68, 69, 71n2, 72n11, 89, 125, 132–45 *passim*, 149, 155, 164, 165n1–2, 166n6, 178, 180, 356
Witzum, A. 173
Wolowski, L. 209, 216, 217, 218
women: employment in nineteenth century 454–5 in canon 451–73; dearth of 6, 451, 469–73
Women in Sociology 453
Women and Work 461
Woodbury, H. *see* Sumner, H.
Wootton, B. 473
Works and Correspondence of David Ricardo, The 4, 43, 244, 245, 270
Wright, F. 455, 461
Wunderlich, F. 466

Yi, Y-A. 462, 463, 464
Young, J. T. 125, 135–6, 137, 140, 149, 158, 160, 174–5

Zahn, L. 468
Zeyss, R. 176, 180
Zinsser, J. P. 451, 472
Zuckerman, M. E. 462
Zur Dynamik des Statkapitalismus 465
Zur Kritik Moderner Krisentheorien 466